WILEY CPA EXAM REVIEW

WILEY CPA EXAM REVIEW 2009

Regulation

O. Ray Whittington, CPA, PhD

Patrick R. Delaney, CPA, PhD

WILEY

JOHN WILEY & SONS, INC.

CONTENTS

			Page number		
			Outlines and study guides	*Problems and solutions*	*Other*
CHAPTER	**1. BEGINNING YOUR CPA REVIEW PROGRAM**				1
	2. EXAMINATION GRADING				15
	3. THE SOLUTIONS APPROACH				17
	4. TAKING THE EXAMINATION				29
	5. REGULATION				33
	Modules and Abbreviations:[1]				
	6. PROFESSIONAL RESPONSIBILITIES AND BUSINESS LAW				37
21	Professional Responsibilities	RESP	41	73	
22	Federal Securities Acts	FEDE	90	108	
23	Contracts	CONT	121	143	
24	Sales	SALE	160	172	
25	Commercial Paper	CPAP	186	203	
26	Secured Transactions	SECU	220	227	
27	Bankruptcy	BANK	235	247	
28	Debtor-Creditor Relationships	DBCR	258	268	
29	Agency	AGEN	276	283	
30	Regulation of Employment and Environment	EMEN	291	306	
31	Property	PROP	316	332	
32	Insurance	INSU	344	347	
	7. FEDERAL TAXATION				**355**
33	Individual	ITAX	360	417	
34	Transactions in Property	TPRO	490	505	
35	Partnership	PTAX	522	535	
36	Corporate	CTAX	562	586	
37	Gift and Estate	GETX	645	654	
APPENDIX A: REGULATION SAMPLE EXAMINATION					**676**
APPENDIX B: SAMPLE TESTLETS RELEASED BY THE AICPA					**699**
APPENDIX C: 2008 RELEASED AICPA QUESTIONS					**705**
INDEX					**722**

[1] *As explained in Chapter 1, this book is organized into 17 modules (manageable study units). The numbering of the modules commences with number 21 to correspond with the numbering system used in our two-volume set.*

PREFACE

Passing the CPA exam upon your first attempt is possible! The *Wiley CPA Examination Review* preparation materials provide you with the necessary materials (visit our Web site at www.wiley.com/cpa for more information). It's up to you to add the hard work and commitment. Together we can beat the pass rate on each section of about 40% All Wiley CPA products are continuously updated to provide you with the most comprehensive and complete knowledge base. Choose your products from the Wiley preparation materials and you can proceed confidently. You can select support materials that are exam-based and user-friendly. You can select products that will help you pass!

Remaining current is one of the keys to examination success. Here is a list of what's new in *Wiley CPA Examination Review Regulation* text:

- The AICPA Content Specification Outlines on Regulation for the computerized CPA Examination
- AICPA questions released in 2008
- Tax law changes for 2008 (tested on the 2009 examination)
- Coverage of latest business law legislation
- Latest coverage of the AICPA and PCAOB ethics rules

The objective of this work is to provide you with the knowledge to pass Regulation portion of the Uniform Certified Public Accounting (CPA) Exam. The text is divided up into seventeen areas of study called modules. Each module contains written text with discussion, examples, and demonstrations of the key exam concepts. Following each text area, actual American Institute of Certified Public Accountants (AICPA) unofficial questions and answers are presented to test your knowledge. We are indebted to the AICPA for permission to reproduce and adapt examination materials from past examinations. Author constructed questions and simulations are provided for new areas or areas that require updating. All author constructed questions and simulations are modeled after AICPA question formats. The multiple-choice questions are grouped into topical areas, giving candidates a chance to assess their areas of strength and weakness. Selection and inclusion of topical content is based upon current AICPA Content Specification Outlines. Only testable topics are presented. If the CPA exam does not test it, this text does not present it.

The CPA exam is one of the toughest exams you will ever take. It will not be easy. But if you follow our guidelines and focus on your goal, you will be thrilled with what you can accomplish.

Ray Whittington
November 2008

**Don't forget to visit our Web site at www.wiley.com/cpa
for supplements and updates.**

ABOUT THE AUTHORS

Ray Whittington, PhD, CPA, CMA, CIA, is the dean of the College of Commerce at DePaul University. Prior to joining the faculty at DePaul, Professor Whittington was the Director of Accountancy at San Diego State University. From 1989 through 1991, he was the Director of Auditing Research for the American Institute of Certified Public Accountants (AICPA), and he previously was on the audit staff of KPMG. He previously served as a member of the Auditing Standards Board of the AICPA and as a member of the Accounting and Review Services Committee and the Board of Regents of the Institute of Internal Auditors. Professor Whittington has published numerous textbooks, articles, monographs, and continuing education courses.

Patrick R. Delaney, deceased, was the dedicated author and editor of the Wiley CPA Exam Review books for twenty years. He was the Arthur Andersen LLP Alumni Professor of Accountancy and Department Chair at Northern Illinois University. He received his PhD in Accountancy from the University of Illinois. He had public accounting experience with Arthur Andersen LLP and was coauthor of *GAAP: Interpretation and Application*, also published by John Wiley & Sons, Inc. He served as Vice President and a member of the Illinois CPA Society's Board of Directors, and was Chairman of its Accounting Principles Committee; was a past president of the Rockford Chapter, Institute of Management Accountants; and had served on numerous other professional committees. He was a member of the American Accounting Association, American Institute of Certified Public Accountants, and Institute of Management Accountants. Professor Delaney was published in *The Accounting Review* and was a recipient of the Illinois CPA Society's Outstanding Educator Award, NIU's Excellence in Teaching Award, and Lewis University's Distinguished Alumnus Award. He was involved in NIU's CPA Review Course as director and instructor.

ABOUT THE CONTRIBUTORS

Duane R. Lambert, JD, MBA, CPA, is a Professor of Business Administration at California State University, Hayward, where he teaches courses in Business Law and Accounting. He also has been, on different occasions, a Visiting Lecturer and Visiting Professor at the University of California, Berkeley. Professor Lambert has "Big Five" experience and also has several years experience teaching CPA review courses and helping examinees prepare successfully for the CPA examination. He wrote and revised the Business Law Modules. He also prepared answer explanations for the multiple-choice questions and other objective questions.

Edward C. Foth, PhD, CPA, Administrator of the Master of Science in Taxation Program at DePaul University. Professor Foth is the author of CCH Incorporated's *Study Guide for Federal Tax Course, Study Guide for CCH Federal Taxation: Comprehensive Topics*, and coauthor of their *S Corporation Guide*. Professor Foth prepared the answer explanations to the multiple-choice and other objective questions in Income Taxes, wrote new questions, selected the mix of questions, and updated items to reflect revisions in the tax law.

2 EXAMINATION GRADING

Setting the Passing Standard of the Uniform		Multiple-Choice Grading	15
CPA Examination	15	Simulation Grading	15
Grading the Examination	15		

All State Boards of Accountancy use the AICPA advisory grading service. As your grade is to be determined by this process, it is very important that you understand the AICPA grading process and its **implications for your preparation program and for the solution techniques you will use during the examination**.

The AICPA has a full-time staff of CPA examination personnel under the supervision of the AICPA Board of Examiners, which has responsibility for the CPA examination.

This chapter contains a description of the AICPA grading process including a determination of the passing standard.

Setting the Passing Standard of the Uniform CPA Examination

As a part of the development of any licensing process, the passing score on the licensing examination must be established. This passing score must be set to distinguish candidates who are qualified to practice from those who are not. After conducting a number of studies of methods to determine passing scores, the Board of Examiners decided to use candidate-centered methods to set passing scores for the computer-based Uniform CPA Examination. In candidate-centered methods, the focus is on looking at actual candidate answers and making judgments about which sets of answers represent the answers of qualified entry-level CPAs. To make these determinations, the AICPA convened panels of CPAs during 2003 to examine candidate responses and set the passing scores for multiple-choice questions and simulations. The data from these panels provide the basis for the development of question and problem points (relative weightings). **As with the previous pencil-and-paper exam, a passing score on the computer-based examination is 75%.**

Grading the Examination

Most of the responses on the computer-based CPA examination are objective in nature. Obviously, this includes the responses to the multiple-choice questions. However, it also includes most of the responses to the requirements of simulations. Requirements of simulations include responses involving check boxes, entries into spreadsheets, form completion, graphical responses, drag and drop, and written communications. All of these responses, with the exception of written communications, are computer graded. Therefore, no consideration is given to any comments or explanations outside of the structured responses.

Graders are used to score the responses involving written communication, (e.g., a written memorandum). These responses are graded for the quality of the written communication, but not for technical accuracy. However, the response must address the requirement to be graded at all.

Multiple-Choice Grading

Regulation exams contain three multiple-choice testlets of 24 questions each. **Four of these questions will be pretest questions that will not be considered in the candidate's score.** Also, the possible score on a question and on a testlet will vary based on the difficulty of the questions. The makeup of the second testlet provided to a candidate will be determined based upon the candidate's performance on the first testlet, and the makeup of the third testlet will be determined by the candidate's performance on the first two testlets. Therefore, you should not be discouraged if you a get a difficult set of questions; it may merely mean that you performed very well on the previous testlet(s). Also, you will receive more raw points for hard and medium questions than for easy questions.

Your answers to the multiple-choice questions are graded by the computer. Your grade is based on the total number of correct answers weighted by their difficulty, and with no penalty for incorrect answers. As mentioned earlier, four of the multiple-choice questions are pretest items that are not included in the candidate's grade.

Simulation Grading

As indicated previously, the majority of the responses to the simulations will be computer graded. They will typically involve checking a box, selecting a response from a list, or dragging and dropping an answer.

The responses involving written communication will be graded for writing skills. These responses are scored based on the following criteria:

1. Organization: structure, ordering of ideas, and linking of one idea to another

    - Overview/thesis statement
    - Unified paragraphs (topic and supporting sentences)
    - Transitions and connectives

2. Development: supporting evidence/information to clarify thoughts

    - Details
    - Definitions
    - Examples
    - Rephrasing

3. Expression: use of standard business English

    - Grammar
    - Punctuation
    - Word usage
    - Capitalization
    - Spelling

A communication response is not graded for technical accuracy. However, it must be on point to be graded at all. For example, if the requirement is to write a memorandum to describe the rules regarding the deductibility of contributions to an individual retirement account, the response must address the limitations regarding deductibility but does not have to be complete or technically accurate. The response must include information that is helpful to the intended user.

As with the multiple-choice questions, a small percentage of the simulation requirements will be pretest items that will not be included in the candidate's grade.

Chapter 3 will provide detailed suggestions on ways that you may use the information about grading to maximize your score.

**NOW IS THE TIME
TO MAKE YOUR COMMITMENT**

3 THE SOLUTIONS APPROACH

Multiple-Choice Screen Layout   17
Multiple-Choice Question Solutions Approach
    Algorithm   18
Multiple-Choice Question Solutions Approach
    Example   18
Simulations   19

Simulations Solutions Approach Algorithm   21
Research Components of Simulations   22
Communication Requirements of Simulations   23
Methods for Improving Your Writing Skills   25
Time Requirements for the Solutions Approach   27

The solutions approach is a systematic problem-solving methodology. The purpose is to assure efficient, complete solutions to CPA exam questions, some of which are complex and confusing relative to most undergraduate accounting problems. This is especially true with regard to the new simulation type problems. Unfortunately, there appears to be a widespread lack of emphasis on problem-solving techniques in accounting courses. Most accounting books and courses merely provide solutions to specific types of problems. Memorization of these solutions for examinations and preparation of homework problems from examples is "cookbooking." "Cookbooking" is perhaps a necessary step in the learning process, but it is certainly not sufficient training for the complexities of the business world. Professional accountants need to be adaptive to a rapidly changing complex environment. For example, CPAs have been called on to interpret and issue reports on new concepts such as price controls, energy allocations, and new taxes. These CPAs rely on their problem-solving expertise to understand these problems and to formulate solutions to them.

The steps outlined below are only one of many possible series of solution steps. Admittedly, the procedures suggested are **very** structured; thus, you should adapt the suggestions to your needs. You may find that some steps are occasionally unnecessary, or that certain additional procedures increase your own problem-solving efficiency. Whatever the case, substantial time should be allocated to developing an efficient solutions approach before taking the examination. You should develop your solutions approach by working previous CPA questions and problems.

Note that the steps below relate to any specific question or problem; overall examination or section strategies are discussed in Chapter 4.

Multiple-Choice Screen Layout

The following is a computer screenshot that illustrates the manner in which multiple-choice questions will be presented:

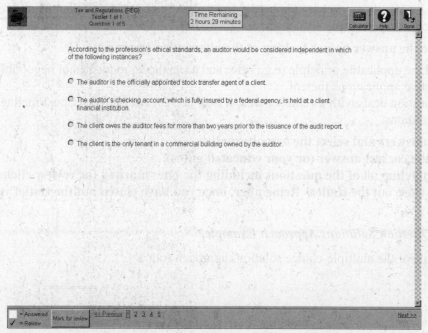

As indicated previously, multiple-choice questions will be presented in three individual testlets of 25 to 30 questions each. Characteristics of the computerized testlets of multiple-choice questions include the following:

1. You may move freely within a particular testlet from one question to the next or back to previous questions until you click the "Done" button. Once you have indicated that you have finished the testlet by clicking on the "Done" button, you can never return to that set of questions.
2. A button on the screen will allow you to mark a question for review if you wish to come back to it later.
3. A four-function computer calculator is available as a tool.
4. The time remaining for the entire exam section is shown on the screen.
5. The number of the questions out of the total in the testlet is shown on the screen.
6. The "Help" button will provide you with help in navigating and completing the testlet.

The screenshot above was obtained from the AICPA's tutorial at www.cpa-exam.org. Candidates are urged to complete the tutorial and other example questions on the AICPA's Web site to obtain additional experience with the computer-based testing.

Multiple-Choice Question Solutions Approach Algorithm

1. **Work individual questions in order.**

   a. If a question appears lengthy or difficult, skip it until you can determine that extra time is available. Mark it for review to remind you to return to a question that you have skipped or need to review.

2. **Read the stem of the question without looking at the answers.**

   a. The answers are sometimes misleading and may cause you to misread or misinterpret the question.

3. **Read each question *carefully* to determine the topical area.**

   a. Study the requirements **first** so you know which data are important.
   b. Note keywords and important data.
   c. Identify pertinent information.
   d. Be especially careful to note when the requirement is an **exception** (e.g., "Which of the following is **not** an effective disclaimer of the implied warranty of merchantability?").
   e. If a set of data is the basis for two or more questions, read the requirements of each of the questions first before beginning to work the first question (sometimes it is more efficient to work the questions out of order).
   f. Be alert to read questions as they are, not as you would like them to be. You may encounter a familiar looking item; do not jump to the conclusion that you know what the answer is without reading the question completely.

4. **Anticipate the answer before looking at the alternative answers.**

   a. Recall the applicable principle (e.g., offer and acceptance, requisites of negotiability, etc.) and the respective applications thereof.
   b. If a question deals with a complex area, it may be very useful to set up a timeline or diagram using abbreviations.

5. **Read the answers and select the *best* alternative.**
6. **Click on the correct answer (or your educated guess).**
7. **After completing all of the questions including the ones marked for review click on the "Done" button to close out the testlet. Remember, once you have closed out the testlet you can never return to it.**

Multiple-Choice Question Solutions Approach Example

A good example of the multiple-choice solutions approach follows.

Step 3:

Topical area? Contracts—Revocation and Attempted Acceptance

Step 4:

Principle? An offer may be revoked at any time prior to acceptance and is effective when received by offeree

Step 5:

a. Incorrect - Mason's acceptance was ineffective because the offer had been revoked prior to Mason's acceptance.

b. Incorrect - Same as a.

c. **Correct**   - Peters' offer was effectively revoked when Mason learned that the lawn mower had been sold to Bronson.

d. Incorrect - Peters' was not obligated to keep the offer open because no consideration had been paid by Mason. Note that if consideration had been given, an option contract would have been formed and the offer would have been irrevocable before June 20.

13. On June 15, Peters orally offered to sell a used lawn mower to Mason for $125. Peters specified that Mason had until June 20 to accept the offer. On June 16, Peters received an offer to purchase the lawn mower for $150 from Bronson, Mason's neighbor. Peters accepted Bronson's offer. On June 17, Mason saw Bronson using the lawn mower and was told the mower had been sold to Bronson. Mason immediately wrote to Peters to accept the June 15 offer.

Which of the following statements is correct?

a. Mason's acceptance would be effective when received by Peters.

b. Mason's acceptance would be effective when mailed.

c. Peters' offer had been revoked and Mason's acceptance was ineffective.

d. Peters was obligated to keep the June 15 offer open until June 20.

Currently, all multiple-choice questions are scored based on the number correct, weighted by a difficulty rating (i.e., there is no penalty for guessing). The rationale is that a "good guess" indicates knowledge. Thus, you should answer all multiple-choice questions.

Simulations

Simulations are case-based multiple-part problems designed to

- Test integrated knowledge
- More closely replicate real-world problems
- Assess research, written communication, and other skills

Each simulation will be designed to take from 30 to 50 minutes.

The parts of simulations are separated by computer tabs. Typically they begin with directions and/or a situation and continue with various tabs requiring responses and possibly a resource tab. An example is shown below.

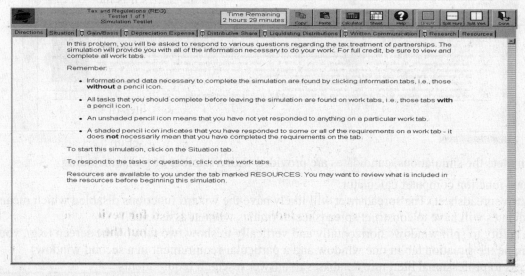

While the tabs without the pencils are informational in nature, the tabs with pencils require a response.

Any of the following types of responses might be required on simulation parts:

- Multiple selection
- Drop-down selection
- Numeric and monetary inputs
- Formula answers

- Check box response
- Enter spreadsheet formulas
- Research results
- Written communications

The screenshot below illustrates a part that requires the candidate to input amounts and formulas.

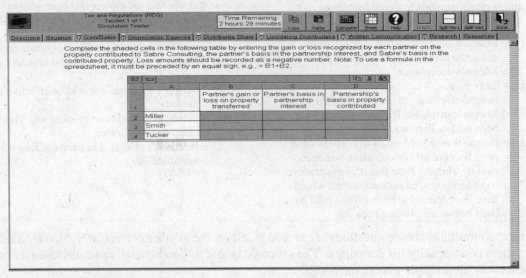

The screenshot below illustrates a requirement to complete a tax form.

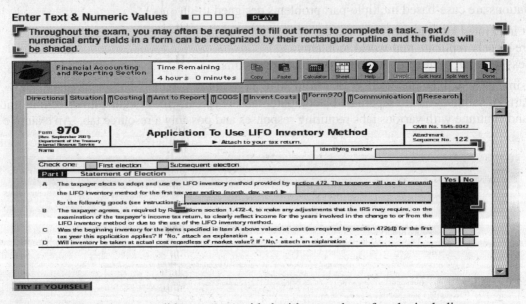

To complete the simulations, candidates are provided with a number of tools, including

- A four-function computer calculator
- Scratch spreadsheet (The spreadsheet will likely have the wizard functions disabled which means that candidates will have to construct spreadsheet formulas without assistance.)
- The ability to split windows horizontally and vertically to show two tabs on the screen (e.g., you can examine the situation tab in one window and a particular requirement in a second window)
- Access to professional literature databases to answer research requirements
- Copy and paste functions
- A spellchecker to correct written communications
- The research screen now has a "back" button to allow you to go back to previously viewed screens

In addition, the resource tab provides other resources that may be needed to complete the problem. For example, a resource tab might contain a depreciation schedule for use in answering a tax problem.

5 REGULATION EXAM CONTENT

Preparing for the Regulation Exam

Regulation is a section of the exam that was added with the computerization of the exam in April 2004. Its content consists of most of the material that was previously in the Business Law and Professional Responsibilities combined with the Taxation topics that were included in the Accounting and Reporting section. **In preparing for the Regulation exam, you should take a systematic approach such as the one detailed in Chapter 1.**

First, in approaching your study, you should become acquainted with the nature of the Regulation exam itself. The content specification outlines are printed below.

Relatedly, you should evaluate your competence by working 10 to 20 multiple-choice questions from each of the modules (21-37) in Volume 2. This diagnostic routine will acquaint you with the specific nature of the questions tested on each topic as well as indicate the amount of study required per topic. You should work toward an 80% correct response rate as a minimum on each topic.

Second, study the content of modules 21-37 emphasizing the concepts of each topic such as legal liability of accountants, elements of a contract, and taxable income. You may have to refer to your textbooks, etc., for topics to which you have had no previous exposure.

Third, work the multiple-choice and simulations under examination conditions.

AICPA Content Specification Outline

The AICPA Content Specification Outline of the coverage of Regulation appears below. This outline was issued by the AICPA, effective as of 2005.

AICPA CONTENT SPECIFICATION OUTLINE: REGULATION

I. Ethics and Professional and Legal Responsibilities **(15%-20%)**

  A. Code of Professional Conduct
  B. Proficiency, Independence, and Due Care
  C. Ethics and Responsibilities in Tax Practice
  D. Licensing and Disciplinary Systems Imposed by the Profession and State Regulatory Bodies
  E. Legal Responsibilities and Liabilities

    1. Common Law Liability to Clients and Third Parties
    2. Federal Statutory Liability

  F. Privileged Communications and Confidentiality

II. Business Law **(20%-25%)**

  A. Agency

    1. Formation and Termination
    2. Duties and Authority of Agents and Principals
    3. Liabilities and Authority of Agents and Principals

  B. Contracts

    1. Formation
    2. Performance
    3. Third-Party Assignments
    4. Discharge, Breach, and Remedies

  C. Debtor-Creditor Relationships

    1. Rights, Duties, and Liabilities of Debtors, Creditors, and Guarantors

    2. Bankruptcy

  D. Government Regulation of Business

    1. Federal Securities Acts
    2. Other Government Regulation (Antitrust, Pension, and Retirement Plans, Union and Employee Relations, and Legal Liability for Payroll and Social Security Taxes)

  E. Uniform Commercial Code

    1. Negotiable Instruments and Letters of Credit
    2. Sales
    3. Secured Transactions
    4. Documents of Title and Title Transfer

  F. Real Property, Including Insurance

III. Federal Tax Procedures and Accounting Issues **(8%-12%)**

  A. Federal Tax Procedures
  B. Accounting Periods
  C. Accounting Methods Including Cash, Accrual, Percentage-of-Completion, Completed-Contract, and Installment Sales
  D. Inventory Methods, Including Uniform Capitalization Rules

IV. Federal Taxation of Property Transactions **(8%-12%)**

  A. Types of Assets
  B. Basis of Assets
  C. Depreciation and Amortization

D. Taxable and Nontaxable Sales and Exchanges

E. Income, Deductions, Capital Gains and Capital Losses, Including Sales and Exchanges of Business Property and Depreciation Recapture

V. Federal Taxation—Individuals (**12%-18%**)

A. Gross Income—Inclusions and Exclusions

B. Reporting of Items from Pass-Through Entities, Including Passive Activity Losses

C. Adjustments and Deductions to Arrive at Taxable Income

D. Filing Status and Exemptions

E. Tax Computations, Credits, and Penalties

F. Alternative Minimum Tax

G. Retirement Plans

H. Estate and Gift Taxation, Including Transfers Subject to the Gift Tax, Annual Exclusion, and Items Includible and Deductible from Gross Estate

VI. Federal Taxation—Entities (**22%-28%**)

A. Similarities and Distinctions in Tax Reporting Among Such Entities as Sole Proprietorships, General and Limited Partnerships, Subchapter C Corporations, Subchapter S Corporations, Limited Liability Companies, and Limited Liability Partnerships

B. Subchapter C Corporations

1. Determination of Taxable Income and Loss, and Reconciliation of Book Income to Taxable Income

2. Tax Computations, Credits, and Penalties, Including Alternative Minimum Tax

3. Net Operating Losses

4. Consolidated Returns

5. Entity/Owner Transactions, Including Contributions and Distributions

C. Subchapter S Corporations

1. Eligibility and Election

2. Determination of Ordinary Income, Separately Stated Items, and Reconciliation of Book Income to Taxable Income

3. Basis of Shareholder's Interest

4. Entity/Owner Transactions, Including Contributions and Liquidating and Nonliquidating Distributions

5. Built-In Gains Tax

D. Partnerships

1. Determination of Ordinary Income, Separately State Items, and Reconciliation of Book Income to Taxable Income

2. Basis of Partner's Interest and Basis of Assets Contributed to the Partnership

3. Partnership and Partner Elections

4. Partner Dealing with Own Partnership

5. Treatment of Partnership Liabilities

6. Distribution of Partnership Assets

7. Ownership Changes and Liquidation and Termination of Partnership

E. Trusts

1. Types of Trusts

2. Income and Deductions

3. Determination of Beneficiary's Share of Taxable Income

RESEARCHING INCOME TAX ISSUES[1]

Research components of Regulation section will involve a research database that includes the Internal Revenue Code.

The Internal Revenue Code of 1986, as Amended (commonly called IRC, or simple the Code) is the most important source of federal income tax law. The IRC is actually Title 26 of the United States Code. The US Code is the complete set of laws passed by Congress. All laws dealing with one topic are consolidated under one title of the US Code. For example, Title 10 of the US Code contains all of the military laws of the United States.

Any changes when Congress passes a new tax law are integrated in the Code. The Code has been amended almost every year since it was reformed in 1986. Prior to that, the Code was reorganized in 1954, and from then until 1986, it was known as the Internal Revenue Code of 1954, as Amended. Before the IRC of 1954, the tax law was contained in the Internal Revenue Code of 1939, the first IRC. Before 1939, the tax law was an unorganized series of tax acts.

Code Organization

There are many different subdivision to the Code, each with a different purpose and name. The Code is divided into subtitles, chapters, parts, subparts, and sections. Some common subtitles of the Code are

Subtitle A	Income Taxes
Subtitle B	Estate and Gift Taxes
Subtitle C	Employment Taxes
Subtitle D	Miscellaneous Excise Taxes

---

[1] *This section was prepared by Gerald E. Whittenburg, Ph.D., CPA. For more information about tax research refer to West's Federal Tax Research, 6th Edition (Thomas South-Western)*

Subtitle E   Alcohol, Tobacco, and Certain Excise Taxes
Subtitle F   Procedures and Administration

Each Subtitle is divided into chapters. The chapters contained in Subtitle A are

Chapter 1   Normal and Surtaxes
Chapter 2   Tax on Self-Employment Income
Chapter 3   Withholding Tax and Nonresident Aliens and Foreign Corporations
Chapter 4   [Repealed]
Chapter 5   Tax on Transfers to Avoid Income Tax
Chapter 6   Consolidated Returns

The chapters are again subdivided into numerous subchapters. Some of the notable subchapters of Chapter 1 are

Subchapter A   Determination of Tax Liability
Subchapter B   Computation of Taxable Income
Subchapter C   Corporate Distributions and Adjustments
Subchapter E   Accounting Periods and Methods
Subchapter I   Natural Resources
Subchapter K   Partners and Partnerships
Subchapter N   International Taxation
Subchapter S   Tax Treatment of S Corporations

Each subchapter may be further divided into parts and subparts, as needed.

The smallest unique part of the Code is the section. The section is normally the basic reference when citing a provision of the Internal Revenue Code. In day-to-day tax practice, reference to larger divisions of the Code such as subtitles and chapters are generally disregarded. Currently, the sections in the Code are numbered from 1 to over 9,000, albeit many numbers are skipped to allow for future expansion of the tax law. Each Code section may be further subdivided into subsections, paragraphs, subparagraphs, and clauses. As an example, the following Code section reference is to the definition of the term medical for purposes of the medical care deduction:

Citation: Section 213(d)(1)(A), where

213 is the Section Number
(d) is the Subdivision
(1) is the Paragraph
(A) is the Subparagraph

The tax practitioner can be assured that there is only one Section 213 in the Code and that this is a specific tax reference that cannot be confused with any other provision of the Code.

Database Searching

Searching a database consists of the following five steps:

1. Define the issue. What is the research question to be answered?
2. Select the database to search (e.g., the IRC).
3. Choose a keyword or table of contents search.
4. Execute the search. Enter the keyword(s) or click on the appropriate table of contents item and complete the search.
5. Evaluate the results. Evaluate the research to see if an answer has been found. If not, try a new search.

EXAMPLE: Bill and Betty support their 18-year old daughter and her husband who live with and are supported by them. Both the daughter and her husband are full-time students at a local community college and have no income. Bill and Betty would like to know if their daughter's husband qualifies as a dependent on their tax return. The research database search would be as follows:

    1.   Define the issue. Does a daughter's husband qualify as a relative for dependant purposes?
    2.   Select the database to search. Internal Revenue Code.
    3.   Choose appropriate keywords. "Son-in-law," or "dependent"
    4.   Execute the search. A search should find Section 152(a)(8)
    5.   Evaluate the results. A son-in-law is a qualified relative.

Advanced Searches

When performing advanced searches it is useful to understand Boolean operators. Boolean operators allow you to make more precise queries of a database.

1. The Boolean "AND" narrows your search by retrieving only cites that contain every one of the keywords listed.

    EXAMPLE: Dependent AND son-in-law

    This query would only retrieve cites that include both dependent and son-in-law.

2. The Boolean "OR" actually expands your search by retrieving all cites that contain either or both of the keywords.

    EXAMPLE: Real property OR tangible property

    This query would retrieve cites that include either real property or tangible property, or both.

3. The Boolean "NOT" narrows your search by retrieving only cites that containing the first keyword but not the second.

    EXAMPLE: Capital gains NOT short-term

    This query would retrieve cites that include capital gains but not short-term.

6 PROFESSIONAL RESPONSIBILITIES AND BUSINESS LAW

	Page no.		Page no.

Module 21/Professional Responsibilities (RESP)

Overview	41	E. Responsibilities of Auditors under Private Securities Litigation Reform Act	68
A. Code of Conduct and Other Responsibilities	41		
B. Accountant's Legal Liabilities	60	F. New Responsibilities and Provisions under Sarbanes-Oxley Actuarial	69
C. Legal Considerations Affecting the Accountant's Responsibility	66	G. Additional Statutory Liability Against Accountants	72
D. Criminal Liability	68		

	Page no.	
	Problem	Answer
66 Multiple-Choice	73	81
2 Simulation Problems	80	88

Module 22/Federal Securities Acts and Antitrust Law (FEDE)

Overview	90	F. State "Blue-Sky" Laws	103
A. Securities Act of 1933	90	G. Antitrust Law	103
B. Securities Exchange Act of 1934	97	H. Sherman Act of 1890	104
C. Sarbanes-Oxley Act of 2002	101	I. Clayton Act of 1914	105
D. Internet Securities Offering	102	J. Federal Trade Commission Act of 1914	106
E. Electronic Signatures and Electronic Records	102	K. Robinson-Patman Act of 1936	107

	Page no.	
	Problem	Answer
44 Multiple-Choice	108	115
2 Simulation Problems	112	119

Module 23/Contracts (CONT)

Overview	121	F. Performance of Contract	139
A. Essential Elements of a Contract	121	G. Discharge of Contracts	140
B. Types of Contracts	121	H. Remedies	141
C. Discussion of Essential Elements of a Contract	122	I. Statute of Limitations	141
D. Assignment and Delegation	138	J. Jurisdiction over Defendant for Online Transactions	141
E. Third-Party Beneficiary Contracts	139	K. Interference with Contractual Relations	142

	Page no.	
	Problem	Answer
57 Multiple-Choice	143	151
2 Simulation Problems	149	157

Module 24/Sales (SALE)

Overview	160	E. Performance and Remedies under Sales Law	167
A. Contracts for Sale of Goods	160		
B. Product Liability	161	F. Leases under UCC	169
C. Transfer of Property Rights	164	G. Contracts for the International Sales of Goods	170
D. Risk of Loss and Title	165		

	Page no.	
	Problem	Answer
47 Multiple-Choice	172	179
2 Simulation Problems	177	184

Module 25/Commercial Paper (CPAP)

Overview	186	
A. General Concepts of Commercial Paper	186	
B. Types of Commercial Paper	186	
C. Requirements of Negotiability	187	
D. Interpretation of Ambiguities in Negotiable Instruments	189	
E. Negotiation	190	
F. Holder in Due Course	192	

G. Rights of a Holder in Due Course	193	
H. Liability of Parties	195	
I. Additional Issues	198	
J. Banks	199	
K. Electronic Fund Transfer Act and Regulation E	200	
L. Fund Transfers under UCC Article 4A	200	
M. Transfer of Negotiable Documents of Title	200	
N. Agencies Involved in Banking	201	

	Page no.	
	Problem	*Answer*
50 Multiple-Choice	203	212
2 Simulation Problems	209	217

Module 26/Secured Transactions (SECU)

Overview	220
A. Scope of Secured Transactions	220
B. Attachment of Security Interests	220
C. Perfecting a Security Interest	221

D. Other Issues under Secured Transactions	223
E. Priorities	224
F. Rights of Parties upon Default	225
G. Other Rights of Parties	226

	Page no.	
	Problem	*Answer*
30 Multiple-Choice	227	231
1 Simulation Problem	230	234

Module 27/Bankruptcy (BANK)

Overview	235
A. Alternatives to Bankruptcy Proceedings	235
B. Bankruptcy in General	235
C. Chapter 7 Voluntary Bankruptcy Petitions	235
D. Chapter 7 Involuntary Bankruptcy Petitions	237
E. Chapter 7 Bankruptcy Proceedings	237
F. Claims	240
G. Discharge of a Bankrupt	241

H. Debts Not Discharged by Bankruptcy	242
I. Revocation of Discharge	243
J. Reaffirmation	243
K. Business Reorganization—Chapter 11	243
L. Debts Adjustment Plans—Chapter 13	244
M. The Bankruptcy Abuse Prevention and Consumer Protection Act of 2005	245
N. Bankruptcy Specialists Fees	246

	Page no.	
	Problem	*Answer*
31 Multiple-Choice	247	253
2 Simulation Problems	251	256

Module 28/Debtor-Creditor Relationships (DBCR)

Overview	258
A. Rights and Duties of Debtors and Creditors	258
B. Nature of Suretyship and Guaranty	260
C. Creditor's Rights and Remedies	262

D. Surety's and Guarantor's Rights and Remedies	263
E. Surety's and Guarantor's Defenses	263
F. Cosureties	265
G. Surety Bonds	266

	Page no.	
	Problem	*Answer*
27 Multiple-Choice	268	272
1 Simulation Problem	271	275

Module 29/Agency (AGEN)

Overview	276
A. Characteristics	276
B. Methods of Creation	278
C. Authority	279

D. Capacity to Be Agent or Principal	279
E. Obligations and Rights	280
F. Termination of Principal-Agent Relationship	281

	Page no.	
	Problem	*Answer*
25 Multiple-Choice	283	287
1 Simulation Problem	286	290

Page no.   *Page no.*

Module 30/Regulation of Employment and Environment (EMEN)

Overview	291	K. Pensions 299
A. Federal Social Security Act	291	L. Worker Adjustment and Retraining
B. Workers' Compensation Act	294	Notification Act 300
C. Torts of Employee	296	M. Federal Employee Polygraph Protection
D. Employee Safety	296	Act 300
E. Employment Discrimination	297	N. Employer Rights to E-mail 300
F. Federal Fair Labor Standards Act	299	O. Environmental Regulation 301
G. National Labor Relations Act	299	P. Telephone Consumer Protection Act 305
H. Taft-Hartley Act	299	Q. Federal Telecommunications Act 305
I. Landrum-Griffin Act	299	R. Identity Theft 305
J. Federal Consolidated Budget Reconciliation		
Act	299	

	Problem	Answer
44 Multiple-Choice	306	311
1 Simulation Problem	310	315

Page no.

Module 31/Property (PROP)

Overview	316	G. Types of Deeds 326
A. Distinctions between Real and Personal		H. Executing a Deed 326
Property	316	I. Recording a Deed 326
B. Personal Property	317	J. Title Insurance 327
C. Bailments	317	K. Adverse Possession 327
D. Intellectual Property and Computer		L. Easement by Prescription 328
Technology Rights	318	M. Mortgages 328
E. Interests in Real Property	323	N. Lessor—Lessee 330
F. Contracts for Sale of Land	325	

	Problem	Answer
43 Multiple-Choice	332	338
1 Simulation Problem	336	342

Page no.

Module 32/Insurance (INSU)

Overview	344	C. Subrogation 345
A. General Considerations	344	D. Liability Insurance 345
B. Insurance Contract	344	E. Fire Insurance 346

	Problem	Answer
8 Multiple-Choice	347	351
2 Simulation Problems	348	352

Regulation Sample Examination	676
Regulation AICPA Sample Testlets	699
Regulation 2008 Released AICPA Questions	705

(1) Compliance with Rule 202 and 203 obligations
(2) Compliance with enforceable subpoena or summons
(3) AICPA review of professional practice
(4) Initiating complaint or responding to inquiry made by a recognized investigative or disciplinary body

Interpretation 301-1. (Deleted)

Interpretation 301-2. (Deleted)

Interpretation 301-3. A member who is considering selling his/her practice, or merging with another CPA, may allow that CPA to review confidential client information without the specific consent of the client.

(1) The member should take appropriate precautions (e.g., obtain a written confidentiality agreement) so that the prospective purchaser does not disclose such information.

*NOTE: This exception only relates to a review in conjunction with a purchase or merger. It **does not** apply to the review of working papers **after** a CPA has purchased another's practice. AU 315, discussed in detail later in this module, requires that the successor who wishes to review predecessor auditor working papers should request the client to authorize the predecessor to make such working papers available.*

Rule 302 Contingent Fees.

(1) A member in public practice shall not

(a) Perform for a contingent fee any professional services when the member or member's firm also performs any of the following services for that client:

1] Audits or reviews of financial statements
2] Compilations when the member is independent and expects that a third party may use the financial statements
3] Examinations of prospective financial information

(b) Prepare an original or amended tax return or claims for a tax refund for a contingent fee for any client

(2) Solely for purposes of this rule, (a) fees fixed by courts or other public authorities, or (b) in tax matters, fees determined based on the results of a judicial proceeding or findings of governmental agency, are not regarded as contingent and are therefore permitted.

Interpretation 302-1. Examples related to contingent fees

(1) A contingent fee **would be permitted** in various circumstances in which the amounts due are not clear; examples are

(a) Representing a client in an examination by a revenue agent
(b) Filing amended tax returns based on a tax issue that is the subject of a test case **involving a different taxpayer**

(2) A contingent fee **would not be permitted** for preparing an amended tax return for a client claiming a refund that is clearly due to the client because of an inadvertent omission.

Rule 301, 302 Ethics Rulings

1. A member may utilize outside computer services to process tax returns as long as there is no release of confidential information.
2. With client permission, a member may provide P&L percentages to a trade association.
3. A CPA withdrawing from a tax engagement due to irregularities on the client's return should urge successor CPA to have client grant permission to reveal reasons for withdrawal.
6. A member may be engaged by a municipality to verify taxpayer's books and records for the purpose of assessing property tax. The member must maintain confidentiality.

7. Members may reveal the names of clients without client consent unless such disclosure releases confidential information.
14. A member has a responsibility to honor confidential relationships with nonclients. Accordingly, members may have to withdraw from consulting services engagements where the client will not permit the member to make recommendations without disclosing confidential information about other clients or nonclients.
15. If the member has conducted a similar consulting services study with a negative outcome, the member should advise potential clients of the previous problems providing that earlier confidential relationships

are not disclosed. If the earlier confidential relationship may be disclosed (through client knowledge of other clients), the member should seek approval from the first client.

16. In divorce proceedings a member who has prepared joint tax returns for the couple should consider both individuals to be clients for purposes of requests for confidential information relating to prior tax returns. Under such circumstances the CPA should consider reviewing the legal implications of disclosure with an attorney.

17. A contingent fee or a commission is considered to be "received" when the performance of the related services is complete and the fee or commission is determined.

18. Identical to Ruling 85 under Rule 101.

19. A member's spouse may provide services to a member's attest client for a contingent fee and may refer products or services for a commission.

20. When a member learns of a potential claim against him/her, the member may release confidential client information to member's liability carrier used solely to defend against claim.

21. Identical to Ruling 99 under Rule 102.

23. A member may disclose confidential client information to the member's attorney or a court in connection with actual or threatened litigation.

24. A member's fee for investment advisory services for an attest client that is based on a percentage of the portfolio would be considered contingent and a violation of Rule 302, unless

   a. The fee is determined as a specified percentage of the portfolio,
   b. The dollar amount of the portfolio is determined at the beginning of each quarterly period (or longer) and is adjusted only for additions or withdrawals by the client, and
   c. The fee arrangement is not renewed with the client more frequently than on a quarterly basis.

25. A member who provides for a contingent fee investment advisory service, or refers for a commission products or services to the owners, officers, or employees of an attest client would not violate Rule 302 with respect to the client.

Rule 501 Acts Discreditable. A member shall not commit an act discreditable to the profession.

Interpretation 501-1. Retention of client records after client has demanded them is discreditable.

(1) A CPA may keep analyses and schedules prepared by the client for the CPA and need not make them available to the client.

(2) A CPA may keep workpapers with information not reflected in the client's books (adjusting, closing, consolidating entries, etc.) until payment of fees due is received.

Interpretation 501-2. Discrimination on basis of race, color, religion, sex, age, or national origin is discreditable.

Interpretation 501-3. In audits of governmental grants, units, or other recipients of governmental monies, failure to follow appropriate governmental standards, procedures, etc. is discreditable.

Interpretation 501-4. Negligently making (or permitting or directing another to make) false or misleading journal entries is discreditable.

Interpretation 501-5. When a governmental body, commission, or other regulatory agency has requirements beyond those required by GAAS, members are required to follow them.

(1) Failure to follow these requirements is considered an act discreditable to the profession, unless the member discloses in the report that such requirements were not followed and the reasons therefor.

Interpretation 501-6. Member who solicits or discloses May 1996 or later Uniform CPA Examination question(s) and/or answer(s) without AICPA written authorization has committed an act discreditable to profession in violation of Rule 501.

Interpretation 501-7. A member who fails to comply with applicable federal, state, or local laws and regulations regarding the timely filing of his or her personal tax returns, or the timely remittance of all payroll and other taxes collected on behalf of others has committed an act discreditable to the profession.

Interpretation 501. In some engagements, government regulators prohibit indemnification or limitation of liability agreements. If the CPA engages in such agreements when they are prohibited, he or she has committed an act discreditable to the profession.

Rule 502 Advertising and Other Forms of Solicitation. In public practice, shall not seek to obtain clients by false, misleading, deceptive advertising or other forms of solicitation.

Interpretation 502-1. (Deleted)

Interpretation 502-2. Advertising that is false, misleading or deceptive is prohibited, including advertising that

(1) Creates false or unjustified expectations
(2) Implies ability to influence a court, tribunal, regulatory agency or similar body or official
(3) Contains unrealistic estimates of future fees
(4) Would lead a reasonable person to misunderstand or be deceived

Interpretations 502-3, 4. (Deleted)

Interpretation 502-5. CPA may render services to clients of third parties as long as all promotion efforts are within Code.

Rule 503 Commissions and Referral Fees.

(1) A member in public practice may not accept a commission for recommending a product or service to a client when the member or member's firm also performs any of the following services for that client:

    (a) Audits or reviews of financial statements
    (b) Compilations when the member is independent and expects that a third party may use the financial statements
    (c) Examinations of prospective financial information

(2) A member who receives a commission [not prohibited in (1) above] shall disclose that fact to the client.
(3) A member who accepts a referral fee for recommending or referring any service of a CPA to any person or entity, or who pays a referral fee to obtain a client, must disclose such acceptance or payment to the client.

Rule 504. (Deleted)

Rule 505 Form of Practice and Name.
Member may practice public accounting in form of proprietorship, partnership, professional corporation, etc. and may not practice under a misleading name.

(1) May include past partners.
(2) An individual may practice in name of a former partnership for up to two years (applies when all other partners have died or withdrawn).
(3) A firm name may include a fictitious name or indicate specialization if name is not misleading.
(4) Firm may not designate itself as member of AICPA unless all partners or shareholders are members.
(5) Appendix B to Code of Professional Conduct allows non-CPA ownership of CPA firms under certain conditions.

    (a) 66 2/3% (super majority) of ownership (both voting rights and financial interest) must belong to CPAs. Non-CPA owners must be involved in own principal occupation, not practice accounting, and not hold selves out as CPAs.
    (b) CPAs must have ultimate responsibility in firm, not non-CPAs.
    (c) Non-CPA owners must abide by AICPA Code of Professional Conduct, CPE requirements and hold a baccalaureate degree.
    (d) Non-CPAs not eligible to be members of AICPA.

Interpretation 505-1. (Deleted)

Interpretation 505-2. Applicability of rules to members who operate a separate business that provides accounting services.

(1) A member in public practice who participates in the operation of a separate business that performs accounting, tax, etc. services must observe all of the Rules of Conduct.

(2) A member not otherwise in the practice of public accounting must observe the Rules of Conduct if the member holds out as a CPA and performs for a client any professional services included in public accounting.

Interpretation 505-3. CPAs with attest practices that are organized as alternative practice structures must remain financially and otherwise responsible for the attest work.

Rule 501, 502, 503, 505 Ethics Rulings and Other Responsibilities Ethics Rulings

Due to rescinding the advertising and solicitation prohibition, the majority of the ethics rulings have been suspended.

2. A member may permit a bank to collect notes issued by a client in payment of fees.

3. A CPA employed by a firm with non-CPA practitioners must comply with the rules of conduct. If a partner of such a firm is a CPA, the CPA is responsible for all persons associated with the firm to comply with the rules of conduct.

33. A member who is a course instructor has the responsibility to determine that the advertising materials promoting the course are within the bounds of Rule 502.

38. A member who is controller of a bank may place his CPA title on bank stationery and in paid advertisements listing the officers and directors of the bank.

78. CPAs who are also attorneys may so indicate on their letterhead.

108. Members interviewed by the press should observe the Code of Professional Conduct and not provide the press with any information for publication that the member could not publish himself.

117. A member may be a director of a consumer credit company if he is not the auditor.

134. Members who share offices, employees, etc., may not indicate a partnership exists unless a partnership agreement **is** in effect.

135. CPA firms that are members of an association cannot use letterhead that indicates a partnership rather than an association.

136. Where a firm consisting of a CPA and a non-CPA is dissolved, and an audit is continued to be serviced by both, the audit opinion should be signed by both individuals, such that a partnership is not indicated.

137. The designation "nonproprietary partner" should not be used to describe personnel as it may be misleading.

138. A member may be a partner of a firm of public accountants when all other personnel are not certified, and at the same time practice separately as a CPA.

140. A partnership practicing under the name of the managing partner who is seeking election to high office may continue to use the managing partner's name plus "and Company" if the managing partner is elected and withdraws from the partnership.

141. A CPA in partnership with a non-CPA is ethically responsible for all acts of the partnership and those of the non-CPA partner.

144. A CPA firm may use an established firm name in a different state even though there is a difference in the roster of partners.

145. Newly merged CPA firms may practice under a title that includes the name of a previously retired partner from one of the firms.

176. A CPA firm's name, logo, etc., may be imprinted on newsletters and similar publications if the CPA has a reasonable basis to conclude that the information is not fake, misleading, or deceptive.

177. Performing centralized billing services for a doctor is a public accounting service and must be conducted in accordance with the Code.

179. CPA firms which are members of an association (for purposes of joint advertising, training, etc.) should practice in their own names, although they may indicate membership in the association.

183. A CPA firm may designate itself "Accredited Personal Financial Specialists" on its letterhead and in marketing materials if all partners or shareholders of the firm currently have the AICPA-awarded designation.

184. Identical to Ruling 18 under Rule 302.

185. A member may purchase a product from a supplier and resell it to a client at a profit without disclosing the profit to the client.

186. A member may contract for support services from a computer-hardware maintenance servicer and bill them to a client at a profit without disclosing the profit to the client.

187. Identical to Ruling 19 under Rule 302.

188. When a member refers products to clients through distributors and agents, the member may not perform for those clients the services described in Rule 503 [part (1) of the outline of Rule 503].

189. When individuals associated with a client entity have an internal dispute, and have separately asked a member for client records, the member need only supply them once, and to the individual who previously has been designated or held out as the client's representative.

190. A member who is in a partnership with non-CPAs may sign reports with the firm name and below it affix his own signature with the designation "Certified Public Accountant" providing it is clear that the partnership is not being held out as composed entirely of CPAs.

191. If a member (not an owner) of a firm is terminated, he/she may not take copies of the firm's client files without the firm's permission.

192. A member who provides for a contingent fee investment advisory services, or refers for a commission products or services to the owners, officers, or employees of an attest client would not violate Rule 302 or Rule 503 with respect to the client.

4. Responsibilities in Consulting Services

    a. In January of 1991 a new series of pronouncements on consulting services, *Statements on Standards for Consulting Services* (SSCS), became effective. This series of pronouncements replaces the three *Statements on Standards for Management Advisory Services*. These standards apply to CPAs in public practice who provide consulting services.

    b. Outline of SSCS 1 Definitions and Standards

       (1) Comparison of consulting and attest services

          (a) **Attest services**—Practitioner expresses a conclusion about the reliability of a written assertion that is the responsibility of another party (the asserter)

          (b) **Consulting services**—Practitioner develops the findings, conclusions and recommendations presented, generally only for the use and benefit of the client; the nature of the work is determined solely by agreement between the practitioner and the client

          (c) Performance of consulting services **for an attest client** requires that the practitioner maintain independence and does not in and of itself impair independence

          NOTE: While one must remain objective in performing consulting services, independence is not required unless the practitioner also performs attest (e.g., audit) services for that client.

       (2) Definitions

          (a) **Consulting services practitioner**—A CPA holding out as a CPA (i.e., a CPA in public practice) while engaged in the performance of a consulting service for a client

          (b) **Consulting process**—Analytical approach and process applied in a consulting service

             1] This definition **excludes** services subject to other AICPA technical standards on auditing (SAS), other attest services (SSAE), compilations and reviews (SSARS), most tax engagements, and recommendations made during one of these engagements as a direct result of having performed these excluded services

          (c) **Consulting services**—Professional services that employ the practitioner's technical skills, education, observations, experiences, and knowledge of the consulting process

       (3) Types of consulting services

          (a) **Consultations**—Provide counsel in a short time frame, based mostly, if not entirely, on existing personal knowledge about the client

             1] Examples: reviewing and commenting on a client business plan, suggesting software for further client investigation

          (b) **Advisory services**—Develop findings, conclusions and recommendations for client consideration and decision making

             1] Examples: Operational review and improvement study, analysis of accounting system, strategic planning assistance, information system advice

          (c) **Implementation services**—Place an action plan into effect

             1] Examples: Installing and supporting computer system, executing steps to improve productivity, assisting with mergers

          (d) **Transaction services**—Provide services related to a specific client transaction, generally with a third party

             1] Examples: Insolvency services, valuation services, information related to financing, analysis of a possible merger or acquisition, litigation services

          (e) **Staff and other support services**—Provide appropriate staff and possibly other support to perform tasks specified by client

             1] Examples: Data processing facilities management, computer programming, bankruptcy trusteeship, controllership activities

          (f) **Product services**—Provide client with a product and associated support services

1] Examples: Sale, delivery, installation, and implementation of training programs, computer software, and systems development

(4) Standards for Consulting Services

(a) General Standards of Rule 201 of Code of Professional Conduct

1] Professional competence
2] Due professional care
3] Planning and supervision
4] Sufficient relevant data

(b) Additional standards established for this area (under Rule 202 of Code of Professional Conduct)

1] Client interest—Must serve client interest while maintaining **integrity** and **objectivity**
2] Understanding with client—Establish either in **writing or orally**
3] Communication with client—Inform client of any conflicts of interest, significant reservations about engagement, significant engagement findings

(c) Professional judgment must be used in applying SSCS

1] Example: Practitioner not required to decline or withdraw from a consulting engagement when there are mutually agreed upon limitations with respect to gathering relevant data

5. Responsibilities in Personal Financial Planning

a. Definition, scope and standards of personal financial planning

(1) Personal financial planning engagements are only those that involve developing strategies and making recommendations to assist a client in defining and achieving personal financial goals

(2) Personal financial planning engagements involve all of following

(a) Defining engagement objectives
(b) Planning specific procedures appropriate to engagement
(c) Developing basis for recommendations
(d) Communicating recommendations to client
(e) Identifying tasks for taking action on planning decisions

(3) Other engagements may also include

(a) Assisting client to take action on planning decisions
(b) Monitoring client's progress in achieving goals
(c) Updating recommendations and helping client revise planning decisions

(4) Personal financial planning does not include services that are limited to, for example

(a) Compiling personal financial statements
(b) Projecting future taxes
(c) Tax compliance, including, but not limited to, preparation of tax returns
(d) Tax advice or consultations

(5) CPA should act in conformity with AICPA Code of Professional Conduct

(a) Rule 102, Integrity and Objectivity

1] A member shall maintain objectivity and integrity, be free of conflicts of interest, and not knowingly misrepresent facts or subordinate his/her judgment to others

(b) Rule 201

1] A member shall undertake only those professional services that member can reasonably expect to be completed with professional competence, shall exercise due professional care in the performance of professional services, shall adequately plan and supervise performance of professional services, and shall obtain sufficient relevant data to afford a reasonable basis for conclusions or recommendations

(c) Rule 301, Confidential Client Information

    e. Company must disclose several items if a director has resigned or refused to stand for reelection because of disagreement with company's practices, operations or policies, or if director has been removed for cause

      (1) Company must disclose such items as circumstances regarding disagreement with company

    f. If new executive officer is appointed, company must disclose information such as his or her name, the position, and description of any material terms of employment agreement between company and officer

5. Act lists several specific service categories that issuer's public accounting firm cannot legally do, even if approved by audit committee, such as

    a. Bookkeeping or other services relating to financial statements or accounting records
    b. Financial information systems design and/or implementation
    c. Appraisal services
    d. Internal audit outsourcing services
    e. Management functions
    f. Actuarial services
    g. Investment or broker-dealer services
    h. Certain tax services, such as tax planning for potentially abusive tax shelters
    i. Board permitted to exempt (on case by case basis) services of audit firm for audit client

Note that Act does **not** restrict auditor from performing these services to nonaudit clients or to private companies. Also, the Act permits auditor as a registered public accounting firm to perform nonaudit services not specifically prohibited (e.g., tax services) when approved by issuer's audit committee

6. Act requires that both assigned audit partner having primary responsibility for a certain audit and audit partner who reviews audit can do the audit services for that issuer for only five consecutive years

    a. If public company has hired employee of an audit firm to be its CEO, CFO, or CAO within previous year, that audit firm may not audit that public company

7. Act requires increased disclosure of off-balance-sheet transactions
8. Act mandates that pro forma financial disclosures be reconciled with figures done under GAAP
9. Act creates new federal laws against destruction or tampering with audit workpapers or documents that are to be used in official proceedings
10. Act increases protection of whistleblowers by better protections from retaliation because of participation in proceedings against securities fraud

    a. Also, provides that employees may report securities fraud directly to audit committee to provide information anonymously and confidentially

11. Public Companies may not make or modify personal loans to officers or directors with few exceptions
12. Annual reports filed with SEC that contain financial statements need to incorporate all material corrections noted by CPA firms
13. Each company must disclose on current basis information on financial condition that SEC determines is useful to public
14. SEC authorized to discipline professionals practicing before SEC

    a. SEC may censure, temporarily bar or permanently bar him/her for

      (1) Lack of qualifications needed
      (2) Improper professional conduct
      (3) Willful violation of helping another violate securities laws or regulations

15. Public Company Accounting Oversight Board set up to register CPAs providing auditing services to public entities
16. Auditor reports to audit committee
17. Auditors to retain workpapers for five years

    a. Failure to do so is punishable by prison term of up to ten years

18. Sarbanes-Oxley Act directed SEC to perform various tasks including several studies to formulate regulations; some of these studies have deadlines in the future and are expected to be used to promul-

gate new important regulations—others have been completed, resulted in regulations by SEC and have force of law including the following

   a. Require disclosure of differences between pro forma financial results and GAAP
   b. Require that "critical" accounting policies be reported from auditors to audit committee
   c. SEC will tell NYSE and NASDAQ to prohibit any public company from being listed whose audit committee does not meet specified requirements on auditor appointment, oversight, and compensation

       (1) Only independent directors can serve on audit committee

   d. Companies required to disclose if they have adopted a code of ethics
   e. Names of "financial experts" required who serve on companies' audit committees
   f. Actions prohibited that fraudulently manipulate or mislead auditors
   g. New conflict of interest rules for analysts
   h. SEC may petition courts to freeze payments by companies that are extraordinary

19. CEOs and CFOs of most large companies listed on public stock exchanges are now required to certify financial statements filed with SEC

   a. This generally means that they certify that information "fairly represents in all material respects the financial conditions and results of operations" of those companies and that

       (1) Signing officer reviewed report
       (2) Company's report does not contain any untrue statements of material facts or does not omit any statements of material facts to the best of his/her knowledge
       (3) Officers have internal control system in place to allow honest certification of financial statements

          (a) Or if any deficiencies in internal control exist, they must be disclosed to auditors

20. Blackout periods established for issuers of certain security transaction types that limit companies' purchase, sale, or transfer of funds in individual accounts
21. Stiffer penalties for other white-collar crimes including federal law covering mail fraud and wire fraud

G. Additional Statutory Liability against Accountants

   1. Auditors are required to use adequate procedures to uncover illegal activity of client
   2. Civil liability is proportional to degree of responsibility

     a. One type of responsibility is through auditors' own carelessness
     b. Another type of responsibility is based on auditor's assisting in improper activities that s/he is aware or should be aware of

MULTIPLE-CHOICE QUESTIONS (1-66)

1. Which of the following best describes what is meant by the term generally accepted auditing standards?
   a. Rules acknowledged by the accounting profession because of their universal application.
   b. Pronouncements issued by the Auditing Standards Board.
   c. Measures of the quality of the auditor's performance.
   d. Procedures to be used to gather evidence to support financial statements.

2. For which of the following can a member of the AICPA receive an automatic expulsion from the AICPA?

   I. Member is convicted of a felony.
   II. Member files his own fraudulent tax return.
   III. Member files fraudulent tax return for a client knowing that it is fraudulent.

   a. I only.
   b. I and II only.
   c. I and III only.
   d. I, II, and III.

3. Which of the following is an example of a safeguard implemented by the client that might mitigate a threat to independence?
   a. Required continuing education for all attest engagement team members.
   b. An effective corporate governance structure.
   c. Required second partner review of an attest engagement.
   d. Management selection of the CPA firm.

4. Which of the following is a "self review" threat to member independence?
   a. An engagement team member has a spouse that serves as CFO of the attest client.
   b. A second partner review is required on all attest engagements.
   c. An engagement team member prepares invoices for the attest client.
   d. An engagement team member has a direct financial interest in the attest client.

5. According to the standards of the profession, which of the following circumstances will prevent a CPA performing audit engagements from being independent?
   a. Obtaining a collateralized automobile loan from a financial institution client.
   b. Litigation with a client relating to billing for consulting services for which the amount is immaterial.
   c. Employment of the CPA's spouse as a client's director of internal audit.
   d. Acting as an honorary trustee for a not-for-profit organization client.

6. The profession's ethical standards most likely would be considered to have been violated when a CPA represents that specific consulting services will be performed for a stated fee and it is apparent at the time of the representation that the

   a. Actual fee would be substantially higher.
   b. Actual fee would be substantially lower than the fees charged by other CPAs for comparable services.
   c. CPA would **not** be independent.
   d. Fee was a competitive bid.

7. According to the ethical standards of the profession, which of the following acts is generally prohibited?
   a. Issuing a modified report explaining a failure to follow a governmental regulatory agency's standards when conducting an attest service for a client.
   b. Revealing confidential client information during a quality review of a professional practice by a team from the state CPA society.
   c. Accepting a contingent fee for representing a client in an examination of the client's federal tax return by an IRS agent.
   d. Retaining client records after an engagement is terminated prior to completion and the client has demanded their return.

8. According to the profession's ethical standards, which of the following events may justify a departure from a Statement of Financial Accounting Standards?

	New legislation	Evolution of a new form of business transaction
a.	No	Yes
b.	Yes	No
c.	Yes	Yes
d.	No	No

9. May a CPA hire for the CPA's public accounting firm a non-CPA systems analyst who specializes in developing computer systems?
   a. Yes, provided the CPA is qualified to perform each of the specialist's tasks.
   b. Yes, provided the CPA is able to supervise the specialist and evaluate the specialist's end product.
   c. No, because non-CPA professionals are **not** permitted to be associated with CPA firms in public practice.
   d. No, because developing computer systems is **not** recognized as a service performed by public accountants.

10. Stephanie Seals is a CPA who is working as a controller for Brentwood Corporation. She is not in public practice. Which statement is true?
    a. She may use the CPA designation on her business cards if she also puts her employment title on them.
    b. She may use the CPA designation on her business cards as long as she does not mention Brentwood Corporation or her title as controller.
    c. She may use the CPA designation on company transmittals but not on her business cards.
    d. She may not use the CPA designation because she is not in public practice.

11. According to the standards of the profession, which of the following activities would most likely **not** impair a CPA's independence?

a. Providing advisory services for a client.
b. Contracting with a client to supervise the client's office personnel.
c. Signing a client's checks in emergency situations.
d. Accepting a luxurious gift from a client.

12. Which of the following reports may be issued only by an accountant who is independent of a client?

    a. Standard report on an examination of a financial forecast.
    b. Report on consulting services.
    c. Compilation report on historical financial statements.
    d. Compilation report on a financial projection.

13. According to the standards of the profession, which of the following activities may be required in exercising due care?

	Consulting with experts	Obtaining specialty accreditation
a.	Yes	Yes
b.	Yes	No
c.	No	Yes
d.	No	No

14. Larry Sampson is a CPA and is serving as an expert witness in a trial concerning a corporation's financial statements. Which of the following is(are) true?

I. Sampson's status as an expert witness is based upon his specialized knowledge, experience, and training.
II. Sampson is required by AICPA ruling to present his position objectively.
III. Sampson may regard himself as acting as an advocate.

    a. I only.
    b. I and II only.
    c. I and III only.
    d. III only.

15. According to the ethical standards of the profession, which of the following acts is generally prohibited?

    a. Purchasing a product from a third party and reselling it to a client.
    b. Writing a financial management newsletter promoted and sold by a publishing company.
    c. Accepting a commission for recommending a product to an audit client.
    d. Accepting engagements obtained through the efforts of third parties.

16. To exercise due professional care an auditor should

    a. Critically review the judgment exercised by those assisting in the audit.
    b. Examine all available corroborating evidence supporting managements assertions.
    c. Design the audit to detect all instances of illegal acts.
    d. Attain the proper balance of professional experience and formal education.

17. Kar, CPA, is a staff auditor participating in the audit engagement of Fort, Inc. Which of the following circumstances impairs Kar's independence?

    a. During the period of the professional engagement, Fort gives Kar tickets to a football game worth $75.
    b. Kar owns stock in a corporation that Fort's 401(k) plan also invests in.
    c. Kar's friend, an employee of another local accounting firm, prepares Fort's tax returns.
    d. Kar's sibling is director of internal audit at Fort.

18. On June 1, 2006, a CPA obtained a $100,000 personal loan from a financial institution client for whom the CPA provided compilation services. The loan was fully secured and considered material to the CPA's net worth. The CPA paid the loan in full on December 31, 2007. On April 3, 2007, the client asked the CPA to audit the client's financial statements for the year ended December 31, 2007. Is the CPA considered independent with respect to the audit of the client's December 31, 2007 financial statements?

    a. Yes, because the loan was fully secured.
    b. Yes, because the CPA was **not** required to be independent at the time the loan was granted.
    c. No, because the CPA had a loan with the client during the period of a professional engagement.
    d. No, because the CPA had a loan with the client during the period covered by the financial statements.

19. Which of the following statements is(are) correct regarding a CPA employee of a CPA firm taking copies of information contained in client files when the CPA leaves the firm?

I. A CPA leaving a firm may take copies of information contained in client files to assist another firm in serving that client.
II. A CPA leaving a firm may take copies of information contained in client files as a method of gaining technical expertise.

    a. I only.
    b. II only.
    c. Both I and II.
    d. Neither I nor II.

20. Which of the following statements is correct regarding an accountant's working papers?

    a. The accountant owns the working papers and generally may disclose them as the accountant sees fit.
    b. The client owns the working papers but the accountant has custody of them until the accountant's bill is paid in full.
    c. The accountant owns the working papers but generally may **not** disclose them without the client's consent or a court order.
    d. The client owns the working papers but, in the absence of the accountant's consent, may **not** disclose them without a court order.

21. According to the profession's standards, which of the following would be considered consulting services?

	Advisory services	Implementation services	Product services
a.	Yes	Yes	Yes
b.	Yes	Yes	No
c.	Yes	No	Yes
d.	No	Yes	Yes

22. According to the standards of the profession, which of the following events would require a CPA performing a consulting services engagement for a nonaudit client to withdraw from the engagement?

 I. The CPA has a conflict of interest that is disclosed to the client and the client consents to the CPA continuing the engagement.
 II. The CPA fails to obtain a written understanding from the client concerning the scope of the engagement.

    a.   I only.
    b.   II only.
    c.   Both I and II.
    d.   Neither I nor II.

23. Which of the following services may a CPA perform in carrying out a consulting service for a client?

 I. Analysis of the client's accounting system.
 II. Review of the client's prepared business plan.
 III. Preparation of information for obtaining financing.

    a.   I and II only.
    b.   I and III only.
    c.   II and III only.
    d.   I, II, and III.

24. Under the Statements on Standards for Consulting Services, which of the following statements best reflects a CPA's responsibility when undertaking a consulting services engagement? The CPA must

    a.   Not seek to modify any agreement made with the client.
    b.   Not perform any attest services for the client.
    c.   Inform the client of significant reservations concerning the benefits of the engagement.
    d.   Obtain a written understanding with the client concerning the time for completion of the engagement.

25. Which of the following services is a CPA generally required to perform when conducting a personal financial planning engagement?

    a.   Assisting the client to identify tasks that are essential in order to act on planning decisions.
    b.   Assisting the client to take action on planning decisions.
    c.   Monitoring progress in achieving goals.
    d.   Updating recommendations and revising planning decisions.

26. Cable Corp. orally engaged Drake & Co., CPAs, to audit its financial statements. Cable's management informed Drake that it suspected the accounts receivable were materially overstated. Though the financial statements Drake audited included a materially overstated accounts receivable balance, Drake issued an unqualified opinion. Cable used the financial statements to obtain a loan to expand its operations. Cable defaulted on the loan and incurred a substantial loss.

If Cable sues Drake for negligence in failing to discover the overstatement, Drake's best defense would be that Drake did **not**

    a.   Have privity of contract with Cable.
    b.   Sign an engagement letter.
    c.   Perform the audit recklessly or with an intent to deceive.
    d.   Violate generally accepted auditing standards in performing the audit.

27. Which of the following statements best describes whether a CPA has met the required standard of care in conducting an audit of a client's financial statements?

    a.   The client's expectations with regard to the accuracy of audited financial statements.
    b.   The accuracy of the financial statements and whether the statements conform to generally accepted accounting principles.
    c.   Whether the CPA conducted the audit with the same skill and care expected of an ordinarily prudent CPA under the circumstances.
    d.   Whether the audit was conducted to investigate and discover all acts of fraud.

28. Ford & Co., CPAs, issued an unqualified opinion on Owens Corp.'s financial statements. Relying on these financial statements, Century Bank lent Owens $750,000. Ford was unaware that Century would receive a copy of the financial statements or that Owens would use them to obtain a loan. Owens defaulted on the loan.

To succeed in a common law fraud action against Ford, Century must prove, in addition to other elements, that Century was

    a.   Free from contributory negligence.
    b.   In privity of contract with Ford.
    c.   Justified in relying on the financial statements.
    d.   In privity of contract with Owens.

29. When performing an audit, a CPA
    a.   Must exercise the level of care, skill, and judgment expected of a reasonably prudent CPA under the circumstances.
    b.   Must strictly adhere to generally accepted accounting principles.
    c.   Is strictly liable for failing to discover client fraud.
    d.   Is **not** liable unless the CPA commits gross negligence or intentionally disregards generally accepted auditing standards.

30. When performing an audit, a CPA will most likely be considered negligent when the CPA fails to

    a.   Detect all of a client's fraudulent activities.
    b.   Include a negligence disclaimer in the client engagement letter.
    c.   Warn a client of known internal control weaknesses.
    d.   Warn a client's customers of embezzlement by the client's employees.

31. A CPA's duty of due care to a client most likely will be breached when a CPA

    a.   Gives a client an oral instead of written report.
    b.   Gives a client incorrect advice based on an honest error of judgment.
    c.   Fails to give tax advice that saves the client money.
    d.   Fails to follow generally accepted auditing standards.

32. Which of the following elements, if present, would support a finding of constructive fraud on the part of a CPA?

    a.   Gross negligence in applying generally accepted auditing standards.
    b.   Ordinary negligence in applying generally accepted accounting principles.

    c.   Identified third-party users.
    d.   Scienter.

33. If a CPA recklessly departs from the standards of due care when conducting an audit, the CPA will be liable to third parties who are unknown to the CPA based on
    a.   Negligence.
    b.   Gross negligence.
    c.   Strict liability.
    d.   Criminal deceit.

34. In a common law action against an accountant, lack of privity is a viable defense if the plaintiff
    a.   Is the client's creditor who sues the accountant for negligence.
    b.   Can prove the presence of gross negligence that amounts to a reckless disregard for the truth.
    c.   Is the accountant's client.
    d.   Bases the action upon fraud.

35. A CPA audited the financial statements of Shelly Company. The CPA was negligent in the audit. Sanco, a supplier of Shelly, is upset because Sanco had extended Shelly a high credit limit based on the financial statements which were incorrect. Which of the following statements is the most correct?
    a.   In most states, both Shelly and Sanco can recover from the CPA for damages due to the negligence.
    b.   States that use the Ultramares decision will allow both Shelly and Sanco to recover.
    c.   In most states, Sanco cannot recover as a mere foreseeable third party.
    d.   Generally, Sanco can recover but Shelly cannot.

36. Under the Ultramares rule, to which of the following parties will an accountant be liable for negligence?

	Parties in privity	Foreseen parties
a.	Yes	Yes
b.	Yes	No
c.	No	Yes
d.	No	No

Items 37 and 38 are based on the following:

    While conducting an audit, Larson Associates, CPAs, failed to detect material misstatements included in its client's financial statements. Larson's unqualified opinion was included with the financial statements in a registration statement and prospectus for a public offering of securities made by the client. Larson knew that its opinion and the financial statements would be used for this purpose.

37. In a suit by a purchaser against Larson for common law negligence, Larson's best defense would be that the
    a.   Audit was conducted in accordance with generally accepted auditing standards.
    b.   Client was aware of the misstatements.
    c.   Purchaser was **not** in privity of contract with Larson.
    d.   Identity of the purchaser was **not** known to Larson at the time of the audit.

38. In a suit by a purchaser against Larson for common law fraud, Larson's best defense would be that

    a.   Larson did **not** have actual or constructive knowledge of the misstatements.
    b.   Larson's client knew or should have known of the misstatements.
    c.   Larson did **not** have actual knowledge that the purchaser was an intended beneficiary of the audit.
    d.   Larson was **not** in privity of contract with its client.

39. Quincy bought Teal Corp. common stock in an offering registered under the Securities Act of 1933. Worth & Co., CPAs, gave an unqualified opinion on Teal's financial statements that were included in the registration statement filed with the SEC. Quincy sued Worth under the provisions of the 1933 Act that deal with omission of facts required to be in the registration statement. Quincy must prove that
    a.   There was fraudulent activity by Worth.
    b.   There was a material misstatement in the financial statements.
    c.   Quincy relied on Worth's opinion.
    d.   Quincy was in privity with Worth.

40. Beckler & Associates, CPAs, audited and gave an unqualified opinion on the financial statements of Queen Co. The financial statements contained misstatements that resulted in a material overstatement of Queen's net worth. Queen provided the audited financial statements to Mac Bank in connection with a loan made by Mac to Queen. Beckler knew that the financial statements would be provided to Mac. Queen defaulted on the loan. Mac sued Beckler to recover for its losses associated with Queen's default. Which of the following must Mac prove in order to recover?

    I.   Beckler was negligent in conducting the audit.
   II.   Mac relied on the financial statements.

    a.   I only.
    b.   II only.
    c.   Both I and II.
    d.   Neither I nor II.

Items 41 and 42 are based on the following:

    Dart Corp. engaged Jay Associates, CPAs, to assist in a public stock offering. Jay audited Dart's financial statements and gave an unqualified opinion, despite knowing that the financial statements contained misstatements. Jay's opinion was included in Dart's registration statement. Larson purchased shares in the offering and suffered a loss when the stock declined in value after the misstatements became known.

41. In a suit against Jay and Dart under the Section 11 liability provisions of the Securities Act of 1933, Larson must prove that
    a.   Jay knew of the misstatements.
    b.   Jay was negligent.
    c.   The misstatements contained in Dart's financial statements were material.
    d.   The unqualified opinion contained in the registration statement was relied on by Larson.

42. If Larson succeeds in the Section 11 suit against Dart, Larson would be entitled to
    a.   Damages of three times the original public offering price.
    b.   Rescind the transaction.

  c.   Monetary damages only.
  d.   Damages, but only if the shares were resold before the suit was started.

Items 43 and 44 are based on the following:

Under the liability provisions of Section 11 of the Securities Act of 1933, a CPA may be liable to any purchaser of a security for certifying materially misstated financial statements that are included in the security's registration statement.

43. Under Section 11, a CPA usually will **not** be liable to the purchaser
  a.   If the purchaser is contributorily negligent.
  b.   If the CPA can prove due diligence.
  c.   Unless the purchaser can prove privity with the CPA.
  d.   Unless the purchaser can prove scienter on the part of the CPA.

44. Under Section 11, which of the following must be proven by a purchaser of the security?

	Reliance on the financial statements	Fraud by the CPA
a.	Yes	Yes
b.	Yes	No
c.	No	Yes
d.	No	No

45. Ocean and Associates, CPAs, audited the financial statements of Drain Corporation. As a result of Ocean's negligence in conducting the audit, the financial statements included material misstatements. Ocean was unaware of this fact. The financial statements and Ocean's unqualified opinion were included in a registration statement and prospectus for an original public offering of stock by Drain. Sharp purchased shares in the offering. Sharp received a copy of the prospectus prior to the purchase but did not read it. The shares declined in value as a result of the misstatements in Drain's financial statements becoming known. Under which of the following Acts is Sharp most likely to prevail in a lawsuit against Ocean?

	Securities Exchange Act of 1934, Section 10(b), Rule 10b-5	Securities Act of 1933, Section 11
a.	Yes	Yes
b.	Yes	No
c.	No	Yes
d.	No	No

46. Danvy, a CPA, performed an audit for Lank Corporation. Danvy also performed an S-1 review to review events subsequent to the balance sheet date. If Danvy fails to further investigate suspicious facts, under which of these can he be found negligent?
  a.   The audit but not the review.
  b.   The review but not the audit.
  c.   Neither the audit nor the review.
  d.   Both the audit and the review.

47. Dart Corp. engaged Jay Associates, CPAs, to assist in a public stock offering. Jay audited Dart's financial statements and gave an unqualified opinion, despite knowing that the financial statements contained misstatements. Jay's opinion was included in Dart's registration statement. Larson purchased shares in the offering and suffered a loss

when the stock declined in value after the misstatements became known.

In a suit against Jay under the antifraud provisions of Section 10(b) and Rule 10b-5 of the Securities Exchange Act of 1934, Larson must prove all of the following **except**
  a.   Larson was an intended user of the false registration statement.
  b.   Larson relied on the false registration statement.
  c.   The transaction involved some form of interstate commerce.
  d.   Jay acted with intentional disregard of the truth.

48. Under the antifraud provisions of Section 10(b) of the Securities Exchange Act of 1934, a CPA may be liable if the CPA acted
  a.   Negligently.
  b.   With independence.
  c.   Without due diligence.
  d.   Without good faith.

49. Under Section 11 of the Securities Act of 1933, which of the following standards may a CPA use as a defense?

	Generally accepted accounting principles	Generally accepted fraud detection standards
a.	Yes	Yes
b.	Yes	No
c.	No	Yes
d.	No	No

50. Dart Corp. engaged Jay Associates, CPAs, to assist in a public stock offering. Jay audited Dart's financial statements and gave an unqualified opinion, despite knowing that the financial statements contained misstatements. Jay's opinion was included in Dart's registration statement. Larson purchased shares in the offering and suffered a loss when the stock declined in value after the misstatements became known.

If Larson succeeds in the Section 10(b) and Rule 10b-5 suit, Larson would be entitled to
  a.   Only recover the original public offering price.
  b.   Only rescind the transaction.
  c.   The amount of any loss caused by the fraud.
  d.   Punitive damages.

51. Which of the following statements is correct with respect to ownership, possession, or access to a CPA firm's audit working papers?
  a.   Working papers may **never** be obtained by third parties unless the client consents.
  b.   Working papers are **not** transferable to a purchaser of a CPA practice unless the client consents.
  c.   Working papers are subject to the privileged communication rule which, in most jurisdictions, prevents any third-party access to the working papers.
  d.   Working papers are the client's exclusive property.

52. Which of the following statements is correct regarding a CPA's working papers? The working papers must be
  a.   Transferred to another accountant purchasing the CPA's practice even if the client hasn't given permission.
  b.   Transferred permanently to the client if demanded.
  c.   Turned over to any government agency that requests them.
  d.   Turned over pursuant to a valid federal court subpoena.

53. To which of the following parties may a CPA partnership provide its working papers, without being lawfully subpoenaed or without the client's consent?

    a.   The IRS.

    b.   The FASB.

    c.   Any surviving partner(s) on the death of a partner.

    d.   A CPA before purchasing a partnership interest in the firm.

54. To which of the following parties may a CPA partnership orvide its working papers without either the client's consent or a lawful subpoena?

	The IRS	The FASB
a.	Yes	Yes
b.	Yes	No
c.	No	Yes
d.	No	No

55. A CPA is permitted to disclose confidential client information without the consent of the client to

   I.   Another CPA who has purchased the CPA's tax practice.

   II.   Another CPA firm if the information concerns suspected tax return irregularities.

   III.   A state CPA society voluntary quality control review board.

    a.   I and III only.

    b.   II and III only.

    c.   II only.

    d.   III only.

56. Thorp, CPA, was engaged to audit Ivor Co.'s financial statements. During the audit, Thorp discovered that Ivor's inventory contained stolen goods. Ivor was indicted and Thorp was subpoenaed to testify at the criminal trial. Ivor claimed accountant-client privilege to prevent Thorp from testifying. Which of the following statements is correct regarding Ivor's claim?

    a.   Ivor can claim an accountant-client privilege only in states that have enacted a statute creating such a privilege.

    b.   Ivor can claim an accountant-client privilege only in federal courts.

    c.   The accountant-client privilege can be claimed only in civil suits.

    d.   The accountant-client privilege can be claimed only to limit testimony to audit subject matter.

57. A violation of the profession's ethical standards most likely would have occurred when a CPA

    a.   Issued an unqualified opinion on the 2002 financial statements when fees for the 2001 audit were unpaid.

    b.   Recommended a controller's position description with candidate specifications to an audit client.

    c.   Purchased a CPA firm's practice of monthly write-ups for a percentage of fees to be received over a three-year period.

    d.   Made arrangements with a financial institution to collect notes issued by a client in payment of fees due for the current year's audit.

58. Which of the following statements concerning an accountant's disclosure of confidential client data is generally correct?

    a.   Disclosure may be made to any state agency without subpoena.

    b.   Disclosure may be made to any party on consent of the client.

    c.   Disclosure may be made to comply with an IRS audit request.

    d.   Disclosure may be made to comply with generally accepted accounting principles.

59. McGee is auditing Nevus Corporation and detects probable criminal activity by one of the employees. McGee believes this will have a material impact on the financial statements. The financial statements of Nevus Corporation are under the Securities Exchange Act of 1934. Which of the following is correct?

    a.   McGee should report this to the Securities Exchange Commission.

    b.   McGee should report this to the Justice Department.

    c.   McGee should report this to Nevus Corporation's audit committee or board of directors.

    d.   McGee will discharge his duty by requiring that a note of this be included in the financial statements.

60. Which of the following is an auditor not required to establish procedures for under the Private Securities Litigation Reform Act?

    a.   To develop a comprehensive internal control system.

    b.   To evaluate the ability of the firm to continue as a going concern.

    c.   To detect material illegal acts.

    d.   To identify material related-party transactions.

61. Which of the following is an auditor required to do under the Private Securities Litigation Reform Act concerning audits under the Federal Securities Exchange Act of 1934?

   I.   Establish procedures to detect material illegal acts of the client being audited.

   II.   Evaluate the ability of the firm being audited to continue as a going concern.

    a.   Neither I nor II.

    b.   I only.

    c.   II only.

    d.   Both I and II.

62. Lin, CPA, is auditing the financial statements of Exchange Corporation under the Federal Securities Exchange Act of 1934. He detects what he believes are probable material illegal acts. What is his duty under the Private Securities Litigation Reform Act?

    a.   He must inform the principal shareholders within ten days.

    b.   He must inform the audit committee or the board of directors.

    c.   He need not inform anyone, beyond requiring that the financial statements are presented fairly.

    d.   He should not inform anyone since he owes a duty of confidentiality to the client.

63. The Private Securities Litigation Reform Act

    a.   Applies only to securities not purchased from a stock exchange.

    b.   Does not apply to common stock of a publicly held corporation.

c. Amends the Federal Securities Act of 1933 and the Federal Securities Exchange Act of 1934.

d. Does not apply to preferred stock of a publicly held corporation.

64. Bran, CPA, audited Frank Corporation. The shareholders sued both Frank and Bran for securities fraud under the Federal Securities Exchange Act of 1934. The court determined that there was securities fraud and that Frank was 80% at fault and Bran was 20% at fault due to her negligence in the audit. Both Frank and Bran are solvent and the damages were determined to be $1 million. What is the maximum liability of Bran?

a. $0

b. $ 200,000

c. $ 500,000

d. $1,000,000

65. Which of the following nonattest services are auditors allowed to perform for a public company?

a. Bookkeeping services.

b. Appraisal services.

c. Tax services.

d. Internal audit services.

66. Which of the following Boards has the responsibility to regulate CPA firms that audit public companies?

a. Auditing Standards Board.

b. Public Oversight Board.

c. Public Company Accounting Oversight Board.

d. Accounting Standards Board.

2. Definitions

  a. Security—any note, stock, bond certificate of interest, debenture, investment contract, etc., or any interest or instrument commonly known as a security

    (1) General idea is that investor intends to make a profit on the investment through the efforts of others rather than through his/her own efforts

> *EXAMPLE: W is a general partner of WDC partnership in Washington, D.C. Usually, W's interest would not be considered a security because a general partner's interest typically involves participation in the business rather than mere investment.*

      (a) Includes limited partnership interests

      (b) Includes rights and warrants to subscribe for the above

      (c) Includes treasury stock

      (d) Investment contract is a security when money is invested in a common enterprise with profits to be derived from the effort of others

> *EXAMPLE: Blue Corporation in Florida owns several acres of orange trees. Blue is planning on selling a large portion of the land with the orange trees to several individuals in various states on a row-by-row basis. Each purchaser gets a deed and is required to purchase a management contract whereby Blue Corporation maintains all the land and oranges and then remits the net profits to the various purchasers. Even though it may appear that each individual purchased separately the land with the oranges and a management contract, the law looks at the "big picture" here. Since in reality the individuals are investing their money, and the profits are derived from the efforts of others, the law treats the above fact pattern as involving securities. Therefore, the Securities Acts apply.*

  b. Person—individual, corporation, partnership, unincorporated association, business trust, government

  c. Controlling person—has power, direct/indirect, to influence the management and/or policies of an issuer, whether by stock ownership, contract, position, or otherwise

> *EXAMPLE: A 51% stockholder is a controlling person by virtue of a majority ownership.*

> *EXAMPLE: A director of a corporation also owns 10% of that same corporation. By virtue of the stock ownership and position on the board of directors, he has a strong voice in the management of the corporation. Therefore, he is a controlling person.*

  d. Insiders—(applies to the Securities Exchange Act of 1934) include officers, directors, and owners of more than 10% of any class of issuer's equity securities

    (1) Note that debentures not included because not equity securities

    (2) For purposes of this law to avoid a "loophole," insiders include "beneficial owners" of more than 10% of the equity stock of issuer

      (a) To determine amount of "beneficial ownership," add to the individual's equity ownership, equity stock owned by

        1] Owner's spouse

        2] Owner's minor children

        3] Owner's relative in same house

        4] Owner's equity stock held in trust in which owner is beneficiary

> *EXAMPLE: X owns 6% of the common stock of ABC Company in Philadelphia. Her spouse owns 3% of ABC Company's common stock. Stock was also placed in the name of their two minor children, each owning 1% of ABC Company's common stock. X has beneficial ownership of 11% of the equity securities of ABC Company so she is an insider for the 1934 Act. Note that her husband also qualifies as an insider.*

> *EXAMPLE: Use the same facts as in the previous example except that all four individuals owned debentures of ABC Company. Since these are not equity securities, none qualifies as an insider.*

> *EXAMPLE: L is an officer who owns 4% of the common stock of XYZ Company in Washington, DC. Since L is an officer, s/he is an insider even though the ownership level is below 10%.*

  e. Underwriter—any person who has purchased from issuer with a view to the public distribution of any security or participates in such undertaking

    (1) Includes any person who offers or sells for issuer in connection with the distribution of any security

    (2) Does not include person who sells or distributes on commission for underwriter (i.e., dealers)

    f.   Sales of securities are covered by these laws

        (1) Issuance of securities as part of business reorganization (e.g., merger or consolidation) consti-tutes a sale and must be registered with SEC unless the issue otherwise qualifies as an exemption from the registration requirements of 1933 Act

        (2) Issuance of stock warrants is considered a sale so that requirements of 1933 Act must be met

        (3) Employee stock purchase plan is a sale and therefore must comply with the provisions of the 1933 Act

           (a) Company must also supply a prospectus to each employee to whom stock is offered

        (4) Stock dividends or splits are not sales

    g.   Registration statement—the statement required to be filed with SEC before initial sale of securities in interstate commerce

        (1) Includes financial statements and all other relevant information about the registrant's property, business, directors, principal officers, together with prospectus

        (2) Also, includes any amendment, report, or document filed as part of the statement or incorpo-rated therein by reference

        (3) It is against law to sell, offer to sell, or offer to purchase securities before filing registration statement

        (4) Registration statement and prospectus become public upon filing

           (a) Effective date of registration statement is 20th day after filing

           (b) Against law to sell securities until effective date but issuer may **offer** securities upon filing registration statement.

           (c) Such offers may be made

               1] Orally

               2] By tombstone ads that identify security, its price, and who will take orders

               3] By a "red-herring prospectus"

                   a] Legend in red ink (thus, red-herring) is printed on this preliminary prospectus in-dicating that the prospectus is "preliminary" and that a registration statement has been filed but has not become effective.

    h.   Prospectus—any notice, circular, advertisement, letter, or communication offering any security for sale (or merger)

        (1) May be a written, radio, or television communication

           (a) SEC adopted new "plain English" rule for important sections of companies' prospectuses, including risk factor sections

        (2) After the effective date of registration statement, communication (written or oral) will not be considered a prospectus if

           (a) Prior to or at same time, a written prospectus was also sent, or

           (b) If it only states from whom written prospectus is available, identifies security, states price, and who will execute orders for it (i.e., tombstone ad)

3. Registration requirements

    a.   Registration is required under the Act if

        (1) The securities are to be offered, sold, or delivered in interstate commerce or through the mail

           (a) Interstate commerce means trade, commerce, transportation, or communication (e.g., tele-phone call) among more than one state or territory of US

               1] Interpreted very broadly to include trade, commerce, etc. that is within one state but affects interstate commerce

                   EXAMPLE: A corporation issues securities to individuals living only in Philadelphia. It is further shown that this issuance affects trade in Delaware. Interstate commerce is affected because although Philadelphia is of course in one state, the effects on at least one other state allow the Federal Securities Acts to take effect under our Constitution. Therefore, registration of these securities is required under the Federal Law unless exemptions are found as discussed later.

    (2) Unless it is an exempted security or exempted transaction as discussed later

b. Issuer has primary duty of registration

    (1) Any person who sells unregistered securities that should have been registered may be liable to a purchaser (unless transaction or security is exempt)

    (2) Liability cannot be disclaimed in writing or orally by issuer

    (3) This liability not dischargeable in bankruptcy

c. Information required, in general, in registration statements

    (1) Financial statements audited by independent CPA

    (2) Names of issuer, directors, officers, general partners, underwriters, large stockholders, counsel, etc.

    (3) Risks associated with the securities

    (4) Description of property, business, and capitalization of issuer

    (5) Information about management of issuer

    (6) Description of security to be sold and use to be made by issuer of proceeds

d. Prospectus is also filed as part of registration statement

    (1) Generally must contain same information as registration statement, but it may be condensed or summarized

e. Registration statement and prospectus are examined by SEC

    (1) Amendments are almost always required by SEC

    (2) SEC may issue stop-order suspending effectiveness of registration if statement appears incomplete or misleading

    (3) Otherwise registration becomes effective on 20th day after filing (or on 20th day after filing amendment)

        (a) Twenty-day period is called the waiting period

    (4) It is unlawful for company to sell the securities prior to approval (effective registration date)

        (a) However, preliminary prospectuses are permitted once registration statement is filed

f. Applies to both corporate and noncorporate issuers

g. Registration covers a single distribution, so second distribution must also be registered

h. Shelf registration is exception to requirement that each new distribution of nonexempt securities requires a new filing

    (1) Allows certain qualified issuers to register securities once and then offer and sell them on a delayed or continuous basis "off the shelf"

    (2) Advantage is that issuer can respond better to changing market conditions affecting stock

i. Different registration forms are available

    (1) Form S-1

        (a) This is basic long-form registration statement

    (2) Additional forms now required based on Sarbanes-Oxley Act that require non-GAAP financial measures to be presented so that they reconcile to the most directly comparable GAAP financial measure

        (a) Goal is to reduce concerns regarding improper use of non-GAAP financial measures

    (3) Forms S-2 and S-3

        (a) These forms adopted by SEC to ease much of burden of disclosures required under federal securities regulation

        (b) Require less detailed disclosures than Form S-1

        (c) Integrate information required under 1933 and 1934 Acts

            1] Firms already on file with SEC under 1934 Act may incorporate much information by reference to avoid additional disclosure

    (4) Forms SB-1 and SB-2

       (a) These forms permitted for small businesses under Regulation S-B

         1] Reduce amount of financial and nonfinancial information required when registering under 1933 Act and when reporting quarterly information under 1934 Act

         2] Small business issuer is generally one that has revenues less than $25 million

4. Exempt securities (need not be registered but still subject to antifraud provisions under the Act)

   a. Commercial paper (e.g., note, draft, check, etc.) with a maturity of nine months or less

     (1) Must be for commercial purpose and not investment

> *EXAMPLE: OK Corporation in Washington, DC, wishes to finance a short-term need for more cash for current operations. OK will do this by issuing some short-term notes which all have a maturity of nine months or less. These are exempt from the registration requirements.*

   b. Intrastate issues—securities offered and sold only within one state

     (1) Issuer must be resident of state and doing 80% of business in the state and must use at least 80% of sale proceeds in connection with business operations in the state

     (2) All offerees and purchasers must be residents of state

     (3) For nine months after last sale by issuer, resales can only be made to residents of state

     (4) All of particular issue must qualify under this rule or this exemption cannot be used for any sale of the issue

> *EXAMPLE: A regional corporation in need of additional capital makes an offer to the residents of the state in which it is incorporated to purchase a new issue of its stock. The offer expressly restricts sales to only residents of the state and all purchasers are residents of the state.*

   c. Small issues (Regulation A)—issuances up to $5,000,000 by issuer in twelve-month period may be exempt if

     (1) There is a notice filed with SEC

     (2) An offering circular (containing financial information about the corporation and descriptive information about offered securities) must be provided to offeree. Financial statements in offering circular need not be audited.

     (3) Note that an offering circular (statement) is required under Regulation A instead of the more costly and time-consuming prospectus

     (4) Nonissuers can sell up to $1,500,000 in twelve-month period

   d. Securities of governments, banks, quasi governmental authorities (e.g., local hospital authorities), savings and loan associations, farmers, co-ops, and common carriers regulated by ICC

     (1) Public utilities are not exempt

   e. Security exchanged by issuer exclusively with its existing shareholders so long as

     (1) No commission is paid

     (2) Both sets of securities must have been issued by the same person

> *EXAMPLE: A stock split is an exempt transaction under the 1933 Act and thus, the securities need not be registered at time of split.*

   f. Securities of nonprofit religious, educational, or charitable organizations

   g. Certificates issued by receiver or trustee in bankruptcy

   h. Insurance and annuity contracts

5. Exempt transactions or offerings (still subject, however, to antifraud provisions of the Act; may also be subject to reporting requirements of the 1934 Act)

   a. Sale or offer to sell by any person **other than** an issuer, underwriter, or dealer

     (1) Generally covers sales by individual investors on their own account

     (2) May be transaction by broker on customer's order

       (a) Does not include solicitation of these orders

     (3) Exemption does not apply to sales by controlling persons because considered an underwriter or issuer

   b. **Regulation D** establishes three important exemptions in Rules 504, 505, and 506 under the 1933 Act

(1) Rule 504 exempts an issuance of securities up to $1,000,000 sold in twelve-month period to any number of investors (this is also known as seed capital exemption)

    (a) General offering and solicitations are permitted under Rule 504 as long as they are restricted to "accredited investors," such as banks, insurance companies, high-worth individuals, etc.

    (b) Issuer need not restrict purchasers' right to resell securities

    (c) No specific disclosure is required

    (d) Must send notice of offering to SEC within fifteen days of first sale of securities

(2) Rule 505 exempts issuance of up to $5,000,000 in twelve-month period

    (a) No general offering or solicitation is permitted within twelve-month period

    (b) Permits sales to thirty-five unaccredited (nonaccredited term sometimes used) investors and to unlimited number of accredited investors within twelve months

        1] Accredited investors are, for example, banks, savings and loan associations, credit unions, insurance companies, broker dealers, certain trusts, partnerships and corporations, also natural persons having joint or individual net worth exceeding $1,000,000 or having joint or individual net income of $200,000 for two most recent years

        2] SEC must be notified within fifteen days of first sale

    (c) The issuer must restrict the purchasers' right to resell the securities; in general must be held for two years or else exemption is lost

    (d) These securities typically state that they have not been registered and that they have resale restrictions

    (e) Unlike under Rule 504, if nonaccredited investor purchases these securities, audited balance sheet must be supplied (i.e., disclosure is required) as well as other financial statements or information, if readily available

        1] If purchased only by accredited investors, no disclosure required

(3) Rule 506 allows private placement of unlimited amount of securities

    (a) In general, same rules apply here as outlined under Rule 505

    (b) However, an additional requirement is that the unaccredited investors (up to thirty-five) must be sophisticated investors (individuals with knowledge and experience in financial matters) or be represented by individual with such knowledge and experience

        EXAMPLE: A growing corporation is in need of additional capital and decides to make a new issuance of its stock. The stock is only offered to ten of the president's friends who regularly make financial investments of this sort. They are interested in purchasing the stock for an investment and each of them is provided with the type of information that is regularly included in a registration statement.

(4) Disclosures for offerings under $2,000,000 have been simplified to be similar to disclosures under Regulation A

(5) A controlling person who sells restricted securities may be held to be an underwriter (and thus subject to the registration provisions) unless requirements of Rule 144 are met when controlling person is selling through a broker

    (a) If the following are met, the security can be sold without registration

        1] Broker performs no services beyond those of typical broker who executes orders and receives customary fee

        2] Ownership (including beneficial ownership) for at least two years

        3] Only limited amounts of stock may be sold—based on a specified formula

        4] Public must have available adequate disclosure of issuer corporation

        5] Notice of sale must be filed with SEC

(6) Small issuers sometimes use offerings over internet to investors

    (a) Often use Regulation A to avoid registration

    (b) Must avoid violating Rules 505 and 506 of Regulation D which prohibits public solicitations to investors

    (c) Some have used Rule 504 to avoid registration

c. Postregistration transactions by dealer (i.e., dealer is not required to deliver prospectus)

(1) If transaction is made at least forty days after first date security was offered to public, or

   (2) After ninety days if it is issuer's first public issue

   (3) Does not apply to sales of securities that are leftover part of an allotment from the public issue

 6. Antifraud provisions

  a. Apply even if securities are exempt or the transactions are exempt as long as interstate commerce is used (use of mail or telephone qualifies) to sell or offer to sell securities

  b. Included are schemes to defraud purchaser or making sale by use of untrue statement of material fact or by omission of material fact

   (1) Proof of negligence is sometimes sufficient rather than proof of scienter

   (2) Protects purchaser, not seller

 7. Civil liability (i.e., private actions brought by purchasers of securities)

  a. Purchaser may recover if can establish that

   (1) Was a purchase of a security issued under a registration statement containing a misleading statement or omission of a material fact, and

    (a) May also recover if issuer or any person sold unregistered securities for which there is no exemption

   (2) Suffered economic loss

   (3) Privity of contract is **not** necessary

    EXAMPLE: *Third parties who have never dealt with issuer but bought securities from another party have a right to recover when the above is established despite lack of privity.*

   (4) Need **not** prove that defendant intended to deceive

   (5) Purchaser need **not** rely on registration statement to recover

  b. Purchaser of securities may recover from

   (1) The issuer

   (2) Any directors, partners, or underwriters of issuer

   (3) Anyone who signed registration statement

   (4) Experts of authorized statements (e.g., attorneys, accountants, engineers, appraisers)

   (5) Loss not dischargeable in bankruptcy

  c. Burden of proof is shifted to defendant in most cases; however, except for the issuer, defendant may use "due diligence" defense

   (1) Due diligence defense can be used successfully by defendant by proving that

    (a) As an expert, s/he had reasonable grounds after reasonable investigation to believe that his/her own statements were true and/or did not contain any omissions of material facts by the time the registration statement became effective

     EXAMPLE: *Whitewood, a CPA, performs a reasonable audit and discovers no irregularities.*

    (b) S/he relied on an expert for the part of the registration statement in question and did believe (and had reasonable grounds for such belief) that there were no misstatements or material omissions of fact

     EXAMPLE: *Greenwood, a CPA, relies on an attorney's work as a foundation for his own work on contingent liabilities.*

    (c) S/he did reasonably believe that after a reasonable investigation, statements not in the province of an expert were true or that material omissions did not exist

     EXAMPLE: *Lucky, an underwriter, made a reasonable investigation on the registration statement and did reasonably believe no impropriety existed even though misstatements and omissions of material facts existed. Note that the issuer is liable even if s/he exercised the same care and held the same reasonable belief because the issuer is liable without fault and cannot use the due diligence defense.*

  d. Seller of security is liable to purchaser

   (1) If interstate commerce or mail is used, and

   (2) If registration is not in effect and should be, or

   (3) If registration statement contains misstatements or omissions of material facts

   (4) For amount paid plus interest less any income received by purchaser

36. Which of the following situations would require Link to be subject to the reporting provisions of the 1934 Act?

	Shares listed on a national securities exchange	More than one class of stock
a.	Yes	Yes
b.	Yes	No
c.	No	Yes
d.	No	No

37. Which of the following documents must Link file with the SEC?

	Quarterly reports (Form 10-Q)	Proxy Statements
a.	Yes	Yes
b.	Yes	No
c.	No	Yes
d.	No	No

38. Which of the following reports must also be submitted to the SEC?

	Report by any party making a tender offer to purchase Link's stock	Report of proxy solicitations by Link stockholders
a.	Yes	Yes
b.	Yes	No
c.	No	Yes
d.	No	No

39. Which of the following events must be reported to the SEC under the reporting provisions of the Securities Exchange Act of 1934?

	Tender offers	Insider trading	Soliciting proxies
a.	Yes	Yes	Yes
b.	Yes	Yes	No
c.	Yes	No	Yes
d.	No	Yes	Yes

40. Adler, Inc. is a reporting company under the Securities Exchange Act of 1934. The only security it has issued is voting common stock. Which of the following statements is correct?

a. Because Adler is a reporting company, it is **not** required to file a registration statement under the Securities Act of 1933 for any future offerings of its common stock.

b. Adler need **not** file its proxy statements with the SEC because it has only one class of stock outstanding.

c. Any person who owns more than 10% of Adler's common stock must file a report with the SEC.

d. It is unnecessary for the required annual report (Form 10-K) to include audited financial statements.

41. Which of the following is correct concerning annual reports (Form 10-K) and quarterly reports (Form 10-Q)?

a. Both Form 10-K and Form 10-Q must be certified by independent public accountants and both must be filed with the SEC.

b. Both Form 10-K and Form 10-Q must be certified by independent public accountants but neither need be filed with the SEC.

c. Although both Form 10-K and Form 10-Q must be filed with the SEC, only Form 10-K need be certified by independent public accountants.

d. Form 10-K must be certified by independent public accountants and must also be filed with the SEC; however, Form 10-Q need not be certified by independent public accountants nor filed with the SEC.

42. Burk Corporation has issued securities that must be registered with the Securities Exchange Commission under the Securities Exchange Act of 1934. A material event took place a week ago, that is, there was a change in the control of Burk Corporation. Which of the following statements is correct?

a. Because of this material event, Burk Corporation is required to file with the SEC, Forms 10-K and 10-Q.

b. Because of this material event, Burk Corporation is required to file Form 8-K.

c. Burk Corporation need not file any forms with the SEC concerning this material event if the relevant facts are fully disclosed in the audited financial statements.

d. Burk Corporation need not file any form concerning the material event if Burk Corporation has an exemption under Rules 504, 505, or 506 of Regulation D.

43. Loop Corp. has made a major breakthrough in the development of a micropencil. Loop has patented the product and is seeking to maximize the profit potential. In this effort, Loop can legally

a. Require its retailers to sell only Loop's products, including the micropencils, and **not** sell similar competing products.

b. Require its retailers to take stipulated quantities of its other products in addition to the micropencils.

c. Sell the product at whatever price the traffic will bear even though Loop has a monopoly.

d. Sell the product to its retailers upon condition that they do not sell the micropencils to the public for less than a stated price.

44. Robinson's pricing policies have come under attack by several of its retailers. In fact, one of those retailers, Patman, has instigated legal action against Robinson alleging that Robinson charges other favored retailers prices for its products which are lower than those charged to it. Patman's legal action against Robinson

a. Will fail unless Patman can show that there has been an injury to competition.

b. Will be sufficient if the complaint alleges that Robinson charged different prices to different customers and there is a reasonable possibility that competition may be adversely affected.

c. Is groundless since one has the legal right to sell at whatever price one wishes as long as the price is determined unilaterally.

d. Is to be tested under the Rule of Reason and if the different prices charged are found to be reasonable, the complaint will be dismissed.

SIMULATION PROBLEMS

Simulation Problem 1   (10 to 15 minutes)

Situation			
	Rule 504	Rule 506	Rule 505

You will have 15 questions based on the following information:

Butler Manufacturing Corp. planned to raise capital for a plant expansion by borrowing from banks and making several stock offerings. Butler engaged Weaver, CPA, to audit its December 31, 2007 financial statements. Butler told Weaver that the financial statements would be given to certain named banks and included in the prospectuses for the stock offerings.

In performing the audit, Weaver did not confirm accounts receivable and, as a result, failed to discover a material overstatement of accounts receivable. Also, Weaver was aware of a pending class action product liability lawsuit that was not disclosed in Butler's financial statements. Despite being advised by Butler's legal counsel that Butler's potential liability under the lawsuit would result in material losses, Weaver issued an unqualified opinion on Butler's financial statements.

In May 2008, Union Bank, one of the named banks, relied on the financial statements and Weaver's opinion in giving Butler a $500,000 loan.

Butler raised an additional $16,450,000 through the following stock offerings, which were sold completely:

- June 2008—Butler made a $450,000 unregistered offering of Class B nonvoting common stock under Rule 504 of Regulation D of the Securities Act of 1933. This offering was sold over one year to twenty accredited investors by general solicitation. The SEC was notified eight days after the first sale of this offering.
- September 2008—Butler made a $10,000,000 unregistered offering of Class A voting common stock under Rule 506 of Regulation D of the Securities Act of 1933. This offering was sold over one year to 200 accredited investors and thirty nonaccredited investors through a private placement. The SEC was notified fourteen days after the first sale of this offering.
- November 2008—Butler made a $6,000,000 unregistered offering of preferred stock under Rule 505 of Regulation D of the Securities Act of 1933. This offering was sold during a one-year period to forty nonaccredited investors by private placement. The SEC was notified eighteen days after the first sale of this offering.

Shortly after obtaining the Union loan, Butler began experiencing financial problems but was able to stay in business because of the money raised by the offerings. Butler was found liable in the product liability suit. This resulted in a judgment Butler could not pay. Butler also defaulted on the Union loan and was involuntarily petitioned into bankruptcy. This caused Union to sustain a loss and Butler's stockholders to lose their investments. As a result

- The SEC claimed that all three of Butler's offerings were made improperly and were not exempt from registration.
- Union sued Weaver for

  - Negligence
  - Common Law Fraud

- The stockholders who purchased Butler's stock through the offerings sued Weaver, alleging fraud under Section 10(b) and Rule 10b-5 of the Securities Exchange Act of 1934.

These transactions took place in a jurisdiction providing for accountant's liability for negligence to known and intended users of financial statements.

	Rule 504		
Situation		Rule 506	Rule 505

Items 1 through 5 are questions related to the June 2008 offering made under Rule 504 of Regulation D of the Securities Act of 1933. For each item, indicate your answer by choosing either Yes or No.

	Yes	*No*
1. Did the offering comply with the dollar limitation of Rule 504?	O	O
2. Did the offering comply with the method of sale restrictions?	O	O
3. Was the offering sold during the applicable time limit?	O	O
4. Was the SEC notified timely of the first sale of the securities?	O	O
5. Was the SEC correct in claiming that this offering was not exempt from registration?	O	O

	Rule 506	
Situation	Rule 504	Rule 505

Items 1 through 5 are questions related to the September 2008 offering made under Rule 506 of Regulation D of the Securities Act of 1933. For each item, indicate your answer by choosing either Yes or No.

	Yes	*No*
1. Did the offering comply with the dollar limitation of Rule 506?	○	○
2. Did the offering comply with the method of sale restrictions?	○	○
3. Was the offering sold to the correct number of investors?	○	○
4. Was the SEC notified timely of the first sale of the securities?	○	○
5. Was the SEC correct in claiming that this offering was not exempt from registration?	○	○

		Rule 505
Situation	Rule 504	Rule 506

Items 1 through 5 are questions related to the November 2008 offering made under Rule 505 of Regulation D of the Securities Act of 1933. For each item, indicate your answer by choosing either Yes or No.

	Yes	*No*
1. Did the offering comply with the dollar limitation of Rule 505?	○	○
2. Was the offering sold during the applicable time limit?	○	○
3. Was the offering sold to the correct number of investors?	○	○
4. Was the SEC notified timely of the first sale of the securities?	○	○
5. Was the SEC correct in claiming that this offering was not exempt from registration?	○	○

Simulation Problem 2   (10 to 15 minutes)

Situation	
	Analysis

Coffee Corp., a publicly held corporation, wants to make an $8,000,000 exempt offering of its shares as a private placement offering under Regulation D, Rule 506, of the Securities Act of 1933. Coffee has more than 500 shareholders and assets in excess of $1 billion, and has its shares listed on a national securities exchange.

	Analysis
Situation	

Items 1 through 5 relate to the application of the provisions of the Securities Act of 1933 and the Securities Exchange Act of 1934 to Coffee Corp. and the offering. For each item, select from List II whether only statement I is correct, whether only statement II is correct, whether both statements I and II are correct, or whether neither statement I nor II is correct.

List II
A. I only
B. II only
C. Both I and II
D. Neither I nor II

		(A)	**(B)**	**(C)**	**(D)**
1.	I. Coffee Corp. may make the Regulation D, Rule 506, exempt offering.	○	○	○	○
	II. Coffee Corp., because it is required to report under the Securities Exchange Act of 1934, may **not** make an exempt offering.				
2.	I. Shares sold under a Regulation D, Rule 506, exempt offering may only be purchased by accredited investors.	○	○	○	○
	II. Shares sold under a Regulation D, Rule 506, exempt offering may be purchased by any number of investors provided there are **no** more than thirty-five nonaccredited investors.				

		(A)	(B)	(C)	(D)
3. I.	An exempt offering under Regulation D, Rule 506, must **not** be for more than $10,000,000.	○	○	○	○
II.	An exempt offering under Regulation D, Rule 506, has **no** dollar limit.				
4. I.	Regulation D, Rule 506, requires that all investors in the exempt offering be notified that for nine months after the last sale **no** resale may be made to a nonresident.	○	○	○	○
II.	Regulation D, Rule 506, requires that the issuer exercise reasonable care to assure that purchasers of the exempt offering are buying for investment and are **not** underwriters.				
5. I.	The SEC must be notified by Coffee Corp. within five days of the first sale of the exempt offering securities.	○	○	○	○
II.	Coffee Corp. must include an SEC notification of the first sale of the exempt offering securities in Coffee's next filed Quarterly Report (Form 10-Q).				

MULTIPLE-CHOICE ANSWERS

1. d __ __	11. b __ __	21. c __ __	31. a __ __	41. c __ __
2. d __ __	12. d __ __	22. b __ __	32. c __ __	42. b __ __
3. d __ __	13. a __ __	23. a __ __	33. b __ __	43. c __ __
4. b __ __	14. c __ __	24. b __ __	34. a __ __	44. b __ __
5. a __ __	15. c __ __	25. b __ __	35. c __ __	
6. a __ __	16. d __ __	26. d __ __	36. b __ __	
7. d __ __	17. d __ __	27. c __ __	37. a __ __	
8. d __ __	18. a __ __	28. b __ __	38. a __ __	
9. b __ __	19. c __ __	29. c __ __	39. a __ __	1st: __/44= __%
10. d __ __	20. b __ __	30. b __ __	40. c __ __	2nd: __/44= __%

MULTIPLE-CHOICE ANSWER EXPLANATIONS

A.   Securities Act of 1933

1.   (d)   A preliminary prospectus is usually called a "red-herring" prospectus. The preliminary prospectus indicates that a registration statement has been filed but has not become effective.

2.   (d)   Securities include debentures, stocks, bonds, some notes, and investment contracts. The main idea is that the investor intends to make a profit on the investment through the efforts of others. A certificate of deposit is a type of commercial paper, not a security.

3.   (d)   A tombstone advertisement is allowed to inform potential investors that a prospectus for the given company is available. It is not an offer to sell or the solicitation of an offer to buy the securities. Answer (a) is incorrect because the tombstone ad informs potential purchasers of the prospectus and cannot be used as a substitute for the prospectus. Answer (b) is incorrect because it informs of the availability of the prospectus and cannot be construed as an offer to sell securities. Answer (c) is incorrect because the tombstone ad notifies potential purchasers of the prospectus. It does not notify that the securities have been withdrawn from the market.

4.   (b)   The registration of securities under the Securities Act of 1933 has as its purpose to provide potential investors with full and fair disclosure of all material information relating to the issuance of securities, including such information as the principal purposes for which the offering's proceeds will be used. Answer (a) is incorrect because information on the stockholders of the offering corporation is not required to be reported. Answer (c) is incorrect because the SEC does not guarantee the accuracy of the registration statements. Answer (d) is incorrect because although the SEC does seek to compel full and fair disclosure, it does not evaluate the securities on merit or value, or give any assurances against loss.

5.   (a)   If no exemption is applicable under the Securities Act of 1933, public offerings must be registered with the SEC accompanied by a prospectus. Answer (b) is incorrect because the SEC does not pass on nor rate the securities. Answer (c) is incorrect because the prospectus is given to prospective purchasers of the securities. Answer (d) is incorrect because the SEC does not pass on the merits or accuracy of the prospectus.

6.   (a)   Notes are exempt securities under the Securities Act of 1933 if they have a maturity of nine months or less and if they are also used for commercial purposes rather than investments. The actual dollar amounts in the question

are not a factor. The notes described in II are not exempt for two reasons; they have a maturity of two years and are used for investment purposes. The notes in III are not exempt because the maturity is two years even though they are for commercial purposes.

7.   (d)   Whether the securities are exempt from registration or not, they are still subject to the antifraud provisions of the Securities Act of 1933.

8.   (d)   The definition of a security is very broad under the Securities Act of 1933. The basic idea is that the investor intends to make a profit through the efforts of others rather than through his/her own efforts. Notes, bond certificates of interest, and debentures are all considered securities.

9.   (b)   If an issuer of securities wants to make an offering by using shelf registration, the actual issuance takes place over potentially a long period of time. Therefore, s/he must keep the original registration statement updated. There is no requirement that the offeror must be a first-time issuer of securities.

10.   (d)   Under the 1933 Act, certain securities are exempt. Although insurance and annuity contracts are exempt, securities issued by the insurance companies are not. Answer (a) is incorrect because securities of nonprofit organizations are exempt. Answer (b) is incorrect because securities issued by or guaranteed by domestic government organizations are exempt. Answer (c) is incorrect because securities issued by savings and loan associations are exempt.

11.   (b)   Securities exchanged for other securities by the issuer exclusively with its existing shareholders are exempt from registration under the 1933 Act as long as no commission is paid and both sets of securities are issued by the same issuer. Answer (a) is incorrect because nonvoting common stock is not exempted under the Act. The amount of the par value is irrelevant. Answer (c) is incorrect because although the securities of governments are themselves exempt, the limited partnership interests are not. Answer (d) is incorrect because no such exemption is allowed.

12.   (d)   Even though the issuer may comply with the Federal Securities Act of 1933, it must also comply with any applicable state "blue-sky" laws that regulate the securities at the state level. Answer (a) is incorrect because it is unlawful for the company to offer or sell the securities prior to the effective registration date. Answer (b) is incorrect because registration becomes effective on the twentieth day after filing unless the SEC issues a stop order. Answer (c) is incorrect because a prospectus is any notice, circular, advertisement, letter, or communication offering the security for sale. No general offering or solicitation is allowed under Rules 505 or 506 of Regulation D whether the purchaser is accredited or not.

13. **(a)** Even if the securities are exempt under the Securities Act of 1933, they are still subject to the antifraud provisions. Both the person defrauded and the SEC can challenge the fraud committed in the course of selling the securities.

14. **(c)** The SEC adopted the Forms S-2 and S-3 to decrease the work that issuers have in preparing registration statements by permitting them to give less detailed disclosure under certain conditions than Form S-1 which is the basic long form. Answer (a) is incorrect because these forms decrease, not increase, reporting required. Answer (b) is incorrect because when permitted, these forms are used instead of Form S-1 which is the standard long-form registration statement. Answer (d) is incorrect because the purpose of the forms was not directed at intrastate issues.

A.5.   Exempt Transactions or Offerings

15. **(c)** The issuance described in I is exempt because Rule 504 exempts an issuance of securities up to $1,000,000 sold in a twelve-month period to any number of investors. The issuer is not required to restrict the purchasers' resale. The issuance described in II is also exempt because Rule 505 exempts an issuance up to $5,000,000 sold in a twelve-month period. It permits sales to thirty-five unaccredited investors and to any number of accredited investors. Since there were only ten investors, this is met. The issuer also restricted the purchasers' right to resell for two years as required.

16. **(d)** Under Regulation D, Rule 504 exempts an issuance of securities up to $1,000,000 sold in a twelve-month period. Rule 505 exempts an issuance of up to $5,000,000 in a twelve-month period. So Rule 506 has to be resorted to for amounts over $5,000,000. Regulation A can be used only for issuances up to $1,500,000.

17. **(d)** When more than $5,000,000 in securities are being offered, an exemption from the registration requirements of the Securities Act of 1933 is available under Rule 506 of Regulation D. Securities under the Act include debentures and investment contracts.

18. **(a)** Under Regulation A of the 1933 Act, the issuer must file an offering circular with the SEC. Answer (b) is incorrect because the rules involving sales to unaccredited and accredited investors are in Regulation D, not Regulation A. Answer (c) is incorrect because although financial information about the corporation must be provided to offerees, the financial statements in the offering circular need not be audited. Answer (d) is incorrect because the issuer is not required to provide investors with a proxy registration statement under Regulation A.

19. **(c)** Sales or offers to sell by any person **other than** an issuer, underwriter, or dealer are exempt under the 1933 Act. Answer (a) is incorrect because the Act covers all types of securities including preferred stock. Answer (b) is incorrect because closely held corporations are not automatically exempt. Answer (d) is incorrect because debentures, as debt

securities, are covered under the Act even if they are highly rated or backed by collateral.

20. **(b)** Regulation D of the Securities Act of 1933 establishes three important exemptions in Rules 504, 505, and 506. Although Rules 505 and 506 have some restrictions on sales to nonaccredited investors, all three rules under Regulation D allow sales to both nonaccredited and accredited investors with varying restrictions. Answer (a) is incorrect because although Rules 505 and 506 allow sales to up to thirty-five nonaccredited investors, all three rules allow sales to an unlimited number of accredited investors. Answer (c) is incorrect because Rule 506 has no dollar limitation. Rule 505 has a $5,000,000 limitation in a twelve-month period and Rule 504 has a $1,000,000 limitation in a twelve-month period. Answer (d) is incorrect because Regulation D is not restricted to only small corporations.

21. **(c)** Under Rule 505 of Regulation D, the issuer must notify the SEC of the offering within fifteen days after the first sale of the securities. Answer (a) is incorrect because under Rule 505, the issuer may sell to an unlimited number of **accredited** investors and to thirty-five unaccredited investors. Answer (b) is incorrect because no general offering or solicitation is permitted. Answer (d) is incorrect because the accredited investors need not receive any formal information. The unaccredited investors, however, must receive a formal registration statement that gives a description of the offering.

22. **(b)** The private placement exemption permits sales of an unlimited number of securities for any dollar amount when sold to accredited investors. This exemption also allows sales to up to thirty-five nonaccredited investors if they are also sophisticated investors under the Act. Resales of these securities are restricted for two years after the date that the issuer sells the last of the securities. Answer (a) is incorrect because there is no such restriction of sale. Answer (c) is incorrect because sales may be made to an unlimited number of accredited investors and up to thirty-five nonaccredited investors. Answer (d) is incorrect because sales can be made to up to thirty-five nonaccredited investors.

23. **(a)** When the issuer is a resident of that state, doing 80% of its business in that state, and only sells or offers the securities to residents of the same state, the offering qualifies for an exemption under the 1933 Act as an intrastate issue. Answer (b) is incorrect as the offering also qualifies for an exemption under the 1934 Act. Therefore, as the offering is exempted from both the 1933 and 1934 Acts, it would not be regulated by the SEC. Answer (d) is incorrect because resales can only be made to residents of that state nine months after the issuer's last sale.

24. **(b)** Rule 506 permits sales to thirty-five unaccredited investors and to an unlimited number of accredited investors. The unaccredited investors must also be sophisticated investors (i.e., individuals with knowledge and experience in financial matters).

25. **(b)** Under Regulation A, an offering statement is required instead of the more costly disclosure requirements of full registration under the Securities Act of 1933. Answer (a) is incorrect because not all intrastate offerings are exempt. They must meet specified requirements to be exempt. Answer (c) is incorrect because many securities sold under Regulation D cannot be resold for two years. An-

EXAMPLE: Same as above except that B and S agree to let N decide what the price will be for the pears. This is a valid contract.

EXAMPLE: Un D. Sided and Tube Issy agree on a contract for 1,000 bushels of avocados to be delivered in three months for a price that they will decide in one month. If they fail to agree on the price, the contract will be for the market value at delivery.

    (b) Open place of delivery term—seller's place of business, if any

        1] Otherwise, seller's residence or if identified goods are elsewhere and their location is known to both parties at time of contracting, then at that location

    (c) Open time of shipment or delivery—becomes a reasonable time

    (d) Open time for payment—due at time and place of delivery of goods or at time and place of delivery of documents of title, if any

        1] If on credit, credit period begins running at time of shipment

  (8) What is a reasonable price or reasonable time becomes a jury question to interpret contract if parties to contract already formed cannot agree on interpretation

  (9) Even if writings do not establish a contract, conduct by parties recognizing a contract will establish one

    (a) The terms will be those on which writings agree and those provided for in UCC where not agreed on (e.g., reasonable price, place of delivery)

    (b) Often occurs when merchants send preprinted forms to each other with conflicting terms and forms are not read for more than quantity and price

l. Auctions

  (1) Bid is offer

  (2) Bidder may retract bid until auctioneer announces sale completed

  (3) If auction is "with reserve," auctioneer may withdraw goods before s/he announces completion of sale

  (4) If auction "without reserve," goods may not be withdrawn unless no bid made within reasonable time

  (5) Auctions are "with reserve" unless specified otherwise

m. Online auctions

  (1) Many individuals and businesses are conducting auctions online

    (a) Becoming increasingly popular as buyers and sellers rely on fluidity of contract-making abilities

3. Consideration—an act, promise, or forbearance that is offered by one party and accepted by another as inducement to enter into agreement

  a. A party binds him/herself to do (or actually does) something s/he is not legally obligated to do, or when s/he surrenders legal right

EXAMPLE: B pays S $500 for S's stereo that he hands over to B. B's consideration is the $500. S's consideration is the stereo.

EXAMPLE: S gives B a stereo today. B promises to pay S $500 in one week. The promise to pay $500, rather than the $500 itself, is the consideration. Thus, the element of consideration is met today.

EXAMPLE: A hits and injures P with his car. P agrees not to sue A when A agrees to settle out of court for $10,000. A's promise to pay the money is consideration. P's promise to refrain from bringing a lawsuit is consideration on his/her side.

EXAMPLE: Using the fact pattern above, further assume that it is not clear whether A is at fault. The settlement (contract) is still enforceable if made in good faith because of possible liability.

  b. Legal detriment does not have to be economic (e.g., giving up drinking, smoking, and swearing)

    (1) If party agrees to have something accomplished but has someone else do it, this is consideration

  c. Consideration must be bargained for (this is essential)

  d. Preexisting legal duty is not sufficient as consideration because no new legal detriment is suffered by performing prior obligation

(1) Agreement to accept from debtor a lesser sum than owed is unenforceable if the debt is a liquidated (undisputed) debt

> *EXAMPLE: C agrees to accept $700 for a $900 debt that D owes C. The amount is not disputed. D still owes C the additional $200.*

   (a) But if debtor incurs a detriment in addition to paying, creditor's promise to accept lesser sum will be binding

> *EXAMPLE: X owes Y $1,000. Y agrees to accept $500 and X will also install Y's new furnace at no additional cost.*

   (b) Note that agreement to accept a lesser sum is enforceable if amount of debt is unliquidated (disputed) because both parties give up right to more favorable sum

> *EXAMPLE: C claims that D owes him $1,000. D claims that the amount owed is $600. If C and D agree to settle this for $700, the agreement is supported by consideration since C gave up right to attempt to collect more than $700 and D gave up right to attempt settlement for a lesser sum.*

(2) Promise to pay someone for refraining from doing something s/he has no right to do is unenforceable

(3) Promise to pay someone to do something s/he is already obligated to do is not enforceable.

> *EXAMPLE: Agreement to pay police officer $200 to recover stolen goods is unenforceable.*

> *EXAMPLE: X promises to pay Y, a jockey, $50 to ride as hard as he can in the race. Y already owes his employer, Z, that duty so there is no consideration to enforce the agreement.*

   (a) Agreement to pay more to finish a job, such as building a house, is unenforceable unless unforeseen difficulties are encountered (e.g., underground stream or marshy land under a house)

e. Past consideration (consideration for a prior act, forbearance, or agreement) is not sufficient for new contract because it is not bargained for

f. Moral obligation is not consideration

(1) In majority of states these following need no consideration

   (a) Promise to pay debt barred by statute of limitations.

   (b) Promise to pay debt barred by bankruptcy. Promise must adhere to strict rules stated in Bankruptcy Reform Act of 1978 concerning reaffirmations of dischargeable debts.

g. Consideration must be legally sufficient

(1) This does not refer to amount of consideration but refers to validity of consideration

> *EXAMPLE: C does not have a CPA license. For $1,000 he promises not to hire himself out as a CPA. This promise is not supported by legally sufficient consideration because C has no right to hire himself out as a CPA.*

h. Adequacy of consideration—courts generally do not look into amount of exchange as long as it is legal consideration and **bargained for**

i. In majority of states, seals placed on contracts are not substitutes for consideration

j. Modifying existing contracts

(1) Modification of contract needs new consideration on both sides to be legally binding

> *EXAMPLE: S agrees in a written contract to sell a piece of land to P for $40,000. S later changes his mind and demands $50,000 for the same piece of land. The original contract is enforceable (at $40,000) even if P agrees to the increased price because although P has agreed to give more consideration, S has not given any new consideration.*

(2) Under UCC, a contract for sale of goods may be modified orally or in writing without consideration if in good faith

> *EXAMPLE: S agrees to sell P 300 pairs of socks for $1.00 each. Due to rapid price increases in S's costs, he asks P if he will modify the price to $1.20 each. P agrees. The contract as modified is enforceable because it is covered under the UCC and does not need new consideration on both sides.*

k. Requirements contracts

(1) If one party agrees to supply what other party requires, agreement is supported by consideration because supplying party gives up right to sell to another; purchasing party gives up right to buy from another

(a) Cannot be required to sell amounts unreasonably disproportionate to normal requirements

(b) Law requires good faith on performance of parties

l. Output contract

(1) If one party agrees to sell all his/her output to another, agreement is supported by consideration because s/he gives up right to sell that output to another

(a) Law requires good faith of parties on performance

(b) However, illusory contracts are not supported by consideration (e.g., party agrees to sell all s/he wishes)

m. Best-efforts contracts are contacts which parties are to use best efforts to complete contract's objectives

n. Promissory estoppel may act as substitute for consideration and renders promise enforceable—promisor is estoppel from asserting lack of consideration

(1) Elements

(a) Detrimental reliance on promise

(b) Reliance is reasonable and foreseeable

(c) Damage results (injustice) if promise is not enforced

(2) Usually applied to gratuitous promises but trend is to apply to commercial transactions. At least recovery of expenses is allowed.

EXAMPLE: A wealthy man in the community promises to pay for a new church if it is built. The church committee reasonably (and in good faith) relies on the promise and incurs the expenses.

o. Mutuality of obligation—means both parties must be bound or neither is bound

(1) Both parties must give consideration by paying or promising to pay for the act, promise, or forbearance of the other with something of legal value

p. Promise to donate to charity is enforceable based on public policy reasons

4. Legal Capacity

a. An agreement between parties in which one or both lack the capacity to contract is void or, in some cases, voidable

b. Minors (persons under age eighteen or twenty-one)

(1) A minor may contract, but agreement is voidable by minor

(a) Adult is held to contract unless minor disaffirms

(2) If minor has purchased nonnecessaries, when minor disaffirms, s/he is required to give back any part s/he still has

(a) Minor may recover all of consideration given

(b) In most courts, minor need not pay for what s/he cannot return

(3) Minor is liable for reasonable value of necessaries furnished to him/her

(a) Minor may disaffirm contract if it is executory (i.e., not completed)

(b) Necessaries include food, clothing, shelter, education, etc., considering his/her age and position in life

(c) Many states have passed laws which make certain contracts enforceable against minors such as contracts which involve

1] Medical care

2] Life insurance

3] Psychological care

4] Loans for education

(4) Minor may disaffirm contract at any time until a reasonable time after reaching majority age

(a) Failure to disaffirm within reasonable time after reaching majority acts as ratification (e.g., one year is too long in the absence of very special circumstances such as being out of the country)

(5) Minor may choose to ratify within a reasonable time after reaching age of majority

    (a) By words, either orally or in writing but must ratify all, or

    (b) By actions that indicate ratification

    (c) Ratification prior to majority is not effective

(6) If minor misrepresents his/her age when making contract, courts are split on effect

    (a) Some courts allow minor to disaffirm contract anyway but allow other party to sue for fraud

    (b) Some allow minor to disaffirm if minor returns consideration in similar condition

    (c) Other courts will not allow minor to disaffirm especially if it was a business contract

(7) A minor usually is liable for own torts (civil wrongs), but this may depend on his/her age (above 14 commonly liable)

    (a) Parents are not liable for torts of minors unless they direct or condone certain conduct or were negligent themselves

c.   Incompetent persons

    (1) Contract by person adjudicated insane is void

      (a) Insane person need not return consideration

    (2) If contract is made before adjudication of insanity, it may be voidable by incompetent person

      (a) Where courts hold such agreements voidable, restitution is condition precedent to disaffirmance

d.   Legal capacity of one intoxicated is determined by his/her ability to understand and by degree of intoxication

    (1) Contracts are enforceable, in general, unless extent of intoxication at time contract made was so great that intoxicated party did not understand terms or nature of contract—then contract voidable at option of one intoxicated if s/he returns items under contract

e.   Corporations contract through agents and are limited by their charters

5.   Legality

   a.   Agreement is unenforceable if it is illegal or violates public policy

   b.   When both parties are guilty, neither will be aided by court (i.e., if one party had already given some consideration, s/he will not get it back)

    (1) But if one party repudiates prior to performance, s/he may recover his/her consideration

> EXAMPLE: *X contracts to buy stolen goods from Y. If X pays Y but then repents and refuses to accept the stolen goods, X may recover the money he paid Y.*

   c.   When one party is innocent, s/he will usually be given relief

    (1) A member of a class of people designed to be protected by statute is considered innocent (e.g., purchaser of stock issued in violation of blue-sky laws)

   d.   Types of illegal contracts

    (1) Agreement to commit crime or tort

      (a) If agreement calls for intentional wrongful interference with a valid contractual relationship, it is an illegal agreement

        1] However, a sale of a business containing a covenant prohibiting seller from owning or operating similar business as well as the termination of an employee who has agreed not to compete are legal and enforceable provided the agreement

          a] Protects legitimate interests of buyer or employer without creating too large a burden on seller or employee (based on ability to find other work)

          b] Is reasonable as to length of time under the circumstances to protect those interests

          c] Is reasonable as to area to protect interests of same area

> EXAMPLE: *Seller of a small bakery agrees not to compete in Washington, DC, for six months.*

(2) An agreement to not press criminal charges for consideration is illegal

> *EXAMPLE: A has embezzled money from his employer. The employer agrees to not press charges if A pays back all of the money.*

(3) Services rendered without a license when statute requires a license

    (a) Two types of licensing statutes

        1] Regulatory licensing statute—one that seeks to protect public from incapable, unskilled, or dishonest persons

           a] Contract is unenforceable by either party

           b] Even if work done, other need not pay because not a contract

> *EXAMPLE: X, falsely claiming to have a CPA license, performs an audit for ABC Company. Upon learning the true facts, ABC may legally refuse to pay X any fees or expenses.*

        2] Revenue-seeking statute—purpose is to raise revenue for government

           a] Contract is enforceable

> *EXAMPLE: Y, based on a contract, performed extensive yard work for M. M then finds out that Y failed to obtain a license required by the local government to raise revenue. M is obligated to pay Y the agreed-upon amount.*

(4) Usury (contract for greater than legal interest rate)

(5) Contracts against public policy

    (a) Contracts in restraint of trade such as covenant not to compete after end of an employment contract

        1] Courts must balance need of former employer such as protection of trade secrets or customer base with need of employee to practice his/her line of work

        2] Typically, contract will restrict employee from competing in named areas for stated period of time

        3] Employer must show that covenant not to compete is needed to protect interests of employer and that restraints are reasonable as to geographical area and as to time period

    (b) Upon sale of business, seller agrees to not compete with sold type of business in named areas for stated period of time

        1] Courts will look at reasonableness as to geographical area, reasonableness as to time, and whether covenant is unduly restrictive for public's need

    (c) Exculpatory clauses are clauses found in contracts in which one party tries to avoid liability for own negligence

        1] These are generally against public policy and not enforceable unless both parties have relatively equal bargaining power

> *EXAMPLE: An automobile dealership agrees to fix the engine of a car brought in by a consumer for repair. A clause in the contract provides that the dealer will not be liable for any mistakes it may make during the repair.*

6. Reality of Consent—If one of the following concepts is present, a contract may be void (i.e., no contract) or voidable (i.e., enforceable until party having right decides to pull out).

  a. Fraud—includes following elements

    (1) Misrepresentation of a material fact

        (a) Can be falsehood or concealment of defect

        (b) Silence is not misrepresentation unless there is duty to speak, for example,

           1] Fiduciary relationship between parties

           2] Seller of property knows there is a dangerous latent (hidden) defect

        (c) Must be statement of past or present fact

           1] Opinion (e.g., of value) is not fact

               a] Experts' opinion does constitute fraud

> *EXAMPLE: An expert appraiser of jewelry appraises a diamond to be worth $500 when he knows it is actually worth $1,500. This fulfills the "misrepresentation of a material fact" element and also scienter element. If the remaining elements of fraud are met, then there is fraud.*

2] Opinions about what will happen in future (expert or not) do not satisfy fact requirement

> *EXAMPLE: A real estate agent tells a prospective buyer that the income property she is considering purchasing will earn at least 50% more next year than last year.*

3] Puffing or sales talk is not fact

> *EXAMPLE: A seller claims her necklace is worth $1,000. The buyer pays $1,000 and later finds out that he can buy a very similar necklace from another seller for $700. Even if the other elements of fraud are present, this opinion does not constitute fraud.*

4] Presently existing intention in mind of the speaker is fact

(2) Intent to mislead—"scienter"

    (a) Need knowledge of falsity with intent to mislead, **or**

    (b) Reckless disregard for truth can be substituted

        1] If all elements (1) through (4) are present but reckless disregard is proven instead of actual knowledge of falsity, then it is called constructive fraud

(3) Reasonable reliance by injured party

    (a) One who knows the truth or might have learned it by a reasonable inquiry may not recover

    (b) One cannot reasonably rely on opinions about future

(4) Resulting in injury to others

(5) Remedies for fraud

    (a) Defrauded party may affirm agreement and sue for damages under tort of deceit, or if party is sued on contract, then s/he may set up fraud in reduction of damages, or

    (b) Defrauded party may rescind contract and sue for damages that result from the fraud

(6) Fraud may occur

    (a) In the inducement

        1] The misrepresentation occurs during contract negotiations

        2] Creates voidable contract at option of defrauded party

> *EXAMPLE: A represents to B that A's car has been driven 50,000 miles when in fact it has been driven for 150,000 miles. If B purchases A's car in reliance on this misrepresentation, fraud in the inducement is present, creating a voidable contract at B's option.*

    (b) In the execution

        1] Misrepresentation occurs in actual form of agreement

        2] Creates void contract

> *EXAMPLE: Larry Lawyer represents to Danny that Danny is signing his will, when in fact he is signing a promissory note payable to Larry. This promissory note is void because fraud in the execution is present.*

(7) Fraud is also called intentional misrepresentation

b. Innocent misrepresentation

(1) An innocent misstatement made in good faith (i.e., no scienter)

(2) All other elements same as fraud

(3) Creates right of rescission (cancellation) in other party—to return both parties to their precontract positions to extent practically possible

    (a) Does not allow aggrieved party to sue for damages

c. Mistake—an act done under an erroneous conviction

(1) Mutual mistake (i.e., by both parties) about material characteristics of subject matter in contract makes contract voidable by either party

> *EXAMPLE: S and B make a contract in which B agrees to buy a boat from S. Although neither party knew it at the time, this boat had been destroyed before this contract was made. This is a mutual mistake about the*

existence of the boat; therefore, either party may void this contract by law. Note that legally either party may pull out although usually only one party may wish to do so.

    (a) Also exists when both parties reasonably attach different meanings to word or phrase

    (b) Also called bilateral mistake

    (c) Mistake about value of subject matter is not grounds for voiding contract

  (2) Unilateral mistake generally does not allow party to void contract

    (a) Major exception for mistakes in computations for bids

      1] Contract based on mistake is voidable by party making mistake if calculation is far enough off so that other party should have known that a mistake was made

d. Duress—a contract entered into because of duress can be voided because of invalid consent

  (1) Any acts or threats of violence or extreme pressure against party or member of party's family, which in fact deprives party of free will and causes him/her to agree, is duress

    EXAMPLE: X threatens to criminally prosecute Y unless he signs contract. This contract is made under duress.

    (a) May involve coercion that is social or economic that leaves him/her with no reasonable alternative

  (2) Physical duress in which party agrees to contract under physical force

  (3) Extreme duress causes agreement to be void

  (4) Ordinary duress creates voidable agreement

e. Undue influence—unfair persuasion of one person over another which prevents understanding or voluntary action

  (1) Usually occurs when very dominant person has extreme influence over weaker person

    (a) Weakness can result from physical, mental, or emotional weakness or combinations of these

  (2) Also occurs through abuse of fiduciary relationship (e.g., CPA, attorney, guardian, trustee, etc.)

  (3) Normally causes agreement to be voidable

f. Changes in weather conditions, economic conditions, etc., that cause hardship to one party will not create voidable contracts when conditions are not so extreme that the parties could have contemplated them

    EXAMPLE: B had a contract to purchase 50,000 gallons of heating oil from S at specified prices. B refuses to take more than 40,000 gallons because the weather was warmer than normal. B is obligated on all 50,000 gallons because the warmer weather could have been contemplated by the parties.

g. Infancy, incompetency, and noncompliance with Statute of Frauds may also create voidable contract

h. Adhesion contract—offeror is in position to say "take it or leave it" because of superior bargaining power

  (1) Usually occurs when large business entity requires its customers to use their standard form contract without allowing modification

i. Traditionally under US law, central theory of contract law has been freedom of contract

  (1) Is still central to contract law, but state and federal governments have been enacting increased statutes protecting consumers, debtors, and others from unfair contracts

  (2) Also, courts have been increasingly using some common law ideas to allow some unjust or oppressive contracts to be unenforced

  (3) This modern law of contracts encourages more government regulation over freedom of contract

    (a) Trend is encouraged by sellers' use of more form contracts being used now that frequently offer goods and services to buyers on a take-it-or-leave-it basis

      1] Sellers today frequently have more power over contracts than they historically did

7. Conformity with the Statute of Frauds

a. Contracts required to be in writing and signed by party to be charged—these are said to be within the Statute

(1) An agreement to sell land or any interest in land

  (a) Includes buildings, easements, and contracts to sell real estate

  (b) Part performance typically satisfies Statute even though real estate contract was oral, but this requires

    1] Possession of the land

    2] Either part payment or making of improvements on real estate

    3] Many courts require all three

(2) An agreement that cannot be performed within one year from the making of agreement

  (a) Contract that can be performed in exactly one year or less may be oral

    EXAMPLE: W agrees to hire X for ten months starting in four months. This contract must be in writing because it cannot be performed until fourteen months after the agreement is made.

  (b) Any contract which can conceivably be completed in one year, irrespective of how long the task actually takes, may be oral

    EXAMPLE: A agrees to paint B's portrait for $400. It actually is not completed until over a year later. This contract did not have to be in writing because it was possible to complete it within one year.

  (c) If performance is contingent on something which could take place in less than one year, agreement may be oral

    EXAMPLE: "I will employ you as long as you live." Party could possibly die in less than one year.

  (d) But if its terms call for more than one year, it must be written even if there is possibility of taking place in less than one year

    EXAMPLE: "I will employ you for five years." The employee's death could occur before the end of five years, but the terms call for the writing requirement under the Statute of Frauds.

  (e) Generally, if one side of performance is complete but other side cannot be performed within year, it is not within Statute (i.e., may be oral). Especially true if performance has been accepted and all that remains is the payment of money.

    EXAMPLE: X agrees to pay E $6,000 salary per month and a bonus of $50,000 if he works for at least two years. After two years, X refuses to pay the bonus. The $50,000 is payable and the Statute of Frauds is no defense here.

(3) An agreement to answer for debt or default of another (contract of guaranty)

  (a) A secondary promise is within this section of the Statute of Frauds (i.e., must be in writing)

    EXAMPLE: "If Jack doesn't pay, I will."

  (b) A primary promise is not within this section of the Statute of Frauds because it is in reality the promisor's own contract

    EXAMPLE: "Let Jack have it, and I will pay."

  (c) Promise for benefit of promisor may be oral

    EXAMPLE: Promisor agrees to answer for default of X, because X is promisor's supplier and he needs X to stay in business to keep himself in business.

  (d) Promise of indemnity (will pay based on another's fault, for example, insurance) is not within Statute

(4) Agreement for sale of goods for $500 or more is required to be in writing under UCC

    EXAMPLE: Oral contract for the sale of fifty calculators for $10 each is not enforceable.

    EXAMPLE: Oral contract to perform management consulting services over the next six months for $100,000 is enforceable because the $500 rule does not apply to contracts that come under common law.

    EXAMPLE: Same as previous example except that the agreed time was for fourteen months. This one was required to be in writing to be enforceable because of the one-year rule.

  (a) Exceptions to writing requirement (these are important)

1] Oral contract involving specially manufactured goods (i.e., not saleable in ordinary course of business) if seller has made substantial start in their manufacture (or even made a contract for necessary raw materials) is enforceable

2] Oral contract is enforceable against party who admits it in court but not beyond quantity of goods admitted

3] Goods that have been paid for (if seller accepts payment) or goods which buyer has accepted are part of enforceable contract even if oral

> EXAMPLE: B orally agrees to purchase 10,000 parts from S for $1 each. B later gives S $6,000 for a portion of the parts. S accepts the money. In absence of a written agreement, B may enforce a contract for 6,000 parts but not for the full 10,000 parts.

(b) Modifications of written contracts involve two issues under UCC

1] New consideration on both sides is not required under UCC although it is required under common law

  a] Under UCC, modification must be done in good faith

2] Modified contract must be in writing if contract, as modified, is within Statute of Frauds (i.e., sale of goods for $500 or more)

> EXAMPLE: S agrees orally to sell B 100 widgets for $4.80 each. B later agrees, orally, to pay $5.00 for the 100 widgets due to changed business conditions. The modified contract is not enforceable because it must have been in writing. Therefore, the original contract is enforceable.

> EXAMPLE: Same as above except that the modification is in writing. Now the modified contract is enforceable despite the fact that S is giving no new consideration.

> EXAMPLE: X and Y have a written contract for the sale of goods for $530. They subsequently both agree orally to a price reduction of $40. The modified contract for $490 is enforceable.

(c) Parties may exclude future oral agreements in a signed writing

(5) Agreement for sale of intangibles over $5,000 must be in writing (e.g., patents, copyrights, or contract rights)

(6) Sale of securities must be in writing

(a) Must include price and quantity

b. When a writing is required and the UCC applies, it must

(1) Indicate in writing that a contract for sale has been made

(2) Be signed by party to be charged, and

(3) Specify quantity of goods sold

(4) However, note the following:

(a) Any written form will do (e.g., letter, telegram, receipt, fax)

(b) Need not be single document (e.g., two telegrams)

(c) Need not be made at same time as contract

1] Must be made before suit is brought

2] Need not exist at time of suit (i.e., may have been destroyed)

(d) Signature need not be at end nor be in a special form so long as intent to authenticate existed (e.g., initials, stamp, printed letterhead, etc., of party to be charged)

1] Generally, signature sent by fax is enforceable

(e) May omit material terms (e.g., price, delivery, time for performance) as long as quantity is stated. Reasonable terms will be inferred.

(f) Exception to signature requirement exists under UCC when both parties are merchants—one party may send signed written confirmation stating terms (especially quantity) of oral agreement to other party within reasonable time, then nonsigning party must object within ten days or the contract is enforceable against him/her

> EXAMPLE: B agreed on January 10 to purchase 100 widgets at $6 each from S. They agreed that delivery would take place on January 31. On January 14, B sent S a letter on B's letterhead that stated: "We no longer need the 100 widgets we ordered on January 10. Don't ship them."
> This contract is enforceable against B even though the writing was later than the original oral agreement.

SIMULATION PROBLEMS

Simulation Problem 1   (5 to 10 minutes)

Consideration

For each of the numbered statements or groups of statements select either A, B, or C.

List

A. Both parties have given consideration legally sufficient to support a contract.
B. One of the parties has **not** given consideration legally sufficient to support a contract. The promise, agreement, or transaction is generally **not** enforceable.
C. One of the parties has **not** given consideration legally sufficient to support a contract. However, the promise, agreement, or transaction **is** generally enforceable.

	(A)	(B)	(C)
1. Party S feels a moral obligation because Party F let S stay in his place for free when S attended college. S now promises to pay F for the past kindness.	○	○	○
2. F agrees to deliver all of the sugar that Company S will need in her business for the following year. S agrees to purchase it at the market price.	○	○	○
3. F does not smoke for one year pursuant to S's agreement to pay F $200 if she does not smoke for one year.	○	○	○
4. F dies leaving a valid will which gives S $100,000.	○	○	○
5. F is an auditor of XYZ Company. S is a potential investor of XYZ and offers to pay F $1,000 if F performs a professional, quality audit of XYZ Company. The $1,000 is in addition to the fee F will get from XYZ. F does perform a professional, quality audit.	○	○	○
6. F had agreed, in writing, to work for S for five years for $100,000 per year. After two years, F asks for a 20% raise. S first agrees then later changes his mind. F, while not agreeing to additional duties or changing his position, wants to enforce the raise in salary.	○	○	○
7. S promised to pay F $1,000 if he crosses the Golden Gate Bridge on his hands and knees. F does so.	○	○	○
8. F promised to pay S $200 for a computer worth $2,000. S agreed to the deal.	○	○	○
9. F agreed to purchase all of the parts from S that S can produce in her business for the next six months. S also agreed.	○	○	○
10. S agreed to accept $1,000 from F for a $1,500 debt that is not disputed. S now wants the additional $500. Focus on the agreement to accept the lesser amount.	○	○	○
11. S agreed to accept $1,000 from F for a debt that S claims is $1,500 but F in good faith claims is $800. F agreed to the $1,000 initially, then decides he will pay only $800. Focus on the enforceability of the agreement for $1,000.	○	○	○
12. S agreed to donate $100 to F, a public charity.	○	○	○

Simulation Problem 2   (10 to 15 minutes)

Situation			
	Contractual Relationship	Assignment	Memo

On December 15, Blake Corp. telephoned Reach Consultants, Inc. and offered to hire Reach to design a security system for Blake's research department. The work would require two years to complete. Blake offered to pay a fee of $100,000 but stated that the offer must be accepted in writing, and the acceptance received by Blake no later than December 20.

On December 20, Reach faxed a written acceptance to Blake. Blake's offices were closed on December 20 and Reach's fax was not seen until December 21.

Reach's acceptance contained the following language:

"We accept your $1,000,000 offer. Weaver has been assigned $5,000 of the fee as payment for sums owed Weaver by Reach. Payment of this amount should be made directly to Weaver."

On December 22, Blake sent a signed memo to Reach rejecting Reach's December 20 fax but offering to hire Reach for a $75,000 fee. Reach telephoned Blake on December 23 and orally accepted Blake's December 22 offer.

Situation	Contractual Relationship	Assignment	Memo

Items 1 through 7 relate to whether a contractual relationship exists between Blake and Reach. For each item, determine whether the statement is True or False.

		True	*False*
1.	Blake's December 15 offer had to be in writing to be a legitimate offer.	○	○
2.	Reach's December 20 fax was an improper method of acceptance.	○	○
3.	Reach's December 20 fax was effective when sent.	○	○
4.	Reach's acceptance was invalid because it was received after December 20.	○	○
5.	Blake's receipt of Reach's acceptance created a voidable contract.	○	○
6.	If Reach had rejected the original offer by telephone on December 17, he could not validly accept the offer later.	○	○
7.	Reach's December 20 fax was a counteroffer.	○	○

Situation	Contractual Relationship	Assignment	Memo

Items 1 through 5 relate to the attempted assignment of part of the fee to Weaver. Assume that a valid contract exists between Blake and Reach. For each item, determine whether the statement is True or False.

		True	*False*
1.	Reach is prohibited from making an assignment of any contract right or duty.	○	○
2.	Reach may validly assign part of the fee to Weaver.	○	○
3.	Under the terms of Reach's acceptance, Weaver would be considered a third-party creditor beneficiary.	○	○
4.	In a breach of contract suit by Weaver, against Blake, Weaver would not collect any punitive damages.	○	○
5.	In a breach of contract suit by Weaver, against Reach, Weaver would be able to collect punitive damages.	○	○

Situation	Contractual Relationship	Assignment	Memo

Items 1 through 3 relate to Blake's December 22 signed memo. For each item, determine whether the statement is True or False.

		True	*False*
1.	Reach's oral acceptance of Blake's December 22 memo may be enforced by Blake against Reach.	○	○
2.	Blake's memo is a valid offer even though it contains no date for acceptance.	○	○
3.	Blake's memo may be enforced against Blake by Reach.	○	○

MULTIPLE-CHOICE ANSWERS

1. a	__ __	13. d	__ __	25. a	__ __	37. c	__ __	49. a	__ __
2. b	__ __	14. b	__ __	26. c	__ __	38. d	__ __	50. a	__ __
3. c	__ __	15. c	__ __	27. b	__ __	39. b	__ __	51. c	__ __
4. a	__ __	16. c	__ __	28. b	__ __	40. c	__ __	52. d	__ __
5. d	__ __	17. c	__ __	29. d	__ __	41. c	__ __	53. a	__ __
6. b	__ __	18. d	__ __	30. b	__ __	42. d	__ __	54. a	__ __
7. b	__ __	19. d	__ __	31. a	__ __	43. d	__ __	55. c	__ __
8. a	__ __	20. b	__ __	32. d	__ __	44. a	__ __	56. a	__ __
9. b	__ __	21. c	__ __	33. d	__ __	45. a	__ __	57. b	__ __
10. c	__ __	22. c	__ __	34. c	__ __	46. c	__ __		
11. a	__ __	23. b	__ __	35. c	__ __	47. b	__ __	1st: __/57 = __%	
12. c	__ __	24. d	__ __	36. b	__ __	48. a	__ __	2nd: __/57 = __%	

MULTIPLE-CHOICE ANSWER EXPLANATIONS

C.1. Offer

1. **(a)** Under common law, an offer must be definite and certain as to what will be agreed upon in the contract. Essential terms are the parties involved, the price, the time for performance, and the subject matter (quantity and type). The price element of the contract was not present.

2. **(b)** Advertisements in almost all cases are merely invitations for interested parties to make an offer. Thus, Harris has not made an offer, but is seeking offers through the use of the advertisement.

3. **(c)** Generally an offeror may revoke an offer at any time prior to acceptance by the offeree. Revocation is effective when it is received by the offeree. Revocation also occurs if the offeree learns by a reliable means that the offeror has already sold the subject of the offer. In this situation, Peters' offer was effectively revoked when Mason learned that the lawn mower had been sold to Bronson. Therefore, Mason's acceptance was ineffective. Answers (a) and (b) are incorrect because the offer had been revoked prior to Mason's acceptance. Answer (d) is incorrect because Peters was not obligated to keep the offer open. Note that if consideration had been paid by Mason to keep the offer open, an option contract would exist and the offer could not be revoked before the stated time.

4. **(a)** Drake did not intend to reject the $300,000 offer but is simply seeing if Calistoga might consider selling the home for less. Answer (b) is incorrect because a counteroffer takes place when the original offer is rejected and a new offer takes its place. Answer (c) is incorrect because Drake showed no intention of rejecting the offer by his mere inquiry. Answer (d) is incorrect because ambiguity is not one of the grounds to have an offer terminated by operation of law.

5. **(d)** An offer automatically terminates upon the occurrence of any of the following events: (1) the death or insanity of either the offeror or offeree, (2) bankruptcy or insolvency of either the offeror or offeree, or (3) the destruction of the specific, identified subject matter. Thus the offer automatically terminates at the date of Opal's death. It does not matter whether Larkin received notice of the death. If Larkin had accepted the offer prior to Opal's death, a valid contract would have been formed.

C.2. Acceptance

6. **(b)** Under the mailbox rule, an acceptance is ordinarily effective when sent if transmitted by the means authorized by the offeror, or by the same means used to transmit the offer if no means was authorized. However, the offeror may stipulate that acceptance is effective only when received by the offeror. In this situation, no contract was formed because Moss' acceptance was not received by the date specified in Fine's offer. Under common law, a method of acceptance other than the means specified in the offer or the method used to communicate the offer, is considered effective when received by the offeror.

7. **(b)** Fresno's acceptance by overnight delivery was made by a method other than the methods specified by Harris in the written offer. When acceptance is sent by a method other than the method specified in the offer or different than the method used to transmit the offer, acceptance is considered valid only when actually received by the offeror. Late acceptance is not valid, but instead constitutes a counteroffer. A valid contract would be formed only if the original offeror (Harris) then accepts.

8. **(a)** A unilateral offer exists when the offeror expects acceptance of an offer by action of the offeree. A unilateral contract is then formed when the offeree accepts the contract through performance of the offeror's required action. In this case, a valid contract is formed when Hammer accepts Kay's unilateral offer by obtaining the artifacts within a two-week period. Answers (b) and (d) are incorrect because a quasi contract is an implied-in-law rather than express agreement which results when one of the parties has been unjustly enriched at the expense of the other. The law creates such a contract when there is no binding agreement present to keep the unjust enrichment from occurring. Answer (c) is incorrect because public policy causes enforcement of promises despite lack of any other legal enforcement of the contract. For example, public policy would normally allow enforcement of a promise by a debtor to pay a debt barred by the statute of limitations.

9. **(b)** Common law applies to this contract because it involves real estate. In this situation, Fox's reply on October 2 is a counteroffer and terminates Summers' original offer made on September 27. The acceptance of an offer must conform exactly to the terms of the offer under common law. By agreeing to purchase the vacation home at a price different from the original offer, Fox is rejecting Summers' offer and is making a counteroffer. Answer (a) is incorrect because the fact that Fox failed to return Summers' letter is irrelevant to the formation of a binding contract. Fox's reply constitutes a counteroffer as Fox did not intend to accept Summers' original offer. Answer (c) is incorrect because Summers' offer was rejected by Fox's counteroffer. Answer (d) is incorrect because with rare exceptions, silence does not constitute acceptance.

C.3. Consideration

10. (c)   Both Zake and Wick had a contract that was binding for five years. For them to modify this contract, both of them must give new consideration under common law rules which apply to employment contracts such as this one. When Wick agreed to the raise, only Wick gave new consideration in the form of $20,000 additional each year. Zake did not give new consideration because he would perform in the last three years as originally agreed. Answers (a) and (b) are incorrect because Zake did not give new consideration whether or not the raise was in writing. Answer (d) is incorrect because duress needed to make a contract voidable or void requires more than "some pressure."

11. (a)   Consideration is an act, promise, or forbearance which is offered by one party and accepted by another as inducement to enter into an agreement. A party must bind him/herself to do something s/he is not legally obligated to do. Furthermore, the consideration must be bargained for. Past consideration is not sufficient to serve as consideration for a new contract because it is not bargained for. Answer (b) is incorrect because relinquishment of a legal right constitutes consideration. Answer (c) is incorrect because even though the consideration must be adequate, courts generally do not look into the amount of exchange, as long as it is legal consideration and is bargained for. Answer (d) is incorrect as this performance by a third party is still deemed consideration.

12. (c)   The rebinding of Dunne's books is considered a service and not a sale of goods, therefore, common law applies. Under common law, modification of an existing contract needs new consideration by both parties to be legally binding. Since Dunne has not given any new consideration for Cook's reduction in price, the contract is unenforceable. Additionally, the parol evidence rule prohibits the presentation of evidence of any prior or contemporaneous oral or written statements for the purpose of modifying or changing a written agreement intended by the payor to be the final and complete expression of their contract. However, it does not bar from evidence any oral or written agreements entered into by the parties subsequent to the written contract. Therefore, the agreement between Dunne and Cook is unenforceable, but evidence of the modification is admissible into evidence. Note that if the contract had been for the sale of goods (UCC), modification of the contract terms would have been enforceable. Under the UCC, a contract for the sale of goods may be modified orally or in writing without new consideration if such modification is done in good faith.

13. (d)   A preexisting legal duty is not sufficient as consideration because no new legal detriment is suffered by performing the prior obligation. For example, when a creditor agrees to accept as full payment an amount less than the full amount of the undisputed (liquidated) debt, the agreement lacks valid consideration to be enforceable. However, when the amount of an obligation is disputed, the creditor's promise to accept a lesser amount as full payment of the debt is enforceable. Preexisting legal duties are not valid as consideration.

14. (b)   A promise to donate money to a charity which the charity relied upon in incurring large expenditures is a situation involving promissory estoppel. Promissory estoppel acts as a substitute for consideration and renders the promise enforceable. The elements necessary for promissory estoppel are (1) detrimental reliance on a promise, (2) reliance on the promise is reasonable and foreseeable, and (3) damage results (injustice) if the promise is not enforced. Answer (a) is incorrect because the failure to enforce an employer's promise to make a cash payment to a deceased employee's family will not result in damages, and therefore, promissory estoppel will not apply. Answer (c) is incorrect because the modification of a contract requires consideration, unless the contract involves the sale of goods under the UCC. Answer (d) is incorrect because an irrevocable oral promise by a merchant to keep an offer open for sixty days is an option contract that must be supported by consideration. A firm offer under the UCC requires an offer signed by the merchant.

C.4. Legal Capacity

15. (c)   A minor may disaffirm a contract at any time during his minority and within a reasonable time after reaching the age of majority. When Rail disaffirmed the contract two days after reaching the age of eighteen, he did so within a reasonable time after reaching majority age. Answer (a) is incorrect because Rail could ratify the contract only after reaching the age of majority. Answer (b) is incorrect because although Rail could have transferred good title to a good-faith purchaser for value, Rail's title was still voidable and subject to disaffirmance. Answer (d) is incorrect because Rail could disaffirm the contract only for a reasonable time after reaching the age of majority. Failure to disaffirm within a reasonable time serves to act as ratification.

16. (c)   When a person has previously been adjudicated by a court of law to be incompetent, all of the contracts that s/he makes are void. Answer (a) is incorrect because the contracts are only voidable at the option of Green if there was no formal, previous court determination of incompetence for Green. Answer (b) is incorrect because once the court determines that Green is incompetent, all of the contracts that s/he makes are not valid but are void. Answer (d) is incorrect because the contracts cannot be enforced by either Green or the other contracting party.

17. (c)   Ratification of a contract prior to reaching majority age is not effective. A minor **may** ratify a contract expressly or by actions indicating ratification after reaching the age of majority. Failure to disaffirm within a reasonable time after reaching majority age **does** act as ratification.

C.5. Legality

18. (d)   An agreement is unenforceable if it is illegal or violates public policy. Therefore, if the personal services of the contract are illegal, the party will not have to perform them. Answer (a) is incorrect because the death of the party who is to **receive** the benefits does not terminate the duties under the contract. His/her heirs can still receive and pay for the personal services. Answer (b) is incorrect because

making less profit or losing money are not grounds for getting out of a contract. Answer (c) is incorrect because bankruptcy of the receiver does not discharge the performer from the contract, although it can allow for forgiveness of all or part of the payment.

19. **(d)** An employer's promise not to press criminal charges against an employee-embezzler who agrees to return the embezzled money is not legally binding. The promise not to press charges is an illegal bargain, and, even if the employee returns the money, the employer is free to cooperate in prosecution of the criminal.

C.6. Reality of Consent

20. **(b)** Fraud is the intentional misrepresentation of a material fact upon which a third party reasonably relies to his or her detriment. An intentionally misstated appraised value would be an example of a fraudulent inducement to make a contract. Answers (a) and (c) are incorrect because a third party cannot reasonably rely on a nonexpert opinion or a prediction. Answer (d) is incorrect because by definition, fraud applies to material facts.

21. **(c)** An immaterial unilateral mistake generally does not allow either party to void the contract.

22. **(c)** Undue influence is a defense that makes a contract voidable. Classic situations of this concept involve close relationships in which a dominant person has extreme influence over a weaker person. Answer (a) is incorrect because although fraud in the inducement can make a contract voidable, it typically does not occur between parties that have a close relationship. Answer (b) is incorrect because unconscionability involves an oppressive contract in which one party has taken severe, unfair advantage of another which is often based on the latter's absence of choice or poor education rather than the parties' close relationship. Answer (d) is incorrect because duress involves acts or threats of violence or pressure, which need not result from close relationships.

23. **(b)** An insurance policy is voidable at the option of the insurer if the insured failed to inform the insurer at the time of application of a fact material to the insurer's risk (e.g., failure to disclose a preexisting heart condition on a life insurance application). The insured's concealment causes the policy to be voidable regardless of the type of beneficiary designated or the nature of the insured's death.

24. **(d)** One of the elements needed to prove fraud is a misrepresentation of a material fact. That statement that "it is a great car" is sales talk or puffing and does not establish this element. The fact that the overhaul was done thirteen months earlier instead of the stated one year is not a misrepresentation of a **material** fact.

25. **(a)** A mistake is an understanding that is not in agreement with a fact. A unilateral mistake (made by one party) generally does not allow the party to void the contract. However, a mistake unknown to the party making it becomes voidable if the other party recognizes it as a mistake. Particularly, this is the case in bid contract computations. The contract is voidable by the party making the mistake if the other party knew of the mistake or if the calculation was far enough off that the other party should have known that a mistake was made.

26. **(c)** Duress is any wrongful threat or act of violence made toward a person (or his family) which forces a person to enter into a contract against his will. For duress to be present, a threat must be made and the threatened party must believe that the other party has the ability to carry out the threat. In this situation, Maco's actions did not constitute duress. Kent's safety and property were in no way threatened by Maco and Kent was able to validly consent to the contract. Answers (a) and (b) are incorrect because regardless of Kent's financial problems and the FMV of Kent's services, duress was not present in that Kent was able to enter into the contract at will. Answer (d) is incorrect because Maco does not need to prove that Kent had no other offers to provide financial services.

27. **(b)** To establish a common law action for fraud, the following elements must be present: (1) misrepresentation of a material fact, (2) either knowledge of the falsity with intent to mislead or reckless disregard for the truth (scienter), (3) reasonable reliance by third party, and (4) injury resulted from misrepresentation. If the misrepresentation occurs during contract negotiations, fraud in the inducement is present resulting in a contract voidable at the option of the injured party. Answer (a) is incorrect because the defendant need not be an expert with regard to the misrepresentation to establish fraud in the inducement. Answer (c) is incorrect because the misrepresentation may be written or oral. Answer (d) is incorrect because the presence of fraud in the inducement does not require a fiduciary relationship between the parties.

28. **(b)** There are two remedies for fraud under the UCC Sales Article: (1) the plaintiff may affirm the agreement and sue for damages under the tort of deceit, or (2) the plaintiff may rescind the contract and sue for damages resulting from the fraud. Answer (a) is incorrect because the plaintiff must return any consideration received from the other party when the contract is rescinded. Answer (c) is incorrect because although punitive damages are allowed in fraud actions because they are intentional torts, they do not require physical injuries. Answer (d) is incorrect because without reliance by the plaintiff on the misrepresentation, there is no fraud, and therefore, the plaintiff may not rescind the contract.

C.7. Conformity with the Statute of Frauds

29. **(d)** The Statute of Frauds requires that a contract to answer the debt or default of another be in writing and signed by the party to be charged. The guarantee that Decker made was only oral. Answer (b) is incorrect, as the reason Decker is not liable for the oral guaranty is not because it expires more than one year after June 1, but because a contract of guaranty must be in writing. Decker is not liable regardless of Baker's confirmation letter; thus answer (a) is incorrect. Answer (c) is incorrect because Decker's oral guaranty is not enforceable. The time period between the date of the oral guaranty and the date payment is demanded has no bearing in this situation.

30. **(b)** Any agreement to sell land or any interest in land falls under the requirements of the Statute of Frauds. Agreements within the Statute of Frauds require contracts to be in writing and signed by the party to be charged (the party being sued). An exception to the above rule is "part performance" by the purchaser. Part performance exists when the purchaser of property takes possession of the property with the landowner's consent. Some states also require either partial payment for the property or permanent improvement of the property by the purchaser. Answer (b) is correct because even though Nolan failed to sign a written agreement, the part performance exception has been satisfied. Answer (a) is incorrect because the fact that Nolan simply failed to object to the agreement does not make the contract valid under the Statute of Frauds. Answer (c) is incorrect because the part performance exception has been met and Train will therefore prevail. Answer (d) is incorrect because no such requirement exists to alleviate Nolan's liability. The part performance rule allows Train to prevail. Note that **all** sales of land are covered under the Statute of Frauds, and not just those greater than $500.

31. **(a)** Contracts that cannot be performed within one year must be in writing. In this case Cherry agreed to purchase Picks Company if an audit after one year shows that the company has been profitable. This would take longer than a year to perform. Answer (b) is incorrect because the $500 provision is in the Uniform Commercial Code for a sale of goods. Answer (c) is incorrect because despite the actual profitability, the contract could not be completed within one year of the making of the contract. Answer (d) is incorrect because although promissory estoppel may be used in the absence of a writing, there are not the facts sufficient to show promissory estoppel.

32. **(d)** Contracts which fall within the requirements of the Statute of Frauds are required to be in writing and signed by the party to be charged. It is not required that the contract terms be formalized in a single writing. Two or more documents may be combined to create a writing which satisfies the Statute of Frauds as long as one of the documents refers to the others. Answer (a) is incorrect because the Statute of Frauds requires that agreements for the sale of goods for $500 or more be in writing; however, contracts that come under common law are not included in this requirement. Answer (b) is incorrect because the Statute of Frauds requires that the written contract be signed by the party to be charged, not by all parties to the contract. Answer (c) is incorrect because the Statute of Frauds applies to contracts that **cannot** be performed within one year from the making of the agreement.

33. **(d)** The Statute of Frauds applies to the following types of contracts: (1) an agreement to sell land or any interest in land, (2) an agreement that cannot be performed within one year from the making of the agreement, (3) an agreement to answer for the debt or default of another, and (4) an agreement for the sale of goods for $500 or more. Since the agreement between Carson and Ives meets none of the above requirements, it is an enforceable oral contract under common law. Furthermore, under common law, modification of an existing contract needs new consideration by both parties to be legally binding. Since Ives received the benefit of additional repairs to his book, Carson's increase in the contract price is enforceable. Therefore, Carson will recover $650.

34. **(c)** Under The Statute of Frauds, agreements that can be performed within one year of their making can be oral. In this case the ethics audit need only span ten months and the completion of the report will take less than one additional month for a total of less than one year. We know that the report can be done in less than a month because

Newell points out that even if she delays start for three months, she will still complete the ten-month audit before the fourteen-month deadline. The fact that it might take longer than a year does not require it to be in writing since it **possibly could** be completed within one year. Answer (a) is incorrect because the $500 provision is for sales of goods not services. Answer (b) is incorrect because the contract can be completed within one year. Answer (d) is incorrect because there is no such provision involved here for the Statute of Frauds.

C.7.d.(1) Parol Evidence Rule

35. **(c)** The parol evidence rule provides that a written agreement intended by contracting parties to be a final and complete contract may not be contradicted by previous or contemporaneous oral evidence. The parol evidence rule does not apply to any subsequent oral promises made after the original agreement. Thus, the subsequent oral agreement between Rogers and Lennon regarding Lennon's right to report on a monthly basis will be allowed as evidence in a lawsuit between the parties. Answer (a) is incorrect because the parol evidence rule applies to all written contracts regardless of the applicability of the Statute of Frauds. Answer (b) is incorrect because the parol evidence rule will prevent the admission into evidence of the contemporaneous oral agreement that Lennon could use Rogers' computer. Answer (d) is incorrect because the parol evidence rule does apply to the contemporaneous oral agreement.

36. **(b)** The parol evidence rule provides that any written agreement intended by parties to be final and complete contract may not be contradicted by previous or contemporaneous evidence, written or oral. Thus, previous written agreements are prohibited by the rule. Exceptions to the parol evidence rule include proof to invalidate the contract between the parties, to show terms not inconsistent with writing that parties would not be expected to have included, to explain the intended meaning of an ambiguity, or to show a condition precedent. The parol evidence rule does not apply to subsequent transactions, such as oral promises made after the original agreement.

37. **(c)** The parol evidence rule prohibits the presentation as evidence of any prior or contemporaneous oral statements concerning a written agreement intended by the parties to be the final and complete expression of their contract. Therefore, the evidence related to the oral agreement regarding the payment of utilities would not be allowed. However, the parol evidence rule does **not** bar the admission of evidence which is presented to establish fraud.

C.9. Contracting Online

38. **(d)** Even though this contract falls under the Statute of Frauds and, therefore, generally must be written and signed, most states have passed laws allowing contracts to be made over the Internet to facilitate commerce. The statutes encourage technology to overcome concerns over authenticity of such contracts. Therefore, answer (a) is incorrect. Answer (b) is incorrect because the parol evidence rule does not specify when a contract must be written and signed. Answer (c) is incorrect because a sale of land is governed by common law rules and not the UCC.

D. Assignment and Delegation

39. **(b)** Assignment is the transfer of a right under a contract by one person to another. Almost all contract rights are assignable as long as the parties agree to it, but there are some exceptions. Contracts involving personal services, trust or confidence are not assignable. If assignment would materially change the risk or burden of the obligor, it is not allowed. For example, a contract for insurance against certain risks are not assignable because they were made upon the character of the contracting party (the insured). Assigning the rights to another party would alter the risk. Therefore, malpractice insurance policy rights are not assignable. A further exception is that future rights are not assignable, with the exception under the UCC that future rights for the sale of goods are assignable, whether based on an existing or nonexisting contract. As the assignment of option contract rights does not fall under any exception, they would be assignable.

40. **(c)** Assignment is the transfer of a right under a contract by one person to another. No consideration is needed for valid assignment. Normally an assignment is done in writing, but any act, oral or written, is sufficient if it gives clear intent of the assignment. Only situations included under the Statute of Frauds are required to be in writing. When consideration is given in exchange for an assignment, it is irrevocable. Also, as a general rule a gratuitous assignment is revocable unless it is evidenced by a writing signed by the assignor, effected by a delivery of a writing used as evidence of the right (i.e., bill of lading), and the assignment is executed. A contract right cannot be assigned if it would materially change the risk or burden of the obligor.

41. **(c)** Assignment is the transfer of a right under a contract by one person to another. If the obligor has notice of the assignment, s/he must pay the assignee, not the assignor. The contract between Barton and Egan provided for both payments on the purchase price and the insurance policy in case of Egan's death. Because Barton assigned his contract rights to Vim, Vim was then entitled to payments on the purchase price and the insurance proceeds. Since Barton received payments on the purchase price and insurance proceeds after the assignment, Vim is entitled to sue Barton for these amounts.

E. Third-Party Beneficiary Contracts

42. **(d)** When a debtor contracts with a second party to pay the debt owed to a creditor, the creditor becomes a creditor beneficiary. Barton contracted with Egan for Egan to pay Ness the business' debts. The contract also required Egan to provide a life insurance policy to pay Ness if Egan died. In both the contract and the insurance policy, Ness was a creditor beneficiary. Neither the contract nor the insurance policy were entered into to confer a gift to Ness, and therefore he was not a donee beneficiary.

43. **(d)** Bugle would have received an unintended benefit under the contract between Fargo and ABC Company. Therefore, Bugle is an incidental beneficiary, not an intended beneficiary and, thus, has no legal rights against either Fargo or ABC. No matter who breached the contract, Bugle has no rights against either party.

44. **(a)** In an assignment, the assignee (Clay) acquires the assignor's (Baxter) rights against the obligor (Globe) and has the right to performance. Baxter is still liable to the assignee if Globe does not perform. However, if Clay released Globe from the contract, Baxter would also be released and no longer liable to Clay. Answer (b) is incorrect because if the obligor has no notice of the assignment, s/he may pay the assignor, and the assignee must recover from the assignor. Thus, if Globe was unaware of the assignment and paid Baxter, Clay would have to collect from Baxter. Answers (c) and (d) are incorrect because even if Baxter released Globe or breached the contract, Baxter would still be liable to Clay.

45. **(a)** Mann is a donee beneficiary and, thus, can bring suit against the promissor, Manus, only. He cannot maintain a suit against Mackay, who was just giving a gift. Mann cannot maintain any action against Mackay either alone or in combination with Manus.

46. **(c)** When a debtor contracts with a second party to pay the debt owed to a creditor, the creditor becomes a creditor beneficiary. A creditor beneficiary has the right to enforce the contract which gives him the intended benefits and may commence an action for nonperformance against either of the contracting parties. For this reason, Ferco (creditor beneficiary) will prevail in a lawsuit against Bell because Ferco has an enforceable right to receive payment. Answer (a) is incorrect because Ferco, as a creditor beneficiary, has the right to recover from either Bell or Allied. Answer (b) is incorrect because the creditor beneficiary is not required to give consideration to have an enforceable right. Answer (d) is incorrect because having knowledge of the contract between Bell and Allied at the time the contract was made is not necessary to later enforce this legal action. Ferco must establish that he is a creditor beneficiary to maintain an action for nonperformance.

F. Performance of Contract

47. **(b)** Under the doctrine of substantial performance, a contract obligation may be discharged even though the performance tendered was not in complete conformity with the terms of the agreement. Under this doctrine, if it can be shown that the defect in performance was only minor in nature, that a good-faith effort was made to conform completely with the terms of the agreement, and if the performing party is willing to accept a decrease in compensation equivalent to the amount of the minor defect in performance, the contractual obligation will be discharged. Since the defect in Glaze's performance was only minor in nature, and since Parc refused to allow Glaze to complete the project, Glaze will prevail in its action against Parc. Anticipatory breach applies only to executory bilateral contracts. An executory contract is a contract wherein both parties have yet to perform. In this instance, Glaze has substantially performed its part of the agreement.

48. **(a)** The duty to perform a contract may depend upon a condition. Conditions that could be present include: condition precedent, which is one that must occur before there is duty to perform; condition subsequent, which is one that removes a preexisting duty to perform; or condition concurrent, which is mutually dependent upon performance at nearly the same time.

G. Discharge of Contracts

49.   (a)   Once one party materially breaches the contract, the other party is discharged from performing his or her obligations under the contract. Answer (b) is incorrect because a reasonable delay in the performance of the contract is not a breach unless time was of the essence. Answer (c) is incorrect because tender or offer to pay or perform obligates the other party to do what s/he promised. Answer (d) is incorrect because assignment of rights typically is allowed under contract law.

50.   (a)   The discharge of a contract can come about in several ways. The first is by agreement. Accord and satisfaction involves an agreed substitute for performance under the contract (accord) and the actual performance of that substitute (satisfaction). An agreement can also be entered into by three parties whereby the previous agreement is discharged by the creation of a new agreement (a novation). The second method of discharge is by release of the contract or parties from performance. Another method of discharging a contract is by performance of the specified action becoming impossible, such as destruction of the subject matter, or death of a party where personal service is necessary. Lastly, breach of the contract discharges the injured party.

51.   (c)   Rescission entails canceling a contract and placing the parties in the position they were in before the contract was formed. Answer (a) is incorrect as a novation is an agreement between three parties whereby a previous agreement is discharged by the creation of a new agreement. Answer (b) is incorrect because release is a means of discharging (abandoning) a contract but it does not place the parties in the same position as before the contract. Answer (d) is incorrect because revocation is used by an offeror to terminate an offer.

H.   Remedies

52.   (d)   The remedy of specific performance is used when money damages will not sufficiently compensate the afflicted party due to the unique nature of the subject matter of the contract. In a contract for the sale of land, the buyer has the right to enforce the agreement by seeking the remedy of specific performance because real property is considered unique. Another remedy for this breach of contract would be for the buyer to seek compensatory damages. If the buyer desires, s/he may seek this remedy instead of specific performance. However, in this situation, Hodges could only sue for either specific performance or compensatory damages but would not be entitled to both remedies. An injured party is generally not allowed to seek punitive damages. Punitive damages are awarded only when the court is seeking to punish a party for their improper actions and are not usually granted in breach of contract actions.

53.   (a)   Under the doctrine of substantial performance, a contract obligation may be discharged even though the performance tendered was not in complete conformity with the terms of the agreement. If it can be shown that the defect in performance was only minor in nature, that a good-faith effort was made to conform completely with the terms of the agreement, and if the performing party is willing to accept a decrease in compensation equivalent to the amount of the minor defect in performance, the contractual obligation will be discharged. Because Ames' breach of contract was both inadvertent and not material, the doctrine of substantial per-

formance applies and recovery will be limited to monetary damages. The installation of fixtures other than those specified in the contract constitutes a breach, although the breach is considered immaterial. The doctrine of substantial performance applies in this situation and the contractual obligation will be discharged.

54.   (a)   A liquidated damage clause is a contractual provision which states the amount of damages that will occur if a party breaches the contract. The liquidated damage clause is enforceable if the amount is reasonable in light of the anticipated or actual harm caused by the breach. Excessive liquidated damages will not be enforceable in court even if both parties have agreed in writing. A clause providing for excessive damages is a penalty and the courts will not enforce a penalty. Materiality does not impact the enforceability of liquidated damage provisions.

55.   (c)   The doctrine of anticipatory repudiation allows a party to either sue at once or wait until after performance is due when the other party indicates s/he will not perform. This doctrine is in effect because Nagel told Fields that Nagel had no intention of delivering the goods (i.e., repudiation of the contract) prior to the date of performance. Answer (a) is incorrect because promissory estoppel acts as a substitute for consideration which is an element in the forming of a contract but is not relevant in this fact situation. Answer (b) is incorrect because accord and satisfaction is an agreement wherein a party with an existing duty or performance under a contract promises to do something other than perform the duty originally promised in the contract. Answer (d) is incorrect because the doctrine of substantial performance would allow for a contract obligation to be discharged even though the performance tendered was not in complete conformity with the terms of the agreement. In this case, Fields is suing Nagel for breach of contract.

56.   (a)   Events occurring after a contract is entered into usually do not affect performance. Some exceptions to this rule include subsequent illegality of the performance, death of a party, or destruction of the subject matter, all of which constitute impossibility of performance. In this case, even though Maco's own potatoes were destroyed, it wasn't specified that Maco's own potato crop be used to fulfill the contract. It was not impossible, therefore, for Maco to perform, because he could have purchased potatoes from another grower to deliver to LBC. If there had been a worldwide infestation of the potato crop, Maco would have reason to not perform on the basis of impossibility.

I.   Statute of Limitations

57.   (b)   The statute of limitations bars suit if it is not brought within the statutory period. The period varies for different types of cases and from state to state. The statute begins to run from the time the cause of action accrues (e.g., breach).

SOLUTIONS TO SIMULATION PROBLEMS

Simulation Problem 1

| Consideration |

		(A)	(B)	(C)
1.	Party S feels a moral obligation because Party F let S stay in his place for free when S attended college. S now promises to pay F for the past kindness.	○	●	○
2.	F agrees to deliver all of the sugar that Company S will need in her business for the following year. S agrees to purchase it at the market price.	●	○	○
3.	F does not smoke for one year pursuant to S's agreement to pay F $200 if she does not smoke for one year.	●	○	○
4.	F dies leaving a valid will which gives S $100,000.	○	○	●
5.	F is an auditor of XYZ Company. S is a potential investor of XYZ and offers to pay F $1,000 if F performs a professional, quality audit of XYZ Company. The $1,000 is in addition to the fee F will get from XYZ. F does perform a professional, quality audit.	○	●	○
6.	F had agreed, in writing, to work for S for five years for $100,000 per year. After two years, F asks for a 20% raise. S first agrees then later changes his mind. F, while not agreeing to additional duties or changing his position, wants to enforce the raise in salary.	○	●	○
7.	S promised to pay F $1,000 if he crosses the Golden Gate Bridge on his hands and knees. F does so.	●	○	○
8.	F promised to pay S $200 for a computer worth $2,000. S agreed to the deal.	●	○	○
9.	F agreed to purchase all of the parts from S that S can produce in her business for the next six months. S also agreed.	●	○	○
10.	S agreed to accept $1,000 from F for a $1,500 debt that is not disputed. S now wants the additional $500. Focus on the agreement to accept the lesser amount.	○	●	○
11.	S agreed to accept $1,000 from F for a debt that S claims is $1,500 but F in good faith claims is $800. F agreed to the $1,000 initially, then decides he will pay only $800. Focus on the enforceability of the agreement for $1,000.	●	○	○
12.	S agreed to donate $100 to F, a public charity.	○	○	●

Explanation of solutions

1. (B) Party F gave S a gift in the past. S's promise to now pay for the usage is not enforceable because F's action is past consideration, and the contract needs consideration on both sides. Furthermore, S's feeling of a moral obligation does not create consideration.

2. (A) This is an example of a requirements contract. F has given consideration because s/he gave up the right to sell that sugar to someone else.

3. (A) F refrained from doing something which she had a right to do. This constitutes consideration.

4. (C) This is not enforceable under contract law because S does not give any consideration in return. It is enforceable, however, as a will which does not require the elements of a contract such as consideration, but does require other formalities.

5. (B) F already had a preexisting legal duty to do a professional, quality audit of XYZ Company.

6. (B) F had a contract to work for S for five years for $100,000 per year. F is not giving any new consideration for the raise since during that five years, he already is obligated to complete the contract.

7. (A) F did something which he did not have to do in exchange for the agreed $1,000. This is a unilateral contract.

8. (A) F agreed to pay $200 and in exchange S agreed to sell the computer. Both have given consideration that is **legally** sufficient. Legally sufficient refers to the validity of the consideration, not the amount. Consideration does not have to be of equal value as long as it is legal consideration and bargained for.

9. (A) Both parties have given consideration for this output contract. F gave up the right to buy these parts elsewhere and S gave up the right to sell her output to someone else.

10. (B) F has a preexisting legal duty to pay the full $1,500. When S agreed to accept less, F gave up nothing. F still owes the remaining $500.

11. (A) In this case, both parties gave consideration. S, in agreeing to accept the $1,000, gave up the right to collect more of the disputed amount. F gave up the right to pay less of the disputed amount.

12. (C) Although the charity gave no consideration in exchange for the promised donation, the promise to donate to a charity is generally enforceable based on public policy reasons.

(3) Delivers all copies to seller or destroys them at seller's request

(4) Buyer in error pays all costs of processing and shipping to seller

(5) Note that nonconsumer buyer may not use these more favorable provisions of this Act

> EXAMPLE: *Buyer intends to purchase one copy of a DVD from ABC Company. The buyer, who is purchasing this DVD for consumer use, mistakenly orders ten copies from ABC's Web site. The buyer is protected by following the steps given above.*

    c. Buyer may accept nonconforming goods

        (1) Buyer must pay at contract price but may still recover damages (i.e., deduct damages from price if s/he gives seller notice)

        (2) Buyer may revoke acceptance in a reasonable time if

            (a) Accepted expecting nonconformity to be cured

            (b) Accepted because of difficulty of discovering defect

            (c) Accepted because seller assured conformity

    d. Buyer may recover damages measured by the difference between the contract price and the market value of the goods at the time buyer learns of the breach, plus any incidental damages and consequential damages

        (1) Consequential damages are damages resulting from buyer's needs that the seller was aware of at the time of contracting

        (2) Consequential damages cannot be recovered if buyer could reasonably have prevented these (mitigation of damages)

    e. Buyer has the right of cover

        (1) Buyer can buy substitute goods from another seller—buyer will still have the right to damages after engaging in "cover"

            (a) Damages are difference between cost of cover and contract price, plus incidental and consequential damages

            (b) Failure to cover does not bar other remedies

    f. Once goods to the contract have been identified, buyer obtains rights in those goods

        (1) Identification occurs when goods under contract are

            (a) Shipped

            (b) Marked as part of the contract, or

            (c) In some way designated as part of contract

        (2) Buyer obtains

            (a) Insurable interest in those goods, and

            (b) Right to obtain goods, called replevin, upon offering contract price

                1] Replevin is not allowed if buyer can cover

    g. Buyer may obtain specific performance if goods are unique or in other proper circumstances even if goods are not identified to the contract

        (1) Proper circumstances may exist when other remedies (such as monetary damages or remedy of cover) are inadequate

> EXAMPLE: *S agrees to sell B an antique car of which only one exists. If S later refuses to go through with the contract, B may require S to sell him the unique car under the remedy of specific performance.*

  7. Statute of limitations for sale of goods is four years

    a. An action for breach must be commenced within this period

    b. Parties may agree to reduce to not less than one year but may not extend it

    c. Statute of limitations begins running when the contract is breached

F. Leases under UCC

1. Law governing leases has been slow to develop and has been "tacked on" for various other areas of law such as property law and secured transactions

2. Now Article 2A of the UCC applies to any transaction creating a lease regardless of form

3. Article 2A is now law in majority of states
4. Article 2A is quite lengthy, but for purpose of CPA exam, note that its provisions are similar to Article 2 except that Article 2A applies to leases and Article 2 applies to sales of goods
5. Under Article 2A

   a. Lessor is person who transfers right to possess named goods and to use them in described ways by lessee

6. Note the following provisions where Article 2A is similar to Article 2:

   a. Statute of frauds except that stated minimum is $1,000 instead of $500 that applies to sales of goods

      (1) There are three exceptions to Statute of Frauds whereby leases need not be in writing even if for $1000 or more (note that these are similar to three exceptions to Statute of Frauds for sales of goods)

         (a) Specially manufactured goods when goods are not suitable for sale or lease in the ordinary course of lessor's business
         (b) Lessor or lessee admits to oral lease in court proceedings

            1] Only enforceable up to quantity admitted

         (c) Part acceptance in which lease is enforceable up to amount accepted by lessee

            > EXAMPLE: *E leases under an oral agreement 900 personal computers. A, the lessor, ships 400 of the personal computers to E. After accepting the 400, E decides she does not want to lease the other 500. E is liable for the lease of the 400 personal computers under the part acceptance exception even though the agreement was oral. She would be liable for the lease of the full 900 personal computers if the agreement had been for less than $1,000 which is not the case here.*

   b. Rules on acceptance, revocation of acceptance, and rejection of goods
   c. Remedies are similar to sellers' and buyers' remedies including the important concept of cure
   d. Principles for performance include anticipatory repudiation or breach, (including use of adequate assurance to avoid a breach), and the concept of impracticability
   e. Leases may be assigned
   f. Use general principles of contract and sales law for these

      (1) Warranties
      (2) Parol evidence
      (3) Firm offers
      (4) Risk of loss rules
      (5) Concept of unconscionable agreements

   g. Provision for sublease by lessee
   h. Leased goods may become fixtures
   i. Lessor has right to take possession of leased property after default without requirement of court adjudication

7. Leases under Article 2A of UCC may be in any manner sufficient to show by words or conduct that lessor and lessee intended to form a lease of identified goods
8. Finance lease is three-party transaction in which lessor acquires title or right to possess goods from supplier

   a. Lessor does not manufacture or supply goods for lessee but third-party supplier does according to lease agreement

G. Contracts for the International Sales of Goods (CISG)

1. Contracts for sales of goods between persons or companies of different countries follow the important rules of CISG
2. Many provisions of CISG are similar to UCC provisions but differences are handled under CISG because USA has this treaty with many countries in South America, Central America, North America, and most countries in Europe

   a. By Constitutional Law, CISG has priority over UCC when it applies and when it conflicts with UCC

b. The following are important areas where CISG and UCC are different

  (1) Price terms

    (a) May be left open under UCC, in which case UCC provides that price is reasonable price at time of delivery

      1] Other specified exceptions allowed under UCC

    (b) CISG requires that price term be included for there to be a contract

      1] CISG allows exception if method to determine price in future is clearly specified in contract

  (2) Time contract formed

    (a) Unlike UCC, CISG specifies that contract is formed only when acceptance is received by offeror

    (b) Also under CISG, acceptance happens at moment requested act is performed, not at the time notice is given of acceptance to offeror

  (3) Acceptances

    (a) CISG provides that there is no contract if terms in acceptance are different from terms in offer

      1] Acceptance is effective if differences are not material

        a] However, almost ever term in contract under CISG is considered material

  (4) Irrevocable offers

    (a) UCC allows offers that are not supported by consideration to be irrevocable if they are written and also meet certain other criteria

    (b) CISG allows offeror to make offer irrevocable by orally stating so

  (5) Written contracts

    (a) UCC has $500 rule for sales of goods

    (b) CISG provides that sales contracts may be oral with no rule regarding amount of money

      1] Also provides that proof of contract can be by any reasonable means

  (6) Parties are encouraged to have choice-of-language and choice-of-law clauses in contracts to help settle any disputes

MULTIPLE-CHOICE QUESTIONS (1-47)

1. Under the Sales Article of the UCC, when a written offer has been made without specifying a means of acceptance but providing that the offer will only remain open for ten days, which of the following statements represent(s) a valid acceptance of the offer?

I. An acceptance sent by regular mail the day before the ten-day period expires that reaches the offeror on the eleventh day.

II. An acceptance faxed the day before the ten-day period expires that reaches the offeror on the eleventh day, due to a malfunction of the offeror's printer.

    a. I only.
    b. II only.
    c. Both I and II.
    d. Neither I nor II.

2. Under the Sales Article of the UCC, a firm offer will be created only if the
    a. Offer states the time period during which it will remain open.
    b. Offer is made by a merchant in a signed writing.
    c. Offeree gives some form of consideration.
    d. Offeree is a merchant.

3. On May 2, Mason orally contracted with Acme Appliances to buy for $480 a washer and dryer for household use. Mason and the Acme salesperson agreed that delivery would be made on July 2. On May 5, Mason telephoned Acme and requested that the delivery date be moved to June 2. The Acme salesperson agreed with this request. On June 2, Acme failed to deliver the washer and dryer to Mason because of an inventory shortage. Acme advised Mason that it would deliver the appliances on July 2 as originally agreed. Mason believes that Acme has breached its agreement with Mason. Acme contends that its agreement to deliver on June 2 was not binding. Acme's contention is
    a. Correct, because Mason is not a merchant and was buying the appliances for household use.
    b. Correct, because the agreement to change the delivery date was not in writing.
    c. Incorrect, because the agreement to change the delivery date was binding.
    d. Incorrect, because Acme's agreement to change the delivery date is a firm offer that cannot be withdrawn by Acme.

4. Under the Sales Article of the UCC, which of the following statements is correct?
    a. The obligations of the parties to the contract must be performed in good faith.
    b. Merchants and nonmerchants are treated alike.
    c. The contract must involve the sale of goods for a price of more than $500.
    d. None of the provisions of the UCC may be disclaimed by agreement.

5. Which of the following contracts is handled under common law rules rather than under Article 2 of the Uniform Commercial Code?
    a. Oral contract to have hair styled in which expensive products will be used on the hair.
    b. Oral contract to purchase a textbook for $100.
    c. Written contract to purchase an old handcrafted chair for $600 from a private party.

    d. Written contract to purchase a heater from a dealer to be installed by the buyer in her home.

6. Cookie Co. offered to sell Distrib Markets 20,000 pounds of cookies at $1.00 per pound, subject to certain specified terms for delivery. Distrib replied in writing as follows:

We accept your offer for 20,000 pounds of cookies at $1.00 per pound, weighing scale to have valid city certificate.

Under the UCC
    a. A contract was formed between the parties.
    b. A contract will be formed only if Cookie agrees to the weighing scale requirement.
    c. No contract was formed because Distrib included the weighing scale requirement in its reply.
    d. No contract was formed because Distrib's reply was a counteroffer.

7. EG Door Co., a manufacturer of custom exterior doors, verbally contracted with Art Contractors to design and build a $2,000 custom door for a house that Art was restoring. After EG had completed substantial work on the door, Art advised EG that the house had been destroyed by fire and Art was canceling the contract. EG finished the door and shipped it to Art. Art refused to accept delivery. Art contends that the contract cannot be enforced because it violated the Statute of Frauds by not being in writing. Under the Sales Article of the UCC, is Art's contention correct?
    a. Yes, because the contract was not in writing.
    b. Yes, because the contract cannot be fully performed due to the fire.
    c. No, because the goods were specially manufactured for Art and cannot be resold in EG's regular course of business.
    d. No, because the cancellation of the contract was not made in writing.

8. On May 2, Handy Hardware sent Ram Industries a signed purchase order that stated, in part, as follows:

Ship for May 8 delivery 300 Model A-X socket sets at current dealer price. Terms 2/10/net 30.

Ram received Handy's purchase order on May 4. On May 5, Ram discovered that it had only 200 Model A-X socket sets and 100 Model W-Z socket sets in stock. Ram shipped the Model A-X and Model W-Z sets to Handy without any explanation concerning the shipment. The socket sets were received by Handy on May 8.
  Which of the following statements concerning the shipment is correct?
    a. Ram's shipment is an acceptance of Handy's offer.
    b. Ram's shipment is a counteroffer.
    c. Handy's order must be accepted by Ram in writing before Ram ships the socket sets.
    d. Handy's order can only be accepted by Ram shipping conforming goods.

9. Under the UCC Sales Article, which of the following conditions will prevent the formation of an enforceable sale of goods contract?
    a. Open price.
    b. Open delivery.
    c. Open quantity.
    d. Open acceptance.

10. Webstar Corp. orally agreed to sell Northco, Inc. a computer for $20,000. Northco sent a signed purchase order to Webstar confirming the agreement. Webstar received the purchase order and did not respond. Webstar refused to deliver the computer to Northco, claiming that the purchase order did not satisfy the UCC Statute of Frauds because it was not signed by Webstar. Northco sells computers to the general public and Webstar is a computer wholesaler. Under the UCC Sales Article, Webstar's position is

   a. Incorrect because it failed to object to Northco's purchase order.
   b. Incorrect because only the buyer in a sale-of-goods transaction must sign the contract.
   c. Correct because it was the party against whom enforcement of the contract is being sought.
   d. Correct because the purchase price of the computer exceeded $500.

11. Patch, a frequent shopper at Soon-Shop Stores, received a rain check for an advertised sale item after Soon-Shop's supply of the product ran out. The rain check was in writing and stated that the item would be offered to the customer at the advertised sale price for an unspecified period of time. A Soon-Shop employee signed the rain check. When Patch returned to the store one month later to purchase the item, the store refused to honor the rain check. Under the Sales Article of the UCC, will Patch win a suit to enforce the rain check?

   a. No, because one month is too long a period of time for a rain check to be effective.
   b. No, because the rain check did not state the effective time period necessary to keep the offer open.
   c. Yes, because Soon-Shop is required to have sufficient supplies of the sale item to satisfy all customers.
   d. Yes, because the rain check met the requirements of a merchant's firm offer even though no effective time period was stated.

12. A sheep rancher agreed in writing to sell all the wool shorn during the shearing season to a weaver. The contract failed to establish the price and a minimum quantity of wool. After the shearing season, the rancher refused to deliver the wool. The weaver sued the rancher for breach of contract. Under the Sales Article of the UCC, will the weaver win?

   a. Yes, because this was an output contract.
   b. Yes, because both price and quantity terms were omitted.
   c. No, because quantity cannot be omitted for a contract to be enforceable.
   d. No, because the omission of price and quantity terms prevents the formation of a contract.

13. Under the Sales Article of the UCC, the warranty of title

   a. Provides that the seller cannot disclaim the warranty if the sale is made to a bona fide purchaser for value.
   b. Provides that the seller deliver the goods free from any lien of which the buyer lacked knowledge when the contract was made.
   c. Applies only if it is in writing and assigned by the seller.
   d. Applies only if the seller is a merchant.

14. Under the Sales Article of the UCC, most goods sold by merchants are covered by certain warranties. An example of an express warranty would be a warranty of

   a. Usage of trade.
   b. Fitness for a particular purpose.
   c. Merchantability.
   d. Conformity of goods to sample.

15. Under the Sales Article of the UCC, which of the following statements is correct regarding the warranty of merchantability arising when there has been a sale of goods by a merchant seller?

   a. The warranty must be in writing.
   b. The warranty arises when the buyer relies on the seller's skill in selecting the goods purchased.
   c. The warranty cannot be disclaimed.
   d. The warranty arises as a matter of law when the seller ordinarily sells the goods purchased.

16. On May 2, Handy Hardware sent Ram Industries a signed purchase order that stated, in part, as follows:

> Ship for May 8 delivery 300 Model A-X socket sets at current dealer price. Terms 2/10/net 30.

Ram received Handy's purchase order on May 4. On May 5, Ram discovered that it had only 200 Model A-X socket sets and 100 Model W-Z socket sets in stock. Ram shipped the Model A-X and Model W-Z sets to Handy without any explanation concerning the shipment. The socket sets were received by Handy on May 8.

Assuming a contract exists between Handy and Ram, which of the following implied warranties would result?

  I. Implied warranty of merchantability.
  II. Implied warranty of fitness for a particular purpose.
  III. Implied warranty of title.

   a. I only.
   b. III only.
   c. I and III only.
   d. I, II, and III.

17. Under the UCC Sales Article, an action for breach of the implied warranty of merchantability by a party who sustains personal injuries may be successful against the seller of the product only when

   a. The seller is a merchant of the product involved.
   b. An action based on negligence can also be successfully maintained.
   c. The injured party is in privity of contract with the seller.
   d. An action based on strict liability in tort can also be successfully maintained.

18. Which of the following conditions must be met for an implied warranty of fitness for a particular purpose to arise in connection with a sale of goods?

  I. The warranty must be in writing.
  II. The seller must know that the buyer was relying on the seller in selecting the goods.

   a. I only.
   b. II only.
   c. Both I and II.
   d. Neither I nor II.

19. Under the UCC Sales Article, the implied warranty of merchantability

a. May be disclaimed by a seller's oral statement that mentions merchantability.

b. Arises only in contracts involving a merchant seller and a merchant buyer.

c. Is breached if the goods are **not** fit for all purposes for which the buyer intends to use the goods.

d. Must be part of the basis of the bargain to be binding on the seller.

20. Cook Company, a common carrier trucking company, made a contract to transport some video equipment for Jackson Company. Cook is trying to limit its liability in the contract. In which of the following situations can Cook **not avoid** liability?

I. In transit, the driver of Cook's truck damages the video equipment when the driver causes an accident.

II. An unknown thief steals the video equipment while in transit. Cook committed no negligence in this theft.

III. The video equipment is destroyed when a bridge under the truck collapses because of an earthquake.

a. I only.
b. I and II only.
c. I, II, and III.
d. I and III only.

21. High sues the manufacturer, wholesaler, and retailer for bodily injuries caused by a power saw High purchased. Which of the following statements is correct under strict liability theory?

a. Contributory negligence on High's part will always be a bar to recovery.

b. The manufacturer will avoid liability if it can show it followed the custom of the industry.

c. Privity will be a bar to recovery insofar as the wholesaler is concerned if the wholesaler did **not** have a reasonable opportunity to inspect.

d. High may recover even if he **cannot** show any negligence was involved.

22. To establish a cause of action based on strict liability in tort for personal injuries that result from the use of a defective product, one of the elements the injured party must prove is that the seller

a. Was aware of the defect in the product.
b. Sold the product to the injured party.
c. Failed to exercise due care.
d. Sold the product in a defective condition.

23. A common carrier bailee generally would avoid liability for loss of goods entrusted to its care if the goods are

a. Stolen by an unknown person.
b. Negligently destroyed by an employee.
c. Destroyed by the derailment of the train carrying them due to railroad employee negligence.
d. Improperly packed by the party shipping them.

24. McGraw purchased an antique rocking chair from Tillis by check. The check was dishonored by the bank due to insufficient funds. In the meantime, McGraw sold the rocking chair to Rio who had no knowledge that McGraw's check had been dishonored. Which of the following is correct?

a. Tillis may repossess the rocking chair from Rio.
b. Tillis may recover money damages from Rio.

c. Tillis may recover money damages from McGraw.
d. Tillis may recover damages from McGraw based on fraud.

25. Yancie took her bike in to Pete's Bike Sales and Repair to have it repaired. Pete said he would need to have her leave it for two days. The next day, one of Pete's employees sold Yancie's bike to Jake. Jake paid for the bike with a credit card, unaware that Pete did not own the bike. Which of the following is correct?

a. Yancie can repossess the bike from Jake if she pays Jake. Yancie then recovers the price from Pete.

b. Pete can repossess the bike from Jake and then return it to Yancie.

c. Yancie can sue Jake for monetary damages only.

d. Jake has title to the bike.

26. Under the Sales Article of the UCC, unless a contract provides otherwise, before title to goods can pass from a seller to a buyer, the goods must be

a. Tendered to the buyer.
b. Identified to the contract.
c. Accepted by the buyer.
d. Paid for.

27. Under the Sales Article of the UCC, in an FOB place of shipment contract, the risk of loss passes to the buyer when the goods

a. Are identified to the contract.
b. Are placed on the seller's loading dock.
c. Are delivered to the carrier.
d. Reach the buyer's loading dock.

28. On May 2, Lace Corp., an appliance wholesaler, offered to sell appliances worth $3,000 to Parco, Inc., a household appliances retailer. The offer was signed by Lace's president, and provided that it would not be withdrawn before June 1. It also included the shipping terms: "FOB Parco's warehouse." On May 29, Parco mailed an acceptance of Lace's offer. Lace received the acceptance June 2.

If Lace inadvertently ships the wrong appliances to Parco and Parco rejects them two days after receipt, title to the goods will

a. Pass to Parco when they are identified to the contract.

b. Pass to Parco when they are shipped.

c. Remain with Parco until the goods are returned to Lace.

d. Revert to Lace when they are rejected by Parco.

29. Under the Sales Article of the UCC and the United Nations Convention for the International Sale of Goods (CISG), absent specific terms in an international sales shipment contract, when will risk of loss pass to the buyer?

a. When the goods are delivered to the first carrier for transmission to the buyer.

b. When the goods are tendered to the buyer.

c. At the conclusion of the execution of the contract.

d. At the time the goods are identified to the contract.

30. Which of the following statements applies to a sale on approval under the UCC Sales Article?

a. Both the buyer and seller must be merchants.

b. The buyer must be purchasing the goods for resale.

c. Risk of loss for the goods passes to the buyer when the goods are accepted after the trial period.

d. Title to the goods passes to the buyer on delivery of the goods to the buyer.

31. Under the Sales Article of UCC, which of the following events will result in the risk of loss passing from a merchant seller to a buyer?

	Tender of the goods at the seller's place of business	Use of the seller's truck to deliver the goods
a.	Yes	Yes
b.	Yes	No
c.	No	Yes
d.	No	No

32. Cey Corp. entered into a contract to sell parts to Deck, Ltd. The contract provided that the goods would be shipped "FOB Cey's warehouse." Cey shipped parts different from those specified in the contract. Deck rejected the parts. A few hours after Deck informed Cey that the parts were rejected, they were destroyed by fire in Deck's warehouse. Cey believed that the parts were conforming to the contract. Which of the following statements is correct?

a. Regardless of whether the parts were conforming, Deck will bear the loss because the contract was a shipment contract.

b. If the parts were nonconforming, Deck had the right to reject them, but the risk of loss remains with Deck until Cey takes possession of the parts.

c. If the parts were conforming, risk of loss does **not** pass to Deck until a reasonable period of time after they are delivered to Deck.

d. If the parts were nonconforming, Cey will bear the risk of loss, even though the contract was a shipment contract.

33. Under the Sales Article of the UCC, which of the following factors is most important in determining who bears the risk of loss in a sale of goods contract?

a. The method of shipping the goods.

b. The contract's shipping terms.

c. Title to the goods.

d. How the goods were lost.

34. Bond purchased a painting from Wool, who is not in the business of selling art. Wool tendered delivery of the painting after receiving payment in full from Bond. Bond informed Wool that Bond would be unable to take possession of the painting until later that day. Thieves stole the painting before Bond returned. The risk of loss

a. Passed to Bond at Wool's tender of delivery.

b. Passed to Bond at the time the contract was formed and payment was made.

c. Remained with Wool, because the parties agreed on a later time of delivery.

d. Remained with Wool, because Bond had **not** yet received the painting.

35. Funston, a retailer, shipped goods worth $600 to a customer by using a common carrier. The contract used by the common carrier, and agreed to by Funston, limited liability to $100 unless a higher fee is paid. Funston did not pay the higher fee. The goods were shipped FOB destination point and were destroyed in transit due to a flash flood. Which of the following is correct?

a. Funston will suffer a loss of $500.

b. Funston will suffer a loss of $600.

c. Funston's customer will suffer a loss of $500.

d. Funston's customer will suffer a loss of $600.

36. Under the Sales Article of the UCC, which of the following statements regarding liquidated damages is(are) correct?

I. The injured party may collect any amount of liquidated damages provided for in the contract.

II. The seller may retain a deposit of up to $500 when a buyer defaults even if there is no liquidated damages provision in the contract.

a. I only.

b. II only.

c. Both I and II.

d. Neither I nor II.

37. Under the Sales Article of the UCC, and unless otherwise agreed to, the seller's obligation to the buyer is to

a. Deliver the goods to the buyer's place of business.

b. Hold conforming goods and give the buyer whatever notification is reasonably necessary to enable the buyer to take delivery.

c. Deliver all goods called for in the contract to a common carrier.

d. Set aside conforming goods for inspection by the buyer before delivery.

38. Under the Sales Article of the UCC, which of the following rights is(are) available to a seller when a buyer materially breaches a sales contract?

	Right to cancel the contract	Right to recover damages
a.	Yes	Yes
b.	Yes	No
c.	No	Yes
d.	No	No

39. Under the Sales Article of the UCC, the remedies available to a seller when a buyer breaches a contract for the sale of goods may include

	The right to resell goods identified to the contract	The right to stop a carrier from delivering the goods
a.	Yes	Yes
b.	Yes	No
c.	No	Yes
d.	No	No

40. Lazur Corp. entered into a contract with Baker Suppliers, Inc. to purchase a used word processor from Baker. Lazur is engaged in the business of selling new and used word processors to the general public. The contract required Baker to ship the goods to Lazur by common carrier pursuant to the following provision in the contract: "FOB Baker Suppliers, Inc. loading dock." Baker also represented in the contract that the word processor had been used for only ten hours by its previous owner. The contract included the provision that the word processor was being sold "as is" and this provision was in a larger and different type style than the remainder of the contract.

Assume that Lazur refused to accept the word processor even though it was in all respects conforming to the contract and that the contract is otherwise silent. Under the UCC Sales Article,

EXAMPLE:

> June 5, 2002
>
> *On June 5, 2003, pay to the order of Bob Smith $1,000 plus 10% annual interest from June 5, 2002.*
>
> To: ABC Corporation
>
> (Signed) Sue Van Deventer

The above is a draft in which Sue Van Deventer is the drawer, ABC Corporation is the drawee, and Bob Smith is the payee

    (a) A check

        1] Is a special type of draft that is payable on demand (unless postdated) and drawee must be a bank

            a] Definition of bank includes savings and loan associations, credit unions, and trust companies

        2] One writing check is drawer (and customer of drawee bank)

  b. A note (also called a promissory note)

    (1) Unlike a draft or check, is a two-party instrument

      (a) One party is called the maker—this party promises to pay a specified sum of money to another party called the payee

EXAMPLE:

> July 10, 2002
>
> *I promise to pay to the order of Becky Hoger $5,000 plus 10% annual interest on July 10, 2003.*
>
> (Signed) Bill Jones

The above is a note in which Bill Jones is the maker and Becky Hoger is the payee.

    (2) May be payable on demand or at a definite time

      (a) Certificate of deposit (CD)

        1] Is an acknowledgment by a financial institution of receipt of money and promise to repay it

            a] Most CDs are commercial paper so that they can be easily transferred

        2] Is actually a special type of note in which financial institution is the maker

C. Requirements of Negotiability

  1. All of the following requirements must be on face of instrument for it to be a negotiable instrument (be sure to know these)

  2. To be negotiable, the instrument must

    a. Be written

    b. Be signed by maker or drawer

    c. Contain an unconditional promise or order to pay

    d. State a fixed amount in money

    e. Be payable on demand or at a definite time

    f. Be payable to order or to bearer, unless it is a check

  3. Details of requirements of negotiability

    a. **Must be in writing**

      (1) Satisfied by printing, typing, handwriting or any other reduction to physical form that is relatively permanent and portable

    b. **Must be signed by maker (of a note or CD) or drawer (of a draft or check)**

      (1) Signature includes any symbol used with intent to authenticate instrument

    (a) Rubber stamp, initials, letterhead satisfy signing requirement

    (b) Assumed name or trade name operates as that party's signature

    (c) Signature may be anywhere on face of instrument

c. **Must contain an unconditional promise or order to pay**

    (1) If payment depends upon (is subject to) another agreement or event, then it is conditional and therefore destroys negotiability

> *EXAMPLE: An instrument that is otherwise negotiable states that it is subject to a particular contract. This condition destroys the negotiability of this instrument.*

> *EXAMPLE: An instrument states: "I, Janice Jones, promise to pay to the order of Richard Riley, $1,000 if the stereo delivered to me is not defective." This instrument is not negotiable whether the stereo is defective or not because it contains a conditional promise.*

        (a) However, the following are permitted and do not destroy negotiability

            1] Instrument may state its purpose

> *EXAMPLE: On a check, the drawer writes "for purchase of textbooks."*

            2] Instrument may refer to or state that it arises from another agreement

            3] Instrument is permitted to show that it is secured by a mortgage or by collateral

            4] Instrument is permitted to contain promise to provide extra collateral

            5] Instrument is permitted to limit payment out of particular fund

    (2) An IOU is not a promise or order to pay but an acknowledgement of debt, thus, an IOU is not negotiable

d. **Must state a fixed amount in money—called sum certain under former law**

    (1) Amount of principal but not interest must be determinable from instrument without need to refer to other sources

        (a) Stated interest rates are allowed because amount can be calculated

> *EXAMPLE: A negotiable note states that $1,000 is due one year from October 1, 2001 at 14% interest.*

> *EXAMPLE: A note states that $1,000 is payable on demand and bears interest at 14%. This also is negotiable because once payment is demanded, the amount of interest can be calculated.*

            1] Variable interest rates are allowed and do not now destroy negotiability even if formula for interest rate or amount requires reference to information outside of negotiable instrument

> *EXAMPLE: The following do not destroy negotiability in an otherwise negotiable instrument: Interest rates tied to some published key interest rate, consumer index market rate, etc.*

            2] If interest rate based on legal rate or judgment rate (fixed by statute), then negotiability not destroyed

        (b) Stated different rates of interest before and after default or specified dates are allowed

        (c) Stated discounts or additions if instrument paid before or after payment dates do not destroy negotiability

        (d) Clauses allowing collection costs and attorney's fees upon default are allowed because they reduce the risk of holding instruments and promote transferability

        (e) Must be payable only in money

            1] Option to be payable in money or something else destroys negotiability because of possibility that payment will not be in money

> *EXAMPLE: A note is payable in $1,000 or its equivalent in gold. This note is not negotiable.*

            2] Foreign currency is acceptable even though reference to exchange rates may be needed due to international trade realities

e. **Must be payable on demand or at a definite time**

    (1) On demand includes

        (a) Payable on sight

        (b) Payable on presentation

        (c) No time for payment stated

(2) It is a definite time if payable

    (a) On a certain date, or
    (b) A fixed period after sight, or
    (c) Within a certain time, or
    (d) On a certain date subject to acceleration

        1] For example, when a payment is missed, total balance may become due at once

    (e) On a certain date subject to an extension of time if

        1] At option of holder, or
        2] At option of maker or drawer only if extension is limited to a definite amount of time

(3) It is not definite if payable on an act or event that is not certain as to time of occurrence

> EXAMPLE: *An instrument contains a clause stating that it is payable ten days after drawer obtains a bank loan. This destroys negotiability.*

f. **Must be payable to order or to bearer unless it is a check (these are magic words of negotiability and are often a central issue on the CPA exam)**

(1) Instrument is payable to order if made payable to the order of

    (a) Any person, including the maker, drawer, drawee, or payee
    (b) Two persons together or alternatively
    (c) Any entity

(2) Instrument is also payable to order if it is payable "to A or order"
(3) Instrument other than a check is not payable to order if it is only payable to a person (e.g., "Pay John Doe")

> EXAMPLE: *A draft that is otherwise negotiable states: "Pay to XYZ Corporation." This statement destroys negotiability because the draft is not payable "to the order of" XYZ Corporation.*

    (a) It is not negotiable
    (b) "Pay to the order of John Doe" would be negotiable

(4) If a **check** says "pay to A," it is negotiable order paper—this is not true of other instruments
(5) Instrument is payable to bearer if it is payable to

    (a) "Bearer"
    (b) "Cash"
    (c) "A person or bearer" is bearer paper if "bearer" handwritten

        1] However, "pay to John Doe, the bearer" is not negotiable because it is not payable to order or to bearer but to a person and simply refers to him as the bearer

    (d) "Order of bearer" or "order of cash"
    (e) Pay to the order of (payee left blank) is bearer paper unless holder inserts payee's name

(6) Instrument cannot be made payable to persons consecutively (i.e., maker cannot specify subsequent holders)

D. Interpretation of Ambiguities in Negotiable Instruments

1. Contradictory terms

  a. Words control over figures
  b. Handwritten terms control over typewritten and printed (typeset) terms
  c. Typewritten terms control over printed (typeset) terms

2. Omissions

  a. Omission of date does not destroy negotiability unless date necessary to determine when payable

> EXAMPLE: *A check is not dated. It is still negotiable because a check is payable on demand.*

> EXAMPLE: *A draft states that it is payable thirty days after its date. If the date is left off, it is not payable at a definite time and, therefore, it is not negotiable.*

  b. Omission of interest rate is allowed because the judgment rate of interest (rate used on a court judgment) is automatically used

    c. Statement of consideration or where instrument is drawn or payable not required

3. Other issues

    a. Instrument may be postdated or antedated and remain negotiable

      (1) Bank is not liable for damages to customer if it pays on postdated check before date on check unless individual notifies bank not to pay check earlier in a separate written document

      (2) Once customer does this, bank is liable for any damages caused by early payment

    b. Instrument may have a provision that by endorsing or cashing it, the payee acknowledges full satisfaction of debt and remain negotiable

    c. If an instrument is payable to order of more than one person

      (1) Either payee may negotiate or enforce it if payable to him/her in the alternative

          EXAMPLE: "Pay $100 to the order of X or Y." Either X or Y may endorse it.

      (2) All payees must negotiate or enforce it if **not** payable to them in the alternative

    d. If not clear whether instrument is draft or note, holder may treat it as either

    e. UCC requires only that a negotiable instrument need be written, must lend itself to permanence, and must be easily transferable (i.e., movable).

E. Negotiation

1. There are two methods of transferring commercial paper

    a. By assignment

      (1) Assignment occurs when transfer does not meet all requirements of negotiation

      (2) Assignee can obtain only same rights that assignor had

    b. By negotiation

      (1) One receiving negotiable instrument by negotiation is called a holder

      (2) If holder further qualifies as a holder in due course (as discussed later) s/he can obtain **more rights** than what transferor had

      (3) There are two methods of negotiation

          (a) Negotiating order paper requires both endorsement by transferor and delivery of instrument

             1] Order paper includes negotiable instruments made payable to the order of X

          (b) Negotiating bearer paper may be accomplished by delivery alone (endorsement not necessary)

                EXAMPLE: A check is made payable to the order of cash.

             1] Subsequent parties may require endorsements (even though UCC does not) for identification

             2] Holder may, in any event, endorse it if s/he chooses to do so

      (4) Endorsement (Indorsement) refers to signature of payee, drawee, accommodation endorser, or holder

2. Types of endorsements

    a. Blank endorsement

      (1) Does not specify any endorsee

          EXAMPLE: A check made to the order of M on the front can be endorsed in blank by M writing only his signature on the back.

      (2) Converts order paper into bearer paper

      (3) Note that bearer paper may be negotiated by mere delivery

          EXAMPLE: B endorses a check in blank that had been made payable to his order. He lost it and C found it who delivered it to D. D is a valid holder since C's endorsement was not required.

    b. Special endorsement

      (1) Indicates specific person to whom endorsee wishes to negotiate instrument

EXAMPLE: On the back of a check payable to the order of M. Jordan he signs as follows: Pay to L. Smith, (signed) M. Jordan.

    (a) Note that words "pay to the order of" are not required on back as endorsements—instrument need be payable to order or to bearer on front only

    (b) Also, note that if instrument is not payable to order or to bearer on its face, it **cannot** be turned into a negotiable instrument by using these words in an endorsement on the back

      EXAMPLE: A particular instrument would have been negotiable except that on the front it was payable to A. On the back, A signed it. "Pay to the order of B, (signed) A." This does not convert it into a negotiable instrument.

  (2) Bearer paper may be converted into order paper by use of special endorsement

    EXAMPLE: A check made out to cash is delivered to Carp. Carp writes on the back; Pay to Durn, (signed) Carp. It was bearer paper until this special endorsement.

    EXAMPLE: Continuing the previous example, Durn simply endorses it in blank. The check is bearer paper again.

  (3) If last (or only) endorsement on instrument is a blank endorsement, any holder may convert that bearer paper into order paper by writing "Pay to X," etc., above that blank endorsement

c. Restrictive endorsement

  (1) Requires endorsees to comply with certain conditions

    EXAMPLE: Endorsement reads "For deposit only, (signed) A. Bell."

    EXAMPLE: Another endorsement reads "Pay to X only if X completes work to my satisfaction on my car within three days of the date on this check, (signed) A." Neither X nor any subsequent holder can enforce payment until this condition has been met.

  (2) Note that conditions in restrictive endorsements do not destroy negotiability even though conditions placed on front of instruments do destroy negotiability because they create conditional promises or orders to pay

  (3) Endorsements cannot prohibit subsequent negotiation

    EXAMPLE: Above her endorsement, M wrote: "Pay to N only." This indicates that N is the new endorsee but does not stop further negotiation after N when N endorses.

d. Qualified endorsement

  (1) Normally, endorser, upon signing, promises automatically to pay holder or any subsequent endorser amount of instrument if it is later dishonored

  (2) Qualified endorsement disclaims this liability

    EXAMPLE: Ann Knolls endorses "Without recourse, (signed) Ann Knolls."

  (3) Qualified endorsements, otherwise, have same effects as other endorsements

  (4) Combinations of endorsements occur

    (a) Special qualified endorsement

      EXAMPLE: "Pay to Pete Bell without recourse, (signed) Tom Lack." Tom Lack has limited his liability and also Pete Bell's endorsement is needed to negotiate this instrument further.

    (b) Blank qualified endorsement

      EXAMPLE: "Without recourse, (signed) D. Hamilton."

    (c) Endorsement that is restrictive, qualified, and blank

      EXAMPLE: "For deposit only, without recourse, (signed) Bill Coffey."

    (d) Endorsement that is restrictive, qualified, and special

      EXAMPLE: "Pay to X if she completes work today, without recourse, (signed) D. Magee."

3. If payee's name misspelled, s/he may endorse in proper spelling or misspelling or both

  a. But endorsee may require both

4. If an order instrument is transferred for value without endorsement, transferee may require endorsement from transferor

  a. Upon obtaining endorsement, will become a holder

5. Federal law standardizes endorsements on checks—endorser should turn check over and sign in designated area

    a. Purpose is to avoid interference with bank's endorsements
    b. Endorsements placed outside this area do not destroy negotiability but may delay clearing process.

6. If check has statement that it is nonnegotiable, check is still negotiable

    a. This is not true of other negotiable instruments whereby such statement destroys negotiability

F. Holder in Due Course

1. Concept of **holder in due course** (also called **HDC**) is very important for CPA exam purposes. A HDC is entitled to payment on negotiable instrument **despite most defenses** that maker or drawer of instrument may have

    a. Recall that an assignee of contract rights receives only rights that assignor had (i.e., assignee takes subject to all defenses that could have been asserted against assignor)
    b. Likewise, an ordinary holder of a negotiable instrument has same rights as assignee

2. To be holder in due course, a taker of instrument must

    a. Be a **holder** of a properly negotiated negotiable instrument
    b. Give **value** for instrument

        (1) Holder gives value if s/he

            (a) Pays or performs agreed consideration

                1] An executory promise (promise to give value in the future) is not value until performed

            (b) Takes as a satisfaction of a previous existing debt
            (c) Gives another negotiable instrument
            (d) Acquires a security interest in the instrument (e.g., the holder takes possession of the instrument as collateral for another debt)

        (2) A bank takes for value to the extent that credit has been given for a deposit and withdrawn

            (a) FIFO method is used to determine whether it has been withdrawn (money is considered to be withdrawn from an account in the order in which it was deposited)

        (3) Value does not have to be for full amount of instrument;

            (a) Purchase at a discount is value for full face amount of instrument provided HDC took in good faith (i.e., as long as not too large a discount)

                > EXAMPLE: *Purchase of a $1,000 instrument in good faith for $950 is considered full value, but purchase of the same instrument for $500 is not considered full value when market conditions show that the discount is excessive.*

                > EXAMPLE: *Handy purchases a negotiable note that has a face value of $1,000. She gives $600 in cash now and agrees to pay $350 in one week. Handy has given value only to the extent of $600 and thus can qualify as a HDC for $600. Once she pays the remaining $350, she qualifies as a HDC for the full $1,000. Note that even though she paid only $950, she has HDC status for the entire $1,000 because it was a reasonable discount.*

    c. Take in **good faith**

        (1) Good faith defined as honesty in fact and observance of reasonable commercial standards of fair dealing

    d. Take **without notice** that it is overdue, has been dishonored, or that any person has a defense or claim to it

        (1) Holder has notice when s/he knows or has reason to know (measured by objective "reasonable person" standard)
        (2) Overdue

            > EXAMPLE: *H acquires a note or draft that is three weeks past the due date on the instrument.*

            (a) Instrument not overdue if default is on payment of interest only

(b) Domestic check, although payable on demand, is overdue ninety days after its date

(3) Defense or claim

(a) Obvious signs of forgery or alteration so as to call into question its authenticity
(b) Incomplete or irregular
(c) If purchaser has notice of any party's claim or that all parties have been discharged

(4) There is no notice of a defense or claim if

(a) It is antedated or postdated
(b) S/he knows that there has been a default in payment of interest

(5) But if one acquires notice **after** becoming a holder and giving value, s/he may still be a HDC

(a) That is, once one is a HDC, acquiring notice does not end HDC status

3. Payee of a negotiable instrument may qualify as a HDC if meets all requirements

G. Rights of a Holder in Due Course (HDC)

1. The general rule is that a transfer of a negotiable instrument to a HDC cuts off all **personal defenses** against a HDC

a. Personal defenses are assertable against ordinary holders and assignees of contract rights to avoid payment

EXAMPLE: Art Dobbs negotiates a note to Mary Price in payment of a stereo. Mary negotiates this note to D. Finch who qualifies as a HDC. When Finch seeks payment, Dobbs points out that Price breached the contract by never delivering the stereo. Finch, as a HDC, still has the right to collect because breach of contract is a personal defense. Dobbs then has to seek recourse directly against Price.

b. EXCEPTION—HDC takes subject to all personal defenses of person with whom HDC directly dealt

2. Some defenses are assertable against any party including a HDC—these defenses are called **real (or universal) defenses**

3. Types of **personal defenses**

a. Breach of contract

(1) Includes breach of warranty

b. Lack or failure of consideration

c. Prior payment

EXAMPLE: Maker of a negotiable note pays on the note but does not keep or cancel the note. A subsequent party who qualifies as a HDC seeks to collect on this same note. Maker, having only a personal defense, must pay the HDC even though it was paid previously.

d. Unauthorized completion

EXAMPLE: X signs a check leaving the amount blank. He tells Y to fill in the amount necessary to buy a typewriter. Y fills in $22,000 and negotiates the check to a HDC. The HDC may enforce the full amount of the check against X.

e. Fraud in the inducement

(1) Occurs when person signs a negotiable instrument and knows what s/he is signing; however, s/he was induced into doing so by intentional misrepresentation

f. Nondelivery

(1) Occurs when bearer instrument is lost or stolen

EXAMPLE: M issues a note that is bearer paper. It is stolen by T who sells it to a HDC. The HDC wins against M.

g. Ordinary duress or undue influence

(1) Most types of duress are considered a personal defense unless they become very extreme and thus are considered real defenses

EXAMPLE: Signing a check based on fear of losing a real estate deal constitutes a personal defense.

h. Mental incapacity

Pay to John Smith only
Frank Parker, President of Lake Corp.

John Smith

Pay to the order of Sharp, Inc. without recourse, but only if
Sharp delivers computers purchased by Mary Harris by
March 15, 2001.
Mary Harris

Sarah Sharp, President of Sharp, Inc.

Which of the following statements is correct?
  a. The note became nonnegotiable as a result of
     Parker's endorsement.
  b. Harris' endorsement was a conditional promise to
     pay and caused the note to be nonnegotiable.
  c. Smith's endorsement effectively prevented further
     negotiation of the note.
  d. Harris' signature was **not** required to effectively
     negotiate the note to Sharp.

19. A note is made payable to the order of Ann Jackson on
the front. On the back, Ann Jackson signs it in blank and
delivers it to Jerry Lin. Lin puts "Pay to Jerry Lin" above
Jackson's endorsement. Which of the following statements
is **false** concerning this note?
  a. After Lin wrote "Pay to Jerry Lin," the note be-
     came order paper.
  b. After Jackson endorsed the note but before Lin
     wrote on it, the note was bearer paper.
  c. Lin needs to endorse this note to negotiate it fur-
     ther, even though he personally wrote "Pay to Jerry
     Lin" on the back.
  d. The note is not negotiable because Lin wrote "Pay
     to Jerry Lin" instead of "Pay to the order of Jerry
     Lin."

20. You are examining some negotiable instruments for a
client. Which of the following endorsements can be classified as a special restrictive endorsement?
  a. Pay to Alex Ericson if he completes the contracted
     work within ten days, (signed) Stephanie Sene.
  b. Pay to Alex Ericson without recourse (signed)
     Stephanie Sene.
  c. For deposit only, (signed) Stephanie Sene.
  d. Pay to Alex Ericson, (signed) Stephanie Sene.

21. On February 15, 2001, P.D. Stone obtained the following instrument from Astor Co. for $1,000. Stone was aware
that Helco, Inc. disputed liability under the instrument because of an alleged breach by Astor of the referenced computer purchase agreement. On March 1, 2001, Willard Bank
obtained the instrument from Stone for $3,900. Willard had
no knowledge that Helco disputed liability under the instrument.

February 12, 2001

Helco, Inc. promises to pay to Astor Co. or bearer the sum of
$4,900 (four thousand four hundred and 00/100 dollars) on
March 12, 2001 (maker may elect to extend due date to March 31,
2001) with interest thereon at the rate of 12% per annum.

HELCO, INC.

By: *A. J. Help*

A. J. Help, President

Reference: Computer purchase agreement dated February 12, 2001

The reverse side of the instrument is endorsed as follows:

Pay to the order of Willard Bank, without recourse

P.D. Stone
P.D. Stone

Which of the following statements is correct?
  a. Willard Bank **cannot** be a holder in due course be-
     cause Stone's endorsement was without recourse.
  b. Willard Bank must endorse the instrument to ne-
     gotiate it.
  c. Neither Willard Bank **nor** Stone are holders in due
     course.
  d. Stone's endorsement was required for Willard
     Bank to be a holder in due course.

22. Under the Commercial Paper Article of the UCC, which
of the following circumstances would prevent a person from
becoming a holder in due course of an instrument?
  a. The person was notified that payment was refused.
  b. The person was notified that one of the prior en-
     dorsers was discharged.
  c. The note was collateral for a loan.
  d. The note was purchased at a discount.

23. One of the requirements needed for a holder of a negotiable instrument to be a holder in due course is the value
requirement. Ruper is a holder of a $1,000 check written out
to her. Which of the following would not satisfy the value
requirement?
  a. Ruper received the check from a tax client to pay
     off a four-month-old debt.
  b. Ruper took the check in exchange for a negotiable
     note for $1,200 which was due on that day.
  c. Ruper received the check in exchange for a prom-
     ise to do certain specified services three months
     later.
  d. Ruper received the check for a tax service debt for
     a close relative.

24. Larson is claiming to be a holder in due course of two
instruments. One is a draft that is drawn on Picket Company
and says "Pay to Brunt." The other is a check that says "Pay
to Brunt." Both are endorsed by Brunt on the back and
made payable to Larson. Larson gave value for and acted in
good faith concerning both the draft and the check. Larson
also claims to be ignorant of any adverse claims on either
instrument which are not overdue or have not been dishonored. Which of the following is(are) true?

  I. Larson is a holder in due course of the draft.
 II. Larson is a holder in due course of the check.

  a. I only.
  b. II only.
  c. Both I and II.
  d. Neither I nor II.

25. In order to be a holder in due course, the holder, among
other requirements, must give value. Which of the following will satisfy this value requirement?

  I. An antecedent debt.
 II. A promise to perform services at a future date.

  a. I only.
  b. II only.

    c.   Both I and II.

    d.   Neither I nor II.

26. Bond fraudulently induced Teal to make a note payable to Wilk, to whom Bond was indebted. Bond delivered the note to Wilk. Wilk negotiated the instrument to Monk, who purchased it with knowledge of the fraud and after it was overdue. If Wilk qualifies as a holder in due course, which of the following statements is correct?

    a.   Monk has the standing of a holder in due course through Wilk.

    b.   Teal can successfully assert the defense of fraud in the inducement against Monk.

    c.   Monk personally qualifies as a holder in due course.

    d.   Teal can successfully assert the defense of fraud in the inducement against Wilk.

27. To the extent that a holder of a negotiable promissory note is a holder in due course, the holder takes the note free of which of the following defenses?

    a.   Minority of the maker where it is a defense to enforcement of a contract.

    b.   Forgery of the maker's signature.

    c.   Discharge of the maker in bankruptcy.

    d.   Nonperformance of a condition precedent.

28. Under the Commercial Paper Article of the UCC, in a nonconsumer transaction, which of the following are real defenses available against a holder in due course?

	Material alteration	*Discharge of bankruptcy*	*Breach of contract*
a.	No	Yes	Yes
b.	Yes	Yes	No
c.	No	No	Yes
d.	Yes	No	No

29. On February 15, 2001, P.D. Stone obtained the following instrument from Astor Co. for $1,000. Stone was aware that Helco, Inc. disputed liability under the instrument because of an alleged breach by Astor of the referenced computer purchase agreement. On March 1, 2001, Willard Bank obtained the instrument from Stone for $3,900. Willard had no knowledge that Helco disputed liability under the instrument.

February 12, 2001

Helco, Inc. promises to pay to Astor Co. or bearer the sum of $4,900 (four thousand four hundred and 00/100 dollars) on March 12, 2001 (maker may elect to extend due date to March 31, 2001) with interest thereon at the rate of 12% per annum.

HELCO, INC.

By: *A. J. Help*

A. J. Help, President

Reference: Computer purchase agreement dated February 12, 2001

The reverse side of the instrument is endorsed as follows:

Pay to the order of Willard Bank, without recourse

P.D. Stone

P.D. Stone

If Willard Bank demands payment from Helco and Helco refuses to pay the instrument because of Astor's breach of the computer purchase agreement, which of the following statements would be correct?

    a.   Willard Bank is **not** a holder in due course because Stone was **not** a holder in due course.

    b.   Helco will **not** be liable to Willard Bank because of Astor's breach.

    c.   Stone will be the only party liable to Willard Bank because he was aware of the dispute between Helco and Astor.

    d.   Helco will be liable to Willard Bank because Willard Bank is a holder in due course.

30. Northup made out a negotiable promissory note that was payable to the order of Port. This promissory note was meant to purchase some furniture that Port used to own, but he lied to Northup when he claimed he still owned it. Port immediately negotiated the note to Johnson who knew about Port's lie. Johnson negotiated the note to Kenner who was a holder in due course. Kenner then negotiated the note back to Johnson. When Johnson sought to enforce the promissory note against Northup, she refused claiming fraud. Which of the following is correct?

    a.   Johnson, as a holder through a holder in due course, can enforce the promissory note.

    b.   Northup wins because Johnson does not have the rights of a holder in due course.

    c.   Northup wins because she has a real defense on this note.

    d.   Johnson's knowledge of the lie does not affect his rights on this note.

31. Goran wrote out a check to Ruz to pay for a television set he purchased at a flea market from Ruz. When Goran got home, he found out the box did not have the television set but some weights. Goran immediately gave his bank a stop payment order over the phone. He followed this up with a written stop payment order. In the meantime, Ruz negotiated the check to Schmidt who qualified as a holder in due course. Schmidt gave the check as a gift to Buck. When Buck tried to cash the check, the bank and Goran both refused to pay. Which of the following is correct?

    a.   Buck cannot collect on the check from the bank because Goran has a real defense.

    b.   Buck cannot collect on the check from Goran because Goran has a personal defense.

    c.   Buck can require the bank to pay because Buck is a holder through a holder in due course.

    d.   Buck can require Goran to pay on the check even though the check was a gift.

32. Under the Negotiable Instruments Article of the UCC, which of the following parties will be a holder but **not** be entitled to the rights of a holder in due course?

    a.   A party who, knowing of a real defense to payment, received an instrument from a holder in due course.

    b.   A party who found an instrument payable to bearer.

    c.   A party who received, as a gift, an instrument from a holder in due course.

    d.   A party who, in good faith and without notice of any defect, gave value for an instrument.

33. A holder in due course will take free of which of the following defenses?

a. Infancy, to the extent that it is a defense to a simple contract.
b. Discharge of the maker in bankruptcy.
c. A wrongful filling-in of the amount payable that was omitted from the instrument.
d. Duress of a nature that renders the obligation of the party a nullity.

34. Cobb gave Garson a signed check with the amount payable left blank. Garson was to fill in, as the amount, the price of fuel oil Garson was to deliver to Cobb at a later date. Garson estimated the amount at $700, but told Cobb it would be no more than $900. Garson did not deliver the fuel oil, but filled in the amount of $1,000 on the check. Garson then negotiated the check to Josephs in satisfaction of a $500 debt with the $500 balance paid to Garson in cash. Cobb stopped payment and Josephs is seeking to collect $1,000 from Cobb. Cobb's maximum liability to Josephs will be

a. $0
b. $ 500
c. $ 900
d. $1,000

35. A maker of a note will have a real defense against a holder in due course as a result of any of the following conditions **except**

a. Discharge in bankruptcy.
b. Forgery.
c. Fraud in the execution.
d. Lack of consideration.

36. Which of the following parties has(have) primary liability on a negotiable instrument?

I. Drawer of a check.
II. Drawee of a time draft before acceptance.
III. Maker of a promissory note.

a. I and II only.
b. II and III only.
c. I and III only.
d. III only.

37. Which of the following actions does **not** discharge a prior party to a commercial instrument?

a. Good faith payment or satisfaction of the instrument.
b. Cancellation of that prior party's endorsement.
c. The holder's oral renunciation of that prior party's liability.
d. The holder's intentional destruction of the instrument.

38. Under the Negotiable Instruments Article of the UCC, when an instrument is indorsed "Pay to John Doe" and signed "Faye Smith," which of the following statements is(are) correct?

	Payment of the instrument is guaranteed	The instrument can be further negotiated
a.	Yes	Yes
b.	Yes	No
c.	No	Yes
d.	No	No

39.

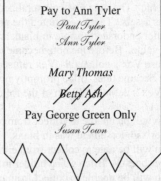

Pay to Ann Tyler
Paul Tyler
Ann Tyler

Mary Thomas
~~*Betty Ash*~~
Pay George Green Only
Susan Town

Susan Town, on receiving the above instrument, struck Betty Ash's endorsement. Under the Commercial Paper Article of the UCC, which of the endorsers of the above instrument will be completely discharged from secondary liability to later endorsers of the instrument?

a. Ann Tyler.
b. Mary Thomas.
c. Betty Ash.
d. Susan Town.

40. A subsequent holder of a negotiable instrument may cause the discharge of a prior holder of the instrument by any of the following actions **except**

a. Unexcused delay in presentment of a time draft.
b. Procuring certification of a check.
c. Giving notice of dishonor the day after dishonor.
d. Material alteration of a note.

41. A check has the following endorsements on the back:

Paul Folk
without recourse
George Hopkins
payment guaranteed
Ann Quarry
collection guaranteed
Rachel Ott

Which of the following conditions occurring subsequent to the endorsements would discharge all of the endorsers?

a. Lack of notice of dishonor.
b. Late presentment.
c. Insolvency of the maker.
d. Certification of the check.

42. Robb, a minor, executed a promissory note payable to bearer and delivered it to Dodsen in payment for a stereo system. Dodsen negotiated the note for value to Mellon by delivery alone and without endorsement. Mellon endorsed the note in blank and negotiated it to Bloom for value. Bloom's demand for payment was refused by Robb because the note was executed when Robb was a minor. Bloom gave prompt notice of Robb's default to Dodsen and Mellon. None of the holders of the note were aware of Robb's minority. Which of the following parties will be liable to Bloom?

	Dodsen	Mellon
a.	Yes	Yes
b.	Yes	No
c.	No	No
d.	No	Yes

43. Vex Corp. executed a negotiable promissory note payable to Tamp, Inc. The note was collateralized by some of Vex's business assets. Tamp negotiated the note to Miller for value. Miller endorsed the note in blank and negotiated it to Bilco for value. Before the note became due, Bilco agreed to release Vex's collateral. Vex refused to pay Bilco when the note became due. Bilco promptly notified Miller and Tamp of Vex's default. Which of the following statements is correct?

- a. Bilco will be unable to collect from Miller because Miller's endorsement was in blank.
- b. Bilco will be able to collect from either Tamp or Miller because Bilco was a holder in due course.
- c. Bilco will be unable to collect from either Tamp or Miller because of Bilco's release of the collateral.
- d. Bilco will be able to collect from Tamp because Tamp was the original payee.

44. Under the Commercial Paper Article of the UCC, which of the following statements best describes the effect of a person endorsing a check "without recourse"?

- a. The person has **no** liability to prior endorsers.
- b. The person makes **no** promise or guarantee of payment on dishonor.
- c. The person gives **no** warranty protection to later transferees.
- d. The person converts the check into order paper.

45. A check is postdated to November 20 even though the check was written out on November 3 of the same year. Which of the following is correct under the Revised Article 3 of the Uniform Commercial Code?

- a. The check is payable on demand on or after November 3 because part of the definition of a check is that it be payable on demand.
- b. The check ceases to be demand paper and is payable on November 20.
- c. The postdating destroys negotiability.
- d. A bank that pays the check is automatically liable for early payment.

46. Stanley purchased a computer from Comp Electronics with a personal check. Later that day, Stanley saw a better deal on the computer so he orally stopped payment on the check with his bank. The bank, however, still paid Comp Electronics when the check was presented three days later. Which of the following is correct?

- a. The bank is liable to Stanley for failure to follow the oral stop payment order.
- b. The bank is not liable to Stanley because the stop payment order was not in writing.
- c. The bank is not liable to Stanley if Comp Electronics qualifies as a holder in due course.
- d. Comp Electronics is liable to Stanley to return the amount of the check.

47. A trade acceptance is an instrument drawn by a

- a. Seller obligating the seller or designee to make payment.
- b. Buyer obligating the buyer or designee to make payment.
- c. Seller ordering the buyer or designee to make payment.
- d. Buyer ordering the seller or designee to make payment.

48. Under the Documents of Title Article of the UCC, which of the following statements is(are) correct regarding a common carrier's duty to deliver goods subject to a negotiable bearer bill of lading?

- I. The carrier may deliver the goods to any party designated by the holder of the bill of lading.
- II. A carrier who, without court order, delivers goods to a party claiming the goods under a missing negotiable bill of lading is liable to any person injured by the misdelivery.

- a. I only.
- b. II only.
- c. Both I and II.
- d. Neither I nor II.

49. Which of the following is **not** a warranty made by the seller of a negotiable warehouse receipt to the purchaser of the document?

- a. The document transfer is fully effective with respect to the goods it represents.
- b. The warehouseman will honor the document.
- c. The seller has **no** knowledge of any facts that would impair the document's validity.
- d. The document is genuine.

50. Under the UCC, a warehouse receipt

- a. Will **not** be negotiable if it contains a contractual limitation on the warehouseman's liability.
- b. May qualify as both a negotiable warehouse receipt and negotiable commercial paper if the instrument is payable either in cash or by the delivery of goods.
- c. May be issued only by a bonded and licensed warehouseman.
- d. Is negotiable if by its terms the goods are to be delivered to bearer or the order of a named person.

SIMULATION PROBLEMS

Simulation Problem 1   (10 to 15 minutes)

Instructions				
	Fact Pattern I	Fact Pattern II	Fact Pattern III	Fact Pattern IV

This simulation has four separate fact patterns, each followed by five legal conclusions relating to the fact pattern preceding those five numbered legal conclusions. Determine whether each conclusion is Correct or Incorrect.

	Fact Pattern I			
Instructions		Fact Pattern II	Fact Pattern III	Fact Pattern IV

An instrument purports to be a negotiable instrument. It otherwise fulfills all the elements of negotiability and it states "Pay to Rich Crane."

		Correct	*Incorrect*
1.	It is negotiable if it is a check and Rich Crane has possession of the check.	O	O
2.	It is negotiable if it is a draft drawn on a corporation.	O	O
3.	It is negotiable if it is a promissory note due one year later with 5% interest stated on its face.	O	O
4.	It is negotiable if it is a certificate of deposit.	O	O
5.	It is negotiable even if it is a cashier's check.	O	O

		Fact Pattern II		
Instructions	Fact Pattern I		Fact Pattern III	Fact Pattern IV

Another instrument fulfills all of the elements of negotiability except possibly one, that is, the instrument does not identify any payee.

		Correct	*Incorrect*
1.	The instrument is **not** negotiable if it is a draft.	O	O
2.	The instrument is bearer paper if it is a check.	O	O
3.	The instrument is negotiable if it is a promissory note.	O	O
4.	The instrument is bearer paper if it is a promissory note.	O	O
5.	The instrument is negotiable only if it also states the word "negotiable" on its face.	O	O

			Fact Pattern III	
Instructions	Fact Pattern I	Fact Pattern II		Fact Pattern IV

A promissory note states that the maker promises to pay to the order of ABC Company $10,000 plus interest at 2% above the prime rate of XYZ Bank in New York City one year from the date on the promissory note.

		Correct	*Incorrect*
1.	The interest rate provision destroys negotiability because the prime rate can fluctuate during the year.	O	O
2.	The interest rate provision destroys negotiability because one has to look outside the note to see what the prime rate of XYZ Bank is.	O	O
3.	The maker is obligated to pay only the $10,000 because the amount of interest is not a sum certain.	O	O
4.	The maker must pay $10,000 plus the judgment rate of interest because the amount of interest cannot be determined without referring to facts outside the instrument.	O	O
5.	Any holder of this note could not qualify as a holder in due course because of the interest provision.	O	O

				Fact Pattern IV
Instructions	Fact Pattern I	Fact Pattern II	Fact Pattern III	

An individual fills out his personal check. He postdates the check for ten days later and notes on the face of the check that it is for "Payment for textbooks."

		Correct	*Incorrect*
1.	The instrument is demand paper because it is a check and is thus payable immediately.	○	○
2.	The check is not payable before the date on its face.	○	○
3.	If a bank pays on this check before its stated date, the bank is liable to the drawer.	○	○
4.	The notation "Payment for textbooks" destroys negotiability because it makes payment conditional.	○	○
5.	The notation "Payment for textbooks" does **not** destroy negotiability but only if the check was actually used to pay for textbooks.	○	○

Simulation Problem 2   (10 to 15 minutes)

Situation		
	Instrument 1	Instrument 2

During an audit of Trent Realty Corp.'s financial statements, Clark, CPA, reviewed two instruments.

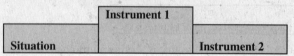

Instrument 1

$300,000	Belle, MD
	April 1, 2004

For value received, ten years after date, I promise to pay to the order of Dart Finance Co. Three Hundred Thousand and 00/100 dollars with interest at 9% per annum compounded annually until fully paid.

This instrument arises out of the sale of land located in MD.

It is further agreed that:

1. Maker will pay all costs of collection including reasonable attorney fees.
2. Maker may prepay the amount outstanding on any anniversary date of this instrument.

$$G.\ Evans$$
G. Evans

The following transactions relate to Instrument 1.

- On March 15, 2005, Dart endorsed the instrument in blank and sold it to Morton for $275,000.
- On July 10, 2005, Evans informed Morton that Dart had fraudulently induced Evans into signing the instrument.
- On August 15, 2005, Trent, which knew of Evans' claim against Dart, purchased the instrument from Morton for $50,000.

Items 1 through 5 relate to Instrument 1. For each item, select from List I the correct answer. An answer may be selected once, more than once, or not at all.

List I

A. Draft	E. Holder in due course	H. Nonnegotiable
B. Promissory Note	F. Holder with rights of a holder in due course under the shelter provision	I. Evans, Morton, and Dart
C. Security Agreement		J. Morton and Dart
D. Holder	G. Negotiable	K. Only Dart

		(A)	**(B)**	**(C)**	**(D)**	**(E)**	**(F)**	**(G)**	**(H)**	**(I)**	**(J)**	**(K)**
1.	Instrument 1 is a (type of instrument)	○	○	○	○	○	○	○	○	○	○	○
2.	Instrument 1 is (negotiability)	○	○	○	○	○	○	○	○	○	○	○
3.	Morton is considered a (type of ownership)	○	○	○	○	○	○	○	○	○	○	○
4.	Trent is considered a (type of ownership)	○	○	○	○	○	○	○	○	○	○	○
5.	Trent could recover on the instrument from [liable party(s)]	○	○	○	○	○	○	○	○	○	○	○

MULTIPLE-CHOICE QUESTIONS (1-30)

1. Under the Revised UCC Secured Transaction Article, when collateral is in a secured party's possession, which of the following conditions must also be satisfied to have attachment?

   a. There must be a written security agreement.
   b. The public must be notified.
   c. The secured party must receive consideration.
   d. The debtor must have rights to the collateral.

2. Under the Revised UCC Secured Transaction Article, which of the following after-acquired property may be attached to a security agreement given to a secured lender?

	Inventory	Equipment
a.	Yes	Yes
b.	Yes	No
c.	No	Yes
d.	No	No

3. Gardner Bank loaned Holland Company $20,000 to purchase some inventory to resell in its store. Gardner had Holland sign a security agreement that listed as collateral all present and future inventory of Holland as well as the proceeds of any sales of the inventory. Later, Boldon Company, who was aware of Gardner's security interest, extended credit to Holland but Holland failed to pay back either Gardner or Boldon. Boldon has sought to defeat the security interest pointing out that Gardner never filled out a financing statement. Which of the following is correct?

   a. Gardner has an enforceable security interest that is valid against Holland and has priority over Boldon's interests.
   b. Gardner does not have an enforceable security interest valid against Holland or against Boldon.
   c. Gardner does have an enforceable security interest valid against Holland but not valid against Boldon.
   d. Gardner does not have an enforceable security interest valid against Holland but does have one valid against Boldon.

4. Article 9 of the UCC which governs security interests has added some items that now are covered by security interests law. Which of the following is true?

   a. Security interests in tort claims already assessed by a court of law are covered.
   b. After-acquired commercial tort claims are covered.
   c. Both a. and b.
   d. Neither a. nor b.

5. Under the Revised Secured Transactions Article of the UCC, which of the following requirements is necessary to have a security interest attach?

	Debtor had rights in the collateral	Proper filing of a security agreement	Value given by the creditor
a.	Yes	Yes	Yes
b.	Yes	Yes	No
c.	Yes	No	Yes
d.	No	Yes	Yes

6. Under the Revised UCC Secured Transaction Article, which of the following events will always prevent a security interest from attaching?

   a. Failure to have a written security agreement.
   b. Failure of the creditor to have possession of the collateral.
   c. Failure of the debtor to have rights in the collateral.
   d. Failure of the creditor to give present consideration for the security interest.

7. Perfection of a security interest permits the secured party to protect its interest by

   a. Avoiding the need to file a financing statement.
   b. Preventing another creditor from obtaining a security interest in the same collateral.
   c. Establishing priority over the claims of most subsequent secured creditors.
   d. Denying the debtor the right to possess the collateral.

8. Under the Revised UCC Secured Transaction Article, what is the effect of perfecting a security interest by filing a financing statement?

   a. The secured party can enforce its security interest against the debtor.
   b. The secured party has permanent priority in the collateral even if the collateral is removed to another state.
   c. The debtor is protected against all other parties who acquire an interest in the collateral after the filing.
   d. The secured party has priority in the collateral over most creditors who acquire a security interest in the same collateral after the filing.

9. A secured creditor wants to file a financing statement to perfect its security interest. Under the Revised UCC Secured Transaction Article, which of the following must be included in the financing statement?

   a. A listing or description of the collateral.
   b. An after-acquired property provision.
   c. The creditor's signature.
   d. The collateral's location.

10. Which of the following transactions would illustrate a secured party perfecting its security interest by taking possession of the collateral?

   a. A bank receiving a mortgage on real property.
   b. A wholesaler borrowing to purchase inventory.
   c. A consumer borrowing to buy a car.
   d. A pawnbroker lending money.

11. Under the Revised UCC Secured Transaction Article, which of the following actions will best perfect a security interest in a negotiable instrument against any other party?

   a. Filing a security agreement.
   b. Taking possession of the instrument.
   c. Perfecting by attachment.
   d. Obtaining a duly executed financing statement.

12. Grey Corp. sells computers to the public. Grey sold and delivered a computer to West on credit. West executed and delivered to Grey a promissory note for the purchase price and a security agreement covering the computer. West purchased the computer for personal use. Grey did not file a financing statement. Is Grey's security interest perfected?

   a. Yes, because Grey retained ownership of the computer.
   b. Yes, because it was perfected at the time of attachment.
   c. No, because the computer was a consumer good.

d. No, because Grey failed to file a financing statement.

13. In which of the following cases does a seller have automatic perfection of a security interest as soon as attachment takes place?

I. Purchase money security interest in consumer goods.
II. Purchase money security interest in inventory.
III. Purchase money security interest in equipment.

    a. I only.
    b. I and II only.
    c. II and III only.
    d. I, II and III.

14. Mars, Inc. manufactures and sells VCRs on credit directly to wholesalers, retailers, and consumers. Mars can perfect its security interest in the VCRs it sells without having to file a financing statement or take possession of the VCRs if the sale is made to
    a. Retailers.
    b. Wholesalers that sell to distributors for resale.
    c. Consumers.
    d. Wholesalers that sell to buyers in the ordinary course of business.

15. Under the Revised Secured Transaction Article of the UCC, which of the following purchasers will own consumer goods free of a perfected security interest in the goods?
    a. A merchant who purchases the goods for resale.
    b. A merchant who purchases the goods for use in its business.
    c. A consumer who purchases the goods from a consumer purchaser who gave the security interest.
    d. A consumer who purchases the goods in the ordinary course of business.

16. Under the Revised UCC Secured Transaction Article, what is the order of priority for the following security interests in store equipment?

I. Security interest perfected by filing on April 15, 2001.
II. Security interest attached on April 1, 2001.
III. Purchase money security interest attached April 11, 2001 and perfected by filing on April 20, 2001.

    a. I, III, II.
    b. II, I, III.
    c. III, I, II.
    d. III, II, I.

17. Noninventory goods were purchased and delivered on June 15, 2001. Several security interests exist in these goods. Which of the following security interests has priority over the others?
    a. Security interest in future goods attached June 10, 2001.
    b. Security interest attached June 15, 2001.
    c. Security interest perfected June 20, 2001.
    d. Purchase money security interest perfected June 24, 2001.

18. Under the Revised Secured Transaction Article of the UCC, what would be the order of priority for the following security interests in consumer goods?

I. Financing agreement filed on April 1.
II. Possession of the collateral by a creditor on April 10.
III. Financing agreement perfected on April 15.

    a. I, II, III.
    b. II, I, III.
    c. II, III, I.
    d. III, II, I.

19. A party who filed a security interest in inventory on April 1, 2001, would have a superior interest to which of the following parties?
    a. A holder of a mechanic's lien whose lien was filed on March 15, 2001.
    b. A holder of a purchase money security interest in after-acquired property filed on March 20, 2001.
    c. A purchaser in the ordinary course of business who purchased on April 10, 2001.
    d. A judgment lien creditor who filed its judgment on April 15, 2001.

20. W & B, a wholesaler, sold on credit some furniture to Broadmore Company, a retailer. W & B perfected its security interest by filing a financing statement. Lean purchased some furniture from Broadmore for his home. He was unaware of W & B's perfected security interest. McCoy purchased some furniture from Broadmore for her home. She was aware that Broadmore's inventory was subject to security interests since Broadmore was having financial problems and had to buy the furniture on credit. Norsome purchased some furniture from Broadmore for use in his business. Broadmore defaults on its loans from W & B, who wants to repossess the furniture purchased and delivered to Lean, McCoy, and Norsome. From which parties can W & B legally repossess the furniture?
    a. McCoy.
    b. Lean and McCoy.
    c. Norsome.
    d. None of these parties.

21. Rand purchased a sofa from Abby Department Store for use in her home. Abby had her sign a security agreement for the balance Rand owed. Rand did not pay the balance and sold the sofa to her neighbor, Gram, for use in his home. Gram did not realize that Rand had not paid off the balance. Abby filed a financing statement after Rand defaulted. This filing was also after Gram purchased the sofa from Rand. Which of the following is correct?
    a. Abby can repossess the sofa from Gram since it has a written security agreement covering the sofa.
    b. Abby can repossess the sofa from Gram since it perfected its security agreement by filing.
    c. Abby can repossess the sofa from Gram since it obtained automatic perfection.
    d. Abby has no right to repossess the sofa from Gram.

22. Wine purchased a computer using the proceeds of a loan from MJC Finance Company. Wine gave MJC a security interest in the computer. Wine executed a security agreement and financing statement, which was filed by MJC. Wine used the computer to monitor Wine's personal investments. Later, Wine sold the computer to Jacobs, for Jacobs' family use. Jacobs was unaware of MJC's security interest. Wine now is in default under the MJC loan. May MJC repossess the computer from Jacobs?
    a. No, because Jacobs was unaware of the MJC security interest.
    b. No, because Jacobs intended to use the computer for family or household purposes.

    c.   Yes, because MJC's security interest was perfected before Jacobs' purchase.

    d.   Yes, because Jacobs' purchase of the computer made Jacobs personally liable to MJC.

23. Rally Co. has purchased some inventory from Kantar Corporation to sell to customers who will use the inventory primarily for consumer use. Which of the following is **not** correct?

    a.   If Kantar sells the inventory to Rally on credit and takes out a security interest using the inventory as collateral, this a purchase money security interest.

    b.   If Kantar sells the inventory to Rally on credit and takes out a security interest using the inventory as collateral, this is a purchase money security interest in consumer goods.

    c.   If Kantar sells the inventory to Rally but Rally pays for it by getting a loan from a bank who takes out a security interest using the inventory as collateral, this is a purchase money security interest.

    d.   If a customer purchases some inventory on credit from Rally for home use and signs a written security agreement presented by Rally that lists the inventory as collateral for the credit, this is a purchase money security interest in consumer goods.

24. On June 15, Harper purchased equipment for $100,000 from Imperial Corp. for use in its manufacturing process. Harper paid for the equipment with funds borrowed from Eastern Bank. Harper gave Eastern a security agreement and financing statement covering Harper's existing and after-acquired equipment. On June 21, Harper was petitioned involuntarily into bankruptcy under Chapter 7 of the Federal Bankruptcy Code. A bankruptcy trustee was appointed. On June 23, Eastern filed the financing statement. Which of the parties will have a superior security interest in the equipment?

    a.   The trustee in bankruptcy, because the filing of the financing statement after the commencement of the bankruptcy case would be deemed a preferential transfer.

    b.   The trustee in bankruptcy, because the trustee became a lien creditor before Eastern perfected its security interest.

    c.   Eastern, because it had a perfected purchase money security interest without having to file a financing statement.

    d.   Eastern, because it perfected its security interest within the permissible time limits.

Items 25 and 26 are based on the following:

Drew bought a computer for personal use from Hale Corp. for $3,000. Drew paid $2,000 in cash and signed a security agreement for the balance. Hale properly filed the security agreement. Drew defaulted in paying the balance of the purchase price. Hale asked Drew to pay the balance. When Drew refused, Hale peacefully repossessed the computer.

25. Under the Revised UCC Secured Transaction Article, which of the following remedies will Hale have?

    a.   Obtain a deficiency judgment against Drew for the amount owed.

    b.   Sell the computer and retain any surplus over the amount owed.

    c.   Retain the computer over Drew's objection.

    d.   Sell the computer without notifying Drew.

26. Under the Revised UCC Secured Transaction Article, which of the following rights will Drew have?

    a.   Redeem the computer after Hale sells it.

    b.   Recover the sale price from Hale after Hale sells the computer.

    c.   Force Hale to sell the computer.

    d.   Prevent Hale from selling the computer.

27. Under the Revised UCC Secured Transaction Article, which of the following statements is correct concerning the disposition of collateral by a secured creditor after a debtor's default?

    a.   A good-faith purchaser for value and without knowledge of any defects in the sale takes free of any subordinate liens or security interests.

    b.   The debtor may not redeem the collateral after the default.

    c.   Secured creditors with subordinate claims retain the right to redeem the collateral after the collateral is sold to a third party.

    d.   The collateral may only be disposed of at a public sale.

28. Bean defaulted on a promissory note payable to Gray Co. The note was secured by a piece of equipment owned by Bean. Gray perfected its security interest on May 29, 2001 Bean had also pledged the same equipment as collateral for another loan from Smith Co. after he had given the security interest to Gray. Smith's security interest was perfected on June 30, 2001. Bean is current in his payments to Smith. Subsequently, Gray took possession of the equipment and sold it at a private sale to Walsh, a good-faith purchaser for value. Walsh will take the equipment

    a.   Free of Smith's security interest because Bean is current in his payments to Smith.

    b.   Free of Smith's security interest because Walsh acted in good faith and gave value.

    c.   Subject to Smith's security interest because the equipment was sold at a private sale.

    d.   Subject to Smith's security interest because Smith is a purchase money secured creditor.

29. Under the Revised Secured Transactions Article of the UCC, which of the following remedies is available to a secured creditor when a debtor fails to make a payment when due?

	Proceed against the collateral	Obtain a general judgment against the debtor
a.	Yes	Yes
b.	Yes	No
c.	No	Yes
d.	No	No

30. In what order are the following obligations paid after a secured creditor rightfully sells the debtor's collateral after repossession?

  I.   Debt owed to any junior security holder.

 II.   Secured party's reasonable sale expenses.

III.   Debt owed to the secured party.

    a.   I, II, III.

    b.   II, I, III.

    c.   II, III, I.

    d.   III, II, I.

SIMULATION PROBLEM

Simulation Problem 1   (10 to 15 minutes)

Situation	
	Analysis

On January 2, 2004, Gray Interiors Corp., a retailer of sofas, contracted with Shore Furniture Co. to purchase 150 sofas for its inventory. The purchase price was $250,000. Gray paid $50,000 cash and gave Shore a note and security agreement for the balance. On March 1, 2004, the sofas were delivered. On March 10, 2004, Shore filed a financing statement.

On February 1, 2004, Gray negotiated a $1,000,000 line of credit with Float Bank, pledged its present and future inventory as security, and gave Float a security agreement. On February 20, 2004, Gray borrowed $100,000 from the line of credit. On March 5, 2004, Float filed a financing statement.

On April 1, 2004, Dove, a consumer purchaser in the ordinary course of business, purchased a sofa from Gray. Dove was aware of both security interests.

	Analysis
Situation	

Items 1 through 6 refer to the fact pattern. For each item, determine whether (A), (B), or (C) is correct.

	(A)	**(B)**	**(C)**
1. Shore's security interest in the sofas attached on A. January 2, 2004. B. March 1, 2004. C. March 10, 2004.	○	○	○
2. Shore's security interest in the sofas was perfected on A. January 2, 2004. B. March 1, 2004. C. March 10, 2004.	○	○	○
3. Float's security interest in Gray's inventory attached on A. February 1, 2004. B. March 1, 2004. C. March 5, 2004.	○	○	○
4. Float's security interest in Gray's inventory was perfected on A. February 1, 2004. B. February 20, 2004. C. March 5, 2004.	○	○	○
5. A. Shore's security interest has priority because it was a purchase money security interest. B. Float's security interest has priority because Float's financing statement was filed before Shore's. C. Float's security interest has priority because Float's interest attached before Shore's.	○	○	○
6. A. Dove purchased the sofa subject to Shore's security interest. B. Dove purchased the sofa subject to both the Shore and Float security interests. C. Dove purchased the sofa free of either the Shore or Float security interests.	○	○	○

MULTIPLE-CHOICE ANSWERS

1. d __ __	8. d __ __	15. d __ __	22. c __ __	29. a __ __	
2. a __ __	9. a __ __	16. c __ __	23. b __ __	30. c __ __	
3. a __ __	10. d __ __	17. d __ __	24. d __ __		
4. a __ __	11. b __ __	18. a __ __	25. a __ __		
5. c __ __	12. b __ __	19. d __ __	26. c __ __		
6. c __ __	13. a __ __	20. d __ __	27. a __ __	1st: __/30 = __%	
7. c __ __	14. c __ __	21. d __ __	28. b __ __	2nd: __/30 = __%	

MULTIPLE-CHOICE ANSWER EXPLANATIONS

B.   Attachment of Security Interests

1.   (d)   Under the Revised Article 9 on Secured Transactions, attachment of a security interest takes place when the secured party gives value, the debtor has rights in the collateral, and one of the following three is true:

   a.   The secured party must possess the collateral if the debtor agrees to it
   b.   The secured party must have control of certain types of collateral, or
   c.   The secured party must have a signed security agreement (or an authenticated electronic transmission).

2.   (a)   An after-acquired property clause in a security agreement allows the secured party's interest in such property to attach once the debtor acquires the property, without the need to make a new security agreement. These clauses are typically used for inventory and accounts receivable, and can also be used for equipment.

3.   (a)   The security interest did attach because there was a signed security agreement, Gardner gave value, and Holland had rights in the collateral. Upon attachment, Gardner's security interest is fully enforceable against Holland. Even though Gardner never perfected the security interest, it still has priority over Boldon's interests because Boldon was aware of the security interest.

4.   (a)   Security interests in tort claims are covered under the Revised UCC Secured Transactions Article; this is not true of after-acquired commercial tort claims.

5.   (c)   In order for attachment of a security interest to occur, three elements must take place. First, the secured party must give value, second, the debtor must have rights in the collateral, and third, there must be a security agreement. This security agreement may be oral if the secured party has possession or control of the collateral. Otherwise, it must be in writing and signed by the debtor. An exception to the signature requirement is made if it is an authenticated electronic transmission.

6.   (c)   In order for a security interest to attach, there must be a valid security agreement, the secured party must have given value, and the debtor must have rights in the collateral. If any one of these items is missing, attachment cannot take place. Answer (a) is incorrect because the security interest may be oral if the secured party has possession or control of the collateral. Answer (b) is incorrect because if the security agreement is in writing, the secured party does not need possession of the collateral to achieve attachment. Answer (d) is incorrect because the secured party must give value, not necessarily consideration. A preexisting claim, although not consideration, does count as value.

C.4.   Filing a Financing Statement

7.   (c)   Perfection of a security interest is important in that it establishes for a secured party priority over the claims that may be made by most subsequent secured creditors. Answer (a) is incorrect because there are three methods of obtaining perfection and one of them is filing a financing statement. Answer (b) is incorrect because subsequent creditors may still obtain security interests in the same collateral although they will normally obtain a lower priority. Answer (d) is incorrect because of times the debtor retains possession of the collateral.

8.   (d)   Perfection by filing a financing statement will not defeat all other parties who acquire an interest in the same collateral; rather, perfection by filing gives the secured party most possible rights in the collateral. Note, purchasers from a merchant in the ordinary course of business take the collateral free from any prior perfected security interest. The only time a purchaser would take the collateral subject to a prior perfected security interest would be when the purchaser knew that the merchant was selling the goods in violation of a financing statement. A creditor need not perfect the security interest in order to enforce it against the debtor. The filing of a financing statement does not protect the debtor's rights but rather the creditor's rights.

9.   (a)   Filing a financing statement is one method of perfecting a security interest in personal property. Under the Revised UCC Secured Transaction Article, a financing statement must include the following: the names of the debtor and creditor, and a listing or description of the collateral. An after-acquired property provision, the creditor's signature, and the collateral's location are not required to be included in the financing statement.

C.5.   Perfection by Possession

10.   (d)   One way to perfect a security interest is for the secured party to take possession of the collateral in addition to attaining attachment. A pawnbroker lending money is such a case. There is a security agreement which may be oral since the secured party has possession of the collateral. The secured party gives value by lending the money. The third step in attachment is that the debtor has rights in the collateral such as ownership. Since these steps constitute attachment, perfection is accomplished by the pawnbroker, the secured party, taking possession of the collateral. The secured transactions laws apply to security interests in personal property, not real property. The wholesaler (car buyer), not the secured party, will have possession of the collateral.

11.   (b)   In general, the best way to perfect a security interest in a negotiable instrument is to take possession of the instrument. This is true because negotiable instruments are easily negotiated to other holders who can become holders in due course. Answer (a) is incorrect because a holder can become a holder in due course even if a security agreement is filed. Answer (c) is incorrect because perfecting by attachment requires a purchase money security interest in consumer goods. Answer (d) is incorrect because this cannot even accomplish perfection until it is filed.

C.6. Automatic Perfection

12. **(b)** Since West purchased the computer for personal use and the computer itself was the collateral for the security agreement, the fact pattern involves a purchase money security interest in consumer goods. Therefore, once attachment took place, perfection was automatic. Answer (c) is incorrect because since the computer was a consumer good, perfection was automatic upon attachment. Answer (d) is incorrect because filing a financing statement is not required for perfecting a purchase money security interest in consumer goods. Answer (a) is incorrect because retaining or obtaining possession, not ownership, by the secured party is a way to perfect. In any event, Grey Corp. did not retain either ownership or possession since they sold and delivered the computer to West.

13. **(a)** Automatic perfection (perfection by attachment) takes place in the case of a purchase money security interest (PMSI) in consumer goods only. Answers (b), (c), and (d) are incorrect because they include PMSI in inventory or equipment which do not qualify for automatic perfection.

14. **(c)** Mars holds a purchase money security interest in the goods sold, which allowed the buyers of these goods to secure the credit for their purchase. When a purchase money security interest is in consumer goods, the secured party (Mars) obtains perfection when attachment takes place without the need to file a financing statement or take possession or control of the collateral. Answers (a), (b), and (d) are incorrect because in those cases the goods comprise inventory, not consumer goods.

E. Priorities

15. **(d)** Buyers in the ordinary course of business take goods free of any security interest whether perfected or not. The buyer can be, but need not be, a consumer. Answer (a) is incorrect because a merchant who purchases consumer goods for resale may not be buying in the ordinary course of business. Answer (b) is incorrect because the merchant who buys the consumer goods for use in his/her business may not be buying in the ordinary course of business. Answer (c) is incorrect because although a consumer can take goods free of a security interest when buying from another consumer, this requires certain facts along with a purchase money security interest in consumer goods. There are no facts in the question to show this.

16. **(c)** In general, a purchase money security interest in noninventory has priority over nonpurchase money security interests if it was perfected within 20 days after the debtor received the collateral. Item III, therefore, has the first priority because the purchase money security interest was perfected on April 20, 2001, which was within twenty days of the attachment. Item I has priority over Item II because the security interest in Item I was perfected, while the security interest in Item II was not.

17. **(d)** A purchase money security interest in noninventory goods has a special rule. Since it was perfected within twenty days after the debtor got possession of the collateral, it has priority over all of the others. Answers (a) and (b) are incorrect because unperfected security interests have a lower priority than perfected security interests. Answer (c) is incorrect because although this security interest was perfected before the purchase money security interest, the latter has priority if perfected within twenty days of the debtor taking possession of the collateral.

18. **(a)** Since security interest I was perfected first when the financing agreement was filed on April 1, it has the first priority. Security interest II was perfected on April 10 when the creditor took possession of the collateral. It has the second priority. Security interest III has the third priority since it was perfected last on April 15.

19. **(d)** The party perfected by filing a security interest in inventory on April 1, 2001. S/he would therefore have priority over a judgment lien creditor who filed later on April 15, 2001. Answer (a) is incorrect because the mechanic's lien was filed on March 15 before the perfection of the security interest. Therefore, the mechanic's lien has priority over the perfected security interest. Answer (b) is incorrect because the holder of the purchase money security interest in after-acquired property filed and perfected before April 1. Answer (c) is incorrect because a purchaser in the ordinary course of business is free of other security interests even if they are perfected before s/he purchases the inventory.

20. **(d)** Lean, McCoy, and Norsome all purchased the furniture in the ordinary course of business. As such, all three parties take free of the security interest even if it was perfected. This is true whether they purchased the furniture for consumer or business use and whether they knew of the security agreement or not.

21. **(d)** Abby had a perfected security agreement because of the purchase money security interest in consumer goods. This, however, is not effective against a good-faith purchaser for value who buys from a consumer for consumer use as in the case of Gram. Perfection by filing is, however, effective in such a case but only if the filing is done before Gram purchases the sofa. Answer (a) is incorrect because the attachment of the written security interest makes it enforceable against Rand, not Gram. Answer (b) is incorrect because the filing of the financing statement took place after Gram bought the sofa. Answer (c) is incorrect because, although Abby did accomplish automatic perfection by way of the PMSI in consumer goods, this type of perfection was not effective against Gram because he was a good-faith purchaser for value who bought it from a consumer (Rand) for consumer use.

22. **(c)** MJC obtained a security interest in the computer purchased by Wine and perfected it by filing. Even though when Jacobs later purchased it for consumer use he was unaware of MJC's security interest, MJC still has priority. This is true because the filing is constructive notice to all subsequent parties. MJC has priority and may repossess the computer even if Jacobs was unaware of the filed security interest. The filing gives MJC priority over Jacob despite his intended use for family. Jacobs is not personally liable to MJC because he made no contract and did not agree to take on liability with MJC.

23.   (b)   Because Kantar has a security interest in the inventory it sold and is also using the same inventory as collateral for the credit, this is a purchase money security interest. However, because the items Rally purchased are inventory, not consumer goods, in **Rally's** hands, this is not a PMSI in consumer goods. Answer (a) is not chosen because this does describe a PMSI since Kantar retained a security interest in the same items sold on credit to secure payment. Answer (c) is not chosen because a PMSI includes a third party giving a loan who retains a security interest in the same items purchased by the loan. Answer (d) is not chosen because this is a PMSI in consumer goods since the customer purchased the items for his/her home use.

24.   (d)   When a purchase money security interest uses noninventory as collateral, it has priority over prior competing interests as long as it is perfected within twenty days of the debtor obtaining possession of the collateral. Since the collateral in this fact pattern was equipment, and Eastern filed within twenty days, Eastern has priority over the trustee in bankruptcy. Perfection was not automatic since it was a purchase money security interest in equipment, not in consumer goods. Furthermore, since the secured party did not have possession of the collateral, the way to perfect this security interest is by filing a financing statement.

F.   Rights of Parties upon Default

25.   (a)   After Hale repossesses the computer and sells it in a commercially reasonable fashion, Hale may obtain a deficiency judgment for the amount still owed after the proceeds from the sale pay the expenses of repossession and sale and the debt owed to Hale. Any remaining proceeds go to the debtor after repossession and sale expenses and secured parties are paid. For consumer goods, such as the personal computer in this fact pattern, the goods must be sold if the debtor has paid more than 60% of the debt secured by the consumer goods. In this fact pattern, Drew paid two-thirds of the debt. Hale must notify Drew in writing of the impending sale unless Drew had agreed otherwise in writing.

26.   (c)   Since Drew has paid two-thirds of the price, which is over 60% payment on the secured debt for consumer goods, Hale is obligated to sell the computer rather than keep it in satisfaction of the debt. The debtor may redeem before, not after, the sale. Hale may keep the proceeds needed to pay off repossession and sale expenses and the debt owed to Hale. Any excess would go to Drew. Hale has the right to sell the repossessed computer to pay off the secured debt unless Drew properly redeems the interest s/he has in the computer.

27.   (a)   Upon the debtor's default, the secured party may take possession of the collateral and sell it. A good-faith purchaser for value buys the collateral free of any liens or security interests. Answer (b) is incorrect because the debtor has the right to redeem the collateral before the secured party disposes of it. The debtor does this by paying the debt in full as well as the secured party's reasonable expenses. Answer (c) is incorrect as a good-faith purchaser of the collateral takes it free of the debtor's rights and any secured interest or lien subordinate to it. Answer (d) is incorrect because although the collateral may be disposed of by a

public sale, it also may be disposed of by a private sale if the sale uses commercially reasonable practices.

28.   (b)   A good-faith purchaser for value at a private sale will take the property free from any security interest or subordinate liens in the property, but remains subject to security interests which are senior to that being discharged at the sale. In this case, Smith perfected his security interest later than Gray and has a subordinate interest in the property. Thus, Walsh takes the equipment free from this subordinate security interest. The fact that Bean is current in his payments to Smith would not affect Smith's interest in the property. As long as Walsh is a good-faith purchaser for value, it doesn't matter if the equipment is sold at a public or private sale. Smith is not a purchase money secured creditor since the proceeds of Smith's loan to Bean were not used to purchase the equipment acting as collateral.

29.   (a)   If the debtor defaults on the debt, the secured party may proceed against the collateral. This extra protection is one of the main reasons for having secured transactions. If the creditor chooses, s/he may obtain a general judgment against the debtor.

30.   (c)   Under the UCC, after a secured creditor rightfully sells the debtor's collateral after repossession, the secured party's reasonable sale expenses are paid first. Next, the debt owed to the secured party is paid. Any junior security holders then get paid to the extent of any money remaining.

    i.   If composition were involved, then discharge bars another discharge for six years unless debtor paid 70% of debts covered

M. The Bankruptcy Abuse Prevention and Consumer Protection Act of 2005

1. Amends various parts of US Bankruptcy Code including consumer bankruptcies and business bankruptcies
2. Needs-based bankruptcy

   a. Individuals who make more than the median income of state they live in will not anymore be able to file under Chapter 7 unless they meet a strict formula

      (1) Filings now subject to audit in ways similar to tax returns
      (2) Formula considers things such as

         (a) Expenses paid that are reasonably necessary for safety of debtor or debtor's family
         (b) Expenses incurred by debtor for care of chronically ill, disabled, or elderly household member
         (c) In other situations, Act heavily restricts amount of expenses

   b. Provides for materials to educate debtors on how to better manage their finances
   c. Debtor cannot receive a Chapter 7 or Chapter 11 discharge in bankruptcy unless debtor has completed an approved course with credit counseling
   d. Essentially requires attorneys to guarantee correct use of formula to file under Chapter 7 or be subject to civil penalties

      (1) Attorneys' signatures on bankruptcy petitions certify that they are well-based on facts

   e. Newly defined Debt Relief Agencies include attorneys and other professionals who assist consumer debtors with their bankruptcy cases and must provide debtors with additional ways to avoid bankruptcy

3. Enhanced consumer protection

   a. Provides penalties for abusive creditor practices

   > *EXAMPLE: Bad creditor refuses to negotiate a reasonable repayment schedule proposed by an approved credit counseling agency on behalf of the debtor*

   b. Certain claims for domestic child support obligations are placed in the first priority claim category
   c. Debts for certain qualified educational loans are dischargeable when those loans create an undue hardship on debtor or debtor's dependent.

4. Prohibits debtor from using household exemptions from protecting such items as electronic entertainment equipment, works of art, antiques or jewelry worth more than $550, more than one personal computer, aircraft, watercraft, or motorized recreational devices.
5. Provisions under new Act allow trade creditors to treat large portions, sometimes most or even all of vendors' claims as being administrative expenses, significantly increasing their priority status.
6. This Act creates a new Bankruptcy Code section that imposes limits on the payment of severance pay or retention bonuses to key employees in a Chapter 11 case

   a. Retention bonuses are permitted only if key employees have good-faith offers from other businesses at the same or greater compensation

7. For consumer cases, the time between discharges has been increased so that Bankruptcy Code will deny discharge to a Chapter 7 debtor if that debtor received either a Chapter 7 or Chapter 11 discharge in a case filed within 8 years of filing of pending case

   a. Prior law said 6 years between such discharges under Chapter 7 or Chapter 11
   b. Under the new act, Chapter 13 debtors have a few different time limitations when combined with the various chapters.

8. Makes more types of debts nondischargeable in bankruptcy

   a. Generally, the following debts are now nondischargeable:

      (1) Debts for luxury goods and services owed to any one creditor under certain conditions within 60 days of filing

(2) Cash advances under various conditions

(3) Death or injury caused while intoxicated further expanded to include any motor vehicles, vessels or aircraft

(4) Nondischargeable student loans now include for-profit and nongovernmental entities

(5) Pension and profit-sharing debts

(6) Homeowner Association, condo and cooperative fees

(7) Debts to pay fines and penalties

  (a) Including those on prisoners

(8) Debts to pay local and state taxes

(9) Nonsupport obligations for separation or divorce

(10) Debts due to violation of securities law are nondischargeable

9. This Bankruptcy Abuse Prevention and Consumer Protection Act of 2005 creates a new Chapter 15 of the US Bankruptcy Code on cross-border insolvency cases

  a. Meant to make bankruptcy proceedings across international borders more functional

  (1) Favors and promotes cooperation and communication with both foreign courts and foreign representatives

N. Bankruptcy Fees

1. In recent years, bankruptcy specialists have made much larger fees. Rising fees have elicited major objections coming from

  a. Federal watchdogs
  b. Organized labor
  c. Major creditors of bankrupt companies

2. Major complaint is that lawyers and other advisors have been taking too many fees and leaving less money for others in the bankruptcy

3. Thus bankruptcy is more likely testable on CPA Exam because it is now on minds of many

MULTIPLE-CHOICE QUESTIONS (1-31)

1. Which of the following statements is correct concerning the voluntary filing of a petition in bankruptcy?
   a. If the debtor has twelve or more creditors, the unsecured claims must total at least $13,475.
   b. The debtor must be insolvent.
   c. If the debtor has less than twelve creditors, the unsecured claims must total at least $13,475.
   d. The petition may be filed jointly by spouses.

2. A voluntary petition filed under the liquidation provisions of Chapter 7 of the Federal Bankruptcy Code
   a. Is **not** available to a corporation unless it has previously filed a petition under the reorganization provisions of Chapter 11 of the Federal Bankruptcy Code.
   b. Automatically stays collection actions against the debtor **except** by secured creditors.
   c. Will be dismissed unless the debtor has twelve or more unsecured creditors whose claims total at least $13,475.
   d. Does **not** require the debtor to show that the debtor's liabilities exceed the fair market value of assets.

3. On February 28, 2008, Master, Inc. had total assets with a fair market value of $1,200,000 and total liabilities of $990,000. On January 15, 2008, Master made a monthly installment note payment to Acme Distributors Corp., a creditor holding a properly perfected security interest in equipment having a fair market value greater than the balance due on the note. On March 15, 2008, Master voluntarily filed a petition in bankruptcy under the liquidation provisions of Chapter 7 of the Federal Bankruptcy Code. One year later, the equipment was sold for less than the balance due on the note to Acme.

If a creditor challenged Master's right to file, the petition would be dismissed
   a. If Master had less than twelve creditors at the time of filing.
   b. Unless Master can show that a reorganization under Chapter 11 of the Federal Bankruptcy Code would have been unsuccessful.
   c. Unless Master can show that it is unable to pay its debts in the ordinary course of business or as they come due.
   d. If Master is an insurance company.

4. Which of the following conditions, if any, must a debtor meet to file a voluntary bankruptcy petition under Chapter 7 of the Federal Bankruptcy Code?

	Insolvency	*Three or more creditors*
a.	Yes	Yes
b.	Yes	No
c.	No	Yes
d.	No	No

5. Brenner Corporation is trying to avoid bankruptcy but its four creditors are trying to force Brenner into bankruptcy. The four creditors are owed the following amounts:

Anteed Corporation	-	$6,000 of unsecured debt
Bounty Corporation	-	$5,000 of unsecured debt and $8,500 of secured debt
Courtney Corporation	-	$2,000 of unsecured debt
Dauntless Corporation	-	$1,000 of unsecured debt

Which of the creditors must sign the petition to force Brenner into bankruptcy?
   a. Bounty is sufficient.
   b. At least Anteed and Bounty are needed.
   c. At least Bounty, Courtney, and Dauntless are needed.
   d. All of these four creditors are needed.

Items 6 through 10 are based on the following:

Dart Inc., a closely held corporation, was petitioned involuntarily into bankruptcy under the liquidation provisions of Chapter 7 of the Federal Bankruptcy Code. Dart contested the petition.

Dart has not been paying its business debts as they became due, has defaulted on its mortgage loan payments, and owes back taxes to the IRS. The total cash value of Dart's bankruptcy estate after the sale of all assets and payment of administration expenses is $100,000.

Dart has the following creditors:

- Fracon Bank is owed $75,000 principal and accrued interest on a mortgage loan secured by Dart's real property. The property was valued at and sold, in bankruptcy, for $70,000.
- The IRS has a $12,000 recorded judgment for unpaid corporate income tax.
- JOG Office Supplies has an unsecured claim of $3,000 that was timely filed.
- Nanstar Electric Co. has an unsecured claim of $1,200 that was not timely filed.
- Decoy Publications has a claim of $16,000, of which $2,000 is secured by Dart's inventory that was valued and sold, in bankruptcy, for $2,000. The claim was timely filed.

6. Which of the following statements would correctly describe the result of Dart's opposing the petition?
   a. Dart will win because the petition should have been filed under Chapter 11.
   b. Dart will win because there are **not** more than 12 creditors.
   c. Dart will lose because it is **not** paying its debts as they become due.
   d. Dart will lose because of its debt to the IRS.

7. Which of the following events will follow the filing of the Chapter 7 involuntary petition?

	A trustee will be appointed	*A stay against creditor collection proceedings will go into effect*
a.	Yes	Yes
b.	Yes	No
c.	No	Yes
d.	No	No

For **items 8 through 10** assume that the bankruptcy estate was distributed.

8. What dollar amount would Nanstar Electric Co. receive?
   a. $0
   b. $ 800
   c. $1,000
   d. $1,200

9. What total dollar amount would Fracon Bank receive on its secured and unsecured claims?
   a. $70,000

   b. $72,000
   c. $74,000
   d. None of the above.

10. What dollar amount would the IRS receive?
   a. $0
   b. $ 8,000
   c. $10,000
   d. $12,000

11. Which of the following is **not** allowed as a federal exemption under the Federal Bankruptcy Code?
   a. Some specified amount of equity in one motor vehicle.
   b. Unemployment compensation.
   c. Some specified amount of value in books and tools of one's trade.
   d. All of the above are allowed.

12. Flax, a sole proprietor, has been petitioned involuntarily into bankruptcy under the Federal Bankruptcy Code's liquidation provisions. Simon & Co., CPAs, has been appointed trustee of the bankruptcy estate. If Simon also wishes to act as the tax return preparer for the estate, which of the following statements is correct?
   a. Simon is prohibited from serving as both trustee and preparer under any circumstances because serving in that dual capacity would be a conflict of interest.
   b. Although Simon may serve as both trustee and preparer, it is entitled to receive a fee only for the services rendered as a preparer.
   c. Simon may employ itself to prepare tax returns if authorized by the court and may receive a separate fee for services rendered in each capacity.
   d. Although Simon may serve as both trustee and preparer, its fees for services rendered in each capacity will be determined solely by the size of the estate.

13. Which of the following transfers by a debtor, within 90 days of filing for bankruptcy, could be set aside as a preferential payment?
   a. Making a gift to charity.
   b. Paying a business utility bill.
   c. Borrowing money from a bank secured by giving a mortgage on business property.
   d. Prepaying an installment loan on inventory.

Items 14 and 15 are based on the following:

On August 1, 2008, Hall filed a voluntary petition under Chapter 7 of the Federal Bankruptcy Code. Hall's assets are sufficient to pay general creditors 40% of their claims.
   The following transactions occurred before the filing:

- On May 15, 2008, Hall gave a mortgage on Hall's home to National Bank to secure payment of a loan National had given Hall two years earlier. When the loan was made, Hall's twin was a National employee.
- On June 1, 2008, Hall purchased a boat from Olsen for $10,000 cash.
- On July 1, 2008, Hall paid off an outstanding credit card balance of $500. The original debt had been $2,500.

14. The National mortgage was
   a. Preferential, because National would be considered an insider.

   b. Preferential, because the mortgage was given to secure an antecedent debt.
   c. Not preferential, because Hall is presumed insolvent when the mortgage was given.
   d. Not preferential, because the mortgage was a security interest.

15. The payment to Olsen was
   a. Preferential, because the payment was made within ninety days of the filing of the petition.
   b. Preferential, because the payment enabled Olsen to receive more than the other general creditors.
   c. Not preferential, because Hall is presumed insolvent when the payment was made.
   d. Not preferential, because the payment was a contemporaneous exchange for new value.

16. Under the liquidation provisions of Chapter 7 of the Federal Bankruptcy Code, a debtor will be denied a discharge in bankruptcy if the debtor
   a. Fails to list a creditor.
   b. Owes alimony and support payments.
   c. Cannot pay administration expenses.
   d. Refuses to satisfactorily explain a loss of assets.

17. On May 1, 2008, two months after becoming insolvent, Quick Corp., an appliance wholesaler, filed a voluntary petition for bankruptcy under the provisions of Chapter 7 of the Federal Bankruptcy Code. On October 15, 2007, Quick's board of directors had authorized and paid Erly $50,000 to repay Erly's April 1, 2007, loan to the corporation. Erly is a sibling of Quick's president. On March 15, 2008, Quick paid Kray $100,000 for inventory delivered that day.

Which of the following is **not** relevant in determining whether the repayment of Erly's loan is a voidable preferential transfer?
   a. Erly is an insider.
   b. Quick's payment to Erly was made on account of an antecedent debt.
   c. Quick's solvency when the loan was made by Erly.
   d. Quick's payment to Erly was made within one year of the filing of the bankruptcy petition.

18. Brook Corporation has filed for bankruptcy. Of the following debts Brook owes, indicate their priorities from the highest to the lowest.

  I. Federal taxes unpaid for the previous year.
  II. Wages of $3,000 owed to employees.
 III. Balance of $5,000 owed to a creditor that had a security interest. This creditor got paid fully by selling off the collateral except for this $5,000 deficiency.

   a. I, II, III.
   b. I, III, II.
   c. II, I, III.
   d. III, I, II.

19. Kessler Company has filed a voluntary bankruptcy petition. Kessler's debts include administration costs owed to accountants, attorneys, and appraisers. It also owes federal and state taxes. Kessler still owes various employees for the previous month's wages accrued before the petition was filed. None of these wages are owed to the officers and at most total $4,000 per employee. The company also owes several creditors for claims arising in the ordinary course of business. All of these latter claims arose before Kessler filed the bankruptcy petition. What are the priorities from highest to lowest of these listed debts and claims?

a. The claims arising in the ordinary course of business; the administration costs; the employees' wages; the federal and state taxes.

b. The administration costs; the employees' wages; the federal and state taxes; the claims arising in the ordinary course of business.

c. The federal and state taxes; the administration costs; the claims arising in the ordinary course of business; the employees' wages.

d. The claims arising in the ordinary course of business; the federal and state taxes; the administration costs; the employees' wages.

20. Which of the following acts will not bar a general discharge in bankruptcy?

a. The debtor tried to hide some property to prevent the estate from getting it.

b. The debtor intentionally injured a creditor during an argument about the bankruptcy proceedings.

c. The debtor is unwilling to explain satisfactorily why some assets are missing.

d. The debtor intentionally destroyed records of his assets.

21. Chapter 7 of the Federal Bankruptcy Code will deny a debtor a discharge when the debtor

a. Made a preferential transfer to a creditor.

b. Accidentally destroyed information relevant to the bankruptcy proceeding.

c. Obtained a Chapter 7 discharge ten years previously.

d. Is a corporation or a partnership.

22. Eckson was granted an order for relief after having filed a petition in bankruptcy. Which of the following actions would bar a general discharge in bankruptcy?

I. Ten months before the bankruptcy proceedings, Eckson had obtained credit from Cardinal Corporation by using false information on the credit application.

II. Six months before he filed the petition, Eckson removed a vehicle from his land with the intent to defraud a creditor.

III. During the bankruptcy proceedings, Eckson made a false entry on some records pertaining to his assets.

a. I only.

b. I and II only.

c. II and III only.

d. I, II, and III.

23. Which of the following acts by a debtor could result in a bankruptcy court revoking the debtor's discharge?

I. Failure to list one creditor.

II. Failure to answer correctly material questions on the bankruptcy petition.

a. I only.

b. II only.

c. Both I and II.

d. Neither I nor II.

24. Which of the following debts will **not** be discharged by bankruptcy even though a general discharge is allowed?

I. Debt owed to a corporation because the debtor was caught embezzling from it.

II. Money owed to a bank because the debtor was found to have committed fraud about her financial condition to get a loan.

III. Damages owed to a major customer because the debtor intentionally breached an important contract.

a. I only.

b. II only.

c. I and II only.

d. I, II, and III.

25. Which of the following claims will **not** be discharged in bankruptcy?

a. A claim that arises from alimony or maintenance.

b. A claim that arises out of the debtor's breach of contract.

c. A claim brought by a secured creditor that remains unsatisfied after the sale of the collateral.

d. A claim brought by a judgment creditor whose judgment resulted from the debtor's negligent operation of a motor vehicle.

26. By signing a reaffirmation agreement on April 15, 2008, a debtor agreed to pay certain debts that would be discharged in bankruptcy. On June 20, 2008, the debtor's attorney filed the reaffirmation agreement and an affidavit with the court indicating that the debtor understood the consequences of the reaffirmation agreement. The debtor obtained a discharge on August 25, 2008. The reaffirmation agreement would be enforceable only if it was

a. Made after discharge.

b. For debts aggregating less than $5,000.

c. Not for a household purpose debt.

d. Not rescinded before discharge.

27. Strong Corp. filed a voluntary petition in bankruptcy under the reorganization provisions of Chapter 11 of the Federal Bankruptcy Code. A reorganization plan was filed and agreed to by all necessary parties. The court confirmed the plan and a final decree was entered.

Which of the following statements best describes the effect of the entry of the court's final decree?

a. Strong Corp. will be discharged from all its debts and liabilities.

b. Strong Corp. will be discharged only from the debts owed creditors who agreed to the reorganization plan.

c. Strong Corp. will be discharged from all its debts and liabilities that arose before the date of confirmation of the plan.

d. Strong Corp. will be discharged from all its debts and liabilities that arose before the confirmation of the plan, except as otherwise provided in the plan, the order of confirmation, or the Bankruptcy Code.

28. Which of the following statements is correct with respect to the reorganization provisions of Chapter 11 of the Federal Bankruptcy Code?

a. A trustee must always be appointed.

b. The debtor must be insolvent if the bankruptcy petition was filed voluntarily.

c. A reorganization plan may be filed by a creditor anytime after the petition date.

d. The commencement of a bankruptcy case may be voluntary or involuntary.

29. Under Chapter 11 of the Federal Bankruptcy Code, which of the following would **not** be eligible for reorganization?

- a. Retail sole proprietorship.
- b. Advertising partnership.
- c. CPA professional corporation.
- d. Savings and loan corporation.

30. Which of the following is false regarding a Chapter 13 bankruptcy?

- a. Individuals in general need not have regular income.
- b. Creditors may not file involuntary petitions under this chapter.
- c. It is initiated when the debtor files a voluntary petition in a bankruptcy court.
- d. All of the above are true.

31. Under the Bankruptcy Abuse Prevention and Consumer Protection Act of 2005, which of the following type(s) of debts is(are) nondischargeable in bankruptcy?

- I. Death caused while intoxicated when operating an aircraft.
- II. Injury caused while intoxicated when driving any motor vehicle.
- III. Debts for Homeowner Association fees.

- a. Only I.
- b. I and II but not III.
- c. I and III but not II.
- d. I, II, and III.

SIMULATION PROBLEMS

Simulation Problem 1   (10 to 15 minutes)

Situation | Analysis | Transactions

On May 1, 2008, Able Corp. was petitioned involuntarily into bankruptcy under the provisions of Chapter 7 of the Federal Bankruptcy Code.

When the petition was filed, Able had the following unsecured creditors:

Creditor	Amount owed
Cole	$14,000
Lake	2,000
Young	1,500
Thorn	1,000

The following transactions occurred before the bankruptcy petition was filed:

- On February 15, 2008, Able paid Vista Bank the $1,000 balance due on an unsecured business loan.
- On February 28, 2008, Able paid $1,000 to Owen, an officer of Able, who had lent Able money.
- On March 1, 2008, Able bought a computer for use in its business from Core Computer Co. for $2,000 cash.

Analysis | Situation | Transactions

Items 1 through 3 refer to the bankruptcy filing. For each item, determine whether the statement is True or False.

		True	*False*
1.	Able can file a voluntary petition for bankruptcy if it is solvent.	○	○
2.	Lake, Young, and Thorn can file a valid involuntary petition.	○	○
3.	Cole alone can file a valid involuntary petition.	○	○

Transactions | Situation | Analysis

Items 1 through 3 refer to the transactions that occurred before the filing of the involuntary bankruptcy petition. Assuming the bankruptcy petition was validly filed, for each item determine whether the statement is True or False.

		True	*False*
1.	The payment to Vista Bank would be set aside as a preferential transfer.	○	○
2.	The payment to Owen would be set aside as a preferential transfer.	○	○
3.	The purchase from Core Computer Co. would be set aside as a preferential transfer.	○	○

Simulation Problem 2   (10 to 15 minutes)

Situation | Transactions

On March 15, 2008, Rusk Corporation was petitioned involuntarily into bankruptcy. At the time of the filing, Rusk had the following creditors:

- Safe Bank, for the balance due on the secured note and mortgage on Rusk's warehouse.
- Employee salary claims.
- 2005 federal income taxes due.
- Accountant's fees outstanding.
- Utility bills outstanding.

Prior to the bankruptcy filing, but while insolvent, Rusk engaged in the following transactions:

- On January 15, 2008, Rusk repaid all corporate directors' loans made to the corporation.
- On February 1, 2008, Rusk purchased raw materials for use in its manufacturing business and paid cash to the supplier.

Transactions

Situation

Items 1 through 4 relate to Rusk's creditors and the January 15 and February 1 transactions. For each item, select from List I whether only statement I is correct, whether only statement II is correct, whether both statements I and II are correct, or whether neither statement I nor II is correct.

List I

A. I only.
B. II only.
C. Both I and II.
D. Neither I nor II.

		(A)	(B)	(C)	(D)
1.	I. Safe Bank's claim will be the first paid of the listed claims because Safe is a secured creditor.				
	II. Safe Bank will receive the entire amount of the balance of the mortgage due as a secured creditor regardless of the amount received from the sale of the warehouse.	○	○	○	○
2.	I. The claim for 2008 federal income taxes due will be paid as a secured creditor claim.				
	II. The claim for 2008 federal income taxes due will be paid prior to the general creditor claims.	○	○	○	○
3.	I. The January 15 repayments of the directors' loans were preferential transfers even though the payments were made more than ten days before the filing of the petition.				
	II. The January 15 repayments of the directors' loans were preferential transfers because the payments were made to insiders.	○	○	○	○
4.	I. The February 1 purchase and payment was **not** a preferential transfer because it was a transaction in the ordinary course of business.				
	II. The February 1 purchase and payment was a preferential transfer because it occurred within ninety days of the filing of the petition.	○	○	○	○

    a.   Usually issued by companies which for a stated fee assume risk of performance by bonded party

    b.   Performance of act or responsibility by bonded party discharges surety's obligation

2.   Performance bonds are used to have surety guarantee completion of terms of contracts

    a.   Construction bond guarantees builder's obligation to complete construction

       (1) If builder breaches contract, surety can be held liable for damages but not for specific performance (i.e., cannot be required to complete construction)

          (a) Surety may complete construction if chooses to

3.   Fidelity bonds are forms of insurance that protects an employer against losses sustained due to acts of dishonest employees

4.   Surety bonding company retains right of subrogation against bonded party

MULTIPLE-CHOICE QUESTIONS (1-27)

1. A debtor may attempt to conceal or transfer property to prevent a creditor from satisfying a judgment. Which of the following actions will be considered an indication of fraudulent conveyance?

	Debtor remaining in possession after conveyance	Secret conveyance	Debtor retains an equitable benefit in the property conveyed
a.	Yes	Yes	Yes
b.	No	Yes	Yes
c.	Yes	Yes	No
d.	Yes	No	Yes

2. A homestead exemption ordinarily could exempt a debtor's equity in certain property from postjudgment collection by a creditor. To which of the following creditors will this exemption apply?

	Valid home mortgage lien	Valid IRS tax lien
a.	Yes	Yes
b.	Yes	No
c.	No	Yes
d.	No	No

3. Which of the following statements is(are) correct regarding debtors' rights?

I. State exemption statutes prevent all of a debtor's personal property from being sold to pay a federal tax lien.
II. Federal social security benefits received by a debtor are exempt from garnishment by creditors.

    a. I only.
    b. II only.
    c. Both I and II.
    d. Neither I nor II.

4. Under the Federal Fair Debt Collection Practices Act, which of the following would a collection service using improper debt collection practices be subject to?
    a. Abolishment of the debt.
    b. Reduction of the debt.
    c. Civil lawsuit for damages for violating the Act.
    d. Criminal prosecution for violating the Act.

5. Which of the following liens generally require(s) the lienholder to give notice of legal action before selling the debtor's property to satisfy the debt?

	Mechanic's lien	Artisan's lien
a.	Yes	Yes
b.	Yes	No
c.	No	Yes
d.	No	No

6. Which of the following prejudgment remedies would be available to a creditor when a debtor owns **no** real property?

	Writ of attachment	Garnishment
a.	Yes	Yes
b.	Yes	No
c.	No	Yes
d.	No	No

7. Which of the following events will release a noncompensated surety from liability to the creditor?
    a. The principal debtor was involuntarily petitioned into bankruptcy.

    b. The creditor failed to notify the surety of a partial surrender of the principal debtor's collateral.
    c. The creditor was adjudicated incompetent after the debt arose.
    d. The principal debtor exerted duress to obtain the surety agreement.

8. Which of the following involve(s) a suretyship relationship?

I. Transferee of a note requires transferor to obtain an accommodation endorser to guarantee payment.
II. The purchaser of goods agrees to pay for the goods but to have them shipped to another party.
III. The shareholders of a small, new corporation agree in writing to be personally liable on a corporate loan if the corporation defaults.

    a. I only.
    b. II only.
    c. I and II only.
    d. I and III only.

9. Reuter Bank loaned Sabean Corporation $500,000 in writing. As part of the agreement, Reuter required that the three owners of Sabean act as sureties on the loan. The corporation also required that some real estate owned by Sabean Corporation be used as collateral for 40% of the loan. The collateral and suretyship agreements were put in writing and signed by all relevant parties. When the $500,000 loan became due, which of the following rights does Reuter Bank have?

I. May demand payment of the full amount immediately from the sureties whether or not the corporation defaults on the loan.
II. May demand payment of the full amount immediately from the sureties even if Reuter does not attempt to recover any amount from the collateral.
III. May attempt to recover up to $200,000 from the collateral and the remainder from the sureties, even if the remainder is more than $300,000.
IV. Must first attempt to collect the debt from Sabean Corporation before it can resort to the sureties or the collateral.

    a. I and III only.
    b. II only.
    c. I, II, and III only.
    d. IV only.

10. Belmont acts as a surety for a loan to Diablo from Chaffin. In which of the following cases would Belmont be released from liability?

I. Diablo dies.
II. Diablo files bankruptcy.
III. Chaffin modifies Diablo's contract, increasing Diablo's risk of nonpayment.

    a. I only.
    b. III only.
    c. I and III only.
    d. I, II, and III.

11. A party contracts to guaranty the collection of the debts of another. As a result of the guaranty, which of the following statements is correct?
    a. The creditor may proceed against the guarantor without attempting to collect from the debtor.

b. The guaranty must be in writing.
c. The guarantor may use any defenses available to the debtor.
d. The creditor must be notified of the debtor's default by the guarantor.

12. Sorus and Ace have agreed, in writing, to act as guarantors of collection on a debt owed by Pepper to Towns, Inc. The debt is evidenced by a promissory note. If Pepper defaults, Towns will be entitled to recover from Sorus and Ace unless

   a. Sorus and Ace are in the process of exercising their rights against Pepper.
   b. Sorus and Ace prove that Pepper was insolvent at the time the note was signed.
   c. Pepper dies before the note is due.
   d. Towns has **not** attempted to enforce the promissory note against Pepper.

13. Which of the following rights does a surety have?

	Right to compel the creditor to collect from the principal debtor	Right to compel the creditor to proceed against the principal debtor's collateral
a.	Yes	Yes
b.	Yes	No
c.	No	Yes
d.	No	No

14. Under the law of suretyship, which are generally among the rights that the surety may use?

I. Subrogation.
II. Exoneration.
III. Reimbursement from debtor.

   a. I only.
   b. III only.
   c. I and II only.
   d. I, II, and III.

15. Which of the following defenses would a surety be able to assert successfully to limit the surety's liability to a creditor?

   a. A discharge in bankruptcy of the principal debtor.
   b. A personal defense the principal debtor has against the creditor.
   c. The incapacity of the surety.
   d. The incapacity of the principal debtor.

16. Which of the following events will release a non-compensated surety from liability?

   a. Release of the principal debtor's obligation by the creditor but with the reservation of the creditor's rights against the surety.
   b. Modification by the principal debtor and creditor of their contract that materially increases the surety's risk of loss.
   c. Filing of an involuntary petition in bankruptcy against the principal debtor.
   d. Insanity of the principal debtor at the time the contract was entered into with the creditor.

17. Which of the following is **not** a defense that a surety may use to avoid payment of a debtor's obligation to a creditor?

   a. The creditor had committed fraud against the debtor to induce the debtor to take on the debt with this creditor.
   b. The creditor had committed fraud against the surety to induce the surety to guarantee the debtor's payment of a loan.
   c. The statute of limitations has run on the debtor's obligation.
   d. The debtor took out bankruptcy.

18. Which of the following acts always will result in the total release of a compensated surety?

   a. The creditor changes the manner of the principal debtor's payment.
   b. The creditor extends the principal debtor's time to pay.
   c. The principal debtor's obligation is partially released.
   d. The principal debtor's performance is tendered.

19. Green was unable to repay a loan from State Bank when due. State refused to renew the loan unless Green provided an acceptable surety. Green asked Royal, a friend, to act as surety on the loan. To induce Royal to agree to become a surety, Green fraudulently represented Green's financial condition and promised Royal discounts on merchandise sold at Green's store. Royal agreed to act as surety and the loan was renewed. Later, Green's obligation to State was discharged in Green's bankruptcy. State wants to hold Royal liable. Royal may avoid liability

   a. If Royal can show that State was aware of the fraudulent representations.
   b. If Royal was an uncompensated surety.
   c. Because the discharge in bankruptcy will prevent Royal from having a right of reimbursement.
   d. Because the arrangement was void at the inception.

20. Wright cosigned King's loan from Ace Bank. Which of the following events would release Wright from the obligation to pay the loan?

   a. Ace seeking payment of the loan only from Wright.
   b. King is granted a discharge in bankruptcy.
   c. Ace is paid in full by King's spouse.
   d. King is adjudicated mentally incompetent.

21. A distinction between a surety and a cosurety is that only a cosurety is entitled to

   a. Reimbursement (Indemnification).
   b. Subrogation.
   c. Contribution.
   d. Exoneration.

22. Ivor borrowed $420,000 from Lear Bank. At Lear's request, Ivor entered into an agreement with Ash, Kane, and Queen for them to act as cosureties on the loan. The agreement between Ivor and the cosureties provided that the maximum liability of each cosurety was: Ash, $84,000; Kane, $126,000; and Queen, $210,000. After making several payments, Ivor defaulted on the loan. The balance was $280,000. If Queen pays $210,000 and Ivor subsequently pays $70,000, what amounts may Queen recover from Ash and Kane?

   a. $0 from Ash and $0 from Kane.
   b. $42,000 from Ash and $63,000 from Kane.
   c. $70,000 from Ash and $70,000 from Kane.

    d. $56,000 from Ash and $84,000 from Kane.

23. Nash, Owen, and Polk are cosureties with maximum liabilities of $40,000, $60,000 and $80,000, respectively. The amount of the loan on which they have agreed to act as cosureties is $180,000. The debtor defaulted at a time when the loan balance was $180,000. Nash paid the lender $36,000 in full settlement of all claims against Nash, Owen, and Polk. The total amount that Nash may recover from Owen and Polk is

    a. $0
    b. $ 24,000
    c. $ 28,000
    d. $140,000

24. Ingot Corp. lent Flange $50,000. At Ingot's request, Flange entered into an agreement with Quill and West for them to act as compensated cosureties on the loan in the amount of $100,000 each. Ingot released West without Quill's or Flange's consent, and Flange later defaulted on the loan. Which of the following statements is correct?

    a.   Quill will be liable for 50% of the loan balance.
    b.   Quill will be liable for the entire loan balance.
    c.   Ingot's release of West will have **no** effect on Flange's and Quill's liability to Ingot.
    d.   Flange will be released for 50% of the loan balance.

25. Mane Bank lent Eller $120,000 and received securities valued at $30,000 as collateral. At Mane's request, Salem and Rey agreed to act as uncompensated cosureties on the loan. The agreement provided that Salem's and Rey's maximum liability would be $120,000 each.

    Mane released Rey without Salem's consent. Eller later defaulted when the collateral held by Mane was worthless and the loan balance was $90,000. Salem's maximum liability is

    a. $30,000
    b. $45,000
    c. $60,000
    d. $90,000

26. Lane promised to lend Turner $240,000 if Turner obtained sureties to secure the loan. Turner agreed with Rivers, Clark, and Zane for them to act as cosureties on the loan from Lane. The agreement between Turner and the cosureties provided that compensation be paid to each of the cosureties. It further indicated that the maximum liability of each cosurety would be as follows: Rivers $240,000, Clark $80,000, and Zane $160,000. Lane accepted the commitments of the sureties and made the loan to Turner. After paying ten installments totaling $100,000, Turner defaulted. Clark's debts, including the surety obligation to Lane on the Turner loan, were discharged in bankruptcy. Later, Rivers properly paid the entire outstanding debt of $140,000. What amount may Rivers recover from Zane?

    a. $0
    b. $56,000
    c. $70,000
    d. $84,000

27. Which of the following rights does one cosurety generally have against another cosurety?

    a.   Exoneration.
    b.   Subrogation.
    c.   Reimbursement.
    d.   Contribution.

SIMULATION PROBLEM

Simulation Problem 1   (10 to 15 minutes)

| Consideration |

For each of the numbered words or phrases, select the one best phrase or sentence from the list A through J. Each response may be used only once.

- A. Relationship whereby one person agrees to answer for the debt or default of another.
- B. Requires certain contracts to be in writing to be enforceable.
- C. Jointly and severally liable to creditor.
- D. Promises to pay debt on default of principal debtor.
- E. One party promises to reimburse debtor for payment of debt or loss if it arises.
- F. Receives intended benefits of a contract.
- G. Right of surety to require the debtor to pay before surety pays.
- H. Upon payment of more than his/her proportionate share, each cosurety may compel other cosureties to pay their shares.
- I. Upon payment of debt, surety may recover payment from debtor.
- J. Upon payment, surety obtains same rights against debtor that creditor had.

	(A)	(B)	(C)	(D)	(E)	(F)	(G)	(H)	(I)	(J)
1. Indemnity contract	○	○	○	○	○	○	○	○	○	○
2. Suretyship contract	○	○	○	○	○	○	○	○	○	○
3. Surety	○	○	○	○	○	○	○	○	○	○
4. Third-party beneficiary	○	○	○	○	○	○	○	○	○	○
5. Cosurety	○	○	○	○	○	○	○	○	○	○
6. Statute of Frauds	○	○	○	○	○	○	○	○	○	○
7. Right of contribution	○	○	○	○	○	○	○	○	○	○
8. Reimbursement	○	○	○	○	○	○	○	○	○	○
9. Subrogation	○	○	○	○	○	○	○	○	○	○
10. Exoneration	○	○	○	○	○	○	○	○	○	○

MULTIPLE-CHOICE ANSWERS

1. a __ __	7. b __ __	13. d __ __	19. a __ __	25. b __ __
2. d __ __	8. d __ __	14. d __ __	20. c __ __	26. b __ __
3. b __ __	9. c __ __	15. c __ __	21. c __ __	27. d __ __
4. c __ __	10. b __ __	16. b __ __	22. b __ __	
5. a __ __	11. b __ __	17. d __ __	23. c __ __	1st: __/27 = __%
6. a __ __	12. d __ __	18. d __ __	24. a __ __	2nd: __/27 = __%

MULTIPLE-CHOICE ANSWER EXPLANATIONS

A. Rights and Duties of Debtors and Creditors

1.   (a)   Fraudulent conveyance of property is done with the intent to defraud a creditor, hinder or delay him/her, or put the property out of his/her reach. If the debtor maintains possession of the property, secretly transfers or hides the property, or retains an equitable interest in the property, then a fraudulent conveyance has occurred as all of the three actions prevent the creditor from receiving the full property.

2.   (d)   Although a homestead exemption can exempt a debtor's equity in certain property from postjudgment collection by a creditor, the collections to which it applies vary among the states. The best answer is that it does not apply to valid home mortgage liens or valid IRS tax liens.

3.   (b)   Under garnishment procedures, creditors may attach a portion of the debtor's wages to pay off a debt. There are legal limits as to how much of the wages can be garnished. Likewise, federal social security benefits are protected from garnishment by creditors. Therefore, statement II is correct. Statement I, however, is incorrect because federal tax liens can be used to sell a debtor's personal property to pay taxes.

4.   (c)   The Federal Fair Debt Collection Practices Act was passed to prevent debt collectors from using unfair or abusive collection methods. The Federal Trade Commission is charged with enforcement of this Act but aggrieved parties may also use a civil lawsuit against the debt collector who violates this Act. Answers (a) and (b) are incorrect because the remedy is a suit for damages or a suit for up to $1,000 for violation of the Act if damages are not proven. The remedy is not a reduction or abolishment of the debt. Answer (d) is incorrect because this Act does not provide for criminal prosecution.

5.   (a)   Liens are used by creditors to secure payment for services or materials, in the case of a mechanic's lien, or for repairs, in the case of an artisan's lien. They require that notice be given to the debtor before the creditor can sell the property to satisfy the debt.

6.   (a)   When a creditor wishes to collect a past-due debt from the debtor, s/he may use a writ of attachment. This is a prejudgment remedy in which the creditor is allowed to take into possession some personal property of the debtor prior to getting a judgment in a lawsuit for the past-due debt. The debtor may also wish to collect the debt by use of garnishment. This allows the creditor to obtain property of the debtor that is held by a third party. Typical examples include garnishing wages owed by the employer to the employee-debtor or garnishing the debtor's bank account. To avoid abuses, there are limitations on both of these remedies.

B. Nature of Suretyship and Guaranty

7.   (b)   Any acts of the creditor that materially affect the surety's obligation will release the surety. In this case, the surety was not notified that the creditor partially surrendered the principal debtor's collateral. The surety will not have this collateral as a possible partial protection and the law allows the noncompensated surety to be released. Answer (a) is incorrect—bankruptcy is a personal defense of the debtor and is not a defense for the surety. Answer (c) is incorrect because this is a debt that is voidable at the option of the creditor. Answer (d) is incorrect because there is a possible wrong against the debtor but this does not release the surety.

8.   (d)   Statement I illustrates a suretyship relationship in which the endorser of the note is the surety. Statement II illustrates a third-party beneficiary contract, not a suretyship relationship. The purchaser has agreed to pay for the goods as his/her own debt. The party to receive the goods is the third-party beneficiary. Statement III illustrates a suretyship relationship in which the shareholders are sureties.

C. Creditor's Rights and Remedies

9.   (c)   The creditor, Reuter Bank, has a lot of flexibility in remedies. Although Reuter may attempt to collect from Sabean when the loan is due, it is not required to but instead may resort to the sureties or to the collateral up to the 40% agreed upon, or both.

10.   (b)   When the creditor modifies the debtor's contract, increasing the surety's risk, the surety is released. Note that death of the principal debtor or the debtor's filing bankruptcy are personal defenses of the debtor that the surety cannot use. Such risks are some of the reasons creditors prefer sureties.

11.   (b)   Under the Statute of Frauds under contract law, a surety's (guarantor's) agreement to answer for the debt or default of another must be in writing. Answer (a) is incorrect, as a guarantor of collection's liability is conditioned on the creditor notifying the guarantor of the debtor's default and the creditor first attempting to collect from the debtor. Answer (c) is incorrect as the guarantor may not use the debtor's personal defenses, such as death or insolvency. Answer (d) is incorrect because it is the creditor that must notify the guarantor of the debtor's default, not vice versa.

12.   (d)   A guarantor's liability is conditioned on the creditor notifying the guarantor of the debtor's default and the creditor first attempting to collect from the debtor. In this case, if Towns has not attempted to collect against Pepper, then Towns would not yet be able to collect against Sorus and Ace. Answer (a) is incorrect because Sorus' and Ace's performance of the right of reimbursement from Pepper does not preclude Towns' recovery from Sorus and Ace.

Answers (b) and (c) are incorrect because insolvency of the debtor and death of the debtor are not valid defenses of the guarantor against the creditor.

D.   Surety's and Guarantor's Rights and Remedies

13.   (d)   The surety is primarily liable on the debt of the principal debtor. Therefore, the creditor can seek payment directly from the surety as soon as the debt is due. For this reason, the surety cannot require the creditor to collect from the debtor nor can s/he compel the creditor to proceed against any collateral the principal debtor may have.

14.   (d)   Upon payment, the surety obtains the right of subrogation which is the ability to use the same rights the creditor had. Also, the surety may resort to the right of exoneration by requiring the debtor to pay when s/he is able if the creditor has not demanded immediate payment directly from the surety. If the surety has paid the debtor's obligation, the surety may attempt reimbursement from the debtor.

E.   Surety's and Guarantor's Defenses

15.   (c)   The surety may use his/her own defenses of incapacity of the **surety** or bankruptcy of the **surety** to limit his/her own liability. Although the surety may use most defenses that the **debtor** has to limit his/her (surety's) liability, the surety may not use the **personal** defenses of the debtor. These include the debtor's bankruptcy and the debtor's incapacity.

16.   (b)   A modification by the principal debtor and creditor in the terms and conditions of their original contract without the surety's consent will automatically release the surety if the surety's risk of loss is thereby materially increased. Note that a noncompensated surety is discharged even if the creditor does not change the surety's risk. However, a compensated surety is discharged only if the modification causes a material increase in risk. Answers (c) and (d) are incorrect because a surety may not exercise the principal debtor's personal defenses (i.e., insolvency and insanity). Answer (a) is incorrect because although a release of the principal debtor without the surety's consent will usually discharge the surety, there is no discharge if the creditor expressly reserves rights against the surety.

17.   (d)   Personal defenses that the debtor has such as bankruptcy or death of the debtor cannot be used by the surety to avoid payment of the debtor's obligation to the creditor. Answer (a) is incorrect because the surety may generally exercise the defenses on the contract that the debtor has against the creditor. Answer (b) is incorrect because the surety may take advantage of his/her own personal defenses such as fraud by the creditor against the surety. Answer (c) is incorrect because the surety generally may exercise the defenses on the contract that would be available to the debtor such as the running of the statute of limitations.

18.   (d)   A compensated surety will be released from an obligation to the creditor upon tender of performance by either the principal debtor or the surety. A compensated surety will also be completely released if modifications are made to the principal debtor's contract which materially increase risk to the surety. However, if the risk is not materially increased, the surety is not completely released but rather his/her obligation is reduced by the amount of loss due to modification. The surety also is not released if the modifications are beneficial to the surety. Answers (a)

and (b) are incorrect because these modifications will not necessarily result in a material increase in the surety's risk or could even be beneficial to the surety. Answer (c) is incorrect because partial release of the principal debtor's obligation will result in partial release of the surety.

19.   (a)   Normally, fraud by the debtor on the surety to induce him/her to act as a surety will not release the surety. However, when the creditor is aware of the debtor's fraudulent misrepresentation, then the surety can avoid liability. Answer (b) is incorrect because the above principle is true whether the surety is compensated or not. Answer (c) is incorrect because the risk of bankruptcy is one of the reasons that the creditor desires a surety. Answer (d) is incorrect because fraudulent misrepresentations do not make a contract void but can make it voidable.

20.   (c)   Once the debt is paid by someone, both the principal debtor and the cosigner are released from obligations to pay the loan. Answer (a) is incorrect because the creditor may proceed against the cosigner without needing to proceed against the principal debtor. Answer (b) is incorrect because the possibility that the principal debtor may qualify for bankruptcy is one of the reasons that the creditor may desire a cosigner. Answer (d) is incorrect because even if the main debtor is adjudicated mentally incompetent, this can allow the main debtor to escape liability but not the cosigner.

F.   Cosureties

21.   (c)   A suretyship relationship exists when one party agrees to answer for the obligations of another. Cosureties exist when there is more than one surety guaranteeing the same obligation of the principal debtor. Both sureties and cosureties are entitled to reimbursement from the debtor if the surety pays the obligation. Sureties and cosureties both have the right of subrogation in that upon making payment, the surety has the same rights against the principal debtor that the creditor had. Both are also entitled to exoneration. Sureties and cosureties both may require the debtor to pay the obligation for which they have given promise if the debtor is able to do so. The right of contribution, however, exists only among cosureties. If a cosurety pays more than his/her proportionate share of the total liability, he/she is entitled to be compensated by the other cosureties for the excess amount paid.

22.   (b)   The right of contribution arises when one cosurety, in performance of the principal debtor's obligation, pays more than his/her proportionate share of the total liability. The right of contribution allows the performing cosurety to receive reimbursement from the other cosureties for their pro rata shares of the liability. The pro rata shares of the cosureties are determined as follows:

	Surety's pro rata share		Remaining liability		Surety's liability
Queen	(210,000/420,000)	×	210,000	=	105,000
Ash	(84,000/420,000)	×	210,000	=	42,000
Kane	(126,000/420,000)	×	210,000	=	63,000

Thus, Queen is entitled to receive $42,000 from Ash and $63,000 from Kane.

23.   (c)   A surety relationship is present when one party agrees to answer for the obligation of another. When there is more than one surety guaranteeing the same obligation of the principal debtor, the sureties become cosureties jointly and severally liable to the claims of the creditor. A right of contribution arises when one cosurety, in performance of the debtor's obligation, pays more than his proportionate share of the total liability. The right of contribution entitles the performing cosurety to reimbursement from the other cosureties for their pro rata shares of the liability. The pro rata shares of the cosureties are determined as follows:

	Surety's pro rata share		Remaining liability		Surety's liability
Nash	(40,000/180,000)	×	36,000	=	8,000
Owen	(60,000/180,000)	×	36,000	=	12,000
Polk	(80,000/180,000)	×	36,000	=	16,000

Thus, Nash is entitled to recover $12,000 from Owen and $16,000 from Polk for a total of $28,000.

24. (a) A discharge or release of one cosurety by a creditor results in a reduction of liability of the remaining cosurety. The remaining cosurety is released to the extent of the released cosurety's pro rata share of debt liability, unless there is a reservation of rights by the creditor against the remaining cosurety. Quill and West each had maximum liability of $100,000. Thus, Ingot's release of West will result in Quill's liability being reduced by West's pro rata share of the total debt liability, which was one-half. Therefore, Quill's liability has been reduced to $25,000 (i.e., 50% of the loan balance) due to the release of West as a cosurety. Answer (c) is therefore incorrect. Answer (d) is incorrect because the release of the cosurety does not release the principal debtor since the debtor's obligation is not affected in any way by Ingot's release of West. Answer (b) is incorrect because as discussed above, Quill's liability has been reduced due to Ingot's release of West.

25. (b) The discharge or release of one cosurety by the creditor results in a reduction of liability of the remaining cosurety. This reduction of liability is limited to the released cosurety's pro rata share of debt liability (unless there is a reservation of rights by the creditor against the remaining cosurety). Since Mane released Rey without reserving rights against Salem, Salem is released to the extent of Rey's pro rata share of the $90,000 liability. Salem's maximum liability can be calculated as follows:

Rey's %	$\dfrac{\$120,000}{\$240,000} = .50$
Loan balance	$ 90,000
× Rey's %	× .50
	$ 45,000
Loan balance	$ 90,000
Rey's pro rata share	(45,000)
Salem's maximum liability	$ 45,000

26. (b) The right of contribution arises when one cosurety, in performance of debtor's obligation, pays more than his proportionate share of the total liability. The right of contribution entitles the performing cosurety to reimbursement from the other cosureties for their pro rata shares of the liability. Since Clark's debts have been discharged in bankruptcy, River may only exercise his right of contribution against Zane, and may recover nothing from Clark. Zane's pro rata share of the remaining $140,000 would be determined as follows:

$$\dfrac{\text{Dollar amount guaranteed by Zane}}{\substack{\text{Total amount of risk assumed by} \\ \text{remaining cosureties}}} \times \text{Remaining obligation}$$

$$\frac{160,000}{160,000 + 240,000} \times 140,000 = 56,000$$

27. (d) Cosureties are jointly and severally liable to the creditor up to the amount of liability each agreed to. If a cosurety pays more than his/her proportionate share of the debt, s/he may seek contribution from the other cosureties for the excess. Answer (a) is incorrect because the right of exoneration refers to the surety requiring the debtor to pay the debt when able. Answer (b) is incorrect because subrogation refers to the right of the surety to obtain the same rights against the debtor that the creditor had, once the surety pays the creditor. Answer (c) is incorrect because the right of reimbursement allows the surety to recover payments from the debtor that the surety has made to the creditor.

SOLUTION TO SIMULATION PROBLEM

Simulation Problem 1

| Consideration |

	(A)	(B)	(C)	(D)	(E)	(F)	(G)	(H)	(I)	(J)
1. Indemnity contract	○	○	○	○	●	○	○	○	○	○
2. Suretyship contract	●	○	○	○	○	○	○	○	○	○
3. Surety	○	○	○	●	○	○	○	○	○	○
4. Third-party beneficiary	○	○	○	○	○	●	○	○	○	○
5. Cosurety	○	○	●	○	○	○	○	○	○	○
6. Statute of Frauds	○	●	○	○	○	○	○	○	○	○
7. Right of contribution	○	○	○	○	○	○	○	●	○	○
8. Reimbursement	○	○	○	○	○	○	○	○	●	○
9. Subrogation	○	○	○	○	○	○	○	○	○	●
10. Exoneration	○	○	○	○	○	○	●	○	○	○

Explanation of solutions

1. **(E)** An indemnity contract is not a suretyship contract. Instead it is a contract involving two parties in which the first party agrees to indemnify and reimburse the second party for covered debts or losses should they take place.

2. **(A)** The suretyship contract involves three parties. The surety agrees with the creditor to pay for the debt or default if the debtor does not.

3. **(D)** The surety is the party that agrees to pay the creditor if the debtor defaults.

4. **(F)** When two parties make a contract that intends to benefit a third party, that party is a third-party beneficiary.

5. **(C)** When two or more sureties agree to be sureties for the same obligation to the same creditor, they are known as co-sureties. They have joint and several liability.

6. **(B)** The Statute of Frauds sets out rules that require certain contracts to be in writing, such as those in which a surety agrees to answer for the debt or default of another.

7. **(H)** Cosureties are liable in contribution for their proportionate shares of the debt. If a cosurety pays more than this amount, s/he may seek contribution for the excess from the other cosureties.

8. **(I)** The right of reimbursement is against the debtor to collect any amounts paid by the surety.

9. **(J)** When the surety pays the creditor, it "steps into the shoes of the creditor" and obtains the same rights against the debtor that the creditor had.

10. **(G)** If the debtor is able to pay, the surety may require the debtor to pay before the surety pays. This is called exoneration.

AGENCY

Overview

Agency is a relationship in which one party (agent) is authorized to act on behalf of another party (principal). The law of agency is concerned with the rights, duties, and liabilities of the parties in an agency relationship. Important to this relationship is the fact that the agent has a fiduciary duty to act in the best interest of the principal.

A good understanding of this module is important because partnership law is a special application of agency law.

The CPA exam emphasizes the creation and termination of the agency relationship, the undisclosed as well as the disclosed principal relationship, unauthorized acts or torts committed by the agent within the course and scope of the agency relationship and principal's liability for agent's unauthorized contracts.

A. Characteristics

1. Agency is a relationship between two parties, whereby one party (agent) agrees to act on behalf of the other party (principal). A contract is not required but is frequently present.

   a. Agent is subject to control of principal
   b. Agent is a fiduciary and must act for the benefit of principal
   c. Agent's specific authority is determined by the principal but generally agent has authority to bind the principal contractually with third parties

2. Employee (servant)

   a. Employee is a type of agent in which employee's physical conduct is subject to control by employer (master)

      (1) Employer is a type of principal and may be called such when the agent is an employee
      (2) Employer is generally liable for employee's torts if committed within course and scope of employment relationship

         (a) Known as doctrine of respondeat superior (vicarious liability)

            EXAMPLE: S is an employee of M. One day while delivering inventory for M, she negligently hits a third party with the delivery truck. Although S is liable because she committed the tort, M is also liable.

         (b) Course and scope of employment is defined broadly

            1] Note that this makes employer liable for torts of employee even if employer not actually negligent him/herself

               EXAMPLE: M, the employer, gives S $30 and asks him to go buy donuts for the employees who are working overtime. He takes his own car and injures a third party through his own negligence. The employer is also liable for this tort.

         (c) Employee need not be following instructions of employer (i.e., rule applies even if employee violated employer's instructions in committing tort)

            EXAMPLE: P works for Q delivering widgets. One rule that Q has is that all employees must look behind the truck before backing out after all deliveries. P violated this rule and injured R. Q is still liable even s/he though had taken steps to prevent this type of accident.

         (d) Employer liable if employee fails to notify employer of dangerous condition that results in injury to a third party
         (e) Contributory negligence (i.e., third party's negligence) is generally a defense for both the agent and his/her principal

            1] Some jurisdictions have adopted comparative negligence which means that defendant at fault pays but that amount of damages is determined by comparing each party's negligence

3. Independent contractor distinguished from employee

   a. Not subject to control of employer as to methods of work
   b. Not subject to regular supervision as an employee
   c. Employer controls results only (independent contractor controls the methods)
   d. Generally, employer is not liable for torts committed by independent contractor

      (1) Unless independent contractor is employed to do something inherently dangerous (e.g., blasting)
      (2) Unless employer was negligent in hiring independent contractor

check is not liable on the negotiable instrument. Answers (a) and (b) are incorrect because the third party can elect to hold either the agent or the principal liable when the agent makes a contract for an undisclosed principal. Answer (d) is incorrect because the party who signs a check is liable on it.

F. Termination of Principal-Agent Relationship

23. **(c)** The declaration of Ogden's incapacity constitutes the termination of the agency relationship by operation of law. When an agency relationship is terminated by operation of law, the agent's authority to enter into a binding agreement on behalf of the principal ceases. There is no requirement that notice be given to third parties when the agency relationship is terminated by operation of law. In this case, Ogden will not be liable to Datz because Thorp was without authority to enter into the contract. Answer (a) is incorrect because insanity of the principal terminates the agency relationship even though the third parties are unaware of the principal's insanity. Answer (b) is incorrect because Thorp's authority terminated upon the declaration of Ogden's incapacity. Answer (d) is incorrect because an undisclosed principal is liable unless the third party holds the agent responsible, the agent has fully performed the contract, the undisclosed principal is expressly excluded by contract or the contract is a negotiable instrument. However, Ogden will not be liable as Thorp was without authority to enter into the agreement.

24. **(c)** An agency relationship is terminated by operation of law if the subject of the agreement becomes illegal or impossible, the principal or the agent dies or becomes insane, or the principal becomes bankrupt. Answers (a), (b), and (d) are incorrect because they will cause the termination of an agency relationship by operation of law. Answer (c), agent's renunciation of the agency, will not cause the termination of an agency relationship.

25. **(c)** When the agency relationship is terminated by an act of the principal and/or agent, third parties are entitled to notice of the termination from the principal. Failure of the principal to give the required notice gives the agent apparent authority to act on behalf of the principal. Specifically, the principal must give actual notice to all parties who had prior dealings with the agent or principal. Constructive or public notice must be given to parties who knew of the existence of the agency relationship, but did not actually have business dealings with the agent or principal. Since Bolt Corp. did not give proper constructive notice to Young Corp., Ace had apparent authority to bind the principal and, therefore, Young Corp. will win. Accordingly, answer (a) is incorrect. Answer (b) is incorrect because although Ace lacked express authority, apparent authority was present due to the inadequacy of Bolt's notice. Answer (d) is incorrect because a principal is not an absolute insurer of his agent's acts. A principal is liable for his agent's torts only if the principal expressly authorizes the conduct or the tort is committed within the scope of the agent's employment.

SOLUTION TO SIMULATION PROBLEM

Simulation Problem 1

	Relationships
Situation	

		(A)	(B)	(C)	(D)
1.	I. Lace's agreement with Banks had to be in writing for it to be a valid agency agreement. II. Lace's agreement with Banks empowered Banks to act as Lace's agent.	○	●	○	○
2.	I. Clear was entitled to rely on Banks' implied authority to customize Lace's software. II. Clear was entitled to rely on Banks' express authority when buying the computer.	●	○	○	○
3.	I. Lace's agreement with Banks was automatically terminated by Banks' sale of the computer. II. Lace must notify Clear before Banks' apparent authority to bind Lace will cease.	○	●	○	○
4.	I. Lace is **not** bound by the agreement made by Banks with Clear. II. Lace may unilaterally amend the agreement made by Banks to prevent a loss on the sale of the computer to Clear.	○	○	○	●
5.	I. Lace, as a disclosed principal, is solely contractually liable to Clear. II. Both Lace and Banks are contractually liable to Clear.	●	○	○	○

Explanation of solutions

1. **(B)** Statement I is incorrect because normally an agency agreement need not be in writing unless the agency contract cannot be completed in one year. Statement II is correct because Lace authorized Banks to be Lace's agent.

2. **(A)** Statement I is correct because Banks was given actual, express authority by Lace to perform Lace's customers' service calls and to customize Lace's software to the customer's needs. As an extension to this actual, express authority, Clear can also rely on what is customary and ordinary for such an agent to be able to do under implied authority. Statement II is incorrect because Banks did not have express authority to sell the computer. In fact, Banks was told **not** to sell Lace's computers.

3. **(B)** Banks breached his/her fiduciary duty to Lace and breached his/her duty to follow instructions when s/he sold the computer. This, however, does not automatically terminate their agreement. Statement II is correct because Banks had dealt with Clear before as Lace's agent. Therefore, Clear must receive actual notice to terminate the apparent authority.

4. **(D)** Statement I is incorrect because Banks had apparent authority to sell the computer even though Banks did not have actual authority to do so. Statement II is incorrect because Lace is bound by the contract with Clear. Any modification of the contract must be made by both parties to the contract, not just one.

5. **(A)** Statement I is correct because since Lace was a disclosed principal, only Lace, the principal, is liable under the contract to Clear, the third party. Banks, the agent, is not. For the same reason, statement II is incorrect.

REGULATION OF EMPLOYMENT AND ENVIRONMENT

Overview

Issues on this topic are based on the Workers' Compensation Laws and Federal Social Security Rules including the Federal Insurance Contributions Act (FICA) and the Federal Unemployment Tax Act (FUTA). These laws supplement the law of agency. In this area, emphasis is placed on the impact that state and federal laws have on the regulation of employment.

To adequately understand these materials, you should emphasize the theory and purpose underlying the Work-

ers' Compensation Laws. You should also focus on the effect that these laws have on employers and employees. Notice the changes these laws have made on common law.

Upon looking at the Federal Social Security Laws, emphasize the coverage and benefits of the respective programs.

Also, emphasize the various discrimination and environmental laws.

A. Federal Social Security Act

1. Main purpose of Act is as name implies (i.e., attainment of the social security of people in our society)

    a. Basic programs include

        (1) Old age insurance
        (2) Survivor's and disability insurance
        (3) Hospital insurance (Medicare)
        (4) Unemployment insurance

    b. Sources of financing for these programs

        (1) Old-age, survivor's, disability, and hospital insurance programs are financed out of taxes paid by employers, employees, and self-employed under provisions of Federal Insurance Contributions Act and Self-Employment Contributions Act
        (2) Unemployment insurance programs are financed out of taxes paid by employers under the Federal Unemployment Tax Act and various state unemployment insurance laws

2. Federal Insurance Contributions Act (FICA)

    a. Imposes social security tax on employees, self-employed, and employers
    b. Social security tax applies to compensation received that is considered to be wages
    c. In general, tax rates are same for both employer and employee

        (1) Rates changed from time to time

    d. Taxes are paid only up to base amount that is also changed frequently

        (1) If employee pays FICA tax on more than base amount, s/he has right to refund for excess

            (a) May happen when employee works for two or more employers

                1] These two or more employers do not get refunds

    e. FICA is also used to fund Medicare

        (1) Base rate on this Medicare portion has been set at a higher amount

    f. It is employer's duty to withhold employee's share of FICA from employee's wages and remit both employee's amount and employer's equal share to government

        (1) Employer subject to fines for failure to make timely FICA deposits

            (a) Also, employer subject to fine for failure to supply taxpayer identification number

        (2) Employer is required to match FICA contributions of employees on dollar-for-dollar basis
        (3) If employer neglects to withhold, employer may be liable for both employee's and employer's share of taxes (i.e., to pay double tax)

            (a) Once employer pays, s/he has right to collect employee's share from employee
            (b) Employer may voluntarily pay not only its share but also employee's share

                1] Employee's share is deductible by employer as additional compensation and is taxable to the employee as compensation

        (4) Employer is required to furnish employee with written statement of wages paid and FICA contributions withheld during calendar year

    g. Taxes paid by employer are deducted on tax return of employer

        (1) But employee may not deduct taxes paid on his/her tax return

    h. Neither pension plans nor any other programs may be substituted for FICA coverage

        (1) Individuals receiving payments from private pension plans may also receive social security payments

3. Self-Employment Contributions Act

    a. Self-employed persons are required to report their own taxable earnings and pay required social security tax

    b. Self-employment income is net earnings from self-employment

    c. Tax rates paid on self-employment income up to base amount

        (1) Since self-employed does not have employer to match the rate, tax rate is that of employer and employee combined

        (2) Base amount and tax rate are subject to amendment

        (3) Base rate is reduced by any wages earned during year because wages are subject to FICA

        (4) Self-employed can deduct half of FICA tax paid on his/her income tax form

4. Unemployment Insurance (Federal Unemployment Tax Act—FUTA)

    a. Tax is used to provide unemployment compensation benefits to workers who lose jobs and cannot find replacement work

    b. Federal unemployment tax must be paid by employer if employer employs one or more persons covered by Act

        (1) Deductible as business expense on employer's federal income tax return

        (2) Not deductible by employee because not paid by employee

    c. Employer must also pay a state unemployment tax

        (1) An employer is entitled to credit against his/her federal unemployment tax for state unemployment taxes paid

        (2) State unemployment tax may be raised or lowered according to number of claims against employer

        (3) If employer pays a low state unemployment tax because of good employment record, then employer is entitled to additional credit against federal unemployment tax

5. Coverage under Social Security Act is mandatory for qualifying employees

    a. Person may not elect to avoid coverage

    b. Part-time and full-time employees are covered

    c. Compensation received must be "wages"

6. Definitions

    a. Wages—all compensation for employment

        (1) Include

            (a) Money wages

            (b) Contingent fees

            (c) Compensation in general even though not in cash

            (d) Base pay of those in the service

            (e) Bonuses and commissions

            (f) Most tips

            (g) Vacation and dismissal allowances

        (2) Exclude

            (a) Wages greater than base amount

            (b) Reimbursed travel expenses

            (c) Employee medical and hospital expenses paid by employer

            (d) Employee insurance premiums paid by employer

            (e) Payment to employee retirement plan by employer

b.   Employee—person whose performance is subject to physical control by employer not only as to results but also as to methods of accomplishing those results

    (1)   Partners, self-employed persons, directors of corporations, and independent contractors are not covered by unemployment compensation provisions since they are not "employees"

        (a)   Are covered as self-employed persons for old-age, survivor's, and disability insurance program purposes

    (2)   Independent contractor distinguished from an employee

        (a)   Independent contractor not subject to control of employer or regular supervision as employee

        (b)   That is, employer seeks results only and contractor controls method

           EXAMPLE: A builder of homes has only to produce the results.

    (3)   Officers and directors of corporations are "employees" if they perform services and receive remuneration for these services from corporation

c.   Employment—all service performed by employee for person employing him/her

    (1)   Must be continuing or recurring work

    (2)   Services from following are exempt from coverage

        (a)   Student nurses

        (b)   Certain public employees

        (c)   Nonresident aliens

    (3)   Services covered if performed by employee for employer without regard to residence or citizenship

        (a)   Unless employer not connected with US

    (4)   Domestic workers, agricultural workers, government employees, and casual workers are governed by special rules

d.   Self-employment—carrying on trade or business either as individual or in partnership

    (1)   Wages greater than base amount are excluded

    (2)   Can be both employed (in one job) and self-employed (another business), but must meet requirements of trade or business (i.e., not a hobby, occasional investment, etc.)

e.   Employer

    (1)   For Federal Unemployment Tax Act (FUTA) need only employ one person or more for some portion of a day for twenty weeks, or pays $1,500 or more in wages in any calendar quarter

    (2)   In general, may be individual, corporation, partnership, trust, or other entity

7.   Old-age, survivor's, and disability insurance benefits

a.   Availability of benefits depends upon attainment by individual of "insured status"

    (1)   Certain lengths of working time are required to obtain insured status

b.   An individual who is "fully insured" is eligible for following benefits

    (1)   Survivor benefits for widow or widower and dependents

    (2)   Benefits for disabled worker and his/her dependents

    (3)   Old-age retirement benefits payable to retired worker and dependents

        (a)   Reduced benefits for retirement at age sixty-two

    (4)   Lump-sum death benefits

c.   Individual who is "currently insured" is eligible for following benefits

    (1)   Limited survivor benefits

        (a)   In general, limited to dependent minors or those caring for dependent minors

    (2)   Benefits for disabled worker and his/her dependents

    (3)   Lump-sum death benefits

(4) Survivors or dependents need not have paid in program to receive benefits

(5) Divorced spouses may receive benefits

d. Amount of benefits defined by statute which changes from time to time and depends upon

(1) Average monthly earnings, and

(2) Relationship of beneficiary to retired, deceased, or disabled worker

(a) For example, husband, wife, child, grandchild—may be entitled to different benefits

(3) Benefits increased based on cost of living

(4) Benefits increased for delayed retirement

8. Reduction of social security benefits

a. Early retirement results in reduced benefits

(1) Retirement age is increasing in steps

b. Returning to work after retirement can affect social security benefits

(1) Income from private pension plans, savings, investments, or insurance does not affect benefits because not earned income

(2) Income from limited partnership is considered investment income rather than self-employment income

9. Unemployment benefits

a. Eligibility for and amount of unemployment benefits governed by state laws

b. Does not include self-employed

c. Generally available only to persons unemployed through no fault of their own; however, not available to seasonal workers if paid on yearly basis (e.g., professional sports player in off-season)

d. One must have worked for specified period of time and/or earned specified amount of wages

B. Workers' Compensation Act

1. Workers' compensation is a form of strict liability whereby employer is liable to employee for injuries or diseases sustained by employee which arise out of and in course of employment

a. Also may include those only partially sustained in course of employment

b. Employee is worker subject to control and supervision of employer

c. Distinguish independent contractor

(1) Details of work not supervised

(2) Final result can of course be monitored (based on contract law)

2. Purpose

a. To give employees and their dependents benefits for job-related injuries or diseases with little difficulty

(1) Previously, employee had to sue employer for negligence to receive any benefits in form of damages

(2) Employee usually cannot waive his/her right to benefits

b. Cost is passed on as an expense of production

c. **No fault need be shown;** payment is automatic upon satisfaction of requirements

(1) Removes employer's common law defenses of

(a) Assumption of risk

(b) Negligence of a fellow employee—employer formerly could avoid liability by proving it was another employee's fault

(c) Contributory negligence—injured employee was also negligent

3. Regulated by states

a. Except that federal government employees are covered by federal statute

b. Each state has its own statute

4. Generally, there are two types of statutes

    a. Elective statutes

        (1) If employer rejects, s/he loses the three common law defenses against employee's common law suit for damages so most accept

    b. Compulsory statutes

        (1) Require that all employers within coverage of statute provide benefits
        (2) Majority of states have compulsory coverage

5. Insurance used to provide benefits

    a. In lieu of insurance policy, employer may assume liability for workers' compensation claims but must show proof of financial responsibility to carry own risk

6. Legislative scope

    a. Workers' compensation coverage extends to all employees who are injured on the job or in the course of the employment (i.e., while acting in furtherance of employer's business purpose)
    b. Coverage also extends to occupational diseases and preexisting diseases that are aggravated by employment
    c. Coverage does not extend to employee while traveling to or from work
    d. Out-of-state work may be covered if it meets above mentioned criteria
    e. All states have workers' compensation law; most employees covered
    f. Must be employee; coverage does not extend to independent contractors
    g. Public employees are often covered

7. Legal action for damages

    a. Employers covered by workers' compensation insurance are generally exempt from lawsuits by employees

        (1) If employee does not receive benefits covered under workers' compensation, s/he may sue insurance company that agreed to cover workers

    b. Benefits under workers' compensation laws received by employee are in lieu of action for damages against employer and such a suit is barred

        (1) Employer assumes liability in exchange for employee giving up his/her common law rights to sue employer for damages caused by the job (e.g., suit based on negligence)
        (2) When employee is covered by workers' compensation law, his/her sole remedy against employer is that which is provided for under appropriate workers' compensation act
        (3) However, if employer **intentionally** injures employee, employee may proceed against employer based on intentional tort in addition to recovering under workers' compensation benefits

    c. Employee is entitled to workers' compensation benefits **without regard to fault**

        (1) Negligence or even gross negligence of injured employee is not a bar to recovery
        (2) Employee's negligence plays no role in determination of amount of benefits awarded
        (3) Failure of employee to follow employer's rules is not a bar to recovery
        (4) However, injuries caused by intentional self-infliction, or intoxication of employee, can bar recovery

    d. When employer fails to provide workers' compensation insurance or when employer's coverage is inadequate, injured employee may sue in common law for damages, and employer cannot resort to usual common law defenses

        (1) When employer uninsured, many states have a fund to pay employee for job-related injuries

            (a) State then proceeds against uninsured company
            (b) Penalties imposed

8. Actions against third parties

    a. Employee's acceptance of workers' compensation benefits does not bar suit against third party whose negligence or unreasonably dangerous product caused injury

(1) Enforced by both EPA and Department of Commerce

(2) Protects both endangered as well as threatened species

s. Pollution Prevention Act

(1) Provides incentives to industry to prevent some pollution from initially being formed

t. SEC requires that companies report in financial statements their environmental liabilities

3. Environmental Compliance Audits

a. These are systematic, objective reviews designed to evaluate compliance with federal and state regulations and laws on environment

(1) Some states have environmental audit privilege laws

b. Purposes of audit

(1) To discover violations or questionable practices to allow company to avoid litigation

(2) Voluntary discovery to avoid criminal sanctions

(3) To meet disclosure requirements under securities laws

P. Telephone Consumer Protection Act

1. Restricts use of prerecorded messages
2. Act requires that in order to use prerecorded messages, a live person must introduce prerecorded message and receive from telephoned person permission to play that message

a. Act exempts calls by nonprofit organizations, calls made for emergencies, and calls to businesses

b. Act does not cover personal phone calls

Q. Federal Telecommunications Act

1. Prevents local or state governments from preventing entry of the growing telecommunications industry

R. Identity Theft

1. Hackers can collect much information on individuals to piece together information on them to, in many cases, obtain credit or make purchases or obtain government benefits
2. Increased penalties for identity theft to help reduce it
3. FTC is appointed to help victims of identity theft to restore credit and minimize impacts of identity theft
4. All banks, savings associations, and credit unions are required to have an identity theft prevention program

MULTIPLE-CHOICE QUESTIONS (1-44)

1. Taxes payable under the Federal Unemployment Tax Act (FUTA) are
   a. Calculated as a fixed percentage of all compensation paid to an employee.
   b. Deductible by the employer as a business expense for federal income tax purposes.
   c. Payable by employers for all employees.
   d. Withheld from the wages of all covered employees.

2. An unemployed CPA generally would receive unemployment compensation benefits if the CPA
   a. Was fired as a result of the employer's business reversals.
   b. Refused to accept a job as an accountant while receiving extended benefits.
   c. Was fired for embezzling from a client.
   d. Left work voluntarily without good cause.

3. After serving as an active director of Lee Corp. for twenty years, Ryan was appointed an honorary director with the obligation to attend directors' meetings with no voting power. In 2001, Ryan received an honorary director's fee of $5,000. This fee is
   a. Reportable by Lee as employee compensation subject to social security tax.
   b. Reportable by Ryan as self-employment income subject to social security self-employment tax.
   c. Taxable as "other income" by Ryan, **not** subject to any social security tax.
   d. Considered to be a gift **not** subject to social security self-employment or income tax.

4. Syl Corp. does **not** withhold FICA taxes from its employees' compensation. Syl voluntarily pays the entire FICA tax for its share and the amounts that it could have withheld from the employees. The employees' share of FICA taxes paid by Syl to the IRS is
   a. Deductible by Syl as additional compensation that is includible in the employees' taxable income.
   b. Not deductible by Syl because it does **not** meet the deductibility requirement as an ordinary and necessary business expense.
   c. A nontaxable gift to each employee, provided that the amount is less than $1,000 annually to each employee.
   d. Subject to prescribed penalties imposed on Syl for its failure to withhold required payroll taxes.

5. Social security benefits may include all of the following **except**
   a. Payments to divorced spouses.
   b. Payments to disabled children.
   c. Medicare payments.
   d. Medicaid payments.

6. Which of the following forms of income, if in excess of the annual exempt amount, will cause a reduction in a retired person's social security benefits?
   a. Annual proceeds from an annuity.
   b. Director's fees.
   c. Pension payments.
   d. Closely held corporation stock dividends.

7. Which of the following payments are deducted from an employee's salary?

	Unemployment compensation insurance	Worker's compensation insurance
a.	Yes	Yes
b.	Yes	No
c.	No	Yes
d.	No	No

8. Which of the following types of income is subject to taxation under the provisions of the Federal Insurance Contributions Act (FICA)?
   a. Interest earned on municipal bonds.
   b. Capital gains of $3,000.
   c. Car received as a productivity award.
   d. Dividends of $2,500.

9. Under the Federal Insurance Contributions Act (FICA), which of the following acts will cause an employer to be liable for penalties?

	Failure to supply taxpayer identification numbers	Failure to make timely FICA deposits
a.	Yes	Yes
b.	Yes	No
c.	No	Yes
d.	No	No

10. Which of the following parties generally is ineligible to collect workers' compensation benefits?
   a. Minors.
   b. Truck drivers.
   c. Union employees.
   d. Temporary office workers.

11. Kroll, an employee of Acorn, Inc., was injured in the course of employment while operating a forklift manufactured and sold to Acorn by Trell Corp. The forklift was defectively designed by Trell. Under the state's mandatory workers' compensation statute, Kroll will be successful in

	Obtaining workers' compensation benefits	A negligence action against Acorn
a.	Yes	Yes
b.	Yes	No
c.	No	Yes
d.	No	No

12. Which of the following provisions is basic to all workers' compensation systems?
   a. The injured employee must prove the employer's negligence.
   b. The employer may invoke the traditional defense of contributory negligence.
   c. The employer's liability may be ameliorated by a coemployee's negligence under the fellow-servant rule.
   d. The injured employee is allowed to recover on strict liability theory.

13. Workers' Compensation Acts require an employer to
   a. Provide coverage for all eligible employees.
   b. Withhold employee contributions from the wages of eligible employees.
   c. Pay an employee the difference between disability payments and full salary.
   d. Contribute to a federal insurance fund.

14. Generally, which of the following statements concerning workers' compensation laws is correct?
   a. The amount of damages recoverable is based on comparative negligence.
   b. Employers are strictly liable without regard to whether or **not** they are at fault.
   c. Workers' compensation benefits are **not** available if the employee is negligent.
   d. Workers' compensation awards are payable for life.

15. Workers' compensation laws provide for all of the following benefits **except**
   a. Burial expenses.
   b. Full pay during disability.
   c. The cost of prosthetic devices.
   d. Monthly payments to surviving dependent children.

16. Which of the following claims is(are) generally covered under workers' compensation statutes?

	Occupational disease	Employment aggravated preexisting disease
a.	Yes	Yes
b.	Yes	No
c.	No	Yes
d.	No	No

17. Under which of the following conditions is an on-site inspection of a workplace by an investigator from the Occupational Safety and Health Administration (OSHA) permissible?
   a. Only if OSHA obtains a search warrant after showing probable cause.
   b. Only if the inspection is conducted after working hours.
   c. At the request of employees.
   d. After OSHA provides the employer with at least twenty-four hours notice of the prospective inspection.

18. Which of the following Acts prohibit(s) an employer from discriminating among employees based on sex?

	Equal Pay Act	Title VII of the Civil Rights Act
a.	Yes	Yes
b.	Yes	No
c.	No	Yes
d.	No	No

19. Under the Age Discrimination in Employment Act, which of the following remedies is(are) available to a covered employee?

	Early Retirement	Back pay
a.	Yes	Yes
b.	Yes	No
c.	No	Yes
d.	No	No

20. Which of the following company policies would violate the Age Discrimination in Employment Act?
   a. The company will not hire any accountant below twenty-five years of age.
   b. The office staff must retire at age sixty-five or younger.
   c. Both of the above.
   d. None of the above.

21. Under the provisions of the Americans With Disabilities Act of 1990, in which of the following areas is a disabled person protected from discrimination?

	Public transportation	Privately operated public accommodations
a.	Yes	Yes
b.	Yes	No
c.	No	Yes
d.	No	No

22. Under the Americans with Disabilities Act, which is(are) true?
   I. The Act requires that companies with at least ten employees set up a specified plan to hire people with disabilities.
   II. The Act requires companies to make reasonable accommodations for disabled persons unless this results in undue hardship on the operations of the company.
   a. I only.
   b. II only.
   c. Both I and II.
   d. Neither I nor II.

23. The Americans With Disabilities Act has as a purpose to give remedies for discrimination to individuals with disabilities. Which of the following is(are) true of this Act?
   I. It protects most individuals with disabilities working for companies but only if the companies do not need to incur any expenses to modify the work environment to accommodate the disability.
   II. It may require a company to modify work schedules to accommodate persons with disabilities.
   III. It may require a company to purchase equipment at company expense to accommodate persons with disabilities.
   a. I only.
   b. I and II only.
   c. II and III only.
   d. III only.

24. Which of the following is **not** true under the Family and Medical Leave Act?
   a. An employee has a right to take a leave from work for the birth and care of her child for one month at half of her regular pay.
   b. An employee has a right to take a leave from work for twelve workweeks to care for his/her seriously ill parent.
   c. An employee, upon returning under the provisions of the Act, must get back the same or equivalent position in the company.
   d. This Act does not cover all employees.

25. The Family Medical Leave Act provides for
   I. Unpaid leave for the employee to care for a newborn baby.
   II. Unpaid leave for the employee to care for the serious health problem of his or her parent.
   III. Paid leave for the employee to care for a serious health problem of his or her spouse.
   a. I only.
   b. II only.
   c. I and II but not III.
   d. III but not I or II.

26. Under the Fair Labor Standards Act, which of the following pay bases may be used to pay covered, nonexempt employees who earn, on average, the minimum hourly wage?

	Hourly	*Weekly*	*Monthly*
a.	Yes	Yes	Yes
b.	Yes	Yes	No
c.	Yes	No	Yes
d.	No	Yes	Yes

27. Under the Fair Labor Standards Act, if a covered, nonexempt employee works consecutive weeks of forty-five, forty-two, thirty-eight, and thirty-three hours, how many hours of overtime must be paid to the employee?

a. 0
b. 7
c. 18
d. 20

28. Which of the following employee benefits is(are) exempt from the provisions of the National Labor Relations Act?

	Sick pay	*Vacation pay*
a.	Yes	Yes
b.	Yes	No
c.	No	Yes
d.	No	No

29. Under the Federal Consolidated Budget Reconciliation Act of 1985 (COBRA), when an employee voluntarily resigns from a job, the former employee's group health insurance coverage that was in effect during the period of employment with the company

a. Automatically ceases for the former employee and spouse, if the resignation occurred before normal retirement age.
b. Automatically ceases for the former employee's spouse, but continues for the former employee for an eighteen-month period at the former employer's expense.
c. May be retained by the former employee at the former employee's expense for at least eighteen months after leaving the company, but must be terminated for the former employee's spouse.
d. May be retained for the former employee and spouse at the former employee's expense for at least eighteen months after leaving the company.

30. Under the Employee Retirement Income Security Act of 1974 (ERISA), which of the following areas of private employer pension plans is(are) regulated?

	Employee vesting	*Plan funding*
a.	Yes	Yes
b.	Yes	No
c.	No	Yes
d.	No	No

31. Under the provisions of the Employee Retirement Income Security Act of 1974 (ERISA), which of the following statements is correct?

a. Employees are entitled to have an employer established pension plan.
b. Employers are prevented from unduly delaying an employee's participation in a pension plan.
c. Employers are prevented from managing retirement plans.

d. Employees are entitled to make investment decisions.

32. Under the Comprehensive Environmental Response, Compensation, and Liability Act (CERCLA), commonly known as Superfund, which of the following parties would be liable to the Environmental Protection Agency (EPA) for the expense of cleaning up a hazardous waste disposal site?

I. The current owner or operator of the site.
II. The person who transported the wastes to the site.
III. The person who owned or operated the site at the time of the disposal.

a. I and II.
b. I and III.
c. II and III.
d. I, II, and III.

33. Which of the following activities is(are) regulated under the Federal Water Pollution Control Act (Clean Water Act)?

	Discharge of heated water by nuclear power plants	*Dredging of wetlands*
a.	Yes	Yes
b.	Yes	No
c.	No	Yes
d.	No	No

34. Environmental Compliance Audits are used for which of the following purpose(s)?

I. To voluntarily discover violations to avoid criminal sanctions.
II. To discover violations to avoid civil litigation.
III. To meet disclosure requirements to the SEC under the securities laws.

a. I only.
b. I and II only.
c. II only.
d. I, II and III.

35. Which of the following is(are) true under the Federal Insecticide, Fungicide, and Rodenticide Act?

I. Herbicides and pesticides must be certified and can be used only for applications that are approved.
II. Herbicides and pesticides must be registered under the Act before companies can sell them.
III. Pesticides, when used on food crops, can only be used in quantities that are limited under the Act.

a. I only.
b. I and II only.
c. II and III only.
d. I, II, and III.

36. Under the Comprehensive Environmental Response, Compensation and Liability Act as amended by the Superfund Amendments, which of the following is(are) true?

I. The present owner of land can be held liable for cleanup of hazardous chemicals placed on the land by a previous owner.
II. An employee of a company that had control over the disposal of hazardous substances on the company's land can be held personally liable for cleanup costs.

a. I only.
b. II only.
c. Both I and II.
d. Neither I nor II.

37. The National Environmental Policy Act was passed to enhance and preserve the environment. Which of the following is **not** true?

    a.   The Act applies to all federal agencies.

    b.   The Act requires that an environmental impact statement be provided if any proposed federal legislation may significantly affect the environment.

    c.   Enforcement of the Act is primarily accomplished by litigation of persons who decide to challenge federal government decisions.

    d.   The Act provides generous tax breaks to those companies that help accomplish national environmental policy.

38. Under the federal statutes governing water pollution, which of the following areas is(are) regulated?

	Dredging of coastal or freshwater wetlands	Drinking water standards
a.	Yes	Yes
b.	Yes	No
c.	No	Yes
d.	No	No

39. The Clean Air Act provides for the enforcement of standards for

  I. The emissions of radioactive particles from private nuclear power plants.

  II. The emissions of pollution from privately owned automobiles.

  III. The emissions of air pollution from factories.

    a.   I and II only.

    b.   I and III only.

    c.   II and III only.

    d.   I, II and III.

40. Under the Clean Air Act, which of the following statements is(are) correct regarding actions that may be taken against parties who violate emission standards?

  I. The federal government may require an automobile manufacturer to recall vehicles that violate emission standards.

  II. A citizens' group may sue to force a coal burning power plant to comply with emission standards.

    a.   I only.

    b.   II only.

    c.   Both I and II.

    d.   Neither I nor II.

41. The Environmental Protection Agency is an administrative agency in the federal government that aids in the protection of the environment. Which of the following is **not** a purpose or function of this agency?

    a.   It adopts regulations to protect the quality of water.

    b.   It aids private citizens to make cases for private civil litigation.

    c.   It may refer criminal matters to the Department of Justice.

    d.   It may refer civil cases to the Department of Justice.

42. Whenever a federal agency recommends actions or legislation that may affect the environment, the agency must prepare an environmental impact statement. Which of the following is **not** required in the environmental impact statement?

    a.   A description of the source of funds to accomplish the action without harming the environment.

    b.   An examination of alternate methods of achieving the goals of the proposed actions or legislation.

    c.   A description in detail of the proposed actions or legislation on the environment.

    d.   A description of any unavoidable adverse consequences.

43. Which of the following is(are) possible when a company violates the Clean Air Act?

  I. The company can be assessed a criminal fine.

  II. Officers of the company can be imprisoned.

  III. The Environmental Protection Agency may assess a civil penalty equal to the savings of costs by the company for noncompliance.

    a.   I only.

    b.   I or II only.

    c.   III only.

    d.   I, II or III.

44. Green, a former owner of Circle Plant, caused hazardous waste pollution at the Circle Plant site two years ago. Sason purchased the plant and caused more hazardous waste pollution. It can be shown that 20% of the problem was caused by Green and that 80% of the problem was caused by Sason. Sason went bankrupt recently. The government wishes to clean up the site and hold Green liable. Which of the following is true?

    a.   The most Green can be held liable for is 20%.

    b.   Green is not liable for any of the cleanup costs since the site was sold.

    c.   Green is not liable for any of the cleanup costs because Green was responsible for less than half of the problem.

    d.   Green can be held liable for all the cleanup costs even if Sason has some funds.

SIMULATION PROBLEM

Simulation Problem 1   (5 to 10 minutes)

> **Consideration**

    For each of the numbered items, indicate: Yes, this item is considered to be wages under the Social Security Act, or No, this item is **not** considered to be wages under the Social Security Act.

		Yes	*No*
1.	Wages, paid in money, to a construction worker.	O	O
2.	Reimbursed normal travel expenses of a salesperson.	O	O
3.	Compensation not paid in cash.	O	O
4.	Commissions of a salesperson.	O	O
5.	Bonuses paid to employees.	O	O
6.	Employee insurance premiums paid by the employer.	O	O
7.	Wages paid to a secretary who is working part time.	O	O
8.	Vacation allowance pay given to employees who are working full time.	O	O
9.	Wages paid to a full-time secretary who wishes to elect not to be covered under the Social Security Act.	O	O
10.	Tips of a waitress.	O	O

(2) Under a race-notice type (notice-race) statute, the subsequent bona fide purchaser wins over a previous purchaser only if s/he also records first (i.e., a "race" to file first)

> *EXAMPLE: X sells some property to Y and then to Z, a good-faith purchaser. After the sale to Z, Y records the purchase and then Z records the purchase. Although Y wins in a state having a race-notice statute, Z wins in a state having a notice-type statute.*

> *EXAMPLE: Same as above except that Z does not record, both results above are not affected.*

(3) Under a race statute, the first to record deed wins

c. Notice refers to actual knowledge of prior sale or constructive knowledge (i.e., one is deemed to be aware of what is filed in records)

d. To be a purchaser, one must give value that does not include antecedent debts

J. Title Insurance

1. Generally used to insure that title is good and to cover the warranties by seller

a. Not required if contract does not require it

2. Without title insurance, purchaser's only recourse is against grantor and s/he may not be able to satisfy the damages

a. Standard insurance policies generally insure against all defects of record and defects grantee may be aware of, but not defects disclosed by survey and physical inspection of premises

b. Title insurance company is liable for any damages or expenses if there is a title defect or encumbrance that is insured against

(1) Certain defects are not insured by the title policy

(a) These exceptions must be shown on face of policy

c. Title insurance does not pass to subsequent purchasers

K. Adverse Possession

1. Possessor of land who was not owner may acquire title if s/he holds it for the statutory period

a. The statutory period is the running of the statute of limitations. Varies by state from five to twenty years.

b. The statute begins to run upon the taking of possession

c. True owner must commence legal action before statute runs or adverse possessor obtains title

d. Successive possessors may tack (cumulate required time together)

(1) Each possessor must transfer to the other. One cannot abandon or statute begins over again for the next possessor.

e. True owner of a future interest (e.g., a remainder, is not affected by adverse possession)

> *EXAMPLE: X dies and leaves his property to A for life, remainder to B. A pays little attention to the property and a third party acquires it by adverse possession. When A dies, B is entitled to the property regardless of the adverse possession but the statute starts running against B.*

2. Necessary elements

a. Open and notorious possession

(1) Means type of possession that would give reasonable notice to owner

b. Hostile possession

(1) Must indicate intentions of ownership

(a) Does not occur when possession started permissively or as cotenants

(b) Not satisfied if possessor acknowledges other's ownership

(2) Color of title satisfies this requirement. When possession is taken under good-faith belief in a defective instrument or deed purporting to convey the land.

c. Actual possession

(1) Possession of land consistent with its normal use (e.g., farm land is being farmed)

d. Continuous possession

      (1) Need not be constant, but possession as normally used

   e. Exclusive possession

      (1) Possession to exclusion of all others

L. Easement by Prescription

1. Person obtains right to use another's land (i.e., easement) in way similar to adverse possession
2. Same elements are used as for adverse possession except for exclusive possession—state laws require several years to obtain this

> *EXAMPLE: X cuts across Y's land for several years in such a way that s/he meets all of the same requirements as those needed for adverse possession except for exclusive possession. X obtains an easement to use the path even if Y later tries to stop X.*

M. Mortgages

1. Lien on real property to secure payment of loan

   a. Mortgage is an interest in real property and thus must satisfy Statute of Frauds

      (1) Must be in writing and signed by party to be charged

         (a) Party to be charged in this case is mortgagor (i.e., party taking out mortgage)

      (2) Must include description of property and debt to be incurred

   b. Debt is usually evidenced by a promissory note which is incorporated into mortgage
   c. Mortgage must be delivered to mortgagee (i.e., lender)
   d. Mortgage may be given to secure future advances
   e. Purchase-money mortgage is created when seller takes a mortgage from buyer at time of sale

      (1) Or lender furnishes money with which property is purchased

2. Mortgage may be recorded and receives the same benefits as recording a deed or recording an assignment of contract

   a. Gives constructive notice of the mortgage

      (1) But mortgage **is effective** between mortgagor and mortgagee and third parties, who have actual notice, even without recording

   b. Protects mortgagee against subsequent mortgagees, purchasers, or other takers
   c. Recording statutes for mortgages are like those used for recording deeds

      (1) Under a notice-type statute, a subsequent good-faith mortgagee has priority over previous mortgagee who did not file

         (a) This is true whether subsequent mortgagee files or not; but of course if s/he does not file, a subsequent good-faith mortgagee will have priority.

> *EXAMPLE: Banks A, B, and C, in that order, grant a mortgage to a property owner. None of these record the mortgage and none knows of the others. Between A and B, B has priority. However, C has priority over B.*

> *EXAMPLE: Same facts as before, however, B does record before C grants the mortgage. B has priority over A again. B also has priority over C because now C has constructive notice of B and thus has lower priority.*

         (b) Notice is either actual notice or constructive notice based on recording

      (2) Under a race-notice type (notice-race) statute, the subsequent good-faith mortgagee wins over a previous mortgagee only if s/he also records first

      (3) Under a race statute, the first mortgagee to record mortgage wins

      (4) First mortgage to have priority is satisfied in full (upon default) before next mortgage to have priority is satisfied

         (a) Second mortgagee can require first mortgagee to resort to other property for payment if first mortgagee has other property available as security

3. When mortgaged property is sold the buyer may

   a. Assume the mortgage

       (1) If "assumed," the buyer becomes personally liable (mortgage holder is third-party beneficiary)

       (2) Seller remains liable (unless released by mortgagee by a novation)

          (a) Mortgagee may hold either seller or buyer liable on mortgage

       (3) Normally the mortgagee's consent is needed due to "due on sale clauses"

          (a) Terms of mortgage may permit acceleration of principal or renegotiation of interest rate upon transfer of the property

   b. Take subject to the mortgage

       (1) If buyer takes "subject to" then buyer accepts **no** liability for mortgage and seller is still primarily liable

       (2) Mortgagee may still foreclose on the property even in the hands of buyer

          (a) Buyer may pay mortgage if s/he chooses to avoid foreclosure

       (3) Mortgagee's consent to allow buyer to take subject to the mortgage is not needed unless stipulated in mortgage

   c. Novation—occurs when purchaser assumes mortgage and mortgagee (lender) releases in writing the seller from the mortgage

> *EXAMPLE: O has mortgaged Redacre. He sells Redacre to T. T agrees to assume mortgage and mortgagee bank agrees in writing to substitute T as the only liable party in place of O. Because of this novation, O is no longer liable on the mortgage.*

4. Rights of parties

   a. Mortgagor (owner, debtor) retains possession and right to use land

       (1) May transfer land encumbered by mortgage

   b. Mortgagee (creditor) has a lien on the land

       (1) Even if mortgagor transfers land, it is still subject to the mortgage if it has been properly recorded

   c. Mortgagee has right to assign mortgage to third party without mortgagors' consent

   d. Upon mortgagor's default, mortgagee may assign mortgage to third parties or mortgagee may foreclose on the land

       (1) Foreclosure requires judicial action that directs foreclosure sale

          (a) Court will refuse to confirm sale if price is so low as to raise a presumption of unfairness

          (b) However, court will not refuse to confirm sale merely because higher price might have been received at a later time

       (2) Mortgagor usually can save real estate (redeem the property) by use of equity of redemption

          (a) Pays interest, debt, and expenses

          (b) Exists until foreclosure sale

          (c) Cannot be curtailed by prior agreement

       (3) After foreclosure sale debtor has right of redemption if state law grants statutory right of redemption

          (a) Affords mortgagor one last chance to redeem property

          (b) Pays off loan within statutory period

       (4) If mortgagee forecloses and sells property and mortgagor does not use equity of redemption or right of redemption

          (a) Mortgagee must return any excess proceeds from sale to mortgagor

             1] Equity above balance due does not give right to mortgagor to retain possession of property

          (b) If proceeds from sale are insufficient to pay note, mortgagor is still indebted to the mortgagee for deficiency

             1] Grantee of the mortgagor who **assumed** mortgage would also be liable for deficiency, but one who took **subject to** the mortgage would not be personally liable

5. Mortgage lenders are regulated by Real Estate Settlement Procedures Act (RESPA)

    a. Provides home buyers with extensive information about settlement process and helps protect them from high settlement fees

6. Deed of trust—also a nonpossessory lien on real property to secure a debt

    a. Like a mortgage, debtor retains possession of land and creditor has a lien on it

    b. Legal title is given to a trustee to hold

        (1) Upon default, trustee may sell the land for the benefit of creditor

7. Sale on contract

    a. Unlike a mortgage or a deed of trust, the seller retains title to property

    b. Purchaser takes possession and makes payments on the contract

    c. Purchaser gets title when debt fully paid

8. When mortgaged property is sold or destroyed, the proceeds from sale or insurance go to mortgagee with highest priority until it is completely paid, then the proceeds, if any, go to any mortgagees or other interest holders, with the next highest priority, etc.

N. Lessor-Lessee

1. A lease is a contract and a conveyance

    a. Contract is the primary source of rights and duties

    b. Contract must contain essential terms including description of leased premises

    c. May be oral if less than one year

        (1) Some states require all leases to be in writing when they involve land

2. Types of leaseholds

    a. Periodic tenancy

        (1) Lease is for a fixed time such as a month or year but it continues from period to period until proper notice of termination

        (2) Notice of termination normally must be given in the same amount of time as rent or tenancy period (i.e., if tenancy is from month to month then the landlord or tenant usually must give at least one month's notice)

    b. Tenancy for a term (also called tenancy for years)

        (1) Lease is for a fixed amount of time (e.g., lease of two years or six months)

        (2) Ends automatically at date of termination

    c. Tenancy at sufferance

        (1) Created when tenant remains in property after lease expires

        (2) Landlord has option of treating tenant as trespasser and ejecting him/her or treating him/her as tenant and collecting rent

    d. Tenancy at will

        (1) Property is leased for indefinite period of time

        (2) Either party may terminate lease at will

3. Lessor covenants (promises) and tenant's rights

    a. Generally, lessor's covenants are independent of lessee's rights; therefore, lessor's breach does not give lessee right to breach

    b. Right to possession—lessor makes premises available to lessee

        (1) Residential lease for real estate entitles tenant to exclusive possession of property during period of lease unless otherwise agreed in lease

    c. Quiet enjoyment—neither lessor nor a third party with a valid claim will evict lessee unless tenant has breached lease contract

    d. Fitness for use—premises are fit for human occupation (i.e., warranty of habitability)

    e. In general, if premises are destroyed through no fault of either party, then contract is terminated

EXAMPLE: Landlord's building is destroyed by a sudden flood. Tenant cannot hold landlord liable for loss of use of building.

    f.   Lessee may assign or sublease unless prohibited or restricted in lease

       (1) Assignment is transfer by lessee of his/her entire interest reserving no rights

          (a) Assignee is in privity of contract with lessor and lessor may proceed against him/her for rent and breaches under lease agreement

          (b) Assignor (lessee) is still liable to lessor unless there is a novation or release

          (c) Lease may have clause that requires consent of lessor for subleases

             1] In which case, consent to each individual sublease is required

             2] Lack of consent makes sublease voidable

          (d) Clause prohibiting sublease does not prohibit assignment

       (2) A sublease is the transfer by lessee of less than his/her entire interest (e.g., for three months during summer, then lessee returns to it in the fall)

          (a) Lessee (sublessor) is still liable on lease

          (b) Lessor has no privity with sublessee and can take no action against him/her for rent, but certain restrictions of original lease run with the land and are enforceable against sublessee

          (c) Sublessee can assume obligations in sublease and be liable to pay landlord

          (d) Clause prohibiting assignment does not prohibit sublease

    g.   Subject to lease terms, trade fixtures attached by lessee may be removed if can be removed without substantial damage to premises

    h.   Tenant can use premises for any legal purpose unless lease restricts

4. Lessee's duties and lessor's rights

    a.   Rent—due at end of term or period of tenancy unless otherwise agreed in lease

       (1) No right to withhold rent even if lessor is in breach (unless so provided by lease or by statute)

       (2) Nonpayment gives lessor right to sue for it or to bring an eviction suit or both

    b.   Lessee has obligation to make ordinary repairs. Lease or statute may make lessor liable.

       (1) Structural repairs are lessor's duty

    c.   If tenant wrongfully retains possession after termination, lessor may

       (1) Evict lessee, or

       (2) Treat as holdover tenant and charge with fair rental value, or

       (3) Tenancy becomes one of period-to-period, and lessee is liable for rent the same as in expired lease

5. Termination

    a.   Expiration of lease

    b.   Proper notice in a tenancy from period-to-period

    c.   Surrender by lessee and acceptance by lessor

    d.   Death of lessee terminates lease except for a lease for a period of years

       (1) Death of lessor generally does not terminate lease

    e.   Eviction

       (1) Actual eviction—ousting directly

       (2) Constructive eviction—allowing conditions which make property unusable if lessor is liable for condition of premises

    f.   Transfer of property does not affect tenancy

       (1) New owner cannot rightfully terminate lease unless old owner could have (e.g., breach by tenant)

          (a) However, if tenant purchases property then lease terminates

MULTIPLE-CHOICE QUESTIONS (1-43)

1. Which of the following items is tangible personal property?
   a.   Share of stock.
   b.   Trademark.
   c.   Promissory note.
   d.   Oil painting.

2. What is an example of property that can be considered either personal property or real property?
   a.   Air rights.
   b.   Mineral rights.
   c.   Harvested crops.
   d.   Growing crops.

3. Which of the following factors help determine whether an item of personal property is a fixture?
   I. Degree of the item's attachment to the property.
   II. Intent of the person who had the item installed.

   a.   I only.
   b.   II only.
   c.   Both I and II.
   d.   Neither I nor II.

4. Getty owned some personal property which was later found by Morris. Both Getty and Morris are claiming title to this personal property. In which of the following cases will Getty win over Morris?
   I. Getty had mislaid the property and had forgotten to take it with him.
   II. Getty had lost the property out of his van while driving down a road.
   III. Getty had abandoned the property but later changed his mind after Morris found it.

   a.   I only.
   b.   II only.
   c.   I and II only.
   d.   I, II, and III.

5. Rand discarded an old rocking chair. Stone found the rocking chair and, realizing that it was valuable, took it home. Later, Rand learned that Stone had the rocking chair and wanted it back. Rand subsequently put a provision in his will that his married daughter Walters will get the rocking chair. Who has the actual title to the rocking chair?

	Stone has title	Rand, while living, has title	Walters obtains title upon Rand's death
a.	No	Yes	Yes
b.	No	Yes	No
c.	Yes	Yes	Yes
d.	Yes	No	No

6. Which of the following standards of liability best characterizes the obligation of a common carrier in a bailment relationship?
   a.   Reasonable care.
   b.   Gross negligence.
   c.   Shared liability.
   d.   Strict liability.

7. Multicomp Company wishes to protect software it has developed. It is concerned about others copying this software and taking away some of its profits. Which of the following is true concerning the current state of the law?
   a.   Computer software is generally copyrightable.

   b.   To receive protection, the software must have a conspicuous copyright notice.
   c.   Software in human readable source code is copyrightable but in machine language object code is not.
   d.   Software can be copyrighted for a period not to exceed twenty years.

8. Which of the following is **not** correct concerning computer software purchased by Gultch Company from Softtouch Company? Softtouch originally created this software.
   a.   Gultch can make backup copies in case of machine failure.
   b.   Softtouch can typically copyright its software for at least seventy-five years.
   c.   If the software consists of compiled computer databases it cannot be copyrighted.
   d.   Computer programs are generally copyrightable.

9. Which of the following statements is correct?
   a.   Patent law is largely based on state law.
   b.   Accessing a digital work is protected by the fair use doctrine.
   c.   Financial and business models used over the internet can be patented.
   d.   All of the above statements are incorrect.

10. Professor Bell runs off fifteen copies to distribute to his accounting class using his computer from a database in some software he had purchased for his personal research. The creator of this software is claiming a copyright. Which of the following is correct?
   a.   This is an infringement of a copyright since he bought the software for personal use.
   b.   This is not an infringement of a copyright since databases cannot be copyrighted.
   c.   This is not an infringement of a copyright because the copies were made using a computer.
   d.   This is not an infringement of a copyright because of the fair use doctrine.

11. Intellectual property rights included in software may be protected under which of the following?
   a.   Patent law.
   b.   Copyright law.
   c.   Both of the above.
   d.   None of the above.

12. Which of the following statements is **not** true of the law of trademarks in the United States?
   a.   Trademark law may protect distinctive shapes as well as distinctive packaging.
   b.   Trademark protection can be lost if the trademark becomes so popular that its use becomes commonplace.
   c.   Trademarks to receive protection need not be registered.
   d.   Trademarks are valid for twenty years after their formation.

13. Diane Trucco recently wrote a novel which is an excellent work of art. She wishes to copyright and publish this novel. Which of the following is correct?
   a.   Her copyright is valid for her life plus seventy years.
   b.   She must register her copyright to receive protection under the law.

a. There must be a relationship between the insured and the insured event so that if the event occurs insured will suffer substantial loss

b. In property, there must be both a legal interest and a possibility of pecuniary loss

(1) Legal interest may be ownership or a security interest (e.g., general creditors do not have an insurable interest but judgment lien creditors and mortgagees do)

> EXAMPLE: *G takes out a fire insurance policy on a building owned by A. G did this because he frequently does some business with A. Although A generally pays his bills as they are due, A owes G $20,000. G, as a general creditor only, has no insurable interest in A's building.*

(2) Insurable interest need not be present at inception of the policy so long as it is present at time of the loss

(3) One can insure only to extent one has an insurable interest (e.g., mortgagee can insure only amount still due)—otherwise could be considered a form of gambling

(4) Contract to purchase or possession of property can give an insurable interest

(5) Goods identified with contract create insurable interest

c. For life insurance, one has an insurable interest in one's own life and the lives of close family relatives or individuals whose death could result in pecuniary loss

(1) Company or person has insurable interest in key personnel or key employees

(2) For life insurance, insurable interest need be present at inception of policy but not at time of death

> EXAMPLE: *Same as example above except that G takes out a life insurance policy on A's life. G does not have an insurable interest.*

> EXAMPLE: *M and N are partners in a firm in which the skills of both M and N are important. M and N take out life insurance policies on each other. There are valid insurable interests for these policies.*

> EXAMPLE: *Same as previous example except that M and N terminate their partnership. They do not, however, terminate the life insurance policies on each other's lives. Upon M's death, N can collect on the life insurance policy.*

d. Insurance offered for identity fraud or identity theft

(1) Typically covers fees paid to help restore bad credit trail left behind affecting person's name such as lost wages for work lost in correcting fraud, attorney's fees, reapplication fees, telephone charges

C. Subrogation

1. This is the right of insurer to step into the shoes of insured as to any cause of action relating to a third party whose conduct caused the loss

> EXAMPLE: *While driving his car, X is hit by Y. If X's insurance company pays X, the insurance company is subrogated to X's claim against Y.*

a. Applies to accident, automobile collision, and fire policies

2. A general release of a third party, who caused the loss, by insured will release insurer from his/her obligation

> EXAMPLE: *While driving his car, X is hit by Y. Y talks X into signing a statement that X releases Y from all liability. X will not be able to recover on his insurance. X's insurance company is released when Y is released.*

a. Because insurer's right of subrogation has been cut off

b. A partial release will release insurer to that extent

D. Liability Insurance

1. Insurer agrees to protect insured against liability for accidental damage to persons or property

a. Usually includes duty to defend in a lawsuit brought by third parties

b. Intentional wrongs not covered (e.g., fraud)

c. Insurer has no rights against insured for causing the loss because this is what the insurance is to protect against

2. Malpractice—a form of personal liability

a. Used by accountants, doctors, lawyers

    b. Protects against liability for harm caused by errors or negligence in work

    c. Does not protect against intentional wrongs (e.g., fraud)

E. Fire Insurance

1. Generally covers direct fire damage and also damage as a result of fire such as smoke, water, or chemicals
2. Blanket policy applies to a class of property that may be changing (inventory) rather than a specific piece of property (specific policy)
3. Valued policy predetermines value of property that becomes the face value of the policy
4. Recovery limited to face value of policy
5. Unvalued (open) policy determines value of property at time of loss which is amount insured collects—maximum amount usually set
6. **Coinsurance clause**

    a. The insured agrees to maintain insurance equal to a specified percentage of the value of his/her property. Then when a loss occurs, insurer only pays a proportionate share if insured has not carried the specified percentage.

    b. Formula

$$\text{Total recovery} = \text{Actual loss} \times \frac{\text{Amount of insurance}}{\text{Coinsurance \% } \times \text{FMV of property at time of loss}}$$

    EXAMPLE: Insured owns a building valued at $100,000. He obtains two insurance policies for $20,000 each and they both contain 80% coinsurance clauses. There is a fire and his loss is $40,000. He will only collect $20,000 ($10,000 each) on his insurance, calculated as follows:

$$\$40,000 \ \times \ \frac{\$20,000 + \$20,000}{80\% \text{ of } \$100,000}$$

    c. This formula is used even though the insured does not maintain insurance equal to specified coverage; in such cases, this formula provides a lower recovery than actual losses

       (1) Therefore, this encourages insured to insure property for amount up to fair market value multiplied by the specified coinsurance percentage

    d. Does not apply when insured property is totally destroyed

    EXAMPLE: On October 10, Harry's warehouse was totally destroyed by fire. At the time of the fire, the warehouse had a value of $500,000 and was insured against fire for $300,000. The policy contained an 80% coinsurance clause. Harry will recover $300,000, the face value of the policy, because total destruction occurred and the coinsurance clause would not apply. If the warehouse had been only partially destroyed, with damages amounting to $300,000, Harry would only recover $225,000 (based on the formula above), because the coinsurance clause would apply.

7. Pro rata clause

    a. Someone who is insured with multiple policies can only collect, from each insurer, the proportionate amount of the loss

       (1) Proportion is the amount insured by each insurer to total amount of insurance

    EXAMPLE: Insured incurs a loss due to fire on property and is entitled to a $10,000 recovery. The property is covered by two insurance policies, one for $8,000 from Company A and one for $12,000 from Company B. Consequently, total insurance coverage on the property was $20,000. Company A will be liable for 40% ($8,000/$20,000) of fire loss, that is, $4,000 (40% × $10,000). Company B will be liable for 60% ($12,000/$20,000) of fire loss, that is, $6,000 (60% × $10,000).

8. Proof of loss

    a. Insured must give insurer a statement of amount of loss, cause of loss, etc., within a specified time

       (1) Failure to comply will excuse insurer's liability unless performance is made impracticable (e.g., death of insured)

9. Mortgagor and mortgagee have insurable interests, and mortgagees usually require insurance for their protection
10. Fire policies are usually not assignable because risk may have changed

    a. Even if property is sold, there can be no assignment of insurance without insurer's consent

    b. A claim against an insurer may be assigned (e.g., house burns and insurance company has not yet paid)

MULTIPLE-CHOICE QUESTIONS (1-8)

1. Which of the following statements correctly describes the requirement of insurable interest relating to property insurance? An insurable interest

    a. Must exist when any loss occurs.

    b. Must exist when the policy is issued and when any loss occurs.

    c. Is created only when the property is owned in fee simple.

    d. Is created only when the property is owned by an individual.

2. In which of the following cases would Brown not have an insurable interest?

    a. Brown is a general creditor of Winfield Corporation which is having financial problems.

    b. Brown is a mortgagee on some real property purchased by Wilson.

    c. Brown, as an owner of Winfield Company, wishes to insure the life of an officer critical to Winfield.

    d. Brown wishes to take out a life insurance policy on his partner of a partnership in which both Brown and his partner have important skills for that partnership.

3. Which of the following parties has an insurable interest?

  I. A corporate retailer in its inventory.

  II. A partner in the partnership property.

    a. I only.

    b. II only.

    c. Both I and II.

    d. Neither I nor II.

4. Massaro is hit by Lux in a two-car accident that is later determined to be completely Lux's fault. Massaro's auto insurance policy paid her for the complete damages to her car and her person. Can Massaro's insurance company collect the amount it paid from another party?

    a. No, because Massaro's insurance company had been paid for the risk it took.

    b. Yes, it can recover from Lux or Lux's insurance company based on the right of subrogation.

    c. Yes, it can recover from Lux's insurance company, if insured, based on the right of contribution.

    d. Yes, it can recover from Lux or Lux's insurance company, if insured, based on the right of contribution.

5. On February 1, Papco Corp. entered into a contract to purchase an office building from Merit Company for $500,000 with closing scheduled for March 20. On February 2, Papco obtained a $400,000 standard fire insurance policy from Abex Insurance Company. On March 15, the office building sustained a $90,000 fire loss. On March 15, which of the following is correct?

  I. Papco has an insurable interest in the building.

  II. Merit has an insurable interest in the building.

    a. I only.

    b. II only.

    c. Both I and II.

    d. Neither I nor II.

6. Clark Corp. owns a warehouse purchased for $150,000 in 1995. The current market value is $200,000. Clark has the warehouse insured for fire loss with Fair Insurance Corp. and Zone Insurance Co. Fair's policy is for $150,000 and Zone's policy is for $75,000. Both policies contain the standard 80% coinsurance clause. If a fire totally destroyed the warehouse, what total dollar amount would Clark receive from Fair and Zone?

    a. $225,000

    b. $200,000

    c. $160,000

    d. $150,000

Items 7 and 8 are based on the following:

In 1997, Pod bought a building for $220,000. At that time, Pod purchased a $150,000 fire insurance policy with Owners Insurance Co. and a $50,000 fire insurance policy with Group Insurance Corp. Each policy contained a standard 80% coinsurance clause. In 2001, when the building had a fair market value of $250,000, it was damaged in a fire.

7. How much would Pod recover from Owners if the fire caused $180,000 in damage?

    a. $ 90,000

    b. $120,000

    c. $135,000

    d. $150,000

8. How much would Pod recover from Owners and Group if the fire totally destroyed the building?

    a. $160,000

    b. $200,000

    c. $220,000

    d. $250,000

SIMULATION PROBLEMS

Simulation Problem 1   (10 to 15 minutes)

Situation				
	Anderson vs. Harvest	Anderson vs. Beach	Anderson vs. Edge	Foreclosure Proceeds

On June 1, 2002, Anderson bought a one-family house from Beach for $240,000. At the time of the purchase, the house had a market value of $200,000 and the land was valued at $40,000. Anderson assumed the recorded $150,000 mortgage Beach owed Long Bank, gave a $70,000 mortgage to Rogers Loan Co., and paid $20,000 cash. Rogers did not record its mortgage. Rogers did not know about the Long mortgage.

Beach gave Anderson a quitclaim deed that failed to mention a recorded easement on the property held by Dalton, the owner of the adjacent piece of property. Anderson purchased a title insurance policy from Edge Title Insurance Co. Edge's policy neither disclosed nor excepted Dalton's easement.

On August 1, 2003, Anderson borrowed $30,000 from Forrest Finance to have a swimming pool dug. Anderson gave Forrest a $30,000 mortgage on the property. Forrest, knowing about the Long mortgage but not the Rogers mortgage, recorded its mortgage on August 10, 2003. After the digging began, Dalton sued to stop the work claiming violation of the easement. The court decided in Dalton's favor.

At the time of the purchase, Anderson had taken out two fire insurance policies; a $120,000 face value policy with Harvest Fire Insurance Co., and a $60,000 face value policy with Grant Fire Insurance Corp. Both policies contained a standard 80% coinsurance clause.

On December 1, 2003, a fire caused $180,000 damage to the house. At that time, the house had a market value of $250,000. Harvest and Grant refused to honor the policies, claiming that the house was underinsured.

Anderson made no mortgage payments after the fire and on April 4, 2004, after the house had been rebuilt, the mortgages were foreclosed. The balances due for principal and accrued interest were as follows: Long, $140,000; Rogers, $65,000; and Forrest, $28,000. At a foreclosure sale, the house and land were sold. After payment of all expenses, $200,000 of the proceeds remained for distribution. As a result of the above events, the following actions took place:

- Anderson sued Harvest and Grant for the face values of the fire insurance policies.
- Anderson sued Beach for failing to mention Dalton's easement in the quitclaim deed.
- Anderson sued Edge for failing to disclose Dalton's easement.
- Long, Rogers, and Forrest all demanded full payment of their mortgages from the proceeds of the foreclosure sale.

The preceding took place in a notice-race jurisdiction.

	Anderson vs. Harvest			
Situation		Anderson vs. Beach	Anderson vs. Edge	Foreclosure Proceeds

Items 1 through 3 relate to Anderson's suit against Harvest and Grant. For each item, select from List I the dollar amount Anderson will receive.

List I

A.	$0	G.	$ 96,000
B.	$ 20,000	H.	$108,000
C.	$ 48,000	I.	$120,000
D.	$ 54,000	J.	$144,000
E.	$ 60,000	K.	$162,000
F.	$ 80,000	L.	$180,000

(A) (B) (C) (D) (E) (F) (G) (H) (I) (J) (K) (L)

1. What will be the dollar amount of Anderson's total fire insurance recovery?   ○ ○ ○ ○ ○ ○ ○ ○ ○ ○ ○ ○

2. What dollar amount will be payable by Harvest?   ○ ○ ○ ○ ○ ○ ○ ○ ○ ○ ○ ○

3. What dollar amount will be payable by Grant?   ○ ○ ○ ○ ○ ○ ○ ○ ○ ○ ○ ○

		Anderson vs. Beach		
Situation	Anderson vs. Harvest		Anderson vs. Edge	Foreclosure Proceeds

Items 1 through 3 relate to Anderson's suit against Beach. For each item, determine whether that statement is True or False.

	True	False
1. Anderson will win the suit against Beach.	○	○
2. A quitclaim deed conveys only the grantor's interest in the property.	○	○
3. A warranty deed protects the purchaser against any adverse title claim against the property.	○	○

Situation	Anderson vs. Harvest	Anderson vs. Beach	Anderson vs. Edge	Foreclosure Proceeds

Items 1 through 3 relate to Anderson's suit against Edge. For each item, determine whether that statement is True or False.

	True	False
1. Anderson will win the suit against Edge.	○	○
2. Edge's policy should insure against all title defects of record.	○	○
3. Edge's failure to disclose Dalton's easement voids Anderson's contract with Beach.	○	○

Situation	Anderson vs. Harvest	Anderson vs. Beach	Anderson vs. Edge	Foreclosure Proceeds

Items 1 through 3 relate to the demands Long, Rogers, and Forrest have made to have their mortgages satisfied out of the foreclosure proceeds. For each item, select from List II the dollar amount to be paid.

List II
A. $0
B. $ 28,000
C. $ 32,000
D. $ 65,000
E. $107,000
F. $135,000
G. $140,000

	(A)	(B)	(C)	(D)	(E)	(F)	(G)
1. What dollar amount of the foreclosure proceeds will Long receive?	○	○	○	○	○	○	○
2. What dollar amount of the foreclosure proceeds will Rogers receive?	○	○	○	○	○	○	○
3. What dollar amount of the foreclosure proceeds will Forrest receive?	○	○	○	○	○	○	○

Simulation Problem 2   (10 to 15 minutes)

Situation	
	Analysis

On January 12, 2004, Frank, Inc. contracted in writing to purchase a factory building from Henderson for $250,000 cash. Closing took place on March 15, 2004. Henderson had purchased the building in 1997 for $225,000 and had, at that time, taken out a $180,000 fire insurance policy with Summit Insurance Co.

On January 15, 2004, Frank took out a $140,000 fire insurance policy with Unity Insurance Co. and a $70,000 fire insurance policy with Imperial Insurance, Inc.

On March 16, 2004, a fire caused $150,000 damage to the building. At that time the building had a market value of $250,000. All fire insurance policies contain a standard 80% coinsurance clause. The insurance carriers have refused any payment to Frank or Henderson alleging lack of insurable interest and insufficient coverage. Frank and Henderson have sued to collect on the policies.

Analysis

Situation

Items 1 through 6 relate to the suits by Frank and Henderson. For each item, determine whether the statement is True or False.

	True	*False*
1. Frank had an insurable interest at the time the Unity and Imperial policies were taken out.	○	○
2. Henderson had an insurable interest at the time of the fire.	○	○
3. Assuming Frank had an insurable interest, Frank's coverage would be insufficient under the Unity and Imperial coinsurance clauses.	○	○
4. Assuming Henderson had an insurable interest, Henderson's coverage would be insufficient under the Summit coinsurance clause.	○	○
5. Assuming only Frank had an insurable interest, Frank will recover $100,000 from Unity and $50,000 from Imperial.	○	○
6. Assuming only Henderson had an insurable interest, Henderson will recover $135,000 from Summit.	○	○

MULTIPLE-CHOICE ANSWERS

1.	a	__ __	3.	c	__ __	5.	c	__ __	7.	c	__ __	1st: __/8 = __%
2.	a	__ __	4.	b	__ __	6.	b	__ __	8.	b	__ __	2nd: __/8 = __%

MULTIPLE-CHOICE ANSWER EXPLANATIONS

B.6. Insurable Interest

1. **(a)** In the case of property insurance, the insurable interest must exist when the loss occurs. It need not exist when the policy is issued. Therefore, answer (b) is incorrect. Answers (c) and (d) are incorrect because there are no such requirements that the property be owned in fee simple or by individuals.

2. **(a)** To have an insurable interest in property, there must be both a legal interest and a possibility of pecuniary loss. Although a legal interest may involve ownership or a security interest, general creditors do not have the requisite interest to have an insurable interest. Answer (b) is incorrect because a mortgagee has an insurable interest for the mortgage balance still owed. Answer (c) is incorrect because Brown has an insurable interest in key company personnel whose death could result in pecuniary loss for Brown. Answer (d) is incorrect because Brown has an insurable interest in his partner whose death could cause him great monetary loss.

3. **(c)** An insurable interest in property exists if the insured has both a legal interest in the property and the possibility of incurring a pecuniary loss. The legal interest may be ownership or a security interest. A corporate retailer has an ownership interest in its inventory, and the possibility of incurring a monetary loss. A partner also has an ownership interest in partnership property, with the possibility of incurring a monetary loss.

C. Subrogation

4. **(b)** Once the insurance company pays its insured, Massaro, it steps into Massaro's shoes and obtains the same rights against third parties that Massaro had. Since Lux was at fault in this accident, the insurance company has rights against Lux as well as any insurance company that has insured Lux. Answer (a) is incorrect because the insurance company can nevertheless recover from third parties based on the right of subrogation. Answer (c) is incorrect because the insurance company has the right to collect from Lux as well as an insurer. Answer (d) is incorrect because the relevant concept is the right of subrogation, not contribution.

E. Fire Insurance

5. **(c)** An important element of a property insurance contract is the existence of an insurable interest. The insurable interest requirement is met when an entity has both a legal interest in the property and a possibility of monetary loss if the property is damaged. Since Merit still owns the office building at the time of the fire, they fulfill both these requirements. Papco also has an insurable interest which began on February 1 when they entered into the contract to purchase the building. Papco's legal interest results from their contract to purchase the building. Papco's monetary interest results from their potential loss of future use of the building. Thus, in this situation, both Papco and Merit have an insurable interest.

E.6. Coinsurance Clause

6. **(b)** Although Clark has insurance coverage exceeding the fair value of the warehouse, he may only recover the actual amount of his loss. The coinsurance clause does not apply when the insured property is totally destroyed. Fair Insurance will pay 150/225 of the $200,000 loss, or $133,333, while Zone Insurance will pay 75/225 of the $200,000 loss, or $66,667. Thus, Clark will receive a total of $200,000 from Fair and Zone.

7. **(c)** The recoverable loss is calculated using the coinsurance formula.

$$\text{Actual loss} \times \frac{\text{Amount of insurance}}{\text{Coinsurance \%} \times \text{FMV of property at time of loss}}$$

The amount recoverable from Owners is calculated as follows:

$$\$180,000 \times \frac{\$150,000}{80\% \times \$250,000} = \$135,000$$

8. **(b)** When property is covered by a coinsurance clause, the insured party agrees to maintain insurance equal to a given percentage of the value of the property, usually 80%. If the percentage of coverage is less than the specified percentage and partial destruction of the property occurs, then the insured will be liable for a portion of the loss. However, a coinsurance clause applies only when there has been partial destruction of property. If the insured property is totally destroyed, the coinsurance clause does not apply and the insured party will recover the face value of the insurance policy. Thus, Pod will recover $150,000 from Owners Insurance Co. and $50,000 from Group Insurance Co. for a total of $200,000.

SOLUTIONS TO SIMULATION PROBLEMS

Simulation Problem 1

Situation	Anderson vs. Harvest	Anderson vs. Beach	Anderson vs. Edge	Foreclosure Proceeds

	(A)	(B)	(C)	(D)	(E)	(F)	(G)	(H)	(I)	(J)	(K)	(L)
1. What will be the dollar amount of Anderson's total fire insurance recovery?	○	○	○	○	○	○	○	○	○	○	●	○
2. What dollar amount will be payable by Harvest?	○	○	○	○	○	○	○	●	○	○	○	○
3. What dollar amount will be payable by Grant?	○	○	○	●	○	○	○	○	○	○	○	○

Explanation of solutions

1. **(K)** In order to calculate the dollar amount of Anderson's total fire insurance recovery, use the coinsurance clause formula, adding together the amount of insurance for both Harvest and Grant, as follows:

$$\text{Recovery} = \text{Actual loss} \times \frac{\text{Amount of insurance}}{\text{Coinsurance \%} \times \text{FMV of property at time of loss}}$$

$$\text{Recovery} = \$180,000 \times \frac{\$120,000 + \$60,000}{80\% \times \$250,000}$$

$$\text{Recovery} = \$162,000$$

2. **(H)** In order to calculate the dollar amount that will be payable to Harvest only, use the coinsurance clause formula.

$$\text{Recovery} = \$180,000 \times \frac{\$120,000}{80\% \times \$250,000}$$

$$\text{Recovery} = \$108,000$$

3. **(D)** In order to calculate the dollar amount payable to Grant only, use the same coinsurance clause formula.

$$\$180,000 \times \frac{\$60,000}{80\% \times \$250,000} = \$54,000$$

Situation	Anderson vs. Harvest	Anderson vs. Beach	Anderson vs. Edge	Foreclosure Proceeds

	True	False
1. Anderson will win the suit against Beach.	○	●
2. A quitclaim deed conveys only the grantor's interest in the property.	●	○
3. A warranty deed protects the purchaser against any adverse title claim against the property.	●	○

Explanation of solutions

1. **(F)** Since Beach had given Anderson a quitclaim deed, Anderson loses in the suit against Beach for failing to mention Dalton's easement in the quitclaim deed.

2. **(T)** Unlike a warranty deed, a quitclaim deed conveys only whatever interest in land the grantor has. No warranty concerning title or easements is given.

3. **(T)** A warranty deed contains covenants that generally protect the grantee against any adverse title claim against the property.

Situation	Anderson vs. Harvest	Anderson vs. Beach	Anderson vs. Edge	Foreclosure Proceeds

	True	*False*
1. Anderson will win the suit against Edge.	●	○
2. Edge's policy should insure against all title defects of record.	●	○
3. Edge's failure to disclose Dalton's easement voids Anderson's contract with Beach.	○	●

Explanation of solutions

1. **(T)** This statement is true because Edge failed to mention a recorded easement on the property. Note that when Edge failed to disclose the recorded easement, this allows Anderson to recover from Edge but does not void the contract between Anderson and the seller of the property.

2. **(T)** Standard title insurance policies generally insure against all title defects of record. This would be true of the title insurance policy that Anderson purchased from Edge.

3. **(F)** Since Edge failed to disclose the recorded easement, this allows Anderson to recover from Edge. However, it does not void the contract between Anderson and Beach.

Situation	Anderson vs. Harvest	Anderson vs. Beach	Anderson vs. Edge	Foreclosure Proceeds

	(A)	(B)	(C)	(D)	(E)	(F)	(G)
1. What dollar amount of the foreclosure proceeds will Long receive?	○	○	○	○	○	○	●
2. What dollar amount of the foreclosure proceeds will Rogers receive?	○	○	●	○	○	○	○
3. What dollar amount of the foreclosure proceeds will Forrest receive?	○	●	○	○	○	○	○

Explanation of solutions

1. **(G)** Under a notice-race statute, the subsequent good-faith mortgagee wins over a previous mortgagee only if s/he also records first. In this fact pattern, Long has the first priority because its mortgage was recorded before mortgages were given to Forrest or Rogers. Since $200,000 remained to be distributed, Long gets all of its $140,000.

2. **(C)** Forrest has the second priority because although its mortgage was granted after Rogers, Rogers did not record its mortgage and Forrest was unaware of it when its mortgage was given. Therefore, Rogers has the third priority. After Long received his $140,000, there is $60,000 left. Forrest has second priority and will receive his full $28,000. Since there is not enough left to pay Rodgers the full $65,000, Rogers only gets the balance remaining of $32,000.

3. **(B)** Forrest has the second priority because although its mortgage was granted after Rogers, Rogers did not record its mortgage and Forrest was unaware of it when its mortgage was given. Therefore, Rogers has the third priority. After Long received his $140,000, there is $60,000 left. Forrest has second priority and will receive his full $28,000.

Simulation Problem 2

Situation	Analysis

	True	*False*
1. Frank had an insurable interest at the time the Unity and Imperial policies were taken out.	●	○
2. Henderson had an insurable interest at the time of the fire.	○	●
3. Assuming Frank had an insurable interest, Frank's coverage would be insufficient under the Unity and Imperial coinsurance clauses.	○	●
4. Assuming Henderson had an insurable interest, Henderson's coverage would be insufficient under the Summit coinsurance clause.	●	○
5. Assuming only Frank had an insurable interest, Frank will recover $100,000 from Unity and $50,000 from Imperial.	●	○
6. Assuming only Henderson had an insurable interest, Henderson will recover $135,000 from Summit.	●	○

    b. An individual who elects to exclude the housing cost amount can exclude only the lesser of (1) the housing cost amount attributable to employer-provided amounts, or (2) the individual's foreign earned income for the year.

    c. Housing cost amounts not provided by an employer can be deducted for AGI, but deduction is limited to the excess of the taxpayer's foreign earned income over the applicable foreign earned income exclusion.

C. Items to Be Included in Gross Income

Gross income includes all income from any source except those specifically excluded. The more common items of gross income are listed below. Those items requiring a detailed explanation are discussed on the following pages.

1. Compensation for services, including wages, salaries, bonuses, commissions, fees, and tips

    a. Property received as compensation is included in income at FMV on date of receipt.

    b. Bargain purchases by an employee from an employer are included in income at FMV less price paid.

    c. Life insurance premiums paid by employer must be included in an employee's gross income except for group-term life insurance coverage of $50,000 or less.

    d. Employee expenses paid or reimbursed by the employer unless the employee has to account to the employer for these expenses and they would qualify as deductible business expenses for employee.

    e. **Tips** must be included in gross income

        (1) If an individual receives less than $20 in tips while working for one employer during one month, the tips do not have to be reported to the employer, but the tips must be included in the individual's gross income when received.

        (2) If an individual receives $20 or more in tips while working for one employer during one month, the individual must report the total amount of tips to the employer by the tenth day of the following month for purposes of withholding of income tax and social security tax. Then the total amount of tips must be included in the individual's gross income for the month in which reported to the employer.

2. Gross income derived from business or profession

3. Distributive share of partnership or S corporation income

4. Gain from the sale or exchange of real estate, securities, or other property

5. Rents and royalties

6. Dividends

7. **Interest** including

    a. Earnings from savings and loan associations, mutual savings banks, credit unions, etc.

    b. Interest on bank deposits, corporate or US government bonds, and Treasury bills

        (1) Interest from US obligations is included, while interest on state and local obligations is generally excluded.

        (2) If a taxpayer elects to amortize the bond premium on taxable bonds acquired after 1987, any bond premium amortization is treated as an offset against the interest earned on the bond. The amortization of bond premium reduces taxable income (by offsetting interest income) as well as the bond's basis.

    c. **Interest on tax refunds**

    d. Imputed interest from interest-free and low-interest loans

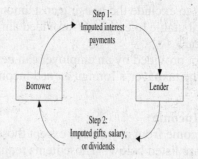

(1) Borrower is treated as making imputed interest payments (subject to the same deduction restrictions as actual interest payments) which the lender reports as interest income.

(2) Lender is treated as making gifts (for personal loans) or paying salary or dividends (for business-related loans) to the borrower.

(3) Rate used to impute interest is tied to average yield on certain federal securities; if the federal rate is greater than the interest rate charged on a loan (e.g., a low-interest loan), impute interest only for the excess.

   (a) For demand loans, the deemed transfers are generally treated as occurring at the end of each year, and will fluctuate with interest rates.

   (b) For term loans, the interest payments are determined at the date of the loan and then allocated over the term of the loan; lender's payments are treated as made on date of loan.

(4) No interest is imputed to either the borrower or the lender for any day on which the aggregate amount of loans between such individuals (and their spouses) does not exceed $10,000.

(5) For any day that the aggregate amount of loans between borrower and lender (and their spouses) does not exceed $100,000, imputed interest is limited to borrower's "net investment income"; no interest is imputed if borrower's net investment income does not exceed $1,000.

> *EXAMPLE: Parents make a $200,000 interest-free demand loan to their unmarried daughter on January 1, 2008. Assume the average federal short-term rate is 6% for 2008. If the loan is outstanding for the entire year, under Step 1, the daughter is treated as making a $12,000 ($200,000 × 6%) interest payment on 12/31/08, which is included as interest income on the parents' 2008 tax return. Under Step 2, the parents are treated as making a $12,000 gift to their daughter on 12/31/08. (Note that the gift will be offset by annual exclusions totaling $24,000 for gift tax purposes as discussed in Module 37.)*

8. **Alimony** and separate maintenance payments

  a. Alimony is included in the recipient's gross income and is deductible toward AGI by the payor. In order for a payment to be considered as alimony, the payment must

    (1) Be made **pursuant to a decree** of divorce or written separation instrument

    (2) Be made in **cash** and received **by or on behalf** of the payee's spouse

    (3) **Terminate upon death** of the recipient

    (4) Not be made to a member of the same household at the time the payments are made

    (5) Not be made to a person with whom the taxpayer is filing a joint return

    (6) Not be characterized in the decree or written instrument as other than alimony

  b. **Alimony recapture** may occur if payments sharply decline in the second or third years. This is accomplished by making the payor report the recaptured alimony from the first and second years as income (and allowing the payee to deduct the same amount) in the third year.

    (1) Recapture for the second year occurs to the extent that the alimony paid in the second year exceeds the third-year alimony by more than $15,000.

    (2) Recapture for the first year occurs to the extent that the alimony paid in the first year exceeds the average alimony paid in the second year (reduced by the recapture for that year) and third year by more than $15,000.

    (3) Recapture will not apply to any year in which payments terminate as a result of the death of either spouse or the remarriage of the payee.

    (4) Recapture does not apply to payments that may fluctuate over three years or more and are not within the control of the payor spouse (e.g., 20% of the net income from a business).

> EXAMPLE: If a payor makes alimony payments of $50,000 in 2006 and no payments in 2007 or 2008, $50,000 – $15,000 = $35,000 will be recaptured in 2008 (assuming none of the exceptions apply).

> EXAMPLE: If a payor makes alimony payments of $50,000 in 2006, $20,000 in 2007, and nothing in 2008, the recapture amount for 2007 is $20,000 – $15,000 = $5,000. The recapture amount for 2006 is $50,000 – ($15,000 + $7,500) = $27,500. The $7,500 is the average payments for 2007 and 2008 after reducing the $20,000 year 2007 payment by the $5,000 of recapture for 2007. The recapture amounts for 2006 and 2007 total $32,500 and are reported in 2008.

c. Any amounts specified as **child support** are not treated as alimony.

   (1) Child support is not gross income to the payee and is not deductible by the payor.

   (2) If the decree or instrument specifies both alimony and child support, but **less is paid than required,** then amounts are first allocated to child support, with any remainder allocated to alimony.

   (3) If a specified amount of alimony is to be reduced upon the happening of some **contingency relating to a child,** then an amount equal to the specified reduction will be treated as child support rather than alimony.

> EXAMPLE: A divorce decree provides that payments of $1,000 per month will be reduced by $400 per month when a child reaches age twenty-one. Here, $400 of each $1,000 monthly payment will be treated as child support.

9. **Social security,** pensions, annuities (other than excluded recovery of capital)

a. Up to 50% of social security retirement benefits may be included in gross income if the taxpayer's provisional income (AGI + tax-exempt income + 50% of the social security benefits) exceeds a threshold that is $32,000 for a joint return, $0 for married taxpayers filing separately, and $25,000 for all other taxpayers. The amount to be included in gross income is the lesser of

   (1) 50% of the social security benefits, or

   (2) 50% of the excess of the taxpayer's provisional income over the base amount.

> EXAMPLE: A single taxpayer with AGI of $20,000 received tax-exempt interest of $2,000 and social security benefits of $7,000. The social security to be included in gross income is the lesser of

> 1/2 ($ 7,000) = $3,500; or
> 1/2 ($25,500 – $25,000) = $250.

b. **Up to 85%** of social security retirement benefits may be included in gross income for taxpayers with provisional income above a higher second threshold that is $44,000 for a joint return, $0 for married taxpayers filing separately, and $34,000 for all other taxpayers. The amount to be included in gross income is the lesser of

   (1) 85% of the taxpayer's social security benefits, or

   (2) The sum of (a) 85% of the excess of the taxpayer's provisional income above the applicable higher threshold amount plus (b) the smaller of (i) the amount of benefits included under a. above, or (ii) $4,500 for single taxpayers or $6,000 for married taxpayers filing jointly.

c. **Rule of thumb:** Social security retirement benefits are fully excluded by low-income taxpayers (i.e., provisional income less than $25,000); 85% of benefits must be included in gross income by high-income taxpayers (i.e., provisional income greater than $60,000).

d. **Lump-sum distributions** from qualified pension, profit-sharing, stock bonus, and Keogh plans (but not IRAs) may be eligible for special tax treatment.

   (1) The portion of the distribution allocable to pre-1974 years is eligible for long-term capital gain treatment.

   (2) If the employee was born before 1936, the employee may elect ten-year averaging.

   (3) Alternatively, the distribution may be rolled over tax-free (within sixty days) to a traditional IRA, but subsequent distributions from the IRA will be treated as ordinary income.

10. **Income in respect of a decedent** is income that would have been income of the decedent before death but was not includible in income under the decedent's method of accounting (e.g., installment payments that are paid to a decedent's estate after his/her death). Such income has the same character as it would have had if the decedent had lived and must be included in gross income by the person who receives it.

11. Employer supplemental unemployment benefits or strike benefits from union funds
12. Fees, including those received by an executor, administrator, director, or for jury duty or precinct election board duty
13. Income from discharge of indebtedness unless specifically excluded (see page 364)
14. **Stock options**

   a. An **incentive stock option** receives favorable tax treatment.

      (1) The option must meet certain technical requirements to qualify.
      (2) No income is recognized by employee when option is granted or exercised.
      (3) If employee holds the stock acquired through exercise of the option at least two years from the date the option was granted, and holds the stock itself at least one year, the

         (a) Employee's realized gain will be long-term capital gain
         (b) Employer receives no deduction

      (4) If the holding period requirements above are not met, the employee has ordinary income to the extent that the FMV at date of exercise exceeds the option price.

         (a) Remainder of gain is short-term or long-term capital gain.
         (b) Employer receives a deduction equal to the amount employee reports as ordinary income.

      (5) An incentive stock option may be treated as a nonqualified stock option if a corporation so elects at the time the option is issued.

   b. A **nonqualified stock option** is included in income when received if option has a determinable FMV.

      (1) If option has no ascertainable FMV when received, then income arises when option is exercised; to the extent of the difference between the FMV when exercised and the option price.
      (2) Amount recognized (at receipt or when exercised) is treated as ordinary income to employee; employer is allowed a deduction equal to amount included in employee's income.

   c. An **employee stock purchase plan** that does not discriminate against rank and file employees

      (1) No income when employee receives or exercises option
      (2) If the employee holds the stock at least two years after the option is granted and at least one year after exercise, then

         (a) Employee has ordinary income to the extent of the lesser of

            1] FMV at time option granted over option price, or
            2] FMV at disposition over option price

         (b) Capital gain to the extent realized gain exceeds ordinary income

      (3) If the stock is not held for the required time, then

         (a) Employee has ordinary income at the time of sale for the difference between FMV when exercised and the option price. This amount also increases basis.
         (b) Capital gain or loss for the difference between selling price and increased basis

15. **Prizes and awards** are generally taxable.

   a. Prizes and awards received for religious, charitable, scientific, educational, artistic, literary, or civic achievement can be excluded only if the recipient

      (1) Was selected without any action on his/her part,
      (2) Is not required to render substantial future services, and
      (3) Designates that the prize or award is to be transferred by the payor to a governmental unit or a tax-exempt charitable, educational, or religious organization
      (4) The prize or award is excluded from the recipient's income, but no charitable deduction is allowed for the transferred amount.

   b. **Employee achievement awards** are excluded from an employee's income if the cost to the employer of the award does not exceed the amount allowable as a deduction (generally from $400 to $1,600 see page 373).

    (1) The award must be for length of service or safety achievement and must be in the form of tangible personal property (cash does not qualify).

    (2) If the cost of the award exceeds the amount allowable as a deduction to the employer, the employee must include in gross income the greater of

        (a) The portion of cost not allowable as a deduction to the employer, or

        (b) The excess of the award's FMV over the amount allowable as a deduction.

16. **Tax benefit rule.** A recovery of an item deducted in an earlier year must be included in gross income to the extent that a tax benefit was derived from the prior deduction of the recovered item.

    a. A tax benefit was derived if the previous deduction reduced the taxpayer's income tax.

    b. A recovery is excluded from gross income to the extent that the previous deduction did not reduce the taxpayer's income tax.

    (1) A deduction would not reduce a taxpayer's income tax if the taxpayer was subject to the alternative minimum tax in the earlier year and the deduction was not allowed in computing AMTI (e.g., state income taxes).

    (2) A recovery of state income taxes, medical expenses, or other items deductible on Schedule A (Form 1040) will be excluded from gross income if an individual did not itemize deductions for the year the item was paid.

> EXAMPLE: Individual X, a single taxpayer, did not itemize deductions but instead used the standard deduction of $5,350 for 2007. In 2008, a refund of $300 of 2007 state income taxes is received. X would exclude the $300 refund from income in 2008.

> EXAMPLE: Individual Y, a single taxpayer, had total itemized deductions of $5,450 for 2007, including $800 of state income taxes. In 2008, a refund of $400 of 2007 state income taxes is received. Y must include $100 ($5,450 − $5,350) of the refund in income for 2008.

17. Embezzled or other illegal income
18. **Gambling winnings**
19. **Unemployment compensation** is fully included in gross income by the recipient.

D. Tax Accounting Methods

    Tax accounting methods often affect the period in which an item of income or deduction is recognized. Note that the classification of an item is not changed, only the time for its inclusion in the tax computation.

1. Cash method or accrual method is commonly used.

    a. **Cash method** recognizes income when first received or constructively received; expenses are deductible when paid.

    (1) **Constructive receipt** means that an item is unqualifiedly available without restriction (e.g., interest on bank deposit is income when credited to account).

    (2) Not all receipts are income (e.g., loan proceeds, return of investment); not all payments are deductible (e.g., loan repayment, expenditures benefiting future years generally must be capitalized and deducted over cost recovery period).

    b. The cash method cannot generally be used if inventories are necessary to clearly reflect income, and cannot generally be used by C corporations, partnerships that have a C corporation as a partner, tax shelters, and certain tax-exempt trusts. However, the following may use the cash method:

    (1) A qualified personal service corporation (e.g., corporation performing services in health, law, engineering, accounting, actuarial science, performing arts, or consulting) if at least 95% of stock is owned by specified shareholders including employees.

    (2) An entity (other than a tax shelter) if for every year it has average annual gross receipts of **$5 million or less** for any prior three-year period and provided it does not have inventories for sale to customers.

    (3) A **small business taxpayer** with average annual gross receipts of **$1 million or less** for any prior three-year period can use the cash method and is excepted from the requirements to account for inventories and use the accrual method for purchases and sales of merchandise.

(4) A **small business taxpayer** is eligible to use the cash method of accounting if, in addition to having average gross receipts of more than $1 million and less than $10 million, the business meets any one of three requirements.

    (a) The principal business activity is **not** retailing, wholesaling, manufacturing, mining, publishing, or sound recording;

    (b) The principal business activity is the provision of services, or custom manufacturing; or

    (c) Regardless of the principal business activity, a taxpayer may use the cash method with respect to any separate business that satisfies (a) or (b) above.

(5) A taxpayer using the accrual method who meets the requirements in (3) or (4) can change to the cash method but must treat merchandise inventory as a material or supply that is not incidental (i.e., only deductible in the year actually consumed or used in the taxpayer's business).

c. **Accrual method** must be used by taxpayers (other than small business taxpayers) for purchases and sales when inventories are required to clearly reflect income.

(1) **Income** is recognized when "all events" have occurred that fix the taxpayer's right to receive the item of income and the amount can be determined with reasonable accuracy.

(2) An **expense** is deductible when "all events" have occurred that establish the fact of the liability and the amount can be determined with reasonable accuracy. The all-events test is not satisfied until **economic performance** has taken place.

    (a) For property or services to be provided **to the taxpayer,** economic performance occurs when the property or services are actually provided by the other party.

    (b) For property or services to be provided **by the taxpayer,** economic performance occurs when the property or services are physically provided by the taxpayer.

(3) An exception to the economic performance rule treats certain **recurring items of expense** as incurred in advance of economic performance provided

    (a) The all-events test, without regard to economic performance, is satisfied during the tax year;

    (b) Economic performance occurs within a reasonable period (but in no event more than 8.5 months after the close of the tax year);

    (c) The item is recurring in nature and the taxpayer consistently treats items of the same type as incurred in the tax year in which the all-events test is met; and

    (d) Either the amount is not material or the accrual of the item in the year the all-events test is met results in a better matching against the income to which it relates.

2. **Special rules** regarding methods of accounting

a. **Rents and royalties received in advance** are included in gross income in the year received under both the cash and accrual methods.

(1) A **security deposit** is included in income when not returned to tenant.

(2) An amount called a "security deposit" that may be used as final payment of rent is considered to be advance rent and included in income when received.

> EXAMPLE: *In 2008, a landlord signed a five-year lease. During 2008, the landlord received $5,000 for that year's rent, and $5,000 as advance rent for the last year (2012) of the lease. All $10,000 will be included in income for 2008.*

b. Dividends are included in gross income in the year received under both the cash and accrual methods.

c. No advance deduction is generally allowed for accrual method taxpayers for estimated or contingent expenses; the obligation must be "fixed and determinable."

3. The **installment method** applies to gains (not losses) from the disposition of property where at least one payment is to be received after the year of sale. The installment method does not change the character of the gain to be reported (e.g., ordinary, capital, etc.), and is required unless the taxpayer makes a negative election to report the full amount of gain in year of sale.

2. Contributions to a **Roth IRA** are not deductible, but qualified distributions of earnings are tax-free. Individuals making contributions to a Roth IRA can still make contributions to a deductible or nondeductible IRA, but maximum contributions to all IRAs is limited to $5,000 for 2008. ($6,000 if the individual is at least age 50).

   a. Eligibility for a Roth IRA is phased out for single taxpayers with AGI between $101,000 and $116,000, and for joint filers with AGI between $159,000 and $169,000.

   b. Unlike traditional IRAs contributions may be made to Roth IRAs even after the individual reaches age 70 1/2.

   c. Qualified distributions from a Roth IRA are not included in gross income and are not subject to the 10% early withdrawal penalty. A qualified distribution is a distribution that is made after the five-year period beginning with the first tax year for which a contribution was made and the distribution is made (1) after the individual reaches age 59 1/2, (2) to a beneficiary (or the individual's estate) after the individual's death, (3) after the individual becomes disabled, or (4) for the first-time homebuyer expenses of the individual, individual's spouse, children, grandchildren, or ancestors ($10,000 lifetime cap).

   d. Nonqualified distributions are includible in income to the extent attributable to earnings and generally subject to the 10% early withdrawal penalty. Distributions are deemed to be made from contributed amounts first.

   e. Taxpayers with AGI of less than $100,000 can convert assets in traditional IRAs to a Roth IRA at any time without paying the 10% tax on early withdrawals, although the deemed distributions of IRA assets will be included in income.

3. Contributions can be made to an **education IRA** (Coverdell Education Savings Account) of up to $2,000 per beneficiary (until the beneficiary reaches age eighteen), to pay the costs of a beneficiary's higher education.

   a. Contributions are not deductible, but withdrawals to pay the cost of a beneficiary's education expenses are tax-free.

   b. Any earnings of an education IRA that are distributed but are not used to pay a beneficiary's education expenses must be included in the distributee's gross income and are subject to a 10% penalty tax.

   c. Under a special rollover provision, the amount left in an education IRA before the beneficiary reaches age 30 can be rolled over to another family member's education IRA without triggering income taxes or penalties.

   d. Eligibility is phased out for single taxpayers with modified AGI between $95,000 and $110,000, and for married taxpayers with modified AGI between $190,000 and $220,000.

   e. Expenses that may be paid tax-free from an education IRA include expenses for enrollment (including room and board, uniforms, transportation, computers, and Internet access services) in elementary or secondary schools, whether public, private, or religious. Furthermore, taxpayers may take advantage of the exclusion for distributions from education IRAs, the Hope and lifetime learning credits, and the qualified tuition program in the same year.

4. **Self-employed** individuals (sole proprietors and partners) may contribute to a qualified retirement plan (called H.R.-10 or Keogh Plan).

   a. The maximum contribution and deduction to a defined-contribution self-employed retirement plan is the lesser of

      (1) $46,000, or 100% of earned income for 2008
      (2) The definition of "earned income" includes the retirement plan and self-employment tax deductions (i.e., earnings from self-employment must be reduced by the retirement plan contribution and the self-employment tax deduction for purposes of determining the maximum deduction).

   b. A taxpayer may elect to treat contributions made up until the due date of the tax return (including extensions) as made for the taxable year for which the tax return is being filed, if the retirement plan was established by the end of that year.

5. An employer's contributions to an employee's **simplified employee pension (SEP) plan** are deductible by the employer, limited to the lesser of 25% of compensation (up to a compensation ceiling of $230,000 for 2008) or $46,000.

   a. The employer's SEP contributions are excluded from the employee's gross income.
   b. In addition, the employee may make deductible IRA contributions subject to the IRA phaseout rules (discussed in 2.c. above).

6. A **savings incentive match plan for employees (SIMPLE)** is not subject to the nondiscrimination rules (including top-heavy provisions) and certain other complex requirements generally applicable to qualified plans, and may be structured as an IRA or as a 401(k) plan.

   a. Limited to employers with 100 or fewer employees who received at least $5,000 in compensation from the employer in the preceding year.

      (1) Plan allows employees to make elective contributions of up to $10,500 of their pretax salaries per year (expressed as a percentage of compensation, not a fixed dollar amount) and requires employers to match a portion of the contributions.
      (2) Eligible employees are those who earned at least $5,000 in any two prior years and who may be expected to earn at least $5,000 in the current year.

   b. Employers must satisfy one of two contribution formulas.

      (1) Matching contribution formula generally requires an employer to match the employee contribution dollar-for-dollar up to 3% of the employee's compensation for the year.
      (2) Alternatively, an employer can make a nonelective contribution of 2% of compensation for each eligible employee who has at least $5,000 of compensation from the employer during the year.

   c. Contributions to the plan are immediately vested, but a 25% penalty applies to employee withdrawals made within two years of the date the employee began participating in the plan.

G. Deduction for Interest on Education Loans

1. An individual is allowed to deduct **up to $2,500** for interest on qualified education loans. However, the deduction is not available if the individual is claimed as a dependent on another taxpayer's return.
2. A *qualified education loan* is any debt incurred to pay the qualified higher education expenses of the taxpayer, taxpayer's spouse, or dependents (as of the time the debt was incurred), and the education expenses must relate to a period when the student was enrolled on at least a half-time basis. However, any debt owed to a related party is not a qualified educational loan (e.g., education debt owed to family member).
3. Qualified education expenses include such costs as tuition, fees, room, board, and related expenses.
4. The deduction is phased out for single taxpayers with modified AGI between $55,000 and $70,000, and for married taxpayers with modified AGI between $115,000 and $145,000.

H. Deduction for Qualified Tuition and Related Expenses

1. For 2007, individuals are allowed to deduct qualified higher education expenses in arriving at AGI. The deduction is limited to $4,000 for individuals with AGI at or below $65,000 ($130,000 for joint filers). The deduction is limited to $2,000 for individuals with AGI above $65,000, but equal to or less than $80,000 ($130,000 and $160,000 respectively for joint filers).
2. Taxpayers with AGI above these levels, married individuals filing separately, and an individual who can be claimed as a dependent are not entitled to any deduction.
3. *Qualified tuition and related expenses* means tuition and fees required for enrollment of the taxpayer, taxpayer's spouse, or dependent at a postsecondary educational institution. Such term does not include expenses with respect to any course involving sports, games, or hobbies, or any noncredit course, unless such course is part of the individual's degree program. Also excluded are nonacademic fees such as student activity fees, athletic fees, and insurance expenses.
4. The deduction is allowed for expenses paid during the tax year, in connection with enrollment during the year or in connection with an academic term beginning during the year or the first three months of the following year.

5. If a taxpayer takes a Hope credit or lifetime learning credit with respect to a student, the qualified higher education expenses of that student for the year are not deductible under this provision.

I. Penalties for Premature Withdrawals from Time Deposits

1. Full amount of interest is included in gross income.
2. Forfeited interest is then subtracted "above the line."

J. Alimony or Separate Maintenance Payments Are Deducted "Above the Line."

K. Jury Duty Pay Remitted to Employer

1. An employee is allowed to deduct the amount of jury duty pay that was surrendered to an employer in return for the employer's payment of compensation during the employee's jury service period.
2. Both regular compensation and jury duty pay must be included in gross income.

L. Costs Involving Discrimination Suits

1. Attorneys' fees and court costs incurred by, or on behalf of, an individual in connection with any action involving a claim for unlawful discrimination (e.g., age, sex, or race discrimination) are allowable as a deduction from gross income in arriving at AGI.
2. The amount of deduction is limited to the amount of judgment or settlement included in the individual's gross income for the tax year.

M. Expenses of Elementary and Secondary Teachers

1. For 2007, eligible educators are allowed an above-the-line deduction for up to $250 for unreimbursed expenses for books, supplies, computer equipment (including related software and services) and supplementary materials used in the classroom.
2. An eligible educator is a kindergarten through grade 12 teacher, instructor, counselor, principal, or aide working in a school for at least 900 hours during the school year.

III. ITEMIZED DEDUCTIONS FROM ADJUSTED GROSS INCOME

Itemized deductions reduce adjusted gross income, and are sometimes referred to as "below the line" deductions because they are deducted from adjusted gross income. Itemized deductions (or a standard deduction) along with personal exemptions are subtracted from adjusted gross income to arrive at taxable income.

A taxpayer will itemize deductions only if the taxpayer's total itemized deductions exceed the applicable standard deduction that is available to nonitemizers. The amount of the standard deduction is based on the filing status of the taxpayer, whether the taxpayer is a dependent, and is indexed for inflation. Additional standard deductions are allowed for age and blindness.

		Basic standard deduction
Filing status		*2008*
a)	Married, filing jointly; or surviving spouse	$10,900
b)	Married, filing separately	5,450
c)	Head of household	8,000
d)	Single	5,450

A dependent's basic standard deduction is limited to the lesser of (1) the basic standard deduction for single taxpayers of $5,450 for 2008; or (2) the greater of (a) $900, or (b) the dependent's earned income plus $300.

An unmarried individual who is not a surviving spouse, and is either age sixty-five or older or blind, receives an additional standard deduction of $1,350 for 2008. The standard deduction is increased by $2,700 for 2008 if the individual is both elderly and blind. The increase is $1,050 for 2008 for each married individual who is age sixty-five or older or blind. The increase for a married individual who is both elderly and blind is $2,100 for 2008. An elderly or blind individual who may be claimed as a dependent on another taxpayer's return may claim the basic standard deduction plus the additional standard deduction(s). For example, for 2008 an unmarried dependent, age sixty-five, with only unearned income would have a standard deduction of $900 + $1,350 = $2,250.

The major itemized deductions are outlined below. It should be remembered that some may be deducted in arriving at AGI if they are incurred by a self-employed taxpayer in a trade or business, or for the production of rents or royalties.

A. Medical and Dental Expenses

1. Medical and dental expenses paid by taxpayer for himself, spouse, or dependent (relationship, support, and citizenship tests are met) are deductible in year of payment, if not reimbursed by insurance, employer, etc. A child of divorced or separated parents is treated as a dependent of both parents for this purpose.

2. Computation—unreimbursed medical expenses (including *prescribed* medicine and insulin, and medical insurance premiums) are deducted to the extent **in excess of 7.5%** of adjusted gross income.

   > EXAMPLE: *Ralph and Alice Jones, who have Adjusted Gross Income of $20,000, paid the following medical expenses: $900 for hospital and doctor bills (above reimbursement), $250 for prescription medicine, and $600 for medical insurance. The Joneses would compute their medical expense deduction as follows:*
   >
   > | | |
   > |---|---:|
   > | Prescribed medicine | $ 250 |
   > | Hospital, doctors | 900 |
   > | Medical insurance | 600 |
   > | | $1,750 |
   > | Less 7.5% of AGI | −1,500 |
   > | Medical expense deduction | $ 250 |

3. Deductible medical care does not include **cosmetic surgery** or other procedures, unless the surgery or procedure is necessary to ameliorate a deformity arising from, or directly related to, a congenital abnormality, a personal injury resulting from an accident or trauma, or a disfiguring disease. In addition, to be deductible, the procedure must promote proper body function or prevent or treat illness or disease (e.g., LASIK and radial keratotomy are deductible; teeth whitening is not deductible).

   a. Cosmetic surgery is defined as any procedure directed at improving the patient's appearance and does not meaningfully promote the proper function of the body or prevent or treat illness or disease.

   b. If expenses for cosmetic surgery are not deductible under this provision, then amounts paid for insurance coverage for such expenses are not deductible, and an employer's reimbursement of such expenses under a health plan is not excludable from the employee's gross income.

4. Expenses incurred by physically handicapped individuals for **removal of structural barriers** in their residences to accommodate their handicapped condition are fully deductible as medical expenses. Qualifying expenses include constructing entrance or exit ramps, widening doorways and hallways, the installation of railings and support bars, and other modifications.

5. **Capital expenditures** for special equipment (other than in 4. above) installed for medical reasons in a home or automobile are deductible as medical expenses to the extent the expenditures exceed the increase in value of the property.

6. **Deductible** medical expenses include

   a. Fees for doctors, surgeons, dentists, osteopaths, ophthalmologists, optometrists, chiropractors, chiropodists, podiatrists, psychiatrists, psychologists, and Christian Science practitioners

   b. Fees for hospital services, therapy, nursing services (including nurses' meals you pay for), ambulance hire, and laboratory, surgical, obstetrical, diagnostic, dental, and X-ray services

   c. Meals and lodging provided by a hospital during medical treatment, and meals and lodging provided by a center during treatment for alcoholism or drug addiction

   d. Amounts paid for lodging (but not meals) while away from home primarily for medical care provided by a physician in a licensed hospital or equivalent medical care facility. Limit is $50 per night for each individual.

   e. Medical and hospital insurance premiums

   f. *Prescribed* medicines and insulin

   g. Transportation for needed medical care. Actual auto expenses can be deducted, or taxpayer can use standard rate of 19¢ per mile beginning January 1, 2008, through June 30; 27¢ per mile beginning July 1 and ending December 31, 2008 (plus parking and tolls).

   h. Special items and equipment, including false teeth, artificial limbs, eyeglasses, hearing aids, crutches, guide dogs, motorized wheelchairs, hand controls on a car, and special telephones for deaf

   i. The cost of stop-smoking programs and the cost of participation in a weight-loss program as a treatment for the disease of obesity qualify. However, the costs of reduced-calorie diet foods are not deductible if these foods merely substitute for food the individual would normally consume.

7. Items **not deductible** as medical expenses include

    a. Bottled water, maternity clothes, and diaper service
    b. Household help, and care of a normal and healthy baby by a nurse (but a portion may qualify for child or dependent care tax credit)
    c. Toothpaste, toiletries, cosmetics, etc.
    d. Weight-loss expenses that are not for the treatment of obesity or other disease
    e. Trip, social activities, or health club dues for general improvement of health
    f. Nonprescribed medicines and drugs (e.g., over-the-counter medicines)
    g. Illegal operation or treatment
    h. Funeral and burial expenses

8. Reimbursement of expenses deducted in an earlier year may have to be included in gross income in the period received under the tax benefit rule.

9. Reimbursement in excess of expenses is includible in income to the extent the excess reimbursement was paid by policies provided by employer.

B. Taxes

1. The following taxes are **deductible as a tax** in year paid if they are imposed on the taxpayer:

    a. **Income tax** (state, local, or foreign)

        (1) The deduction for state and local taxes includes amounts withheld from salary, estimated payments made during the year, and payments made during the year on a tax for a prior year.
        (2) A refund of a prior year's taxes is not offset against the current year's deduction, but is generally included in income under the tax benefit rule.

    b. For tax years beginning after December 31, 2003, and before January 1, 2008, an individual may elect to deduct state and local general sales taxes in lieu of state and local income taxes. The amount that can be deducted is either the total of actual general sales taxes paid as substantiated by receipts, or an amount from IRS-provided tables, plus the amount of general sales taxes paid with regard to the purchase of a motor vehicle, boat, or other items prescribed in Pub. 600.

        (1) The sales taxes imposed on food, clothing, medical supplies, and motor vehicles may be deducted even if imposed at a rate lower than the general rate.
        (2) In the case of sales taxes on motor vehicles that are higher than the general rate, only an amount up to the general rate is allowed. The sales tax on boats is deductible only if imposed at the general sales tax rate.

    c. **Real property taxes** (state, local, or foreign) are deductible by the person on whom the taxes are imposed.

        (1) When real property is sold, the deduction is apportioned between buyer and seller on a daily basis within the real property tax year, even if parties do not apportion the taxes at the closing.
        (2) **Assessments** for improvements (e.g., special assessments for streets, sewers, sidewalks, curbing) are generally not deductible, but instead must be added to the basis of the property. However, the portion of an assessment that is attributable to repairs or maintenance, or to meeting interest charges on the improvements, is deductible as taxes.

    d. **Personal property taxes** (state or local, not foreign) are deductible if ad valorem (i.e., assessed in relation to the value of property). A motor vehicle tax based on horsepower, weight, or model year is not deductible.

2. The following taxes are **deductible only as an expense** incurred in a trade or business or in the production of income (above the line):

    a. Social security and other employment taxes paid by employer
    b. Federal excise taxes on automobiles, tires, telephone service, and air transportation
    c. Customs duties and gasoline taxes
    d. State and local taxes not deductible as such (stamp or cigarette taxes) or charges of a primarily regulatory nature (licenses, etc.)

3. The following taxes are **not deductible**:

a. Federal income taxes
b. Federal, state, or local estate or gift taxes
c. Social security and other federal employment taxes paid by employee (including self-employment taxes)
d. Social security and other employment taxes paid by an employer on the wages of an employee who only performed domestic services (i.e., maid, etc.)

C. Interest Expense

1. The classification of interest expense is generally determined by tracing the use of the borrowed funds. Interest expense is not deductible if loan proceeds were used to produce tax-exempt income (e.g., purchase municipal bonds).
2. No deduction is allowed for prepaid interest; it must be capitalized and deducted in the future period(s) to which it relates. However, an individual may elect to deduct *mortgage points* when paid if the points represent interest and mortgage proceeds were used to buy, build, or substantially improve a principal residence. Otherwise points must be capitalized and deducted over the term of the mortgage.
3. **Personal interest.** No deduction is allowed for personal interest.

    a. Personal interest **includes** interest paid or incurred to purchase an asset for personal use, credit card interest for personal purchases, interest incurred as an employee, and interest on income tax underpayments.
    b. Personal interest **excludes** qualified residence interest, investment interest, interest allocable to a trade or business (other than as an employee), interest incurred in a passive activity, and interest on deferred estate taxes.

       > EXAMPLE: X, a **self-employed** consultant, finances a new automobile used 80% for business and 20% for personal use. X would treat 80% of the interest as deductible business interest expense (toward AGI), and 20% as nondeductible personal interest.

       > EXAMPLE: Y, an **employee**, finances a new automobile used 80% for use in her employer's business and 20% for personal use. All of the interest expense on the auto loan would be considered nondeductible personal interest.

4. **Qualified residence interest.** The disallowance of personal interest above does not apply to interest paid or accrued on acquisition indebtedness or home equity indebtedness secured by a security interest perfected under local law on the taxpayer's principal residence or a second residence owned by the taxpayer.

    a. **Acquisition indebtedness.** Interest is deductible on up to $1,000,000 ($500,000 if married filing separately) of loans secured by the residence if such loans were used to acquire, construct, or substantially improve the home.

       (1) Acquisition indebtedness is reduced as principal payments are made and cannot be restored or increased by refinancing the home.
       (2) If the home is refinanced, the amount qualifying as acquisition indebtedness is limited to the amount of acquisition debt existing at the time of refinancing plus any amount of the new loan that is used to substantially improve the home.

    b. **Home equity indebtedness.** Interest is deductible on up to $100,000 ($50,000 if married filing separately) of loans secured by the residence (other than acquisition indebtedness) regardless of how the loan proceeds are used (e.g., automobile, education expenses, medical expenses, etc.). The amount of home equity indebtedness cannot exceed the FMV of the home as reduced by any acquisition indebtedness.

       > EXAMPLE: Allan purchased a home for $380,000, borrowing $250,000 of the purchase price that was secured by a fifteen-year mortgage. In 2008, when the home was worth $400,000 and the balance of the first mortgage was $230,000, Allan obtained a second mortgage on the home in the amount of $120,000, using the proceeds to purchase a car and to pay off personal loans. Allan may deduct the interest on the balance of the first mortgage acquisition indebtedness of $230,000. However, Allan can deduct interest on only $100,000 of the second mortgage as qualified residence interest because it is considered home equity indebtedness (i.e., the loan proceeds were not used to acquire, construct, or substantially improve a home). The interest on the remaining $20,000 of the second mortgage is nondeductible personal interest.

    c. The term "residence" includes houses, condominiums, cooperative housing units, and any other property that the taxpayer uses as a dwelling unit (e.g., mobile home, motor home, boat, etc.).

    b. For personal property placed in service after 1986, the difference between regular tax depreciation and depreciation using the 150% declining balance method (switching to straight-line when necessary to maximize the deduction).

    c. Excess of stock's FMV over amount paid upon exercise of incentive stock options.

    d. The medical expense deduction is computed using a 10% floor (instead of the 7.5% floor used for regular tax).

    e. No deduction is allowed for home mortgage interest if the loan proceeds were not used to buy, build, or improve the home.

    f. No deduction is allowed for personal, state, and local taxes, and for miscellaneous itemized deductions subject to the 2% floor for regular tax purposes.

    g. No deduction is allowed for personal exemptions and the standard deduction.

    h. For long-term contracts, the excess of income under the percentage-of-completion method over the amount reported using the completed-contract method.

    i. The installment method cannot be used for sales of dealer property.

6. **Preference items.** The following are examples of preference items added to taxable income (as adjusted above) in computing AMTI:

    a. Tax-exempt interest on certain private activity bonds reduced by related interest expense that is disallowed for regular tax purposes

    b. Accelerated depreciation on real property and leased personal property placed in service before 1987—excess of accelerated depreciation over straight-line

    c. The excess of percentage of depletion over the property's adjusted basis

    d. 7% of the amount of excluded gain from Sec. 1202 small business stock

7. **Tax credits.** Generally, an individual's tax credits are allowed to reduce regular tax liability, but only to the extent that regular income tax liability exceeds tentative minimum tax liability.

    a. For tax years beginning in 2007, the nonrefundable personal credits (e.g., dependent care credit, credit for the elderly and disabled, the adoption credit, the nonrefundable portion of the child tax credit, the Hope and lifetime learning credits, credit for qualified retirement savings contributions) are allowed to offset both regular tax liability and the alternative minimum tax.

    b. An individual's AMT is reduced by the alternative minimum tax foreign tax credit, the alcohol fuels credit, and the credit for electricity or refined coal.

8. **Minimum tax credit.** The amount of AMT paid (net of exclusion preferences) is allowed as a credit against regular tax liability in future years.

    a. The amount of the AMT credit to be carried forward is the excess of the AMT paid over the AMT that would be paid if AMTI included only exclusion preferences (e.g., disallowed itemized deductions and the preferences for excess percentage of depletion, tax-exempt interest, and charitable contributions).

    b. The credit can be carried forward indefinitely, but not carried back.

    c. The AMT credit can only be used to reduce regular tax liability, **not** future AMT liability.

E. Other Taxes

1. **Social security** (FICA) tax is imposed on both employers and employees (withheld from wages). The FICA tax has two components: old age, survivor, and disability insurance (OASDI) and medicare hospital insurance (HI). The OASDI rate is 6.2% and the HI rate is 1.45%, resulting in a combined rate of 7.65%. For 2008, the OASDI portion (6.2%) is capped at $102,000, while the HI portion (1.45%) applies to all wages.

2. **Federal unemployment** (FUTA) tax is imposed only on employers at a rate of 6.2% of the first $7,000 of wages paid to each employee. A credit of up to 5.4% is available for unemployment taxes paid to a state, leaving a net federal tax of 0.8%.

3. **Self-employment** tax is imposed on individuals who work for themselves (e.g., sole proprietor, independent contractor, partner). The combined self-employment tax rate is 15.3%, of which the medicare portion is 2.9%.

    a. The full self-employment tax (15.3%) is capped at $102,000 for 2008, while the medicare portion (2.9%) applies to all self-employment earnings.

b. Income from self-employment generally includes all items of business income less business deductions. Does not include personal interest, dividends, rents, capital gains and losses, and gains and losses on the disposition of business property.

c. Wages subject to FICA tax are deducted from $102,000 for 2008 in determining the amount of income subject to self-employment tax.

d. No tax if net earnings from self-employment are less than $400.

e. A deduction equal to one-half of the self-employment tax rate (7.65%) multiplied by the taxpayer's self-employment income (without regard to this deduction) is allowed in computing the taxpayer's net earnings from self-employment.

(1) This deemed deduction is allowed in place of deducting one-half of the amount of self-employment tax that is actually paid.

(2) The purpose of this deduction is to allow the amount on which the self-employment tax is based to be adjusted downward to reflect the fact that employees do not pay FICA tax on the amount of the FICA tax that is paid by their employers.

> EXAMPLE: A taxpayer has self-employment income of $50,000 before the deemed deduction for 2008. The deemed deduction is $50,000 × 7.65% = $3,825, resulting in net earnings from self-employment of $50,000 – $3,825 = $46,175 and a self-employment tax of $46,175 × 15.30% = $7,065. In computing AGI, the taxpayer is allowed to deduct one-half of the self-employment tax actually paid, $7,065 × 50% = $3,533.

> EXAMPLE: A taxpayer has self-employment income of $120,000 before the deemed deduction for 2008. The deemed deduction is $120,000 × 7.65% = $9,180, resulting in net earnings from self-employment of $120,000 – $9,180 = $110,820. The taxpayer's self-employment tax will be ($102,000 × 15.3%) + [($110,820 – $102,000) × 2.9%] = $15,862. In computing AGI, the taxpayer is allowed to deduct one-half of the self-employment tax actually paid, $15,862 × 50% = $7,931.

VI. TAX CREDITS/ESTIMATED TAX PAYMENTS

Tax credits directly reduce tax liability. The tax liability less tax credits equals taxes payable. Taxes that have already been withheld on wages and estimated tax payments are credited against tax liability without limitation, even if the result is a refund due to the taxpayer.

A. General Business Credit

1. It is comprised of numerous credits including the (1) investment credit (energy, rehabilitation, and reforestation), (2) work opportunity credit, (3) welfare-to-work credit, (4) alcohol fuels credit, (5) research credit, (6) low-income housing credit, (7) enhanced oil recovery credit, (8) disabled access credit, (9) renewable resources electricity production credit, (10) empowerment zone employment credit, (11) Indian employment credit, (12) employer social security credit, (13) orphan drug credit, (14) new markets tax credit, (15) small-employer pension plan startup cost credit, (16) the employer-provided child care credit, and (17) the new energy-efficient home credit.

2. The general business credit is allowed to the extent of "net income tax" less the greater of (1) the tentative minimum tax or (2) 25% of "net regular tax liability" above $25,000.

a. "Net income tax" means the amount of the regular income tax plus the alternative minimum tax, and minus nonrefundable tax credits (except the alternative minimum tax credit).

b. "Net regular tax liability" is the taxpayer's regular tax liability reduced by nonrefundable tax credits (except the alternative minimum tax credit).

> EXAMPLE: An individual (not subject to the alternative minimum tax) has a net income tax of $65,000. The individual's general business credit cannot exceed $65,000 – [25% × ($65,000 – $25,000)] = $55,000.

3. A general business credit in excess of the limitation amount is carried back one year and forward twenty years.

B. Business Energy Credit

1. The business energy credit is 10% to 30% for qualified investment in property that uses solar, geothermal, or ocean thermal energy. The property must be constructed by the taxpayer, or if acquired, the taxpayer must be the first person to use the property.

2. The recoverable basis of energy property must be reduced by 50% of the amount of business energy credit.

C. Credit for Rehabilitation Expenditures

1. Special investment credit (in lieu of regular income tax credits and energy credits) for qualified expenditures incurred to substantially rehabilitate old buildings. Credit percentages are (1) 10% for nonresidential buildings placed in service before 1936 (other than certified historic structures), and (2) 20% for residential and nonresidential certified historic structures.
2. **To qualify** for credit on other than certified historic structures

   a. 75% of external walls must remain in place as external or internal walls
   b. 50% or more of existing external walls must be retained in place as external walls
   c. 75% or more of existing internal structural framework must be retained in place
3. A building's recoverable basis must be reduced by 100% of the amount of rehabilitation credit.

D. Work Opportunity Credit

1. Credit is generally 40% of the first $6,000 of qualified first year wages paid to each qualified new employee who begins work before September 1, 2011. For qualified summer youth employees, the credit is 40% of the first $3,000 of wages for services performed during any ninety-day period between May 1 and September 15.
2. Qualified new employees include a (1) qualified IV-A recipient, (2) qualified veteran, (3) qualified ex-felon, (4) designated community resident, (5) vocational rehabilitation referral, (6) qualified summer youth employee, (7) qualified food stamp recipient, (8) qualified SSI recipient, and (9) long-term family assistance recipient.
3. Employer's deduction for wages is reduced by the amount of credit.
4. Taxpayer may elect not to claim credit (to avoid reducing wage deduction).

E. Alcohol Fuels Credit

1. A ten cents per gallon tax credit is allowed for the production of up to fifteen million gallons per year of ethanol by an eligible small ethanol producer (i.e., one having a production capacity of up to sixty million gallons of alcohol per year).
2. The tax credit for ethanol blenders is sixty cents per gallon for 190 or greater proof ethanol and forty-five cents per gallon for 150 to 190 proof ethanol.

F. Low-Income Housing Credit

1. The amount of credit for owners of low-income housing projects depends upon (1) whether the taxpayer acquires existing housing or whether the housing is newly constructed or rehabilitated, and (2) whether or not the housing project is financed by tax-exempt bonds or other federally subsidized financing. The applicable credit rates are the appropriate percentages issued by the IRS for the month in which the building is placed in service.
2. The amount on which the credit is computed is the portion of the total depreciable basis of a qualified housing project that reflects the portion of the housing units within the project that are occupied by qualified low-income individuals.
3. The credit is claimed each year (for a ten-year period) beginning with the year that the property is placed in service. The first-year credit is prorated to reflect the date placed in service.

G. Disabled Access Credit

1. A tax credit is available to an eligible small business for expenditures incurred to make the business accessible to disabled individuals. The amount of this credit is equal to 50% of the amount of the eligible access expenditures for a year that exceed $250 but do not exceed $10,250.
2. An eligible small business is one that either (1) had gross receipts for the preceding tax year that did not exceed $1 million, or (2) had no more than 30 full-time employees during the preceding tax year, and (3) elects to have this credit apply.
3. Eligible access expenditures are amounts incurred to comply with the requirements of the Americans with Disabilities Act of 1990 and include amounts incurred for the purpose of removing architectural, communication, physical, or transportation barriers that prevent a business from being accessible to, or usable by, disabled individuals; amounts incurred to provide qualified readers to visually impaired individuals, and amounts incurred to acquire or modify equipment or devices for disabled individuals. Expenses incurred in connection with new construction are not eligible for the credit.

4. This credit is included as part of the general business credit; no deduction or credit is allowed under any other Code provision for any amount for which a disabled access credit is allowed.

H. Empowerment Zone Employment Credit

1. The credit is generally equal to 20% of the first $15,000 of wages paid to each employee who is a resident of a designated empowerment zone and performs substantially all services within the zone in an employer's trade or business.
2. The deduction for wages must be reduced by the amount of credit.

I. Employer Social Security Credit

1. Credit allowed to food and beverage establishments for the employer's portion of FICA tax (7.65%) attributable to reported tips in excess of those tips treated as wages for purposes of satisfying the minimum wage provisions of the Fair Labor Standards Act.
2. No deduction is allowed for any amount taken into account in determining the credit.

J. Employer-Provided Child Care Credit

1. Employers who provide child care facilities to their employees during normal working hours are eligible for a credit equal to 25% of qualified child care expenditures, and 10% of qualified child care resource and referral expenditures. The maximum credit is $150,000 per year, and is subject to a ten-year recapture rule.
2. *Qualified child care expenditures* include amounts paid to acquire, construct, and rehabilitate property which is to be used as a qualified child care facility (e.g., training costs of employees, scholarship programs, compensation for employees with high levels of child care training).
3. To prevent a double benefit, the basis of qualifying property is reduced by the amount of credit, and the amount of qualifying expenditures that would otherwise be deductible must be reduced by the amount of credit.

K. Credit for the Elderly and the Disabled

1. Eligible taxpayers are those who are either (1) 65 or older or (2) permanently and totally disabled.

   a. Permanent and total disability is the inability to engage in substantial gainful activity for a period that is expected to last for a continuous twelve-month period.
   b. Married individuals must file a joint return to claim the credit unless they have not lived together at all during the year.
   c. Credit cannot be claimed if Form 1040A or 1040EZ is filed.

2. Credit is **15%** of an initial amount reduced by certain amounts excluded from gross income and AGI in excess of certain levels. The amount of credit is limited to the amount of tax liability.

   a. Initial amount varies with filing status.

      (1) $5,000 for single or joint return where only one spouse is 65 or older
      (2) $7,500 for joint return where both spouses are 65 or older
      (3) $3,750 for married filing a separate return
      (4) Limited to disability income for taxpayers under age 65

   b. Reduced by annuities, pensions, social security, or disability income that is excluded from gross income
   c. Also reduced by 50% of the excess of AGI over

      (1) $7,500 if single
      (2) $10,000 if joint return
      (3) $5,000 for married individual filing separate return

   > EXAMPLE: H, age 67, and his wife, W, age 65, file a joint return and have adjusted gross income of $12,000. H received social security benefits of $2,000 during the year. The computation of their credit would be as follows:

Initial amount		$7,500
Less: social security	$2,000	
50% of AGI over $10,000	1,000	3,000

Balance	*4,500*
	× 15%
Amount of credit (limited to tax liability)	*$ 675*

L. Child and Dependent Care Credit

1. For 2008, the credit may vary from **20% to 35%** of the amount paid for qualifying household and dependent care expenses incurred to enable taxpayer to be gainfully employed or look for work. Credit is 35% if AGI is $15,000 or less, but is reduced by 1 percentage point for each $2,000 (or portion thereof) of AGI in excess of $15,000 (but not reduced below 20%).

   EXAMPLE: Able, Baker, and Charlie have AGIs of $10,000, $20,000, and $50,000 respectively, and each incurs child care expenses of $2,000. Able's child care credit is $700 (35% × $2,000); Baker's credit is $640 (32% × $2,000); and Charlie's credit is $400 (20% × $2,000).

2. **Eligibility** requirements include

   a. Expenses must be incurred on behalf of a qualifying individual and must enable taxpayer to be gainfully employed or look for work
   b. Married taxpayer must file joint return. If divorced or separated, credit available to parent having custody longer time during year
   c. A **qualifying individual** must have the same principal place of abode as the taxpayer for more than one-half of the tax year. A qualifying individual includes

      (1) The taxpayer's qualifying child (e.g., taxpayer's child, stepchild, sibling, step-sibling, or descendant of any of these) under age thirteen, or
      (2) Dependent or spouse who is physically or mentally incapable of self-care

   d. **Qualifying expenses** are those incurred for care of qualifying individual and for household services that were partly for care of qualifying individual to enable taxpayer to work or look for work

      (1) Expenses incurred outside taxpayer's household qualify only if incurred for a qualifying individual who regularly spends at least eight hours each day in taxpayer's household
      (2) Payments to taxpayer's child under age nineteen do not qualify
      (3) Payments to a relative do not qualify if taxpayer is entitled to a dependency exemption for that relative

3. **Maximum amount of expenses** that qualify for credit is the least of

   a. Actual expenses incurred, or
   b. **$3,000** for one, **$6,000** for two or more qualifying individuals, or
   c. Taxpayer's earned income (or spouse's earned income if smaller)
   d. If spouse is a student or incapable of self-care and thus has little or no earned income, spouse is treated as being gainfully employed and having earnings of not less than $250 per month for one, $500 per month for two or more qualifying individuals

   EXAMPLE: Husband and wife have earned income of $15,000 each, resulting in AGI of $30,000. They have one child, age 3. They incurred qualifying household service expenses of $1,500 and child care expenses at a nursery school of $2,200.

Household expenses	*$1,500*
Add child care outside home	*2,200*
Total employment-related expenses	*$3,700*
Maximum allowable expenses	*$3,000*
Credit = 27% × $3,000	*$ 810*

M. Foreign Tax Credit

1. Foreign income taxes on US taxpayers can either be deducted or used as a credit at the option of the taxpayer each year.
2. The credit is limited to the overall limitation of

$$\frac{\text{TI from all foreign countries}}{\text{Taxable income + Exemptions}} \times (\text{US tax} - \text{Credit for elderly})$$

3. The limitation must be computed separately for passive income (i.e., dividends, interest, royalties, rents, and annuities).

4. Foreign tax credit in excess of the overall limitation is subject to a one-year carryback and a ten-year carryforward.
5. There is no limitation if foreign taxes are used as a deduction.

N. Earned Income Credit

1. The earned income credit is a **refundable** tax credit for eligible low-income workers. Earned income includes wages, salaries, and other employee compensation (including union strike benefits), plus earnings from self-employment (after the deduction for one-half self-employment taxes). Earned income excludes income from pensions and annuities, and investment income such as interest and dividends.
2. For 2008, the earned income credit is allowed at a rate of 34% of the first $8,580 of earned income for taxpayers with one qualifying child, and is allowed at a rate of 40% on the first $12,060 of earned income for taxpayers with two or more qualifying children. The maximum credit is reduced by 15.98% (21.06% for two or more qualifying children) of the amount by which earned income (or AGI if greater) exceeds $15,740 ($18,740 for married taxpayers filing jointly).
3. To be eligible for the credit an individual must

    a. Have earned income and a return that covers a twelve-month period
    b. Maintain a household for more than half the year for a qualifying child in the US
    c. Have a filing status other than married filing a separate return
    d. Not be a qualifying child of another person
    e. Not claim the exclusion for foreign earned income
    f. Not have disqualified income in excess of $2,950

4. A **qualifying child** must be

    a. The taxpayer's child, adopted child, eligible foster child, stepchild, sibling, step-sibling or descendant of any of these who has the same principal place of abode as the taxpayer for more than one-half of the tax year, and is
    b. Under age nineteen, or a full-time student under age twenty-four, or permanently and totally disabled.
    c. If a custodial parent would be entitled to a child's dependency exemption but for having released it to the noncustodial parent for purposes of the earned income credit.

5. **Disqualified income** includes both taxable and tax-exempt interest, dividends, net rental and royalty income, net capital gain income, and net passive income.
6. A **reduced earned income credit** is available to an individual who does not have qualifying children if (1) the individual's principal place of abode for more than half the tax year is in the US, (2) the individual (or spouse) is at least age twenty-five (but under sixty-five) at the end of the tax year, and (3) the individual does not qualify as a dependency exemption on another taxpayer's return. For 2008, the maximum credit is 7.65% of the first $5,720 of earned income, and is reduced by 7.65% of earned income (or AGI if greater) in excess of $7,160 ($10,160 for married taxpayers filing jointly).
7. The earned income credit is refundable if the amount of credit exceeds the taxpayer's tax liability. Individuals with qualifying children who expect a refund because of the earned income credit may arrange to have up to 60% of the credit added to paychecks.

O. Credit for Adoption Expenses

1. A nonrefundable credit of up to $11,650 (for 2008) for qualified adoption expenses incurred for each eligible child (including a child with special needs).

    a. An *eligible child* is an individual who has not attained the age of 18 as of the time of the adoption, or who is physically or mentally incapable of self-care.
    b. Married taxpayers generally must file a joint return to claim the credit.
    c. The credit is phased out ratably for modified AGI between $174,730 and $214,730.

2. *Qualified adoption expenses* are taken into account in the year the adoption becomes final and include all reasonable and necessary adoption fees, court costs, attorney fees, and other expenses that are directly related to the legal adoption by the taxpayer of an eligible child. However, expenses incurred in carrying out a surrogate parenting arrangement or in adopting a spouse's child do not qualify for the credit.

3. Any portion of the credit not allowed because of the limitation based on tax liability may be carried forward for up to five years.

P. Child Tax Credit (CTC)

1. The amount of the credit is $1,000 per qualifying child for 2008.
2. A *qualifying child* is a US citizen or resident who is the taxpayer's child, adopted child, eligible foster child, stepchild, step-sibling, or descendant of any of these who is less than seventeen years old as of the close of the calendar year in which the tax year of the taxpayer begins.
3. The child tax credit begins to phase out when modified adjusted gross income reaches $110,000 for joint filers, $55,000 for married taxpayers filing separately, and $75,000 for single taxpayers and heads of households. The credit is reduced by $50 for each $1,000, or fraction thereof, of modified AGI above the thresholds.
4. The CTC is refundable to the extent of 15% of the taxpayer's earned income in excess of $12,050 (for 2008), up to the per child credit amount of $1,000 per child. Taxpayers with more than two children may calculate the refundable portion of the credit using the excess of their social security taxes (i.e., taxpayer's share of FICA taxes and one-half of self-employment taxes) over their earned income credit, if it results in a larger amount. The amount of refundable CTC reduces the amount of nonrefundable CTC.

Q. Hope Scholarship Credit

1. For the *first two years* of a postsecondary school program, qualifying taxpayers may elect to take a nonrefundable tax credit of 100% for the first $1,200 of qualified tuition and related expenses (not room and board), and a 50% credit for the next $1,200 of such expenses, for a total credit of up to $1,800 a year per student for 2008.
2. The credit is available on a *per student basis* and covers tuition payments for the taxpayer as well as the taxpayer's spouse and dependents.
   a. To be eligible for the credit, the student must be enrolled on at least a half-time basis for one academic period during the year.
   b. If a student is claimed as a dependent of another taxpayer, only that taxpayer may claim the education credit for the student's qualified tuition and related expenses. However, if the taxpayer is eligible to, but does **not** claim the student as a dependent, only the student may claim the education credit for the student's qualified tuition and related expenses.
3. The credit is phased out for single taxpayers with modified AGI between $48,000 and $58,000, and for joint filers with a modified AGI between $96,000 and $116,000.
4. For a tax year, a taxpayer may elect only one of the following with respect to one student: (1) the Hope credit, or (2) the lifetime learning credit.

R. Lifetime Learning Credit

1. A nonrefundable 20% tax credit is available for up to $10,000 of qualified tuition and related expenses per year for graduate and undergraduate courses at an eligible educational institution.
2. The credit may be claimed for an unlimited number of years, is available on a *per taxpayer basis*, covers tuition payments for the taxpayer, spouse, and dependents.
3. Similar to the Hope credit, if a student is claimed as a dependent of another taxpayer, only that taxpayer may claim the education credit for the student's qualified tuition and related expenses. However, if the taxpayer is eligible to, but does **not** claim the student as a dependent, only the student may claim the education credit for the student's qualified tuition and related expenses.
4. The credit is phased out for single taxpayers with a modified AGI between $48,000 and $58,000, and for joint filers with modified AGI between $96,000 and $116,000.
5. For a tax year, a taxpayer may elect only one of the following with respect to one student: (1) the Hope credit, or (2) the lifetime learning credit.

> EXAMPLE: *Alan paid qualified tuition and related expenses for his dependent, Betty, to attend college. Assuming all other relevant requirements are met, Alan may claim either a Hope Scholarship credit or lifetime learning credit with respect to his dependent, Betty, but not both.*

> EXAMPLE: *Cathy paid $2,000 in qualified tuition and related expenses for her dependent, Doug, to attend college. Also during the year, Cathy paid $600 in qualified tuition to attend a continuing education course to improve her job*

skills. Assuming all relevant requirements are met, Cathy may claim the Hope Scholarship credit for the $2,000 paid for her dependent, Doug, and a lifetime learning credit for the $600 of qualified tuition that she paid for the continuing education course to improve her job skills.

*EXAMPLE:　The facts are the same as in the preceding example, except that Cathy paid $3,500 in qualified tuition and related expenses for her dependent, Doug, to attend college. Although a Hope Scholarship credit is available only with respect to the first $2,400 of qualified tuition and related expenses paid with respect to Doug, Cathy **cannot** add the $1,100 of excess expenses to her $600 of qualified tuition in computing the amount of her lifetime learning credit.*

*EXAMPLE:　Ernie has one dependent, Frank. During the current year, Ernie paid qualified tuition and related expenses for Frank to attend college. Although Ernie is eligible to claim Frank as a dependent on Ernie's federal income tax return, Ernie does **not** do so. Therefore, assuming all other relevant requirements are met, Frank is allowed an education credit on Frank's federal income tax return for his qualified tuition and related expenses paid by Ernie, and Ernie is not allowed an education credit with respect to Frank's education expenses. The result would be the same if Frank had paid his qualified tuition expenses himself.*

S.　Credit for Qualified Retirement Savings

1.　The amount of nonrefundable credit is from 10% to 50% of up to $2,000 of elective contributions to IRAs and most retirement plans. The credit rate (10% to 50%) is based on AGI, and the credit is in addition to any deduction or exclusion that would otherwise apply to the contributions.

2.　Only individuals filing joint returns with AGI of $53,000 or less, filing as a head of household with AGI of $39,750 or less, and filing other returns with AGI of $26,500 or less qualify for the credit.

3.　The credit is available to an individual taxpayer at least eighteen years old at the close of the tax year who is not a full-time student nor claimed as a dependent on another taxpayer's return.

T.　Estimated Tax Payments

1.　An individual whose regular and alternative minimum tax liability is not sufficiently covered by withholding on wages must pay estimated tax in quarterly installments or be subject to penalty.

2.　Quarterly payments of estimated tax are due by the 15th day of the 4th, 6th, and 9th month of the taxable year, and by the 15th day of the 1st month of the following year.

3.　For 2008, individuals (other than high-income individuals) will incur no penalty if the amount of tax withheld plus estimated payments are at least equal to the lesser of

　　a.　90% of the current year's tax,
　　b.　90% of the tax determined by annualizing current-year taxable income through each quarter, or
　　c.　100% of the prior year's tax.

4.　For 2008, high-income individuals must use 110% (instead of 100%) if they base their estimates on their prior year's tax. A person is a high-income individual if the AGI shown on the individual's return for the preceding tax year exceeds $150,000 ($75,000 for a married individual filing separately).

5.　The penalty is based on the difference between the required annual payment (i.e., lesser of a., b., or c. above) and the amount paid.

6.　Generally no penalty if

　　a.　Total tax due was less than $1,000;
　　b.　Taxpayer had no tax liability for prior year (i.e., total tax was zero), prior year was a twelve-month period, and taxpayer was a US citizen or resident for entire year; or
　　c.　IRS waives penalty because failure to pay was the result of casualty, disaster, or other unusual circumstances.

VII.　FILING REQUIREMENTS

A.　Form 1040 must generally be filed if gross income at least equals the sum of the taxpayer's standard deduction plus personal exemptions allowable (e.g., generally $5,450 + $3,500 = $8,950 for single taxpayer for 2008).

1.　The additional standard deduction for age ($1,350 for 2008) is included in determining an individual's filing requirement; the additional standard deduction for blindness and dependency exemptions are not included.

　　*EXAMPLE:　A single individual age 65 and blind who **cannot** be claimed as a dependency exemption by another taxpayer must file a return for 2008 if the individual's gross income is at least $5,450 + $3,500 + $1,350 = $10,300*

2.　An individual who can be claimed as a dependency exemption by another taxpayer must file a return if the individual either has (1) unearned income in excess of the sum of $900 plus any additional standard deductions allowed for age and blindness, or (2) total gross income in excess of the individual's standard deduction (i.e., earned income plus $300 up to the normal amount of the basic standard deduction—$5,450 for single taxpayer—plus additional standard deductions for age and blindness).

> *EXAMPLE: A single individual age 65 who can be claimed as a dependency exemption by another taxpayer must file a return for 2008 if the individual has unearned income (e.g., interest and dividends) in excess of $900 + $1,350 = $2,250.*

3. Self-employed individual must file if net earnings from self-employment are **$400** or more.
4. A married individual filing separately must file if gross income is $3,500 or more.

B. Return must be filed by 15th day of 4th calendar month following close of taxable year.

C. An automatic four-month extension of time for filing the return can be obtained by filing Form 4868 by the due date of the return, and paying any estimated tax due.

VIII. FARMING INCOME AND EXPENSES

A. A farming business involves the cultivating of land or raising or harvesting of any agricultural or horticultural commodity. It does not include contract harvesting, or the buying or reselling of plants or animals grown or raised by another person.

B. An individual engaged in farming must file Schedule F (Form 1040), Farm Income and Expenses. Additionally, a farmer must also file Schedule SE in order to compute self-employment tax on farm earnings. Completing Schedule F for farming is similar to completing a Schedule C which is used by sole proprietors. Partnerships engaged in farming must file Form 1065, while corporations engaged in farming must file the appropriate Form 1120.

C. The income and expenses from farming are generally treated in the same manner as the income and expenses from any other business. Similarly, the general rules that apply to all cash and accrual taxpayers also apply to farming businesses.

1. A cash-basis farmer who receives insurance proceeds as a result of the destruction or damage to crops may elect to include the proceeds in income for the year after the year of damage if the farmer can show that the income from the crops would normally have been reported in the following year.

2. Income from the sale of a crop is normally reported in the year of sale. However, if the farmer has pledged all of part of the crop production to secure a Commodity Credit Corporation loan, the farmer may elect to report the loan proceeds as income in the year received rather than reporting income in the year the crop is sold. The amount reported as income becomes the farmer's basis for the crop and is used to determine gain or loss upon the sale of the crop.

3. A farmer may generally deduct soil and water conservation expenditures that are consistent with a conservation plan approved by a federal or state agency. However, the deduction is annually limited to 25% of the farmer's gross income from farming. Excess expenses can be carried over for an unlimited number of years subject to the 25 % limitation in each carryover year.

   a. Expenses related to the draining of wetlands or to land preparation for the installation of center pivot irrigation systems may not be deducted under this provision.
   b. Land clearing expenses must be capitalized and added to the farmer's basis in the land.

   > *EXAMPLE: A farmer had gross income from Farm A of $25,000 and gross income from Farm B of $19,000 for the current year. During the year the farmer spent $16,000 on Farm B for soil and water conservation expenditures under a plan approved by a state agency. For the current year, the farmer's deduction of the $16,000 of soil and water conservation expenditures would be limited to ($25,000 + $19,000) × 25% =$11,000.*

4. Cash-basis farmers can generally deduct prepaid feed costs in the year of payment if the deduction does not materially distort income. However, no deduction is allowed for advance payments for feed, seed, fertilizer, or other supplies to the extent such prepayments exceed 50% of total deductible farming expenses (excluding the prepaid items).

   > *EXAMPLE: During December 2007, a calendar-year farmer purchased a 6-month supply of feed for $6,000 and also purchased $2,000 of seed to be used in the subsequent spring planting season. The farmer's other farm expenses totaled $9,000. In this case the farmer's 2007 deduction for prepaid feed and seed would be limited to 50% × $9,000 = $4,500.*

5. The cost of tangible personal property used in a farming business cannot be depreciated under the 200% declining balance method, but instead is generally recovered using the MACRS 150% declining balance method.

6. An individual engaged in farming can elect to determine current year tax liability by averaging, over the previous three years, all or part of his/her current year income from farming.

IX. TAX PROCEDURES

A. Audit and Appeal Procedures

1. Taxpayer makes determination of tax when return is filed.
2. Examination of questionable returns may be conducted by correspondence, in an IRS office (i.e., office audit), or at taxpayer's place of business (i.e., field audit).
3. If taxpayer does not agree with the changes proposed by the examiner and the examination was made in an IRS office or by correspondence, the taxpayer may request a meeting with the examiner's supervisor.
4. If no agreement is reached, or if the examination was conducted in the field, the IRS will send the taxpayer a copy of the examination report and a letter stating the proposed changes (**thirty-day letter**).
5. A taxpayer has thirty days to (1) accept deficiency, (2) appeal the examiner's findings, or (3) may disregard the thirty-day letter and wait for a statutory notice of deficiency (**ninety-day letter**).
6. If taxpayer has appealed and agreement is not reached at appellate level of IRS, a ninety-day letter is sent.
7. Taxpayer has ninety days to file a petition in the Tax Court.
   a. Assessment and collection are prohibited so long as the taxpayer can petition the Tax Court. Payment of deficiency is not required before going to Tax Court.
   b. If a petition is not filed within ninety days, the tax deficiency is assessed and the amount is subject to collection if not paid within ten days.

B. Assessments

1. The normal period for assessment of a tax deficiency is **three years** after the due date of the return or three years after the return is filed, whichever is later.
2. The assessment period is extended to **six years** if gross income omissions exceed 25% of the gross income stated on the return.
3. There is no time limit for assessment if no return is filed, if the return is fraudulent, or if there is a willful attempt to evade taxes.
4. If a taxpayer fails to include any required information on a tax return or statement relating to a listed transaction, the statute of limitations with respect to that listed transaction will not expire until one year after the date the information is provided to the IRS.
5. Assessment period (normally three years) is suspended for 150 days after timely mailing of deficiency notice (90-day letter) to taxpayer.
6. Within sixty days after making the assessment, the IRS is required to provide a notice and demand for payment. If tax is not paid, the tax may be collected by levy or by court proceedings started within ten years of assessment.

C. Collection from Transferees and Fiduciaries

1. Transferee provisions are a method of collecting a predetermined tax that the transferor taxpayer cannot pay.
2. Generally transferor must be insolvent, or no longer in existence (e.g., corporation was dissolved).
3. Generally transferees are liable only to the extent of property received from the transferor taxpayer.

D. Closing Agreement and Compromise

1. A closing agreement is a final determination of tax liability that is binding on both the IRS and taxpayer.
2. A compromise is a writing-down of the tax liability. The IRS has broad authority to compromise in the event that doubt exists as to the existence of actual tax liability or because of the taxpayer's inability to pay.

E. Claims for Refund

1. An income tax refund claim is made on Form 1040X. Form 843 should be used to file a refund claim for taxes other than income taxes. Form 1045 may be used to file for a tentative adjustment or refund

of taxes when an overpayment of taxes for a prior year results from the carryback of a current year's net operating loss.

2. Period for filing refund claims

a. Refund claim must be filed within **three years** from date return was filed, or **two years** from payment of tax, whichever is later. If return filed before due date, the return is treated as filed on due date.

b. Three-year period is extended to seven years for claims resulting from bad debts or worthless securities.

c. If refund claim results from a carryback (e.g., NOL), the three-year period begins with the return for the year in which the carryback arose.

3. Suit for refund

a. Only recourse from IRS's disallowance of refund claim is to begin suit in court within two years of notice of disallowance.

b. If IRS fails to act on refund claim within six months, the taxpayer may treat it as disallowed.

F. Interest

1. Interest is allowed on overpayments from date of overpayment to thirty days before date of refund check.

a. If an overpayment, amounts of tax withheld and estimated payments are deemed paid on due date of return.

b. No interest is allowed if refund is made within forty-five days of later of (1) return due date or (2) actual filing of return.

2. For underpayments of tax, the interest rate is equal to the three-month Treasury bill rate plus three percentage points. For overpayments, the interest rate is equal to the federal short-term rate plus two percentage points.

G. Taxpayer Penalties

1. Penalties may be imposed for late filing or failure to file, and late payment of tax.

a. **Late filing** or failure to file penalty is 5% of the net tax due per month (up to 25%).

b. **Late payment** of tax penalty is 1% of the net tax due per month (up to 25%).

   (1) For any month to which both of the above apply, the late filing penalty is reduced by the late payment penalty so that the maximum is 5% per month (up to 25%).

   (2) For returns not filed within sixty days of due date (including extensions), the IRS may assess a minimum late filing penalty which is the lesser of $100 or the amount of net tax due.

2. An **accuracy-related penalty of 20%** of the underpayment applies if the underpayment of tax is attributable to one or more of the following: (1) negligence or disregard of rules and regulations, (2) any substantial understatement of income tax, (3) any substantial valuation overstatement, (4) any substantial overstatement of pension liabilities, or (5) any substantial gift or estate tax valuation understatement.

a. Accuracy-related penalty does not apply if the underpayment is due to reasonable cause, or there is adequate disclosure and the position has a reasonable basis for being sustained.

b. **Negligence penalty** applies to any careless, reckless, or intentional disregard of rules or regulations, and any failure to make a reasonable attempt to comply with the provisions of the tax law. Penalty is imposed only on the portion of tax liability due to negligence, and can be avoided by adequate disclosure of a position that has a reasonable basis.

c. **Substantial understatement of income tax penalty** applies if the understatement exceeds the greater of (1) 10% of the tax due, or (2) $5,000 ($10,000 for most corporations). Penalty can be avoided by adequate disclosure of a position that has a reasonable basis, or if there is substantial authority for the position taken.

d. **Substantial valuation misstatement penalty** may be imposed if the value (or adjusted basis) of property stated on the return is 150% or more of the amount determined to be correct.

      (1) Penalty applies to the extent resulting income tax underpayment exceeds $5,000 ($10,000 for most corporations).

      (2) Penalty is applied at a 40% rate if gross overvaluation is 200% or more of the amount determined to be correct.

    e. **Substantial overstatement of pension liabilities penalty** applies if the amount of stated pension liabilities is 200% or more of the amount determined to be correct. Penalty is 40% if misstatement is 400% or more, but penalty is not applicable if resulting underpayment is $1,000 or less.

    f. **Gift or estate tax valuation misstatement penalty** applies if the value of property on a gift or estate return is 50% or less of the amount determined to be correct.

      (1) Penalty is 40% if valuation used is 25% or less of amount determined to be correct.

      (2) No penalty if resulting understatement of tax is $5,000 or less.

3. A separate accuracy-related penalty applies to **tax shelter transactions**. The penalty is 30% of the tax understatement if the taxpayer fails to disclose a listed transaction or other reportable transaction with a significant tax-avoidance purpose. A lower penalty of 20% of the tax understatement applies if there is disclosure.

    a. The penalty may be waived for reasonable cause if the taxpayer made adequate disclosure, the position is (or was) supported by substantial authority, and the taxpayer reasonably believed the position was more-likely-than-not correct.

    b. Even if a taxpayer reasonably believed that its position was correct, the penalty cannot be waived if there was no disclosure.

4. **Civil fraud penalty** is 75% of the portion of underpayment attributable to fraud. The accuracy-related penalty does not apply to the portion of underpayment subject to the fraud penalty.

X. SOURCES OF FEDERAL TAX AUTHORITY

A. The Internal Revenue Code (IRC) is the basic foundation of federal tax law, and represents a codification of the federal tax laws of the United States.

1. A series of self-contained revenue acts were first codified into an organized framework with the Internal Revenue Code of 1939. Subsequently, the 1939 IRC was reorganized and replaced with the 1954 IRC. In 1986, the Code's name was changed to the IRC of 1986, and has been frequently amended since then (e.g., Jobs and Growth Tax Relief Reconciliation Act of 2004).

2. The Internal Revenue Code of 1986 is actually Title 26 of the United States Code, and is generally divided into an orderly framework as follows: Subtitles; Chapters; Subchapters; Parts; Subparts; Sections; and Subsections.

3. **Subtitles** are denoted with a capital letter, with most pertaining to a general area of tax law as follows:

Subtitle	*Topic*
A	Income Taxes
B	Estate and Gift Taxes
C	Employment Taxes
D	Miscellaneous Excise Taxes
E	Alcohol, Tobacco, and Certain Other Excise Taxes
F	Procedure and Administration
G	The Joint Committee on Taxation
H	Financing of Presidential Election Campaigns
I	Trust Fund Code
J	Coal Industry Health Benefits
K	Group Health Plan Requirements

4. Each subtitle generally contains a number of **chapters** that are numbered in ascending order throughout the Code. Each chapter generally contains the tax rules that relate to a more narrowly defined area of law than is addressed by a subtitle. For example, Subtitle A—Income Taxes is divided as follows:

Chapter	*Topic*
1	Normal Taxes and Surtaxes
2	Tax on Self-Employment Income

d. $8,000

120. Sara Harding is a cash-basis taxpayer who itemized her deductions. The following information pertains to Sara's state income taxes for the taxable year 2008:

Withheld by employer in 2008		$2,000
Payments on 2008 estimate:		
4/15/08	$300	
6/15/08	300	
9/15/08	300	
1/15/09	300	1,200
Total paid and withheld		$3,200
Actual tax, per state return		3,000
Overpayment		$ 200

There was no balance of tax or refund due on Sara's 2007 state tax return. How much is deductible for state income taxes on Sara's 2008 federal income tax return?

- a. $2,800
- b. $2,900
- c. $3,000
- d. $3,200

121. During 2008, Jack and Mary Bronson paid the following taxes:

Taxes on residence (for period January 1 to	
December 31, 2008)	$2,700
State motor vehicle tax on value of the car	360

The Bronsons sold their house on June 30, 2008, under an agreement in which the real estate taxes were not prorated between the buyer and sellers. What amount should the Bronsons deduct as taxes in calculating itemized deductions for 2008?

- a. $1,350
- b. $1,695
- c. $2,160
- d. $3,060

122. George Granger sold a plot of land to Albert King on July 1, 2008. Granger had not paid any realty taxes on the land since 2006. Delinquent 2007 taxes amounted to $600, and 2008 taxes amounted to $700. King paid the 2007 and 2008 taxes in full in 2008, when he bought the land. What portion of the $1,300 is deductible by King in 2008?

- a. $ 352
- b. $ 700
- c. $ 952
- d. $1,300

123. During 2008 Mr. and Mrs. West paid the following taxes:

Property taxes on residence	$1,800
Special assessment for installation of a sewer system	
in their town	1,000
State personal property tax on their automobile	600
Property taxes on land held for long-term	
appreciation	300

What amount can the Wests deduct as property taxes in calculating itemized deductions for 2008?

- a. $2,100
- b. $2,700
- c. $3,100
- d. $3,700

124. Alex and Myra Burg, married and filing joint income tax returns, derive their entire income from the operation of their retail candy shop. Their 2008 adjusted gross income was $50,000. The Burgs itemized their deductions on

Schedule A for 2008. The following unreimbursed cash expenditures were among those made by the Burgs during 2008:

State income tax	$1,200
Self-employment tax	7,650

What amount should the Burgs deduct for taxes in their itemized deductions on Schedule A for 2008?

- a. $1,200
- b. $3,825
- c. $5,025
- d. $7,650

125. The 2008 deduction by an individual taxpayer for interest on investment indebtedness is

- a.   Limited to the investment interest paid in 2008.
- b.   Limited to the taxpayer's 2008 interest income.
- c.   Limited to the taxpayer's 2008 net investment income.
- d.   Not limited.

126. The Browns borrowed $20,000, secured by their home, to purchase a new automobile. At the time of the loan, the fair market value of their home was $400,000, and it was unencumbered by other debt. The interest on the loan qualifies as

- a.   Deductible personal interest.
- b.   Deductible qualified residence interest.
- c.   Nondeductible interest.
- d.   Investment interest expense.

127. On January 2, 2005, the Philips paid $50,000 cash and obtained a $200,000 mortgage to purchase a home. In 2008 they borrowed $15,000 secured by their home, and used the cash to add a new room to their residence. That same year they took out a $5,000 auto loan.

The following information pertains to interest paid in 2008:

Mortgage interest	$17,000
Interest on room construction loan	1,500
Auto loan interest	500

For 2008, how much interest is deductible, prior to any itemized deduction limitations?

- a. $17,000
- b. $17,500
- c. $18,500
- d. $19,000

128. Jackson owns two residences. The second residence, which has never been used for rental purposes, is the only residence that is subject to a mortgage. The following expenses were incurred for the second residence in 2008:

Mortgage interest	$5,000
Utilities	1,200
Insurance	6,000

For regular income tax purposes, what is the maximum amount allowable as a deduction for Jackson's second residence in 2008?

- a. $6,200 in determining adjusted gross income.
- b. $11,000 in determining adjusted gross income.
- c. $5,000 as an itemized deduction.
- d. $12,200 as an itemized deduction.

129. Robert and Judy Parker made the following payments during 2008:

Interest on a life insurance policy loan (the loan
proceeds were used for personal use) $1,200
Interest on home mortgage for period January 1
to October 4, 2008   3,600
Penalty payment for prepayment of home
mortgage on October 4, 2008   900

How much can the Parkers utilize as interest expense in calculating itemized deductions for 2008?

   a. $5,700
   b. $4,620
   c. $4,500
   d. $3,600

130. Charles Wolfe purchased the following long-term investments at par during 2008:

$20,000 general obligation bonds of Burlington County (wholly tax-exempt)
$10,000 debentures of Arrow Corporation

Wolfe financed these purchases by obtaining a $30,000 loan from the Union National Bank. For the year 2008, Wolfe made the following interest payments:

Union National Bank $3,600
Interest on home mortgage   3,000
Interest on credit card charges (items pur-
chased for personal use)   500

What amount can Wolfe utilize as interest expense in calculating itemized deductions for 2008?

   a. $3,000
   b. $4,200
   c. $5,400
   d. $7,100

131. During 2008, William Clark was assessed a deficiency on his 2006 federal income tax return. As a result of this assessment he was required to pay $1,120 determined as follows:

Additional tax $900
Late filing penalty   60
Negligence penalty   90
Interest   70

What portion of the $1,120 would qualify as itemized deductions for 2008?

   a. $0
   b. $ 14
   c. $150
   d. $220

132. Smith, a single individual, made the following charitable contributions during the current year. Smith's adjusted gross income is $60,000.

Donation to Smith's church $5,000
Artwork donated to the local art museum. Smith purchased it for $2,000 four months ago. A local art
dealer appraised it for   3,000
Contribution to a needy family   1,000

What amount should Smith deduct as a charitable contribution?

   a. $5,000
   b. $7,000
   c. $8,000
   d. $9,000

133. Stein, an unmarried taxpayer, had adjusted income of $80,000 for the year and qualified to itemize deductions. Stein had no charitable contribution carryovers and only made one contribution during the year. Stein do-

nated stock, purchased seven years earlier for $17,000, to a tax-exempt educational organization. The stock was valued at $25,000 when it was contributed. What is the amount of charitable contributions deductible on Stein's current year income tax return?

   a. $17,000
   b. $21,000
   c. $24,000
   d. $25,000

134. Moore, a single taxpayer, had $50,000 in adjusted gross income for 2008. During 2008 she contributed $18,000 to her church. She had a $10,000 charitable contribution carryover from her 2007 church contributions. What was the maximum amount of properly substantiated charitable contributions that Moore could claim as an itemized deduction for 2008?

   a. $10,000
   b. $18,000
   c. $25,000
   d. $28,000

135. Spencer, who itemizes deductions, had adjusted gross income of $60,000 in 2008. The following additional information is available for 2008:

Cash contribution to church $4,000
Purchase of art object at church bazaar (with a fair
market value of $800 on the date of purchase)   1,200
Donation of used clothing to Salvation Army
(fair value evidenced by receipt received)   600

What is the maximum amount Spencer can claim as a deduction for charitable contributions in 2008?

   a. $5,400
   b. $5,200
   c. $5,000
   d. $4,400

136. Ruth Lewis has adjusted gross income of $100,000 for 2008 and itemizes her deductions. On September 1, 2008, she made a contribution to her church of stock held for investment for two years that cost $10,000 and had a fair market value of $70,000. The church sold the stock for $70,000 on the same date. Assume that Lewis made no other contributions during 2008 and made no special election in regard to this contribution on her 2008 tax return. How much should Lewis claim as a charitable contribution deduction for 2008?

   a. $50,000
   b. $30,000
   c. $20,000
   d. $10,000

137. On December 15, 2008, Donald Calder made a contribution of $500 to a qualified charitable organization, by charging the contribution on his bank credit card. Calder paid the $500 on January 20, 2009, upon receipt of the bill from the bank. In addition, Calder issued and delivered a promissory note for $1,000 to another qualified charitable organization on November 1, 2008, which he paid upon maturity six months later. If Calder itemizes his deductions, what portion of these contributions is deductible in 2008?

   a. $0
   b. $ 500
   c. $1,000
   d. $1,500

138. Under a written agreement between Mrs. Norma Lowe and an approved religious exempt organization, a ten-year-old girl from Vietnam came to live in Mrs. Lowe's home on August 1, 2008, in order to be able to start school in the US on September 3, 2008. Mrs. Lowe actually spent $500 for food, clothing, and school supplies for the student during 2008, without receiving any compensation or reimbursement of costs. What portion of the $500 may Mrs. Lowe deduct on her 2008 income tax return as a charitable contribution?

    a. $0
    b. $200
    c. $250
    d. $500

139. During 2008, Vincent Tally gave to the municipal art museum title to his private collection of rare books that was assessed and valued at $60,000. However, he reserved the right to the collection's use and possession during his lifetime. For 2008, he reported an adjusted gross income of $100,000. Assuming that this was his only contribution during the year, and that there were no carryovers from prior years, what amount can he deduct as contributions for 2008?

    a. $0
    b. $30,000
    c. $50,000
    d. $60,000

140. Jimet, an unmarried taxpayer, qualified to itemize 2008 deductions. Jimet's 2008 adjusted gross income was $30,000 and he made a $2,000 cash donation directly to a needy family. In 2008, Jimet also donated stock, valued at $3,000, to his church. Jimet had purchased the stock four months earlier for $1,500. What was the maximum amount of the charitable contribution allowable as an itemized deduction on Jimet's 2008 income tax return?

    a. $0
    b. $1,500
    c. $2,000
    d. $5,000

141. Taylor, an unmarried taxpayer, had $90,000 in adjusted gross income for 2008. During 2008, Taylor donated land to a church and made no other contributions. Taylor purchased the land in 1997 as an investment for $14,000. The land's fair market value was $25,000 on the day of the donation. What is the maximum amount of charitable contribution that Taylor may deduct as an itemized deduction for the land donation for 2008?

    a. $25,000
    b. $14,000
    c. $11,000
    d. $0

142. In 2008, Joan Frazer's residence was totally destroyed by fire. The property had an adjusted basis and a fair market value of $130,000 before the fire. During 2008, Frazer received insurance reimbursement of $120,000 for the destruction of her home. Frazer's 2008 adjusted gross income was $70,000. Frazer had no casualty gains during the year. What amount of the fire loss was Frazer entitled to claim as an itemized deduction on her 2008 tax return?

    a. $ 2,900
    b. $ 8,500
    c. $ 8,600
    d. $10,000

143. Alex and Myra Burg, married and filing joint income tax returns, derive their entire income from the operation of their retail candy shop. Their 2008 adjusted gross income was $50,000. The Burgs itemized their deductions on Schedule A for 2008. The following unreimbursed cash expenditures were among those made by the Burgs during 2008:

> Repair of glass vase accidentally broken in home by
>   dog; vase cost $500 in 2005; fair value $600 before
>   accident and $200 after accident $90

Without regard to the $100 "floor" and the adjusted gross income percentage threshold, what amount should the Burgs deduct for the casualty loss in their itemized deductions on Schedule A for 2008?

    a. $0
    b. $ 90
    c. $300
    d. $400

144. Hall, a divorced person and custodian of her twelve-year-old child, filed her 2008 federal income tax return as head of a household. During 2008 Hall paid a $490 casualty insurance premium on her personal residence. Hall does not rent out any portion of the home, nor use it for business.

    The casualty insurance premium of $490 is

    a.   Allowed as an itemized deduction subject to the $100 floor and the 10% of adjusted gross income floor.
    b.   Allowed as an itemized deduction subject to the 2% of adjusted gross income floor.
    c.   Deductible in arriving at adjusted gross income.
    d.   Not deductible in 2008.

Items 145 and 146 are based on the following selected 2008 information pertaining to Sam and Ann Hoyt, who filed a joint federal income tax return for the calendar year 2008. The Hoyts had adjusted gross income of $34,000 and itemized their deductions for 2008. Among the Hoyts' cash expenditures during 2008 were the following:

> $2,500 repairs in connection with 2008 fire damage to the Hoyt
>   residence. This property has a basis of $50,000. Fair market
>   value was $60,000 before the fire and $55,000 after the fire.
>   Insurance on the property had lapsed in 2007 for nonpayment
>   of premium.
> $800 appraisal fee to determine amount of fire loss.

145. What amount of fire loss were the Hoyts entitled to deduct as an itemized deduction on their 2008 return?

    a. $5,000
    b. $2,500
    c. $1,600
    d. $1,500

146. The appraisal fee to determine the amount of the Hoyts' fire loss was

    a.   Deductible from gross income in arriving at adjusted gross income.
    b.   Subject to the 2% of adjusted gross income floor for miscellaneous itemized deductions.
    c.   Deductible after reducing the amount by $100.
    d.   Not deductible.

147. Which of the following is **not** a miscellaneous itemized deduction?

    a.   Legal fee for tax advice related to a divorce.
    b.   IRA trustee's fees that are separately billed and paid.

c. Appraisal fee for a charitable contribution.
d. Check-writing fees for a personal checking account.

148. Hall, a divorced person and custodian of her twelve-year-old child, submitted the following information to the CPA who prepared her 2008 return:

> The divorce agreement, executed in 2005, provides for Hall to receive $3,000 per month, of which $600 is designated as child support. After the child reaches eighteen, the monthly payments are to be reduced to $2,400 and are to continue until remarriage or death. However, for the year 2008, Hall received a total of only $5,000 from her former husband. Hall paid an attorney $2,000 in 2008 in a suit to collect the alimony owed.

The $2,000 legal fee that Hall paid to collect alimony should be treated as

a. A deduction in arriving at adjusted gross income.
b. An itemized deduction subject to the 2% of adjusted gross income floor.
c. An itemized deduction **not** subject to the 2% of adjusted gross income floor.
d. A nondeductible personal expense.

149. Hall, a divorced person and custodian of her twelve-year-old child, submitted the following information to the CPA who prepared her 2008 return:

> During 2008, Hall spent a total of $1,000 for state lottery tickets. Her lottery winnings in 2008 totaled $200.

Hall's lottery transactions should be reported as follows:

	Other income on page 1	Schedule A—itemized deductions Other miscellaneous deductions Subject to 2% AGI floor	Not subject to 2% AGI floor
a.	$0	$0	$0
b.	$200	$0	$200
c.	$200	$200	$0
d.	$200	$0	$0

150. Joel Rich is an outside salesman, deriving his income solely from commissions, and personally bearing all expenses without reimbursement of any kind. During 2008, Joel paid the following expenses pertaining directly to his activities as an outside salesman:

Travel	$10,000
Secretarial	7,000
Telephone	1,000

How should these expenses be deducted in Joel's 2008 return?

	From gross income, in arriving at adjusted gross income	As itemized deductions
a.	$18,000	$0
b.	$11,000	$ 7,000
c.	$10,000	$ 8,000
d.	$0	$18,000

151. Magda Micale, a public school teacher with adjusted gross income of $10,000, paid the following items in 2008 for which she received no reimbursement:

Initiation fee for membership in teachers' union	$100
Dues to teachers' union	180
Voluntary unemployment benefit fund contributions to union-established fund	72

How much can Magda claim in 2008 as allowable miscellaneous deductions on Schedule A of Form 1040?

a. $ 80
b. $280

c. $252
d. $352

152. Harold Brodsky is an electrician employed by a contracting firm. His adjusted gross income is $25,000. During the current year he incurred and paid the following expenses:

Use of personal auto for company business (reimbursed by employer for $200)	$300
Specialized work clothes	550
Union dues	600
Cost of income tax preparation	150
Preparation of will	100

If Brodsky were to itemize his personal deductions, what amount should he claim as miscellaneous deductible expenses?

a. $ 800
b. $ 900
c. $1,500
d. $1,700

153. Which items are **not** subject to the phaseout of the amount of certain itemized deductions that may be claimed by high-income individuals?

a. Qualified residence interest.
b. Charitable contributions.
c. Investment interest expenses.
d. Real estate taxes.

154. For 2008, Dole's adjusted gross income exceeds $500,000. After the application of any other limitation, itemized deductions are reduced by

a. The **lesser** of 3% of the excess of adjusted gross income over the applicable amount or 80% of **certain** itemized deductions.
b. The **lesser** of 3% of the excess of adjusted gross income over the applicable amount or 80% of **all** itemized deductions.
c. The **greater** of 3% of the excess of adjusted gross income over the applicable amount or 80% of **certain** itemized deductions.
d. The **greater** of 3% of the excess of adjusted gross income over the applicable amount or 80% of **all** itemized deductions.

155. Which one of the following is **not** included in determining the total support of a dependent?

a. Fair rental value of dependent's lodging.
b. Medical insurance premiums paid on behalf of the dependent.
c. Birthday presents given to the dependent.
d. Nontaxable scholarship received by the dependent.

156. In 2008, Smith, a divorced person, provided over one-half the support for his widowed mother, Ruth, and his son, Clay, both of whom are US citizens. During 2008, Ruth did not live with Smith. She received $9,000 in social security benefits. Clay, a full-time graduate student, and his wife lived with Smith. Clay had no income but filed a joint return for 2008, owing an additional $500 in taxes on his wife's income. How many exemptions was Smith entitled to claim on his 2008 tax return?

a. 4
b. 3
c. 2

d. 1

157. Jim and Kay Ross contributed to the support of their two children, Dale and Kim, and Jim's widowed parent, Grant. For 2008, Dale, a twenty-year-old full-time college student, earned $4,500 from a part-time job. Kim, a twenty-three-year-old bank teller, earned $18,000. Grant received $5,000 in dividend income and $4,000 in nontaxable social security benefits. Grant, Dale, and Kim are US citizens and were over one-half supported by Jim and Kay. How many exemptions can Jim and Kay claim on their 2008 joint income tax return?

    a. Two
    b. Three
    c. Four
    d. Five

158. Joe and Barb are married, but Barb refuses to sign a 2008 joint return. On Joe's separate 2008 return, an exemption may be claimed for Barb if

    a. Barb was a full-time student for the entire 2008 school year.
    b. Barb attaches a written statement to Joe's income tax return, agreeing to be claimed as an exemption by Joe for 2008.
    c. Barb was under the age of nineteen.
    d. Barb had **no** gross income and was **not** claimed as another person's dependent in 2008.

159. Al and Mary Lew are married and filed a joint 2008 income tax return in which they validly claimed the $3,500 personal exemption for their dependent seventeen-year-old daughter, Doris. Since Doris earned $5,400 in 2008 from a part-time job at the college she attended full-time, Doris was also required to file a 2008 income tax return. What amount was Doris entitled to claim as a personal exemption in her 2008 individual income tax return?

    a. $0
    b. $ 850
    c. $3,500
    d. $5,450

160. During 2008 Robert Moore, who is fifty years old and unmarried, maintained his home in which he and his widower father, age seventy-five, resided. His father had $3,700 interest income from a savings account and also received $2,400 from social security during 2008. Robert provided 60% of his father's total support for 2008. What is Robert's filing status for 2008, and how many exemptions should he claim on his tax return?

    a. Head of household and two exemptions.
    b. Single and two exemptions.
    c. Head of household and one exemption.
    d. Single and one exemption.

161. John and Mary Arnold are a childless married couple who lived apart (alone in homes maintained by each) the entire year 2008. On December 31, 2008, they were legally separated under a decree of separate maintenance. Which of the following is the only filing status choice available to them when filing for 2008?

    a. Single.
    b. Head of household.
    c. Married filing separate return.
    d. Married filing joint return.

162. Albert and Lois Stoner, age sixty-six and sixty-four, respectively, filed a joint tax return for 2008. They provided all of the support for their blind nineteen-year-old son, who has no gross income. Their twenty-three-year-old daughter, a full-time student until her graduation on June 14, 2008, earned $4,900, which was 40% of her total support during 2008. Her parents provided the remaining support. The Stoners also provided the total support of Lois' father, who is a citizen and lifelong resident of Peru. How many exemptions can the Stoners claim on their 2008 income tax return?

    a. 4
    b. 5
    c. 6
    d. 7

163. Jim Planter, who reached age sixty-five on January 1, 2008, filed a joint return for 2008 with his wife Rita, age fifty. Mary, their twenty-one-year-old daughter, was a full-time student at a college until her graduation on June 2, 2008. The daughter had $6,500 of income and provided 25% of her own support during 2008. In addition, during 2008 the Planters were the sole support for Rita's niece, age 27, who had no income. How many exemptions should the Planters claim on their 2008 tax return?

    a. 2
    b. 3
    c. 4
    d. 5

164. In 2008, Sam Dunn provided more than half the support for his wife, his father's brother, and his cousin. Sam's wife was the only relative who was a member of Sam's household. None of the relatives had any income, nor did any of them file an individual or a joint return. All of these relatives are US citizens. Which of these relatives should be claimed as a dependent or dependents on Sam's 2008 return?

    a. Only his wife.
    b. Only his father's brother.
    c. Only his cousin.
    d. His wife, his father's brother, and his cousin.

165. In 2008, Alan Kott provided more than half the support for his following relatives, none of whom qualified as a member of Alan's household:

> Cousin
> Niece
> Foster parent

None of these relatives had any income, nor did any of these relatives file an individual or joint return. All of these relatives are US citizens. Which of these relatives could be claimed as a dependent on Alan's 2008 return?

    a. No one.
    b. Niece.
    c. Cousin.
    d. Foster parent.

166. Sara Hance, who is single and lives alone in Idaho, has no income of her own and is supported in full by the following persons:

	Amount of support	Percent of total
Alma (an unrelated friend)	$2,400	48
Ben (Sara's brother)	2,150	43
Carl (Sara's son)	450	9
	$5,000	100

Under a multiple support agreement, Sara's dependency exemption can be claimed by

a. No one.
b. Alma.
c. Ben.
d. Carl.

167. Mr. and Mrs. Vonce, both age sixty-two, filed a joint return for 2008. They provided all the support for their daughter, who is nineteen, legally blind, and who has no income. Their son, age twenty-one and a full-time student at a university, had $6,200 of income and provided 70% of his own support during 2008. How many exemptions should Mr. and Mrs. Vonce have claimed on their 2008 joint income tax return?

a. 2
b. 3
c. 4
d. 5

168. Which of the following is(are) among the requirements to enable a taxpayer to be classified as a "qualifying widow(er)"?

I. A dependent has lived with the taxpayer for six months.
II. The taxpayer has maintained the cost of the principal residence for six months.

a. I only.
b. II only.
c. Both I and II.
d. Neither I nor II.

169. For head of household filing status, which of the following costs are considered in determining whether the taxpayer has contributed more than one-half the cost of maintaining the household?

	Insurance on the home	Rental value of home
a.	Yes	Yes
b.	No	No
c.	Yes	No
d.	No	Yes

170. A husband and wife can file a joint return even if

a. The spouses have different tax years, provided that both spouses are alive at the end of the year.
b. The spouses have different accounting methods.
c. Either spouse was a nonresident alien at any time during the tax year, provided that at least one spouse makes the proper election.
d. They were divorced before the end of the tax year.

171. Emil Gow's wife died in 2006. Emil did not remarry, and he continued to maintain a home for himself and his dependent infant child during 2007 and 2008, providing full support for himself and his child during these years. For 2006, Emil properly filed a joint return. For 2008, Emil's filing status is

a. Single.
b. Head of household.
c. Qualifying widower with dependent child.
d. Married filing joint return.

172. Nell Brown's husband died in 2005. Nell did not remarry, and continued to maintain a home for herself and her dependent infant child during 2006, 2007, and 2008, providing full support for herself and her child during these three years. For 2005, Nell properly filed a joint return. For 2008, Nell's filing status is

a. Single.
b. Married filing joint return.
c. Head of household.
d. Qualifying widow with dependent child.

173. Mrs. Irma Felton, by herself, maintains her home in which she and her unmarried twenty-six-year-old son reside. Her son, however, does not qualify as her dependent. Mrs. Felton's husband died in 2007. What is Mrs. Felton's filing status for 2008?

a. Single.
b. Qualifying widow with dependent child.
c. Head of household.
d. Married filing jointly.

174. Poole, forty-five years old and unmarried, is in the 15% tax bracket. He had 2008 adjusted gross income of $20,000. The following information applies to Poole:

Medical expenses	$7,000
Standard deduction	5,450
Personal exemption	3,500

Poole wishes to minimize his income tax. What is Poole's 2008 total income tax?

a. $3,000
b. $1,733
c. $1,650
d. $1,455

175. Which of the following itemized deductions are deductible when computing the alternative minimum tax for individuals?

a. State income taxes.
b. Home equity mortgage interest when the loan proceeds were used to purchase an auto.
c. Unreimbursed employee expenses in excess of 2% of adjusted gross income.
d. Gambling losses.

176. Randy Lowe reported the following items in computing his regular federal income tax for 2008:

Personal exemption	$3,500
Itemized deduction for state taxes	1,500
Cash charitable contributions	1,250
Net long-term capital gain	700
Excess of accelerated depreciation over straight-line depreciation on real property placed in service prior to 1987	600
Tax-exempt interest from private activity bonds	400

What are the amounts of tax preference items and adjustments that must be added to or subtracted from regular taxable income in order to compute Lowe's alternative minimum taxable income for 2008?

	Preferences	Adjustments
a.	$1,000	$5,000
b.	$1,000	$5,600
c.	$1,700	$6,150
d.	$2,250	$5,400

5. Life insurance proceeds

6. Jury duty pay

7. Gambling winnings

Situation	Filing Status	Adjusted Gross Income	Tax Treatment		Research	Communication

During 2008 the following payments were made or losses were incurred. For **items 1 through 14,** select the appropriate tax treatment. A tax treatment may be selected once, more than once, or not at all.

Tax treatment

A. Not deductible.

B. Deductible in Schedule A—Itemized Deductions, subject to threshold of 7.5% of adjusted gross income.

C. Deductible in Schedule A—Itemized Deductions, subject to threshold of 2% of adjusted gross income.

D. Deductible on page 1 of Form 1040 to arrive at adjusted gross income.

E. Deductible in full in Schedule A—Itemized Deductions.

F. Deductible in Schedule A—Itemized Deductions, subject to maximum of 50% of adjusted gross income.

	(A)	(B)	(C)	(D)	(E)	(F)
1. Premiums on Mr. Vick's personal life insurance policy.	O	O	O	O	O	O
2. Penalty on Mrs. Vick's early withdrawal of funds from a certificate of deposit.	O	O	O	O	O	O
3. Mrs. Vick's substantiated cash donation to the American Red Cross.	O	O	O	O	O	O
4. Payment of estimated state income taxes.	O	O	O	O	O	O
5. Payment of real estate taxes on the Vick home.	O	O	O	O	O	O
6. Loss on the sale of the family car.	O	O	O	O	O	O
7. Cost in excess of the increase in value of residence, for the installation of a stairlift in January 2008, related directly to the medical care of Mr. Vick.	O	O	O	O	O	O
8. The Vicks' health insurance premiums for hospitalization coverage.	O	O	O	O	O	O
9. CPA fees to prepare the 2007 tax return.	O	O	O	O	O	O
10. Amortization over the life of the loan of points paid to refinance the mortgage at a lower rate on the Vick home.	O	O	O	O	O	O
11. One-half the self-employment tax paid by Mrs. Vick.	O	O	O	O	O	O
12. Mrs. Vick's $100 in gambling losses.	O	O	O	O	O	O
13. Mrs. Vick's union dues.	O	O	O	O	O	O
14. 2007 federal income tax paid with the Vicks' tax return on April 15, 2008.	O	O	O	O	O	O

Situation	Filing Status	Adjusted Gross Income	Tax Treatment	Research		Communication

Mrs. Vick is considering making contributions to a qualified tuition program to provide savings for her daughter's college education. However, Mrs. Vick is concerned that the contributions will be considered a gift of a future interest and result in a taxable gift. Which code section and subsection provide the gift tax treatment for contributions to a qualified tuition program? Indicate the reference to that citation in the shaded boxes below.

Section	Subsection
§ [ ]	([ ])

Situation	Filing Status	Adjusted Gross Income	Tax Treatment	Research	Communication

Describe the results of your research in a memorandum to Mrs. Vick.

To: Mrs. Vick
From: CPA Candidate
Re: College savings plan

Simulation Problem 6   (40 to 45 minutes)

Situation					
	Income and Loss	Adjustments	Tax Treatments	Communication	Research

Tom and Joan Moore, both CPAs, filed a joint 2008 federal income tax return showing $70,000 in taxable income. During 2008, Tom's daughter Laura, age sixteen, resided with Tom's former spouse. Laura had no income of her own and was not Tom's dependent.

	Income and Loss				
Situation		Adjustments	Tax Treatments	Communication	Research

For **items 1 through 10,** determine the amount of income or loss, if any, that should be included on page one of the Moores' 2008 Form 1040.

1. The Moores had no capital loss carryovers from prior years. During 2008 the Moores had the following stock transactions that resulted in a net capital loss:

	Date acquired	Date sold	Sales price	Cost
Revco	2/1/08	3/17/08	$15,000	$25,000
Abbco	2/18/07	4/1/08	8,000	4,000

2. In 2005, Joan received an acre of land as an inter vivos gift from her grandfather. At the time of the gift, the land had a fair market value of $50,000. The grandfather's adjusted basis was $60,000. Joan sold the land in 2008 to an unrelated third party for $56,000.

3. The Moores received a $500 security deposit on their rental property in 2008. They are required to return the amount to the tenant.

4. Tom's 2008 wages were $53,000. In addition, Tom's employer provided group-term life insurance on Tom's life in excess of $50,000. The value of such excess coverage was $2,000.

5. During 2008, the Moores received a $2,500 federal tax refund and a $1,250 state tax refund for 2007 overpayments. In 2007, the Moores were not subject to the alternative minimum tax and were not entitled to any credit against income tax. The Moores' 2007 adjusted gross income was $80,000 and itemized deductions were $1,450 in excess of the standard deduction. The state tax deduction for 2007 was $2,000.

6. In 2008, Joan received $1,300 in unemployment compensation benefits. Her employer made a $100 contribution to the unemployment insurance fund on her behalf.

7. The Moores received $8,400 in gross receipts from their rental property during 2008. The expenses for the residential rental property were

Bank mortgage interest	$1,200
Real estate taxes	700
Insurance	500
MACRS depreciation	3,500

8. The Moores received a stock dividend in 2008 from Ace Corp. They had the option to receive either cash or Ace stock with a fair market value of $900 as of the date of distribution. The par value of the stock was $500.

9. In 2008, Joan received $3,500 as beneficiary of the death benefit that was provided by her brother's employer. Joan's brother did not have a nonforfeitable right to receive the money while living, and the death benefit does not represent the proceeds of life insurance.

10. Tom received $10,000, consisting of $5,000 each of principal and interest, when he redeemed a Series EE savings bond in 2008. The bond was issued in his name in 1999 and the proceeds were used to pay for Laura's college tuition. Tom had not elected to report the yearly increases in the value of the bond.

Situation	Income and Loss	Adjustments	Tax Treatments	Communication	Research

Determine the amount of the adjustment, if any, to arrive at adjusted gross income.

As required by a 2003 divorce agreement, Tom paid an annual amount of $8,000 in alimony and $10,000 in child support during 2008.

Situation	Income and Loss	Adjustments	Tax Treatments	Communication	Research

During 2008, the following events took place. For **items 1 through 12,** select the appropriate tax treatment. A tax treatment may be selected once, more than once, or not at all.

Tax treatment

A. Not deductible on Form 1040.

B. Deductible in full in Schedule A—Itemized Deductions.

C. Deductible in Schedule A—Itemized Deductions, subject to a threshold of 7.5% of adjusted gross income.

D. Deductible in Schedule A—Itemized Deductions, subject to a limitation of 50% of adjusted gross income.

E. Deductible in Schedule A—Itemized Deductions, subject to a $100 floor and a threshold of 10% of adjusted gross income.

F. Deductible in Schedule A—Itemized Deductions, subject to a threshold of 2% of adjusted gross income.

	(A)	(B)	(C)	(D)	(E)	(F)
1. On March 23, 2008, Tom sold fifty shares of Zip stock at a $1,200 loss. He repurchased fifty shares of Zip on April 15, 2008.	○	○	○	○	○	○
2. Payment of a personal property tax based on the value of the Moores' car.	○	○	○	○	○	○
3. Used clothes were donated to church organizations.	○	○	○	○	○	○
4. Premiums were paid covering insurance against Tom's loss of earnings.	○	○	○	○	○	○
5. Tom paid for subscriptions to accounting journals.	○	○	○	○	○	○
6. Interest was paid on a $10,000 home-equity line of credit secured by the Moores' residence. The fair market value of the home exceeded the mortgage by $50,000. Tom used the proceeds to purchase a sailboat.	○	○	○	○	○	○
7. Amounts were paid in excess of insurance reimbursement for prescription drugs.	○	○	○	○	○	○
8. Funeral expenses were paid by the Moores for Joan's brother.	○	○	○	○	○	○
9. Theft loss was incurred on Joan's jewelry in excess of insurance reimbursement. There were no 2008 personal casualty gains.	○	○	○	○	○	○
10. Loss on the sale of the family's sailboat.	○	○	○	○	○	○
11. Interest was paid on the $300,000 acquisition mortgage on the Moores' home. The mortgage is secured by their home.	○	○	○	○	○	○
12. Joan performed free accounting services for the Red Cross. The estimated value of the services was $500.	○	○	○	○	○	○

Situation	Income and Loss	Adjustments	Tax Treatments	Communication	Research

The Moores contact you and indicate that they are considering buying a more expensive home, as well as using a home equity loan to purchase an automobile. They want to know what possible limitations might apply to their deduction for the interest expense that will result from these purchases. Write a letter to the Moores explaining the limitations that would apply to their deduction for the interest expense they might incur.

To: Tom and Joan Moore
From: CPA Candidate
Re: Interest expense deduction limitations

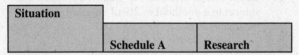

Situation	Income and Loss	Adjustments	Tax Treatments	Communication	Research

Adjustments must be made to regular taxable income in order to compute an individual's alternative minimum taxable income (AMTI). Which code section and subsection provide the adjustments that only apply to individuals when computing the alternative minimum tax? Indicate the reference to that citation in the shaded boxes below.

Section	Subsection
§	( )

Simulation Problem 7   (30 to 35 minutes)

Situation		
	Schedule A	Research

Fred (social security number 123-67-5489) and Laura Shaw provided you with the following tax return data. The amount from Form 1040, line 38 is $80,000.

Medical and dental expenses

Medical insurance premiums	$3,600
Disability income insurance premiums	800
Prescription drugs	825
Nonprescription medicine	280
Dr. Jones – neurologist	2,250
Dentist	750
Dr. Smith – LASIK surgery	900
Insurance reimbursement for medical bills	2,000
Transportation to and from doctors	80

Taxes

Balance of state income taxes due for 2006 paid on April 15, 2007	$ 225
State income taxes withheld for 2007	975
Real estate taxes on principal residence	7,000
Real estate taxes on summer residence	3,000
County personal property tax	410
Registration fee for automobiles	160

Interest

Mortgage interest on principal residence	$5,500
Mortgage interest on summer residence	2,200
Interest paid on automobile loan	800
Interest paid on personal use credit cards	500

Contributions

Cash donated to church	$2,500
Stock donated to church. (The Shaws purchased it for $3,000 18 months ago)	4,000

Miscellaneous payments

Legal fee for preparation of a will	$ 350
Rent for safety-deposit box containing stocks and bonds	120
Union dues	600
Subscriptions to investment publications	300
Life insurance premiums	2,800
Transportation to and from work	2,400
Fee paid for tax return preparation	400
Unreimbursed business travel away from home overnight	900
Contribution to a national political party	200
Repairs to principal residence	2,000

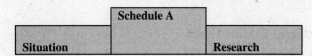

Complete the following 2007 Form 1040 Schedule A-Itemized Deductions for Fred and Laura Shaw.

The Shaws are considering donating a painting to a state university for display in the university's library. The Shaws acquired the painting six months ago for $90,000 and believe that the painting is now worth $105,000. Which code section and subsection determine the amount of charitable contribution to which the Shaws will be entitled if they donate the painting at the present time? Indicate the reference to that citation in the shaded boxes below.

Section	Subsection
§	( )

SCHEDULES A&B	Schedule A—Itemized Deductions	OMB No. 1545-0074
(Form 1040)	(Schedule B is on back)	**2007**
Department of the Treasury Internal Revenue Service	▶ **Attach to Form 1040.** ▶ **See Instructions for Schedules A&B (Form 1040).**	Attachment Sequence No. **07**

Name(s) shown on Form 1040 | Your social security number

Medical and Dental Expenses

Caution. Do not include expenses reimbursed or paid by others.

1 Medical and dental expenses (see page A-1) . . . | **1**
2 Enter amount from Form 1040, line 38 | **2** |
3 Multiply line 2 by 7.5% (.075) . . . . | **3**
4 Subtract line 3 from line 1. If line 3 is more than line 1, enter -0- . . . . . | **4**

Taxes You Paid

(See page A-2.)

5 State and local (check only one box):
   a ☐ Income taxes, **or**
   b ☐ General sales taxes } . . . . . . | **5**
6 Real estate taxes (see page A-5) . . . . . | **6**
7 Personal property taxes . . . . | **7**
8 Other taxes. List type and amount ▶................................ | **8**
9 Add lines 5 through 8 . . . . | **9**

Interest You Paid

(See page A-5.)

Note. Personal interest is not deductible.

10 Home mortgage interest and points reported to you on Form 1098 | **10**
11 Home mortgage interest not reported to you on Form 1098. If paid to the person from whom you bought the home, see page A-6 and show that person's name, identifying no., and address ▶

   ---------------------------------- | **11**
12 Points not reported to you on Form 1098. See page A-6 for special rules . . . . | **12**
13 Qualified mortgage insurance premiums (See page A-7) . | **13**
14 Investment interest. Attach Form 4952 if required. (See page A-7.) . . . . | **14**
15 Add lines 10 through 14 . . . . | **15**

Gifts to Charity

If you made a gift and got a benefit for it, see page A-8.

16 Gifts by cash or check. If you made any gift of $250 or more, see page A-8 . . . . . . | **16**
17 Other than by cash or check. If any gift of $250 or more, see page A-8. You **must** attach Form 8283 if over $500 | **17**
18 Carryover from prior year . . . . | **18**
19 Add lines 16 through 18 . . . . | **19**

Casualty and Theft Losses

20 Casualty or theft loss(es). Attach Form 4684. (See page A-9.) . . . . | **20**

Job Expenses and Certain Miscellaneous Deductions

(See page A-9.)

21 Unreimbursed employee expenses—job travel, union dues, job education, etc. Attach Form 2106 or 2106-EZ if required. (See page A-9.) ▶.................... | **21**
22 Tax preparation fees . . . . | **22**
23 Other expenses—investment, safe deposit box, etc. List type and amount ▶............................
   ---------------------------------- | **23**
24 Add lines 21 through 23 . . . . - | **24**
25 Enter amount from Form 1040, line 38 | **25** |
26 Multiply line 25 by 2% (.02) . . . . . . | **26**
27 Subtract line 26 from line 24. If line 26 is more than line 24, enter -0- . . . . | **27**

Other Miscellaneous Deductions

28 Other—from list on page A-10. List type and amount ▶ ....
---------------------------------- | **28**

Total Itemized Deductions

29 Is Form 1040, line 38, over $156,400 (over $78,200 if married filing separately)?
   ☐ **No.**   Your deduction is not limited. Add the amounts in the far right column for lines 4 through 28. Also, enter this amount on Form 1040, line 40. } ▶ | **29**
   ☐ **Yes.** Your deduction may be limited. See page A-10 for the amount to enter.
30 If you elect to itemize deductions even though they are less than your standard deduction, check here ▶ ☐

For Paperwork Reduction Act Notice, see Form 1040 instructions.   Cat. No. 11330X   Schedule A (Form 1040) 2007

property's basis. Here, the stock worth $3,000 was purchased for $1,500 just four months earlier. Since its holding period did not exceed twelve months, a sale of the stock would result in a short-term capital gain, and the amount of allowable contribution deduction is limited to the stock's basis of $1,500. Additionally, to be deductible, a contribution must be made to a qualifying **organization**. As a result, the $2,000 cash given directly to a needy family is not deductible.

141. (a) The requirement is to determine the maximum amount of charitable contribution deductible as an itemized deduction on Taylor's tax return for 2008. The donation of appreciated land purchased for investment and held for more than twelve months is a contribution of real capital gain property (property that would result in long-term capital gain if sold). The amount of contribution is the land's FMV of $25,000, limited in deductibility for the current year to 30% of AGI. In this case, since 30% of AGI would be 30% × $90,000 = $27,000, the full amount of the land contribution ($25,000) is deductible for 2008.

III.E. Personal Casualty and Theft Gains and Losses

142. (a) The requirement is to determine the amount of the fire loss to her personal residence that Frazer can claim as an itemized deduction. The amount of a personal casualty loss is computed as the lesser of (1) the adjusted basis of the property ($130,000), or (2) the decline in the property's fair market value resulting from the casualty ($130,000 – $0 = $130,000); reduced by any insurance recovery ($120,000), and a $100 floor. Since Frazer had no casualty gains during the year, the net casualty loss is then deductible as an itemized deduction to the extent that it exceeds 10% of adjusted gross income.

Fire loss	$ 130,000
Insurance proceeds	(120,000)
$100 floor	(100)
10% of $70,000 AGI	(7,000)
Casualty loss itemized deduction	$ 2,900

143. (a) The requirement is to determine the amount the Burgs should deduct for the casualty loss (repair of glass vase accidentally broken by their dog) in their itemized deductions. A casualty is the damage, destruction, or loss of property resulting from an identifiable event that is sudden, unexpected, or unusual. Deductible casualty losses may result from earthquakes, tornadoes, floods, fires, vandalism, auto accidents, etc. However, a loss due to the accidental breakage of household articles such as glassware or china under normal conditions is not a casualty loss. Neither is a loss due to damage caused by a family pet.

144. (d) The requirement is to determine the proper treatment of the $490 casualty insurance premium. Casualty insurance premiums on an individual's personal residence are considered nondeductible personal expenses. Even though a casualty is actually incurred during the year, no deduction is available for personal casualty insurance premiums.

145. (d) The requirement is to determine the amount of the fire loss damage to their personal residence that the Hoyts can deduct as an itemized deduction. The amount of a nonbusiness casualty loss is computed as the lesser of (1) the adjusted basis of the property, or (2) the property's decline in FMV; reduced by any insurance recovery, and a $100 floor. If an individual has a net casualty loss for the year, it is then deductible as an itemized deduction to the extent that it exceeds 10% of adjusted gross income.

Lesser of:		
Adjusted basis	= $50,000	
Decline in FMV		
($60,000 – $55,000)	= $ 5,000	$ 5,000
Reduce by:		
Insurance recovery		(0)
$100 floor		(100)
10% of $34,000 AGI		(3,400)
Casualty loss itemized deduction		$ 1,500

Note that the $2,500 spent for repairs is not included in the computation of the loss.

146. (b) The requirement is to determine the proper treatment for the $800 appraisal fee that was incurred to determine the amount of the Hoyts' fire loss. The appraisal fee is considered an expense of determining the Hoyts' tax liability; it is not a part of the casualty loss itself. Thus, the appraisal fee is deductible as a miscellaneous itemized deduction subject to a 2% of adjusted gross income floor.

III.F. Miscellaneous Deductions

147. (d) The requirement is to determine which item is **not** a miscellaneous itemized deduction. A legal fee for tax advice related to a divorce, IRA trustee's fees that are separately billed and paid, and an appraisal fee for valuing a charitable contribution qualify as miscellaneous itemized deductions subject to the 2% of AGI floor. On the other hand, the check writing fees for a personal checking account are a personal expense and not deductible.

148. (b) The requirement is to determine the proper treatment of the $2,000 legal fee that was incurred by Hall in a suit to collect the alimony owed her. The $2,000 legal fee is considered an expenditure incurred in the production of income. Expenses incurred in the production of income are deductible as miscellaneous itemized deductions subject to the 2% of adjusted gross income floor.

149. (b) The requirement is to determine the proper reporting of Hall's lottery transactions. Hall's lottery winnings of $200 must be reported as other income on page 1 of Hall's Form 1040. Hall's $1,000 expenditure for state lottery tickets is deductible as a miscellaneous itemized deduction not subject to the 2% of AGI floor, but is limited in amount to the $200 of lottery winnings included in Hall's gross income.

150. (d) The requirement is to determine how expenses pertaining to business activities should be deducted by an outside salesman. An outside salesman is an employee who principally solicits business for his employer while away from the employer's place of business. All unreimbursed business expenses of an outside salesman are deducted as miscellaneous itemized deductions, subject to a 2% of AGI floor. Deductible expenses include business travel, secretarial help, and telephone expenses.

151. (a) The requirement is to determine the amount that can be claimed as miscellaneous itemized deductions. Both the initiation fee and the union dues are fully deductible. The voluntary benefit fund contribution is not deductible. Miscellaneous itemized deductions are generally deductible only to the extent they exceed 2% of AGI. In this case the deductible amount is $80 [$280 – (.02 × $10,000)].

152. (b)   The requirement is to compute the amount of miscellaneous itemized deductions. The cost of uniforms not adaptable to general use (specialized work clothes), union dues, unreimbursed auto expenses, and the cost of income tax preparation are all miscellaneous itemized deductions. The preparation of a will is personal in nature, and is not deductible. Thus, the computation of Brodsky's miscellaneous itemized deductions in excess of the 2% of AGI floor is as follows:

Unreimbursed auto expenses	$ 100
Specialized work clothes	550
Union dues	600
Cost of income tax preparation	150
	$1,400
Less (2% × $25,000)	(500)
Deduction allowed	$ 900

III.G.   Reduction of Itemized Deductions

153. (c)   The requirement is to determine the item that is not subject to the phaseout of itemized deductions for high-income individuals. An individual whose adjusted gross income exceeds a threshold amount ($159,950 for 2008) is required to reduce the amount of allowable itemized deductions by 3% of the excess of adjusted gross income over the threshold amount. All itemized deductions are subject to this reduction **except** medical expenses, nonbusiness casualty losses, investment interest expense, and gambling losses.

154. (a)   The requirement is to determine the correct statement regarding the reduction in itemized deductions. For an individual whose AGI exceeds a threshold amount, the amount of otherwise allowable itemized deductions is reduced by the lesser of (1) 3% of the excess of AGI over the threshold amount, or (2) 80% of certain itemized deductions. The itemized deductions that are subject to reduction include taxes, qualified residence interest, charitable contributions, and miscellaneous itemized deductions (other than gambling losses). The reduction of these itemized deductions can not exceed 80% of the amount that is otherwise allowable.

IV. Exemptions

155. (d)   The requirement is to determine which item is not included in determining the total support of a dependent. Support includes food, clothing, FMV of lodging, medical, recreational, educational, and certain capital expenditures made on behalf of a dependent. Excluded from support is life insurance premiums, funeral expenses, nontaxable scholarships, and income and social security taxes paid from a dependent's own income.

156. (c)   The requirement is to determine the number of exemptions that Smith was entitled to claim on his 2008 tax return. Smith will be allowed one exemption for himself and one exemption for his dependent mother. Smith is entitled to an exemption for his mother because he provided over half of her support, and her gross income ($0) was less than $3,500. Note that her $9,000 of social security benefits is excluded from her gross income, and that she did not have to live with Smith because she is related to him. No exemption is available to Smith for his son, Clay, because his son filed a joint return on which there was a tax liability.

157. (b)   The requirement is to determine how many exemptions Jim and Kay can claim on their 2008 joint income tax return. Jim and Kay are entitled to one personal exemption each on their joint return. They also are entitled to one exemption for their son, Dale, since he is a *qualifying child* (i.e., Dale did not provide more than half of his own support, and Dale is a full-time student under age twenty-four). However, no dependency exemptions are available for Kim and Grant. Kim is not a qualifying child because she is at least age 19 and not a full-time student, and she is not a qualifying relative because her gross income was at least $3,500. Similarly, Grant is not a qualifying relative because his gross income was at least $3,500.

158. (d)   The requirement is to determine the requirements which must be satisfied in order for Joe to claim an exemption for his spouse on Joe's separate return for 2008. An exemption can be claimed for Joe's spouse on Joe's separate 2008 return only if the spouse had **no** gross income and was **not** claimed as another person's dependent in 2008.

159. (a)   The requirement is to determine the amount of personal exemption on a dependent's tax return. No personal exemption is allowed on an individual's tax return if the individual can be claimed as a dependency exemption by another taxpayer.

160. (d)   The requirement is to determine Robert's filing status and the number of exemptions that he should claim. Robert's father does not qualify as Robert's dependent because his father's gross income (interest income of $3,700) was not less than $3,500. Social security is not included in the gross income test. Since his father does not qualify as his dependent, Robert does not qualify for head-of-household filing status. Thus, Robert will file as single with one exemption.

161. (a)   The requirement is to determine the filing status of the Arnolds. Since they were legally separated under a decree of separate maintenance on the last day of the taxable year and do not qualify for head-of-household status, they must each file as single.

162. (a)   Mr. and Mrs. Stoner are entitled to one exemption each. They are entitled to one exemption for their daughter since she is a qualifying child (i.e., she did not provide more than half of her own support, and she is a full-time student under age twenty-four). An exemption can be claimed for their son because he is a qualifying relative (i.e., they provided more than half of his support, and his gross income was less than $3,500). No exemption is allowable for Mrs. Stoner's father since he was neither a US citizen nor resident of the US, Canada, or Mexico. There is no additional exemption for being age sixty-five or older.

163. (c)   The requirement is to determine the number of exemptions the Planters may claim on their joint tax return. There is one exemption for Mr. Planter, and one exemption for his spouse. In addition there is one dependency exemption for their daughter who is a qualifying child (i.e., she did not provide more than half of her own support, and she is a full-time student under age twenty-four). There is also one dependency exemption for their niece who is a qualifying relative (i.e., they provided more than half of her support, and her gross income was less than $3,500). However, there is no additional exemption for being age sixty-five or older.

164. (b) The requirement is to determine which of the relatives can be claimed as a dependent (or dependents) on Sam's 2008 return. A taxpayer's own spouse is never a dependent of the taxpayer. Although a personal exemption is generally available for a taxpayer's spouse on the taxpayer's return, it is not a "dependency exemption." Generally, a dependency exemption is available for a qualifying relative if (1) the taxpayer furnishes more than 50% of the dependent's support, (2) the dependent's gross income is less than $3,500, (3) the dependent is of specified relationship to the taxpayer or lives in the taxpayer's household for the entire year, (4) the dependent is a US citizen or resident of the US, Canada, or Mexico, and (5) the dependent does not file a joint return. Here, the support, gross income, US citizen, and joint return tests are met with respect to both Sam's cousin and his father's brother (i.e., Sam's uncle). However, Sam's cousin is not of specified relationship to Sam as defined in the IRC, and could only be claimed as a dependent if the cousin lived in Sam's household for the entire year. Since Sam's cousin did not live in Sam's household, Sam cannot claim a dependency exemption for his cousin. On the other hand, Sam's uncle is of specified relationship to Sam as defined in the IRC and can be claimed as a dependency exemption by Sam.

165. (b) The requirement is to determine which relative could be claimed as a dependent. One of the requirements that must be satisfied to claim a dependency exemption for a person as a qualifying relative is that the person must be (1) of specified relationship to the taxpayer, or (2) a member of the taxpayer's household. Cousins and foster parents are not of specified relationship and only qualify if a member of the taxpayer's household. Since Alan's cousin and foster parent do not qualify as members of Alan's household, only Alan's niece can be claimed as a dependent.

166. (c) The requirement is to determine who can claim Sara's dependency exemption under a multiple support agreement. A multiple support agreement can be used if (1) no single taxpayer furnishes more than 50% of a dependent's support, and (2) two or more persons, each of whom would be able to take the exemption but for the support test, together provide more than 50% of the dependent's support. Then, any taxpayer who provides more than 10% of the dependent's support can claim the dependent if (1) the other persons furnishing more than 10% agree not to claim the dependent as an exemption, and (2) the other requirements for a dependency exemption are met. One of the other requirements that must be met is that the dependent be related to the taxpayer or live in the taxpayer's household. Alma is not eligible for the exemption because Sara is unrelated to Alma and did not live in Alma's household. Carl is not eligible for the exemption because he provided only 9% of Sara's support. Ben is eligible to claim the exemption for Sara under a multiple support agreement because Ben is related to Sara and has provided more than 10% of her support.

167. (b) The requirement is to determine the number of exemptions allowable in 2008. Mr. and Mrs. Vonce are entitled to one exemption each. They are also entitled to one exemption for their dependent daughter since they provided over one half of her support and she had less than $3,500 of gross income. An exemption is not available for their son because he provided over one-half of his own support.

V.C. Filing Status

168. (d) The requirement is to determine which statements (if any) are among the requirements to enable a taxpayer to be classified as a "qualifying widow(er)." Qualifying widow(er) filing status is available for the two years following the year of a spouse's death if (1) the surviving spouse was eligible to file a joint return in the year of the spouse's death, (2) does not remarry before the end of the current year, and (3) the surviving spouse pays **over 50%** of the cost of maintaining a household that is the principal home for the **entire year** of the surviving spouse's dependent child.

169. (c) The requirement is to determine which items are considered in determining whether an individual has contributed more than one half the cost of maintaining the household for purposes of head of household filing status. The cost of maintaining a household includes such costs as rent, mortgage interest, taxes, insurance on the home, repairs, utilities, and food eaten in the home. The cost of maintaining a household does **not** include the cost of clothing, education, medical treatment, vacations, life insurance, transportation, the rental value of a home an individual owns, or the value of an individual's services or those of any member of the household.

170. (b) The requirement is to determine the correct statement regarding the filing of a joint tax return. A husband and wife can file a joint return even if they have different accounting methods. Answer (a) is incorrect because spouses must have the same tax year to file a joint return. Answer (c) is incorrect because if either spouse was a nonresident alien at any time during the tax year, **both** spouses must elect to be taxed as US citizens or residents for the entire tax year. Answer (d) is incorrect because taxpayers cannot file a joint return if divorced before the end of the year.

171. (c) The requirement is to determine Emil Gow's filing status for 2008. Emil should file as a "Qualifying widower with dependent child" (i.e., surviving spouse) which will entitle him to use the joint return tax rates. This filing status is available for the two taxable years following the year of a spouse's death if (1) the surviving spouse was eligible to file a joint return in the year of the spouse's death, (2) does not remarry before the end of the current tax year, and (3) the surviving spouse pays over 50% of the cost of maintaining a household that is the principal home for the entire year of the surviving spouse's dependent child.

172. (c) The requirement is to determine Nell's filing status for 2008. Nell qualifies as a head of household because she is unmarried and maintains a household for her infant child. Answer (a) is incorrect because although Nell is single, head of household filing status provides for lower tax rates. Answer (b) is incorrect because Nell is unmarried at the end of 2008. Since Nell's spouse died in 2005, answer (d) is incorrect because the filing status of a "qualifying widow" is only available for the two years following the year of the spouse's death.

173. (a) Mrs. Felton must file as a single taxpayer. Even though she is unmarried, Mrs. Felton does not qualify as a head of household because her son is neither a qualifying child (because of his age) nor a qualifying relative (because he is not her dependent). Answer (b) is incorrect because in order for Mrs. Felton to qualify, her son must qualify as a dependent, which he does not. Although Mrs. Felton would have qualified as married filing jointly, answer (d), in 2007 (the year of her husband's death), the problem requirement is her 2008 filing status.

174. (c) The requirement is to determine the 2008 income tax for Poole, an unmarried taxpayer in the 15% bracket with $20,000 of adjusted gross income. To determine Poole's taxable income, his adjusted gross income must be reduced by the greater of his itemized deductions or a standard deduction, and a personal exemption. Since Poole's medical expenses of $7,000 are deductible to the extent in excess of 7.5% of his AGI of $20,000, his itemized deductions of $5,500 exceed his available standard deduction of $5,450. Poole's tax computation is as follows:

Adjusted gross income		$20,000
Less:		
Itemized deductions	$5,500	
Personal exemption	3,500	9,000
Taxable income		$11,000
Tax rate		× 15%
Income tax		$ 1,650

V.D. Alternative Minimum Tax (AMT)

175. (d) The requirement is to determine the itemized deduction that is deductible when computing an individual's alternative minimum tax (AMT). For purposes of computing an individual's AMT, no deduction is allowed for personal, state, and local income taxes, and miscellaneous itemized deductions subject to the 2% of adjusted gross income threshold. Similarly, no deduction is allowed for home mortgage interest if the loan proceeds were not used to buy, build, or substantially improve the home.

176. (a) The requirement is to determine the amount of tax preferences and adjustments that must be included in the computation of Randy's alternative minimum tax. The tax preferences include the $600 of excess depreciation on real property placed in service prior to 1987, and the $400 of tax-exempt interest on private activity bonds. These must be added to regular taxable income in arriving at alternative minimum taxable income (AMTI). The adjustments include the $3,500 personal exemption and $1,500 of state income taxes that are deductible in computing regular taxable income but are not deductible in computing AMTI.

177. (d) The requirement is to determine the amount of Karen's unused alternative minimum tax credit that will carry over to 2009. The amount of alternative minimum tax paid by an individual that is attributable to timing preferences and adjustments is allowed as a tax credit (i.e., minimum tax credit) that can be applied against regular tax liability in future years. The minimum tax credit is computed as the excess of the AMT actually paid over the AMT that would have been paid if AMTI included only exclusion preferences and adjustments (e.g., disallowed itemized deductions, excess percentage depletion, tax-exempt private activity bond interest). Since the minimum tax credit can only be used to reduce future regular tax liability, the credit can only reduce regular tax liability to the point at which it equals the taxpayer's tentative minimum tax. In this case, Karen's payment of $20,000 of alternative minimum tax in 2007 generates a minimum tax credit of $20,000 – $9,000 = $11,000 which is carried forward to 2008. Since Karen's 2008 regular tax liability of $50,000 exceeded her tentative

minimum tax of $45,000, $5,000 of Karen's minimum tax credit would be used to reduce her 2008 tax liability to $45,000. Therefore, $11,000 – $5,000 = $6,000 of unused minimum tax credit would carry over to 2009.

178. (c) The requirement is to determine the amount that Mills should report as alternative minimum taxable income (AMTI) before the AMT exemption. Certain itemized deductions, although allowed for regular tax purposes, are not deductible in computing an individual's AMTI. As a result, no AMT deduction is allowed for state, local, and foreign income taxes, real and personal property taxes, and miscellaneous itemized deductions subject to the 2% of AGI floor. Also, the deduction for medical expenses is computed using a 10% floor (instead of the 7.5% floor used for regular tax), and no deduction is allowed for qualified residence interest if the mortgage proceeds were **not** used to buy, build, or substantially improve the taxpayer's principal residence or a second home. Additionally, no AMT deduction is allowed for personal exemptions and the standard deduction.

Here, Mills' $5,000 of state and local income taxes and $2,000 of miscellaneous itemized deductions that were deducted for regular tax purposes must be added back to his $70,000 of regular taxable income before personal exemption to arrive at Mills' AMTI before AMT exemption of ($70,000 + $5,000 + $2,000)= $77,000. Note that no adjustment was necessary for the mortgage interest because the mortgage loan was used to acquire his residence.

179. (c) The requirement is to determine whether a net capital gain and home equity interest expense are adjustments for purposes of computing the alternative minimum tax. Although an excess of net long-term capital gain over net short-term capital loss may be subject to a reduced maximum tax rate, the excess is neither a tax preference nor an adjustment in computing the alternative minimum tax. On the other hand, home equity interest expense where the home equity loan proceeds were not used to buy, build, or improve the home is an adjustment because the interest expense, although deductible for regular tax purposes, is not deductible for purposes of computing an individual's alternative minimum tax.

180. (d) The requirement is to determine the proper treatment for the credit for prior year alternative minimum tax (AMT). The amount of AMT paid by an individual taxpayer that is attributable to timing differences can be carried forward indefinitely as a minimum tax credit to offset the individual's future regular tax liability (not future AMT liability). The amount of AMT credit to be carried forward is the excess of the AMT actually paid over the AMT that would have been paid if AMTI included only exclusion preferences (e.g., disallowed itemized deductions, preferences for excess percentage depletion, and tax-exempt private activity bond interest).

181. (b) The requirement is to determine the correct statement regarding the computation of the alternative minimum tax (AMT). A taxpayer is subject to the AMT only if the taxpayer's tentative AMT exceeds the taxpayer's regular tax. Thus, the alternative minimum tax is computed as the excess of the tentative AMT over the regular tax.

V.E. Other Taxes

182. (b)   The requirement is to determine the amount of net earnings from self-employment that would be multiplied by the self-employment tax rate to compute Diamond's self-employment tax for 2008. Since self-employment earnings generally represent earnings derived from a trade or business carried on as a sole proprietor, the $10,000 of interest income from personal investments would be excluded from the computation. On the other hand, a self-employed taxpayer is allowed a deemed deduction equal to 7.65% of self-employment earnings in computing the amount of net earnings upon which the tax is based. The purpose of this deemed deduction is to reflect the fact that employees do not pay FICA tax on the corresponding 7.65% FICA tax paid by their employers.

Gross receipts from business	$150,000
Cost of goods sold	(80,000)
Operating expenses	(40,000)
Self-employment earnings	$ 30,000
Less deemed deduction (100%- 7.65%)	× 92.35%
Net earnings to be multiplied by self-employment tax rate	$ 27,705

183. (c)   The requirement is to determine the amount of Freeman's income that is subject to self-employment tax. The self-employment tax is imposed on self-employment income to provide Social Security and Medicare benefits for self-employed individuals. Self-employment income includes an individual's net earnings from a trade or business carried on as sole proprietor or as an independent contractor. The term also includes a partner's distributive share of partnership ordinary income or loss from trade or business activities, as well as guaranteed payments received by a partner for services rendered to a partnership. Self-employment income excludes gains and losses from the disposition of property used in a trade or business, as well as a shareholder's share of ordinary income from an S corporation.

184. (a)   The requirement is to determine the amount of Rich's net self-employment income. Income from self-employment generally includes all items of business income less business deductions. Excluded from the computation would be estimated income taxes on self-employment income, charitable contributions, investment income, and gains and losses on the disposition of property used in a trade or business. An individual's charitable contributions can only be deducted as an itemized deduction. Rich's net self-employment income would be

Business receipts	$20,000
Air conditioning parts	(2,500)
Yellow Pages listing	(2,000)
Business telephone calls	(400)
	$15,100

185. (c)   The requirement is to determine the correct statement regarding the self-employment tax. The self-employment tax is imposed at a rate of 15.3% on individuals who work for themselves (e.g., sole proprietor, independent contractor, partner). One-half of an individual's self-employment tax is deductible from gross income in arriving at adjusted gross income.

186. (c)   The requirement is to determine the correct statement with regard to social security tax (FICA) withheld in an amount greater than the maximum for a particular year. If an individual works for more than one employer, and combined wages exceed the maximum used for FICA purposes, too much FICA tax will be withheld. In such case, since the excess results from correct withholding by two or more employers, the excess should be claimed as a credit against income tax. Answer (a) is incorrect because the excess cannot be used as an itemized deduction. Answer (b) is incorrect because if employers withhold correctly, no reimbursement can be obtained from the employers. Answer (d) is incorrect because if the excess FICA tax withheld results from incorrect withholding by any one employer, the employer must reimburse the excess and it cannot be claimed as a credit against tax.

187. (b)   The requirement is to determine Berger's gross income from self-employment for 2008. Self-employment income represents the net earnings of an individual from a trade or business carried on as a proprietor or partner, or from rendering services as an independent contractor. The director's fee is self-employment income since it is related to a trade or business, and Berger is not an employee. Fees received by a fiduciary (e.g., executor) are generally not related to a trade or business and not self-employment income. However, executor's fees may constitute self-employment income if the executor is a professional fiduciary or carries on a trade or business in the administration of an estate.

188. (d)   The requirement is to determine Smith's gross income from self-employment. Self-employment income represents the net earnings of an individual from a trade or business carried on as a sole proprietor or partner, or from rendering services as an independent contractor (i.e., not an employee). The $8,000 consulting fee and the $2,000 of director's fees are self-employment income because they are related to a trade or business and Smith is not an employee.

VI.A. General Business Credit

189. (c)   The requirement is to determine which credit is not a component of the general business credit. The general business credit is a combination of several credits that provide uniform rules for current and carryback-carryover years. The general business credit is composed of the investment credit, work opportunity credit, alcohol fuels credit, research credit, low-income housing credit, enhanced oil recovery credit, disabled access credit, renewable electricity production credit, empowerment zone employment credit, Indian employment credit, employer social security credit, orphan drug credit, the new markets credit, the small employer pension plan start-up costs credit, and the employer-provided child care facilities credit. A general business credit in excess of the limitation amount is carried back one year and forward twenty years to offset tax liability in those years.

190. (a)   The requirement is to determine which tax credit is a combination of credits to provide for uniform rules for the current and carryback-carryover years. The general business credit is composed of the investment credit, work opportunity credit, welfare-to-work credit, alcohol fuels credit, research credit, low-income housing credit, enhanced oil recovery credit, disabled access credit, renewable electricity production credit, empowerment zone employment credit, Indian employment credit, employer social security credit, orphan drug credit, the new markets credit, the small employer pension plan start-up costs credit, and the employer-provided child care facilities credit. A general business credit in excess of the limitation amount is carried back one year and forward twenty years to offset tax liability in those years.

VI.K. Credit for the Elderly and the Disabled

191. (a) The requirement is to determine the amount that can be claimed as a credit for the elderly. The amount of credit (limited to tax liability) is 15% of an initial amount reduced by social security and 50% of AGI in excess of $10,000. Here, the credit is the lesser of (1) the taxpayers' tax liability of $60, or (2) 15% [$7,500 − $3,000 − (.50)($20,200 − $10,000)] = $0.

VI.L. Child and Dependent Care Credit

192. (c) The requirement is to compute Nora's child care credit for 2008. Since she has two dependent preschool children, all $6,000 paid for child care qualifies for the credit. The credit is 35% of qualified expenses, but is reduced by one percentage point for each $2,000 (or fraction thereof) of AGI over $15,000 down to a minimum of 20%. Since Nora's AGI is $44,000, her credit is 20% × $6,000 = $1,200.

193. (b) The requirement is to determine the amount of the child care credit allowable to the Jasons. The credit is from 20% to 35% of certain dependent care expenses limited to the lesser of (1) $3,000 for one qualifying individual, $6,000 for two or more; (2) taxpayer's earned income, or spouse's if smaller; or (3) actual expenses. The $2,500 paid to the Union Day Care Center qualifies, as does the $1,000 paid to Wilma Jason. Payments to relatives qualify if the relative is not a dependent of the taxpayer. Since Robert and Mary Jason only claimed three exemptions, Wilma was not their dependent. The $500 paid to Acme Home Cleaning Service does not qualify since it is *completely* unrelated to the care of their child. To qualify, expenses must be at least partly for the care of a qualifying individual. Since qualifying expenses exceed $3,000, the Jasons' credit is 20% × $3,000 = $600.

194. (b) The requirement is to determine the qualifications for the child care credit that at least one spouse must satisfy on a joint return. The child care credit is a percentage of the amount paid for qualifying household and dependent care expenses incurred to enable an individual to be gainfully employed or look for work. To qualify for the child care credit on a joint return, at least one spouse must be gainfully employed or be looking for work when the related expenses are incurred. Note that it is not required that at least one spouse be gainfully employed, but only needs to be looking for work when the expenses are incurred. Additionally, at least one spouse must have earned income during the year. However, there is no limit as to the maximum amount of earned income or adjusted gross income reported on the joint return.

VI.M. Foreign Tax Credit

195. (a) The requirement is to determine which factor(s) may affect the amount of Sunex's foreign tax credit available in its current year corporate income tax return. Since US taxpayers are subject to US income tax on their worldwide income, they are allowed a credit for the income taxes paid to foreign countries. The applicable foreign tax rate will affect the amount of foreign taxes paid, and thereby affect the amount available as a foreign tax credit. Addi-

tionally, since the amount of credit that can be currently used cannot exceed the amount of US tax attributable to the foreign-source income, the income source will affect the amount of available foreign tax credit for the current year if the limitation based on the amount of US tax is applicable.

196. (b) The requirement is to determine the amount of foreign tax credit that Wald Corp. may claim for 2008. Since US taxpayers are subject to US income tax on their worldwide income, they are allowed a credit for the income taxes paid to foreign countries. However, the amount of credit that can be currently used cannot exceed the amount of US tax that is attributable to the foreign income. This foreign tax credit limitation can be expressed as follows:

$$\frac{\text{Foreign TI}}{\text{Worldwide TI}} \times (\text{US tax}) = \text{Foreign tax credit limitation}$$

One limitation must be computed for foreign source passive income (e.g., interest, dividends, royalties, rents, annuities), with a separate limitation computed for all other foreign source taxable income.

In this case, the foreign income taxes paid on other foreign source taxable income of $27,000 is fully usable as a credit in 2008 because it is less than the applicable limitation amount (i.e., the amount of US tax attributable to the income).

$$\frac{\$90,000}{\$300,000} \times (\$96,000) = \$28,000$$

On the other hand, the credit for the $12,000 of foreign income taxes paid on non-business-related interest is limited to the amount of US tax attributable to the foreign interest income, $9,600.

$$\frac{\$30,000}{\$300,000} \times (\$96,000) = \$9,600$$

Thus, Wald Corp.'s foreign tax credit for 2008 totals $27,000 + $9,600 = $36,600. The $12,000 − $9,600 = $2,400 of unused foreign tax credit resulting from the application of the limitation on foreign taxes attributable to foreign source interest income can be carried back one year and forward ten years to offset US income tax in those years.

197. (a) The requirement is to determine the correct statement regarding a corporation's foreign income taxes. Foreign income taxes paid by a corporation may be claimed either as a credit or as a deduction, at the option of the corporation.

VI.N. Earned Income Credit

198. (c) The requirement is to determine the credit that can result in a refund even if an individual had no income tax liability. The earned income credit is a refundable credit and can result in a refund even if the individual had no tax withheld from wages.

199. (a) The requirement is to choose the correct statement regarding Kent's earned income credit. The earned income credit could result in a refund even if Kent had no tax withheld from wages. Since the credit is refundable, answer (c) is incorrect because there will never be any unused credit to carry back or forward. Answer (d) is incorrect because the credit is a direct subtraction from the computed tax.

200. (c) The requirement is to determine the correct statement regarding the earned income credit. The earned income credit is a refundable credit and can result in a refund even if the individual had no tax withheld from wages. To qualify, an individual must have earned income, but the amount of earned income does not have to equal adjusted gross income. For purposes of the credit, earned income excludes workers' compensation benefits. Additionally, the credit is available only if the tax return covers a full twelve-month period.

201. **(b)**   The requirement is to determine the tax credit that cannot be claimed by a corporation. The foreign tax credit, alternative fuel production credit, and general business credit may be claimed by a corporation. The earned income credit cannot be claimed by a corporation; it is available only to individuals.

VI.O.   Credit for Adoption Expenses

202. **(c)**   The requirement is to determine the correct statement regarding the credit for adoption expenses. The adoption expenses credit is a nonrefundable credit for up to $11,650 (for 2008) of expenses (including special needs children) incurred to adopt an eligible child. An eligible child is one who is under eighteen years of age at time of adoption, or physically or mentally incapable of self-care. Qualified adoption expenses are taken as a credit in the year the adoption becomes final.

VI.P.   Child Tax Credit

203. **(c)**   The requirement is to determine the incorrect statement concerning the child tax credit. Individual taxpayers are permitted to take a tax credit based solely on the number of their dependent children under age seventeen. The amount of the credit is $1,000 per qualifying child, but is subject to reduction if adjusted gross income exceeds certain income levels. A qualifying child must be a US citizen or resident.

VI.Q.   Hope Scholarship Credit

204. **(c)**   The requirement is to determine the incorrect statement concerning the Hope scholarship credit. The Hope scholarship credit provides for a maximum credit of $1,650 per year (100% of the first $1,100, plus 50% of the next $1,100 of tuition expenses) for the first two years of postsecondary education. The credit is available on a per student basis and covers tuition paid for the taxpayer, spouse, and dependents. To be eligible, the student must be enrolled on at least a part-time basis for one academic period during the year. If a parent claims a child as a dependent, only the parent can claim the credit and any qualified expenses paid by the child are deemed paid by the parent.

VI.R.   Lifetime Learning Credit

205. **(d)**   The requirement is to determine the incorrect statement concerning the lifetime learning credit. The lifetime learning credit provides a credit of 20% of up to $10,000 of tuition and fees paid by a taxpayer for one or more students for graduate and undergraduate courses at an eligible educational institution. The credit may be claimed for an unlimited number of years, is available on a per taxpayer basis, and covers tuition paid for the taxpayer, spouse, and dependents.

VI.S.   Estimated Tax Payments

206. **(a)**   The requirement is to determine which statement(s) describe how Baker may avoid the penalty for the underpayment of estimated tax for the 2008 tax year. An individual whose regular and alternative minimum tax liability is not sufficiently covered by withholding from wages must pay estimated tax in quarterly installments or be subject to penalty. Individuals will incur no underpayment penalty for 2008 if the amount of tax withheld plus estimated payments are at least equal to the lesser of (1) 90% of the current year's tax; (2) 100% of the prior year's tax; or (3) 90% of the tax determined by annualizing current year taxable income through each quarter. However, note that for 2008, high-income individuals (i.e., individuals whose adjusted gross income for the preceding year exceeds $150,000) must use 110% (instead of 100%) if they wish to base their estimated tax payments on their prior year's tax liability.

207. **(a)**   The requirement is to determine what amount would be subject to penalty for the underpayment of estimated taxes. A taxpayer will be subject to an underpayment of estimated tax penalty if the taxpayer did not pay enough tax either through withholding or by estimated tax payments. For 2007, there will be no penalty if the total tax shown on the return less the amount paid through withholding (including excess social security tax withholding) is less than $1,000. Additionally, for 2007, individuals will incur no penalty if the amount of tax withheld plus estimated payments are at least equal to the lesser of (1) 90% of the current year's tax (determined on the basis of actual income or annualized income), or (2) 100% of the prior year's tax. In this case, since the tax shown on Krete's return ($16,500) less the tax paid through withholding ($16,000) was less than $1,000, there will be no penalty for the underpayment of estimated taxes.

VII.   Filing Requirements

208. **(d)**   The requirement is to determine the original due date for a decedent's federal income tax return. The final return of a decedent is due on the same date the decedent's return would have been due had death not occurred. An individual's federal income tax return is due on the 15th day of the fourth calendar month following the close of the tax year (e.g., April 15 for a calendar-year taxpayer).

209. **(a)**   The requirement is to determine Birch's filing requirement. A self-employed individual must file an income tax return if net earnings from self-employment are $400 or more.

VIII.B.   Assessments

210. **(c)**   The requirement is to determine the date on which the statute of limitations begins for Jackson Corp.'s 2008 tax return. Generally, any tax that is imposed must be assessed within three years of the filing of the return, or if later, the due date of the return. Since Jackson Corp.'s 2007 return was filed on March 13, 2008, and the return was due on March 15, 2008, the statute of limitations expires on March 15, 2011. This means that the statute of limitations begins on March 16, 2008.

211. **(c)**   The requirement is to determine the latest date that the IRS can assert a notice of deficiency for a 2007 calendar-year return if the taxpayer neither committed fraud nor omitted amounts in excess of 25% of gross income. The normal period for assessment is the later of three years after a return is filed, or three years after the due date of the return. Since the 2007 calendar-year return was filed on March 20, 2008, and was due on April 15, 2008, the IRS must assert a deficiency no later than April 15, 2011.

212. **(d)**   A six-year statute of limitations applies if gross income omitted from the return exceeds 25% of the gross income reported on the return. For this purpose, gross income of a business includes total gross receipts before subtracting cost of goods sold and deductions. Thus, a six-year statute of limitations will apply to Thompson if he omitted from gross income an amount in excess of ($400,000 + $36,000) × 25% = $109,000.

213. **(d)**   The requirement is to determine the maximum period during which the IRS can issue a notice of deficiency if the gross income omitted from a taxpayer's return exceeds 25% of the gross income reported on the return. A **six-year** statute of limitations applies if gross income omitted from the return exceeds 25% of the gross income reported on the return. Additionally, a tax return filed **before** its due date is treated as filed **on** its due date. Thus, if a return is filed before its due date, and the gross income omitted from the return exceeds 25% of the gross income reported on the return, the IRS has **six** years from the due date of the return to issue a notice of deficiency.

VIII.E.   Claims for Refund

214. **(c)**   The requirement is to determine the form that must be filed by an individual to claim a refund of erroneously paid income taxes. Form 1040X, Amended US Individual Income Tax Return, should be used to claim a refund of erroneously paid income taxes. Form 843 should be used to file a refund claim for taxes other than income taxes. Form 1139 may be used by a corporation to file for a tentative adjustment or refund of taxes when an overpayment of taxes for a prior year results from the carryback of a current year's net operating loss or net capital loss. Form 1045 may be used by taxpayers other than corporations to apply for similar adjustments.

215. **(a)**   The requirement is to determine the date by which a refund claim must be filed if an individual paid income tax during 2007 but did not file a tax return. An individual must file a claim for refund within three years from the date a return was filed, or two years from the date of payment of tax, whichever is later. If no return was filed, the claim for refund must be filed within two years from the date that the tax was paid.

216. **(c)**   The requirement is to determine the date by which a taxpayer must file an amended return to claim a refund of tax paid on a calendar-year 2006 return. A taxpayer must file an amended return to claim a refund within three years from the date a return was filed, or two years from the date of payment of tax, whichever is later. If a return is filed before its due date, it is treated as filed on its due date. Thus, the taxpayer's 2006 calendar-year return that was filed on March 15, 2007, is treated as filed on April 15, 2007. Therefore, an amended return to claim a refund must be filed not later than April 15, 2010.

217. **(d)**   The requirement is to determine the date by which a refund claim due to worthless security must be filed. The normal three-year statute of limitations is extended to seven years for refund claims resulting from bad debts or worthless securities. Since the securities became

worthless during 2006, and Baker's 2006 return was filed on April 15, 2007, Baker's refund claim must be filed no later than April 15, 2014.

VIII.G.   Taxpayer Penalties

218. **(b)**   The requirement is to determine the amount on which the penalties for late filing and late payment would be computed. The late filing and late payment penalties are based on the amount of net tax due. If a taxpayer's tax return indicated a tax liability of $50,000, and $45,000 of taxes were withheld, the late filing and late payment penalties would be based on the $5,000 of tax that is owed.

219. **(c)**   An accuracy-related penalty equal to 20% of the underpayment of tax may be imposed if the underpayment of tax is attributable to one or more of the following: (1) negligence or disregard of the tax rules and regulations; (2) any substantial understatement of income tax; (3) any substantial valuation overstatement; (4) any substantial overstatement of pension liabilities; or (5) any substantial gift or estate tax valuation understatement. The penalty for gift or estate tax valuation understatement may apply if the value of property on a gift or estate tax return is 50% or less of the amount determined to be correct. The penalty for a substantial income tax valuation overstatement may apply if the value (or adjusted basis) of property is 200% or more of the amount determined to be correct.

SOLUTIONS TO SIMULATION PROBLEMS

Simulation Problem 1

	Tax Treatment		
Situation		Research	Communication

Transactions	(A)	(B)	(C)	(D)	(E)	(F)	(G)	(H)	(I)	(J)	(K)	(L)	(M)	(N)	(O)	(P)
1. Fees received for jury duty.	○	●	○	○	○	○	○	○	○	○	○	○	○	○	○	○
2. Interest income on mortgage loan receivable.	●	○	○	○	○	○	○	○	○	○	○	○	○	○	○	○
3. Penalty paid to bank on early withdrawal of savings.	○	○	○	●	○	○	○	○	○	○	○	○	○	○	○	○
4. Write-offs of uncollectible accounts receivable from accounting practice.	○	○	○	○	○	○	○	○	○	○	○	○	○	○	○	●
5. Cost of attending review course in preparation for the Uniform CPA Examination.	○	○	○	○	○	○	○	○	○	○	○	○	○	○	○	●
6. Fee for the biennial permit to practice as a CPA.	○	○	○	○	○	○	○	●	○	○	○	○	○	○	○	○
7. Costs of attending CPE courses in fulfillment of state board requirements.	○	○	○	○	○	○	○	●	○	○	○	○	○	○	○	○
8. Contribution to a qualified Keogh retirement plan.	○	○	○	●	○	○	○	○	○	○	○	○	○	○	○	○
9. Loss sustained from nonbusiness bad debt.	○	○	○	○	○	○	○	○	●	○	○	○	○	○	○	○
10. Loss sustained on sale of "Small Business Corporation" (Section 1244) stock.	○	○	○	○	○	○	○	○	○	○	○	●	○	○	○	○
11. Taxes paid on land owned by Cole and rented out as a parking lot.	○	○	○	○	○	○	○	○	○	○	●	○	○	○	○	○
12. Interest paid on installment purchases of household furniture.	○	○	○	○	○	○	○	○	○	○	○	○	○	○	○	●
13. Alimony paid to former spouse who reports the alimony as taxable income.	○	○	○	●	○	○	○	○	○	○	○	○	○	○	○	○
14. Personal medical expenses charged on credit card in December 2008 but not paid until January 2009.	○	○	○	○	●	○	○	○	○	○	○	○	○	○	○	○
15. Personal casualty loss sustained.	○	○	○	○	○	●	○	○	○	○	○	○	○	○	○	○
16. State inheritance tax paid on bequest received.	○	○	○	○	○	○	○	○	○	○	○	○	○	○	○	●
17. Foreign income tax withheld at source on dividend received.	○	○	○	○	○	○	○	○	○	○	○	○	●	○	○	○
18. Computation of self-employment tax.	○	○	○	○	○	○	○	○	○	○	○	○	○	○	●	○
19. One-half of self-employment tax paid with 2008 return filed in April 2009.	○	○	○	●	○	○	○	○	○	○	○	○	○	○	○	○
20. Insurance premiums paid on Cole's life.	○	○	○	○	○	○	○	○	○	○	○	○	○	○	○	●

Explanation of solutions

1. (B) Fees received for jury duty represent compensation for services and must be included in gross income. Since there is no separate line for jury duty fees, they are taxable as other income on page 1 of Form 1040.

2. (A) Interest income on a mortgage loan receivable must be included in gross income and is taxable as interest income in Schedule B—Interest and Dividend Income.

3. (D) An interest forfeiture penalty for making an early withdrawal from a certificate of deposit is deductible on page 1 of Form 1040 to arrive at adjusted gross income.

4. (P) The problem indicates that Cole is a CPA reporting on the cash basis. Accounts receivable resulting from services rendered by a cash-basis taxpayer have a zero tax basis, because the income has not yet been reported. Therefore, the write-offs of zero basis uncollectible accounts receivable from Cole's accounting practice are not deductible.

5. (P) An educational expense that is part of a program of study that can qualify an individual for a new trade or business is not deductible. This is true even if the individual is not seeking a new job. In this case, the cost of attending a review course in preparation for the CPA examination is a nondeductible personal expense since it qualifies Cole for a new profession.

6. (I) Licensing and regulatory fees paid to state or local governments are an ordinary and necessary trade or business expense and are deductible by a sole proprietor on Schedule C—Profit or Loss from Business. Since Cole is a cash method tax payor, he can deduct the fee for the biennial permit to practice when paid in 2008.

7. (I) All trade or business expenses of a self-employed individual are deductible on Schedule C—Profit or Loss from Business. Education must meet certain requirements before the related expenses can be deducted. Generally, deductible education expenses must not be a part of a program that will qualify the individual for a new trade or business and must (1) be required by an employer or by law to keep the individual's present position, or (2) maintain or improve skills required in the individual's present work. In this case, Cole already is a CPA and is fulfilling state CPE requirements, so his education costs of attending CPE courses are deductible in Schedule C—Profit or Loss from Business.

8. (D) Contributions to a self-employed individual's qualified Keogh retirement plan are deductible on page 1 of Form 1040 to arrive at adjusted gross income. The maximum deduction for contributions to a defined contribution Keogh retirement plan is limited to the lesser of $46,000 (for 2008), or 100% of self-employment income.

9. (J) A loss sustained from a nonbusiness bad debt is always classified as a short-term capital loss. Therefore, Cole's nonbusiness bad debt is deductible in Schedule D—Capital Gains or Losses.

10. (L) A loss sustained on the sale of Sec. 1244 stock is generally deductible as an ordinary loss, with the amount of ordinary loss deduction limited to $50,000. On a joint return, the limit is increased to $100,000, even if the stock was owned by only one spouse. The ordinary loss resulting from the sale of Sec. 1244 stock is deductible in Form 4797—Sales of Business Property. To the extent that a loss on Sec. 1244 stock exceeds the applicable $50,000 or $100,000 limit, the loss is deductible as a capital loss in Schedule D—Capital Gains or Losses. Similarly, if Sec. 1244 stock is sold at a gain, the gain would be reported as a capital gain in Schedule D if the stock is a capital asset.

11. (K) Rental income and expenses related to rental property are generally reported in Schedule E. Here, the taxes paid on land owned by Cole and rented out as a parking lot are deductible in Schedule E—Supplemental Income and Loss. Schedule E also is used to report the income or loss from royalties, partnerships, S corporations, estates, and trusts.

12. (P) The interest paid on installment purchases of household furniture is considered personal interest and is not deductible. Personal interest is any interest that is not qualified residence interest, investment interest, passive activity interest, or business interest. Personal interest generally includes interest on car loans, interest on income tax, underpayments, installment plan interest, credit card finance charges, and late payment charges by a utility.

13. (D) Alimony paid to a former spouse who reports the alimony as taxable income is deductible on page 1 of Form 1040 to arrive at adjusted gross income.

14. (E) Personal medical expenses are generally deductible as an itemized deduction subject to a 7.5% of AGI threshold for the year in which they are paid. Additionally, an individual can deduct medical expenses charged to a credit card in the year the charge is made. It makes no difference when the amount charged is actually paid. Here, Cole's personal medical expenses charged on a credit card in December 2008 but not paid until January 2009 are deductible for 2008 in Schedule A—Itemized Deductions, subject to a threshold of 7.5% of adjusted gross income.

15. (F) If an individual sustains a personal casualty loss, it is deductible in Schedule A—Itemized Deductions subject to a threshold of $100 and an additional threshold of 10% of adjusted gross income.

16. (P) State inheritance taxes paid on a bequest that was received are not deductible. Other taxes not deductible in computing an individual's federal income tax include federal estate and gift taxes, federal income taxes, and social security and other employment taxes paid by an employee.

17. (M) An individual can deduct foreign income taxes as an itemized deduction or can deduct foreign income taxes as a tax credit. Cole's foreign income tax withheld at source on foreign dividends received can be claimed in Form 1116—Foreign Tax Credit, or in Schedule A—Itemized Deductions, at Cole's option.

18. (O) A self-employed individual is subject to a self-employment tax if the individual's net earnings from self-employment are at least $400.

19. (D) An individual's self-employment tax is computed in Schedule SE and is added as an additional tax in arriving at the individual's total tax. One-half of the computed self-employment tax is allowed as a deduction in arriving at adjusted gross income. Here, one-half of Cole's self-employment tax for 2008 is deductible for 2008 on page 1 of Form 1040 to arrive at adjusted gross income, even though the tax was not paid until the return was filed in April 2009.

20. (P) Insurance premiums paid on Cole's life are classified as a personal expense and are not deductible.

Situation	Tax Treatment	Research	Communication

Internal Revenue Code Section 163, subsection (h) provides that interest is deductible on up to $1,000,000 of qualified residence acquisition indebtedness.

Section	Subsection
§ 163	(h)

Situation	Tax Treatment	Research	Communication

To: Mr. Cole
From: CPA Candidate
Re: Deductibility of interest on mortgage

As you requested, I researched the issue of limitations on the deductibility of home mortgage interest. I understand that you plan to purchase a residence for $1,500,000 and finance the purchase with a mortgage totaling $1,150,000.

Internal Revenue Code section 163(h)(3)(B) limits the interest deduction on a primary residence to the interest on $1,000,000 of qualified acquisition indebtedness. However, section 163(h)(3)(C) allows an additional deduction of interest on up to $100,000 of home equity indebtedness. On your proposed transaction, this means that you would be entitled to deduct the interest on all but $50,000 of the mortgage loan.

If you have any additional questions please contact me.

Simulation Problem 2

Situation	Tax Treatment I	Tax Treatment II	Research	Communication

Transactions	(A)	(B)	(C)	(D)	(E)	(F)	(G)	(H)	(I)	(J)	(K)	(L)	(M)	(N)	(O)
1. Retainer fees received from clients.	○	○	●	○	○	○	○	○	○	○	○	○	○	○	○
2. Oil royalties received.	○	○	○	●	○	○	○	○	○	○	○	○	○	○	○
3. Interest income on general obligation state and local government bonds.	○	○	○	○	●	○	○	○	○	○	○	○	○	○	○
4. Interest on refund of federal taxes.	○	●	○	○	○	○	○	○	○	○	○	○	○	○	○
5. Death benefits from term life insurance policy on parent.	○	○	○	○	●	○	○	○	○	○	○	○	○	○	○
6. Interest income on US Treasury bonds.	○	●	○	○	○	○	○	○	○	○	○	○	○	○	○
7. Share of ordinary income from an investment in a limited partnership reported in Form 1065, Schedule K-1.	○	○	○	●	○	○	○	○	○	○	○	○	○	○	○
8. Taxable income from rental of a townhouse owned by Green.	○	○	○	●	○	○	○	○	○	○	○	○	○	○	○
9. Prize won as a contestant on a TV quiz show.	●	○	○	○	○	○	○	○	○	○	○	○	○	○	○
10. Payment received for jury service.	●	○	○	○	○	○	○	○	○	○	○	○	○	○	○
11. Dividends received from mutual funds that invest in tax-free government obligations.	○	○	○	○	●	○	○	○	○	○	○	○	○	○	○
12. Qualifying medical expenses not reimbursed by insurance.	○	○	○	○	○	○	●	○	○	○	○	○	○	○	○
13. Personal life insurance premiums paid by Green.	○	○	○	○	○	○	○	○	○	○	○	○	○	○	●
14. Expenses for business-related meals where clients were present.	○	○	○	○	○	○	○	○	○	○	○	○	●	○	○
15. Depreciation on personal computer purchased in 2008 used for business.	○	○	○	○	○	○	○	○	○	○	○	●	○	○	○
16. Business lodging expenses, while out of town.	○	○	○	○	○	○	○	○	○	○	○	●	○	○	○
17. Subscriptions to professional journals used for business.	○	○	○	○	○	○	○	○	○	○	○	●	○	○	○
18. Self-employment taxes paid.	○	○	○	○	●	○	○	○	○	○	○	○	○	○	○
19. Qualifying contributions to a simplified employee pension plan.	○	○	○	○	●	○	○	○	○	○	○	○	○	○	○

Transactions	(A)	(B)	(C)	(D)	(E)	(F)	(G)	(H)	(I)	(J)	(K)	(L)	(M)	(N)	(O)
20. Election to expense business equipment purchased in 2008.	○	○	○	○	○	○	○	○	○	○	●	○	○	○	○
21. Qualifying alimony payments made by Green.	○	○	○	○	○	●	○	○	○	○	○	○	○	○	○
22. Subscriptions for investment-related publications.	○	○	○	○	○	○	○	○	●	○	○	○	○	○	○
23. Interest expense on a home-equity line of credit for an amount borrowed to finance Green's business.	○	○	○	○	○	○	○	○	○	○	○	●	○	○	○
24. Interest expense on a loan for an auto used 75% for business.	○	○	○	○	○	○	○	○	○	○	○	○	○	●	○
25. Loss on sale of residence.	○	○	○	○	○	○	○	○	○	○	○	○	○	○	●

Explanation of solutions

1. (C) All trade or business income and deductions of a self-employed individual are reported on Schedule C—Profit or Loss from Business. Retainer fees received from clients is reported in Schedule C as trade or business income.

2. (D) Income derived from royalties is reported in Schedule E—Supplemental Income and Loss. Schedule E also is used to report the income or loss from rental real estate, partnerships, S corporations, estates, and trusts.

3. (E) Interest from general obligation state and local government bonds is tax-exempt and is excluded from gross income.

4. (B) The interest income on a refund of federal income taxes must be included in gross income and is reported in Schedule B—Interest and Dividend Income. The actual refund of federal income taxes itself is excluded from gross income.

5. (E) Life insurance proceeds paid by reason of death are generally excluded from gross income. Here, the death benefits received by Green from a term life insurance policy on the life of Green's parent are not taxable.

6. (B) Interest income from US Treasury bonds and treasury bills must be included in gross income and is reported in Schedule B—Interest and Dividend Income.

7. (D) A partner's share of a partnership's ordinary income that is reported to the partner on Form 1065, Schedule K-1 must be included in the partner's gross income and is reported in Schedule E—Supplemental Income and Loss.

8. (D) The taxable income from the rental of a townhouse owned by Green must be included in gross income and is reported in Schedule E—Supplemental Income and Loss.

9. (A) A prize won as a contestant on a TV quiz show must be included in gross income. Since there is no separate line on Form 1040 for prizes, they are taxable as other income on Form 1040.

10. (A) Fees received for jury duty represent compensation for services and must be included in gross income. Since there is no separate line for jury duty fees, they are taxable as other income on Form 1040.

11. (E) An investor in a mutual fund may receive several different kinds of distributions including ordinary dividends, capital gain distributions, tax-exempt interest dividends, and return of capital distributions. A mutual fund may pay tax-exempt interest dividends to its shareholders if it meets certain requirements. These dividends are paid from the tax-exempt state and local obligation interest earned by the fund and retain their tax-exempt character when reported by the shareholder. Thus, Green's dividends received from mutual funds that invest in tax-free government obligations are not taxable.

12. (H) Qualifying medical expenses not reimbursed by insurance are deductible in Schedule A as an itemized deduction to the extent in excess of 7.5% of adjusted gross income.

13. (O) Personal life insurance premiums paid on Green's life are classified as a personal expense and not deductible.

14. (M) All trade or business expenses of a self-employed individual are deductible on Schedule C—Profit or Loss from Business. However, only 50% of the cost of business meals and entertainment is deductible. Therefore, Green's expenses for business-related meals where clients were present are partially deductible in Schedule C.

15. (K) The deduction for depreciation on listed property (e.g., automobiles, cellular telephones, computers, and property used for entertainment etc.) is computed on Form 4562—Depreciation and Amortization. Since Green's personal computer was used in his business as a self-employed consultant, the amount of depreciation computed on Form 4562 is then deductible in Schedule C—Profit or Loss from Business.

16. (L) Lodging expenses while out of town on business are an ordinary and necessary business expense and are fully deductible by a self-employed individual in Schedule C—Profit or Loss from Business.

17. (L) The cost of subscriptions to professional journals used for business are an ordinary and necessary business expense and are fully deductible by a self-employed individual in Schedule C—Profit or Loss from Business.

18. (G) An individual's self-employment tax is computed in Schedule SE and is added as an additional tax in arriving at the individual's total tax liability. One-half of the computed self-employment tax is then allowed as a deduction on Form 1040 in arriving at adjusted gross income.

19. (F) Qualifying contributions to a self-employed individual's simplified employee pension plan are deductible on page 1 of Form 1040 to arrive at adjusted gross income.

20. (K) For 2008, Sec. 179 permits a taxpayer to elect to treat up to $250,000 of the cost of qualifying depreciable personal business property as an expense rather than as a capital expenditure. In this case, Green's election to expense business equipment would be computed on Form 4562—Depreciation and Amortization, and then would be deductible in Schedule C—Profit or Loss from Business.

21. (F) Qualifying alimony payments made by Green to a former spouse are fully deductible on Form 1040 to arrive at adjusted gross income.

22. (I) The costs of subscriptions for investment publications are not related to Green's trade or business, but instead are considered expenses incurred in the production of portfolio income and are reported as miscellaneous itemized deductions in Schedule A—Itemized Deductions. These investment expenses are deductible to the extent that the aggregate of expenses in this category exceed 2% of adjusted gross income.

23. (L) The nature of interest expense is determined by using a tracing approach (i.e., the nature depends upon how the loan proceeds were used). Since the interest expense on Green's home-equity line of credit was for a loan to finance Green's business, the best answer is to treat the interest as a business expense fully deductible in Schedule C—Profit or Loss from Business.

24. (M) The interest expense on a loan for an auto used by a self-employed individual in a trade or business is deductible as a business expense. Since Green's auto was used 75% for business, only 75% of the interest expense is deductible in Schedule C—Profit or Loss from Business. The remaining 25% is considered personal interest expense and is not deductible.

25. (O) The loss resulting from the sale of Green's personal residence is not deductible because the property was held for personal use. Only losses due to casualty or theft are deductible for personal use property.

Situation	Tax Treatment I	Tax Treatment II	Research	Communication

	(A)	(B)	(C)	(D)	(E)	(F)	(G)
1. In 2008, Green paid $2,000 interest on the $25,000 home equity mortgage on his vacation home, which he used exclusively for personal use. The mortgage is secured by Green's vacation home, and the loan proceeds were used to purchase an automobile.	○	●	○	○	○	○	○
2. For 2008, Green had a $30,000 cash charitable contribution carryover from his 2007 cash donation to the American Red Cross. Green made no additional charitable contributions in 2008.	○	○	●	○	○	○	○
3. During 2008, Green had investment interest expense that did not exceed his net investment income.	○	●	○	○	○	○	○
4. Green's 2008 lottery ticket losses were $450. He had no gambling winnings.	●	○	○	○	○	○	○
5. During 2008, Green paid $2,500 in real property taxes on his vacation home, which he used exclusively for personal use.	○	●	○	○	○	○	○
6. In 2008, Green paid a $500 premium for a homeowner's insurance policy on his principal residence.	●	○	○	○	○	○	○
7. For 2008, Green paid $1,500 to an unrelated babysitter to care for his child while he worked.	○	○	○	○	○	○	●
8. In 2008, Green paid $4,000 interest on the $60,000 acquisition mortgage of his principal residence. The mortgage is secured by Green's home.	○	●	○	○	○	○	○
9. During 2008, Green paid $3,600 real property taxes on residential rental property in which he actively participates. There was no personal use of the rental property.	○	○	○	○	○	●	○

Explanation of solutions

1. (B) Interest expense on home equity indebtedness is deductible on up to $100,000 of home equity loans secured by a first or second residence regardless of how the loan proceeds were used.

2. (C) Contributions in excess of applicable percentage limitations can be carried forward for up to five tax years. Here, the $30,000 of charitable contribution carryover from 2007 is deductible as an itemized deduction for 2008 subject to a limitation of 50% of AGI.

3. (B) Investment interest expense is deductible as an itemized deduction to the extent of net investment income. Since Green's investment interest expense did not exceed his net investment income, it is deductible in full.

4. (A) Gambling losses (including lottery ticket losses) are deductible as an itemized deduction to the extent of the gambling winnings included in gross income. Since Green had no gambling winnings, the losses are not deductible.

5. (B) State, local, or foreign real estate taxes imposed on the taxpayer for property held for personal use are fully deductible as an itemized deduction.

6. (A) A premium for a homeowner's insurance policy on a principal residence is a nondeductible personal expense.

7. (G) Payments to an unrelated babysitter to care for his child while Green worked would qualify for the child and dependent care credit. For 2008, the credit may vary from 20% to 35% of up to $3,000 ($6,000 for two or more qualifying individuals) of qualifying household and dependent care expenses incurred to enable the taxpayer to be gainfully employed or look for work.

8. (B) Interest expense on acquisition indebtedness is deductible on up to $1 million of loans secured by the residence if such loans were used to acquire, construct, or substantially improve a principal residence or a second residence.

9. (F) Expenses incurred in the production of rental income (e.g., interest, taxes, depreciation, insurance, utilities) are deductible on Schedule E and are included in the computation of net rental income or loss.

Situation	Tax Treatment I	Tax Treatment II	**Research**	Communication

Internal Revenue Code Section 21, subsection (c) provides that the maximum amount of employment-related expenses that qualify for a credit is limited to $3,000 for one qualifying individual.

Section	Subsection
§ 21	(c)

Situation	Tax Treatment I	Tax Treatment II	Research	**Communication**

To: Mr. Green
From: CPA Candidate
Re: Dependent care payments

     You have requested that I research the effects of the payments to a babysitter for care of your child on your tax liability. The payments will entitle you to a dependent child credit. For 2008, the credit varies from 20% to 35% of qualified employment-related expenses, limited to $3,000 for one qualifying child. Because your adjusted gross income is greater than $45,000, your credit is limited to 20% of $3,000, or $600. Your tax liability will be reduced by that amount.
     If you have any other questions, please contact me.

Simulation Problem 3

Situation	**Deductibility**	Research	Communication

	For AGI (A)	From AGI (No 2%) (B)	From AGI (2% Floor) (C)	Not ded. (D)
1. Smith paid the medical expenses of his mother-in-law. Although Smith provided more than half of her support, she does not qualify as Smith's dependent because she had gross income of $5,000.	○	●	○	○
2. Smith paid the real estate taxes on his rental apartment building.	●	○	○	○
3. Smith paid state sales taxes of $1,500 on an automobile that he purchased for personal use.	○	●	○	○
4. Smith paid the real estate taxes on his mother-in-law's home. She is the owner of the home.	○	○	○	●
5. Smith paid $1,500 of interest on credit card charges. The charges were for items purchased for personal use.	○	○	○	●
6. Smith paid an attorney $500 to prepare Smith's will.	○	○	○	●

	For AGI (A)	From AGI *(No 2%)* (B)	From AGI *(2% Floor)* (C)	*Not ded.* (D)
7. Smith incurred $750 of expenses for business meals and entertainment in his position as an employee of Patton Corporation. Smith's expenses were not reimbursed.	○	○	●	○
8. Smith paid self-employment taxes of $3,000 as a result of earnings from the consulting business that he conducts as a sole proprietor.	●	○	○	○
9. Smith made a contribution to his self-employed retirement plan (Keogh Plan).	●	○	○	○
10. Smith had gambling losses totaling $2,500 for the year. He is including a lottery prize of $5,000 in his gross income this year.	○	●	○	○

Explanation of solutions

1. (B) Deductible medical expenses include amounts paid for the diagnosis, cure, relief, treatment or prevention of disease of the taxpayer, spouse, and dependents. The term **dependent** includes any person who qualifies as a dependency exemption, or would otherwise qualify as a dependency exemption except that the gross income and joint return tests are not met. Therefore, the medical expenses of Smith's mother-in-law are properly deductible from Smith's AGI and are not subject to the 2% limitation.

2. (A) Expenses attributable to property held for the production of rents or royalties are properly deductible "above the line." "Above the line" deductions are subtracted from gross income to determine adjusted gross income. Therefore, expenses incurred from a passive activity such as Smith's rental apartment building are deductible for AGI.

3. (B) For tax years beginning after December 31, 2003, and before January 1, 2009, an individual may elect to deduct state and local general sales taxes in lieu of state and local income taxes. The amount that can be deducted is either the total of actual general sales taxes paid as substantiated by receipts, or an amount from IRS-provided tables, plus the amount of general sales taxes paid with regard to the purchase of a motor vehicle, boat, and specified other items. The deduction for sales taxes is not subject to the 2% of AGI floor.

4. (D) Real estate (real property) taxes are deductible only if imposed on property owned by the taxpayer. Since Smith's mother-in-law is the legal owner of the house, Smith cannot deduct his payment of those real estate taxes.

5. (D) No deduction is allowed for personal interest.

6. (D) Personal legal expenses are not a deductible expense. Only legal counsel obtained for advice concerning tax matters or incurred in the production of income are deductible. Therefore, Smith cannot deduct the $500 incurred to prepare his will.

7. (C) Unreimbursed employee expenses including business meals and entertainment (subject to the 50% rule) are deductible to the extent they exceed 2% of AGI. Therefore, $375 ($750 × 50%) is deductible from AGI, subject to the 2% floor.

8. (A) An individual is allowed to deduct one half of the self-employment tax paid for the taxable year in the computation of AGI. Therefore, $1,500 is deductible for AGI.

9. (A) Contributions by self-employed individuals to a qualified retirement plan (Keogh Plan) are a deduction for AGI.

10. (B) Gambling losses to the extent of gambling winnings are categorized as miscellaneous deductions not subject to the 2% floor. Therefore, the $2,500 of Smith's gambling losses would be deductible in full since he properly included his $5,000 winnings in his gross income for 2008.

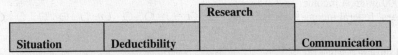

Internal Revenue Code Section 213, subsection (a) provides that the unreimbursed medical expenses of a taxpayer, spouse, and dependents are deductible to the extent in excess of 7.5% of adjusted gross income.

Section	Subsection
§ 213	(a)

place of employment, or if previously unemployed at least fifty miles from his former residence. To satisfy the change of health condition, the taxpayer must be instructed to relocate by a physician for health reasons (e.g., advanced age-related infirmities, severe allergies, emotional problems). Unforeseen circumstances include natural or man-made disasters such as war or acts of terrorism, cessation of employment, death, divorce or legal separation, and multiple births from the same pregnancy.

> EXAMPLE: Harold, an unmarried taxpayer, purchased a home in a suburb of Chicago on October 1, 2006. Eighteen months later his employer transferred him to St. Louis and Harold sold his home for a gain of $200,000. Since Harold sold his home because of a change in place of employment and had owned and used the home as a principal residence for eighteen months, the exclusion of his gain is limited to $250,000 × 18/24 = $187,500.

(7) If a taxpayer was entitled to take depreciation deductions because the residence was used for business purposes or as rental property, the taxpayer cannot exclude gain to the extent of any depreciation allowed or allowable as a deduction after May 6, 1997.

> EXAMPLE: Ron sold his principal residence during 2008 for a gain of $20,000. He used one room of the residence for business and deducted $1,000 of depreciation in 2007. Although Ron meets the ownership and use tests to exclude residence sale gain from income, he can exclude only $20,000 – $1,000 = $19,000 from income. The remaining $1,000 of gain is taxable and must be included in gross income.

(8) Gain from the sale of a principal residence cannot be excluded from gross income if, during the two-year period ending on the date of the sale, the taxpayer sold another residence at a gain and excluded all or part of that gain from income. If the taxpayer cannot exclude the gain, it must be included in gross income.

> EXAMPLE: In September 2005, Anna purchased a new principal residence. In November 2005, Anna sold her old residence for a gain of $50,000. Since she met the ownership and use tests, Anna excluded the $50,000 gain from gross income for 2005. On October 10, 2007, Anna sold the residence she had purchased in September 2005 for a gain of $30,000. The sale was not due to a change in place of employment, health, or unforeseen circumstances. Because Anna had excluded gain from the sale of another residence within the two-year period ending on October 10, 2007, she cannot exclude the gain on this sale.

(9) A loss from the sale of personal residence is not deductible.

d. **Exchange of insurance policies.** No gain or loss is recognized on an exchange of certain life, endowment, and annuity contracts to allow taxpayers to obtain better insurance.

5. **Sales and exchanges of securities**
   a. Stocks and bonds are not included under like-kind exchanges
   b. Exchange of stock of same corporation
      (1) Common for common, or preferred for preferred is nontaxable
      (2) Common for preferred, or preferred for common is taxable, unless exchange qualifies as a recapitalization (see page 583)
   c. Exercise of conversion privilege in convertible stock or bond is generally nontaxable.
   d. The first-in, first-out (FIFO) method is used to determine the basis of securities sold unless the taxpayer can specifically identify the securities sold and uses specific identification.
   e. **Capital gains exclusion for small business stock**
      (1) A noncorporate taxpayer can exclude 50% of capital gains resulting from the sale of qualified small business stock held for more than five years.
      (2) To qualify, the stock must be acquired directly (or indirectly through a pass-through entity) at its original issuance.
      (3) A qualified small business is a C corporation with $50 million or less of capitalization. Generally, personal service, banking, leasing, investing, real estate, farming, mineral extraction, and hospitality businesses do not qualify as eligible small businesses.
      (4) Gains eligible for exclusion are limited to the greater of $10 million, or 10 times the investor's stock basis.
         (a) 7% of the excluded gain is treated as a tax preference item for AMT purposes.
         (b) Only gains net of exclusion are included in determining the investment interest expense and capital loss limitations.
   f. **Rollover of capital gain from publicly traded securities**

(1) An individual or C corporation may elect to roll over an otherwise currently taxable capital gain from the sale of publicly traded securities if the sale proceeds are used to purchase common stock or a partnership interest in a specialized small business investment company (SSBIC) within sixty days of the sale of the securities.

(2) An SSBIC is a partnership or corporation licensed by the Small Business Administration under the Small Business Investment Act of 1958 as in effect on May 13, 1993.

(3) The amount of gain eligible for rollover is limited to $50,000 per year for individuals (lifetime cap of $500,000) and $250,000 per year for corporations (lifetime cap of $1 million).

(4) The taxpayer's basis in the SSBIC stock or partnership interest must be reduced by the gain that is rolled over.

g. **Market discount bonds**

(1) Gain on the disposition of a bond (including a tax-exempt bond) that was acquired for a price that was less than the principal amount of the bond is treated as taxable interest income to the extent of the accrued market discount for bonds purchased after April 30, 1993.

(2) Accrued market discount is the difference between the bond's cost basis and its redemption value at maturity amortized over the remaining life of the bond.

h. **Wash sales**

(1) Wash sale occurs when stock or securities (or options to acquire stock or securities) are sold at a loss and within **thirty days before or after the sale,** substantially identical stock or securities (or options to acquire them) in the same corporation are purchased.

(2) Wash sale loss is not deductible, but is added to the basis of the new stock.

(3) Wash sale rules do not apply to gains.

> EXAMPLE: C purchased 100 shares of XYZ Corporation stock for $1,000. C later sold the stock for $700, and within thirty days acquired 100 shares of XYZ Corporation stock for $800. The loss of $300 on the sale of stock is not recognized. However, the unrecognized loss of $300 is added to the $800 cost of the new stock to arrive at the basis for the new stock of $1,100. The holding period of the new stock includes the period of time the old stock was held.

(4) Does not apply to dealers in stock and securities where loss is sustained in ordinary course of business.

i. **Worthless stock and securities**

(1) Treated as a capital loss as if sold on the last day of the taxable year they become worthless.

(2) Treated as an ordinary loss if stock and securities are those of an **80% or more owned corporate subsidiary** that derived more than 90% of its gross receipts from active-type sources.

6. **Losses on deposits in insolvent financial institutions**

a. Loss resulting from a nonbusiness deposit in an insolvent financial institution is generally treated as a nonbusiness bad debt deductible as a short-term capital loss (STCL) in the year in which a final determination of the amount of loss can be made.

b. As an alternative, if a reasonable estimate of the amount of loss can be made, an individual may elect to

(1) Treat the loss as a personal casualty loss subject to the $100 floor and 10% of AGI limitation. Then no bad debt deduction can be claimed.

(2) In lieu of (1) above, treat up to $20,000 as a miscellaneous itemized deduction subject to the 2% of AGI floor if the deposit was not federally insured. Then remainder of loss is treated as a STCL.

> EXAMPLE: An individual with no capital gains and an AGI of $70,000, incurred a loss on a federally insured deposit in a financial institution of $30,000. The individual may treat the loss as a $30,000 STCL subject to the $3,000 net capital loss deduction limitation, with the remaining $27,000 carried forward as a STCL; or, may treat the loss as a personal casualty loss and an itemized deduction of [($30,000 − $100) − (10% × $70,000)] = $22,900. If the deposit had **not** been federally insured, the individual could also have taken a miscellaneous itemized deduction of [$20,000 − (2% × $70,000)] = $18,600, with the remaining $10,000 treated as a STCL (i.e., $3,000 net capital loss deduction and a $7,000 STCL carryover).

7. **Losses, expenses, and interest between related taxpayers**

a. **Loss is disallowed** on the sale or exchange of property to a related taxpayer.

(1) Transferee's basis is cost; holding period begins when transferee acquires property.

(2) On a later resale, any gain recognized by the transferee is reduced by the disallowed loss (unless the transferor's loss was from a wash sale, in which case no reduction is allowed).

(3) **Related taxpayers** include

    (a) Members of a family, including spouse, brothers, sisters, ancestors, and lineal descendents

    (b) A corporation and a more than 50% shareholder

    (c) Two corporations which are members of the same controlled group

    (d) A person and an exempt organization controlled by that person

    (e) Certain related individuals in a trust, including the grantor or beneficiary and the fiduciary

    (f) A C corporation and a partnership if the same persons own more than 50% of the corporation, and more than 50% of the capital and profits interest in the partnership

    (g) Two S corporations if the same persons own more than 50% of each

    (h) An S corporation and a C corporation if the same persons own more than 50% of each

> EXAMPLE: *During August 2007, Bob sold stock with a basis of $4,000 to his brother Ray for $3,000, its FMV. During June 2008, Ray sold the stock to an unrelated taxpayer for $4,500. Bob's loss of $1,000 is disallowed; Ray recognizes a STCG of ($4,500 – $3,000) – $1,000 disallowed loss = $500.*

(4) **Constructive stock ownership rules** apply in determining if taxpayers are related. For purposes of determining stock ownership

    (a) Stock owned, directly or indirectly, by a corporation, partnership, estate, or trust is considered as being owned proportionately by its shareholders, partners, or beneficiaries.

    (b) An individual is considered as owning the stock owned, directly or indirectly, by his brothers and sisters (whole or half blood), spouse, ancestors, and lineal descendants.

    (c) An individual owning stock in a corporation [other than by (b) above] is considered as owning the stock owned, directly or indirectly, by his partner.

b. The disallowed loss rule in a. above does not apply to transfers between spouses, or former spouses incident to divorce, as discussed below.

c. Any loss from the sale or exchange of property between corporations that are members of the same **controlled group** is deferred (instead of disallowed) until the property is sold outside the group. Use controlled group definition found in Module 36, D.2., but substitute "more than 50%" for "at least 80%."

> EXAMPLE: *Mr. Gudjob is the sole shareholder of X Corp. and Y Corp. During 2007, X Corp. sold nondepreciable property with a basis of $8,000 to Y Corp. for $6,000, its FMV. During 2009, Y Corp. sold the property to an unrelated taxpayer for $6,500. X Corp.'s loss in 2007 is deferred. In 2008, X Corp. recognizes the $2,000 of deferred loss, and Y Corp. recognizes a gain of $500.*

d. An accrual-basis payor is effectively placed on the cash method of accounting for purposes of deducting accrued interest and other expenses owed to a related cash-basis payee.

(1) No deduction is allowable until the year the amount is actually paid.

(2) This rule applies to pass-through entities (e.g., a partnership and **any** partner; two partnerships if the same persons own more than 50% of each; an S corporation and **any** shareholder) in addition to the related taxpayers described in a.(3) above, but does not apply to guaranteed payments to partners. This rule also applies to a personal service corporation and **any** employee-owner.

> EXAMPLE: *A calendar-year S corporation accrued a $500 bonus owed to an employee-shareholder in 2007 but did not pay the bonus until February 2008. The $500 bonus will be deductible by the S corporation in 2008, when the employee-shareholder reports the $500 as income.*

8. **Transfers in part a sale and in part a gift**

a. If a transfer of property is in part a sale and in part a gift, the transferor recognizes gain to the extent that the amount realized exceeds the transferor's adjusted basis for the property transferred. However, no loss can be recognized by the transferor.

b. The basis of the property to the transferee is generally the greater of (1) the amount paid by the transferee for the property, or (2) the transferor's basis for the property at the time of the transfer. However, for purposes of determining a loss, the basis of the property in the hands of the transferee shall not be greater than the fair market value of the property at the time of the transfer.

EXAMPLE: Alan transfers property to his sister, Brianna, for $60,000. The property has a basis of $40,000 and a FMV of $90,000 at date of transfer. Alan must recognize a gain of $60,000 – $40,000 = $20,000, and has made a gift to Brianna of $90,000 – $60,000 = $30,000. Brianna's basis for the property is $60,000.

EXAMPLE: Brenda transfers property to her brother, Carl, for $30,000. The transferred property has a basis of $40,000 and a FMV of $90,000 at date of transfer. Brenda's realized loss of $40,000 – $30,000 = $10,000 cannot be recognized, and she has made a gift to Carl of $90,000 – $30,000 = $60,000. Carl's basis for the property is $40,000.

EXAMPLE: David transfers property to his son, Evan, for $30,000. The property has a basis of $90,000 and a FMV of $60,000 at date of transfer. David's realized loss of $90,000 – $30,000 = $60,000 cannot be recognized, and he has made a gift to Evan of $60,000 – $30,000 = $30,000. Evan's basis for the property is $90,000. However, for purposes of determining a loss on a later sale or other disposition of the property by Evan, the property's basis is limited to its FMV at date of transfer of $60,000.

9. **Transfer between spouses**

a. No gain or loss is generally recognized on the transfer of property from an individual to (or in trust for the benefit of)

   (1) A spouse (other than a nonresident alien spouse), or
   (2) A former spouse (other than a nonresident alien former spouse), if the transfer is related to the cessation of marriage, or occurs within one year after marriage ceases

b. Transfer is treated as if it were a gift from one spouse to the other.
c. Transferee's basis in the property received will be the transferor's basis (even if FMV is less than the property's basis).

> *EXAMPLE: H sells property with a basis of $6,000 to his spouse, W, for $8,000. No gain is recognized to H, and W's basis for the property is $6,000. W's holding period includes the period that H held the property.*

d. If property is transferred to a **trust** for the benefit of a spouse or former spouse (incident to divorce)

   (1) Gain is recognized to the extent that the amount of liabilities assumed exceeds the total adjusted basis of property transferred.
   (2) Gain or loss is recognized on the transfer of installment obligations.

10. Gain from the sale or exchange of property will be entirely ordinary gain (no capital gain) if the property is depreciable in hands of transferee and the sale or exchange is between

a. A person and a more than 50% owned corporation or partnership
b. A taxpayer and any trust in which such taxpayer or spouse is a beneficiary, unless such beneficiary's interest is a remote contingent interest
c. Constructive ownership rules apply; use rules in Section 7.a.(4)(a) and (b) above

B. Capital Gains and Losses

1. Capital gains and losses result from the "sale or exchange of capital assets." The term **capital assets** includes investment property and property held for personal use. The term specifically **excludes**

a. Stock in trade, inventory, or goods held primarily for sale to customers in the normal course of business
b. Depreciable or real property used in a trade or business
c. Copyrights or artistic, literary, etc., compositions created by the taxpayer

   (1) They are capital assets only if purchased by the taxpayer.
   (2) Patents are generally capital assets in the hands of the inventor.

d. Accounts or notes receivable arising from normal business activities
e. US government publications acquired other than by purchase at regular price
f. Supplies of a type regularly used or consumed by a taxpayer in the ordinary course of the taxpayer's trade or business

2. Whether short-term or long-term depends upon the **holding period**

a. Long-term if held more than one year
b. The day property was acquired is excluded and the day it is disposed of is included.
c. Use calendar months (e.g., if held from January 4 to January 4 it is held exactly one year)

d. If stock or securities which are traded on an established securities market (or other property regularly traded on an established market) are sold, any resulting gain or loss is recognized on the date the trade is executed (transaction date) by both cash and accrual taxpayers.

e. The holding period of property received in a nontaxable exchange (e.g., like-kind exchange, involuntary conversion) includes the holding period of the property exchanged, if the property that was exchanged was a capital asset or Sec. 1231 asset.

f. If the basis of property to a prior owner carries over to the present owner (e.g., gift), the holding period of the prior owner "tacks on" to the present owner's holding period.

g. If using the lower FMV on date of gift to determine loss, then holding period begins when the gift is received.

> EXAMPLE: X purchased property on July 14, 2007, for $10,000. X made a gift of the property to Z on June 10, 2008, when its FMV was $8,000. Since Z's basis for gain is $10,000, Z's holding period for a disposition at a gain extends back to July 14, 2007. Since Z's $8,000 basis for loss is determined by reference to FMV at June 10, 2008, Z's holding period for a disposition at a loss begins on June 11.

h. Property acquired from a decedent is always given long-term treatment, regardless of how long the property was held by the decedent or beneficiary, and is treated as property held more than twelve months.

3. Computation of capital gains and losses for **all taxpayers**

a. First net STCG with STCL and net LTCG with LTCL to determine

(1) Net short-term capital gain or loss (NSTCG or NSTCL)
(2) Net long-term capital gain or loss (NLTCG or NLTCL)

b. Then net these two together to determine whether there is a net capital gain or loss (NCG or NCL)

4. The following rules apply to **individuals:**

a. Capital gains offset capital losses, with any remaining net capital gains included in gross income.

b. Net capital gains are subject to tax at various rates, depending on the type of assets sold or exchanged and length of time the assets were held.

(1) Capital gain from assets held one year or less is taxed at the taxpayer's regular tax rates (up to 35%).

(2) Capital gain from the sale of collectibles held more than twelve months (e.g., antiques, metals, gems, stamps, coins) is taxed at a maximum rate of 28%.

(3) Capital gain attributable to unrecaptured depreciation on Sec. 1250 property held more than twelve months is taxed at a maximum rate of 25%.

(4) Capital gain from assets held more than twelve months (other than from collectibles and unrecaptured depreciation on SEC. 1250 property) is taxed at a rate of 15% (or for tax years beginning after December 31, 2008, 0% for individuals in the 10% or 15% tax bracket).

(5) For installment sales of assets held more than twelve months, the date an installment payment is received (not the date the asset was sold) determines the capital gains rate that should be applied

c. Gains and losses (including carryovers) within each of the rate groups are netted to arrive at a net gain or loss. A net loss in any rate group is applied to reduce the net gain in the highest rate group first (e.g., a net short-term capital loss is applied to reduce any net gain from the 28% group, then the 25% group, and finally to reduce gain from the 15% group).

> EXAMPLE: Kim, who is in the 35% tax bracket, had the following capital gains and losses for calendar-year 2008:
>
> | | |
> |---|---:|
> | Net short-term capital loss | $(1,500) |
> | 28% group—collectibles net gain | 900 |
> | 25% group—unrecaptured Sec. 1250 net gain | 2,000 |
> | 15% group—net gain | 5,000 |
> | Net capital gain | $ 6,400 |
>
> In this case, the NSTCL of $1,500 first offsets the $900 of collectibles gain, and then offsets $600 of the unrecaptured Sec. 1250 gain. As a result of this netting procedure, Kim has $1,400 of unrecaptured Sec. 1250 gain that will be taxed at a rate of 25%, and $5,000 of capital gain that will be taxed at a rate of 15%.

d. If there is a **net capital loss** the following rules apply:

(1) A net capital loss is a deduction in arriving at AGI, but limited to the lesser of

    (a) $3,000 ($1,500 if married filing separately), or

    (b) The excess of capital losses over capital gains

(2) Both a NSTCL and a NLTCL are used dollar-for-dollar in computing the capital loss deduction.

> EXAMPLE: An individual had $2,000 of NLTCL and $500 of NSTCL for 2008. The capital losses are combined and the entire net capital loss of $2,500 is deductible in computing the individual's AGI.

(3) Short-term losses are used before long-term losses. The amount of net capital loss that exceeds the allowable deduction may be carried over for an unlimited period of time. Capital loss carryovers retain their identity; short-term losses carry over as short-term losses, and long-term losses carry over as long-term losses in the 28% group. Losses remaining unused on a decedent's final return are extinguished and provide no tax benefit.

> EXAMPLE: An individual has a $4,000 STCL and a $5,000 LTCL for 2008. The $9,000 net capital loss results in a capital loss deduction of $3,000 for 2008, while the remainder is a carryover to 2009. Since $3,000 of the STCL would be used to create the capital loss deduction, there is a $1,000 STCL carryover and a $5,000 LTCL carryover to 2009. The $5,000 LTCL carryover would first offset gains in the 28% group.

(4) For purposes of determining the amount of excess net capital loss that can be carried over to future years, the taxpayer's net capital loss for the year is reduced by the lesser of (1) $3,000 ($1,500 if married filing separately), or (2) adjusted taxable income.

    (a) Adjusted taxable income is taxable income increased by $3,000 ($1,500 if married filing separately) and the amount allowed for personal exemptions.

    (b) An excess of deductions allowed over gross income is taken into account as negative taxable income.

> EXAMPLE: For 2008, a single individual with no dependents had a net capital loss of $8,000, and had allowable deductions that exceeded gross income by $4,000. For 2008, the individual is entitled to a net capital loss deduction of $3,000, and will carry over a net capital loss of $5,500 to 2009. This amount represents the 2008 net capital loss of $8,000 reduced by the lesser of (1) $3,000, or (2) – $4,000 + $3,000 + $3,500 personal exemption = $2,500.

5. **Corporations** have special capital gain and loss rules.

  a. Capital losses are only allowed to offset capital gains, not ordinary income.

  b. A **net capital loss** is carried back three years, and forward five years to offset capital gains in those years. All capital loss carrybacks and carryovers are treated as **short-term** capital losses.

> EXAMPLE: A corporation has a NLTCL of $8,000 and a NSTCG of $2,000, resulting in a net capital loss of $6,000 for 2008. The $6,000 NLTCL is not deductible for 2008, but is first carried back as a STCL to 2005 to offset capital gains. If not used up in 2005, the STCL is carried to 2006 and 2007, and then forward to 2009, 2010, 2011, 2012, and 2013 to offset capital gains in those years.

  c. Although an alternative tax computation still exists for a corporation with a net capital gain, the alternative tax computation applies the highest corporate rate (35%) to a net capital gain and thus provides no benefit.

C. Personal Casualty and Theft Gains and Losses

Gains and losses from casualties and thefts of property held for personal use are separately netted, without regard to the holding period of the converted property.

1. If gains exceed losses (after the $100 floor for each loss), then all gains and losses are treated as capital gains and losses, short-term or long-term depending upon holding period.

> EXAMPLE: An individual incurred a $25,000 personal casualty gain, and a $15,000 personal casualty loss (after the $100 floor) during the current taxable year. Since there was a net gain, the individual will report the gain and loss as a $25,000 capital gain and a $15,000 capital loss.

2. If losses (after the $100 floor for each loss) exceed gains, the losses (1) offset gains, and (2) are an ordinary deduction from AGI to the extent in excess of 10% of AGI.

> EXAMPLE: An individual had AGI of $40,000 (before casualty gains or losses), and also had a personal casualty loss of $25,000 (after the $100 floor) and a personal casualty gain of $15,000. Since there was a net personal casualty loss, the net loss will be deductible as an itemized deduction of [$25,000 – $15,000 – (10% × $40,000)] = $6,000.

exchanges of property between related taxpayers, including family members. Any gain later realized by the related transferee on the subsequent disposition of the property is not recognized to the extent of the transferor's disallowed loss. Here, her father's realized loss of $30,000 – $20,000 = $10,000 was disallowed because he sold the stock to his daughter, Alice. Her basis for the stock is her cost of $20,000. On the subsequent sale of the stock, Alice realizes a gain of $25,000 – $20,000 = $5,000. However, this realized gain of $5,000 is not recognized because of her father's disallowed loss of $10,000.

34. **(b)** The requirement is to determine the amount of gain from the sale of stock to a third party that Martin should report on his 2008 income tax return. Losses are disallowed on sales of property between related taxpayers, including family members. Any gain later realized by the transferee on the disposition of the property is not recognized to the extent of the transferor's disallowed loss. Here, Fay's realized loss of $15,000 – $11,000 = $4,000 is disallowed because she sold the stock to her son, Martin. Martin's basis for the stock is his cost of $11,000. On the subsequent sale of the stock to an unrelated third party, Martin realizes a gain of $16,000 – $11,000 = $5,000. However, this realized gain of $5,000 is recognized only to the extent that it exceeds Fay's $4,000 disallowed loss, or $1,000.

35. **(c)** The requirement is to determine among which of the related individuals are losses from sales and exchanges not recognized for tax purposes. No loss deduction is allowed on the sale or exchange of property between members of a family. For this purpose, an individual's *family* includes only brothers, sisters, half-brothers and half-sisters, spouse, ancestors (parents, grandparents, etc.) and lineal descendants (children, grandchildren, etc.) Since in-laws and uncles are excluded from this definition of a family, a loss resulting from a sale or exchange with an uncle or between in-laws would be recognized.

36. **(a)** Losses are disallowed on sales between related taxpayers, including family members. Thus, Daniel's loss of $3,000 is disallowed on the sale of stock to his son, William. William's basis for the stock is his $7,000 cost. Since William's stock basis is determined by his cost (not by reference to Daniel's cost), there is no "tack-on" of Daniel's holding period. Thus, a later sale of the stock for $6,000 on July 1 generates a $1,000 STCL for William.

37. **(c)** The requirement is to determine the amount of loss that Rego Corp. can deduct on a sale of its trailer to a 50% shareholder. Losses are disallowed on transactions between related taxpayers, including a corporation and a shareholder owning more than 50% of its stock. Since Al Eng owns only 50% (not more than 50%), the loss is recognized by Rego. Since the trailer was held for more than one year and used in Rego's business, the $2,000 loss is a Sec. 1231 loss. Answer (d) is incorrect because Sec. 1245 only applies to gains.

B.   Capital Gains and Losses

38. **(a)** The requirement is to determine when gain or loss on a year-end sale of listed stock arises for a cash basis taxpayer. If stock or securities that are traded on an established securities market are sold, any resulting gain or loss is recognized on the trade date (i.e., the date on which the trade is executed) by both cash and accrual method taxpayers.

39. **(b)** The requirement is to determine the amount of an $8,000 net long-term capital loss that can be offset against Lee's taxable income of $100,000. An individual's net capital loss can be offset against ordinary income up to a maximum of $3,000 ($1,500 if married filing separately). Since a net capital loss offsets ordinary income dollar for dollar, Lee has a $3,000 net capital loss deduction for 2008 and a long-term capital loss carryover of $5,000 to 2009.

40. **(d)** The requirement is to determine the amount of excess of net long-term capital loss over net short-term capital gain that Sol Corp. can offset against ordinary income. A corporation's net capital loss cannot be offset against ordinary income. Instead, a net capital loss is generally carried back three years and forward five years as a STCL to offset capital gains in those years.

41. **(d)** The requirement is to determine the proper treatment for a $24,000 NLTCL for Nam Corp. A corporation's capital losses can only be used to offset capital gains. If a corporation has a net capital loss, the net capital loss cannot be currently deducted, but must be carried back three years and forward five years as a STCL to offset capital gains in those years. Since Nam had not realized any capital gains since it began operations, the $24,000 LTCL can only be carried forward for five years as a STCL.

42. **(b)** The requirement is to determine the holding period for determining long-term capital gains and losses. Long-term capital gains and losses result if capital assets are held more than twelve months.

43. **(a)** The requirement is to determine the treatment for the sale of the antique by Wald. Since the antique was held for personal use, the sale of the antique at a loss is not deductible.

44. **(c)** The requirement is to determine the capital loss carryover to 2009. The NSTCL and the NLTCL result in a net capital loss of $6,000. LTCLs are deductible dollar for dollar, the same as STCLs. Since an individual can deduct a net capital loss up to a maximum of $3,000, the net capital loss of $6,000 results in a capital loss deduction of $3,000 for 2008, and a long-term capital loss carryover to 2009 of $3,000.

B.1.   Capital Assets

45. **(c)** The requirement is to determine the item that is included in the definition of capital assets. The definition of capital assets includes property held as an investment and would include a manufacturing company's investment in US Treasury bonds. In contrast, the definition specifically excludes accounts receivable arising from the sale of inventory, depreciable property used in a trade or business, and property held primarily for sale to customers in the ordinary course of a trade or business.

46. **(b)** The requirement is to determine the amount of Hall's capital assets. The definition of capital assets includes investment property and property held for personal use (e.g., personal residence and furnishings), but excludes property used in a trade or business (e.g., limousine).

47. **(b)** The requirement is to determine the proper treatment for the gain recognized on the sale of a painting that was purchased in 2002 and held for personal use. The definition of "capital assets" includes investment property and property held for personal use (if sold at a gain). Because the painting was held for more than one year, the gain from the sale of the painting must be reported as a long-term capital gain. Note that if personal-use property is sold at a loss, the loss is not deductible.

48. (b) The requirement is to determine the correct treatment for a capital loss incurred by a married couple filing a joint return for 2008. Capital losses first offset capital gains, and then are allowed as a deduction of up to $3,000 against ordinary income, with any unused capital loss carried forward indefinitely. Note that a married taxpayer filing separately can only offset up to $1,500 of net capital loss against ordinary income.

49. (d) The requirement is to determine the proper classification of land used as a parking lot and a shed erected on the lot for customer transactions. The definition of capital assets includes investment property and property held for personal use, but excludes any property used in a trade or business. The definition of Sec. 1231 assets generally includes business assets held more than one year. Since the land and shed were used in conjunction with a parking lot business, they are properly classified as Sec. 1231 assets.

50. (a) The requirement is to determine the classification of Ruth's diamond necklace. The diamond necklace is classified as a capital asset because the definition of "capital asset" includes investment property and *property held for personal use*. Answers (b), (c), and (d) are incorrect because Sec. 1231 generally includes only assets used in a trade or business, while Sections 1245 and 1250 only include depreciable assets.

51. (b) The requirement is to determine which asset is a capital asset. The definition of capital assets includes personal-use property, but excludes property used in a trade or business (e.g., delivery truck, land used as a parking lot). Treasury stock is not considered an asset, but instead is treated as a reduction of stockholders' equity.

52. (a) The requirement is to determine how a lump sum of $30,000 received in 2008, for an agreement not to operate a competing enterprise, should be treated. A covenant not to compete is not a capital asset. Thus, the $30,000 received as consideration for such an agreement must be reported as ordinary income in the year received.

53. (b) The requirement is to determine the amount of furniture classified as capital assets. The definition of capital assets includes investment property and property held for personal use (e.g., kitchen and living room pieces), but excludes property used in a trade or business (e.g., showcases and tables).

C. Personal Casualty and Theft Gains and Losses

54. (a) The requirement is to determine the correct statement regarding the deductibility of an individual's losses on transactions entered into for personal purposes. An individual's losses on transactions entered into for personal purposes are deductible only if the losses qualify as casualty or theft losses. Answer (b) is incorrect because hobby losses are not deductible. Answers (c) and (d) are incorrect because losses (other than by casualty or theft) on transactions entered into for personal purposes are not deductible.

D. Gains and Losses on Business Property

55. (d) The requirement is to determine the characterization of Evon Corporation's $50,000 of net Sec. 1231 gain for its 2008 tax year. Although a net Sec. 1231 gain is generally treated as a long-term capital gain, it instead must be treated as ordinary income to the extent of the taxpayer's nonrecaptured net Sec. 1231 losses for its five preceding taxable years. Here, since the nonrecaptured net Sec. 1231 losses for 2006 and 2007 total $35,000, only $15,000 of the $50,000 net Sec. 1231 gain will be treated as a long-term capital gain.

56. (a) The requirement is to determine which item would not be characterized as Sec. 1231 property. Sec. 1231 property generally includes both depreciable and nondepreciable property used in a trade or business or held for the production of income if held for more than twelve months. Specifically excluded from Sec. 1231 is inventory and property held for sale to customers, as well as accounts and notes receivable arising in the ordinary course of a trade or business.

57. (c) The requirement is to determine the amount of ordinary income that must be recognized by Vermont Corporation from the distribution of the equipment to a shareholder. When a corporation distributes appreciated property, it must recognize gain just as if it had sold the property for its fair market value. As a result Vermont must recognize a gain of $9,000 − $2,000 = $7,000 on the distribution of the equipment. Since the distributed property is depreciable personal property, the gain is subject to Sec. 1245 recapture as ordinary income to the extent of the $6,000 of straight-line depreciation deducted by Vermont. The remaining $1,000 of gain would be treated as Sec. 1231 gain.

58. (c) The requirement is to determine the nature of a loss resulting from the sale of business machinery that had been held sixteen months. Property held for use in a trade or business is specifically excluded from the definition of capital assets, and if held for more than one year is considered Sec. 1231 property. Answer (b) is incorrect because Sec. 1245 only applies to gains.

59. (c) The requirement is to determine the amount of gain from the sale of property that must be recaptured as ordinary income. A gain from the disposition of seven-year tangible property is subject to recapture under Sec. 1245 which recaptures gain to the extent of all depreciation previously deducted. Here, Bates' gain from the sale of the property is determined as follows:

Selling price		$102,000
Cost	$100,000	
Depreciation	− 47,525	
Adjusted basis		− 52,475
Gain		$ 49,525

Under Sec. 1245, Bates Corp's gain is recaptured as ordinary income to the extent of the $47,525 deducted as depreciation. The remaining $2,000 of gain would be classified as Sec. 1231 gain.

60. (b) The requirement is to determine the proper treatment of the $50,000 gain on the sale of the building, which is Sec. 1250 property. Sec. 1250 recaptures gain as ordinary income to the extent of "excess" depreciation (i.e., depreciation deducted in excess of straight-line). The total gain less any depreciation recapture is Sec. 1231 gain. Since straight-line depreciation was used, there is no recapture under Sec. 1250. However, Sec. 291 requires that the amount of ordinary income on the disposition of Sec. 1250 property by corporations be increased by 20% of the additional amount that would have been ordinary income if the property had instead been Sec. 1245 property. If the building had been Sec. 1245 property the amount of recapture would have been $30,000 ($200,000 – $170,000). Thus, the Sec. 291 ordinary income is $30,000 × 20% = $6,000. The remaining $44,000 is Sec. 1231 gain.

61. **(b)** The requirement is to determine McEwing Corporation's taxable income given book income plus additional information regarding items that were included in book income. The loss on sale of the building ($7,000) and gain on sale of the land ($16,000) are Sec. 1231 gains and losses. The resulting Sec. 1231 net gain of $9,000 is then treated as LTCG and will be offset against the LTCL of $8,000 resulting from the sale of investments. Since these items have already been included in book income, McEwing's taxable income is the same as its book income, $120,000.

62. **(a)** The realized gain resulting from the involuntary conversion ($125,000 insurance proceeds – $86,000 adjusted basis = $39,000) is recognized only to the extent that the insurance proceeds are not reinvested in similar property ($125,000 – $110,000 = $15,000). Since the machinery was Sec. 1245 property, the recognized gain of $15,000 is recaptured as ordinary income to the extent of the $14,000 of depreciation previously deducted. The remaining $1,000 is Sec. 1231 gain.

SOLUTIONS TO SIMULATION PROBLEMS

Simulation Problem 1

Situation	Schedule D	Communication	Research

SCHEDULE D (Form 1040) Department of the Treasury Internal Revenue Service	**Capital Gains and Losses** ▶ Attach to Form 1040 or Form 1040NR. ▶ See Instructions for Schedule D (Form 1040). ▶ Use Schedule D-1 to list additional transactions for lines 1 and 8.	OMB No. 1545-0074 **2007** Attachment Sequence No. **12**

Name(s) shown on return Lou Tomsik

Your social security number 324 65 7037

Part I   Short-Term Capital Gains and Losses—Assets Held One Year or Less

(a) Description of property (Example: 100 sh. XYZ Co.)	(b) Date acquired (Mo., day, yr.)	(c) Date sold (Mo., day, yr.)	(d) Sales price (see page D-7 of the instructions)	(e) Cost or other basis (see page D-7 of the instructions)	(f) Gain or (loss) Subtract (e) from (d)
200 shs King Corp.	2·24·07	11·15·07	5,000	4,000	1,000

2 Enter your short-term totals, if any, from Schedule D-1, line 2 . .	**2**	
3 Total short-term sales price amounts. Add lines 1 and 2 in column (d)	**3** 5,000	
4 Short-term gain from Form 6252 and short-term gain or (loss) from Forms 4684, 6781, and 8824	**4**	
5 Net short-term gain or (loss) from partnerships, S corporations, estates, and trusts from Schedule(s) K-1	**5**	
6 Short-term capital loss carryover. Enter the amount, if any, from line 10 of your **Capital Loss Carryover Worksheet** on page D-7 of the instructions	**6** (7,300)	
7 Net short-term capital gain or (loss). Combine lines 1 through 6 in column (f)	**7** (6,300)	

Part II   Long-Term Capital Gains and Losses—Assets Held More Than One Year

(a) Description of property (Example: 100 sh. XYZ Co.)	(b) Date acquired (Mo., day, yr.)	(c) Date sold (Mo., day, yr.)	(d) Sales price (see page D-7 of the instructions)	(e) Cost or other basis (see page D-7 of the instructions)	(f) Gain or (loss) Subtract (e) from (d)
8 100 shs. Copperleaf Ind.	3·1·06	6·20·07	4,200	2,500	1,700

9 Enter your long-term totals, if any, from Schedule D-1, line 9	**9**	
10 Total long-term sales price amounts. Add lines 8 and 9 in column (d)	**10** 4,200	
11 Gain from Form 4797, Part I; long-term gain from Forms 2439 and 6252; and long-term gain or (loss) from Forms 4684, 6781, and 8824	**11**	
12 Net long-term gain or (loss) from partnerships, S corporations, estates, and trusts from Schedule(s) K-1	**12**	
13 Capital gain distributions. See page D-2 of the instructions	**13** 1,500	
14 Long-term capital loss carryover. Enter the amount, if any, from line 15 of your **Capital Loss Carryover Worksheet** on page D-7 of the instructions	**14** ( )	
15 Net long-term capital gain or (loss). Combine lines 8 through 14 in column (f). Then go to Part III on the back	**15** 3,200	

For Paperwork Reduction Act Notice, see Form 1040 or Form 1040NR instructions.   Cat. No. 11338H   Schedule D (Form 1040) 2007

Part III **Summary**

16 Combine lines 7 and 15 and enter the result. **16** (3,100)

If line 16 is:
- A **gain**, enter the amount from line 16 on Form 1040, line 13, or Form 1040NR, line 14. Then go to line 17 below.
- A **loss**, skip lines 17 through 20 below. Then go to line 21. Also be sure to complete line 22.
- **Zero**, skip lines 17 through 21 below and enter -0- on Form 1040, line 13, or Form 1040NR, line 14. Then go to line 22.

17 Are lines 15 and 16 **both** gains?
☐ **Yes.** Go to line 18.
☐ **No.** Skip lines 18 through 21, and go to line 22.

18 Enter the amount, if any, from line 7 of the **28% Rate Gain Worksheet** on page D-8 of the instructions . . . . ▶   **18**

19 Enter the amount, if any, from line 18 of the **Unrecaptured Section 1250 Gain Worksheet** on page D-9 of the instructions . . . . ▶   **19**

20 Are lines 18 and 19 **both** zero or blank?
☐ **Yes.** Complete Form 1040 through line 43, or Form 1040NR through line 40. Then complete the **Qualified Dividends and Capital Gain Tax Worksheet** on page 35 of the Instructions for Form 1040 (or in the Instructions for Form 1040NR). **Do not** complete lines 21 and 22 below.
☐ **No.** Complete Form 1040 through line 43, or Form 1040NR through line 40. Then complete the **Schedule D Tax Worksheet** on page D-10 of the instructions. **Do not** complete lines 21 and 22 below.

21 If line 16 is a loss, enter here and on Form 1040, line 13, or Form 1040NR, line 14, the **smaller** of:

- The loss on line 16 or   }
- ($3,000), or if married filing separately, ($1,500) } **21** (3,000)

Note. When figuring which amount is smaller, treat both amounts as positive numbers.

22 Do you have qualified dividends on Form 1040, line 9b, or Form 1040NR, line 10b?
☐ **Yes.** Complete Form 1040 through line 43, or Form 1040NR through line 40. Then complete the **Qualified Dividends and Capital Gain Tax Worksheet** on page 35 of the Instructions for Form 1040 (or in the Instructions for Form 1040NR).
☒ **No.** Complete the rest of Form 1040 or Form 1040NR.

Situation	Schedule D	Communication	Research

The technical points to be covered in this response should include

Individuals may carry over a net capital loss to future tax years until the loss is used. A capital loss that is carried over to a later tax year retains its short-term or long-term character for the year to which it is carried. A short-term capital loss carryover first offsets short-term gain in the carryover year. If a net short-term capital loss results, this loss first offsets net long-term capital gain and then up to $3,000 of ordinary income. A long-term capital loss carryover first reduces long-term capital gain in the carryover year, then net short-term capital gain, and finally up to $3,000 of ordinary income.

Situation	Schedule D	Communication	Research

Internal Revenue Code Section 1221 provides a definition of capital assets.

PARTNERSHIPS

Partnerships are organizations of two or more persons to carry on business activities for profit. For tax purposes, partnerships also include a syndicate, joint venture, or other unincorporated business through which any business or financial operation is conducted. Partnerships do not pay any income tax, but instead act as a conduit to pass through tax items to the partners. Partnerships file an informational return (Form 1065), and partners report their share of partnership ordinary income or loss and other items on their individual returns. The nature or character (e.g., taxable, nontaxable) of income or deductions is not changed by the pass-through nature of the partnership.

A. Entity Classification

1. Eligible business entities (a business entity other than an entity automatically classified as a corporation) may choose how they will be classified for federal tax purposes by filing Form 8832. A business entity with at least two members can choose to be classified as either an association taxable as a corporation or as a partnership. A business entity with a single member can choose to be classified as either an association taxable as a corporation or disregarded as an entity separate from its owner.

    a. An eligible business entity that does not file Form 8832 will be classified under default rules. Under default rules, an eligible business entity will be classified as a partnership if it has two or more members, or disregarded as an entity separate from its owner if it has a single owner.

    b. Once an entity makes an election, a different election cannot be made for sixty months unless there is more than a 50% ownership change and the IRS consents.

2. **General partnerships** exist when two or more partners join together and do not specifically provide that one or more partners is a limited partner. Since each general partner has unlimited liability, creditors can reach the personal assets of a general partner to satisfy partnership debts, including a malpractice judgment against the partnership even though the partner was not personally involved in the malpractice.

3. **Limited partnerships** have two classes of partners, with at least one general partner (who has the same rights and responsibilities as a partner in a general partnership) and at least one limited partner. A limited partner generally cannot participate in the active management of the partnership, and in the event of losses, generally can lose no more than his or her own capital contribution. A limited partnership is often the preferred entity of choice for real estate ventures requiring significant capital contributions.

4. **Limited liability partnerships** differ from general partnerships in that with an LLP, a partner is not liable for damages resulting from the negligence, malpractice, or fraud committed by other partners. However, each partner is personally liable for his or her own negligence, malpractice, or fraud. LLPs are often used by service providers such as architects, accountants, attorneys, and physicians.

5. **Limited liability companies** that do not elect to be treated as an association taxable as a corporation are subject to the rules applicable to partnerships (a single-member LLC would be disregarded as an entity separate from its owner). An LLC combines the nontax advantage of limited liability for each and every owner of the entity, with the tax advantage of pass-through treatment, and the flexibility of partnership taxation. The LLC structure is generally available to both nonprofessional service providers as well as capital-intensive companies.

6. **Electing large partnerships** are partnerships that have elected to be taxed under a simplified reporting system that does not require as much separate reporting to partners as does a regular partnership. For example, charitable contributions are deductible by the partnership (subject to a 10% of taxable income limitation), and the Sec. 179 expense election is deducted in computing partnership ordinary income and not separately passed through to partners. To qualify, the partnership must not be a service partnership nor engaged in commodity trading, must have at least 100 partners, and must file an election to be taxed as an electing large partnership. A partnership will cease to be an electing large partnership if it has fewer than 100 partners for a taxable year.

7. **Publicly traded partnerships** are partnerships whose interests are traded on an established securities exchange or in a secondary market and are generally taxed as C corporations.

B. Partnership Formation

1. As a general rule, **no gain or loss** is recognized by a partner when there is a contribution of property to the partnership in exchange for an interest in the partnership. There are three situations where gain must be recognized.

    a. A partner must recognize gain when property is contributed which is subject to a liability, and the resulting decrease in the partner's individual liability exceeds the partner's partnership basis.

        (1) The excess of liability over adjusted basis is generally treated as a capital gain from the sale or exchange of a partnership interest.

        (2) The gain will be treated as ordinary income to the extent the property transferred was subject to depreciation recapture under Sec. 1245 or 1250.

        > EXAMPLE: *A partner acquires a 20% interest in a partnership by contributing property worth $10,000 but with an adjusted basis of $4,000. There is a mortgage of $6,000 that is assumed by the partnership. The partner must recognize a gain of $800, and has a zero basis for the partnership interest, calculated as follows:*
        >
        > | | |
        > |---|---:|
        > | Adjusted basis of contributed property | $ 4,000 |
        > | Less: portion of mortgage allocated to other partners (80% × $6,000) | (4,800) |
        > | Partner's basis (not reduced below 0) | $ 0 |

    b. Gain will be recognized on a contribution of property to a partnership in exchange for an interest therein if the partnership would be an investment company if incorporated.

    c. Partner must recognize compensation income when an interest in partnership capital is received in exchange for **services rendered**.

        > EXAMPLE: *X received a 10% capital interest in the ABC Partnership in exchange for services rendered. On the date X was admitted to the partnership, ABC's net assets had a basis of $30,000 and a FMV of $50,000. X must recognize compensation income of $5,000.*

2. Property contributed to the partnership has the same **basis** as it had in the contributing partner's hands (a transferred basis).

    a. The basis for the partner's partnership interest is increased by the adjusted basis of property contributed.

    b. No gain or loss is generally recognized by the partnership upon the contribution.

3. The **partnership's holding period** for contributed property includes the period of time the property was held by the partner.

4. A **partner's holding period** for a partnership interest includes the holding period of property contributed, if the contributed property was a capital asset or Sec. 1231 asset in the contributing partner's hands.

5. Although not a separate taxpaying entity, the partnership must make most elections as to the tax treatment of partnership items. For example, the partnership must select a taxable year and various accounting methods which can differ from the methods used by its partners. Partnership elections include an overall method of accounting, inventory method, the method used to compute depreciation, and the election to expense depreciable assets under Sec. 179.

6. Effective for amounts paid after October 22, 2004, a partnership may elect to deduct up to $5,000 of organizational expenditures for the tax year in which the partnership begins business. The $5,000 amount must be reduced (but not below zero) by the amount by which **organizational expenditures** exceed $50,000. Remaining expenditures can be deducted ratably over the 180-month period beginning with the month in which the partnership begins business.

    a. Similar rules apply to partnership start-up expenditures.

    b. For amounts paid on or before October 22, 2004, a partnership may elect to amortize organizational expenditures and start-up expenditures over not less than 60 months beginning with the month that business begins.

    c. Partnership syndication fees (expenses of selling partnership interests) are neither deductible nor amortizable.

C. Partnership Income and Loss

1. Since a partnership is not a separate taxpaying entity, but instead acts as a conduit to pass-through items of income and deduction to individual partners, the partnership's reporting of income and deductions requires a two-step approach.

2009. In addition, Dale received a $10,000 interest-free loan from the partnership in 2008. This $10,000 is to be offset against Dale's share of 2009 partnership income. What total amount of partnership income is taxable to Dale in 2008?

    a. $27,000
    b. $37,000
    c. $50,000
    d. $60,000

23. At December 31, 2007, Alan and Baker were equal partners in a partnership with net assets having a tax basis and fair market value of $100,000. On January 1, 2008, Carr contributed securities with a fair market value of $50,000 (purchased in 2006 at a cost of $35,000) to become an equal partner in the new firm of Alan, Baker, and Carr. The securities were sold on December 15, 2008, for $47,000. How much of the partnership's capital gain from the sale of these securities should be allocated to Carr?

    a. $0
    b. $ 3,000
    c. $ 6,000
    d. $12,000

24. Gilroy, a calendar-year taxpayer, is a partner in the firm of Adams and Company which has a fiscal year ending June 30. The partnership agreement provides for Gilroy to receive 25% of the ordinary income of the partnership. Gilroy also receives a guaranteed payment of $1,000 monthly which is deductible by the partnership. The partnership reported ordinary income of $88,000 for the year ended June 30, 2008, and $132,000 for the year ended June 30, 2009. How much should Gilroy report on his 2008 return as total income from the partnership?

    a. $25,000
    b. $30,500
    c. $34,000
    d. $39,000

25. On December 31, 2007, Edward Baker gave his son, Allan, a gift of a 50% interest in a partnership in which capital is a material income-producing factor. For the year ended December 31, 2008, the partnership's ordinary income was $100,000. Edward and Allan were the only partners in 2008. There were no guaranteed payments to partners. Edward's services performed for the partnership were worth a reasonable compensation of $40,000 for 2008. Allan has never performed any services for the partnership. What is Allan's distributive share of partnership income for 2008?

    a. $20,000
    b. $30,000
    c. $40,000
    d. $50,000

Items 26 and 27 are based on the following:

Jones and Curry formed Major Partnership as equal partners by contributing the assets below.

	Asset	Adjusted basis	Fair market value
Jones	Cash	$45,000	$45,000
Curry	Land	30,000	57,000

The land was held by Curry as a capital asset, subject to a $12,000 mortgage, that was assumed by Major.

26. What was Curry's initial basis in the partnership interest?

    a. $45,000
    b. $30,000
    c. $24,000
    d. $18,000

27. What was Jones' initial basis in the partnership interest?

    a. $51,000
    b. $45,000
    c. $39,000
    d. $33,000

Items 28 and 29 are based on the following:

Flagg and Miles are each 50% partners in Decor Partnership. Each partner had a $200,000 tax basis in the partnership on January 1, 2008. Decor's 2008 net business income before guaranteed payments was $45,000. During 2008, Decor made a $7,500 guaranteed payment to Miles for deductible services rendered.

28. What total amount from Decor is includible in Flagg's 2008 tax return?

    a. $15,000
    b. $18,750
    c. $22,500
    d. $37,500

29. What is Miles's tax basis in Decor on December 31, 2008?

    a. $211,250
    b. $215,000
    c. $218,750
    d. $222,500

30. Peters has a one-third interest in the Spano Partnership. During 2008, Peters received a $16,000 guaranteed payment, which was deductible by the partnership, for services rendered to Spano. Spano reported a 2008 operating loss of $70,000 before the guaranteed payment. What is(are) the net effect(s) of the guaranteed payment?

  I. The guaranteed payment decreases Peters' tax basis in Spano by $16,000.
  II. The guaranteed payment increases Peters' ordinary income by $16,000.

    a.   I only.
    b.   II only.
    c.   Both I and II.
    d.   Neither I nor II.

31. Dean is a 25% partner in Target Partnership. Dean's tax basis in Target on January 1, 2008, was $20,000. At the end of 2008, Dean received a nonliquidating cash distribution of $8,000 from Target. Target's 2008 accounts recorded the following items:

Municipal bond interest income	$12,000
Ordinary income	40,000

What was Dean's tax basis in Target on December 31, 2008?

    a. $15,000
    b. $23,000
    c. $25,000
    d. $30,000

32. On January 4, 2008, Smith and White contributed $4,000 and $6,000 in cash, respectively, and formed the Macro General Partnership. The partnership agreement allocated profits and losses 40% to Smith and 60% to White.

In 2008, Macro purchased property from an unrelated seller for $10,000 cash and a $40,000 mortgage note that was the general liability of the partnership. Macro's liability

    a.   Increases Smith's partnership basis by $16,000.
    b.   Increases Smith's partnership basis by $20,000.
    c.   Increases Smith's partnership basis by $24,000.
    d.   Has **no** effect on Smith's partnership basis.

33. Gray is a 50% partner in Fabco Partnership. Gray's tax basis in Fabco on January 1, 2008, was $5,000. Fabco made no distributions to the partners during 2008, and recorded the following:

Ordinary income	$20,000
Tax exempt income	8,000
Portfolio income	4,000

What is Gray's tax basis in Fabco on December 31, 2008?

    a. $21,000
    b. $16,000
    c. $12,000
    d. $10,000

34. On January 1, 2008, Kane was a 25% equal partner in Maze General Partnership, which had partnership liabilities of $300,000. On January 2, 2008, a new partner was admitted and Kane's interest was reduced to 20%. On April 1, 2008, Maze repaid a $100,000 general partnership loan. Ignoring any income, loss, or distributions for 2009, what was the **net** effect of the two transactions for Kane's tax basis in Maze partnership interest?

    a.   Has **no** effect.
    b.   Decrease of $35,000.
    c.   Increase of $15,000.
    d.   Decrease of $75,000.

35. Lee inherited a partnership interest from Dale. The adjusted basis of Dale's partnership interest was $50,000, and its fair market value on the date of Dale's death (the estate valuation date) was $70,000. What was Lee's original basis for the partnership interest?

    a. $70,000
    b. $50,000
    c. $20,000
    d. $0

36. Which of the following should be used in computing the basis of a partner's interest acquired from another partner?

	Cash paid by transferee to transferor	Transferee's share of partnership liabilities
a.	No	Yes
b.	Yes	No
c.	No	No
d.	Yes	Yes

37. Hall and Haig are equal partners in the firm of Arosa Associates. On January 1, 2008, each partner's adjusted basis in Arosa was $40,000. During 2008 Arosa borrowed $60,000, for which Hall and Haig are personally liable. Arosa sustained an operating loss of $10,000 for the year ended December 31, 2008. The basis of each partner's interest in Arosa at December 31, 2008, was

    a. $35,000
    b. $40,000
    c. $65,000
    d. $70,000

38. Doris and Lydia are sisters and also are equal partners in the capital and profits of Agee & Nolan. The following information pertains to 300 shares of Mast Corp. stock sold by Lydia to Agee & Nolan.

Year of purchase	2001
Year of sale	2008
Basis (cost)	$9,000
Sales price (equal to fair market value)	$4,000

The amount of long-term capital loss that Lydia recognized in 2008 on the sale of this stock was

    a. $5,000
    b. $3,000
    c. $2,500
    d. $0

39. In March 2008, Lou Cole bought 100 shares of a listed stock for $10,000. In May 2008, Cole sold this stock for its fair market value of $16,000 to the partnership of Rook, Cole & Clive. Cole owned a one-third interest in this partnership. In Cole's 2008 tax return, what amount should be reported as short-term capital gain as a result of this transaction?

    a. $6,000
    b. $4,000
    c. $2,000
    d. $0

40. Kay Shea owns a 55% interest in the capital and profits of Dexter Communications, a partnership. In 2008, Kay sold an oriental lamp to Dexter for $5,000. Kay bought this lamp in 2002 for her personal use at a cost of $1,000 and had used the lamp continuously in her home until the lamp was sold to Dexter. Dexter purchased the lamp as an investment. What is Kay's reportable gain in 2008 on the sale of the lamp to Dexter?

    a. $4,000 ordinary income.
    b. $4,000 long-term capital gain.
    c. $2,200 ordinary income.
    d. $1,800 long-term capital gain.

41. Gladys Peel owns a 50% interest in the capital and profits of the partnership of Peel and Poe. On July 1, 2008, Peel bought land the partnership had used in its business for its fair market value of $10,000. The partnership had acquired the land five years ago for $16,000. For the year ended December 31, 2008, the partnership's net income was $94,000 after recording the $6,000 loss on the sale of land. Peel's distributive share of ordinary income from the partnership for 2008 was

    a. $47,000
    b. $48,500
    c. $49,000
    d. $50,000

42. Under Section 444 of the Internal Revenue Code, certain partnerships can elect to use a tax year different from their required tax year. One of the conditions for eligibility to make a Section 444 election is that the partnership must

    a.   Be a limited partnership.
    b.   Be a member of a tiered structure.
    c.   Choose a tax year where the deferral period is **not** longer than three months.
    d.   Have less than seventy-five partners.

43. Which one of the following statements regarding a partnership's tax year is correct?

a. A partnership formed on July 1 is required to adopt a tax year ending on June 30.

b. A partnership may elect to have a tax year other than the generally required tax year if the deferral period for the tax year elected does **not** exceed three months.

c. A "valid business purpose" can **no** longer be claimed as a reason for adoption of a tax year other than the generally required tax year.

d. Within thirty days after a partnership has established a tax year, a form must be filed with the IRS as notification of the tax year adopted.

44. Without obtaining prior approval from the IRS, a newly formed partnership may adopt

a. A taxable year which is the same as that used by one or more of its partners owning an aggregate interest of more than 50% in profits and capital.

b. A calendar year, only if it comprises a twelve-month period.

c. A January 31 year-end if it is a retail enterprise, and all of its principal partners are on a calendar year.

d. Any taxable year that it deems advisable to select.

45. Irving Aster, Dennis Brill, and Robert Clark were partners who shared profits and losses equally. On February 28, 2008, Aster sold his interest to Phil Dexter. On March 31, 2008, Brill died, and his estate held his interest for the remainder of the year. The partnership continued to operate and for the fiscal year ending June 30, 2008, it had a profit of $45,000. Assuming that partnership income was earned on a pro rata monthly basis and that all partners were calendar-year taxpayers, the distributive shares to be included in 2008 gross income should be

a. Aster $10,000, Brill $0, Estate of Brill $15,000, Clark $15,000, and Dexter $5,000.

b. Aster $10,000, Brill $11,250, Estate of Brill $3,750, Clark $15,000, and Dexter $5,000.

c. Aster $0, Brill $11,250, Estate of Brill $3,750, Clark $15,000, and Dexter $15,000.

d. Aster $0, Brill $0, Estate of Brill $15,000, Clark $15,000, and Dexter $15,000.

46. On January 3, 2008, the partners' interests in the capital, profits, and losses of Able Partnership were

	% of capital profits and losses
Dean	25%
Poe	30%
Ritt	45%

On February 4, 2008, Poe sold her entire interest to an unrelated person. Dean sold his 25% interest in Able to another unrelated person on December 20, 2008. No other transactions took place in 2008. For tax purposes, which of the following statements is correct with respect to Able?

a. Able terminated as of February 4, 2008.

b. Able terminated as of December 20, 2008.

c. Able terminated as of December 31, 2008.

d. Able did **not** terminate.

47. Curry's sale of her partnership interest causes a partnership termination. The partnership's business and financial operations are continued by the other members. What is(are) the effect(s) of the termination?

I. There is a deemed distribution of assets to the remaining partners and the purchaser.

II. There is a hypothetical recontribution of assets to a new partnership.

a. I only.

b. II only.

c. Both I and II.

d. Neither I nor II.

48. Cobb, Danver, and Evans each owned a one-third interest in the capital and profits of their calendar-year partnership. On September 18, 2008, Cobb and Danver sold their partnership interests to Frank, and immediately withdrew from all participation in the partnership. On March 15, 2009, Cobb and Danver received full payment from Frank for the sale of their partnership interests. For tax purposes, the partnership

a. Terminated on September 18, 2008.

b. Terminated on December 31, 2008.

c. Terminated on March 15, 2009.

d. Did **not** terminate.

49. Partnership Abel, Benz, Clark & Day is in the real estate and insurance business. Abel owns a 40% interest in the capital and profits of the partnership, while Benz, Clark, and Day each owns a 20% interest. All use a calendar year. At November 1, 2008, the real estate and insurance business is separated, and two partnerships are formed: Partnership Abel & Benz takes over the real estate business, and Partnership Clark & Day takes over the insurance business. Which one of the following statements is correct for tax purposes?

a. Partnership Abel & Benz is considered to be a continuation of Partnership Abel, Benz, Clark & Day.

b. In forming Partnership Clark & Day, partners Clark and Day are subject to a penalty surtax if they contribute their entire distributions from Partnership Abel, Benz, Clark & Day.

c. Before separating the two businesses into two distinct entities, the partners must obtain approval from the IRS.

d. Before separating the two businesses into two distinct entities, Partnership Abel, Benz, Clark & Day must file a formal dissolution with the IRS on the prescribed form.

50. Under which of the following circumstances is a partnership that is not an electing large partnership considered terminated for income tax purposes?

I. Fifty-five percent of the total interest in partnership capital and profits is sold within a twelve-month period.

II. The partnership's business and financial operations are discontinued.

a. I only.

b. II only.

c. Both I and II.

d. Neither I nor II.

51. David Beck and Walter Crocker were equal partners in the calendar-year partnership of Beck & Crocker. On July 1, 2008, Beck died. Beck's estate became the successor in interest and continued to share in Beck & Crocker's profits until Beck's entire partnership interest was liquidated on April 30, 2009. At what date was the partnership considered terminated for tax purposes?

    a.   April 30, 2009.
    b.   December 31, 2009.
    c.   July 31, 2008.
    d.   July 1, 2008.

52. On December 31, 2008, after receipt of his share of partnership income, Clark sold his interest in a limited partnership for $30,000 cash and relief of all liabilities. On that date, the adjusted basis of Clark's partnership interest was $40,000, consisting of his capital account of $15,000 and his share of the partnership liabilities of $25,000. The partnership has no unrealized receivables or appreciated inventory. What is Clark's gain or loss on the sale of his partnership interest?

    a.   Ordinary loss of $10,000.
    b.   Ordinary gain of $15,000.
    c.   Capital loss of $10,000.
    d.   Capital gain of $15,000.

Items 53 and 54 are based on the following:

The personal service partnership of Allen, Baker & Carr had the following cash basis balance sheet at December 31, 2008:

Assets	Adjusted basis per books	Market value
Cash	$102,000	$102,000
Unrealized accounts receivable	--	420,000
Totals	$102,000	$522,000
Liability and Capital		
Note payable	$ 60,000	$ 60,000
Capital accounts:		
Allen	14,000	154,000
Baker	14,000	154,000
Carr	14,000	154,000
Totals	$102,000	$522,000

Carr, an equal partner, sold his partnership interest to Dole, an outsider, for $154,000 cash on January 1, 2009. In addition, Dole assumed Carr's share of the partnership's liability.

53. What was the total amount realized by Carr on the sale of his partnership interest?

    a. $174,000
    b. $154,000
    c. $140,000
    d. $134,000

54. What amount of ordinary income should Carr report in his 2009 income tax return on the sale of his partnership interest?

    a. $0
    b. $ 20,000
    c. $ 34,000
    d. $140,000

55. On April 1, 2008, George Hart, Jr. acquired a 25% interest in the Wilson, Hart and Company partnership by gift from his father. The partnership interest had been acquired by a $50,000 cash investment by Hart, Sr. on July 1, 2002. The tax basis of Hart, Sr.'s partnership interest was $60,000 at the time of the gift. Hart, Jr. sold the 25% partnership interest for $85,000 on December 17, 2008. What type and amount of capital gain should Hart, Jr. report on his 2008 tax return?

    a.   A long-term capital gain of $25,000.
    b.   A short-term capital gain of $25,000.
    c.   A long-term capital gain of $35,000.
    d.   A short-term capital gain of $35,000.

56. On June 30, 2008, James Roe sold his interest in the calendar-year partnership of Roe & Doe for $30,000. Roe's adjusted basis in Roe & Doe at June 30, 2008, was $7,500 before apportionment of any 2008 partnership income. Roe's distributive share of partnership income up to June 30, 2008, was $22,500. Roe acquired his interest in the partnership in 2002. How much long-term capital gain should Roe report in 2008 on the sale of his partnership interest?

    a. $0
    b. $15,000
    c. $22,500
    d. $30,000

57. Stone and Frazier decided to terminate the Woodwest Partnership as of December 31. On that date, Woodwest's balance sheet was as follows:

Cash	$2,000
Land (adjusted basis)	2,000
Capital—Stone	3,000
Capital—Frazier	1,000

The fair market value of the equipment was $3,000. Frazier's outside basis in the partnership was $1,200. Upon liquidation, Frazier received $1,500 in cash. What gain should Frazier recognize?

    a. $0
    b. $250
    c. $300
    d. $500

58. Curry's adjusted basis in Vantage Partnership was $5,000 at the time he received a nonliquidating distribution of land. The land had an adjusted basis of $6,000 and a fair market value of $9,000 to Vantage. What was the amount of Curry's basis in the land?

    a. $9,000
    b. $6,000
    c. $5,000
    d. $1,000

59. Hart's adjusted basis in Best Partnership was $9,000 at the time he received the following nonliquidating distribution of partnership property:

Cash	$ 5,000
Land	
Adjusted basis	7,000
Fair market value	10,000

What was the amount of Hart's basis in the land?

    a. $0
    b. $ 4,000
    c. $ 7,000
    d. $10,000

60. Day's adjusted basis in LMN Partnership interest is $50,000. During the year Day received a nonliquidating distribution of $25,000 cash plus land with an adjusted basis of $15,000 to LMN, and a fair market value of $20,000. How much is Day's basis in the land?

    a. $10,000
    b. $15,000
    c. $20,000
    d. $25,000

Items 61 and 62 are based on the following:

The adjusted basis of Jody's partnership interest was $50,000 immediately before Jody received a current distribution of $20,000 cash and property with an adjusted basis to the partnership of $40,000 and a fair market value of $35,000.

61. What amount of taxable gain must Jody report as a result of this distribution?
- a. $0
- b. $ 5,000
- c. $10,000
- d. $20,000

62. What is Jody's basis in the distributed property?
- a. $0
- b. $30,000
- c. $35,000
- d. $40,000

63. On June 30, 2008, Berk retired from his partnership. At that time, his capital account was $50,000 and his share of the partnership's liabilities was $30,000. Berk's retirement payments consisted of being relieved of his share of the partnership liabilities and receipt of cash payments of $5,000 per month for eighteen months, commencing July 1, 2008. Assuming Berk makes no election with regard to the recognition of gain from the retirement payments, he should report income of

	2008	2009
a.	$13,333	$26,667
b.	20,000	20,000
c.	40,000	--
d.	--	40,000

64. The basis to a partner of property distributed "in kind" in complete liquidation of the partner's interest is the
- a. Adjusted basis of the partner's interest increased by any cash distributed to the partner in the same transaction.
- b. Adjusted basis of the partner's interest reduced by any cash distributed to the partner in the same transaction.
- c. Adjusted basis of the property to the partnership.
- d. Fair market value of the property.

Items 65 and 66 are based on the following data:

Mike Reed, a partner in Post Co., received the following distribution from Post:

	Post's basis	Fair market value
Cash	$11,000	$11,000
Inventory	5,000	12,500

Before this distribution, Reed's basis in Post was $25,000.

65. If this distribution were nonliquidating, Reed's basis for the inventory would be
- a. $14,000
- b. $12,500
- c. $ 5,000
- d. $ 1,500

66. If this distribution were in complete liquidation of Reed's interest in Post, Reed's recognized gain or loss resulting from the distribution would be
- a. $7,500 gain.
- b. $9,000 loss

- c. $1,500 loss.
- d. $0

67. In 2003, Lisa Bara acquired a one-third interest in Dee Associates, a partnership. In 2008, when Lisa's entire interest in the partnership was liquidated, Dee's assets consisted of the following: cash, $20,000 and tangible property with a basis of $46,000 and a fair market value of $40,000. Dee has no liabilities. Lisa's adjusted basis for her one-third interest was $22,000. Lisa received cash of $20,000 in liquidation of her entire interest. What was Lisa's recognized loss in 2008 on the liquidation of her interest in Dee?
- a. $0.
- b. $2,000 short-term capital loss.
- c. $2,000 long-term capital loss.
- d. $2,000 ordinary loss.

68. For tax purposes, a retiring partner who receives retirement payments ceases to be regarded as a partner
- a. On the last day of the taxable year in which the partner retires.
- b. On the last day of the particular month in which the partner retires.
- c. The day on which the partner retires.
- d. Only after the partner's entire interest in the partnership is liquidated.

69. John Albin is a retired partner of Brill & Crum, a personal service partnership. Albin has not rendered any services to Brill & Crum since his retirement in 2006. Under the provisions of Albin's retirement agreement, Brill & Crum is obligated to pay Albin 10% of the partnership's net income each year. In compliance with this agreement, Brill & Crum paid Albin $25,000 in 2008. How should Albin treat this $25,000?
- a. Not taxable.
- b. Ordinary income.
- c. Short-term capital gain.
- d. Long-term capital gain.

SIMULATION PROBLEM

Simulation Problem 1   (30 to 35 minutes)

Situation				
	Partner's Basis	Concepts	Research	Communication

During 2008, Adams, a general contractor, Brinks, an architect, and Carson, an interior decorator, formed the Dex Home Improvement General Partnership by contributing the assets below.

	Asset	Adjusted basis	Fair market value	% of partner share in capital, profits & losses
Adams	Cash	$40,000	$40,000	50%
Brinks	Land	$12,000	$21,000	20%
Carson	Inventory	$24,000	$24,000	30%

The land was a capital asset to Brinks, subject to a $5,000 mortgage, which was assumed by the partnership.

	Partner's Basis			
Situation		Concepts	Research	Communication

For items 1 and 2, determine and select the initial basis of the partner's interest in Dex.

                                                    (A) (B) (C)
                                                     ○   ○   ○

1. Brinks' initial basis in Dex is
   A. $21,000
   B. $12,000
   C. $ 8,000

                                                    (A) (B) (C)
                                                     ○   ○   ○

2. Carson's initial basis in Dex is
   A. $25,500
   B. $24,000
   C. $19,000

During 2008, the Dex Partnership breaks even but decides to make distributions to each partner.

		Concepts		
Situation	Partner's Basis		Research	Communication

For items 1 through 6, determine whether the statement is True or False.

		True	False
1.	A nonliquidating cash distribution may reduce the recipient partner's basis in his partnership interest below zero.	○	○
2.	A nonliquidating distribution of unappreciated inventory reduces the recipient partner's basis in his partnership interest.	○	○
3.	In a liquidating distribution of property other than money, where the partnership's basis of the distributed property exceeds the basis of the partner's interest, the partner's basis in the distributed property is limited to his predistribution basis in the partnership interest.	○	○
4.	Gain is recognized by the partner who receives a nonliquidating distribution of property, where the adjusted basis of the property exceeds his basis in the partnership interest before the distribution.	○	○
5.	In a nonliquidating distribution of inventory, where the partnership has no unrealized receivables or appreciated inventory, the basis of inventory that is distributed to a partner cannot exceed the inventory's adjusted basis to the partnership.	○	○
6.	The partnership's nonliquidating distribution of encumbered property to a partner who assumes the mortgage, does not affect the other partners' bases in their partnership interests.	○	○

			Research	
Situation	Partner's Basis	Concepts		Communication

The Dex Home Improvement General Partnership is planning to adopt a fiscal year ending September 30, while Brinks (a 20% partner) uses the calendar year as his taxable year. Research the Internal Revenue Code to determine how Brinks should determine the amount of income and other partnership items from the fiscal-year partnership that must be reported on Brinks' calendar-year tax return. Indicate the section and subsection from the IRC in the boxes below.

Section	Subsection
§ ▢	(▢)

				Communication
Situation	**Partner's Basis**	**Concepts**	**Research**	

Write a memorandum to Mr. Brinks describing the results of your research above.

To: Mr. Brinks
From: CPA Candidate
Re: Partnership accounting

Simulation Problem 2   (40 to 45 minutes)

Topic—Partnership Taxation

Situation					
	Form 1065	**Schedule K**	**Schedule K-1**	**Research**	**Communication**

The Madison Restaurant (identification number 86-0806200) was formed as a cash method general partnership to operate the Madison Restaurant, which is located at 6001 Palm Trace Landing in Davie, Florida 33314. Bob Buron (social security number 347-54-1212) manages the restaurant and has a 60% capital and profits interest. His address is 1104 North 8th Court, Plantation, Florida 33324. Ray Hughes owns the remaining 40% partnership interest but is not active in the restaurant business. The partnership made cash distributions of $66,000 and $44,000 to Buron and Hughes respectively, on December 31, 2007, but made no other property distributions. Madison's income statement for the year, ended December 31, 2007, is presented below.

Sales		$980,000
Cost of sales		460,000
Gross profit		520,000
Operating expenses		
Salaries and wages (excluding partners)	$190,000	
Guaranteed payment to Bob Buron	70,000	
Repairs and maintenance	10,000	
Rent expense	24,000	
Amortization of permanent liquor license	2,000	
Annual liquor license fee	1,000	
Depreciation	49,000	
Advertising	20,000	
Charitable contributions (cash)	8,000	
Total expenses		$374,000
Operating profit		$146,000
Other income and losses		
Gain on sale of ABE stock held 13 months	$12,000	
Loss on sale of TED stock held 7 months	(7,000)	
Sec. 1231 gain on sale of land	8,500	
Interest from US Treasury bills	3,000	
Dividends from ABE stock	1,500	
Interest from City of Ft. Lauderdale general obligation bonds	1,000	
Net other income		19,000
Net income		$165,000

Additional information

- Madison Restaurant began business on July 14, 2001, and its applicable business code number is 722110. It files its tax return with the Ogden, Utah IRS Service Center. The partnership had recourse liabilities at the end of the year of $25,000, and total assets of $282,000.
- The guaranteed payment to Bob Buron was for services rendered and was determined without regard to partnership profits. Buron's capital account at the beginning of 2008 totaled $135,000.
- The permanent liquor license was purchased for $10,000 from a café that had gone out of business. This license, which is renewable for an indefinite period, is being amortized per books over the five-year term of Madison's lease.

- The cost of depreciable personal property used in the restaurant operations was $200,000. Madison elected to expense $24,000 of the cost for these Sec. 179 assets. The $49,000 depreciation includes the Sec. 179 expense deduction.
- The gain on the sale of land resulted from the sale of a parking lot that the restaurant no longer needed.

Situation	**Form 1065**		Schedule K	Schedule K-1	Research	Communication

Prepare Madison Restaurant's income and deductions on page 1 of Form 1065, Partnership Return.

Situation	Form 1065	**Schedule K**		Schedule K-1	Research	Communication

Prepare Madison Restaurant's Schedule K, Partners' Shares of Income, Credits, Deductions, etc.

Situation	Form 1065	Schedule K	**Schedule K-1**		Research	Communication

Prepare Bob Buron's Schedule K-1, Partner's Share of Income, Credits, Deductions, etc. (Do **not** prepare a Schedule K-1 for Ray Hughes.)

Situation	Form 1065	Schedule K	Schedule K-1	**Research**		Communication

In 2008, Madison is considering making a proportionate nonliquidating distribution of shares of stock that it owns in CDE Corporation to its partners. Determine the basis that the partners will have for the CDE stock that they receive. Select the applicable Internal Revenue Code sections.

Situation	Form 1065	Schedule K	Schedule K-1	Research	**Communication**	

Buron and Hughes are concerned that the Madison Restaurant will have to recognize gain if it distributes shares of stock in CDE Corporation since the stock has appreciated in value. Write a memo to Buron and Hughes indicating whether the Madison Restaurant will have to recognize gain on the stock distribution to partners.

To: Mr. Buron and Mr. Hughes
From: CPA Candidate

Form **1065**

Department of the Treasury
Internal Revenue Service

U.S. Return of Partnership Income

For calendar year 2007, or tax year beginning ...., 2007, ending ...., 20......
▶ See separate instructions.

OMB No. 1545-0099

2007

A Principal business activity	Use the IRS label. Other-wise, print or type.	Name of partnership	D Employer identification number
B Principal product or service		Number, street, and room or suite no. If a P.O. box, see the instructions.	E Date business started
C Business code number		City or town, state, and ZIP code	F Total assets (see the instructions) $

G Check applicable boxes: **(1)** ☐ Initial return **(2)** ☐ Final return **(3)** ☐ Name change **(4)** ☐ Address change **(5)** ☐ Amended return

H Check accounting method: **(1)** ☐ Cash   **(2)** ☐ Accrual   **(3)** ☐ Other (specify) ▶ ....

I   Number of Schedules K-1. Attach one for each person who was a partner at any time during the tax year ▶ ....

J   Check if Schedule M-3 attached . . . . ☐

Caution. *Include **only** trade or business income and expenses on lines 1a through 22 below. See the instructions for more information.*

Income

1a Gross receipts or sales	**1a**		
b Less returns and allowances	**1b**		**1c**
2 Cost of goods sold (Schedule A, line 8)			**2**
3 Gross profit. Subtract line 2 from line 1c			**3**
4 Ordinary income (loss) from other partnerships, estates, and trusts *(attach statement)*.			**4**
5 Net farm profit (loss) *(attach Schedule F (Form 1040))*			**5**
6 Net gain (loss) from Form 4797, Part II, line 17 *(attach Form 4797)*			**6**
7 Other income (loss) *(attach statement)*			**7**
8 Total income (loss). Combine lines 3 through 7			**8**

Deductions (see the instructions for limitations)

9 Salaries and wages (other than to partners) (less employment credits) . .			**9**
10 Guaranteed payments to partners			**10**
11 Repairs and maintenance			**11**
12 Bad debts			**12**
13 Rent			**13**
14 Taxes and licenses			**14**
15 Interest			**15**
16a Depreciation *(if required, attach Form 4562)*	**16a**		
b Less depreciation reported on Schedule A and elsewhere on return	**16b**		**16c**
17 Depletion **(Do not deduct oil and gas depletion.)**			**17**
18 Retirement plans, etc.			**18**
19 Employee benefit programs			**19**
20 Other deductions *(attach statement)*			**20**
21 Total deductions. Add the amounts shown in the far right column for lines 9 through 20 .			**21**
22 Ordinary business income (loss). Subtract line 21 from line 8			**22**

Sign Here

Under penalties of perjury, I declare that I have examined this return, including accompanying schedules and statements, and to the best of my knowledge and belief, it is true, correct, and complete. Declaration of preparer (other than general partner or limited liability company member manager) is based on all information of which preparer has any knowledge.

▶ _____   ▶ _____
Signature of general partner or limited liability company member manager   Date

May the IRS discuss this return with the preparer shown below (see instructions)? ☐ Yes ☐ No

Paid Preparer's Use Only

Preparer's signature		Date	Check if self-employed ▶ ☐	Preparer's SSN or PTIN
Firm's name (or yours if self-employed), address, and ZIP code	▶		EIN ▶	
			Phone no. ( )	

For Privacy Act and Paperwork Reduction Act Notice, see separate instructions.   Cat. No. 11390Z   Form **1065** (2007)

The tax basis for the partner's capital account is increased by all income items and reduced by all loss and deduction items.

The basis for the capital account is increased by the ordinary income of $108,000, interest of $1,800, dividends of $900, net long-term capital gain of $7,200, net Sec. 1231 gain of $5,100, and tax-exempt income of $600.

The basis for the capital account is decreased by the net short-term capital loss of $4,200, Sec. 179 deduction of $14,400, and other deductions of $4,800. The resulting net change is an increase of $100,200.

Note that the guaranteed payments of $70,000 were already deducted in the computation of ordinary income and are not separately taken into account. Also note that there is only $900 of dividends even though that amount is reported on two lines.

Situation	Form 1065	Schedule K	Schedule K-1	Research	Communication

In researching this issue appropriate keywords include "distributions by partnership." The applicable IRS section is as follows:

SEC. 732. Basis of Distributed Property other than Money.

>   **732(a) Distributions other than Liquidation of a Partner's Interest—**

>   >   **732(a)(1) General Rule**—The basis of property (other than money) distributed by a partnership to a partner other than in liquidation of the partner's interest shall, except as provided in paragraph (2), be its adjusted basis to the partnership immediately before such distribution.

>   >   **732(a)(2) Limitation**—The basis to the distributee partner of property to which paragraph (1) is applicable shall not exceed the adjusted basis of such partner's interest in the partnership reduced by any money distributed in the same transaction.

Situation	Form 1065	Schedule K	Schedule K-1	Research	Communication

To: Mr. Buron and Mr. Hughes
From: CPA Candidate

This memorandum describes the results of my research regarding the recognition of gain if the appreciated CDE stock is distributed by the Madison Restaurant to its partners. A partnership generally recognizes no gain or loss when making a nonliquidating distribution of property to its partners so long as the distribution is proportionate among partners. There is an exception which treats a disproportionate distribution as a sale of property, but that exception will not apply in your situation.

CORPORATIONS

Corporations are separate taxable entities, organized under state law. Although corporations may have many of the same income and deduction items as individuals, corporations are taxed at different rates and some tax rules are applied differently. There also are special provisions applicable to transfers of property to a corporation, and issuance of stock.

A. Transfers to a Controlled Corporation (Sec. 351)

1. **No gain or loss** is recognized if property is transferred to a corporation solely in exchange for stock and immediately after the exchange those persons transferring property control the corporation.

    a. **Property** includes everything but services.

    b. **Control** means ownership of at least 80% of the total combined voting power and 80% of each class of nonvoting stock.

    c. **Receipt of boot** (e.g., cash, short-term notes, securities, etc.) will cause recognition of gain (but not loss).

        (1) Corporation's assumption of liabilities is treated as boot only if there is a tax avoidance purpose, or no business purpose.

        (2) Shareholder recognizes gain if liabilities assumed by corporation exceed the total basis of property transferred by the shareholder.

2. **Shareholder's basis for stock** = Adjusted basis of property transferred

    a. + Gain recognized

    b. – Boot received (assumption of liability always treated as boot for purposes of determining stock basis)

3. **Corporation's basis for property** = Transferor's adjusted basis + Gain recognized to transferor.

    EXAMPLE: *Individuals A, B, & C form ABC Corp. and make the following transfer to their corporation:*

Item transferred	A	B	C
Property – FMV	$10,000	$8,000	$ --
– Adjusted basis	1,500	3,000	--
Liability assumed by ABC Corp.	2,000	--	--
Services	--	--	1,000
Consideration received			
Stock (FMV)	$ 8,000	$7,600	$1,000
Two-year note (FMV)	--	400	--
Gain recognized to shareholder	$ 500[a]	$ 400[b]	$1,000[c]
Basis of stock received	--	3,000	1,000
Basis of property to corp.	2,000	3,400	1,000[d]

    [a] *Liability in excess of basis: $2,000 – $1,500 = $500*
    [b] *Assumes B elects out of the installment method*
    [c] *Ordinary compensation income*
    [d] *Expense or asset depending on nature of services rendered*

    a. For Sec. 351 transactions after October 22, 2004, if the aggregate adjusted basis of transferred property exceeds its aggregate FMV, the corporate transferee's aggregate basis for the property is generally limited to its aggregate FMV immediately after the transaction. Any required basis reduction is allocated among the transferred properties in proportion to their built-in loss immediately before the transaction.

    b. Alternatively, the transferor and the corporate transferee are allowed to make an irrevocable election to limit the basis in the stock received by the transferor to the aggregate FMV of the transferred property.

        EXAMPLE: *Amy transferred Lossacre with a basis of $6,000 (FMV of $2,000) and Gainacre with a basis of $4,000 (FMV of $5,000) to ABE Corp. in exchange for stock in a Sec. 351 transaction. Since the aggregate adjusted basis of the transferred property ($10,000) exceeds its aggregate FMV ($7,000), ABE's aggregate basis for the property is limited to $7,000. The required basis reduction of $3,000 would reduce ABE's basis for Lossacre to $3,000 ($6,000 – $3,000). Amy's basis for her stock would equal the total basis of the transferred property, $10,000.*

        Alternatively, if Amy and ABE elect, ABE's basis for the transferred property will be $6,000 for Lossacre and $4,000 for Gainacre, and Amy's basis for her stock will be limited to its FMV of $7,000.

B.   Section 1244—Small Business Corporation (SBC) Stock

1.   Sec. 1244 stock permits shareholders to deduct an **ordinary loss** on sale or worthlessness of stock.

   a.   Shareholder must be the original holder of stock, and an individual or partnership.

   b.   Stock can be common or preferred, voting or nonvoting, and must have been issued for money or property (other than stock or securities)

   c.   Ordinary loss limited to **$50,000 ($100,000** on joint return); any excess is treated as a capital loss.

   d.   The corporation during the five-year period before the year of loss, received less than 50% of its total gross receipts from royalties, rents, dividends, interest, annuities, and gains from sales or exchanges of stock or securities.

> *EXAMPLE: Jim (married and filing a joint return) incurred a loss of $120,000 from the sale of Sec. 1244 stock during 2008. $100,000 of Jim's loss is deductible as an ordinary loss, with the remaining $20,000 treated as a capital loss.*

2.   If Sec. 1244 stock is received in exchange for property whose FMV is less than its adjusted basis, the stock's basis is reduced to the FMV of the property to determine the amount of ordinary loss.

> *EXAMPLE: Joe made a Sec. 351 transfer of property with an adjusted basis of $20,000 and a FMV of $16,000 in exchange for Sec. 1244 stock. The basis of Joe's stock is $20,000, but solely for purposes of Sec. 1244 the stock's basis is reduced to $16,000. If Joe subsequently sold his stock for $15,000, $1,000 of his loss would be treated as an ordinary loss under Sec. 1244, with the remaining $4,000 treated as a capital loss.*

3.   For purposes of determining the amount of ordinary loss, increases in basis through capital contributions or otherwise are treated as allocable to stock which is not Sec. 1244 stock.

> *EXAMPLE: Jill acquired 100 shares of Sec. 1244 stock for $10,000. Jill later made a $2,000 contribution to the capital of the corporation, increasing her stock basis to $12,000. Jill subsequently sold the 100 shares for $9,000. Of Jill's $3,000 loss, ($10,000 ÷ $12,000) × $3,000 = $2,500 qualifies as an ordinary loss under Sec. 1244, with the remaining ($2,000 ÷ $12,000) × $3,000 = $500 treated as a capital loss.*

4.   SBC is any domestic corporation whose aggregate amount of money and adjusted basis of other property received for stock, as a contribution to capital, and as paid-in surplus, does not exceed $1,000,000. If more than $1 million of stock is issued, up to $1 million of qualifying stock can be designated as Sec. 1244 stock.

C.   Variations from Individual Taxation

1.   Filing and payment of tax

   a.   A corporation generally must file a Form 1120 every year even though it has no taxable income. A short-form Form 1120-A may be filed if gross receipts, total income, and total assets are each less than $500,000.

   b.   The return must be filed by the fifteenth day of the third month following the close of its taxable year (e.g., March 15 for calendar-year corporation).

   (1) An automatic six-month extension may be obtained by filing Form 7004.
   (2) Any balance due on the corporation's tax liability must be paid with the request for extension.

   c.   Estimated tax payments must be made by every corporation whose estimated tax is expected to be $500 or more. A corporation's estimated tax is its expected tax liability (including alternative minimum tax) less its allowable tax credits.

   (1) Quarterly payments are due on the fifteenth day of the fourth, sixth, ninth, and twelfth months of its taxable year (April 15, June 15, September 15, and December 15 for a calendar-year corporation). Any balance due must be paid by the due date of the return.
   (2) No penalty for underpayment of estimated tax will be imposed if payments at least equal the lesser of

   (a) 100% of the current year's tax (determined on the basis of actual income or annualized income), or
   (b) 100% of the preceding year's tax (if the preceding year was a full twelve months and showed a tax liability).

   (3) A corporation with $1 million or more of taxable income in any of its three preceding tax years (i.e., **large corporation**) can use its preceding year's tax only for its first installment and must base its estimated payments on 100% of its current year's tax to avoid penalty.

(4) If any amount of tax is not paid by the original due date, interest must be paid from the due date until the tax is paid.

(5) A failure-to-pay tax delinquency penalty will be owed if the amount of tax paid by the original due date of the return is less than 90% of the tax shown on the return. The failure-to-pay penalty is imposed at a rate of 0.5% per month (or fraction thereof), with a maximum penalty of 25%.

2. Corporations are subject to

   a. **Regular tax rates**

Taxable income	Rate
(1) $0-$50,000	15%
(2) $50,001-$75,000	25
(3) $75,001-$10 million	34
(4) Over $10 million	35

   (5) The less-than-34% brackets are phased out by adding an additional tax of 5% of the excess of taxable income over $100,000, up to a maximum additional tax of $11,750.

   (6) The 34% bracket is phased out for corporations with taxable income in excess of $15 million by adding an additional 3% of the excess of taxable income over $15 million, up to a maximum additional tax of $100,000.

   b. Certain personal service corporations are not eligible to use the less-than-35% brackets and their taxable income is taxed at a flat 35% rate.

   c. **Alternative minimum tax (AMT)**

   (1) **Computation.** The AMT is generally the amount by which 20% of alternative minimum taxable income (AMTI) as reduced by an exemption and the alternative minimum tax foreign tax credit, exceeds the regular tax (i.e., regular tax liability reduced by the regular tax foreign tax credit). AMTI is equal to taxable income computed with specified adjustments and increased by tax preferences.

   (2) **Exemption.** AMTI is offset by a $40,000 exemption. However, the exemption is reduced by 25% of AMTI over $150,000, and completely phased out once AMTI reaches $310,000.

   (3) **AMT formula**

	Regular taxable income before NOL deduction
+	Tax preference items
+(–)	Adjustments (other than ACE and NOL deduction)
	Pre-ACE alternative minimum taxable income (AMTI)
+(–)	ACE adjustment [75% of difference between pre-ACE AMTI and adjusted current earnings (ACE)]
–	AMT NOL deduction [limited to 90% of pre-NOL AMTI]
	Alternative minimum taxable income (AMTI)
–	Exemption ($40,000 less 25% of AMTI over $150,000)
	Alternative minimum tax base
×	20% rate
	Tentative AMT before foreign tax credit
–	AMT foreign tax credit
	Tentative minimum tax (TMT)
–	Regular income tax (less regular tax foreign tax credit)
	Alternative minimum tax (if positive)

   (4) **Preference items.** The following are examples of items added to regular taxable income in computing pre-ACE AMTI:

   (a) Tax-exempt interest on private activity bonds (net of related expenses)

   (b) Excess of accelerated over straight-line depreciation on real property and leased personal property placed in service before 1987

   (c) The excess of percentage depletion deduction over the property's adjusted basis

   (d) The excess of intangible drilling costs using a ten-year amortization over 65% of net oil and gas income

   (5) **Adjustments.** The following are examples of adjustments to regular taxable income in computing pre-ACE AMTI:

(a) For real property placed in service after 1986 and before 1999, the difference between regular tax depreciation and straight-line depreciation over forty years

(b) For personal property placed in service after 1986, the difference between regular tax depreciation and depreciation using the 150% declining balance method

(c) The installment method cannot be used for sales of inventory-type items

(d) Income from long-term contracts must be determined using the percentage of completion method

(6) **Adjusted current earnings (ACE).** ACE is a concept based on a corporation's earnings and profits, and is calculated by making adjustments to pre-ACE AMTI.

> AMTI before ACE adjustment and NOL deduction
> Add: Tax-exempt income on municipal bonds (less expenses)
> Tax-exempt life insurance death benefits (less expenses)
> 70% dividends-received deduction
> Deduct: Depletion using cost depletion method
> Depreciation using ADS straight-line for all property (this adjustment eliminated for property placed in service after 1993)
> Other: Capitalize organizational expenditures and circulation expenses
> Add increase (subtract decrease) in LIFO recapture amount (i.e., excess of FIFO value over LIFO basis)
> Installment method cannot be used for nondealer sales of property
> <u>Amortize intangible drilling costs over five years</u>
> Adjusted current earnings (ACE)
> <u>– Pre-ACE AMTI</u>
> Balance (positive or negative)
> <u>× 75%</u>
> ACE adjustment (positive or negative)

> EXAMPLE: Acme, Inc. has adjusted current earnings of $100,000 and alternative minimum taxable income (before this adjustment) of $60,000. Since adjusted current earnings exceeds pre-ACE AMTI by $40,000, 75% of this amount must be added to Acme's AMTI. Thus, Acme's AMTI for the year is $90,000 [$60,000 + ($40,000 × 75%)].

(a) The ACE adjustment can be positive or negative, but a negative ACE adjustment is limited in amount to prior years' net positive ACE adjustments.

(b) The computation of ACE is not the same as the computation of a corporation's E&P. For example, federal income taxes, penalties and fines, and the disallowed portion of business meals and entertainment would be deductible in computing E&P, but are not deductible in computing ACE.

(7) **Minimum tax credit.** The amount of AMT paid is allowed as a credit against regular tax liability in future years.

(a) The credit can be carried forward indefinitely, but not carried back.

(b) The AMT credit can only be used to reduce regular tax liability, not future AMT liability.

(8) **Small corporation exemption.** A corporation is exempt from the corporate AMT for its first tax year (regardless of income levels). After the first year, it is exempt from AMT if it passes a gross receipts test. It is exempt for its second year if its first year's gross receipts do not exceed $5 million. To be exempt for its third year, the corporation's average gross receipts for the first two years must not exceed $7.5 million. To be exempt for the fourth year (and subsequent years), the corporation's average gross receipts for all prior three-year periods must not exceed $7.5 million.

> EXAMPLE: Zero Corp., a calendar-year corporation, was formed on January 2, 2005, and had gross receipts for its first four taxable years as follows:

Year	Gross receipts
2005	$ 4,500,000
2006	9,000,000
2007	8,000,000
2008	6,500,000

> Zero is automatically exempt from AMT for 2005. It is exempt for 2006 because its gross receipts for 2005 do not exceed $5 million. Zero also is exempt for 2007 because its average gross receipts for 2005-2006 do not exceed $7.5 million. Similarly, it is exempt for 2008 because its average gross receipts for 2005-2007 do not exceed $7.5 million. However, Zero will lose its exemption from AMT for 2009 and all subsequent years because its average gross receipts for 2006-2008 exceed $7.5 million.

      d.   See subsequent discussion for penalty taxes on

          (1) Accumulated earnings

          (2) Personal holding companies

3. **Gross income** for a corporation is quite similar to the rules for an individual taxpayer. However, there are a few differences.

    a.   A corporation does not recognize gain or loss on the **issuance of its own stock** (including treasury stock), or on the lapse or acquisition of an option to buy or sell its stock (including treasury stock).

        (1) It generally recognizes gain (but not loss) if it distributes appreciated property to its shareholders.

        (2) **Contributions to capital** are excluded from a corporation's gross income, whether received from shareholders or nonshareholders.

            (a) If property is received from a shareholder, the shareholder recognizes no gain or loss, the shareholder's basis for the contributed property transfers to the corporation, and the shareholder's stock basis is increased by the basis of the contributed property.

            (b) If property is received as a capital contribution from a nonshareholder, the corporation's basis for the contributed property is zero.

                1] If money is received, the basis of property purchased within one year afterwards is reduced by the money contributed.

                2] Any money not used reduces the basis of the corporation's existing property beginning with depreciable property.

    b.   No gain or loss is recognized on the **issuance of debt**.

        (1) Premium or discount on bonds payable is amortized as income or expense over the life of bonds.

        (2) Ordinary income/loss is recognized by a corporation on the repurchase of its bonds, determined by the relationship of the repurchase price to the net carrying value of the bonds (issue price plus or minus the discount or premium amortized).

        (3) Interest earned and gains recognized in a bond sinking fund are income to the corporation.

    c.   Gains are treated as ordinary income on sales to or from a more than 50% shareholder, or between corporations which are more than 50% owned by the same individual, if the property is subject to depreciation in the hands of the buyer.

4. Deductions for a corporation are much the same as for individuals. However, there are some major differences.

    a.   Adjusted gross income is not applicable to corporations.

    b.   Effective for **organizational expenditures** paid or incurred after October 22, 2004, a corporation may elect to deduct up to $5,000 of organizational expenditures for the tax year in which the corporation begins business. The $5,000 amount must be reduced (but not below zero) by the amount by which organizational expenditures exceed $50,000. Remaining expenditures can be deducted ratably over the 180-month period beginning with the month in which the corporation begins business.

        EXAMPLE: A calendar-year corporation was organized and began business during 2008 incurring $4,800 or organizational expenditures. The corporation may elect to deduct the $4,800 or organizational expenditures for 2008.

        EXAMPLE: A calendar-year corporation was organized during February, 2008 incurring organizational expenditures of $6,000. Assuming the corporation begins business during April, 2008, its maximum deduction for organizational expenditures for 2008 would be $5,000 + [($6,000 - $5,000) × 9/180] = $5,050.

        EXAMPLE: A calendar-year corporation was organized during February, 2008 incurring organizational expenditures of $60,000. Assuming the corporation begins business during April, 2008, its maximum deduction for organizational expenditures for 2008 would be $60,000 × 9/180 = $3,000.

        (1) For amounts paid on or before October 22, 2004, a corporation may elect to amortize organizational expenditures over not less than 60 months, beginning with the month that business begins.

(1) A shareholder's amount at-risk includes amounts borrowed and reloaned to the S corporation if the shareholder is personally liable for repayment of the borrowed amount, or has pledged property not used in the activity as security for the borrowed amount.

(2) A shareholder's amount at-risk does not include any debt of the S corporation to any person other than the shareholder, even if the shareholder guarantees the debt.

c. The deductibility of S corporation losses may also be subject to the **passive activity loss limitations** [Sec. 469]. Passive activity losses are deductible only to the extent of the shareholder's income from other passive activities (See Module 33).

(1) Passive activities include (a) any S corporation trade or business in which the shareholder does not materially participate, and (b) any rental activity.

(2) If a shareholder "actively participates" in a rental activity and owns (together with spouse) at least 10% of the value of an S corporation's stock, up to $25,000 of rental losses may be deductible against earned income and portfolio income.

10. A shareholder's S corporation **stock basis** is **increased** by all income items (including tax-exempt income), plus depletion in excess of the basis of the property subject to depletion; **decreased** by all loss and deduction items, nondeductible expenses not charged to capital, and the shareholder's deduction for depletion on oil and gas wells; and **decreased** by distributions that are excluded from gross income. Stock basis is **adjusted in the following order:**

a. Increased for all income items
b. Decreased for distributions that are excluded from gross income
c. Decreased for nondeductible, noncapital items
d. Decreased for deductible expenses and losses

> EXAMPLE: An S corporation has tax-exempt income of $5,000, and an ordinary loss from business activity of $6,000 for calendar year 2008. Its sole shareholder had a stock basis of $2,000 on January 1, 2008. The $5,000 of tax-exempt income would pass through to the shareholder, increasing the shareholder's stock basis to $7,000, and would permit the pass-through and deduction of the $6,000 of ordinary loss, reducing the shareholder's stock basis to $1,000.

> EXAMPLE: An S corporation had an ordinary loss from business activity of $6,000 and made a $7,000 cash distribution to its sole shareholder during calendar year 2008. The sole shareholder had a stock basis of $8,000 on January 1, 2008. The $7,000 cash distribution would be nontaxable and would reduce stock basis to $1,000. As a result, only $1,000 of the $6,000 ordinary loss would be allowable as a deduction to the shareholder for 2008. The remaining $5,000 of ordinary loss would be carried forward and deducted by the shareholder when there is stock basis to absorb it.

11. The **treatment of distributions** (Cash + FMV of other property) to shareholders is determined as follows:

a. Distributions are **nontaxable** to the extent of the Accumulated Adjustments Account (AAA) and are applied to **reduce the AAA and the shareholder's stock basis**.

(1) The AAA represents the cumulative total of undistributed net income items for S corporation taxable years beginning after 1982.

(2) If there is more than one distribution during the year, a pro rata portion of each distribution is treated as made from the AAA.

(3) The AAA can have a negative balance if expenses and losses exceed income.

(4) No adjustment is made to the AAA for tax-exempt income and related expenses, and Federal taxes attributable to a year in which the corporation was a C corporation. Tax-exempt income and related expenses are reflected in the corporation's Other Adjustments Account (OAA).

(5) For purposes of determining the treatment of a distribution, the amount in the AAA at the close of any taxable year is determined without regard to any **net negative adjustment** (i.e., the excess of reductions over increases to the AAA for the taxable year) for such taxable year.

b. Distributions in excess of the AAA are treated as **ordinary dividends** to the extent of the corporation's **accumulated earnings and profits (AEP).** These amounts represent earnings and profits that were accumulated (and never taxed to shareholders) during C corporation taxable years.

c. Distributions are next **nontaxable** to the extent of **remaining stock basis** and are applied to reduce the OAA and paid-in capital.

d. Distributions **in excess of stock basis** are treated as **gain** from the sale of stock.

> *EXAMPLE: A calendar-year S corporation had subchapter C accumulated earnings and profits of $10,000 at December 31, 2007. During calendar year 2008, the corporation had net income of $20,000, and distributed $38,000 to its sole shareholder on June 20, 2008. Its shareholder had a stock basis of $15,000 at January 1, 2008.*
>
> *The $20,000 of net income passes through and is includible in gross income by the shareholder for 2008. The shareholder's stock basis is increased by the $20,000 of income (to $35,000), as is the AAA which is increased to $20,000. Of the $38,000 distribution, the first $20,000 is nontaxable and (1) reduces stock basis to $15,000, and (2) the AAA to zero; the next $10,000 of distribution is reported as dividend income (no effect on stock basis); while the remaining $8,000 of distribution is nontaxable and reduces stock basis to $7,000.*

12. Health and accident insurance premiums and other **fringe benefits** paid by an S corporation on behalf of a more than 2% shareholder-employee are deductible by the S corporation as compensation and includible in the shareholder-employee's gross income on Form W-2.

13. An S corporation (that previously was a C corporation) is taxed on its **net recognized built-in gain** if the gain is (1) attributable to an excess of the FMV of its assets over their aggregate adjusted basis as of the beginning of its first taxable year as an S corporation, and (2) is recognized within **ten years** after the effective date of its S corporation election.

    a. This provision generally applies to C corporations that make an S corporation election after December 31, 1986.

    b. To determine the tax, (1) take the lesser of (a) the net recognized built-in gain for the taxable year, or (b) taxable income determined as if the corporation were a C corporation (except the NOL and dividends-received deductions are not allowed); (2) subtract any NOL and capital loss carryforwards from C corporation years; (3) multiply the resulting amount by the highest corporate tax rate (currently 35%); and (4) subtract any general business credit carryovers from C corporation years and the special fuels tax credit.

    c. Any net recognized built-in gain that escapes the built-in gains tax because of the taxable income limitation is carried forward and is subject to the built-in gains tax to the extent the corporation subsequently has other taxable income (that is not already subject to the built-in gains tax) for any taxable year within the ten-year recognition period.

    d. Recognized built-in gain **does not include** gain from the disposition of an asset if

       (1) The asset was not held by the corporation when its S election became effective (e.g., an asset was purchased after the first day of its S election), or

       (2) The gain is attributable to appreciation that occurred after the S election became effective (e.g., an asset is sold for a gain of $1,000, but $600 of its appreciation occurred after the first day of its S election; the corporation would be taxed on only $400 of gain).

    e. The total amount of net recognized built-in gain that will be taxed to an S corporation is limited to the aggregate net unrealized built-in gain when the S election became effective.

    f. The **built-in gains tax** that is paid by an S corporation is **treated as a loss** sustained by the S corporation during the taxable year. The character of the loss is determined by allocating the loss proportionately among the recognized built-in gains giving rise to such tax.

       > *EXAMPLE: For 2008, an S corporation has taxable income of $100,000, which includes a $40,000 long-term capital gain that is also a recognized built-in gain. Since its recognized built-in gain of $40,000 is less than its taxable income, its built-in gains tax for 2008 is $40,000 × 35% = $14,000. Since the built-in gain was a long-term capital gain, the built-in gains tax paid of $14,000 is treated as a long-term capital loss. As a result, a net long-term capital gain of $26,000 ($40,000 LTCG – $14,000 LTCL) passes through to shareholders for 2008.*

       > *EXAMPLE: For 2007, an S corporation has taxable income of $10,000, which includes a $40,000 long-term capital gain that is also a recognized built-in gain. Since its taxable income of $10,000 is less than its recognized built-in gain of $40,000, its built-in gains tax for 2007 is limited to $10,000 × 35% = $3,500. As a result, a net long-term capital gain of $40,000 – $3,500 = $36,500 passes through to shareholders for 2007.*
       >
       > *The remaining $30,000 of untaxed recognized built-in gain would be suspended and carried forward to 2008, where it would again be treated as a recognized built-in gain. If the S corporation has at least $30,000 of taxable income in 2008 that is not already subject to the built-in gains tax, the suspended gain from 2007 will be taxed. As a result, the amount of built-in gains tax paid by the S corporation for 2008 will be $30,000 × 35% = $10,500, and will pass through to shareholders as a long-term capital loss, since the original gain in 2007 was a long-term capital gain.*

14. If an S corporation has subchapter C accumulated earnings and profits, and its **passive investment income exceeds 25% of gross receipts,** a tax is imposed at the highest corporate rate on the lesser of (1) excess net passive income (ENPI), or (2) taxable income.

a. $ENPI = \left(\dfrac{\text{Net passive}}{\text{income}}\right) \times \left(\dfrac{\text{Passive investment income } - (25\% \text{ of Gross receipts})}{\text{Passive investment income}}\right)$

b.   **Passive investment income** means gross receipts derived from dividends, interest, royalties, rents, annuities, and gains from the sale or exchange of stock or securities. However, dividends from an affiliated C corporation subsidiary are not treated as passive investment income to the extent the dividends are attributable to the earnings and profits derived from the active conduct of a trade or business by the C corporation.

c.   The tax paid reduces the amount of passive investment income passed through to shareholders

> EXAMPLE: *An S corporation has gross receipts of $80,000, of which $50,000 is interest income. Expenses incurred in the production of this passive income total $10,000. The ENPI is $24,000.*

$$ENPI = \left(\$50,000 - \$10,000\right) \times \left(\dfrac{\$50,000 - (25\% \times \$80,000)}{\$50,000}\right) = \$24,000$$

H. Corporate Reorganizations

Certain exchanges, usually involving the exchange of one corporation's stock for the stock or property of another, result in deferral of gain or loss.

1.   There are seven different **types** of reorganizations which generally result in nonrecognition treatment.

   a.   Type A—statutory mergers or consolidations

   (1) Merger is one corporation absorbing another by operation of law
   (2) Consolidation is two corporations combining in a new corporation, the former ones dissolving

   b.   Type B—the use of solely voting stock of the acquiring corporation (or its parent) to acquire at least 80% of the voting power and 80% of each class of nonvoting stock of the target corporation

   (1) No boot can be used by the acquiring corporation to acquire the target's stock
   (2) Results in the acquisition of a controlled subsidiary

   c.   Type C—the use of solely voting stock of the acquiring corporation (or its parent) to acquire substantially all of the target's properties

   (1) In determining whether the acquisition is made for solely voting stock, the assumption by the acquiring corporation of a liability of the target corporation, or the fact that the property acquired is subject to a liability is disregarded.
   (2) "Substantially all" means at least 90% of the FMV of the target's net assets, and at least 70% of its gross assets.
   (3) The target (acquired) corporation must distribute the consideration it receives, as well as all of its other properties, in pursuance of the plan of reorganization.

   d.   Type D—a transfer by a corporation of part or all of its assets to another if immediately after the transfer the transferor corporation, or its shareholders, control the transferee corporation (i.e., own at least 80% of the voting power and at least 80% of each class of nonvoting stock)

   (1) Although it may be acquisitive, this type of reorganization is generally used to divide a corporation.
   (2) Generally results in a spin-off, split-off, or split-up

   e.   Type E—a recapitalization to change the capital structure of a single corporation (e.g., bondholders exchange old bonds for new bonds or stock)
   f.   Type F—a mere change in identity, form, or place of organization (e.g., name change, change of state of incorporation)
   g.   Type G—a transfer of assets by an insolvent corporation or pursuant to bankruptcy proceedings, with the result that former creditors often become the owners of the corporation

2.   For the reorganization to be tax-free, it must meet one of the above definitions and the exchange must be made under a plan of reorganization involving the affected corporations as parties to the reorganization. It generally must satisfy the judicial doctrines of continuity of shareholder interest, business purpose, and continuity of business enterprise.

    a. **Continuity of shareholder interest**—The shareholders of the transferor (acquired) corporation must receive stock in the transferee (acquiring) corporation at least equal in value to 50% of the value of all of the transferor's formerly outstanding stock. This requirement does not apply to Type E and Type F reorganizations.

    b. **Continuity of business enterprise**—The transferor's historic business must be continued, or a significant portion (e.g., 1/3) of the transferor's historic assets must be used in a business. This requirement does not apply to Type E and Type F reorganizations.

3. **No gain or loss** is generally recognized to a **transferor corporation** on the transfer of its property pursuant to a plan of reorganization.

    a. The **transferee corporation's basis for property** received equals the transferor's basis plus gain recognized (if any) to the transferor.

    b. Gain is recognized on the distribution to shareholders of any property other than stock or securities of a party to the reorganization (e.g., property the transferor retained and did not transfer to the acquiring corporation), as if such property were sold for its FMV.

4. No gain or loss is recognized by a corporation on the disposition of stock or securities in another corporation that is a party to the reorganization.

    a. No gain or loss is generally recognized on the distribution of stock or securities of a controlled subsidiary in a qualifying spin-off, split-off, or split-up. However, the distributing corporation must recognize gain on the distribution of its subsidiary's stock if immediately after the distribution, any person holds a 50% or greater interest in the distributing corporation or a distributed subsidiary that is attributable to stock acquired by purchase during the five-year period ending on date of distribution.

    b. Gain is recognized on the distribution of appreciated boot property.

5. If a **shareholder receives boot** in a reorganization, gain is recognized (but not loss).

    a. Boot includes the FMV of an excess of principal (i.e., face) amount of securities received over the principal amount of securities surrendered.

> *EXAMPLE: In a recapitalization, a bondholder exchanges a bond with a face amount and basis of $1,000, for a new bond with a face amount of $1,500 and a fair market value of $1,575. Since an excess face amount of security ($500) has been received, the bondholder's realized gain of $575 will be recognized to the extent of the fair market value of the excess [($500/$1,500) × $1,575] = $525.*

    b. Recognized gain will be treated as a dividend to the extent of the shareholder's ratable share of earnings and profits of the acquired corporation if the receipt of boot has the effect of the distribution of a dividend.

        (1) Whether the receipt of boot has the effect of a dividend is determined by applying the Sec. 302(b) redemption tests based on the shareholder's stock interest in the acquiring corporation (i.e., as if only stock had been received, and then the boot was used to redeem the stock that was not received).

        (2) The receipt of boot will generally not have the effect of a dividend, and will thus result in capital gain.

6. A shareholder's **basis for stock and securities received** equals the basis of stock and securities surrendered, plus gain recognized, and minus boot received.

> *EXAMPLE: Pursuant to a merger of Corporation T into Corporation P, Smith exchanged 100 shares of T that he had purchased for $1,000, for 80 shares of P having a FMV of $1,500 and also received $200 cash. Smith's realized gain of $700 is recognized to the extent of the cash received of $200, and is treated as a capital gain. Smith's basis for his P stock is $1,000 ($1,000 + $200 recognized gain – $200 cash received).*

7. **Carryover of tax attributes**

    a. The tax attributes of the acquired corporation (e.g., NOL carryovers, earnings and profits, accounting methods, etc.) generally carry over to the acquiring corporation in an acquisitive reorganization.

    b. The amount of an **acquired corporation's NOL** carryovers that can be utilized by the acquiring corporation for its first taxable year ending after the date of acquisition is **limited by Sec. 381** to

$$\text{Acquiring corporation's TI before} \atop \text{NOL deduction} \quad \times \quad \frac{\text{Days after acquisition date}}{\text{Total days in taxable year}}$$

EXAMPLE: Corporation P (on a calendar year) acquired Corporation T in a statutory merger on October 19, 2008, with the former T shareholders receiving 60% of P's stock. If T had an NOL carryover of $70,000, and P has taxable income (before an NOL deduction) of $91,500, the amount of T's $70,000 NOL carryover that can be deducted by P for 2008 would be limited to

$$\$91,500 \quad \times \quad \frac{73}{365} \quad = \$18,300$$

c.   If there is a **more than 50% change in ownership** of a loss corporation, the taxable income for any year of the new loss (or surviving) corporation may be reduced by an NOL carryover from the old loss corporation only to the extent of the value of the old loss corporation's stock on the date of the ownership change multiplied by the "long-term tax-exempt rate" (**Sec. 382 limitation**).

(1) An ownership change has occurred when the percentage of stock owned by an entity's 5% or more shareholders has increased by more than 50 percentage points relative to the lowest percentage owned by such shareholders at any time during the preceding three-year testing period.

(2) For the year of acquisition, the Sec. 382 limitation amount is available only to the extent allocable to days after the acquisition date.

$$\text{Section 382 limitation} \quad \times \quad \frac{\text{Days after acquisition date}}{\text{Total days in taxable year}}$$

EXAMPLE: If T's former shareholders received only 30% of P's stock in the preceding example, there would be a more than 50 percentage point change in ownership of T Corporation, and T's NOL carryover would be subject to a Sec. 382 limitation. If the FMV of T's stock on October 19, 2008, was $500,000 and the long-term tax-exempt rate were 5%, the Sec. 382 limitation for 2008 would be ($500,000 × 5%) × (73/365 days) = $5,000.

Thus, only $5,000 of T's NOL carryover could be deducted by P for 2008. The remaining $70,000 – $5,000 = $65,000 of T's NOL would be carried forward by P and could be used to offset P's taxable income for 2009 to the extent of the Sec. 382 limitation (i.e., $500,000 × 5% = $25,000).

MULTIPLE-CHOICE QUESTIONS (1-163)

1. Alan, Baker, and Carr formed Dexter Corporation during 2009. Pursuant to the incorporation agreement, Alan transferred property with an adjusted basis of $30,000 and a fair market value of $45,000 for 450 shares of stock, Baker transferred cash of $35,000 in exchange for 350 shares of stock, and Carr performed services valued at $25,000 in exchange for 250 shares of stock. Assuming the fair market value of Dexter Corporation stock is $100 per share, what is Dexter Corporation's tax basis for the property received from Alan?

- a. $0
- b. $30,000
- c. $45,000
- d. $65,000

2. Clark and Hunt organized Jet Corp. with authorized voting common stock of $400,000. Clark contributed $60,000 cash. Both Clark and Hunt transferred other property in exchange for Jet stock as follows:

| | Other property | | |
	Adjusted basis	Fair market value	Percentage of Jet stock acquired
Clark	$ 50,000	$100,000	40%
Hunt	120,000	240,000	60%

What was Clark's basis in Jet stock?

- a. $0
- b. $100,000
- c. $110,000
- d. $160,000

3. Adams, Beck, and Carr organized Flexo Corp. with authorized voting common stock of $100,000. Adams received 10% of the capital stock in payment for the organizational services that he rendered for the benefit of the newly formed corporation. Adams did not contribute property to Flexo and was under no obligation to be paid by Beck or Carr. Beck and Carr transferred property in exchange for stock as follows:

	Adjusted basis	Fair market value	Percentage of Flexo stock acquired
Beck	5,000	20,000	20%
Carr	60,000	70,000	70%

What amount of gain did Carr recognize from this transaction?

- a. $40,000
- b. $15,000
- c. $10,000
- d. $0

4. Jones incorporated a sole proprietorship by exchanging all the proprietorship's assets for the stock of Nu Co., a new corporation. To qualify for tax-free incorporation, Jones must be in control of Nu immediately after the exchange. What percentage of Nu's stock must Jones own to qualify as "control" for this purpose?

- a. 50.00%
- b. 51.00%
- c. 66.67%
- d. 80.00%

5. Feld, the sole stockholder of Maki Corp., paid $50,000 for Maki's stock in 2002. In 2008, Feld contributed a parcel of land to Maki but was not given any additional stock for this contribution. Feld's basis for the land was $10,000, and its fair market value was $18,000 on the date of the transfer of title. What is Feld's adjusted basis for the Maki stock?

- a. $50,000
- b. $52,000
- c. $60,000
- d. $68,000

6. Rela Associates, a partnership, transferred all of its assets, with a basis of $300,000, along with liabilities of $50,000, to a newly formed corporation in return for all of the corporation's stock. The corporation assumed the liabilities. Rela then distributed the corporation's stock to its partners in liquidation. In connection with this incorporation of the partnership, Rela recognizes

- a. No gain or loss on the transfer of its assets nor on the assumption of Rela's liabilities by the corporation.
- b. Gain on the assumption of Rela's liabilities by the corporation.
- c. Gain or loss on the transfer of its assets to the corporation.
- d. Gain, but **not** loss, on the transfer of its assets to the corporation.

7. Roberta Warner and Sally Rogers formed the Acme Corporation on October 1, 2008. On the same date Warner paid $75,000 cash to Acme for 750 shares of its common stock. Simultaneously, Rogers received 100 shares of Acme's common stock for services rendered. How much should Rogers include as taxable income for 2008 and what will be the basis of her stock?

	Taxable income	Basis of stock
a.	$0	$0
b.	$0	$10,000
c.	$10,000	$0
d.	$10,000	$10,000

8. Jackson, a single individual, inherited Bean Corp. common stock from Jackson's parents. Bean is a qualified small business corporation under Code Sec. 1244. The stock cost Jackson's parents $20,000 and had a fair market value of $25,000 at the parents' date of death. During the year, Bean declared bankruptcy and Jackson was informed that the stock was worthless. What amount may Jackson deduct as an ordinary loss in the current year?

- a. $0
- b. $ 3,000
- c. $20,000
- d. $25,000

9. Which of the following is **not** a requirement for stock to qualify as Sec. 1244 small business corporation stock?

- a. The stock must be issued to an individual or to a partnership.
- b. The stock was issued for money or property (other than stock and securities).
- c. The stock must be common stock.
- d. The issuer must be a domestic corporation.

10. During the current year, Dinah sold Sec. 1244 small business corporation stock that she owned for a loss of $125,000. Assuming Dinah is married and files a joint income tax return for 2008, what is the character of Dinah's recognized loss from the sale of the stock?

a. $125,000 capital loss.
b. $25,000 capital loss; $100,000 ordinary loss.
c. $75,000 capital loss; $50,000 ordinary loss.
d. $0 capital loss; $125,000 ordinary loss.

11. Nancy, who is single, formed a corporation during 2003 using a tax-free asset transfer that qualified under Sec. 351. She transferred property having an adjusted basis of $80,000 and a fair market value of $60,000, and in exchange received Sec. 1244 small business corporation stock. During February 2008, Nancy sold all of her stock for $35,000. What is the amount and character of Nancy's recognized loss resulting from the sale of the stock in 2008?

a. $0 ordinary loss; $45,000 capital loss.
b. $25,000 ordinary loss; $10,000 capital loss.
c. $25,000 ordinary loss; $20,000 capital loss.
d. $45,000 ordinary loss; $0 capital loss.

12. A civil fraud penalty can be imposed on a corporation that underpays tax by

a. Omitting income as a result of inadequate record-keeping.
b. Failing to report income it erroneously considered **not** to be part of corporate profits.
c. Filing an incomplete return with an appended statement, making clear that the return is incomplete.
d. Maintaining false records and reporting fictitious transactions to minimize corporate tax liability.

13. Bass Corp., a calendar-year C corporation, made qualifying 2007 estimated tax deposits based on its actual 2006 tax liability. On March 15, 2008, Bass filed a timely automatic extension request for its 2007 corporate income tax return. Estimated tax deposits and the extension payment totaled $7,600. This amount was 95% of the total tax shown on Bass' final 2007 corporate income tax return. Bass paid $400 additional tax on the final 2007 corporate income tax return filed before the extended due date. For the 2007 calendar year, Bass was subject to pay

I. Interest on the $400 tax payment made in 2008.
II. A tax delinquency penalty.

a. I only.
b. II only.
c. Both I and II.
d. Neither I nor II.

14. Edge Corp., a calendar-year C corporation, had a net operating loss and zero tax liability for its 2007 tax year. To avoid the penalty for underpayment of estimated taxes, Edge could compute its first quarter 2008 estimated income tax payment using the

	Annualized income method	Preceding year method
a.	Yes	Yes
b.	Yes	No
c.	No	Yes
d.	No	No

15. A corporation's tax year can be reopened after all statutes of limitations have expired if

I. The tax return has a 50% nonfraudulent omission from gross income.
II. The corporation prevails in a determination allowing a deduction in an open tax year that was taken erroneously in a closed tax year.

a. I only.
b. II only.
c. Both I and II.
d. Neither I nor II.

16. A corporation's penalty for underpaying federal estimated taxes is

a. Not deductible.
b. Fully deductible in the year paid.
c. Fully deductible if reasonable cause can be established for the underpayment.
d. Partially deductible.

17. Blink Corp., an accrual-basis calendar-year corporation, carried back a net operating loss for the tax year ended December 31, 2008. Blink's gross revenues have been under $500,000 since inception. Blink expects to have profits for the tax year ending December 31, 2009. Which method(s) of estimated tax payment can Blink use for its quarterly payments during the 2009 tax year to avoid underpayment of federal estimated taxes?

I. 100% of the preceding tax year method
II. Annualized income method

a. I only.
b. Both I and II.
c. II only.
d. Neither I nor II.

18. When computing a corporation's income tax expense for estimated income tax purposes, which of the following should be taken into account?

	Corporate tax credits	Alternative minimum tax
a.	No	No
b.	No	Yes
c.	Yes	No
d.	Yes	Yes

19. Finbury Corporation's taxable income for the year ended December 31, 2007, was $2,000,000 on which its tax liability was $680,000. In order for Finbury to escape the estimated tax underpayment penalty for the year ending December 31, 2008, Finbury's 2008 estimated tax payments must equal at least

a. 90% of the 2008 tax liability.
b. 93% of the 2008 tax liability.
c. 100% of the 2008 tax liability.
d. The 2007 tax liability of $680,000.

20. Kisco Corp.'s taxable income for 2008 before taking the dividends received deduction was $70,000. This includes $10,000 in dividends from a 15%-owned taxable domestic corporation. Given the following tax rates, what would Kisco's income tax be before any credits?

Taxable income partial rate table	Tax rate
Up to $50,000	15%
Over $50,000 but not over $75,000	25%

a. $10,000
b. $10,750
c. $12,500
d. $15,750

21. Green Corp. was incorporated and began business in 2006. In computing its alternative minimum tax for 2007, it determined that it had adjusted current earnings (ACE) of $400,000 and alternative minimum taxable income (prior to the ACE adjustment) of $300,000. For 2008, it had adjusted current earnings of $100,000 and alternative minimum taxable income (prior to the ACE adjustment) of $300,000. What is the amount of Green Corp.'s adjustment for adjusted current earnings that will be used in calculating its alternative minimum tax for 2008?

- a. $ 75,000
- b. $ (75,000)
- c. $(100,000)
- d. $(150,000)

22. Eastern Corp., a calendar-year corporation, was formed during 2007. On January 3, 2008, Eastern placed five-year property in service. The property was depreciated under the general MACRS system. Eastern did not elect to use the straight-line method, and elected not to use bonus depreciation. The following information pertains to Eastern:

Eastern's 2008 taxable income	$300,000
Adjustment for the accelerated depreciation taken on 2008 5-year property	1,000
2008 tax-exempt interest from private activity bonds	5,000

What was Eastern's 2008 alternative minimum taxable income before the adjusted current earnings (ACE) adjustment?

- a. $306,000
- b. $305,000
- c. $304,000
- d. $301,000

23. If a corporation's tentative minimum tax exceeds the regular tax, the excess amount is

- a. Carried back to the first preceding taxable year.
- b. Carried back to the third preceding taxable year.
- c. Payable in addition to the regular tax.
- d. Subtracted from the regular tax.

24. Rona Corp.'s 2008 alternative minimum taxable income was $200,000. The exempt portion of Rona's 2008 alternative minimum taxable income was

- a. $0
- b. $12,500
- c. $27,500
- d. $52,500

25. A corporation's tax preference items that must be taken into account for 2008 alternative minimum tax purposes include

- a. Use of the percentage-of-completion method of accounting for long-term contracts.
- b. Casualty losses.
- c. Tax-exempt interest on private activity bonds.
- d. Capital gains.

26. In computing its 2008 alternative minimum tax, a corporation must include as an adjustment

- a. The dividends received deduction.
- b. The difference between regular tax depreciation and straight-line depreciation over forty years for real property placed in service in 1998.
- c. Charitable contributions.
- d. Interest expense on investment property.

27. A corporation will not be subject to the alternative minimum tax for calendar year 2008 if

- a. The corporation's net assets do not exceed $7.5 million.

- b. The corporation's average annual gross receipts do not exceed $10 million.
- c. The corporation has less then ten shareholders.
- d. 2008 is the corporation's first tax year.

28. Bradbury Corp., a calendar-year corporation, was formed on January 2, 2005, and had gross receipts for its first four taxable years as follows:

Year	Gross receipts
2005	$4,500,000
2006	9,000,000
2007	9,500,000
2008	6,500,000

What is the first taxable year that Bradbury Corp. is **not exempt** from the alternative minimum tax (AMT)?

- a. 2006
- b. 2007
- c. 2008
- d. Bradbury is exempt from AMT for its first four taxable years.

29. Which of the following entities must include in gross income 100% of dividends received from unrelated taxable domestic corporations in computing regular taxable income?

	Personal service corporations	Personal holding companies
a.	Yes	Yes
b.	No	No
c.	Yes	No
d.	No	Yes

30. Andi Corp. issued $1,000,000 face amount of bonds in 2000 and established a sinking fund to pay the debt at maturity. The bondholders appointed an independent trustee to invest the sinking fund contributions and to administer the trust. In 2008, the sinking fund earned $60,000 in interest on bank deposits and $8,000 in net long-term capital gains. All of the trust income is accumulated with Andi's periodic contributions so that the aggregate amount will be sufficient to pay the bonds when they mature. What amount of trust income was taxable to Andi in 2008?

- a. $0
- b. $ 8,000
- c. $60,000
- d. $68,000

31. The following information pertains to treasury stock sold by Lee Corp. to an unrelated broker in 2008:

Proceeds received	$50,000
Cost	30,000
Par value	9,000

What amount of capital gain should Lee recognize in 2008 on the sale of this treasury stock?

- a. $0
- b. $ 8,000
- c. $20,000
- d. $30,500

32. During 2008, Ral Corp. exchanged 5,000 shares of its own $10 par common stock for land with a fair market value of $75,000. As a result of this exchange, Ral should report in its 2008 tax return

- a. $25,000 Section 1245 gain.
- b. $25,000 Section 1231 gain.
- c. $25,000 ordinary income.
- d. No gain.

33. Pym, Inc., which had earnings and profits of $100,000, distributed land to Kile Corporation, a stockholder, as a dividend in kind. Pym's adjusted basis for this land was $3,000. The land had a fair market value of $12,000 and was subject to a mortgage liability of $5,000, which was assumed by Kile Corporation. The dividend was declared and paid during March 2008.

How much of the distribution would be reportable by Kile as a dividend, before the dividends received deduction?

- a. $0
- b. $ 3,000
- c. $ 7,000
- d. $12,000

34. Which of the following costs are deductible organizational expenditures?

- a. Professional fees to issue the corporation's stock.
- b. Commissions paid by the corporation to underwriters for stock issue.
- c. Printing costs to issue the corporation's stock.
- d. Expenses of temporary directors meetings.

35. Brown Corp., a calendar-year taxpayer, was organized and actively began operations on July 1, 2008, and incurred the following costs:

Legal fees to obtain corporate charter	$40,000
Commission paid to underwriter	25,000
Temporary directors' meetings	15,000
State incorporation fees	4,400

For 2008, what amount should Brown Corp. deduct for organizational expenses?

- a. $1,980
- b. $2,814
- c. $5,940
- d. $6,812

36. The costs of organizing a corporation during 2008

- a. May be deducted in full in the year in which these costs are incurred if they do not exceed $5,000.
- b. May be deducted only in the year in which these costs are paid.
- c. May be amortized over a period of not less than sixty months even if these costs are capitalized on the company's books.
- d. Are nondeductible capital expenditures.

37. Silo Corp. was organized on March 1, 2008, began doing business on September 1, 2008, and elected to file its income tax return on a calendar-year basis. The following qualifying organizational expenditures were incurred in organizing the corporation:

July 1, 2008	$3,000
September 3, 2008	5,600

The maximum allowable deduction for organizational expenditures for 2008 is

- a. $ 600
- b. $3,000
- c. $5,000
- d. $5,080

38. During 2008, Jackson Corp. had the following income and expenses:

Gross income from operations	$100,000
Dividend income from taxable domestic 20%-owned corporations	10,000
Operating expenses	35,000
Officers' salaries	20,000
Contributions to qualified charitable organizations	8,000
Net operating loss carryforward from 2007	30,000

What is the amount of Jackson Corp.'s charitable contribution carryover to 2009?

- a. $0
- b. $2,500
- c. $5,500
- d. $6,300

39. In 2008, Cable Corp., a calendar-year C corporation, contributed $80,000 to a qualified charitable organization. Cable's 2008 taxable income before the deduction for charitable contributions was $820,000 after a $40,000 dividends received deduction. Cable also had carryover contributions of $10,000 from the prior year. In 2008, what amount can Cable deduct as charitable contributions?

- a. $90,000
- b. $86,000
- c. $82,000
- d. $80,000

40. Tapper Corp., an accrual-basis calendar-year corporation, was organized on January 2, 2008. During 2008, revenue was exclusively from sales proceeds and interest income. The following information pertains to Tapper:

Taxable income before charitable contributions for the year ended December 31, 2008	$500,000
Tapper's matching contribution to employee-designated qualified universities made during 2008	10,000
Board of Directors' authorized contribution to a qualified charity (authorized December 1, 2008, made February 1, 2009)	30,000

What is the maximum allowable deduction that Tapper may take as a charitable contribution on its tax return for the year ended December 31, 2008?

- a. $0
- b. $10,000
- c. $30,000
- d. $40,000

41. Lyle Corp. is a distributor of pharmaceuticals and sells only to retail drug stores. During 2008, Lyle received unsolicited samples of nonprescription drugs from a manufacturer. Lyle donated these drugs in 2008 to a qualified exempt organization and deducted their fair market value as a charitable contribution. What should be included as gross income in Lyle's 2008 return for receipt of these samples?

- a. Fair market value.
- b. Net discounted wholesale price.
- c. $25 nominal value assigned to gifts.
- d. $0.

42. During 2008, Nale Corp. received dividends of $1,000 from a 10%-owned taxable domestic corporation. When Nale computes the maximum allowable deduction for contributions in its 2008 return, the amount of dividends to be included in the computation of taxable income is

- a. $0
- b. $ 200
- c. $ 300
- d. $1,000

43. Gero Corp. had operating income of $160,000, after deducting $10,000 for contributions to State University, but not including dividends of $2,000 received from nonaffiliated taxable domestic corporations.

In computing the maximum allowable deduction for contributions, Gero should apply the percentage limitation to a base amount of

    a. $172,000
    b. $170,400
    c. $170,000
    d. $162,000

44. Norwood Corporation is an accrual-basis taxpayer. For the year ended December 31, 2008, it had book income before tax of $500,000 after deducting a charitable contribution of $100,000. The contribution was authorized by the Board of Directors in December 2008, but was not actually paid until March 1, 2009. How should Norwood treat this charitable contribution for tax purposes to minimize its 2008 taxable income?

    a.   It cannot claim a deduction in 2008, but must apply the payment against 2009 income.
    b.   Make an election claiming a deduction for 2008 of $50,000 and carry the remainder over a maximum of five succeeding tax years.
    c.   Make an election claiming a deduction for 2008 of $60,000 and carry the remainder over a maximum of five succeeding tax years.
    d.   Make an election claiming a 2008 deduction of $100,000.

45. In 2008, Best Corp., an accrual-basis calendar-year C corporation, received $100,000 in dividend income from the common stock that it held in a 15%-owned domestic corporation. The stock was not debt-financed, and was held for over a year. Best recorded the following information for 2008:

Loss from Best's operations	$ (10,000)
Dividends received	100,000
Taxable income (before dividends received deduction)	$ 90,000

Best's dividends received deduction on its 2008 tax return was

    a. $100,000
    b. $ 80,000
    c. $ 70,000
    d. $ 63,000

46. In 2008, Acorn, Inc. had the following items of income and expense:

Sales	$500,000
Cost of sales	250,000
Dividends received	25,000

The dividends were received from a corporation of which Acorn owns 30%. In Acorn's 2008 corporate income tax return, what amount should be reported as income before special deductions?

    a. $525,000
    b. $505,000
    c. $275,000
    d. $250,000

47. The corporate dividends received deduction

    a.   Must exceed the applicable percentage of the recipient shareholder's taxable income.
    b.   Is affected by a requirement that the investor corporation must own the investee's stock for a specified minimum holding period.
    c.   Is unaffected by the percentage of the investee's stock owned by the investor corporation.
    d.   May be claimed by S corporations.

48. In 2008, Ryan Corp. had the following income:

Income from operations	$300,000
Dividends from unrelated taxable domestic corporations less than 20% owned	2,000

Ryan had no portfolio indebtedness. In Ryan's 2008 taxable income, what amount should be included for the dividends received?

    a. $ 400
    b. $ 600
    c. $1,400
    d. $1,600

49. In 2008, Daly Corp. had the following income:

Profit from operations	$100,000
Dividends from 20%-owned taxable domestic corporation	1,000

In Daly's 2008 taxable income, how much should be included for the dividends received?

    a. $0
    b. $ 200
    c. $ 800
    d. $1,000

50. Cava Corp., which has **no** portfolio indebtedness, received the following dividends in 2008:

From a mutual savings bank	$1,500
From a 20%-owned unaffiliated domestic taxable corporation	7,500

How much of these dividends qualifies for the 80% dividends received deduction?

    a. $9,000
    b. $7,500
    c. $1,500
    d. $0

51. During 2008, Stark Corp. reported gross income from operations of $350,000 and operating expenses of $400,000. Stark also received dividend income of $100,000 (not included in gross income from operations) from an investment in a taxable domestic corporation in which it owns 10% of the stock. Additionally, Stark had a net operating loss carryover from 2007 of $30,000. What is the amount of Stark Corp.'s net operating loss for 2008?

    a. $0
    b. $(20,000)
    c. $(30,000)
    d. $(50,000)

52. A C corporation's net capital losses are

    a.   Carried forward indefinitely until fully utilized.
    b.   Carried back three years and forward five years.
    c.   Deductible in full from the corporation's ordinary income.
    d.   Deductible from the corporation's ordinary income only to the extent of $3,000.

53. For the year ended December 31, 2008, Taylor Corp. had a net operating loss of $200,000. Taxable income for the earlier years of corporate existence, computed without reference to the net operating loss, was as follows:

	Taxable income
2003	$ 5,000
2004	$10,000
2005	$20,000
2006	$30,000
2007	$40,000

If Taylor makes **no** special election to waive a net operating loss carryback period, what amount of net operating loss will be available to Taylor for the year ended December 31, 2009?

- a. $200,000
- b. $130,000
- c. $110,000
- d. $ 95,000

54. When a corporation has an unused net capital loss that is carried back or carried forward to another tax year,

- a. It retains its original identity as short-term or long-term.
- b. It is treated as a short-term capital loss whether or not it was short-term when sustained.
- c. It is treated as a long-term capital loss whether or not it was long-term when sustained.
- d. It can be used to offset ordinary income up to the amount of the carryback or carryover.

55. For the year ended December 31, 2008, Haya Corp. had gross business income of $600,000 and expenses of $800,000. Contributions of $5,000 to qualified charities were included in expenses. In addition to the expenses, Haya had a net operating loss carryover of $9,000. What was Haya's net operating loss for 2008?

- a. $209,000
- b. $204,000
- c. $200,000
- d. $195,000

56. Dorsett Corporation's income tax return for 2008 shows deductions exceeding gross income by $56,800. Included in the tax return are the following items:

Net operating loss deduction (carryover from 2007)	$15,000
Dividends received deduction	6,800

What is Dorsett's net operating loss for 2008?

- a. $56,800
- b. $50,000
- c. $41,800
- d. $35,000

57. Ram Corp.'s operating income for the year ended December 31, 2008, amounted to $100,000. Also in 2008, a machine owned by Ram was completely destroyed in an accident. This machine's adjusted basis immediately before the casualty was $15,000. The machine was not insured and had no salvage value.

In Ram's 2008 tax return, what amount should be deducted for the casualty loss?

- a. $ 5,000
- b. $ 5,400
- c. $14,900
- d. $15,000

58. For the first taxable year in which a corporation has qualifying research and experimental expenditures, the corporation

- a. Has a choice of either deducting such expenditures as current business expenses, or capitalizing these expenditures.
- b. Has to treat such expenditures in the same manner as they are accounted for in the corporation's financial statements.
- c. Is required to deduct such expenditures currently as business expenses or lose the deductions.
- d. Is required to capitalize such expenditures and amortize them ratably over a period of not less than sixty months.

59. For the year ended December 31, 2008, Kelly Corp. had net income per books of $300,000 before the provision for federal income taxes. Included in the net income were the following items:

Dividend income from a 5%-owned domestic taxable corporation (taxable income limitation does not apply and there is no portfolio indebtedness)	$50,000
Bad debt expense (represents the increase in the allowance for doubtful accounts)	80,000

Assuming no bad debt was written off, what is Kelly's taxable income for the year ended December 31, 2008?

- a. $250,000
- b. $330,000
- c. $345,000
- d. $380,000

60. For the year ended December 31, 2008, Maple Corp.'s book income, before federal income tax, was $100,000. Included in this $100,000 were the following:

Provision for state income tax	$1,000
Interest earned on US Treasury Bonds	6,000
Interest expense on bank loan to purchase US Treasury Bonds	2,000

Maple's taxable income for 2008 was

- a. $ 96,000
- b. $ 97,000
- c. $100,000
- d. $101,000

61. For the year ended December 31, 2008, Dodd Corp. had net income per books of $100,000. Included in the computation of net income were the following items:

Provision for federal income tax	$27,000
Net long-term capital loss	5,000
Keyman life insurance premiums (corporation is beneficiary)	3,000

Dodd's 2008 taxable income was

- a. $127,000
- b. $130,000
- c. $132,000
- d. $135,000

62. For the year ended December 31, 2008, Bard Corp.'s income per accounting records, before federal income taxes, was $450,000 and included the following:

State corporate income tax refunds	$ 4,000
Life insurance proceeds on officer's death	15,000
Net loss on sale of securities bought for investment in 2006	20,000

Bard's 2008 taxable income was

- a. $435,000

b. $451,000
c. $455,000
d. $470,000

63. Dewey Corporation's book income before federal income taxes was $520,000 for the year ended December 31, 2008. Dewey was incorporated during 2008 and began business in June. Organization costs of $257,400 were expensed for financial statement purposes during 2008. For tax purposes these costs are being written off over the minimum allowable period. For the year ended December 31, 2008, Dewey's taxable income was

a. $520,000
b. $747,900
c. $767,390
d. $778,000

64. Bishop Corporation reported taxable income of $700,000 on its federal income tax return for calendar year 2008. Selected information for 2008 is available from Bishop's records as follows:

Provision for federal income tax per books	$280,000
Depreciation claimed on the tax return	130,000
Depreciation recorded in the books	75,000
Life insurance proceeds on death of corporate officer	100,000

Bishop reported net income per books for 2008 of

a. $855,000
b. $595,000
c. $575,000
d. $475,000

65. For the year ended December 31, 2008, Ajax Corporation had net income per books of $1,200,000. Included in the determination of net income were the following items:

Interest income on municipal bonds	$ 40,000
Damages received from settlement of patent infringement lawsuit	200,000
Interest paid on loan to purchase municipal bonds	8,000
Provision for federal income tax	524,000

What should Ajax report as its taxable income for 2008?

a. $1,492,000
b. $1,524,000
c. $1,684,000
d. $1,692,000

66. For its taxable year 2008, Farve Corp. had net income per books of $80,000, which included municipal bond interest of $5,000, dividend income of $10,000, a deduction for a net capital loss of $6,000, a deduction for business meals of $4,000, and a deduction for federal income taxes of $18,000. What is the amount of income that would be shown on the last line of Schedule M-1 (Reconciliation of Income [Loss] Per Books with Income [Loss] Per Return) of Farve Corp.'s corporate income tax return for 2008?

a. $ 90,000
b. $ 93,000
c. $ 99,000
d. $101,000

67. In 2008, Starke Corp., an accrual-basis calendar-year corporation, reported book income of $380,000. Included in that amount was $50,000 municipal bond interest income, $170,000 for federal income tax expense, and $2,000 interest expense on the debt incurred to carry the municipal bonds. What amount should Starke's taxable income be as

reconciled on Starke's Schedule M-1 of Form 1120, US Corporation Income Tax Return?

a. $330,000
b. $500,000
c. $502,000
d. $550,000

68. Would the following expense items be reported on Schedule M-1 of the corporation income tax return (Form 1120) showing the reconciliation of income per books with income per return?

	Lodging expenses for executive out-of-town travel	*Deduction for a net capital loss*
a.	Yes	Yes
b.	No	No
c.	Yes	No
d.	No	Yes

69. In the reconciliation of income per books with income per return

a.   Only temporary differences are considered.
b.   Only permanent differences are considered.
c.   Both temporary and permanent differences are considered.
d.   Neither temporary nor permanent differences are considered.

70. Media Corp. is an accrual-basis, calendar-year C corporation. Its 2008 reported book income included $6,000 in municipal bond interest income. Its expenses included $1,500 of interest incurred on indebtedness used to carry municipal bonds and $8,000 in advertising expense. What is Media's net M-1 adjustment on its 2008 Form 1120, US Corporation Income Tax Return, to reconcile to its 2008 taxable income?

a. $(4,500)
b. $ 1,500
c. $ 3,500
d. $ 9,500

71. Barbaro Corporation's retained earnings at January 1, 2008, was $600,000. During 2008 Barbaro paid cash dividends of $150,000 and received a federal income tax refund of $26,000 as a result of an IRS audit of Barbaro's 2005 tax return. Barbaro's net income per books for the year ended December 31, 2008, was $274,900 after deducting federal income tax of $183,300. How much should be shown in the reconciliation Schedule M-2, of Form 1120, as Barbaro's retained earnings at December 31, 2008?

a. $443,600
b. $600,900
c. $626,900
d. $750,900

72. Olex Corporation's books disclosed the following data for the calendar year 2008:

Retained earnings at beginning of year	$50,000
Net income for year	70,000
Contingency reserve established at end of year	10,000
Cash dividends paid during year	8,000

What amount should appear on the last line of reconciliation Schedule M-2 of Form 1120?

a. $102,000
b. $120,000

c. $128,000
d. $138,000

73. Bank Corp. owns 80% of Shore Corp.'s outstanding capital stock. Shore's capital stock consists of 50,000 shares of common stock issued and outstanding. Shore's 2008 net income was $140,000. During 2008, Shore declared and paid dividends of $60,000. In conformity with generally accepted accounting principles, Bank recorded the following entries in 2008:

	Debit	*Credit*
Investment in Shore Corp. common stock	$112,000	
Equity in earnings of subsidiary		$112,000
Cash	48,000	
Investment in Shore Corp. common stock		48,000

In its 2008 consolidated tax return, Bank should report dividend revenue of
a. $48,000
b. $14,400
c. $ 9,600
d. $0

74. In 2008, Portal Corp. received $100,000 in dividends from Sal Corp., its 80%-owned subsidiary. What net amount of dividend income should Portal include in its 2008 consolidated tax return?
a. $100,000
b. $ 80,000
c. $ 70,000
d. $0

75. Potter Corp. and Sly Corp. file consolidated tax returns. In January 2007, Potter sold land, with a basis of $60,000 and a fair value of $100,000, to Sly for $100,000. Sly sold the land in June 2008 for $125,000. In its 2008 and 2007 tax returns, what amount of gain should be reported for these transactions in the consolidated return?

	2008	*2007*
a.	$25,000	$40,000
b.	$25,000	$0
c.	$40,000	$25,000
d.	$65,000	$0

76. When a consolidated return is filed by an affiliated group of includible corporations connected from inception through the requisite stock ownership with a common parent
a.   Intercompany dividends are excludable to the extent of 80%.
b.   Operating losses of one member of the group offset operating profits of other members of the group.
c.   Each of the subsidiaries is entitled to an alternative minimum tax exemption.
d.   Each of the subsidiaries is entitled to an accumulated earnings tax credit.

77. Dana Corp. owns stock in Seco Corp. For Dana and Seco to qualify for the filing of consolidated returns, at least what percentage of Seco's total voting power and total value of stock must be directly owned by Dana?

	Total voting power	*Total value of stock*
a.	51%	51%
b.	51%	80%
c.	80%	51%
d.	80%	80%

78. Consolidated returns may be filed
a.   Either by parent-subsidiary corporations or by brother-sister corporations.
b.   Only by corporations that formally request advance permission from the IRS.
c.   Only by parent-subsidiary affiliated groups.
d.   Only by corporations that issue their financial statements on a consolidated basis.

79. Parent Corporation and Subsidiary Corporation file consolidated returns on a calendar-year basis. In January 2007, Subsidiary sold land, which it had used in its business, to Parent for $50,000. Immediately before this sale, Subsidiary's basis for the land was $30,000. Parent held the land primarily for sale to customers in the ordinary course of business. In July 2008, Parent sold the land to Adams, an unrelated individual. In determining consolidated taxable income for 2008, how much should Subsidiary take into account as a result of the 2007 sale of the land from Subsidiary to Parent?
a. $0
b. $20,000
c. $30,000
d. $50,000

80. At the beginning of the year, Westwind, a C corporation, had a deficit of $45,000 in accumulated earnings and profits. For the current year, Westwind reported earnings and profits of $15,000. Westwind distributed $12,000 during the year. What was the amount of Westwind's accumulated earnings and profits deficit at year-end?
a. $(30,000)
b. $(42,000)
c. $(45,000)
d. $(57,000)

81. At the beginning of the year, Cable, a C corporation, had accumulated earnings and profits of $100,000. Cable reported the following items on its current year tax return:

Taxable income	$50,000
Federal income taxes paid	5,000
Current year charitable contributions in excess of 10% limitation	1,000
Net capital loss for current year	2,000

What is Cable's accumulated earnings and profits at the end of the year?
a. $142,000
b. $145,000
c. $147,000
d. $150,000

82. On January 1, 2008, Locke Corp., an accrual-basis, calendar-year C corporation, had $30,000 in accumulated earnings and profits. For 2008, Locke had current earnings and profits of $20,000 and made two $40,000 cash distributions to its shareholders, one in April and one in September of 2008. What amount of the 2008 distributions is classified as dividend income to Locke's shareholders?
a. $0
b. $20,000
c. $50,000
d. $80,000

83. Chicago Corp., a calendar-year C corporation, had accumulated earnings and profits of $100,000 as of January 1, 2008 and had a **deficit** in its current earnings and profits for the entire 2008 tax year in the amount of $140,000. Chicago Corp. distributed $30,000 cash to its shareholders on December 31, 2008. What would be the balance of Chicago Corp.'s accumulated earnings and profits as of January 1, 2009?

     a. $0
     b. $(30,000)
     c. $(40,000)
     d. $(70,000)

84. Salon, Inc. distributed cash and personal property to its sole shareholder. Using the following facts, determine the amount of gain that would be recognized by Salon, Inc. as the result of making the distribution to its shareholder?

Item	*Amount*
Cash	$20,000
Personal property:	
Fair market value	6,000
Adjusted basis	3,000
Liability on property assumed by	
shareholder	10,000

     a. $ 3,000
     b. $ 4,000
     c. $ 7,000
     d. $23,000

85. Kent Corp. is a calendar-year, accrual-basis C corporation. In 2008, Kent made a nonliquidating distribution of property with an adjusted basis of $150,000 and a fair market value of $200,000 to Reed, its sole shareholder. The following information pertains to Kent:

Reed's basis in Kent stock at January 1, 2008	$500,000
Accumulated earnings and profits at January 1, 2008	125,000
Current earnings and profits for 2008	60,000

What was taxable as dividend income to Reed for 2008?

     a. $ 60,000
     b. $150,000
     c. $185,000
     d. $200,000

86. Ridge Corp., a calendar-year C corporation, made a nonliquidating cash distribution to its shareholders of $1,000,000 with respect to its stock. At that time, Ridge's current and accumulated earnings and profits totaled $750,000 and its total paid-in capital for tax purposes was $10,000,000. Ridge had no corporate shareholders. Ridge's cash distribution

   I. Was taxable as $750,000 of dividend income to its shareholders.
   II. Reduced its shareholders' adjusted bases in Ridge stock by $250,000.

     a.   I only.
     b.   II only.
     c.   Both I and II.
     d.   Neither I nor II.

87. Tour Corp., which had earnings and profits of $400,000, made a nonliquidating distribution of property to its shareholders in 2008 as a dividend in kind. This property, which had an adjusted basis of $30,000 and a fair market value of $20,000 at date of distribution, did not constitute assets used in the active conduct of Tour's business. How much <u>loss</u> did Tour recognize on this distribution?

     a. $30,000
     b. $20,000

     c. $10,000
     d. $0

88. On January 1, 2008, Kee Corp., a C corporation, had a $50,000 deficit in earnings and profits. For 2008 Kee had current earnings and profits of $10,000 and made a $30,000 cash distribution to its stockholders. What amount of the distribution is taxable as dividend income to Kee's stockholders?

     a. $30,000
     b. $20,000
     c. $10,000
     d. $0

89. Dahl Corp. was organized and commenced operations in 1998. At December 31, 2008, Dahl had accumulated earnings and profits of $9,000 before dividend declaration and distribution. On December 31, 2008, Dahl distributed cash of $9,000 and a vacant parcel of land to Green, Dahl's only stockholder. At the date of distribution, the land had a basis of $5,000 and a fair market value of $40,000. What was Green's taxable dividend income in 2008 from these distributions?

     a. $ 9,000
     b. $14,000
     c. $44,000
     d. $49,000

90. Pym, Inc. which had earnings and profits of $100,000, distributed land to Alex Rowe, a stockholder, as a dividend in kind. Pym's adjusted basis for this land was $3,000. The land had a fair market value of $12,000 and was subject to a mortgage liability of $5,000, which was assumed by Rowe. The dividend was declared and paid during November 2008. How much of the distribution was taxable to Rowe as a dividend?

     a. $9,000
     b. $7,000
     c. $4,000
     d. $3,000

91. On June 30, 2008, Ral Corporation had retained earnings of $100,000. On that date, it sold a plot of land to a noncorporate stockholder for $50,000. Ral had paid $40,000 for the land in 2000, and it had a fair market value of $80,000 when the stockholder bought it. The amount of dividend income taxable to the stockholder in 2008 is

     a. $0
     b. $10,000
     c. $20,000
     d. $30,000

92. On December 1, 2008, Gelt Corporation declared a dividend and distributed to its sole shareholder, as a dividend in kind, a parcel of land that was not an inventory asset. On the date of the distribution, the following data were available:

Adjusted basis of land	$ 6,500
Fair market value of land	14,000
Mortgage on land	5,000

For the year ended December 31, 2008, Gelt had earnings and profits of $30,000 without regard to the dividend distribution. By how much should the dividend distribution reduce the earnings and profits for 2008?

     a. $ 1,500
     b. $ 6,500

c. $ 9,000
d. $14,000

93. Two unrelated individuals, Mark and David, each own 50% of the stock of Pike Corporation, which has accumulated earnings and profits of $250,000. Because of his inactivity in the business in recent years, Mark has decided to retire from the business and wishes to sell his stock. Accordingly, Pike will distribute cash of $500,000 in redemption of all of the stock owned by Mark. If Mark's adjusted basis for his stock at date of redemption is $300,000, what will be the tax effect of the redemption to Mark?
a. $125,000 dividend.
b. $200,000 dividend.
c. $200,000 capital gain.
d. $250,000 dividend.

94. How does a noncorporate shareholder treat the gain on a redemption of stock that qualifies as a partial liquidation of the distributing corporation?
a.   Entirely as capital gain.
b.   Entirely as a dividend.
c.   Partly as capital gain and partly as a dividend.
d.   As a tax-free transaction.

95. In 2008, Kara Corp. incurred the following expenditures in connection with the repurchase of its stock from shareholders to avert a hostile takeover:

Interest on borrowings used to repurchase stock	$100,000
Legal and accounting fees in connection with the repurchase	400,000

The total of the above expenditures deductible in 2008 is
a. $0
b. $100,000
c. $400,000
d. $500,000

96. A corporation was completely liquidated and dissolved during 2008. The filing fees, professional fees, and other expenditures incurred in connection with the liquidation and dissolution are
a.   Deductible in full by the dissolved corporation.
b.   Deductible by the shareholders and not by the corporation.
c.   Treated as capital losses by the corporation.
d.   Not deductible either by the corporation or shareholders.

97. What is the usual result to the shareholders of a distribution in complete liquidation of a corporation?
a.   No taxable effect.
b.   Ordinary gain to the extent of cash received.
c.   Ordinary gain or loss.
d.   Capital gain or loss.

98. Par Corp. acquired the assets of its wholly owned subsidiary, Sub Corp., under a plan that qualified as a tax-free complete liquidation of Sub. Which of the following of Sub's unused carryovers may be transferred to Par?

	Excess charitable contributions	Net operating loss
a.	No	Yes
b.	Yes	No
c.	No	No
d.	Yes	Yes

99. Kappes Corp. distributed marketable securities in a pro rata redemption of its stock in a complete liquidation. These securities, which had been purchased in 2000 for $150,000, had a fair market value of $100,000 when distributed. What loss does Kappes recognize as a result of the distribution?
a. $0.
b. $50,000 long-term capital loss.
c. $50,000 Section 1231 loss.
d. $50,000 ordinary loss.

100. When a parent corporation completely liquidates its 80%-owned subsidiary, the parent (as stockholder) will ordinarily
a.   Be subject to capital gains tax on 80% of the long-term gain.
b.   Be subject to capital gains tax on 100% of the long-term gain.
c.   Have to report any gain on liquidation as ordinary income.
d.   Not recognize gain or loss on the liquidating distributions.

101. Lark Corp. and its wholly owned subsidiary, Day Corp., both operated on a calendar year. In January 2008, Day adopted a plan of complete liquidation. Two months later, Day paid all of its liabilities and distributed its remaining assets to Lark. These assets consisted of the following:

Cash	$50,000
Land (at cost)	10,000

Fair market value of the land was $30,000. Upon distribution of Day's assets to Lark, all of Day's capital stock was canceled. Lark's basis for the Day stock was $7,000. Lark's recognized gain in 2008 on receipt of Day's assets in liquidation was
a. $0
b. $50,000
c. $53,000
d. $73,000

102. On June 1, 2008, Green Corp. adopted a plan of complete liquidation. The liquidation was completed within a twelve-month period. On August 1, 2008, Green distributed to its stockholders installment notes receivable that Green had acquired in connection with the sale of land in 2007. The following information pertains to these notes:

Green's basis	$ 90,000
Fair market value	162,000
Face amount	185,000

How much gain must Green recognize in 2008 as a result of this distribution?
a. $0
b. $23,000
c. $72,000
d. $95,000

103. Carmela Corporation had the following assets on January 2, 2008, the date on which it adopted a plan of complete liquidation:

	Adjusted basis	Fair market value
Land	$ 75,000	$150,000
Inventory	43,500	66,000
Totals	$118,500	$216,000

The land was sold on June 30, 2008, to an unrelated party at a gain of $75,000. The inventory was sold to various customers during 2008 at an aggregate gain of $22,500. On

			Communication
Situation	Tax Return Amounts	Research	

Ray Lathan, the CEO of Ral Corp., has indicated that Ral is considering purchasing 8% of the outstanding stock of Diamond Corporation, one of its suppliers. However, because of a cash shortage, Ral would have to borrow $320,000 of the projected $400,000 cost of the Diamond stock. Ral projects that it will receive dividends totaling $20,000 from its stock investment in Diamond during 2009, and will have to pay $23,000 of interest expense on the funds borrowed to purchase the Diamond stock during that period. Write a letter to Lathan explaining the tax effect that the proposed investment will have on Ral's income and deductions for its 2009 tax year.

Dear Mr. Lathan:

Simulation Problem 4   (35 to 40 minutes)

Situation			
	Tax Return Amounts	Research	Communication

Lan Corp., an accrual-basis calendar-year repair service corporation, was formed and began business on January 7, 2008. Lan's valid S corporation election took effect retroactively on January 7, 2008. Since the question requires a numeric answer, a list of numeric amounts would be provided for the candidate to select from.

	Tax Return Amounts		
Situation		Research	Communication

For **items 1 through 4,** determine the amount, if any, using the fact pattern for each item.

1. Assume the following facts:

    Lan's 2008 books recorded the following items:

Gross receipts	$7,260
Interest income on investments	50
Charitable contributions	1,000
Supplies	1,120

    What amount of net business income should Lan report on its 2008 Form 1120S, US Income Tax Return for an S Corporation, Schedule K?

2. Assume the following facts:

    As of January 7, 2008, Taylor and Barr each owned 100 shares of the 200 issued shares of Lan stock. On January 31, 2008, Taylor and Barr each sold twenty shares to Pike. No election was made to terminate the tax year. Lan had net business income of $14,400 for the year ended December 31, 2008, and made no distributions to its shareholders. Lan's 2008 calendar year had 360 days.

    What amount of net business income should have been reported on Pike's 2008 Schedule K-1 from Lan? (2008 is a 360-day tax year.) Round the answer to the nearest hundred.

3. Assume the following facts:

    Pike purchased forty Lan shares on January 31, 2008, for $4,000. Lan made no distributions to shareholders, and Pike's 2008 Schedule K-1 from Lan reported

Ordinary business loss	$(1,000)
Municipal bond interest income	150

    What was Pike's basis in his Lan stock at December 31, 2008?

4. Assume the following facts:

    On January 6, 2008, Taylor and Barr each owned 100 shares of the 200 issued shares of Lan stock. Taylor's basis in Lan shares on that date was $10,000. Taylor sold all of his Lan shares to Pike on January 31, 2008, and Lan made a valid election to terminate its tax year. Taylor's share of ordinary income from Lan prior to the sale was $2,000. Lan made a cash distribution of $3,000 to Taylor on January 30, 2008.

    What was Taylor's basis in Lan shares for determining gain or loss from the sale to Pike?

		Research		
Situation	Tax Return Amounts			Communication

Mr. Perry is the sole shareholder of Arrow, Inc., a calendar-year S corporation. Due to the pass-through of losses in previous years, Perry's aggregate basis for the Arrow stock and debt that he owns has been reduced to zero. For its calendar year 2008, Arrow expects to incur another large loss which Perrry wishes to deduct on his 2008 Form 1040 tax return. What Internal Revenue Code section and subsection limits a shareholder's deduction of an S corporation's losses to the shareholder's basis for stock and debt?

Section	Subsection
§ [＿＿＿＿]	([＿＿＿＿])

			Communication
Situation	Tax Return Amounts	Research	

Perry contacts you and asks what he can do to enable him to deduct the pass-through of Arrow's projected loss for 2008. Specifically, Perry wants to know whether contributing his own note to Arrow, or guaranteeing Arrow's loan from the Fifth-First Bank will allow him to deduct Arrow's loss for 2008. Write a letter to Perry explaining what options are available to him that will allow him to deduct Arrow's loss on his 2008 Form 1040.

Dear Mr. Perry:

Simulation Problem 5　　　　　　　　　　　　　　(40 to 45 minutes)

Introduction						
	Schedule M-1 Adjustments	Deductibility	Taxability	Alternative Minimum Tax	Communication	Research

Reliant Corp., an accrual-basis calendar-year C corporation, filed its 2008 federal income tax return on March 15, 2009.

	Schedule M-1 Adjustments					
Introduction		Deductibility	Taxability	Alternative Minimum Tax	Communication	Research

The following **two** responses are required for each of the **items 1 through 6**.

- Determine the amount of Reliant's 2008 Schedule M-1 adjustment.
- Indicate if the adjustment increases, decreases, or has no effect, on Reliant's 2008 taxable income.

Selections

I.　Increases Reliant's 2008 taxable income.
D.　Decreases Reliant's 2008 taxable income.
N.　Has no effect on Reliant's 2008 taxable income.

	Schedule M-1 Adjustment	(I)	(D)	(N)
1. Reliant's disbursements included reimbursed employees' expenses in 2008 for travel of $100,000, and business meals of $30,000. The reimbursed expenses met the conditions of deductibility and were properly substantiated under an accountable plan. The reimbursement was not treated as employee compensation.	＿＿＿＿	○	○	○
2. Reliant's books expensed $7,000 in 2008 for the term life insurance premiums on the corporate officers. Reliant was the policy owner and beneficiary.	＿＿＿＿	○	○	○
3. Reliant's books indicated an $18,000 state franchise tax expense for 2008. Estimated state tax payments for 2008 were $15,000.	＿＿＿＿	○	○	○

	Schedule M-1 Adjustment	(I)	(D)	(N)

4. Book depreciation on computers for 2008 was $10,000. These computers, which cost $50,000, were placed in service on January 2, 2007. Tax depreciation used MACRS with the half-year convention. No election was made to expense part of the computer cost or to use a straight-line method.   ○ ○ ○

_____

5. For 2008, Reliant's books showed a $4,000 short-term capital gain distribution from a mutual fund corporation and a $5,000 loss on the sale of Retro stock that was purchased in 2006. The stock was an investment in an unrelated corporation. There were no other 2008 gains or losses and no loss carryovers from prior years.   ○ ○ ○

_____

6. Reliant's 2008 taxable income before the charitable contribution and the dividends received deductions was $500,000. Reliant's books expensed $15,000 in board of director authorized charitable contributions that were paid on January 5, 2009. Charitable contributions paid and expensed during 2008 were $35,000. All charitable contributions were properly substantiated. There were no net operating losses or charitable contributions that were carried forward.   ○ ○ ○

_____

Introduction	Schedule M-1 Adjustments	**Deductibility**	Taxability	Alternative Minimum Tax	Communication	Research

For the following, indicate if the expenses are fully deductible, partially deductible, or nondeductible for regular tax purposes on Reliant's 2008 federal income tax return.

Selections

F. Fully taxable for regular tax purposes on Reliant's 2008 federal income tax return.
P. Partially taxable for regular tax purposes on Reliant's 2008 federal income tax return.
N. Nontaxable for regular tax purposes on Reliant's 2008 federal income tax return.

	(F)	(P)	(N)

1. Reliant purchased theater tickets for its out of town clients. The performances took place after Reliant's substantial and bona fide business negotiations with its clients.   ○ ○ ○

2. Reliant accrued advertising expenses to promote a new product line. Ten percent of the new product line remained in ending inventory.   ○ ○ ○

3. Reliant incurred interest expense on a loan to purchase municipal bonds.   ○ ○ ○

4. Reliant paid a penalty for the underpayment of 2007 estimated taxes.   ○ ○ ○

5. On December 9, 2008, Reliant's board of directors voted to pay a $500 bonus to each nonstockholder employee for 2008. The bonuses were paid on February 3, 2009.   ○ ○ ○

Introduction	Schedule M-1 Adjustments	Deductibility	**Taxability**	Alternative Minimum Tax	Communication	Research

For the following, indicate if the items are fully taxable, partially taxable, or nontaxable for regular tax purposes on Reliant's 2008 federal income tax return. All transactions occurred during 2008.

Selections

F. Fully taxable for regular tax purposes on Reliant's 2008 federal income tax return.
P. Partially taxable for regular tax purposes on Reliant's 2008 federal income tax return.
N. Nontaxable for regular tax purposes on Reliant's 2008 federal income tax return.

Items are based on the following:

Reliant filed an amended federal income tax return for 2006 and received a refund that included both the overpayment of the federal taxes and interest.

	(F)	(P)	(N)

1. The portion of Reliant's refund that represented the overpayment of the 2006 federal taxes.   ○ ○ ○

2. The portion of Reliant's refund that is attributable to the interest on the overpayment of federal taxes.   ○ ○ ○

3. Reliant received dividend income from a mutual fund that solely invests in municipal bonds.   ○ ○ ○

			(F) (P) (N)

4. Reliant, the lessor, benefited from the capital improvements made to its property by the lessee in 2008. The lease agreement is for one year ending December 31, 2008, and provides for a reduction in rental payments by the lessee in exchange for the improvements.   ○ ○ ○

5. Reliant collected the proceeds on the term life insurance policy on the life of a debtor who was not a shareholder. The policy was assigned to Reliant as collateral security for the debt. The proceeds exceeded the amount of the debt.   ○ ○ ○

Introduction	Schedule M-1 Adjustments	Deductibility	Taxability	Alternative Minimum Tax	Communication	Research

Indicate if the following items increase, decrease, or have no effect on Reliant's 2008 alternative minimum taxable income (AMTI) **prior to** the adjusted current earnings adjustment (ACE).

Selections

I. Increases Reliant's 2008 AMTI.
D. Decreases Reliant's 2008 AMTI.
N. Has no effect on Reliant's 2008 AMTI.

	(I) (D) (N)

1. Reliant used the 70% dividends received deduction for regular tax purposes.   ○ ○ ○

2. Reliant received interest from a state's general obligation bonds.   ○ ○ ○

3. Reliant used MACRS depreciation on seven-year personal property placed into service January 3, 2008, for regular tax purposes. No expense election was made, and Reliant elected not to use bonus depreciation.   ○ ○ ○

4. Depreciation on nonresidential real property placed into service on January 3, 2008, was under the general MACRS depreciation system for regular tax purposes.   ○ ○ ○

5. Reliant had only cash charitable contributions for 2008.   ○ ○ ○

Introduction	Schedule M-1 Adjustments	Deductibility	Taxability	Alternative Minimum Tax	Communication	Research

The owner of Reliant Corporation, Mary Evans, contacts you and indicates that Reliant expects to form a wholly owned subsidiary, Surety Corporation, to conduct business unrelated to Reliant's current operations. Mary wants to have Surety expense the costs of formation, including the amounts paid for legal fees and the cost of issuing stock. Write a letter to Mary Evans explaining the appropriate tax treatment of the costs of forming Surety Corporation.

Reminder: Your response will be graded for both technical content and writing skills. For writing skills, you should demonstrate the ability to develop your ideas, organize them, and express them clearly.

Dear Ms. Evans:

Introduction	Schedule M-1 Adjustments	Deductibility	Taxability	Alternative Minimum Tax	Communication	Research

What Internal Revenue Code section, subsection, and paragraph limits a corporation's deduction for charitable contributions to a percentage of its taxable income before specified deductions?

Section	Subsection	Paragraph
§ _____	(_____)	_____

Simulation Problem 6   (40 to 45 minutes)

Situation						
	Schedule M-1 Adjustments	Taxability	Deductibility	Alternative Minimum Tax	Communication	Research

Capital Corp., an accrual-basis calendar-year C corporation, began operations on January 2, 2006. Capital timely filed its 2008 federal income tax return on March 15, 2009.

	Schedule M-1 Adjustments					
Situation		Taxability	Deductibility	Alternative Minimum Tax	Communication	Research

The following items each require **two** responses:

- For each item below, determine the amount of Capital's 2008 Schedule M-1 adjustment necessary to reconcile book income to taxable income. On the CPA exam, a list of numeric answers would be presented for the candidate to select from.
- In addition, determine if the Schedule M-1 adjustment necessary to reconcile book income to taxable income increases, decreases, or has no effect on Capital's 2008 taxable income. An answer may be selected once, more than once, or not at all.

Selections

I.   Increases Capital's 2008 taxable income.
D. Decreases Capital's 2008 taxable income.
N. Has no effect on Capital's 2008 taxable income.

	Amount of Adjustment	(I)	(D)	(N)
1. At its corporate inception in 2006, Capital incurred and paid $41,100 in organizational costs for legal fees to draft the corporate charter. In 2006, Capital correctly elected, for book purposes, to expense the organizational costs and to amortize the organizational expenditures over the minimum allowable period on its federal income tax return. For 2008, no organizational costs were deducted on its books.	_____	○	○	○
2. Capital's 2008 disbursements included $10,000 for reimbursed employees' expenses for business meals and entertainment. The reimbursed expenses met the conditions of deductibility and were properly substantiated under an accountable plan. The reimbursement was not treated as employee compensation.	_____	○	○	○
3. Capital's 2008 disbursements included $15,000 for life insurance premium expense paid for its executives as part of their taxable compensation. Capital is neither the direct nor the indirect beneficiary of the policy, and the amount of the compensation is reasonable.	_____	○	○	○
4. In 2008, Capital increased its allowance for uncollectible accounts by $10,000. No bad debt was written off in 2008.	_____	○	○	○

		Taxability				
Situation	Schedule M-1 Adjustments		Deductibility	Alternative Minimum Tax	Communication	Research

Sunco Corp., an accrual-basis calendar-year C corporation, timely filed its 2008 federal income tax return on March 15, 2009. Determine if the following items are fully taxable, partially taxable, or nontaxable for regular income tax purposes on Sunco's 2008 federal income tax return. An answer may be selected once, more than once, or not at all.

Selections

F. Fully taxable for regular income tax purposes on Sunco's 2008 federal income tax return.
P. Partially taxable for regular income tax purposes on Sunco's 2008 federal income tax return.
N. Nontaxable for regular income tax purposes on Sunco's 2008 federal income tax return.

	(F)	(P)	(N)
1. In 2008, Sunco received dividend income from a 35%-owned domestic corporation. The dividends were not from debt-financed portfolio stock, and the taxable income limitation did not apply.	○	○	○
2. In 2008, Sunco received a $2,800 lease cancellation payment from a three-year lease tenant.	○	○	○

Situation	Schedule M-1 Adjustments	Taxability	Deductibility	Alternative Minimum Tax	Communication	Research

Quest Corp., an accrual-basis calendar-year C corporation, timely filed its 2008 federal income tax return on March 15, 2009. Determine if the following items are fully deductible, partially deductible, or nondeductible for regular income tax purposes on Quest's 2008 federal income tax return. An answer may be selected once, more than once, or not at all.

Selections

F.   Fully deductible for regular income tax purposes on Quest's 2008 federal income tax return.
P.   Partially deductible for regular income tax purposes on Quest's 2008 federal income tax return.
N.   Nondeductible for regular income tax purposes on Quest's 2008 federal income tax return.

                                                                                            (F) (P) (N)

1. Quest's 2008 taxable income before charitable contributions and dividends received deduction was $200,000. Quest's Board of Directors authorized a $38,000 contribution to a qualified charity on December 1, 2008. The payment was made on February 1, 2009. All charitable contributions were properly substantiated.   ○   ○   ○

2. During 2008 Quest was assessed and paid a $300 uncontested penalty for failure to pay its 2007 federal income taxes on time.   ○   ○   ○

Situation	Schedule M-1 Adjustments	Taxability	Deductibility	Alternative Minimum Tax	Communication	Research

On its 2008 federal income tax return, Gelco Corp., an accrual-basis calendar-year C corporation, reported the same amounts for regular income tax and alternative minimum tax purposes. Determine if each item, taken separately, contributes to overstating, understating, or correctly stating Gelco's 2008 alternative minimum taxable income (AMTI) prior to the adjusted current earnings adjustment (ACE). An answer may be selected once, more than once, or not at all.

Selections

O.   Overstating Gelco's 2008 AMTI prior to the ACE.
U.   Understating Gelco's 2008 AMTI prior to the ACE.
C.   Correctly stating Gelco's 2008 AMTI prior to the ACE.

                                                                                            (O) (U) (C)

1. For regular tax purposes, Gelco deducted the maximum MACRS depreciation on seven-year personal property placed in service on January 2, 2008. Gelco did not elect to expense any part of the cost of the property under Sec. 179, and elected not to take bonus depreciation.   ○   ○   ○

2. For regular income tax purposes, Gelco depreciated nonresidential real property placed in service on January 2, 1998, under the general MACRS depreciation system for a thirty-nine-year depreciable life.   ○   ○   ○

3. Gelco excluded state highway construction general obligation bond interest income earned in 2008 for regular income tax and alternative minimum tax (AMT) purposes.   ○   ○   ○

Situation	Schedule M-1 Adjustments	Taxability	Deductibility	Alternative Minimum Tax	Communication	Research

Dan King contacts you and indicates that he is considering incorporating a business by transferring investment property with a fair market value of $500,000 and an adjusted basis of $150,000. In the exchange, King would receive all of the corporation's stock and the corporation would assume a $180,000 recourse liability on the transferred property that was incurred when the property was acquired. King is concerned that the assumption of the liability by the corporation may cause him to recognize gain and wants to know what can be done in the incorporation process to avoid recognition of gain. Write a letter to King addressing his concerns regarding the transfer of the liability.

Dear Mr. King:

117. (d) The requirement is to determine the correct statement concerning the accumulated earnings tax (AET). Answer (d), "The accumulated earnings tax can **not** be imposed on a corporation that has undistributed earnings and profits of less than $150,000," is correct because every corporation (even a personal service corporation) is eligible for an accumulated earnings credit of at least $150,000. Answer (a) is incorrect because the AET is not self-assessing, but instead is assessed by the IRS after finding a tax avoidance intent on the part of the taxpayer. Answer (b) is incorrect because the AET may be imposed regardless of the number of shareholders that a corporation has. Answer (c) is incorrect because the AET cannot be imposed on a corporation for any year in which an S corporation election is in effect because an S corporation's earnings pass through and are taxed to shareholders regardless of whether the earnings are actually distributed.

118. (d) The requirement is to determine the amount on which Kee Holding Corp.'s liability for personal holding company (PHC) tax will be based. To be classified as a personal holding company, a corporation must meet both a "stock ownership test" and an "income test." The "stock ownership test" requires that more than 50% of the stock must be owned (directly or indirectly) by five or fewer individuals. Since Kee has eighty unrelated equal shareholders, the stock ownership test is not met. Thus, Kee is not a personal holding company and has no liability for the PHC tax.

119. (b) The accumulated earnings tax (AET) can be avoided by sufficient dividend distributions. The imposition of the AET does not depend on a stock ownership test, nor is it self-assessing requiring the filing of a separate schedule attached to the regular tax return. The AET cannot be imposed on personal holding companies.

120. (c) The personal holding company (PHC) tax may be imposed if more than 50% of a corporation's stock is owned by five or fewer individuals. The PHC tax cannot be imposed on partnerships. Additionally, small business investment companies licensed by the Small Business Administration are excluded from the tax. If a corporation's gross income arises solely from rents, the rents will not be PHC income (even though no services are rendered to lessees) and thus, the PHC tax cannot be imposed.

121. (d) A net capital loss for the current year is allowed as a deduction in determining accumulated taxable income for purposes of the accumulated earnings tax. A capital loss carryover from a prior year, a dividends received deduction, and a net operating loss deduction would all be added back to taxable income in arriving at accumulated taxable income.

122. (d) The minimum accumulated earnings credit is $250,000 for nonservice corporations; $150,000 for service corporations.

123. (a) The requirement is to determine Daystar's allowable accumulated earnings credit for 2008. The credit is the greater of (1) the earnings and profits of the tax year retained for reasonable business needs of $20,000; or (2) $150,000 less the accumulated earnings and profits at the end of the preceding year of $45,000. Thus, the credit is $150,000 – $45,000 = $105,000.

H. S Corporations

124. (c) The requirement is to determine Stahl's basis for his S corporation stock at the end of the year. A shareholder's basis for S corporation stock is increased by the pass-through of all income items (including tax-exempt income) and is decreased by distributions that are excluded from the shareholder's gross income, as well as the pass-through of all loss and deduction items (including nondeductible items). Here, Stahl's beginning stock basis of $65,000 is increased by the $6,000 of municipal interest income and $4,000 of long-term capital gain, and is decreased by the ordinary loss of $10,000 and short-term capital loss of $9,000, resulting in a stock basis of $56,000 at the end of the year.

125. (b) The requirement is to determine the amount of the $30,000 distribution from an S corporation that is taxable to Baker. If an S corporation has no accumulated earnings and profits from C years, distributions to shareholders are generally nontaxable and reduce a shareholder's stock basis. To the extent that distributions exceed stock basis, they result in capital gain. A shareholder's basis for S corporation stock is first increased by the pass through of income, then reduced by distributions that are excluded from gross income, and finally reduced by the pass through of losses and deductions. Here, Baker's beginning stock basis of $25,000 would first be increased by the pass through of the $1,000 of ordinary income, to $26,000. Then the $30,000 cash distribution would be a nontaxable return of stock basis to the extent of $26,000, with the remaining $4,000 in excess of stock basis taxable to Baker as capital gain. Baker will not be able to deduct the long-term capital loss of $3,000 this year because the cash distribution reduced his stock basis to zero. Instead, the $3,000 loss will be carried forward and will be available as a deduction when Baker has sufficient basis to absorb the loss.

126. (d) The requirement is to determine the amount of the $7,200 of health insurance premiums paid by Lane, Inc. (an S corporation) to be included in gross income by Mill. Compensation paid by an S corporation includes fringe benefit expenditures made on behalf of officers and employees owning more than 2% of the S corporation' stock. Since Mill is a 10% shareholder-employee, Mill's compensation income reported on his W-2 from Lane must include the $7,200 of health insurance premiums paid by Lane for health insurance covering Mill, his spouse, and dependents. Note that Mill may qualify to deduct 100% of the $7,200 for AGI as a self-employed health insurance deduction.

127. (b) The requirement is to determine Lazur's tax basis for the Beck Corp. stock after the distribution. A shareholder's basis for stock of an S corporation is increased by the pass-through of all income items (including tax-exempt income) and is decreased by distributions that are excluded from the shareholder's gross income. Here, Lazur's beginning basis of $12,000 is increased by his 50% share of Beck's ordinary business income ($40,500) and tax-exempt income ($5,000) and is decreased by the $51,000 cash distribution excluded from his gross income, resulting in a stock basis of $6,500.

128. (d) The requirement is to determine the amount of income from Graphite Corp. (an S corporation) that should be included in Smith's 2008 adjusted gross income. An S corporation is a pass-through entity and its items of income and deduction flow through to be reported on shareholders' returns. Since Smith is a 50% shareholder, half of the ordinary business income ($80,000 × 50% = $40,000) and half of the tax-exempt interest ($6,000 × 50% = $3,000) would pass through to Smith. Since the income passed through to Smith would retain its character, Smith must include the $40,000 of ordinary income in gross income, while the $3,000 of tax-exempt interest retains its exempt characteristic and would be excluded from Smith's gross income. Smith's $12,000 of stock basis at the beginning of the year would be increased by the pass-through of the $40,000 of ordinary income as well as the $3,000 of tax-exempt income, to $55,000. As a result, the $53,000 cash distribution received by Smith would be treated as a nontaxable return of stock basis and would reduce the basis of Smith's stock to $2,000.

129. (a) The requirement is to determine the effect of the revocation statement on Dart Corp.'s S corporation election. A revocation of an S election will be effective if it is signed by shareholders owning more than 50% of the S corporation's outstanding stock. For this purpose, both voting and nonvoting shares are counted. Here Dart Corp. has a total of 100,000 shares outstanding. As a result, the revocation statement consented to by shareholders holding a total of 40,000 shares, would not be effective and would not terminate Dart Corp.'s S corporation election.

130. (d) The requirement is to determine the incorrect statement regarding S corporation eligibility requirements. The eligibility requirements restrict S corporation shareholders to individuals (other than nonresident aliens), estates, and certain trusts. Partnerships and C corporations are not permitted to own stock in an S corporation. However, an S corporation is permitted to be a partner in a partnership, and may own any percentage of stock of a C corporation, as well as own 100% of the stock of a qualified subchapter S subsidiary.

131. (b) The requirement is to determine the portion of the $310,000 distribution that must be reported as dividend income by Robert. Distributions from an S corporation are generally treated as first coming from its accumulated adjustment account (AAA), and then are treated as coming from its accumulated earnings and profits (AEP). A positive balance in an S corporation's AAA is generally nontaxable when distributed because it represents amounts that have already been taxed to shareholders during S years. In contrast, an S corporation's AEP represents earnings accumulated during C years that have never been taxed to shareholders, and must be reported as dividend income when received. In this case, the beginning balance in the AAA and shareholder stock basis must first be increased by the pass through of the $200,000 of ordinary income that is taxed to Robert for 2008. This permits the first $250,000 of the distribution to be nontaxable and will reduce the balance in the AAA to zero and Robert's stock basis to $50,000. The remaining $60,000 of distribution is a distribution of the corporation's AEP and must be reported as dividend income by Robert.

132. (b) The requirement is to determine the date on which Village Corp.'s S status became effective. A subchapter S election that is filed on or before the 15th day of the third month of a corporation's taxable year is generally

effective as of the beginning of the taxable year in which filed. If the S election is filed after the 15th day of the third month, the election is generally effective as of the first day of the corporation's next taxable year. Here, Village Corp. uses a calendar year and its S election was filed on September 5, 2008, which is beyond the 15th day of the third month of the taxable year (March 15). As a result, Village's subchapter S status becomes effective as of the first day of its next taxable year, January 1, 2009.

133. (d) The requirement is to determine whether a shareholder's basis in the stock of an S corporation is increased by the shareholder's pro rata share of tax-exempt interest and taxable interest. An S corporation is a pass through entity and its items of income and deduction pass through to be reported on shareholder returns. As a result, a shareholder's S corporation stock basis is increased by the pass through of all items of income, including both taxable as well as tax-exempt interest. An S shareholder's stock basis must be increased by tax-exempt interest in order to permit a later distribution of that interest to be nontaxable.

134. (b) The requirement is to determine the amount of income that should be allocated to Zinco Corp.'s short S year when its S election is terminated on April 1, 2008. When a corporation's subchapter S election is terminated during a taxable year, its income for the entire year must be allocated between the resulting S short year and C short year. If no special election is made, the income must be allocated on a daily basis between the S and C short years. In this case, the daily income equals $311,100/366 days = $850 per day. Since the election was terminated on April 1, there would be ninety-one days in the S short year, and $850 × 91 = $77,350 of income would be allocated to the tax return for the S short year to be passed through and taxed to shareholders.

135. (d) The requirement is to determine the correct statement regarding the termination of an S election. Answer (d) is correct because an S election will be terminated if an S corporation has passive investment income in excess of 25% of gross receipts for three consecutive taxable years, if the corporation also has subchapter C accumulated earnings and profits at the end of each of those three years. Answer (a) is incorrect because an S corporation is permitted to have a maximum of one hundred shareholders. Answer (b) is incorrect because a decedent's estate may be a shareholder of an S corporation. Answer (c) is incorrect because S corporations are allowed to make charitable contributions. Contributions separately pass through to shareholders and can be deducted as charitable contributions on shareholder returns.

136. (a) The requirement is to determine the amount of income from Manning (an S corporation) that should be reported on Kane's 2008 tax return. An S corporation's tax items are allocated to shareholders on a per share, per day basis. Since Manning had income of $73,200 for its entire year, its per day income is $73,200/366 = $200. Since there are 100 shares outstanding, Manning's daily income per share is $200/100 = $2. Since Kane sold twenty-five of his shares on the 40th day of 2008 and held his remaining seventy-five shares throughout the year, the amount of income to be reported on Kane's 2008 return would be determined as follows:

75 shares	×	$2	×	366 days	=	$54,900
25 shares	×	$2	×	40 days	=	2,000
						$56,900

137. (d) The requirement is to determine the earliest date on which Ace Corp. (a calendar-year corporation) can be recognized as an S corporation. Generally, an S election will be effective as of the first day of a taxable year if the election is made on or before the 15th day of the third month of the taxable year. Since there was no change in shareholders during the year, all of Ace's shareholders consented to the election, and Ace met all eligibility requirements during the preelection portion of the year, its election filed on February 10, 2008, is effective as of January 1, 2008. Note that if either a shareholder who held stock during the taxable year and before the date of election did not consent to the election, or the corporation did not meet the eligibility requirements before the date of election, then an otherwise valid election would be treated as made for the following taxable year.

138. (c) The requirement is to determine the number of shares of voting and nonvoting stock that must be owned by shareholders making a revocation of an S election. A revocation of an S election may be filed by shareholders owning more than 50% of an S corporation's outstanding stock. For this purpose, both voting and nonvoting shares are counted. In this case, since the S corporation has a total of 50,000 voting and nonvoting shares outstanding, the shareholders consenting to the revocation must own more than 25,000 shares.

139. (b) The requirement is to determine the amount of increase for each shareholder's basis in the stock of Haas Corp., a calendar-year S corporation, for the year ended December 31, 2008. An S corporation shareholder's basis for stock is increased by the pass through of all S corporation income items (including tax-exempt income), and is decreased by all loss and deduction items, as well as nondeductible expenses not charged to capital. Since Haas has two equal shareholders, each shareholder's stock basis will be increased by 50% of the operating income of $50,000, and 50% of the interest income of $10,000, resulting in an increase for each shareholder of $30,000.

140. (d) The requirement is to determine the condition that will prevent a corporation from qualifying as an S corporation. Certain eligibility requirements must be satisfied before a corporation can make a subchapter S election. Generally, in order to be an S corporation, a corporation must have only one class of stock outstanding and have no more than one hundred shareholders, who are either individuals, estates, or certain trusts. An S corporation may own any percentage of the stock of a C corporation, and 100% of the stock of a qualified subchapter S subsidiary.

141. (c) The requirement is to determine the correct statement regarding distributions to shareholders by an S corporation that has no accumulated earnings and profits. S corporations do not generate any earnings and profits, but may have accumulated earnings and profits from prior years as a C corporation. If accumulated earnings and profits are distributed to shareholders, the distributions will be taxed as dividend income to the shareholders. However, if an S corporation has no accumulated earnings and profits, distributions are generally nontaxable and reduce a shareholder's basis for stock. To the extent distributions exceed stock basis, they result in capital gain.

142. (d) The requirement is to determine whether a corporation that has been an S corporation from its inception may have both passive and nonpassive income, and be owned by a bankruptcy estate. To qualify as an S corporation, a corporation must have one hundred or fewer shareholders who are individuals (other than nonresident aliens), certain trusts, or estates (including bankruptcy estates). If a corporation has been an S corporation since its inception, there is no limitation on the amount or type of income that it generates, and it can have both passive and nonpassive income.

143. (b) The requirement is to determine Meyer's share of an S corporation's $36,600 ordinary loss. An S corporation's items of income and deduction are allocated on a daily basis to anyone who was a shareholder during the taxable year. Here, the $36,600 ordinary loss would be divided by 366 days to arrive at a loss of $100 per day. Since Meyer held 50% of the S corporation's stock for forty days, Meyer's share of the loss would be ($100 × 50%) × 40 days = $2,000.

144. (c) The requirement is to determine the period that a calendar-year corporation must wait before making a new S election following the termination of its S status during 2008. Generally, following the revocation or termination of an S election, a corporation must wait five years before reelecting subchapter S status unless the IRS consents to an earlier election.

145. (d) The requirement is to determine which will render a corporation ineligible for S corporation status. Answer (d) is correct because an S corporation is limited to 100 shareholders for tax years beginning after December 31, 2004. Answers (a) and (b) are incorrect because a decedent's estate and a bankruptcy estate are allowed as S corporation shareholders. Although an S corporation may only have one class of stock issued and outstanding, answer (c) is incorrect because a difference in voting rights among outstanding common shares is not treated as having more than one class of stock outstanding.

146. (d) The requirement is to determine the correct statement with regard to the application of the "at-risk" rules to S corporations and their shareholders. The at-risk rules limit a taxpayer's deduction of losses to the amount that the taxpayer can actually lose (i.e., generally the amount of cash and the adjusted basis of property invested by the taxpayer, plus any liabilities for which the taxpayer is personally liable). The at-risk rules apply to S corporation shareholders rather than at the corporate level, with the result that the deduction of S corporation losses is limited to the amount of a shareholder's at-risk investment. The application of the at-risk rules does not depend on the type of income reported by the S corporation, are not subject to any elections made by S corporation shareholders, and are applied without regard to the S corporation's ratio of debt to equity.

147. (d) The requirement is to determine the item that may be deducted by an S corporation. Items having no special tax characteristics can be netted together in the computation of the S corporation's ordinary income or loss, with only the net amount passed through to shareholders. Thus, only ordinary items (e.g., amortization of organizational expenditures) can be deducted by an S corporation. Answer (a) is incorrect because foreign income taxes must be separately passed through to shareholders so that the shareholders can individually elect to treat the payment of foreign income taxes as a deduction or as a credit. Answer (b) is incorrect because a net Sec. 1231 loss must be separately passed through to shareholders so that the Sec. 1231 netting process can take place at the shareholder level. Answer (c) is incorrect because investment interest expense must be separately passed through to shareholders so the deduction limitation (i.e., limited to net investment income) can be applied at the shareholder level.

148. (d) The requirement is to determine the correct statement regarding an S corporation's Accumulated Adjustments Account (AAA). An S corporation that has accumulated earnings and profits must maintain an AAA. The AAA represents the cumulative balance of all items of the undistributed net income and deductions for S corporation years beginning after 1982. The AAA is generally increased by all income items and is decreased by distributions and all loss and deduction items except no adjustment is made for tax-exempt income and related expenses, and no adjustment is made for federal income taxes attributable to a taxable year in which the corporation was a C corporation. The payment of federal income taxes attributable to a C corporation year would decrease an S corporation's accumulated earnings and profits (AEP). Note that the amounts represented in the AAA differ from AEP. A positive AEP balance represents earnings and profits accumulated in C corporation years that have never been taxed to shareholders. A positive AAA balance represents income from S corporation years that has already been taxed to shareholders but not yet distributed. An S corporation will not generate any earnings and profits for taxable years beginning after 1982.

149. (b) The requirement is to determine the due date of a calendar-year S corporation's tax return. An S corporation must file its federal income tax return (Form 1120-S) by the 15th day of the third month following the close of its taxable year. Thus, a calendar-year S corporation must file its tax return by March 15, if an automatic six-month extension of time is not requested.

150. (c) The requirement is to determine the item for which an S corporation is not permitted a deduction. Compensation of officers, interest paid to nonshareholders, and employee benefits for nonshareholders are deductible by an S corporation in computing its ordinary income or loss. However, charitable contributions, since they are subject to percentage limitations at the shareholder level, must be separately stated and are not deductible in computing an S corporation's ordinary income or loss.

151. (d) For tax years beginning after December 31, 2004, an S corporation may have as many as 100 shareholders. However, an S corporation cannot have both common and preferred stock outstanding because an S corporation is limited to a single class of stock. Similarly, a partnership is not permitted to be a shareholder in an S corporation because all S corporation shareholders must be individuals, estates, or certain trusts. Additionally, an S corporation cannot have a nonresident alien as a shareholder.

152. (a) The requirement is to determine which is **not** a requirement for a corporation to elect S corporation status.

An S corporation must generally have only one class of stock, be a domestic corporation, and confine shareholders to individuals, estates, and certain trusts. An S corporation need **not** be a member of a controlled group.

153. (b) The requirement is to determine the amount of loss from an S corporation that can be deducted by each of two equal shareholders. An S corporation loss is passed through to shareholders and is deductible to the extent of a shareholder's basis for stock plus the basis for any debt owed the shareholder by the corporation. Here, each shareholder's allocated loss of $45,000 ($90,000 ÷ 2) is deductible to the extent of stock basis of $5,000 plus debt basis of $15,000, or $20,000. The remainder of the loss ($25,000 for each shareholder) can be carried forward indefinitely by each shareholder and deducted when there is basis to absorb it.

I.   Corporate Reorganizations

154. (b) The requirement is to determine the correct statement regarding King Corp.'s acquisition of 90% of Jaxson Corp.'s voting common stock solely in exchange for 50% of King Corp.'s voting common stock. The acquisition by one corporation, in exchange **solely** for part of its voting stock, of stock of another corporation qualifies as a tax-free type B reorganization if immediately after the acquisition, the acquiring corporation is in control of the acquired corporation. The term **control** means the ownership of at least 80% of the acquired corporation's stock. Since King Corp. will use solely its voting stock to acquire 90% of Jaxson Corp. the acquisition will qualify as a tax-free type B reorganization. Answer (c) is incorrect because there is no requirement concerning the minimum percentage of King Corp. stock that must be used. Answer (d) is incorrect because a type B reorganization involves the acquisition of stock, not assets.

155. (a) The requirement is to determine whether a qualifying reorganization is tax-free to the corporations and their shareholders. Corporate reorganizations are generally nontaxable. As a result, a corporation will not recognize gain or loss on the transfer of its assets, and shareholders do not recognize gain or loss when they exchange stock and securities in parties to the reorganization. Here, Ace and Bate combine and form Carr, the only surviving corporation. This qualifies as a consolidation (Type A reorganization) and is tax-free to Ace and Bate on the transfer of their assets to Carr, and also is tax-free to the shareholders when they exchange their Ace and Bate stock for Carr stock. Similarly, the reorganization is tax-free to Carr when it issues its shares to acquire the Ace and Bate assets.

156. (c) The requirement is to determine whether the statements are applicable to type B reorganizations. In a type B reorganization, the acquiring corporation must use solely voting stock to acquire control of the target corporation immediately after the acquisition. The stock that is used to make the acquisition can be solely voting stock of the acquiring corporation, or solely voting stock of the parent corporation that is in control of the acquiring corporation, but not both. If a subsidiary uses its parent's stock to make the acquisition, the target corporation becomes a second-tier subsidiary of the parent corporation.

157. (d) The requirement is to determine Gow's recognized gain resulting from the exchange of Lad Corp. stock for Rook Corp. stock pursuant to a plan of corporate reorganization. No gain or loss is recognized to a shareholder if stock in one party to a reorganization (Lad Corp.) is exchanged **solely** for stock in another corporation (Rook Corp.) that is a party to the reorganization.

158. (a) The requirement is to determine the item that is defined in the Internal Revenue Code as a corporate reorganization. Corporate reorganizations generally receive nonrecognition treatment. Sec. 368 of the Internal Revenue Code defines seven types of reorganization, one of which is listed. An "F" reorganization is a mere change in identity, form, or place of organization of one corporation. A stock redemption is not a reorganization but instead results in dividend treatment or qualifies for exchange treatment. A change of depreciation method or inventory method is a change of an accounting method.

159. (c) The requirement is to determine the correct statement concerning corporate reorganizations. Answer (b) is incorrect because the reorganization provisions do provide for tax-free treatment for certain corporate transactions. Specifically, shareholders will not recognize gain or loss when they exchange stock or securities in a corporation that is a party to a reorganization solely for stock or securities in such corporation, or in another corporation that is also a party to the reorganization. Thus, securities in corporations not parties to the reorganization are always treated as "boot." Answer (d) is incorrect because the term "a party to the reorganization" includes a corporation resulting from the reorganization (i.e., the consolidated company). Answer (a) is incorrect because a mere change in identity, form, or place of organization of one corporation qualifies as a Type F reorganization.

160. (a) The requirement is to determine which is not a corporate reorganization. A corporate reorganization is specifically defined in Sec. 368 of the Internal Revenue Code. Sec. 368 defines seven types of reorganization, of which 3 are present in this item: Type A, a statutory merger; Type E, a recapitalization; and, Type F, a mere change in identity, form, or place of organization. Answer (a), a stock redemption, is the correct answer because it is not a reorganization as defined by Sec. 368 of the Code.

161. (a) The requirement is to determine the amount of Claudio's net operating loss (NOL) carryover that can be used to offset Stellar's 2008 taxable income. The amount of Claudio's NOL ($270,000) that can be utilized by Stellar for 2008 is limited by Sec. 381 to the taxable income of Stellar for its full taxable year (before a NOL deduction) multiplied by the fraction

$$\frac{\text{Days after acquisition date}}{\text{Total days in the tax table year}}$$

This limitation is 184/366 days × $360,000 = $180,984. Additionally, since there was a more than fifty percentage point change in the ownership of Claudio, Sec. 382 limits the amount of Claudio's NOL carryover that can be utilized by Stellar to the fair market value of Claudio multiplied by the federal long-term tax-exempt rate. $1,500,000 × 3% = $45,000. However, for purposes of applying this limitation for the year of acquisition, the limitation amount is only available to the extent allocable to the days in Stellar's taxable year after the acquisition date.

$$\$45,000 \times 184/366 \text{ days} = \$22,685$$

The remainder of Claudio's NOL ($270,000 − $22,685 = $247,315) can be carried forward and used to offset Stellar's taxable income (subject to the Sec. 382 limitation) in carryforward years.

162. (a) The requirement is to determine the recognized gain to be reported by Mueller on the exchange of her Disco bond for Disco preferred stock. The issuance by Disco Corporation of its preferred stock in exchange for its bonds is a nontaxable "Type E" reorganization (i.e., a recapitalization). Since Mueller did not receive any boot, no part of her $400 realized gain is recognized.

163. (b) The requirement is to determine the amount of recognized gain in a recapitalization. Since a recapitalization is a reorganization, a realized gain will be recognized to the extent that consideration other than stock or securities is received, including the FMV of an excess principal amount of securities received over the principal amount of securities surrendered. Since no securities were surrendered, the entire $10,500 FMV of the securities received by Roberts is treated as boot. However, in this case, Roberts recognized gain is limited to her realized gain ($91,000 + $10,500) − $95,000 = $6,500.

SOLUTIONS TO SIMULATION PROBLEMS

Simulation Problem 1

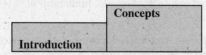

1. A corporation whose income was derived solely from dividends, interest, and royalties, and during the last six months of its year more than 50% of the value of its outstanding stock is owned by five or fewer individuals.

2. The basis used to determine gain on sale of property that was received as a gift.

3. The trade-in of production machinery for new production machinery by a corporation, when the corporation pays additional cash.

4. An unmarried individual whose filing status enables the taxpayer to use a set of income tax rates that are lower than those applicable to other unmarried individuals, but are higher than those applicable to married persons filing a joint return.

5. If income is unqualifiedly available, it will be subject to the income tax even though it is not physically in the taxpayer's possession.

6. A special tax imposed on corporations that accumulate their earnings beyond the reasonable needs of the business.

7. The classification of income from interest, dividends, annuities, and certain royalties.

8. The classification of depreciable assets and real estate used in a trade or business and held for more than one year.

9. This deduction attempts to mitigate the triple taxation that would occur if one corporation paid dividends to a corporate shareholder who, in turn, distributed such amounts to its individual shareholders.

10. Sale of property to a corporation by a shareholder for a selling price that is in excess of the property's fair market value.

	(A)	(B)	(C)	(D)	(E)	(F)	(G)	(H)	(I)	(J)	(K)	(L)	(M)	(N)	(O)	(P)	(Q)	(R)	(S)	(T)	(U)	(V)	(W)	(X)	(Y)	(Z)
1.	○	○	○	○	○	○	○	○	○	○	○	○	○	○	○	○	○	●	○	○	○	○	○	○	○	○
2.	○	○	○	○	○	○	○	○	○	○	○	○	○	○	○	○	○	○	○	○	○	○	○	○	○	●
3.	○	○	○	○	○	○	○	○	○	○	○	○	○	○	○	●	○	○	○	○	○	○	○	○	○	○
4.	○	○	○	○	○	○	○	○	○	○	○	○	○	○	●	○	○	○	○	○	○	○	○	○	○	○
5.	○	○	○	○	○	○	●	○	○	○	○	○	○	○	○	○	○	○	○	○	○	○	○	○	○	○
6.	●	○	○	○	○	○	○	○	○	○	○	○	○	○	○	○	○	○	○	○	○	○	○	○	○	○
7.	○	○	○	○	○	○	○	○	○	○	○	○	○	○	○	○	○	○	○	○	●	○	○	○	○	○
8.	○	○	○	○	○	○	○	○	○	○	○	○	○	○	○	○	○	○	○	○	○	○	●	○	○	○
9.	○	○	○	○	○	○	○	●	○	○	○	○	○	○	○	○	○	○	○	○	○	○	○	○	○	○
10.	○	○	○	○	○	●	○	○	○	○	○	○	○	○	○	○	○	○	○	○	○	○	○	○	○	○

Explanation of solutions

1. **(R)** To be classified as a personal holding company, a corporation must meet two requirements: (1) the corporation must receive at least 60% of its adjusted ordinary gross income as "personal holding company income" such as dividends, interest, rents, royalties, and other passive income; and (2) the corporation must have more than 50% of the value of its outstanding stock directly or indirectly owned by five or fewer individuals during any time in the last half of the tax year.

2. **(Z)** The transferred basis, equal to the basis of the donor plus any gift tax paid attributable to the net appreciation in the value of the gift, is the basis used to determine gain on sale of property that was received as a gift.

3. **(P)** A like-kind exchange, the exchange of business or investment property for property of a like-kind, qualifies as a non-taxable exchange. Thus, the exchange of production machinery for new production machinery when boot (money) is given is a nontaxable exchange.

4. **(O)** Head of household filing status applies to unmarried persons not qualifying for surviving spouse status who maintain a household for more than one-half of the taxable year for a dependent. The tax rates applicable to the head of household status are lower than those applicable to individuals filing as single, but are higher than rates applicable to married individuals filing a joint return.

5. **(G)** Under the doctrine of constructive receipt, income is includable in gross income and subject to income tax for the taxable year in which that income is made unqualifiedly available to the taxpayer without restriction, even though not physically in the taxpayer's possession.

6. **(A)** Corporations may be subject to an accumulated earnings tax, in addition to regular income tax, if a corporation accumulates earnings beyond reasonable business needs in order to avoid shareholder tax on dividend distributions.

7. **(U)** Portfolio income is defined as income from interest, dividends, annuities, and certain royalties.

8. **(W)** Section 1231 assets include depreciable assets and real estate used in a trade or business and held for more than one year.

9. **(J)** The dividends received deduction was enacted by Congress to mitigate the triple taxation that occurs when one corporation pays dividends to a corporate stockholder who, in turn, distributes such amounts to its individual stockholders.

10. **(F)** A constructive dividend results when a shareholder is considered to have received a dividend from a corporation, although the corporation did not specifically declare a dividend. This situation may occur when a shareholder/employee receives an excessive salary from a corporation, when there is a loan to a shareholder where there is no intent to repay the amount loaned, or when a corporation purchases shareholder property for an amount in excess of the property's fair market value. Constructive dividends often result when a transaction between a shareholder and corporation is not an arm's-length transaction.

Simulation Problem 2

Situation	Tax Return Amount		Schedule M-1	Research	Communication

1. **($20,000)** Interest on funds borrowed for working capital is deductible. However, interest incurred on borrowed funds to purchase municipal bonds is not deductible because the resulting income is exempt from tax.

2. **($20,000)** Interest earned on corporate bonds must be included in gross income. However, interest earned on municipal bonds is excluded.

3. **($8,000)** For organizational expenditures incurred or paid after October 22, 2004, a corporation may elect to deduct up to $5,000 for the tax year in which the corporation begins business. This $5,000 amount must be reduced by the amount by which organizational expenditures exceed $50,000. Remaining expenditures are deducted ratably over the 180-month period beginning with the month in which the corporation begins business. Aviator's qualifying expenditures include the legal fees and state incorporation fees, which total $50,000. However, the $15,000 commission for selling stock is neither deductible nor amortizable. The amount of Aviator's deduction for organizational expenditures for 2007 is $5,000 + ($45,000 × 12/180) = $8,000.

4. **($20,000)** All of the capital gains would be included in Aviator's gross income.

5. **($20,000)** Corporate capital losses can only be deducted to the extent of capital gains. Therefore, only $20,000 of capital losses can be deducted on the Aviator, Inc. tax return. Since this is Aviator's first year of existence, the excess of capital losses over capital gains ($10,000) will then be carried forward five years as a short-term capital loss, to offset capital gains.

6. **($35,000)** The dividends received deduction will be based on 70% of its dividends received, since Aviator, Inc. owns less than 20% of the dividend-paying corporation.

7. **($38,000)** A charitable contributions deduction is limited to a maximum of 10% of taxable income before the dividends received deduction and a charitable contributions deduction. Therefore, taxable income before these deductions needs to be calculated to determine the maximum allowable deduction. Taxable income is computed as follows:

Sales	$2,000,000
Dividends	50,000
Interest revenue	20,000
Gains on the sale of stock	20,000
Cost of goods sold	(1,000,000)
Salaries and wages	(400,000)
Depreciation	(260,000)
Losses on the sale of stock	(20,000)
Organizational expenditures	(8,000)
Interest expense	(20,000)
	$ 382,000

The charitable contributions deduction will be limited to $38,200 ($382,000 × 10%). The excess not allowed ($40,000 − $38,200 = $1,800) will be carried forward for up to five years.

Situation	Tax Return Amount	Schedule M-1		Research	Communication

Schedule M-1 of Form 1120 is used to reconcile a corporate taxpayer's income reported per books with income reported on the tax return. Generally, items of income or deduction whose book and tax treatment differ, result in Schedule M-1 items. However, since Schedule M-1 reconciles book income to taxable income before special deductions (line 28, page 1), the dividends received deduction and net operating loss deduction which are special deductions will never be reconciling items on Schedule M-1.

4. The grantor (or nonadverse party) can deal with trust property in a nonfiduciary capacity (e.g., purchase trust assets for less than adequate consideration or borrow trust property at below market rate).

5. The grantor (or grantor's spouse) or nonadverse party controls the beneficial enjoyment of the trust (e.g., ability to change beneficiaries).

G. Termination of Estate or Trust

1. An estate or trust is not entitled to a personal exemption on its final return.

2. Any unused carryovers (e.g., NOL or capital loss) are passed through to beneficiaries for use on their individual tax returns.

3. Any excess deductions for its final year are passed through to beneficiaries and can be deducted as miscellaneous itemized deductions.

IV. TAX RETURN PREPARERS

A. Preparer—an individual who prepares for compensation, or who employs one or more persons to prepare for compensation, any federal tax return, or a substantial portion thereof, including income, employment, excise, exempt organization, gift, and estate tax returns.

1. Preparer need **not** be enrolled to practice before the Internal Revenue Service.

2. Compensation—must be received and can be implied or explicit (e.g., accountant who prepares individual return of the president of a company, for which he performs the audit, for no additional fee as part of a prior agreement **has** been compensated [implied])

3. The performance of the following acts will not classify a person as a preparer:

   a. Preparation of a return for a friend, relative or neighbor free of charge even though the person completing the return receives a gift of gratitude from the taxpayer;

   b. The furnishing of typing, reproducing or other mechanical assistance in preparing a return; and

   c. Preparation by an employee of a return for his or her employer, or an officer of the employer, or for another employee if he or she is regularly employed by that employer.

B. AICPA Statement on Standards for Tax Services

1. **Tax Return Positions**

   a. With respect to tax return positions, a CPA

      (1) Should not recommend a position unless there is a **realistic possibility of it being sustained** administratively or judicially on its merits if challenged.

      (2) Should not prepare or sign a tax return if the CPA knows the return takes a position that the CPA could not recommend under a. above.

      (3) Notwithstanding a. and b., a CPA may recommend a position that is not frivolous so long as the position is adequately disclosed on the return or claim for refund. A frivolous position is one which is knowingly advanced in bad faith and is patently improper (e.g., a return position that is contrary to a clear, unambiguous statute).

      (4) Should advise the client of the potential penalty consequences of any recommended tax position.

   b. A CPA should not recommend a tax position that exploits the IRS audit process, or serves as a mere arguing position advanced solely to obtain leverage in bargaining with the IRS.

   c. A CPA has both the right and the responsibility to be an advocate for the client.

2. **Realistic Possibility Standard**

   a. The CPA should consider the weight of each authority (e.g., Code, Regs., court decisions, well-reasoned treaties, article in professional tax publications, etc.) in determining whether this standard is met, and may rely on well-reasoned treatises and articles in recognized professional tax publications.

   b. Realistic possibility of success may require as much as a **one-third likelihood** of success.

   c. The realistic possibility standard is less stringent than the "more likely than not" and "substantial authority" standards, but is more strict than the "reasonable basis" standard.

3. **Answers to Questions on Returns**

   a. A CPA should make a reasonable effort to obtain from the client and provide appropriate answers to all questions on a tax return before signing as preparer.

   b. When reasonable grounds for omitting an answer exist, the CPA is not required to provide an explanation on the return of the reason for omission. Reasonable grounds for omitting an answer include

   (1) Information is not readily available and the answer is not significant in terms of taxable income or tax liability.

   (2) Uncertainty as to meaning of question.

   (3) Answer is voluminous and return states that data will be supplied upon examination.

4. **Procedural Aspects of Preparing Returns**

   a. A CPA may in good faith rely without verification upon information furnished by the client or by third parties, and is not required to audit, examine, or review books, records, or documents in order to independently verify the taxpayer's information.

   (1) However, the CPA should not ignore implications of information furnished and should make reasonable inquires if information appears incorrect, incomplete, or inconsistent.

   (2) When feasible, the CPA should refer to the client's past returns.

   b. Where the IRS imposes a condition for deductibility or other treatment of an item (e.g., requires supporting documentation), the CPA should make appropriate inquiries to determine whether the condition for deductibility has been met.

   c. When preparing a tax return, a CPA should consider information known from the tax return of another client if that information is relevant to the return being prepared, and such consideration does not violate any rule regarding confidentiality.

5. **Use of Estimates**

   a. Where data is missing (e.g., result of a fire, computer failure), estimates of the missing data may be made by the client.

   b. A CPA may prepare a tax return using estimates if it is impracticable to obtain exact data, and the estimated amounts are reasonable.

   c. An estimate should not imply greater accuracy than actually exists (e.g., estimate $1,000 rather than $999.32).

6. **Departure from Position Previously Concluded in an IRS Proceeding or Court Decision**

   a. Unless the taxpayer is bound to a specified treatment in the later year, such as by a formal closing agreement, the treatment of an item as part of concluding an IRS proceeding or as part of a court decision in a prior year, does not restrict the CPA from recommending a different tax treatment in a later year's return.

   b. Court decisions, rulings, or other authorities more favorable to the taxpayer's current position may have developed since the prior proceeding was concluded or the prior court decision was rendered.

7. **Knowledge of Error: Return Preparation**

   a. The term "error" as used here includes any position, omission, or method of accounting that, at the time the return is filed, fails to meet the standards as outlined in 1. and 2. above. An error does not include an item that has an insignificant effect on the client's tax liability.

   b. A CPA should inform a client promptly upon becoming aware of a material error in a previously filed return or upon becoming aware of a client's failure to file a required return. A CPA

   (1) Should recommend (either orally or in writing) measures to be taken.

   (2) Is not obligated to inform the IRS of the error, and may not do so without the client's permission, except where required by law.

   c. If the CPA is requested to prepare the client's current return, and the client has not taken appropriate action to correct an error in a prior year's return, the CPA should consider whether to continue a professional relationship with the client or withdraw.

8. **Knowledge of Error: Administrative Proceedings**

   a. When a CPA is representing a client in an IRS proceeding (e.g., examination, appellate confer-ence) with respect to a return that contains an error of which the CPA has become aware, the CPA should promptly inform the client and recommend measures to be taken.

   b. The CPA should request the client's permission to disclose the error to the IRS, and lacking such permission, should consider whether to withdraw from representing the client.

9. **Form and Content of Advice to Clients**

   a. No standard format is required in communicating written or oral advice to a client.

   b. Written, rather than oral, communications are recommended for important, unusual, or compli-cated transactions.

   c. A CPA may choose to communicate with a client when subsequent developments affect previous advice. Such communication is only required when the CPA undertakes this obligation by spe-cific agreement with the client.

C. Preparer Penalties

1. A preparer is subject to a penalty equal to the greater of $1,000, or 50% of the income derived (or to be derived) by the preparer with respect to the return or refund claim if any part of an understatement of liability with respect to the return or claim is due to an undisclosed position on the return or refund claim for which there is *not* a reasonable belief that the position would **more likely than not** be sus-tained on its merits.

   a. The *more likely than not* standard requires a more than 50% probability of being sustained on its merits, in contrast to the *realistic possibility of success* standard which requires a one-third likeli-hood of success.

   b. The penalty can be avoided by

      (1) An adequate disclosure of the questionable position on the return or refund claim, and

      (2) A showing that there was a reasonable basis for the position. The reasonable basis standard may require at least a 20% probability of being sustained on its merits.

   c. The penalty can also be avoided if the preparer can show there was a reasonable cause for the understatement and that the return preparer acted in good faith.

2. If any part of an understatement of liability with respect to a return or refund claim is due (1) to a will-ful attempt to understate tax liability by a return preparer with respect to the return or claim, or (2) to any reckless or intentional disregard of rules or regulations, the preparer is subject to a penalty equal to the greater of $5,000, or 50% of the income derived (or to be derived) by the preparer with respect to the return or refund claim.

   a. This penalty is reduced by the penalty paid in 1. above.

   b. Rules and regulations include the Internal Revenue Code, Treasury Regulations, and Revenue Rulings.

3. Additional penalties may be imposed on preparers if they fail to fulfill the following requirements (unless failure is due to reasonable cause):

   a. Preparer must sign returns done for compensation.

   b. Preparer must provide a copy of the return or refund claim to the taxpayer no later than when the preparer presents a copy of the return to the taxpayer for signing.

   c. Returns and claims for refund must contain the social security number of preparer and identifica-tion number of preparer's employer or partnership (if any).

   d. Preparer must either keep a list of those for whom returns were filed with specified information, or copies of the actual returns, for three years.

   e. Employers of return preparers must retain a listing of return preparers and place of employment for three years.

   f. Preparer must not endorse or negotiate a refund check issued to a taxpayer.

   g. Preparer must not disclose information furnished in connection with the preparation of a tax re-turn, unless for quality or peer review, or under an administrative order by a regulatory agency.

MULTIPLE-CHOICE QUESTIONS (1-59)

1. Steve and Kay Briar, US citizens, were married for the entire 2008 calendar year. In 2008, Steve gave a $30,000 cash gift to his sister. The Briars made no other gifts in 2008. They each signed a timely election to treat the $30,000 gift as made one-half by each spouse. Disregarding the applicable credit and estate tax consequences, what amount of the 2008 gift is taxable to the Briars?
    a. $20,000
    b. $8,000
    c. $6,000
    d. $0

2. In 2008, Sayers, who is single, gave an outright gift of $50,000 to a friend, Johnson, who needed the money to pay medical expenses. In filing the 2008 gift tax return, Sayers was entitled to a maximum exclusion of
    a. $0
    b. $11,000
    c. $12,000
    d. $50,000

3. During 2008, Blake transferred a corporate bond with a face amount and fair market value of $20,000 to a trust for the benefit of her sixteen-year old child. Annual interest on this bond is $2,000, which is to be accumulated in the trust and distributed to the child on reaching the age of twenty-one. The bond is then to be distributed to the donor or her successor-in-interest in liquidation of the trust. Present value of the total interest to be received by the child is $8,710. The amount of the gift that is excludable from taxable gifts is
    a. $20,000
    b. $12,000
    c. $ 8,710
    d. $0

4. Under the unified rate schedule for 2008,
    a.   Lifetime taxable gifts are taxed on a noncumulative basis.
    b.   Transfers at death are taxed on a noncumulative basis.
    c.   Lifetime taxable gifts and transfers at death are taxed on a cumulative basis.
    d.   The gift tax rates are 5% higher than the estate tax rates.

5. Which of the following requires filing a gift tax return, if the transfer exceeds the available annual gift tax exclusion?
    a.   Medical expenses paid directly to a physician on behalf of an individual unrelated to the donor.
    b.   Tuition paid directly to an accredited university on behalf of an individual unrelated to the donor.
    c.   Payments for college books, supplies, and dormitory fees on behalf of an individual unrelated to the donor.
    d.   Campaign expenses paid to a political organization.

6. On July 1, 2008, Vega made a transfer by gift in an amount sufficient to require the filing of a gift tax return. Vega was still alive in 2009. If Vega did **not** request an extension of time for filing the 2008 gift tax return, the due date for filing was
    a.   March 15, 2009.

    b.   April 15, 2009.
    c.   June 15, 2009.
    d.   June 30, 2009.

7. Jan, an unmarried individual, gave the following outright gifts in 2008:

Donee	Amount	Use by donee
Jones	$15,000	Down payment on house
Craig	13,000	College tuition
Kande	5,000	Vacation trip

Jan's 2008 exclusions for gift tax purposes should total
    a. $30,000
    b. $29,000
    c. $27,000
    d. $18,000

8. When Jim and Nina became engaged in April 2008, Jim gave Nina a ring that had a fair market value of $50,000. After their wedding in July 2008, Jim gave Nina $75,000 in cash so that Nina could have her own bank account. Both Jim and Nina are US citizens. What was the amount of Jim's 2008 marital deduction?
    a. $ 63,000
    b. $ 75,000
    c. $113,000
    d. $125,000

9. Raff created a joint bank account for himself and his friend's son, Dave. There is a gift to Dave when
    a.   Raff creates the account.
    b.   Raff dies.
    c.   Dave draws on the account for his own benefit.
    d.   Dave is notified by Raff that the account has been created.

10. Fred and Ethel (brother and sister), residents of a non-community property state, own unimproved land that they hold in joint tenancy with rights of survivorship. The land cost $100,000 of which Ethel paid $80,000 and Fred paid $20,000. Ethel died during 2008 when the land was worth $300,000, and $240,000 was included in Ethel's gross estate. What is Fred's basis for the property after Ethel's death?
    a. $140,000
    b. $240,000
    c. $260,000
    d. $300,000

11. Bell, a cash-basis calendar-year taxpayer, died on June 1, 2008. In 2008, prior to her death, Bell incurred $2,000 in medical expenses. The executor of the estate paid the medical expenses, which were a claim against the estate, on July 1, 2008. If the executor files the appropriate waiver, the medical expenses are deductible on
    a.   The estate tax return.
    b.   Bell's final income tax return.
    c.   The estate income tax return.
    d.   The executor's income tax return.

12. If the executor of a decedent's estate elects the alternate valuation date and none of the property included in the gross estate has been sold or distributed, the estate assets must be valued as of how many months after the decedent's death?
    a.   12
    b.   9
    c.   6
    d.   3

13. What amount of a decedent's taxable estate is effectively tax-free if the maximum applicable estate tax credit is taken during 2008?
   a. $ 675,000
   b. $1,000,000
   c. $2,000,000
   d. $3,500,000

14. Which of the following credits may be offset against the gross estate tax to determine the net estate tax of a US citizen dying during 2008?

	Applicable credit	Credit for gift taxes paid on gifts made after 1976
a.	Yes	Yes
b.	No	No
c.	No	Yes
d.	Yes	No

15. Fred and Amy Kehl, both US citizens, are married. All of their real and personal property is owned by them as tenants by the entirety or as joint tenants with right of survivorship. The gross estate of the first spouse to die
   a. Includes 50% of the value of all property owned by the couple, regardless of which spouse furnished the original consideration.
   b. Includes only the property that had been acquired with the funds of the deceased spouse.
   c. Is governed by the federal statutory provisions relating to jointly held property, rather than by the decedent's interest in community property vested by state law, if the Kehls reside in a community property state.
   d. Includes one-third of the value of all real estate owned by the Kehls, as the dower right in the case of the wife or curtesy right in the case of the husband.

16. In connection with a "buy-sell" agreement funded by a cross-purchase insurance arrangement, business associate Adam bought a policy on Burr's life to finance the purchase of Burr's interest. Adam, the beneficiary, paid the premiums and retained all incidents of ownership. On the death of Burr, the insurance proceeds will be
   a. Includible in Burr's gross estate, if Burr owns 50% or more of the stock of the corporation.
   b. Includible in Burr's gross estate only if Burr had purchased a similar policy on Adam's life at the same time and for the same purpose.
   c. Includible in Burr's gross estate, if Adam has the right to veto Burr's power to borrow on the policy that Burr owns on Adam's life.
   d. Excludible from Burr's gross estate.

17. Following are the fair market values of Wald's assets at the date of death:

Personal effects and jewelry	$450,000
Land bought by Wald with Wald's funds five	
years prior to death and held with Wald's sister	
as joint tenants with right of survivorship	1,800,000

The executor of Wald's estate did not elect the alternate valuation date. The amount includible as Wald's gross estate in the federal estate tax return is
   a. $ 450,000
   b. $1,350,000
   c. $1,800,000
   d. $2,250,000

18. Which one of the following is a valid deduction from a decedent's gross estate?
   a. Foreign death taxes.
   b. Income tax paid on income earned and received after the decedent's death.
   c. Federal estate taxes.
   d. Unpaid income taxes on income received by the decedent before death.

19. Eng and Lew, both US citizens, died in 2008. Eng made taxable lifetime gifts of $100,000 that are **not** included in Eng's gross estate. Lew made no lifetime gifts. At the dates of death, Eng's gross estate was $1,600,000, and Lew's gross estate was $1,800,000. A federal estate tax return must be filed for

	Eng	Lew
a.	No	No
b.	No	Yes
c.	Yes	No
d.	Yes	Yes

20. With regard to the federal estate tax, the alternate valuation date
   a. Is required to be used if the fair market value of the estate's assets has increased since the decedent's date of death.
   b. If elected on the first return filed for the estate, may be revoked in an amended return provided that the first return was filed on time.
   c. Must be used for valuation of the estate's liabilities if such date is used for valuation of the estate's assets.
   d. Can be elected only if its use decreases both the value of the gross estate and the estate tax liability.

21. Proceeds of a life insurance policy payable to the estate's executor, as the estate's representative, are
   a. Includible in the decedent's gross estate only if the premiums had been paid by the insured.
   b. Includible in the decedent's gross estate only if the policy was taken out within three years of the insured's death under the "contemplation of death" rule.
   c. Always includible in the decedent's gross estate.
   d. Never includible in the decedent's gross estate.

22. Ross, a calendar-year, cash-basis taxpayer who died in June 2008, was entitled to receive a $10,000 accounting fee that had not been collected before the date of death. The executor of Ross' estate collected the full $10,000 in July 2008. This $10,000 should appear in
   a. Only the decedent's final individual income tax return.
   b. Only the estate's fiduciary income tax return.
   c. Only the estate tax return.
   d. Both the fiduciary income tax return and the estate tax return.

Items 23 and 24 are based on the following data:

   Alan Curtis, a US citizen, died on March 1, 2008, leaving an adjusted gross estate with a fair market value of $2,600,000 at the date of death. Under the terms of Alan's will, $900,000 was bequeathed outright to his widow, free of all estate and inheritance taxes. The remainder of Alan's estate was left to his mother. Alan made no taxable gifts during his lifetime.

23. Disregarding extensions of time for filing, within how many months after the date of Alan's death is the federal estate tax return due?
- a. 2 1/2
- b. 3 1/2
- c. 9
- d. 12

24. In computing the taxable estate, the executor of Alan's estate should claim a marital deduction of
- a. $ 450,000
- b. $ 780,800
- c. $ 900,000
- d. $1,300,000

25. In 2003, Edwin Ryan bought 100 shares of a listed stock for $5,000. In June 2008, when the stock's fair market value was $7,000, Edwin gave this stock to his sister, Lynn. No gift tax was paid. Lynn died in October 2008, bequeathing this stock to Edwin, when the stock's fair market value was $9,000. Lynn's executor did not elect the alternate valuation. What is Edwin's basis for this stock after he inherits it from Lynn's estate?
- a. $0
- b. $5,000
- c. $7,000
- d. $9,000

26. The generation-skipping transfer tax is imposed
- a. Instead of the gift tax.
- b. Instead of the estate tax.
- c. At the highest tax rate under the unified transfer tax rate schedule.
- d. When an individual makes a gift to a grandparent.

27. Under the terms of the will of Melvin Crane, $10,000 a year is to be paid to his widow and $5,000 a year is to be paid to his daughter out of the estate's income during the period of estate administration. No charitable contributions are made by the estate. During 2008, the estate made the required distributions to Crane's widow and daughter and for the entire year the estate's distributable net income was $12,000. What amount of the $10,000 distribution received from the estate must Crane's widow include in her gross income for 2008?
- a. $0
- b. $ 4,000
- c. $ 8,000
- d. $10,000

Items 28 and 29 are based on the following:

Lyon, a cash-basis taxpayer, died on January 15, 2008. In 2008, the estate executor made the required periodic distribution of $9,000 from estate income to Lyon's sole heir. The following pertains to the estate's income and disbursements in 2008:

2008 Estate Income
$20,000   Taxable interest
10,000   Net long-term capital gains allocable to corpus

2008 Estate Disbursements
$5,000   Administrative expenses attributable to taxable income

28. For the 2008 calendar year, what was the estate's distributable net income (DNI)?
- a. $15,000
- b. $20,000
- c. $25,000

- d. $30,000

29. Lyon's executor does not intend to file an extension request for the estate fiduciary income tax return. By what date must the executor file the Form 1041, US Fiduciary Income Tax Return, for the estate's 2008 calendar year?
- a. March 15, 2009.
- b. April 15, 2009.
- c. June 15, 2009.
- d. September 15, 2009.

30. A distribution from estate income, that was **currently** required, was made to the estate's sole beneficiary during its calendar year. The maximum amount of the distribution to be included in the beneficiary's gross income is limited to the estate's
- a. Capital gain income.
- b. Ordinary gross income.
- c. Distributable net income.
- d. Net investment income.

31. A distribution to an estate's sole beneficiary for the 2008 calendar year equaled $15,000, the amount currently required to be distributed by the will. The estate's 2008 records were as follows:

Estate income
$40,000   Taxable interest

Estate disbursements
$34,000   Expenses attributable to taxable interest

What amount of the distribution was taxable to the beneficiary?
- a. $40,000
- b. $15,000
- c. $ 6,000
- d. $0

32. With regard to estimated income tax, estates
- a. Must make quarterly estimated tax payments starting no later than the second quarter following the one in which the estate was established.
- b. Are exempt from paying estimated tax during the estate's first two taxable years.
- c. Must make quarterly estimated tax payments only if the estate's income is required to be distributed currently.
- d. Are not required to make payments of estimated tax.

33. A complex trust is a trust that
- a. Must distribute income currently, but is prohibited from distributing principal during the taxable year.
- b. Invests only in corporate securities and is prohibited from engaging in short-term transactions.
- c. Permits accumulation of current income, provides for charitable contributions, or distributes principal during the taxable year.
- d. Is exempt from payment of income tax since the tax is paid by the beneficiaries.

34. The 2008 standard deduction for a trust or an estate in the fiduciary income tax return is
- a. $0
- b. $650
- c. $750
- d. $800

35. Which of the following fiduciary entities are required to use the calendar year as their taxable period for income tax purposes?

	Estates	*Trusts (except those that are tax exempt)*
a.	Yes	Yes
b.	No	No
c.	Yes	No
d.	No	Yes

36. Ordinary and necessary administration expenses paid by the fiduciary of an estate are deductible

a. Only on the fiduciary income tax return (Form 1041) and never on the federal estate tax return (Form 706).

b. Only on the federal estate tax return and never on the fiduciary income tax return.

c. On the fiduciary income tax return only if the estate tax deduction is waived for these expenses.

d. On both the fiduciary income tax return and on the estate tax return by adding a tax computed on the proportionate rates attributable to both returns.

37. An executor of a decedent's estate that has only US citizens as beneficiaries is required to file a fiduciary income tax return, if the estate's gross income for the year is at least

a. $ 400
b. $ 500
c. $ 600
d. $1,000

38. The charitable contribution deduction on an estate's fiduciary income tax return is allowable

a. If the decedent died intestate.

b. To the extent of the same adjusted gross income limitation as that on an individual income tax return.

c. Only if the decedent's will specifically provides for the contribution.

d. Subject to the 2% threshold on miscellaneous itemized deductions.

39. On January 1, 2008, Carlt created a $300,000 trust that provided his mother with a lifetime income interest starting on January 1, 2008, with the remainder interest to go to his son. Carlt expressly retained the power to revoke both the income interest and the remainder interest at any time. Who will be taxed on the trust's 2008 income?

a. Carlt's mother.
b. Carlt's son.
c. Carlt.
d. The trust.

40. Astor, a cash-basis taxpayer, died on February 3. During the year, the estate's executor made a distribution of $12,000 from estate income to Astor's sole heir and adopted a calendar year to determine the estate's taxable income. The following additional information pertains to the estate's income and disbursements for the year:

Estate income	
Taxable interest	$65,000
Net long-term capital gains allocable to corpus	5,000
Estate disbursements	
Administrative expenses attributable to taxable income	14,000
Charitable contributions from gross income to a public charity, made under the terms of the will	9,000

For the calendar year, what was the estate's distributable net income (DNI)?

a. $39,000
b. $42,000
c. $58,000
d. $65,000

41. For income tax purposes, the estate's initial taxable period for a decedent who died on October 24

a. May be either a calendar year, or a fiscal year beginning on the date of the decedent's death.

b. Must be a fiscal year beginning on the date of the decedent's death.

c. May be either a calendar year, or a fiscal year beginning on October 1 of the year of the decedent's death.

d. Must be a calendar year beginning on January 1 of the year of the decedent's death.

42. Which of the following acts constitute(s) grounds for a tax preparer penalty?

I. Without the taxpayer's consent, the tax preparer disclosed taxpayer income tax return information under an order from a state court.

II. At the taxpayer's suggestion, the tax preparer deducted the expenses of the taxpayers' personal domestic help as a business expense on the taxpayer's individual tax return.

a. I only.
b. II only.
c. Both I and II.
d. Neither I nor II.

43. Vee Corp. retained Water, CPA, to prepare its 2008 income tax return. During the engagement, Water discovered that Vee had failed to file its 2003 income tax return. What is Water's professional responsibility regarding Vee's unfiled 2003 income tax return?

a. Prepare Vee's 2003 income tax return and submit it to the IRS.

b. Advise Vee that the 2003 income tax return has not been filed and recommend that Vee ignore filing its 2003 return since the statute of limitations has passed.

c. Advise the IRS that Vee's 2003 income tax return has not been filed.

d. Consider withdrawing from preparation of Vee's 2008 income tax return until the error is corrected.

44. To avoid tax return preparer penalties for a return's understated tax liability due to an intentional disregard of the regulations, which of the following actions must a tax preparer take?

a. Audit the taxpayer's corresponding business operations.

b. Review the accuracy of the taxpayer's books and records.

c. Make reasonable inquiries if the taxpayer's information is incomplete.

d. Examine the taxpayer's supporting documents.

45. Kopel was engaged to prepare Raff's 2007 federal income tax return. During the tax preparation interview, Raff told Kopel that he paid $3,000 in property taxes in 2007. Actually, Raff's property taxes amounted to only $600. Based on Raff's word, Kopel deducted the $3,000 on Raff's return, resulting in an understatement of Raff's tax liability.

Kopel had no reason to believe that the information was incorrect. Kopel did not request underlying documentation and was reasonably satisfied by Raff's representation that Raff had adequate records to support the deduction. Which of the following statements is correct?

    a.   To avoid the preparer penalty for willful understatement of tax liability, Kopel was obligated to examine the underlying documentation for the deduction.

    b.   To avoid the preparer penalty for willful understatement of tax liability, Kopel would be required to obtain Raff's representation in writing.

    c.   Kopel is **not** subject to the preparer penalty for willful understatement of tax liability because the deduction that was claimed was more than 25% of the actual amount that should have been deducted.

    d.   Kopel is **not** subject to the preparer penalty for willful understatement of tax liability because Kopel was justified in relying on Raff's representation.

46. A penalty for understated corporate tax liability can be imposed on a tax preparer who fails to

    a.   Audit the corporate records.

    b.   Examine business operations.

    c.   Copy all underlying documents.

    d.   Make reasonable inquiries when taxpayer information appears incorrect.

47. A tax return preparer is subject to a penalty for knowingly or recklessly disclosing corporate tax return information, if the disclosure is made

    a.   To enable a third party to solicit business from the taxpayer.

    b.   To enable the tax processor to electronically compute the taxpayer's liability.

    c.   For peer review.

    d.   Under an administrative order by a state agency that registers tax return preparers.

48. A tax return preparer may disclose or use tax return information without the taxpayer's consent to

    a.   Facilitate a supplier's or lender's credit evaluation of the taxpayer.

    b.   Accommodate the request of a financial institution that needs to determine the amount of taxpayer's debt to it, to be forgiven.

    c.   Be evaluated by a quality or peer review.

    d.   Solicit additional nontax business.

49. Which, if any, of the following could result in penalties against an income tax return preparer?

  I. Knowing or reckless disclosure or use of tax information obtained in preparing a return.

 II. A willful attempt to understate any client's tax liability on a return or claim for refund.

    a.   Neither I nor II.

    b.   I only.

    c.   II only.

    d.   Both I and II.

50. Clark, a professional tax return preparer, prepared and signed a client's 2008 federal income tax return that resulted in a $600 refund. Which one of the following statements is correct with regard to an Internal Revenue Code penalty

Clark may be subject to for endorsing and cashing the client's refund check?

    a.   Clark will be subject to the penalty if Clark endorses and cashes the check.

    b.   Clark may endorse and cash the check, without penalty, if Clark is enrolled to practice before the Internal Revenue Service.

    c.   Clark may endorse and cash the check, without penalty, because the check is for less than $500.

    d.   Clark may endorse and cash the check, without penalty, if the amount does **not** exceed Clark's fee for preparation of the return.

51. A CPA who prepares clients' federal income tax returns for a fee must

    a.   File certain required notices and powers of attorney with the IRS before preparing any returns.

    b.   Keep a completed copy of each return for a specified period of time.

    c.   Receive client documentation supporting all travel and entertainment expenses deducted on the return.

    d.   Indicate the CPA's federal identification number on a tax return only if the return reflects tax due from the taxpayer.

52. A CPA owes a duty to

    a.   Provide for a successor CPA in the event death or disability prevents completion of an audit.

    b.   Advise a client of errors contained in a previously filed tax return.

    c.   Disclose client fraud to third parties.

    d.   Perform an audit according to GAAP so that fraud will be uncovered.

53. In general, if the IRS issues a thirty-day letter to an individual taxpayer who wishes to dispute the assessment, the taxpayer

    a.   May, without paying any tax, immediately file a petition that would properly commence an action in Tax Court.

    b.   May ignore the thirty-day letter and wait to receive a ninety-day letter.

    c.   Must file a written protest within ten days of receiving the letter.

    d.   Must pay the taxes and then commence an action in federal district court.

54. A CPA will be liable to a tax client for damages resulting from all of the following actions **except**

    a.   Failing to timely file a client's return.

    b.   Failing to advise a client of certain tax elections.

    c.   Refusing to sign a client's request for a filing extension.

    d.   Neglecting to evaluate the option of preparing joint or separate returns that would have resulted in a substantial tax savings for a married client.

55. According to the AICPA Statement on Standards for Tax Services, which of the following statements is correct regarding the standards a CPA should follow when recommending tax return positions and preparing tax returns?

    a.   A CPA may recommend a position that the CPA concludes is frivolous as long as the position is adequately disclosed on the return.

b. A CPA may recommend a position in which the CPA has a good faith belief that the position has a realistic possibility of being sustained if challenged.

c. A CPA will usually **not** advise the client of the potential penalty consequences of the recommended tax return position.

d. A CPA may sign a tax return as preparer knowing that the return takes a position that will **not** be sustained if challenged.

56. According to the standards of the profession, which of the following statements is(are) correct regarding the action to be taken by a CPA who discovers an error in a client's previously filed tax return?

I. Advise the client of the error and recommend the measures to be taken.

II. Withdraw from the professional relationship regardless of whether or not the client corrects the error.

a. I only.
b. II only.
c. Both I and II.
d. Neither I nor II.

57. According to the profession's ethical standards, a CPA preparing a client's tax return may rely on unsupported information furnished by the client, without examining underlying information, unless the information

a. Is derived from a pass-through entity.
b. Appears to be incomplete on its face.
c. Concerns dividends received.
d. Lists charitable contributions.

58. Which of the following acts by a CPA will **not** result in a CPA incurring an IRS penalty?

a. Failing, without reasonable cause, to provide the client with a copy of an income tax return.
b. Failing, without reasonable cause, to sign a client's tax return as preparer.
c. Understating a client's tax liability as a result of an error in calculation.
d. Negotiating a client's tax refund check when the CPA prepared the tax return.

59. According to the standards of the profession, which of the following sources of information should a CPA consider before signing a client's tax return?

I. Information actually known to the CPA from the tax return of another client.

II. Information provided by the client that appears to be correct based on the client's returns from prior years.

a. I only.
b. II only.
c. Both I and II.
d. Neither I nor II.

SIMULATION PROBLEMS

Simulation Problem 1   (10 to 20 minutes)

During 2008, various clients went to Rowe, CPA, for tax advice concerning possible gift tax liability on transfers they made throughout 2008.

For each client, indicate whether the transfer of cash, the income interest, or the remainder interest is a gift of a present interest, a gift of a future interest, or not a completed gift.

Answer List

P.   Present Interest
F.   Future Interest
N.   Not Completed

Assume the following facts:

Cobb created a $500,000 trust that provided his mother with an income interest for her life and the remainder interest to go to his sister at the death of his mother. Cobb expressly retained the power to revoke both the income interest and the remainder interest at any time.

Items to be answered

		(P)	(F)	(N)
1.	The income interest at the trust's creation.	○	○	○
2.	The remainder interest at the trust's creation.	○	○	○

Kane created a $100,000 trust that provided her nephew with the income interest until he reached forty-five years of age. When the trust was created, Kane's nephew was twenty-five. The income distribution is to start when Kane's nephew is twenty-nine. After Kane's nephew reaches the age of forty-five, the remainder interest is to go to Kane's niece.

		(P)	(F)	(N)
3.	The income interest.	○	○	○

During 2008, Hall, an unmarried taxpayer, made a $10,000 cash gift to his son in May and a further $12,000 cash gift to him in August.

		(P)	(F)	(N)
4.	The cash transfers.	○	○	○

During 2008, Yeats transferred property worth $20,000 to a trust with the income to be paid to her twenty-two-year-old niece Jane. After Jane reaches the age of thirty, the remainder interest is to be distributed to Yeats' brother. The income interest is valued at $9,700 and the remainder interest at $10,300.

		(P)	(F)	(N)
5.	The income interest.	○	○	○
6.	The remainder interest.	○	○	○

Tom and Ann Curry, US citizens, were married for the entire 2008 calendar year. Tom gave a $40,000 cash gift to his uncle, Grant. The Currys made no other gifts to Grant in 2008. Tom and Ann each signed a timely election stating that each made one-half of the $40,000 gift.

		(P)	(F)	(N)
7.	The cash transfers.	○	○	○

Murry created a $1,000,000 trust that provided his brother with an income interest for ten years, after which the remainder interest passes to Murry's sister. Murry retained the power to revoke the remainder interest at any time. The income interest was valued at $600,000.

		(P)	(F)	(N)
8.	The income interest.	○	○	○
9.	The remainder interest.	○	○	○

5.   (P) A return preparer will be subject to penalty if there is a willful attempt in any manner to understate the tax liability of any taxpayer. A preparer is considered to have willfully attempted to understate liability if the preparer disregards information furnished by the taxpayer to wrongfully reduce the tax liability of the taxpayer.

6.   (N) A return preparer will be subject to penalty if the preparer knowingly or recklessly discloses information furnished in connection with the preparation of a tax return, unless such information is furnished for quality or peer review, under an administrative order by a regulatory agency, or pursuant to an order of a court.

7.   (E) Under these facts, a position taken on a return which is consistent with incorrect instructions does not satisfy the realistic possibility standard. However, if the preparer relied on the incorrect instructions and was not aware of the announcement or regulations, the reasonable cause and good faith exception may apply depending upon the facts and circumstances.

8.   (P) A return preparer will be subject to penalty if the preparer knowingly or recklessly discloses information furnished in connection with the preparation of a tax return, unless such information is furnished for quality or peer review, under an administrative order by a regulatory agency, or pursuant to an order of a court.

9.   (P) A return preparer will be subject to penalty if there is a willful attempt in any manner to understate the tax liability of any taxpayer or there is a reckless or intentional disregard of rules or regulations. The penalty will apply if a preparer knowingly deducts the expenses of the taxpayer's domestic help as wages paid in the taxpayer's business.

Simulation Problem 3

For **items 1 through 5,** candidates were asked to identify the federal tax treatment for each item by indicating whether the item was fully includible in Remsen's gross estate (F), partially includible in Remsen's gross estate (P), or not includible in Remsen's gross estate (N).

	(F)	(P)	(N)
1. What is the estate tax treatment of the $7,000 cash gift to each sister?	○	○	●
2. What is the estate tax treatment of the life insurance proceeds?	●	○	○
3. What is the estate tax treatment of the marketable securities?	●	○	○
4. What is the estate tax treatment of the $2,000 tuition payment?	○	○	●
5. What is the estate tax treatment of the $650,000 cash?	●	○	○

Explanation of solutions

1.   (N) Generally, gifts made before death are not includible in the decedent's gross estate, even though the gifts were made within three years of death.

2.   (F) The gross estate includes the value of all property in which the decedent had a beneficial interest at time of death. Here, the life insurance proceeds must be included in Remsen's gross estate because the problem indicates that Remsen was the owner of the policy.

3.   (F) The fair market value of the marketable securities must be included in Remsen's gross estate because Remsen was the owner of the securities at the time of his death.

4.   (N) Generally, gifts made before death are not includible in the decedent's gross estate.

5.   (F) The $650,000 cash that Remsen owned must be included in Remsen's gross estate.

For **items 1 through 5,** candidates were asked to identify the federal tax treatment for each item by indicating whether the item was deductible from Remsen's gross estate to arrive at Remsen's taxable estate (G), deductible on Remsen's 2008 individual income tax return (I), deductible on either Remsen's estate tax return or Remsen's 2008 individual income tax return (E), or not deductible on either Remsen's estate tax return or Remsen's 2008 individual income tax return (N).

	(G)	(I)	(E)	(N)
1. What is the estate tax treatment of the executor's fees?	○	○	○	●
2. What is the estate tax treatment of the cash bequest to Remsen's son?	○	○	○	●
3. What is the estate tax treatment of the life insurance proceeds paid to Remsen's spouse?	●	○	○	○

	(G)	(I)	(E)	(N)

4.   What is the estate tax treatment of the funeral expenses?   ● ○ ○ ○

5.   What is the estate tax treatment of the $10,000 of medical expenses incurred before the
     decedent's death and paid by the executor on December 3, 2008?   ○ ○ ● ○

Explanation of solutions

1.   **(N)** The $15,000 of executor's fees to distribute the decedent's property are deductible on **either** the federal estate tax return (Form 706) or the estate's fiduciary income tax return (Form 1041). Such expenses **cannot** be deducted twice. Since the problem indicates that these expenses were deducted on the fiduciary tax return (Form 1041), they cannot be deducted on the estate tax return.

2.   **(N)** A decedent's gross estate is reduced by funeral and administrative expenses, debts and mortgages, casualty and theft losses, charitable bequests, and a marital deduction for the value of property passing to the decedent's surviving spouse. There is no deduction for bequests to beneficiaries other than the decedent's surviving spouse.

3.   **(G)** Generally, property included in a decedent's gross estate will be eligible for an unlimited marital deduction if the property passes to the decedent's surviving spouse. Here, the life insurance proceeds paid to Remsen's spouse were included in Remsen's gross estate because Remsen owned the policy, and are deductible from Remsen's gross estate as part of the marital deduction in arriving at Remsen's taxable estate.

4.   **(G)** Funeral expenses are deductible only on the estate tax return and include a reasonable allowance for a tombstone, monument, mausoleum, or burial lot.

5.   **(E)** The executor of a decedent's estate may elect to treat medical expenses paid by the estate for the decedent's medical care as paid by the decedent at the time the medical services were provided. To qualify for this election, the medical expenses must be paid within the one-year period after the decedent's death, and the executor must attach a waiver to the decedent's Form 1040 indicating that the expenses will not be claimed as a deduction on the decedent's estate tax return. In this case, the medical expenses qualify for the election because Remsen died on January 9, 2008, and the expenses were paid on December 3, 2008.

Simulation Problem 4

Situation	Gift Tax Treatment

For **items 1 through 7,** candidates were asked to identify the federal gift tax treatment for each item by indicating whether the item is fully taxable (F), partially taxable (P), or not taxable (N) to Lane in 2008 for gift tax purposes after considering the gift tax annual exclusion.

	(F)	(P)	(N)

1.   What is the gift tax treatment of Lane's gift to Kamp?   ○ ○ ●

2.   What is the gift tax treatment of Lane's cash gifts to his child?   ○ ● ○

3.   What is the gift tax treatment of the trust's income interest to Lane's aunt?   ○ ● ○

4.   What is the gift tax treatment of the trust's remainder interest to Lane's cousin?   ● ○ ○

5.   What is the gift tax treatment of the tuition payment to Lane's grandchild's university?   ○ ○ ●

6.   What is the gift tax treatment of the trust's income interest to Lane's brother?   ● ○ ○

7.   What is the gift tax treatment of the $13,000 interest income that Lane's niece received from the
     revocable trust?   ○ ● ○

Explanation of solutions

1.   **(N)** There is no taxable gift because the $12,000 cash gift is a gift of a present interest and is fully offset by a $12,000 annual exclusion.

2.   **(P)** The $20,000 of cash gifts given to his child would be partially offset by a $12,000 annual exclusion, resulting in a taxable gift of $8,000.

3.   **(P)** The gift of the income interest valued at $26,000 to his aunt is a gift of a present interest and would be partially offset by a $12,000 annual exclusion, resulting in a taxable gift of $14,000.

4.   **(F)** Since the remainder interest will pass to Lane's cousin after the expiration of five years, the gift of the remainder interest is a gift of a future interest and is not eligible for an annual exclusion. As a result, the $74,000 value of the remainder interest is fully taxable.

5. **(N)** An unlimited exclusion is available for medical expenses and tuition paid on behalf of a donee. Since Lane paid the $25,000 of tuition directly to his grandchild's university on his grandchild's behalf, the gift is fully excluded and not subject to gift tax.

6. **(F)** Since Lane created the irrevocable trust in 2008 but his brother will not begin receiving the income until 2010, the gift of the income interest to his brother is a gift of a future interest and cannot be offset by an annual exclusion. As a result, the gift is fully taxable for gift tax purposes.

7. **(P)** The creation of a revocable trust is not a completed gift and trust income is taxable to the grantor (Lane). As a result, a gift occurs only as the trust income is actually paid to the beneficiary. Here, the $13,000 of interest income received by the niece during 2008 is a gift of a present interest and would be partially offset by a $12,000 annual exclusion.

Simulation Problem 5

Situation	Research and Communication

Keywords you might have used include, "inheritance," "basis," "holding period," and "capital gains and losses."

To: Client Tax File
From: CPA Candidate
Date: [*today's date*]

Facts

Glen Moore inherited stock when his mother, Ruth, died on September 1, 2008. The stock had cost Ruth $120,000 on May 15, 2008, and had a fair market value of $150,000 on the date of her death. Ruth's estate was too small to require the filing of a Federal estate tax return. Moore may sell the stock for $165,000 in March 2009.

Issues

How much gross income must Moore report for 2008 because of his stock inheritance?
What amount and type of gain will Moore report if he sells the stock for $165,000 in January 2009?

Conclusion

The receipt of the stock will be excluded from Moore's gross income. The sale of the stock for $165,000 would result in a $15,000 long-term capital gain in 2009.

Support

Moore will be able to exclude the receipt of the stock from gross income since Code Sec. 102(a) provides that gross income does **not** include the value of property acquired by gift, bequest, devise, or inheritance. Sec. 1014(a)(1) provides that the basis of property acquired from a decedent shall be its fair market value at the date of decedent's death, which in this case is $150,000. Since the stock is being held as an investment and qualifies as a capital asset under Sec. 1221, a sale of the stock for $165,000 in March 2009 would result in a capital gain of $15,000. In regard to holding period, Sec. 1223(11) provides that if property is acquired from a decedent and its basis is determined under Sec. 1014, and the property is sold within one year after death, then the property shall be considered to have been held for more than one year. Finally, Sec. 1222 provides that the term "long-term capital gain" means gain from sale or exchange of a capital asset held for more than one year. As a result, Moore's gain of $165,000 – $150,000 = $15,000 would be reported as a long-term capital gain if the stock were sold in March 2009.

Action to Be Taken

Prepare letter and review results with client.

REGULATION

TESTLET 1

1. Which of the following statements best describes the ethical standard of the profession pertaining to advertising and solicitation?

    a.   All forms of advertising and solicitation are prohibited.

    b.   There are **no** prohibitions regarding the manner in which CPAs may solicit new business.

    c.   A CPA may advertise in any manner that is **not** false, misleading, or deceptive.

    d.   A CPA may only solicit new clients through mass mailings.

2. Burrow & Co., CPAs, have provided annual audit and tax compliance services to Mare Corp. for several years. Mare has been unable to pay Burrow in full for services Burrow rendered nineteen months ago. Burrow is ready to begin fieldwork for the current year's audit. Under the ethical standards of the profession, which of the following arrangements will permit Burrow to begin the fieldwork on Mare's audit?

    a.   Mare sets up a two-year payment plan with Burrow to settle the unpaid fee balance.

    b.   Mare commits to pay the past due fee in full before the audit report is issued.

    c.   Mare gives Burrow an eighteen-month note payable for the full amount of the past due fees before Burrow begins the audit.

    d.   Mare engages another firm to perform the fieldwork, and Burrow is limited to reviewing the workpapers and issuing the audit report.

3. Which of the following is not a covered member for purposes of application of the independence requirements of the AICPA Code of Professional Conduct?

    a.   A staff person on the attest team.

    b.   A staff person that performs tax services for the attest client.

    c.   The partner in charge of the firm office that performs the attest engagement.

    d.   A partner that performs extensive consulting services for the attest client.

4. CPAs must be concerned with their responsibilities in the performance of professional services. In performing an audit, a CPA

    a.   Is strictly liable for failure to exercise due professional care.

    b.   Is strictly liable for failure to detect management fraud.

    c.   Is **not** liable unless the CPA is found to be grossly negligent.

    d.   Is strictly liable for failure to detect illegal acts.

5. The Apex Surety Company wrote a general fidelity bond covering defalcations by the employees of Watson, Inc. Thereafter, Grand, an employee of Watson, embezzled $18,900 of company funds. When his activities were discovered, Apex paid Watson the full amount in accordance with the terms of the fidelity bond, and then sought recovery against Watson's auditors, Kane & Dobbs, CPAs. Which of the following would be Kane & Dobbs' best defense?

    a.   Apex is not in privity of contract.

    b.   The shortages were the result of clever forgeries and collusive fraud that would not be detected by an examination made in accordance with generally accepted auditing standards.

    c.   Kane & Dobbs were not guilty either of gross negligence or fraud.

    d.   Kane & Dobbs were not aware of the Apex-Watson surety relationship.

6. If a stockholder sues a CPA for common law fraud based on false statements contained in the financial statements audited by the CPA, which of the following, if present, would be the CPA's best defense?

    a.   The stockholder lacks privity to sue.

    b.   The false statements were immaterial.

    c.   The CPA did **not** financially benefit from the alleged fraud.

    d.   The contributory negligence of the client.

7. Mathews is an agent for Sears with the express authority to solicit orders from customers in a geographic area assigned by Sears. Mathews has no authority to grant discounts or to collect payment on orders solicited. Mathews secured an order from Davidson for $1,000 less a 10% discount if Davidson makes immediate payment. Davidson had previously done business with Sears through Mathews but this was the first time that a discount-payment offer had been made. Davidson gave Mathews a check for $900 and, thereafter, Mathews turned in both the check and the order to Sears. The order clearly indicated that a 10% discount had been given by Mathews. Sears shipped the order and cashed the check. Later, Sears attempted to collect $100 as the balance owed on the order from Davidson. Which of the following is correct?

    a.   Sears can collect the $100 from Davidson because Mathews contracted outside the scope of his express or implied authority.

    b.   Sears **cannot** collect the $100 from Davidson because Mathews, as an agent with express authority to solicit orders, had implied authority to give discounts and collect.

    c.   Sears **cannot** collect the $100 from Davidson as Sears has ratified the discount granted and made to Mathews.

    d.   Sears **cannot** collect the $100 from Davidson because, although Mathews had **no** express or implied authority to grant a discount and collect, Mathews had apparent authority to do so.

8. Which of the following regarding workers' compensation is correct?

    a.   A purpose of workers' compensation is for the employer to assume a definite liability in exchange for the employee giving up his common law rights.

    b.   It applies to workers engaged in or affecting interstate commerce only.

    c.   It is optional in most jurisdictions.

    d.   Once workers' compensation has been adopted by the employer, the amount of damages recoverable is based upon comparative negligence.

9. Regulation D of the Securities Act of 1933 is available to issuers without regard to the dollar amount of an offering only when the
   a. Purchasers are all accredited investors.
   b. Number of purchasers who are nonaccredited is thirty-five or less.
   c. Issuer is **not** a reporting company under the Securities Exchange Act of 1934.
   d. Issuer is **not** an investment company.

10. During an audit of Actee Corporation, you examine the following:

   • A check that is postdated and also says "Pay to Acteé Corporation." You are concerned about these two issues but note that all other elements of negotiability are present in the check.
   • A note that is payable on demand and says "Pay to Actee Corporation" on its face. You see that all other issues about negotiability are satisfied.

   You question whether or not the issues raised above destroy negotiability of these two instruments. Which of the instruments is(are) negotiable instruments?

	The check	*The note*
a.	Yes	Yes
b.	Yes	No
c.	No	Yes
d.	No	No

11. Nat purchased a typewriter from Rob. Rob is not in the business of selling typewriters. Rob tendered delivery of the typewriter after receiving payment in full from Nat. Nat informed Rob that he was unable to take possession of the typewriter at that time, but would return later that day. Before Nat returned, the typewriter was destroyed by a fire. The risk of loss
   a. Passed to Nat upon Rob's tender of delivery.
   b. Remained with Rob, since Nat had not yet received the typewriter.
   c. Passed to Nat at the time the contract was formed and payment was made.
   d. Remained with Rob, since title had **not** yet passed to Nat.

12. Marco Auto Inc. made many untrue statements in the course of inducing Rockford to purchase a used auto for $3,500. The car in question turned out to have some serious faults. Which of the following untrue statements made by Marco should Rockford use in seeking recovery from Marco for breach of warranty?
   a. "I refused a $3,800 offer for this very same auto from another buyer last week."
   b. "This auto is one of the best autos we have for sale."
   c. "At this price the auto is a real steal."
   d. "I can guarantee that you will never regret this purchase."

13. On April 14, 2007, Seeley Corp. entered into a written agreement to sell to Boone Corp. 1,200 cartons of certain goods at $.40 per carton, delivery within thirty days. The agreement contained no other terms. On April 15, 2007, Boone and Seeley orally agreed to modify their April 14 agreement so that the new quantity specified was 1,500 cartons, same price and delivery terms. What is the status of this modification?

   a. Enforceable.
   b. Unenforceable under the statute of frauds.
   c. Unenforceable for lack of consideration.
   d. Unenforceable because the change is substantial.

14. Purdy purchased real property from Hart and received a warranty deed with full covenants. Recordation of this deed is
   a. Not necessary if the deed provides that recordation is not required.
   b. Necessary to vest the purchaser's legal title to the property conveyed.
   c. Required primarily for the purpose of providing the local taxing authorities with the information necessary to assess taxes.
   d. Irrelevant if the subsequent party claiming superior title had actual notice of the unrecorded deed.

15. Peters defaulted on a purchase money mortgage held by Fairmont Realty. Fairmont's attempts to obtain payment have been futile and the mortgage payments are several months in arrears. Consequently, Fairmont decided to resort to its rights against the property. Fairmont foreclosed on the mortgage. Peters has all of the following rights **except**
   a. To remain in possession as long as his equity in the property exceeds the amount of debt.
   b. An equity of redemption.
   c. To refinance the mortgage with another lender and repay the original mortgage.
   d. A statutory right of redemption.

16. Richard Brown, who retired on May 31, 2007, receives a monthly pension benefit of $700 payable for life. His life expectancy at the date of retirement is ten years. The first pension check was received on June 15, 2007. During his years of employment, Brown contributed $12,000 to the cost of his company's pension plan. How much of the pension amounts received may Brown exclude from taxable income for the years 2007, 2008, and 2009?

	2007	*2008*	*2009*
a.	$0	$0	$0
b.	$4,900	$4,900	$4,900
c.	$ 700	$1,200	$1,200
d.	$4,900	$8,400	$8,400

17. Lee, an attorney, uses the cash receipts and disbursements method of reporting. In 2007, a client gave Lee 500 shares of a listed corporation's stock in full satisfaction of a $10,000 legal fee the client owed to Lee. This stock had a fair market value of $8,000 on the date it was given to Lee. The client's basis for this stock was $6,000. Lee sold the stock for cash in January 2008. In Lee's 2007 income tax return, what amount of income should be reported in connection with the receipt of the stock?
   a. $10,000
   b. $ 8,000
   c. $ 6,000
   d. $0

18. Don Wolf became a general partner in Gata Associates on January 1, 2007, with a 5% interest in Gata's profits, losses, and capital. Gata is a distributor of auto parts. Wolf does not materially participate in the partnership business. For the year ended December 31, 2007, Gata had an operating loss of $100,000. In addition, Gata earned interest of $20,000 on a temporary investment. Gata has kept the prin-

cipal temporarily invested while awaiting delivery of equipment that is presently on order. The principal will be used to pay for this equipment. Wolf's passive loss for 2007 is

- a. $0
- b. $4,000
- c. $5,000
- d. $6,000

19. In 2007, Don Mills, a single taxpayer, had $70,000 in taxable income before personal exemptions. Mills had no tax preferences. His itemized deductions were as follows:

State and local income taxes	$5,000
Home mortgage interest on loan to acquire residence	6,000
Miscellaneous deductions that exceed 2% of adjusted gross income	2,000

What amount did Mills report as alternative minimum taxable income before the AMT exemption?

- a. $72,000
- b. $75,000
- c. $77,000
- d. $83,000

20. An accuracy-related penalty applies to the portion of tax underpayment attributable to

- I. Negligence or a disregard of the tax rules or regulations.
- II. Any substantial understatement of income tax.

    - a. I only.
    - b. II only.
    - c. Both I and II.
    - d. Neither I nor II.

21. Smith, an individual calendar-year taxpayer, purchased 100 shares of Core Co. common stock for $15,000 on November 15, 2007, and an additional 100 shares for $13,000 on December 30, 2007. On January 3, 2008, Smith sold the shares purchased on November 15, 2007, for $13,000. What amount of loss from the sale of Core's stock is deductible on Smith's 2007 and 2008 income tax returns?

	2007	*2008*
a.	$0	$0
b.	$0	$2,000
c.	$1,000	$1,000
d.	$2,000	$0

22. Strom acquired a 25% interest in Ace Partnership by contributing land having an adjusted basis of $16,000 and a fair market value of $50,000. The land was subject to a $24,000 mortgage, which was assumed by Ace. No other liabilities existed at the time of the contribution. What was Strom's basis in Ace?

- a. $0
- b. $16,000
- c. $26,000
- d. $32,000

Items 23 and 24 are based on the following data:

Mike Reed, a partner in Post Co., received the following distribution from Post:

	Post's basis	*Fair market value*
Cash	$11,000	$11,000
Land	5,000	12,500

Before this distribution, Reed's basis in Post was $25,000.

23. If this distribution were nonliquidating, Reed's recognized gain or loss on the distribution would be

- a. $11,000 gain.
- b. $ 9,000 loss.
- c. $ 1,500 loss.
- d. $0.

24. If this distribution were in complete liquidation of Reed's interest in Post, Reed's basis for the land would be

- a. $14,000
- b. $12,500
- c. $ 5,000
- d. $ 1,500

25. Finbury Corporation's taxable income for the year ended December 31, 2007, was $2,000,000 on which its tax liability was $680,000. In order for Finbury to escape the estimated tax underpayment penalty for the year ending December 31, 2008, Finbury's 2008 estimated tax payments must equal at least

- a. 90% of the 2008 tax liability.
- b. 93% of the 2008 tax liability.
- c. 100% of the 2008 tax liability.
- d. The 2007 tax liability of $680,000.

26. Barbaro Corporation's retained earnings at January 1, 2007, was $600,000. During 2007 Barbaro paid cash dividends of $150,000 and received a federal income tax refund of $26,000 as a result of an IRS audit of Barbaro's 2004 tax return. Barbaro's net income per books for the year ended December 31, 2007, was $274,900 after deducting federal income tax of $183,300. How much should be shown in the reconciliation Schedule M-2, of Form 1120, as Barbaro's retained earnings at December 31, 2007?

- a. $443,600
- b. $600,900
- c. $626,900
- d. $750,900

27. Brooke, Inc., an S corporation, was organized on January 2, 2007, with two equal stockholders who materially participate in the S corporation's business. Each stockholder invested $5,000 in Brooke's capital stock, and each loaned $15,000 to the corporation. Brooke then borrowed $60,000 from a bank for working capital. Brooke sustained an operating loss of $90,000 for the year ended December 31, 2007. How much of this loss can each stockholder claim on his 2007 income tax return?

- a. $ 5,000
- b. $20,000
- c. $45,000
- d. $50,000

28. When Jim and Nina became engaged in April 2008, Jim gave Nina a ring that had a fair market value of $50,000. After their wedding in July 2008, Jim gave Nina $75,000 in cash so that Nina could have her own bank account. Both Jim and Nina are US citizens. What was the amount of Jim's 2008 marital deduction?

- a. $0
- b. $ 75,000
- c. $115,000
- d. $125,000

29. Ross, a calendar-year, cash-basis taxpayer who died in June 2008, was entitled to receive a $10,000 accounting fee that had not been collected before the date of death. The executor of Ross' estate collected the full $10,000 in July 2008. This $10,000 should appear in

a. Only the decedent's final individual income tax return.

b. Only the estate's fiduciary income tax return.

c. Only the estate tax return.

d. Both the fiduciary income tax return and the estate tax return.

30. Kopel was engaged to prepare Raff's 2007 federal income tax return. During the tax preparation interview, Raff told Kopel that he paid $3,000 in property taxes in 2007. Actually, Raff's property taxes amounted to only $600. Based on Raff's word, Kopel deducted the $3,000 on Raff's return, resulting in an understatement of Raff's tax liability. Kopel had no reason to believe that the information was incorrect. Kopel did not request underlying documentation and was reasonably satisfied by Raff's representation that Raff had adequate records to support the deduction. Which of the following statements is correct?

a. To avoid the preparer penalty for willful understatement of tax liability, Kopel was obligated to examine the underlying documentation for the deduction.

b. To avoid the preparer penalty for willful understatement of tax liability, Kopel would be required to obtain Raff's representation in writing.

c. Kopel is **not** subject to the preparer penalty for willful understatement of tax liability because the deduction that was claimed was more than 25% of the actual amount that should have been deducted.

d. Kopel is **not** subject to the preparer penalty for willful understatement of tax liability because Kopel was justified in relying on Raff's representation.

REGULATION

ANSWERS TO TESTLET 1

1. c	5. b	9. b	13. b	17. b	21. a	25. c	29. d
2. b	6. b	10. b	14. d	18. c	22. a	26. d	30. d
3. b	7. c	11. a	15. a	19. c	23. d	27. b	
4. a	8. a	12. a	16. c	20. c	24. a	28. b	

Regulation Hints

1. Advertising must be appropriate.

2. Prior year past due fees impair independence.

3. Only managers or partners performing nonattest services for an attest client may become covered members.

4. Professionals must exercise due professional care.

5. Compliance with GAAS indicates due care.

6. Recall proof requirements.

7. The principal accepted the benefits of the unauthorized act.

8. Employee gives up rights but receives automatic payment.

9. Recall the requirements for a private placement.

10. A note, unlike a draft or a check, is a two-party instrument.

11. Rob is **not** a merchant.

12. An **explicit** declaration of fact forms an express warranty; sales talk and predictions do not.

13. After modification, contract is for >$500.

14. Notice can be constructive or actual.

15. Foreclosure ends the mortgagor's rights in the property.

16. Each payment is part income and part a return of Brown's investment.

17. The amount of compensation is determined from the value of the property received.

18. Interest is generally considered portfolio income.

19. Qualified residence interest in the form of acquisition indebtedness is deductible for AMT purposes.

20. The items listed are two components of the accuracy-related penalty.

21. The acquisition of substantially identical stock within a thirty-day period before or after the date of the loss results in a wash sale.

22. The 75% net reduction in liability is treated as a deemed cash distribution.

23. No loss can be recognized in a nonliquidating distribution.

24. No loss can be recognized in a liquidating distribution if property other than cash, receivables, or inventory is received.

25. Because of taxable income in excess of $1 million, Finbury cannot use its tax for the preceding year as a safe estimate.

26. Schedule M-2 provides a reconciliation of unappropriated retained earnings per books.

27. Shareholders do not receive basis for the corporation's debts to third parties.

28. The taxpayer must be married on the date of gift to qualify for the marital deduction.

29. The fee qualifies as income in respect of a decedent.

30. A preparer is not required to audit or examine a client's books and records.

REGULATION

TESTLET 2

1. Under the ethical standards of the profession, which of the following situations involving independent members of an auditor's family is most likely to impair the auditor's independence?

a. A parent's immaterial investment in a client.

b. A first cousin's loan from a client.

c. A spouse's employment as CEO of a client.

d. A sibling's loan to a director of a client.

2. What body has the responsibility for issuing auditing standards for auditors of public companies?

a. The AICPA's Auditing Standards Board.

b. The Chief Accountant of the Securities and Exchange Commission.

c. The Public Company Accounting Oversight Board.

d. The Financial Accounting Standards Board.

3. According to the ethical standards for the profession, which of the following would impair the independence of an auditor in providing an audit for First State Bank, a nonpublic financial institution?

a. The accountant has an automobile loan with the bank collateralized by the automobile.

b. The accountant has a credit card with the bank with an outstanding balance of $12,000.

c. The accountant has a $20,000 loan at the bank collateralized by a certificate of deposit.

d. The accountant has a demand deposit account of $25,000 with the bank.

4. Hart, CPA, is concerned about the type of fee arrangements that are permissible under the profession's ethical standards. Which of the following professional services may be performed for a contingent fee?

a. A review of financial statements.

b. An examination of prospective financial statements.

c. Preparation of a tax return.

d. Information technology consulting.

5. Rhodes Corp. desired to acquire the common stock of Harris Corp. and engaged Johnson & Co., CPAs, to audit the financial statements of Harris Corp. Johnson failed to discover a significant liability in performing the audit. In a common law action against Johnson, Rhodes at a minimum must prove

a. Gross negligence on the part of Johnson.

b. Negligence on the part of Johnson.

c. Fraud on the part of Johnson.

d. Johnson knew that the liability existed.

6. A debtor will be denied a discharge in bankruptcy if the debtor

a. Failed to timely list a portion of his debts.

b. Unjustifiably failed to preserve his books and records which could have been used to ascertain the debtor's financial condition.

c. Has negligently made preferential transfers to favored creditors within ninety days of the filing of the bankruptcy petition.

d. Has committed several willful and malicious acts that resulted in bodily injury to others.

7. Which of the following is a part of the social security law?

a. A self-employed person must contribute an annual amount that is equal to the combined contributions of an employee and his or her employer.

b. Upon the death of an employee prior to his retirement, his estate is entitled to receive the amount attributable to his contributions as a death benefit.

c. Social security benefits must be fully funded and payments, current and future, must constitutionally come only from social security taxes.

d. Social security benefits are taxable as income when they exceed the individual's total contributions.

8. Duval Manufacturing Industries, Inc. orally engaged Harris as one of its district sales managers for an eighteen-month period commencing April 1, 2007. Harris commenced work on that date and performed his duties in a highly competent manner for several months. On October 1, 2007, the company gave Harris a notice of termination as of November 1, 2007, citing a downturn in the market for its products. Harris sues seeking either specific performance or damages for breach of contract. Duval pleads the Statute of Frauds and/or a justified dismissal due to the economic situation. What is the probable outcome of the lawsuit?

a. Harris will prevail because he has partially performed under the terms of the contract.

b. Harris will lose because his termination was caused by economic factors beyond Duval's control.

c. Harris will lose because such a contract must be in writing and signed by a proper agent of Duval.

d. Harris will prevail because the Statute of Frauds does **not** apply to contracts such as his.

9. Harp Corp. is offering to issue $450,000 of its securities pursuant to Regulation D of the Securities Act of 1933. Harp is not required to deliver a disclosure document in the states where the offering is being conducted. The exemption for small issues of $1,000,000 or less (Rule 504) under Regulation D

a. Requires that the issuer be subject to the reporting requirements of the Securities Exchange Act of 1934.

b. Does **not** require that any specific information be furnished to investors.

c. Permits the use of general solicitation.

d. Requires that each investor be a sophisticated investor or be represented by a purchaser representative.

10. Which of the following will **not** constitute value in determining whether a person is a holder in due course?

a. The taking of a negotiable instrument for a future consideration.

b. The taking of a negotiable instrument as security for a loan.

c. The giving of one's own negotiable instrument in connection with the purchase of another negotiable instrument.

d.   The performance of services rendered the payee of a negotiable instrument who endorses it in payment for services.

11. Kent, a wholesale distributor of cameras, entered into a contract with Williams. Williams agreed to purchase 100 cameras with certain optional attachments. The contract was made on March 1, 2007, for delivery by March 15, 2007; terms: 2/10, net 30. Kent shipped the cameras on March 6, and they were delivered on March 10. The shipment did not conform to the contract, in that one of the attachments was not included. Williams immediately notified Kent that he was rejecting the goods. For maximum legal advantage Kent's most appropriate action is to

a.   Bring an action for the price less an allowance for the missing attachment.

b.   Notify Williams promptly of his intention to cure the defect and make a conforming delivery by March 15.

c.   Terminate his contract with Williams and recover for breach of contract.

d.   Sue Williams for specific performance.

12. If a seller repudiates his contract with a buyer for the sale of 100 radios, what recourse does the buyer have?

a.   He can "cover" (i.e., procure the goods elsewhere and recover the difference).

b.   He must await the seller's performance for a commercially reasonable time after repudiation.

c.   He can obtain specific performance by the seller.

d.   He can recover punitive damages.

13. Wilmont owned a tract of waterfront property on Big Lake. During Wilmont's ownership of the land, several frame bungalows were placed on the land by tenants who rented the land from Wilmont. In addition to paying rent, the tenants paid for the maintenance and insurance of the bungalows, repaired, altered and sold them, without permission or hindrance from Wilmont. The bungalows rested on surface cinderblock and were not bolted to the ground. The buildings could be removed without injury to either the buildings or the land. Wilmont sold the land to Marsh. The deed to Marsh recited that Wilmont sold the land, with buildings thereon, "subject to the rights of tenants, if any, ..." When the tenants attempted to remove the bungalows, Marsh claimed ownership of them. In deciding who owns the bungalows, which of the following is **least** significant?

a.   The leasehold agreement itself, to the extent it manifested the intent of the parties.

b.   The mode and degree of annexation of the buildings to the land.

c.   The degree to which removal would cause injury to the buildings or the land.

d.   The fact that the deed included a general clause relating to the buildings.

14. Smith purchased a tract of land. To protect himself, he ordered title insurance from Valor Title Insurance Company. The policy was the usual one issued by title companies. Accordingly

a.   Valor will not be permitted to take exceptions to its coverage if it agreed to insure and prepared the title abstract.

b.   The title policy is assignable in the event Smith subsequently sells the property.

c.   The title policy provides protection against defects in record title only.

d.   Valor will be liable for any title defect that arises, even though the defect could **not** have been discovered through the exercise of reasonable care.

15. Tremont Enterprises, Inc. needed some additional working capital to develop a new product line. It decided to obtain intermediate term financing by giving a second mortgage on its plant and warehouse. Which of the following is true with respect to the mortgages?

a.   If Tremont defaults on both mortgages and a bankruptcy proceeding is initiated, the second mortgagee has the status of general creditor.

b.   If the second mortgagee proceeds to foreclose on its mortgage, the first mortgagee must be satisfied completely before the second mortgagee is entitled to repayment.

c.   Default on payment to the second mortgagee will constitute default on the first mortgage.

d.   Tremont **cannot** prepay the second mortgage prior to its maturity without the consent of the first mortgagee.

16. Frank Lanier is a resident of a state that imposes a tax on income. The following information pertaining to Lanier's state income taxes is available:

Taxes withheld in 2007	$3,500
Refund received in 2007 of 2006 tax	400
Deficiency assessed and paid in 2007 for 2005:	
Tax	600
Interest	100

What amount should Lanier utilize as state and local income taxes in calculating itemized deductions for his 2007 federal tax return?

a. $3,500

b. $3,700

c. $4,100

d. $4,200

17. Ace Rentals, Inc., an accrual-basis taxpayer, reported rent receivable of $35,000 and $25,000 in its 2007 and 2006 balance sheets, respectively. During 2007, Ace received $50,000 in rent payments and $5,000 in nonrefundable rent deposits. In Ace's 2007 corporate income tax return, what amount should Ace include as rent revenue?

a. $50,000

b. $55,000

c. $60,000

d. $65,000

18. Sol and Julia Crane (both age 41) are married, and filed a joint return for 2007. Sol earned a salary of $110,000 in 2007 from his job at Troy Corp., where Sol is covered by his employer's pension plan. In addition, Sol and Julia earned interest of $3,000 in 2007 on their joint savings account. Julia is not employed, and the couple had no other income. On January 15, 2007, Sol contributed $4,000 to an IRA for himself, and $4,000 to an IRA for his spouse. The allowable IRA deduction in the Cranes' 2007 joint return is

a. $0

b. $4,000

c. $6,000

d. $8,000

19. Spencer, who itemizes deductions, had adjusted gross income of $60,000 in 2007. The following additional information is available for 2007:

Cash contribution to church	$4,000
Purchase of art object at church bazaar (with a fair market value of $800 on the date of purchase)	1,200
Donation of used clothing to Salvation Army (fair value evidenced by receipt received)	600

What is the maximum amount Spencer can claim as a deduction for charitable contributions in 2007?

    a. $5,400
    b. $5,200
    c. $5,000
    d. $4,400

20. The following information pertains to Wald Corp.'s operations for the year ended December 31, 2007:

Worldwide taxable income	$300,000
US source taxable income	180,000
US income tax before foreign tax credit	96,000
Foreign nonbusiness-related interest earned	30,000
Foreign income taxes paid on nonbusiness-related interest earned	12,000
Other foreign source taxable income	90,000
Foreign income taxes paid on other foreign source taxable income	27,000

What amount of foreign tax credit may Wald claim for 2007?

    a. $28,800
    b. $36,600
    c. $38,400
    d. $39,000

21. Platt owns land that is operated as a parking lot. A shed was erected on the lot for the related transactions with customers. With regard to capital assets and Section 1231 assets, how should these assets be classified?

	Land	Shed
a.	Capital	Capital
b.	Section 1231	Capital
c.	Capital	Section 1231
d.	Section 1231	Section 1231

22. At partnership inception, Black acquires a 50% interest in Decorators Partnership by contributing property with an adjusted basis of $80,000. Black recognizes a gain if

  I. The fair market value of the contributed property exceeds its adjusted basis.
  II. The property is encumbered by a mortgage with a balance of $100,000.

    a.   I only.
    b.   II only.
    c.   Both I and II.
    d.   Neither I nor II.

Items 23 and 24 are based on the following data:

The partnership of Hager, Mazer & Slagle had the following cash-basis balance sheet at December 31, 2007:

	Adjusted basis per books	Fair market value
Assets		
Cash	$51,000	$ 51,000
Accounts receivable	--	210,000
Totals	$51,000	$261,000

	Adjusted basis per books	Fair market value
Liabilities and Capital		
Note payable	$30,000	$ 30,000
Capital accounts:		
Hager	7,000	77,000
Mazer	7,000	77,000
Slagle	7,000	77,000
Totals	$51,000	$261,000

Slagle, an equal partner, sold his partnership interest to Burns, an outsider, for $77,000 cash on January 1, 2008. In addition, Burns assumed Slagle's share of partnership liabilities.

23. What was the total amount realized by Slagle on the sale of his partnership interest?

    a. $67,000
    b. $70,000
    c. $77,000
    d. $87,000

24. How much ordinary income should Slagle report in his 2008 income tax return on the sale of his partnership interest?

    a. $0
    b. $10,000
    c. $70,000
    d. $77,000

25. Eastern Corp., a calendar-year corporation, was formed in 2006. On January 2, 2007, it placed five-year property in service. The property was depreciated under the general MACRS system. Eastern did not elect to use the straight-line method. The following information pertains to Eastern:

Eastern's 2007 taxable income	$300,000
Adjustment for the accelerated depreciation taken on 2007 five-year property	1,000
2007 tax-exempt interest from specified private activity bonds issued in 2003	5,000

What was Eastern's 2007 alternative minimum taxable income before the adjusted current earnings (ACE) adjustment?

    a. $306,000
    b. $305,000
    c. $304,000
    d. $301,000

26. Bank Corp. owns 80% of Shore Corp.'s outstanding capital stock. Shore's capital stock consists of 50,000 shares of common stock issued and outstanding. Shore's 2007 net income was $140,000. During 2007, Shore declared and paid dividends of $60,000. In conformity with generally accepted accounting principles, Bank recorded the following entries in 2007:

	Debit	Credit
Investment in Shore Corp. common stock	$112,000	
Equity in earnings of subsidiary		$112,000
Cash	48,000	
Investment in Shore Corp. common stock		48,000

In its 2007 consolidated tax return, Bank should report dividend revenue of

    a. $48,000
    b. $14,400
    c. $ 9,600
    d. $0

SOLUTION TO SIMULATION PROBLEM 2

Situation	Form 2441	Communication	Research

Form **2441**

Department of the Treasury
Internal Revenue Service (99)

Child and Dependent Care Expenses

▶ Attach to Form 1040 or Form 1040NR.

▶ See separate instructions.

OMB No. 1545-0074

2007

Attachment Sequence No. **21**

Name(s) shown on return: **CHRIS + ROBIN RAULF**

Your social security number: **432 89 5567**

Before you begin: Figure the amount of any foreign tax credit you are claiming on Form 1040, line 51, or Form 1040NR, line 46.

Part I   **Persons or Organizations Who Provided the Care—You must complete this part.**
(If you have more than two care providers, see the instructions.)

1	(a) Care provider's name	(b) Address (number, street, apt. no., city, state, and ZIP code)	(c) Identifying number (SSN or EIN)	(d) Amount paid (see instructions)
	HAPPY TIMES CHILD CARE	319 FAIRWAY DRIVE SUPERIOR, CO. 80027	36-4567891	5,200

Did you receive dependent care benefits?

No ⟶ Complete only Part II below.

Yes ⟶ Complete Part III on the back next.

Caution. If the care was provided in your home, you may owe employment taxes. See the instructions for Form 1040, line 62, or Form 1040NR, line 57.

Part II   **Credit for Child and Dependent Care Expenses**

2   Information about your **qualifying person(s).** If you have more than two qualifying persons, see the instructions.

(a) Qualifying person's name First Last		(b) Qualifying person's social security number	(c) Qualified expenses you incurred and paid in 2007 for the person listed in column (a)
COLIN	RAULF	343 04 3413	5,200

3	Add the amounts in column (c) of line 2. **Do not** enter more than $3,000 for one qualifying person or $6,000 for two or more persons. If you completed Part III, enter the amount from line 35	**3**	3,000
4	Enter your **earned income.** See instructions	**4**	24,000
5	If married filing jointly, enter your spouse's earned income (if your spouse was a student or was disabled, see the instructions); **all others,** enter the amount from line 4	**5**	16,000
6	Enter the **smallest** of line 3, 4, or 5	**6**	3,000
7	Enter the amount from Form 1040, line 38, or Form 1040NR, line 36 **7** 41,600		
8	Enter on line 8 the decimal amount shown below that applies to the amount on line 7		

If line 7 is:

Over	But not over	Decimal amount is	Over	But not over	Decimal amount is
$0	15,000	.35	$29,000	31,000	.27
15,000	17,000	.34	31,000	33,000	.26
17,000	19,000	.33	33,000	35,000	.25
19,000	21,000	.32	35,000	37,000	.24
21,000	23,000	.31	37,000	39,000	.23
23,000	25,000	.30	39,000	41,000	.22
25,000	27,000	.29	41,000	43,000	.21
27,000	29,000	.28	43,000	No limit	.20

		8	× .21
9	Multiply line 6 by the decimal amount on line 8. If you paid 2006 expenses in 2007, see the instructions	**9**	630
10	Enter the amount from Form 1040, line 46, or Form 1040NR, line 43 **10** 2,746		
11	Enter the amount from Form 1040, line 51, or Form 1040NR, line 46 **11** 0		
12	Subtract line 11 from line 10. If zero or less, **stop.** You cannot take the credit	**12**	2,746
13	**Credit for child and dependent care expenses.** Enter the **smaller** of line 9 or line 12 here and on Form 1040, line 47, or Form 1040NR, line 44	**13**	630

For Paperwork Reduction Act Notice, see page 4 of the instructions.   Cat. No. 11862M   Form **2441** (2007)

		Communication	
Situation	**Form 2441**		**Research**

The technical points to be covered in this response should include

The term "qualified expenses" for purposes of the child care credit include amounts paid for household services and care of a qualifying person while you work or look for work. Household services are services needed to care for the qualifying person as well as to run the home. For example, they include the services of a cook, maid, babysitter, housekeeper, or cleaning person if the services were partly for the care of the qualifying person. Care of a qualifying person includes the cost of services for the qualifying person's well-being and protection. You can include the cost of care provided outside the home for a dependent under age 13 or any other qualifying person who regularly spends at least eight hours a day in your home. Care does not include the cost of schooling for a child in the first grade or above.

			Research
Situation	**Form 2441**	**Communication**	

Internal Revenue Code Section 21(b) defines a qualifying individual for purposes of the child and dependent care credit.

Section	Subsection
§ 21	(b)

REGULATION TESTLETS RELEASED BY AICPA

1. According to the profession's ethical standards, an auditor would be considered independent in which of the following instances?
   a. The auditor is the officially appointed stock transfer agent of a client.
   b. The auditor's checking account that is fully insured by a federal agency, is held at a client financial institution.
   c. The client owes the auditor fees for more than two years prior to the issuance of the audit report.
   d. The client is the only tenant in a commercial building owned by the auditor.

1. **(b)** The requirement is to identify the instance in which an auditor would be considered independent. Answer (b) is correct because per ET 191.140-.141 the auditor's independence would not be impaired, provided the checking accounts, etc. are fully insured by an appropriate deposit insurance agency. Answer (a) is incorrect because per ET 191.077-.078 an auditor's independence would be impaired since the function of a transfer agent is considered equivalent to that of a member of management. Answer (c) is incorrect because per ET 191.103-.104 an auditor's independence is considered to be impaired if, when the report on the client's current year is issued, fees remain unpaid, whether billed or unbilled, for professional services provided more than one year prior to the date of the report. Answer (d) is incorrect because per ET 191.58 leasing property to a client results in an indirect financial interest in that client. Therefore, an auditor's independence would be considered to be impaired if the indirect financial interest in a client is material to the auditor.

2. Which of the following rights is a holder of a public corporation's cumulative preferred stock always entitled to?
   a. Conversion of the preferred stock into common stock.
   b. Voting rights.
   c. Dividend carryovers from years in which dividends were **not** paid, to future years.
   d. Guaranteed dividends.

2. **(c)** Preferred shares of stock are shares that have a contractual preference over other classes of stock as to liquidations and dividends. If a preferred stock is cumulative, the shareholder would be entitled to dividend carryovers from years in which dividends were not paid, to future years and would receive all dividends in arrears before any dividend is paid to owners of common stock. Answers (a) and (b) are incorrect because in order for a shareholder to be entitled to convert preferred stock into common stock or to have voting rights, it must be stated in the articles of incorporation. These are not rights that a holder of preferred stock would always be entitled to. Answer (d) is incorrect because although a preferred stockholder has preference over other classes of stock as to declared dividends, the board of directors' power to declare dividends is discretionary and thus dividends are not guaranteed.

3. Leker exchanged a van that was used exclusively for business and had an adjusted tax basis of $20,000 for a new van. The new van had a fair market value of $10,000, and Leker also received $3,000 in cash. What was Leker's tax basis in the acquired van?
   a. $20,000
   b. $17,000
   c. $13,000
   d. $ 7,000

3. **(b)** The requirement is to determine the basis for Leker's new van. The exchange of Leker's old van with a basis of $20,000 that was used exclusively for business, for a new van worth $10,000 plus $3,000 cash qualified as a like-kind exchange. Since it is a like-kind exchange, Leker's realized loss of $20,000 – ($10,000 + $3,000) = $7,000 cannot be recognized, but instead is reflected in the basis of the new van. The new van's basis is the adjusted basis of Leker's old van of $20,000 reduced by the $3,000 of cash boot received, resulting in a basis of $17,000.

4. If a corporation's charitable contributions exceed the limitation for deductibility in a particular year, the excess
   a. Is **not** deductible in any future or prior year.
   b. May be carried back or forward for one year at the corporation's election.
   c. May be carried forward to a maximum of five succeeding years.
   d. May be carried back to the third preceding year.

4. **(c)** The requirement is to select the correct statement regarding a corporation's charitable contributions in excess of the limitation for deductibility in a particular year. Corporate charitable contributions in excess of the 10% of taxable income limitation may be carried forward to a maximum of five succeeding years, subject to a 10% limitation in those years.

5. Strom acquired a 25% interest in Ace Partnership by contributing land having an adjusted basis of $16,000 and a fair market value of $50,000. The land was subject to a $24,000 mortgage, which was assumed by Ace. No other liabilities existed at the time of the contribution. What was Strom's basis in Ace?
   a. $0
   b. $16,000
   c. $26,000
   d. $32,000

5. **(a)** The requirement is to determine Strom's initial basis for the 25% interest in Ace Partnership that was received in exchange for land, subject to a mortgage that was assumed by Ace. Strom's initial basis for the 25% partnership interest received consists of the $16,000 basis of the land contributed, less the net reduction in Strom's liabilities resulting from the partnership's assumption of the $24,000 mortgage. Since Strom received a 25% partnership interest, the **net** reduction in Strom's liability is $24,000 × 75% = $18,000. Since Strom cannot have a negative basis, his basis for his 25% interest in Ace is $16,000 – $18,000 = $0. Additionally, note that Strom must recognize a $2,000 gain because the liability reduction exceeded his basis in the transferred land.

SIMULATION 1 (35 to 40 minutes)

Directions							
	Situation	Gain/Basis	Depreciation Expense	Distributive Share	Liquidating Distributions	Written Communication	Research

In this problem, you will be asked to respond to various questions regarding the tax treatment of partnerships. The simulation will provide you with all the information necessary to do your work. For full credit, be sure to view and complete all work tabs.

Remember

- Information and data necessary to complete the simulation are found by clicking information tabs (i.e., those **without a pencil icon**).
- All tasks that you should complete before leaving the simulation are found on work tabs (i.e., those tabs **with** a pencil icon).
- An unshaded pencil icon means that you have not yet responded to anything on a particular work tab.
- A shaded pencil icon indicates that you have responded to some or all of the requirements on a work tab—it does **not** necessarily mean that you have completed the requirements on the tab.

To start this simulation, click on the Situation tab.
To respond to the tasks or questions, click on the work tabs.
Resources are available to you under the tab marked Resources. You may want to review what is included in the resources before beginning this simulation.

	Situation						
Directions		Gain/Basis	Depreciation Expense	Distributive Share	Liquidating Distributions	Written Communication	Research

Miller, Smith, and Tucker decided to form a partnership to perform engineering services. All of the partners have extensive experience in the engineering field and now wish to pool their resources and client contacts to begin their own firm. The new entity, Sabre Consulting, will begin operations on April 1, 2007, and will use the calendar year for reporting purposes.

All of the partners expect to work full time for Sabre and each will contribute cash and other property to the company sufficient to commence operations. The partners have agreed to share all income and losses of the partnership equally. A written partnership agreement, duly executed by the partners, memorializes this agreement among the partners.

The table below shows the estimated values for assets contributed to Sabre by each partner. None of the contributed assets' costs have been previously recovered for tax purposes.

Partner	Cash contribution	Estimated FMV of noncash property contributed	Basis in noncash property contributed
Miller	$15,000	$11,000	$10,000
Smith	10,000	17,000	15,000
Tucker	20,000	6,500	5,000
Totals	45,000	34,500	30,000

		Gain/Basis					
Directions	Situation		Depreciation Expense	Distributive Share	Liquidating Distributions	Written Communication	Research

Complete the shaded cells in the following table by entering the gain or loss recognized by each partner on the property contributed to Sabre Consulting, the partner's basis in the partnership interest, and Sabre's basis in the contributed property. Loss amounts should be recorded as a negative number.

NOTE: To use a formula in the spreadsheet, it must be preceded by an equal sign (e.g., = B1 + B2).

E16	▼	fx		
	A	B	C	D
1		Partner's gain or loss on property transferred	Partner's basis in partnership interest	Partnership's basis in property contributed
2	Miller			
3	Smith			
4	Tucker			

Directions	Situation	Gain/Basis	Depreciation Expense	Distributive Share	Liquidating Distributions	Written Communication	Research

Using the MACRS table (which can be found by clicking the Resources tab) and the partnership basis in the contributed assets calculated on the prior tab, complete the following table to determine Sabre's tax depreciation expense for 2007. Assume that none of the original cost of any asset was expensed by the partnership under the provisions of Section 179.

NOTE: To use a formula in the spreadsheet, it must be preceded by an equal sign (e.g., =B1 + B2).

D15	▼	*fx*		
	A	B	C	D
1	**Partner**	**Asset type**	**Depreciable basis**	**2005 Depreciation expense**
2	Miller	Office furniture		
3	Smith	Pickup truck used 100% for business purposes		
4	Tucker	Computers and printers		

Directions	Situation	Gain/Basis	Depreciation Expense	Distributive Share	Liquidating Distributions	Written Communication	Research

Assume that Sabre had only the items of income and expense show in the following table for the 2007 tax year. Complete the remainder of the table by properly classifying each item of income and expense as ordinary business income that is reportable on page 1, Form 1065, or as a separately stated item that is reportable on Schedule K, Form 1065. Some entries may appear in both columns.

NOTE: To use a formula in the spreadsheet, it must be preceded by an equal sign (e.g., = B1 + B2).

G15	▼	*fx*		
	A	B	C	D
1			**Ordinary Income**	**Separately stated items**
2	Sales revenue	$500,000		
3	Interest income	$4,000		
4	Depreciation expense	$(7,500)		
5	Operating expenses	$(426,000)		
6	Charitable contributions	$(3,000)		
7				
8	Total net ordinary income			

Directions	Situation	Gain/Basis	Depreciation Expense	Distributive Share	Liquidating Distributions	Written Communication	Research

The partners have decided to liquidate Sabre Consulting at December 31, 2007. On that date, Tucker received the following asset as a liquidating distribution in exchange for his entire partnership interest. There were no partnership liabilities at the date of liquidation. Tucker's basis in the partnership interest at the date of liquidation was $3,000.

	Cost	Accumulated depreciation	Estimated FMV
Drafting equipment	$12,000	$8,000	$6,000

Based on the foregoing information, complete the following table. Loss amounts should be recorded as a negative number.

NOTE: To use a formula in the spreadsheet, it must be preceded by an equal sign (e.g., = B1 + B2).

D15	▼	*fx*		🗐 ✂ 🗐
	A			B
1	Gain or loss recognized by partnership on the liquidating distribution			
2	Gain or loss recognized by Tucker on the liquidating distribution			
3	Tucker's basis in the asset received as part of the liquidating distribution			

Directions	Situation	Gain/Basis	Depreciation Expense	Distributive Share	Liquidating Distributions	Written Communication	Research

You also handle Mr. Smith's personal taxes. He received dividends from foreign stocks during the year from which foreign taxes of $50 were withheld. He has requested your help in determining whether it would be more advantageous to claim these foreign taxes paid as an itemized deduction or as a credit against income taxes. For the current year, Mr. Smith is single, has adjusted gross income of $85,000, total itemized deductions of $8,000, and taxable income of $74,000. His marginal tax rate is 30%. Write a letter to Mr. Smith explaining which option would be more advantageous for the tax year based on the above information.

Directions	Situation	Gain/Basis	Depreciation Expense	Distributive Share	Liquidating Distributions	Written Communication	Research

Use the research materials available to you by clicking the Code button to research the answer to the following questions. Find the code section that addresses the question, and enter the section citation in the shaded boxes below. Give the most precise a citation possible (i.e., both code section and subsection, if applicable). Do **not** copy the actual text of the citation.

During its initial tax year, Sabre Consulting incurred $2,000 of legal fees and $750 of accounting fees to organize the partnership. What code section and subsection permits the partnership to elect to deduct these expenses for federal tax purposes?

Section	Subsection
§	( )

TO:

FROM:

Directions	Situation	Taxable Income	Line 26 worksheet	Schedules M-1 and M-2	Communication	Research

In the subsequent year, InterTax, Inc. sold one of its stock investments and realized a loss. What code section and subsection provides the authority regarding treatment by corporate taxpayers of this realized loss?

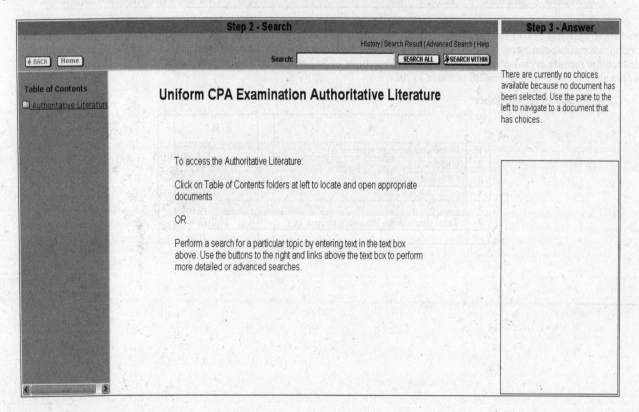

SOLUTION TO SIMULATION 1

Directions	Situation	Taxable Income	Line 26 worksheet	Schedules M-1 and M-2	Communication	Research

The requirement is to complete lines 1a – 30 of Form 1120, US Corporate Income Tax Return for InterTax's first year of operations. (See completed form on the following page.) The amount to be entered on line 26 – Other deductions is to be determined by using the worksheet provided in Tab 4.

Since this is InterTax's first year of operations, the Initial Return box on line E should be checked.

Except for total Other deductions, the amounts to be entered on page 1 of Form 1020 can be found under the Tax column of the Income Statement provided under the Situation Tab.

Although InterTax donated $80,000 to charity during the year, the amount allowable for the tax purposes is limited to 10% of taxable income before the contributions deduction. InterTax's allowable contributions deduction of $62,569 has already been computed and is shown in the Tax column of the Income Statement ($62,569 + $563,124) × 10% = $62,569.

Directions	Situation	Taxable Income	Line 26 worksheet	Schedules M-1 and M-2	Communication	Research

InterTax is required to attach a schedule, listing by type and amount, all allowable deductions that are not deductible elsewhere on Form 1120. The type of deductions that might be found on line 26 include amortization, business start-up and organizational expenditures, supplies, travel, utilities, and 50% of business meals and entertainment. Here, InterTax's Other deductions include organization expenses of $5,707, utilities of $12,000, and office supplies of $7,000, for a total of $24,707 which should be entered on line 26 of Form 1120.

Line 26 Deduction Worksheet

	A	B	
1	Organization expenses	5,707	
2	Utilities	12,000	
3	Office supplies	7,000	
4			
5			
7	Total deductions (transfer to line 26)	24,707	

Form 1120
Department of the Treasury
Internal Revenue Service

U.S. Corporation Income Tax Return

For calendar year 2007 or tax year beginning .... , 2007, ending .... , 20 .....
▶ See separate instructions.

OMB No. 1545-0123

2007

A Check if:
1a Consolidated return (attach Form 851) ☐
b Life/nonlife consolidated return ☐
2 Personal holding co. (attach Sch. PH) ☐
3 Personal service corp. (see instructions) ☐
4 Schedule M-3 attached ☐

Use IRS label. Otherwise, print or type.

Name
InterTax, Inc.

Number, street, and room or suite no. If a P.O. box, see instructions.

City or town, state, and ZIP code

B Employer identification number

C Date incorporated

D Total assets (see instructions)
$

E Check if: (1) ☑ Initial return   (2) ☐ Final return   (3) ☐ Name change   (4) ☐ Address change

Income

1a	Gross receipts or sales	1,880,000	
b	Less returns and allowances	c Bal ▶ 1c	1,880,000
2	Cost of goods sold (Schedule A, line 8)	2	
3	Gross profit. Subtract line 2 from line 1c	3	
4	Dividends (Schedule C, line 19)	4	
5	Interest	5	16,400
6	Gross rents	6	
7	Gross royalties	7	
8	Capital gain net income (attach Schedule D (Form 1120))	8	
9	Net gain or (loss) from Form 4797, Part II, line 17 (attach Form 4797)	9	
10	Other income (see instructions—attach schedule)	10	
11	**Total income.** Add lines 3 through 10 ▶	11	1,896,400

Deductions (See instructions for limitations on deductions.)

12	Compensation of officers (Schedule E, line 4)	12	800,000
13	Salaries and wages (less employment credits)	13	240,000
14	Repairs and maintenance	14	2,000
15	Bad debts	15	
16	Rents	16	76,800
17	Taxes and licenses	17	10,000
18	Interest	18	10,000
19	Charitable contributions	19	62,569
20	Depreciation from Form 4562 not claimed on Schedule A or elsewhere on return (attach Form 4562)	20	75,200
21	Depletion	21	
22	Advertising	22	30,000
23	Pension, profit-sharing, etc., plans	23	
24	Employee benefit programs	24	2,000
25	Domestic production activities deduction (attach Form 8903)	25	
26	Other deductions (attach schedule)	26	24,707
27	**Total deductions.** Add lines 12 through 26 ▶	27	1,333,276
28	Taxable income before net operating loss deduction and special deductions. Subtract line 27 from line 11	28	563,124
29	**Less:** a Net operating loss deduction (see instructions) 29a		
	b Special deductions (Schedule C, line 20) 29b	29c	
30	**Taxable income.** Subtract line 29c from line 28 (see instructions)	30	563,124

Tax and Payments

31	**Total tax** (Schedule J, line 10)	31	
32 a	2006 overpayment credited to 2007 32a		
b	2007 estimated tax payments 32b		
c	2007 refund applied for on Form 4466 32c ( ) d Bal ▶ 32d		
e	Tax deposited with Form 7004 32e		
f	Credits: (1) Form 2439 (2) Form 4136 32f	32g	
33	Estimated tax penalty (see instructions). Check if Form 2220 is attached ▶ ☐	33	
34	**Amount owed.** If line 32g is smaller than the total of lines 31 and 33, enter amount owed	34	
35	**Overpayment.** If line 32g is larger than the total of lines 31 and 33, enter amount overpaid	35	
36	Enter amount from line 35 you want: **Credited to 2008 estimated tax ▶** Refunded ▶	36	

Sign Here

Under penalties of perjury, I declare that I have examined this return, including accompanying schedules and statements, and to the best of my knowledge and belief, it is true, correct, and complete. Declaration of preparer (other than taxpayer) is based on all information of which preparer has any knowledge.

▶ _____ Signature of officer   Date   ▶ _____ Title

May the IRS discuss this return with the preparer shown below (see instructions)? ☐ Yes ☐ No

Paid Preparer's Use Only

	Date	Check if self-employed ☐	Preparer's SSN or PTIN
Preparer's signature ▶			
Firm's name (or yours if self-employed), address, and ZIP code ▶		EIN	
		Phone no. ( )	

For Privacy Act and Paperwork Reduction Act Notice, see separate instructions.   Cat. No. 11450Q   Form **1120** (2007)

Directions	Situation	Taxable Income	Line 26 worksheet	Schedules M-1 and M-2	Communication	Research

Schedule M-1 of Form 1120 is used to reconcile a corporate taxpayer's income reported per books with income reported on the tax return. Generally, items of income or deduction whose book and tax treatment differ, result in Schedule M-1 items. InterTax's M-1 items can be determined by comparing the Tax and Book columns of the Income Statement found under Tab 2.

Line 1. Enter InterTax's net income per books of $396,440.

Line 2. The federal income taxes of $186,560 deducted per books is not deductible for tax purposes and is added back to book income.

Line 5b. Although InterTax deducted charitable contributions of $80,000 per books, only $62,569 is allowable for tax purposes because of the 10% of taxable income limitation. [($62,569 + $563,124) × 10% = $62,569]. The difference, $80,000 − $62,569 = $17, 431, must be added back to book income.

Line 5c. Although InterTax deducted all $15,600 of its organization expenses per books, the amount that can be deducted for tax purposes is limited to $5,707. The difference, $15,600 − $5,707 = $9,893, must be added back to book income. The amount allowable for tax purposes is computed as follows: $5,000 + [($15,600 − $5,000) × 12/180] = $5,707.

Line 7. The $2,400 of tax-exempt interest included in book income is not taxable and must be subtracted from book income.

Line 8a. Since InterTax's allowable depreciation deduction of $75,200 for tax purposes exceeds the depreciation deduction of $30,400 for book purposes, the excess of $44,800 must be subtracted from book income.

Schedule M-2 provides an analysis of unappropriated retained earnings per books between the beginning and end of the year. Since this was InterTax's first year and no shareholder distributions were made during the year, the only item entered in Schedule M-2 is InterTax's net income per books of $396,440.

Schedule M-1   Reconciliation of Income (Loss) per Books With Income per Return

Note: Schedule M-3 required instead of Schedule M-1 if total assets are $10 million or more—see instructions

1	Net income (loss) per books	396,440	7	Income recorded on books this year not included on this return (itemize):	
2	Federal income tax per books	186,560		Tax-exempt interest $ 2,400	
3	Excess of capital losses over capital gains .				
4	Income subject to tax not recorded on books this year (itemize):				2,400
5	Expenses recorded on books this year not deducted on this return (itemize):		8	Deductions on this return not charged against book income this year (itemize):	
a	Depreciation . . . . . $		a	Depreciation . . . . . $ 44,800	
b	Charitable contributions $ 17,431		b	Charitable contributions $	
c	Travel and entertainment $				44,800
	Organization expenses 9,893	27,324	9	Add lines 7 and 8	47,200
6	Add lines 1 through 5 .	610,324	10	Income (page 1, line 28)—line 6 less line 9	563,124

Schedule M-2   Analysis of Unappropriated Retained Earnings per Books (Line 25, Schedule L)

1	Balance at beginning of year	0	5	Distributions: a Cash	0
2	Net income (loss) per books	396,440		b Stock	
3	Other increases (itemize):			c Property	
	....		6	Other decreases (itemize):	
	....		7	Add lines 5 and 6	0
4	Add lines 1, 2, and 3	396,440	8	Balance at end of year (line 4 less line 7)	396,440

Form **1120** (2007)

Directions	Situation	Income & Expense	Depreciation	Self-Employment Tax	Communication	Research

James Dugan
42 Chestnut Street
Anytown, USA

Dear Mr. Dugan:

This letter is in response to the IRS notice that you recently forwarded to me regarding your 2002 tax return. The notice indicated that their records show that you received a Form 1099-DIV from First Investors Brokerage showing ordinary dividend income in the amount of $2,000. The inclusion of this $2,000 in your gross income results in your owing $500 of additional tax for the 2002 tax year.

We will need to do two things in order to determine whether this addition to your gross income is correct. First, we need to review your documentation of transactions with First Investors Brokerage to determine whether the Form 1099-

DIV is in error. Second, we need to review your 2002 tax return to determine whether this $2,000 was already included in your gross income but improperly classified as interest or other income, instead of ordinary dividend income.

It is important that we meet to review your 2002 tax return and supporting documentation so that we can respond to the IRS notice by October 30th. Please call me at your earliest convenience so that we can schedule a time to meet and determine the appropriateness of the IRS's assessment.

Sincerely,

CPA Candidate

Directions	Situation	Income & Expense	Depreciation	Self-Employment Tax	Communication	Research

IRC § 1211(a)

Internal Revenue Code Sec. 1211 subsection (a) provides the authority for the treatment of capital losses by corporate taxpayers. It indicates that losses from sales or exchanges of capital assets shall be allowed only to the extent of gains from such sales or exchanges. In other words, corporate taxpayers are not allowed to deduct a net capital loss.

A

e deductions, 382
ost recovery system
offer, 124
Accident benefits, taxability of, 361
Accommodation party, 197
Accounting methods
   Tax, 369
Accrual basis, 370
Accumulated adjustments account, 581
Accumulated earnings and profits, 573, 581
Accumulated earnings tax, 576
Acquisition indebtedness, 390
   Stock purchase treated as, 575
Active income, 376
Active participation, 377
Actual (compensatory) damages, 141
Adhesion contracts, 133
Adjusted current earnings (ACE), 565
Adjusted gross income, 382, 387
Adjustments to AMTI, 402, 564
Admonishment from AICPA, 41
Adoption expenses
   Credit for, 408
   Paid by employer, 362
Adverse possession, 327
Advisory services, 57
Affiliated corporations, 571
Affirmative action, 298
Age Discrimination in Employment Act, 297
Agency, 276
   Agent
      And third parties, 280
      Authority of, 279
      Capacity to be, 279
      Characteristics of, 276
      Liability of, 281
      Obligations of, 280
      Types of, 278
   Coupled with an interest, 277
   Creation of, 278
   Employer/employee relationships, 276, 293
   Independent contractor, 276
   Principal
      And third parties, 281
      Capacity to be, 279
      Liability of, 280
      Obligations of, 280
      Types of, 277
   Termination of, 281
      Notice of termination, 282
Alcohol fuels credit, 405
Alimony recapture, 366
Alimony, tax treatment
   Payments, 387
   Receipts, 366
Alternate valuation date, 647
Alternative depreciation system (ADS), 378
Alternative minimum tax, 402, 564

Americans with Disabilities Act of 1990, 297, 405
Amortization, tax purposes, 381
Annuities
   Taxability of, 360, 367
Antecedent debt, 239
Anticipatory breach, 140, 167
Anticybersquatting Consumer Protection Act, 322
Arbitration, 141
Artisan's lien, 258
Assessments, tax, 389, 412
Assignment
   For benefit of creditors, 259
   Of contracts, 138
   Of income, 360
   Of negotiable instruments, 190
Assumption of liabilities
   Partnerships, 527
   Sales and exchanges, 492
At-risk limitation, 375, 525, 580
Attachment
   Of security interests, 220
   Perfection by, 221
   Writ of, 258
Attest services, 57
Auctions, 127
Audit and appeal procedures, 412, 414
Automatic expulsion from AICPA, 60
Automatic perfection, 222
Averaging convention, 378
Awards, taxability of, 368

B

Bad debt, deductibility of
   Business, 373, 569
   Nonbusiness, 374
Bailment, 317
Banker's acceptance, 198
Bankruptcy, 194, 235
   Administration costs, 241
   Alternatives to, 235
   Assignment for benefit of creditors, 259
   Automatic stay of other legal proceedings, 237
   Chapter 7, 235, 237
   Chapter 11, 243
   Chapter 13, 244
   Claims to debtor's estate, 240
      Filing of, 240
      Priority of, 241
      Proof of, 240
      Property rights, 241
   Discharge, 241
      Nondischargeable debts, 242
      Reaffirmation of, 243
      Revocation of, 243
   Equity sense vs. bankruptcy sense, 236
   Exempt entities, 236
   Exempt property and benefits, 237
   Fraudulent conveyance, 239
   Involuntary bankruptcy petitions, 235
   Preferential transfers, 239
   Priority of claims, 241

   Proceedings, 237
   Receiverships, 235
   Trustee in bankruptcy, 237
      As a lien creditor, 225
      Duties and powers of, 237, 238
      Exceptions to trustee's power to avoid preferential transfers, 240
   Types of proceedings
      Business reorganizations, 243
      Debt adjustment plans, 244
      Liquidation, 237
   Voluntary bankruptcy petitions, 235
Banks, 199
Bargain and sale deeds, 326
Basis
   Nonliquidating distributions, 531
Basis of accounting
   Accrual, 370
   Cash, 369, 529
Basis of partnership interests, 527
Basis of property
   Carryover, 574
   Estate, 648
   Exchanges, 492
   Gifts, 490, 646
   In general, 490
   In liquidation, 574
   Partnership, 523, 533
Battle of forms, 161
Bearer paper, 189, 191
Beneficiaries, tax treatment of, 650
Bequest, 362
Bilateral offer/contract, 122
Bill of lading, 161, 200
Blank endorsement, 190
Blue-sky laws, 103
Bonds
   Surety, 266
Bonds, market discount, 496
Boot, 492, 562
Breach of contract, 60, 140, 166, 193
Brother-sister corporations, 571
Business energy credit, 404
Business expenses, deductibility of
   By employees, 382, 396
   By proprietor, 371
Business gifts, 373
Business income, tax purposes, 365, 371
Business property, gains and losses on, 501, 503
   Capital gains treatment, 501, 503
   Classification of, 503
   Ordinary, 501, 503
   Recapture rules
      Section 291, 503
      Section 1245, 501
      Section 1250, 502
   Section 1231, 501, 503
Business reorganizations, 243
Business use of home, 375
Buyers in the ordinary course of business, 224

C

Capital assets, 498
Capital expenditures, 388

Capital gains and losses, 498
  Carryovers, 499, 569
  Corporate, 500, 569
  Holding period, 498
  Individual, 365, 394, 499
  Netting of, 499
  Rollover of capital gain
    On securities, 495
Capital gains exclusion for small business stock, 495
Capitalization of interest cost
  Tax purposes, 372
Capitalization of interest, tax purposes, 372
Carryforwards/carrybacks
  Of capital gains and losses, 500, 569
  Of net operating losses, 374, 569
Cash basis, 369, 529
Casualty gains and losses, 394, 500, 569
Charitable gifts, 646
Checks, 187
  Types of, 198
Child care credit, 406
Child support, tax treatment
  Payments, 367
  Receipts, 360, 367
Child tax credit, 409
Civil liability, 96, 100
Civil Rights Act, 297
Claims for refund, 412
Claims to debtor's estate, 240
Clean Air Act, 301
Clean Water Act, 302
Closely held C corporation, 376, 377
Closing agreement, 412
Coinsurance clause, 346
Collateral, 220
  Types, 220
Collection from transferees and fiduciaries, 412
Combined corporations, 572
Compensation, taxability of, 365
Compensatory (actual) damages, 141
Composition agreement, 235, 259
Comprehensive Environmental, Compensation, and Liability Act, 303
Compromise, 412
Computer Matching and Privacy Act, 322
Computer technology rights, 318
Concurrent interest in real property, 324
Conduit, 522, 649
Consent dividends, 576
Consequential damages, 169
Consideration for contract, 127, 193
Consignments, 161, 223
Consolidations, tax treatment, 583
Construction bonds, 267
Constructive eviction, 331
Constructive fraud, 62
Constructive receipt, 369
Constructive stock ownership, 497
Consulting services, 57

Contingent expenses, deductibility of, 370
Contract price, 371
Contracts, 121
  Acceptance of offer, 124
  Against public policy, 131
  Assignment of, 138
  Battle of forms problem, 126, 161
  Consideration for, 127, 193
  Delegation of, 138
  Discharge of, 140
  Essential elements of, 121, 122
  Legal capacity, 129
  Legality of, 130
  Modification of, 128, 135, 161
  Offer, 122
    Auctions, 127
    Counteroffer, 123
    Firm offer, 125, 160
    Option contracts, 123, 125
    Termination of, 122
  Online, 136
  Parol evidence rule, 136
  Performance, 139
  Reality of consent, 131
  Remedies for breach of contract, 141
  Statute of Frauds, 133
  Statute of limitations, 141, 169
  Types of, 121
    Third-party beneficiary contracts, 139, 262
  Uniform Commercial Code Rules, 125, 160
  Void/voidable contracts, 121, 129, 131
Contribution, right of, 266
Contributions
  Deductibility of
    Charitable
      Corporate, 567
      Individual, 391, 396
      Nondeductible, 392
      Qualified organizations, 391
    To retirement plans
      By employer, 570
      By self, 384
Contributory negligence, 62, 163, 276
Controlled corporations, 571
  Transfers to, 562
Controlled group, 497, 571
Controlled partnerships, transactions with, 528
Copyright law, 318
Copyrights, amortization of, 381
Corporate reorganizations, 583
Corporate taxation, 562
  Accumulated earnings tax, 575
  Affiliated corporations, 571
  Alternative minimum tax, 564
  Calculation of tax, 570
  Capital gains and losses, 498, 500, 569
  Controlled corporations, 571
    Transfers to, 562
  Deductions, 566
  Dividends and distributions, 572, 574
  Dividends received deduction, 568
  Earnings and profits, 573

  Filing and payment of tax, 563
  Form 1120, 359, 563, 571
  Gross income, 566
  Individual taxation, variations from, 563
  Liquidations, 574
  Losses
    Capital, 569
    Net operating, 569
    Ordinary, 569
  Personal holding companies, 575
  Reconciling book and tax income, 570
  Reorganization, 583
  Small business corporation stock (Sec. 1244), 563
  Stock redemptions, 573
  Tax rates, 564
Cosureties, 265
Counteroffer, 123
Creditor beneficiary, 139
Creditors' agreement, 259
Credits, tax, 360, 404
Criminal liability, 68, 97, 100
Crummey trust, 646
Current earnings and profits, 573

D

Damages, 62, 64, 66, 141, 168
  Mitigation of, 141, 169
Damages, taxability of, 362
De minimis fringes, 362
Death benefits, taxability of, 361
Debt
  Discharge of
    Taxability of, 364
  Discharge of indebtness, taxability, 364
Debt adjustment plans, 244
Debt-financed portfolio stock, 568
Debtor-creditor relationships, 258
  Attachment, 258
  Composition agreements, 259
  Construction bonds, 267
  Contracts, surety and guaranty, 260
  Cosureties, 265
    Contribution, right of, 266
    Discharge or release of, 266
    Joint and several liability, 266
  Creditors
    Assignment for the benefit of, 259
    Composition agreement with, 259
    Rights and remedies of, 262
  Equal Credit Opportunity Act, 260
  Exoneration, right of, 263, 266
  Fair Credit Billing Act, 260
  Fair Credit Reporting Act, 260
  Fair Debt Collection Practices Act, 259
  Fidelity bonds, 267
  Garnishment, 258
  Guarantor, 261
    Capacity to act as, 262
    Defenses, 263
    Rights and remedies of, 263
  Guaranty, 260
    Contracts, 261
  Homestead exemption, 259

e bonds, 267
ment, right of, 263, 266
uties of, 258
right of, 263, 266
Surety, 266
Bonds, 266
Defenses of, 263
Rights and remedies of, 263
Truth-in-Lending Act, 259
Debts not discharged in bankruptcy, 242
Decedent, 367, 490
Deductions from gross income
Corporate taxation, 566
Individual taxation, 360
Above the line, 382
Business, 371
Itemized, 387
Required reduction of, 397
Standard, 387
Partnership taxation, 523
Deed of trust, 330
Deeds, 326
Default, 225
Defined benefit pension plan, 570
Defined contribution pension plan, 570
Del credere, 277
Delegation of contracts, 138
Dental expenses, deductibility of, 388
Dependent care assistance, 362
Depletion, income tax purposes, 377, 380, 570
Depreciation
Accelerated cost recovery system (ACRS), 378
Recapture, 371, 501
Depreciation, income tax purposes, 377, 570
Accelerated cost recovery system (ACRS), 378
Alternative depreciation system, 378
Modified accelerated cost recovery system (MACRS), 378
Devises, 362
Digital Millennium Copyright Act, 323
Direct Public Offerings (DPO), 102
Disabled access credit, 405
Disabled, credit for elderly and, 406
Discharge
Of bankrupt, 241
Of contractual obligation, 140
Of liability on negotiable instrument, 197
Discharge of indebtedness, 364
Disciplinary systems, 59
Disclaimer of warranty, 163
Disclosed principal, 277, 280
Distributable net income, 650
Distributions, income tax purposes
From corporations, 572
Liquidations, 574
Stock redemptions, 573
From estates/trusts, 649
From partnerships, 531

Dividends
Tax treatment
Payment of, 572
Receipt of
By corporations, 567
By individuals, 361, 363, 365, 370
By partnerships, 524
Dividends received deduction, 568
Doctrine of respondeat superior, 276
Doctrine of substantial performance, 140
Donee beneficiary, 139
Drafts, 186, 198
Due diligence, 96
Due negotiation, 201
Dues, 373
Duress, 133

E

Earned income, 385
Earned income credit, 408
Earnings and profits, 574
Easement by prescription, 328
Economic effect, 525
Education expenses, tax treatment
Paid by self, 396
Paid via assistance, 362, 363, 646
Savings bonds for, 363
Education IRA, 385
Education loans
Deduction for interest on, 386
Elderly credit, 406
Embezzlement income, 369
Emergency Planning, and Community Right-to-Know Act, 304
Employee achievement awards, 368
Employee benefits, 296, 298
Employee benefits, taxability of, 361, 362
Employee business expenses, deductibility of, 382, 396
Employee discount, 362
Employee Retirement Income Security Act (ERISA), 299
Employee safety, 296
Employee stock purchase plan, 368
Employer social security credit, 406
Employer supplemental unemployment benefits, 368
Employer/employee relationships, 276, 293
Employment discrimination, 297
Empowerment zone employment credit, 406
Endangered Species Act, 304
Endorsement of negotiable instruments, 190
Entertainment expenses, deductibility of, 372
Environmental Compliance Audits, 305
Environmental liability, 301
Environmental Protection Agency (EPA), 301
Environmental regulation, 301
Clean Air Act, 301

Clean Water Act, 302
Comprehensive Environmental, Compensation, and Liability Act (CERCLA), 303
Emergency Planning, and Community Right-to-Know Act, 304
Endangered Species Act, 305
Federal Environmental Pesticide Control Act, 303
Federal Insecticide, Fungicide, and Rodenticide Act, 303
International protection of ozone layer, 304
Marine Protection, Research, and Sanctuaries Act, 304
National Environmental Policy Act, 301
Noise Control Act, 303
Nuclear Waste Policy Act, 304
Oil Pollution Act, 302
Pollution Prevention Act, 305
Resource Conservation and Recovery Act, 303
Safe Drinking Water Act, 302
Toxic Substance Control Act, 303
Equal Credit Opportunity Act, 260
Equal Employment Opportunity Commission, 298
Equal Pay Act, 298
Error, knowledge of, 653
E-SIGN Act, 136
Estate tax, 647
Alternate valuation date, 647
Basis of property, 648
Computation of, 647
Deductions, 647
Generation-skipping tax, 648
Gross estate, 647
Income in respect of a decedent, 367
Property acquired from a decedent, 490
Estates
Intestate succession, 317
Estates and trusts, taxation of
Beneficiaries, 649
Computation of tax, 647
Termination of, 651
Estimated tax payments, 410
Estoppel
Agency by, 278, 279
Promissory, 129
Ethics rulings, 50, 52, 56
Exchanges, taxability of, 491
Exclusions from gross income, 360
Exculpatory clause, 131
Exempt securities, 94, 98
Exemptions, 398
Exoneration, right of, 263, 266
Express warranties, 162
Expulsion from AICPA, 41, 59
Extraordinary dividend, 568

F

Fair Credit Billing Act, 260
Fair Credit Reporting Act, 260
Fair Debt Collection Practices Act, 259

Fair Labor Standards Act, 406
Family and Medical Leave Act, 298
Family Educational Rights and
 Privacy Act, 322
Family partnerships, 526
Federal Consolidated Budget
 Reconciliation Act, 299
Federal Counterfeit Access Device
 and Computer Fraud and Abuse
 Act, 321
Federal Employee Polygraph
 Protection Act, 300
Federal Environmental Pesticide
 Control Act, 303
Federal Fair Labor Standards Act,
 299
Federal Insecticide, Fungicide, and
 Rodenticide Act, 303
Federal Insurance Contributions Act
 (FICA), 291
Federal Social Security Act, 291
Federal Unemployment Tax Act
 (FUTA), 292, 403
Fee simple, 323
Fellowships, taxability of, 364
FICA tax, 403
Fictitious payee rule, 198
Fidelity bonds, 267
Field warehousing, 223
Fifty (50%) reduction rule, 372
Filing requirements
 Corporate taxation, 562
 Estate tax, 647
 Estates and trusts, 648
 Gift tax, 645
 Individual taxation, 410
Filing status, 401
Financing statement, filing, 221
Fines, 371
Fire insurance, 346
Firm offer, 125, 160
Fitness for a particular purpose,
 warranty of, 162
Fixed amount, 188
Fixtures, 316
Foreign Corrupt Practices Act, 101
Foreign earned income exclusion, 364
Foreign tax credit, 407
Foreseeable third party, 63
Foreseen third party, 63
Forgery, 194
 Fictitious payee rule, 198
 Imposter rule, 197
Fraud, 61, 131, 194
Fraudulent conveyance, 239
Fringe benefits, taxability of, 362, 582
Future interest in real property, 324

G

Gains and losses, tax treatment
 Between related parties, 496, 528,
  569
 Personal casualty and theft, 394, 500,
  569
Gambling winnings/losses, tax
 treatment, 369, 397

Garnishment, 258
General business credit, 404
Generation-skipping tax, 648
Gift tax
 Annual exclusion, 645
 Basis of property, 646
 Computation of, 645
 Exclusions, 646
 Generation-skipping tax, 648
Gifts, 645
 Basis of, 490
 Deductibility of, 393
  Business gifts, 373
 Taxability of, 362
  Nontaxable gifts, 645
Gifts of property, 317
Gift-splitting, 646
Good faith, 140, 161, 192
Grant deeds, 326
Gross income
 Corporate, 566
 Individual, 360, 365
  Of business, 371
Gross negligence, 62
Group-term life insurance, 361
Guaranteed payments, 526
Guarantor of debt, 374
Guaranty contracts, 134, 261

H

Head of household status, 401
Health benefits, taxability of, 361
Health Insurance Portability and
 Accountability Act, 299
Hobby-loss rules, 374
Holder in due course, 192, 225
 Rights of, 193
Holder through a holder in due
 course, 195
Holding period, 498, 523
Home equity indebtedness, 390
Homestead exemption, 259
Hope Scholarship credit, 409

I

Identification of goods, 165, 169, 345
Illegal income, taxability of, 369
Illegality
 Of commercial paper, 194
 Of contracts, 130
Implementation services, 57
Implied warranties, 162
Imposter rule, 197
Imputed interest, 365
Incentive stock option, 368
Incidental beneficiary, 139
Income distribution deduction, 650
Income in respect of a decedent, 367
Income tax deductibility, 389
Income tax return preparers, 651
Income tax returns
 Form 1040 (Individuals), 358
 Form 1065 (Partnerships), 359, 522
 Form 1120 (Corporations), 359, 563,
  571
Income taxes
 Corporate, 563

Estate, 647
Gift, 645
Individual, 360
Partnerships, 523
Property transactions, 490
Trusts, 649
Incompetence, 130, 133
Indemnity contract, 262
Independence, auditor's, 44, 49
Independent contractor, 276, 293
Individual Retirement Account (IRA),
 384
Individual taxation, 360
 Alternative minimum tax, 402
 Calculation of tax, 400
 Deductions, 360
  Above the line, 382
  Business, 371
   At-risk limitation, 375
  Itemized, 387
   Required reduction of, 397
  Standard, 387
 Depreciation, depletion, and
  amortization, 377
 Estimated tax payments, 410
 Exclusions, 360
 Exemptions, 398
 Filing requirements, 410
 Filing status, 401
 Gross income, 360, 365
  Of a business, 371
 Passive activities, 376
 Tax accounting methods, 369
 Tax procedures, 412
 Tax rate schedules, 400
 Tax tables, 400
Infancy, 133, 194
Inheritances
 Basis of, 490
 Holding period of, 499
 Taxability of, 362
Injunction, 141
Innkeeper's lien, 258
Innocent misrepresentation, 132
Insiders, 91
 Preferential transfers to, 239
 Reporting requirements of, 100
Insolvency, bankruptcy vs. equity
 sense, 236
Insolvent financial institutions, 496
Installment sales method
 Tax reporting, 370
Insurable interest, 169, 344
Insurance, 344
 Coinsurance clause, 346
 Contracts for, 344
 Fire insurance, 346
 Insurable interest, 169, 345
 Liability insurance, 345
 Life insurance, 345
 Malpractice insurance, 67, 345
 Pro rata clause, 346
 Proof of loss, 346
 Self-insurance, 344
 Statute of Frauds, applicability of,
  344
 Subrogation, insurer's right of, 345